AMERICAN

EVANGELICALISM

George M. Marsden. Photo by Lisa Svelmoe.

EDITED BY

Darren Dochuk,

Thomas S. Kidd,

AND

Kurt W. Peterson

AMERICAN
EVANGELICALISM

George Marsden and the State

of American Religious History

UNIVERSITY OF NOTRE DAME PRESS

NOTRE DAME, INDIANA

University of Notre Dame Press
Notre Dame, Indiana 46556
www.undpress.nd.edu
All Rights Reserved

Published in the United States of America

Copyright © 2014 by University of Notre Dame

Paperback edition published in 2017

Library of Congress Cataloging-in-Publication Data

American evangelicalism : George Marsden and the state of American religious history / edited by Darren Dochuk, Thomas S. Kidd, and Kurt W. Peterson.
    pages   cm
Includes bibliographical references and index.
ISBN 978-0-268-03842-7 (hardback)
ISBN 978-0-268-15879-8 (paper)

1. United States—Church history. 2. Marsden, George M., 1939– 3. Evangelicalism—United States—History.   I. Dochuk, Darren, editor.
II. Kidd, Thomas S., editor.   III. Peterson, Kurt W., editor.
BR515.A537   2014
277.3'08—dc23
2014022435

∞ *The paper in this book meets the guidelines for permanence and durability of the Committee on Production Guidelines for Book Longevity of the Council on Library Resources*

For George M. Marsden

CONTENTS

Foreword: George Marsden as Scholar, Christian, and Friend   xi
NATHAN HATCH, MARK NOLL, HARRY STOUT,
AND GRANT WACKER

Acknowledgments   xv

Introduction   1

PART I.   Puritan Beginnings

1   Jonathan Edwards and the Study of His Eighteenth-Century   15
World: George Marsden's Contribution to Colonial American
Religious Historiography
Douglas A. Sweeney

2   *Jonathan Edwards: A Life*   36
Thomas S. Kidd

3   Jonathan Edwards and Francis Asbury   50
John Wigger

PART II.   Protestantism's Century

4   The Evangelical Mind and the Historians   71
Margaret Bendroth

5 *The Evangelical Mind and the New School Presbyterian Experience*   91
Peter J. Wallace

6 The African American Great Awakening and Modernity, 1866–1900   110
Jay R. Case

PART III. Protesting Modernity

7 Marsden and Modern Fundamentalism   141
Barry Hankins

8 *Fundamentalism and American Culture*   166
William L. Svelmoe

9 Reorienting American Religious History in the Age of Global Christianity: The Case of Katharine Bushnell   180
Kristin Kobes Du Mez

10 A Gilded Age Modernist: Reuben A. Torrey and the Roots of Contemporary Conservative Evangelicalism   199
Timothy E. W. Gloege

11 The Interdenominational Evangelicalism of D. L. Moody and the Problem of Fundamentalism   230
Michael S. Hamilton

PART IV. Pluralism's Challenge

12 Marsden and Secularization   283
John Schmalzbauer

13 *The Soul of the American University*   312
Steven M. Nolt

14 More Than a Footnote? Evangelical Ministries and   334
    the Secular University
    John G. Turner

15 The Southernization of the Evangelical Mind   357
    Rick Ostrander

PART V. Pluralism's Blessing

16 Marsden and Fundamentalist Resurgence   381
    Garth M. Rosell

17 *Reforming Fundamentalism*   398
    Darren Dochuk

18 Missionary Realities and the New Evangelicalism in   418
    Post–World War II America
    Kathryn T. Long

19 The Evangelical Left and the Politicization of Evangelicalism 442
    David R. Swartz

    Conclusion: How an Evangelical Won the Bancroft Prize 468
    Mark Noll

    Appendix: List of George Marsden's Doctoral Students   487
    and Their Dissertations

    Selected Bibliography of George Marsden's Works   490

    List of Contributors   500

    Index   507

FOREWORD
George Marsden as Scholar, Christian, and Friend

George Marsden's efforts have opened many doors for many people. At different times and in different ways the four authors of this preface have been able to do what we have done only because George was there first. We find ourselves profoundly indebted to George for many reasons, but three stand out.

First is the sheer magnitude of what he has written—a river flowing unabated for four decades of books, scholarly articles, essay reviews, public addresses, and As We See It op-eds in the late, lamented *Reformed Journal*. Most historians emphasize their specializations, but Marsden's work has spanned U.S. intellectual, cultural, and religious history from the early seventeenth to the early twenty-first centuries. After publishing his Yale dissertation on the origins of New School Presbyterianism in the Age of Jackson, George took in stride the development of fundamentalism, the secularization of the modern university, the philosophy of historical analysis, the life of Jonathan Edwards, and, currently, the twilight of the American Enlightenment after World War II. Two or three historians of our generation might have written (even) more, but none has published as many distinguished landmarks on so many subjects. Each of his books has "defined the conversation." Thoughtful scholars sometimes have disagreed with George's interpretations, but few have dared to ignore them. Each book advanced an argument— keyed to specific questions, circumstances, or individuals—but in every case Marsden also created an agenda that others eagerly engaged. George's work has given new meaning to the aphorism that words should be weighed, not just counted.

Our second debt concerns the clarity and boldness of George's effort to integrate critical historical method with Christian faith. The operative word here is *integrate*. On one hand, his work has met the most rigorous standards of the modern academy. Despite George's quip that historians are expert at building a mountain of speculation on a molehill of evidence, he has known better than anyone that responsible historical publication requires responsible historical research. His books have "smelt of the candle." Yet there is more. He also has known that the evidence must be tortured, as R. G. Collingwood once said, in order to see what conclusions it warrants, and maybe even more important, does not warrant. And then it requires positioning in a compelling vision of what the past has *meant*, both then and now. If there is an antiquarian bone in George's body, he has kept it hidden.

On the other hand, and at the same time, George also showed that responsible historical method could become even more critical if it remained open to ultimate religious questions. Through judicious deployment of his own Reformed and evangelical commitments, he encouraged others who shared his convictions, and many who did not, to engage large questions of meaning directly. This also obliged them to interpret their data empathetically, so that believers of times past would have been able to recognize themselves in the portrait. To make religious commitments transparent is to tempt triumphalism on one side and paternalism on the other. Yet by skirting the special pleading and in-group preoccupations of conventional church history *and* by eschewing the elitist reductionism of anticonventional religious and cultural studies, Marsden has sailed straight between those perils.

A third vitally important feature of George's influence stems from his personal relationships—as a teacher, a mentor of graduate students, and a colleague. What his lectures may have lacked in histrionics, they have more than made up in thought-provoking content. And in the seminar room, George's ability to discern the point of a text, and somehow persuade graduate students that they saw it first, has won universal admiration. Though none of us was his graduate student, we have experienced enough of his personality in small group settings to understand why his style has been so pedagogically effective: modest, ironic, pithy, often self-deprecating, and always laced with bon mots to take down sacred cows. Then, too, the remarkable number of students whom George mentored through PhD programs at Duke and at Notre Dame, the prizes they have won, and the academic positions they have captured—as well as the essays many of them contributed to this volume—define a record worthy of his own Yale teacher, Sydney Ahlstrom. Finally, as George's slightly junior colleagues, we all have benefited from his perennial willingness to break away from his own projects in order to read, critique, and encourage our own. He never has taken the easy route of saying, "I liked your manuscript." Rather, he always has taken the hard one of saying, "I liked your manuscript—but here are some paragraphs you might want to revisit."

We gratefully introduce this collection, reflecting as it does George's lifetime contribution to historical thought and inquiry enacted in the context of his lived faith. More particularly, we celebrate the occasion of this publication as a witness to the meaning of George's friendship to each of us, both as professional historians and as fellow sojourners.

Nathan Hatch
Mark Noll
Harry Stout
Grant Wacker

ACKNOWLEDGMENTS

This book grew out of conversation between George Marsden's graduate students who felt that his mentorship should, upon his retirement from the University of Notre Dame, be honored in published form. Each one of this volume's chapters bears witness to the impact he has had on countless readers through his prodigious research and writing, but none comes close (though a few offer hints) to revealing the true weight of his influence, which came through his teaching. All of the contributors to this volume have benefited directly from George's instruction—whether through coursework, dissertation advising, or scholarly consultation—and have pursued research and writing agendas shaped under his counsel. There is much more that we could say about George's commitment to our intellectual and professional development and about the many admirable characteristics that have made him such a warm and gracious friend as well as adviser to us all. Alas, time and space are too short. We trust, however, that the labor committed to this volume will offer readers at least a glimpse into George's many other strengths and, at least for now, serve as a "thank-you" to someone who has meant so much.

Thanks must also be offered to a few individuals who helped press this volume into publication. Grant Wacker, Harry Stout, and Nathan Hatch were eager from the beginning to see this volume in print, and we are grateful for their encouragement along the way. Mark Noll was especially determined to have us move forward, even when circumstances got in the way, so we owe him our special gratitude. We also appreciate the extremely helpful feedback offered by two external reviewers, one anonymous, the other Jon Butler, a contemporary of George's who has shaped the field of American religious history in similarly fundamental ways. Thanks, finally, to Charles VanHof, our editor, and the entire editorial and production team at the University of Notre Dame Press (especially Susan Berger, Rebecca DeBoer, Elisabeth Magnus, and Wendy McMillen), who patiently assisted us at each turn and ushered this project to completion.

Introduction

For three decades, the study of religious history has been surging in America, a trend reflected in the remarkable results of the American Historical Association's 2009 survey, which showed that religion had become the most common specialty among professional historians. Religious history possessed its greatest number of adherents among younger historians, signaling that this was a development not likely to vanish any time soon.[1] Experts offered various reasons for the survey results, but Yale historian Jon Butler spoke for many when he suggested that the growing popularity of religious history resulted from "the obvious inadequacy of the secularization thesis to explain world history since 1945."[2]

Crude versions of secularization theory posited the inexorable privatization and decline of faith in the withering light of modernity, yet increasingly since World War II religion has seemed to be everywhere: publicly and politically significant, on the rise, not the decline. Around the world vibrant expressions of all major religions have redefined terms of local and international engagement and made the "god factor" a global phenomenon. Christianity's vigor may have faded in western Europe, but elsewhere—in sub-Saharan Africa, Central and South America, and parts of Asia—it has grown at mind-boggling rates. In the United States, meanwhile, many evangelical Christians have become closely connected with political conservatism and recently a "Tea

Party" movement that has countered President Barack Obama at every turn. American evangelicals have not been alone in their growing desire to make religion count in politics and society. During this same recent stretch of time liberal Protestants, Catholics, and Jews have defended Obama's progressive politics, while people of other non-Judeo-Christian traditions have carried out similarly ambitious quests to orient community and country to their spiritual values. Spurred on by new immigration, new media, and a new global economic order, religious citizens have bucked predictions of secularization and stepped out into the public square. As a result, pundits and scholars alike can no longer deny the historical significance or currency of faith in the modern world.

One might expect the history of religion to be torn by the same ideological rifts that have emerged amid this rising tide of religiosity, and to some extent that has happened. Evangelical Christians, for instance, have often turned to nonacademic, entrepreneurial history writers who offer a Christian-inflected version of the American past. Conversely, several academic and journalistic historians have argued for fully secular versions of the American past, and especially of the American founding, in which the faith factor is written out of the narrative or downplayed as only a minor motivation for a few marginal historical actors. But welcome developments in recent decades have offered a way beyond a staunchly ideological history of religion.

First, a number of professional historians with no firm faith commitments themselves have written deeply sympathetic yet critical histories of American religion. The pioneer of this kind of scholarship was Harvard's Perry Miller, who in the mid-twentieth century reinvigorated the serious intellectual study of Puritanism. With noticeable acceleration since the 1990s, historians of Miller's ilk—those who do not necessarily hold to any faith commitment—have joined the rush to incorporate sacred matters in their treatments of American economic, social, cultural, and especially political development. David Hollinger has claimed that "religion is too important to be left in the hands of people who believe in it," and whether or not they have heard this call, historians of late have seemed ready to prove his point. Spurred on by trends in Washington, where movement politics on the right and left have leaned on religion to marshal voters, political historians especially have been eager to integrate religion in their histories of grassroots mobilization, congressional and presidential policy, and inner-Beltway power struggles.

Second, and more to the point of this volume, a number of believing historians have broken out of the constraints of denominational, hagiographical history and engaged with the methods of mainstream academic history, producing sympathetic histories that locate churches and parishioners within their cultural and political milieu. Mark Noll notes in his conclusion to this volume that Timothy Smith, a Nazarene who received his PhD at Harvard before joining the faculty at Johns Hopkins, was the parallel to Perry Miller among believing historians with mainstream academic credentials. Smith's *Revivalism and Social Reform* (1957) remains a standard work for all historians interested in understanding the great nineteenth-century campaigns for social improvement. Thanks to Smith's legacy and the influence of other like-minded chroniclers (such as Noll) who profess faith commitments but write for a wider public, the quest to blend personal belief with rigorous, first-rate scholarship continues to inspire many young, ambitious historians.[3]

George Marsden's illustrious career bears witness to the rise of religion in America's new historical consciousness and the attempt by some scholars to write history from a faith-friendly perspective. Marsden, one could say, was destined for this type of impact. After growing up in a Pennsylvania town and a devout Orthodox Presbyterian family, he attended the Quaker-affiliated Haverford College, attained an MDiv at Westminster Seminary, a leading institution in his denominational tradition, and took his PhD in American studies at Yale University. At Yale, Marsden worked with Edmund Morgan, a student of Perry Miller and arguably the greatest historian of colonial and Revolutionary America since World War II. As Marsden offered in a 2009 reflective piece for *Reviews in American History*, Morgan was his "stylistic idol," the teacher who taught him how to write not just for specialists in his field but also for laypeople—those who (as Morgan put it) "are smarter than you but know nothing about the subject." Considering his work's mass appeal, Marsden obviously internalized Morgan's message. Even more significant for his training in American religious history, however, was the guidance of Sydney Ahlstrom, his doctoral adviser. Ahlstrom's magisterial *A Religious History of the American People* is still one of the standard surveys of religion in America; its volumes appear on many a religious history syllabus and many a graduate student's exam reading list. Ahlstrom trained Marsden and a number of other leading historians to take religion seriously but also to see religion as shaping, and shaped by, broader culture. Marsden's arduous theological preparation within his denominational perspective, and the wider professional training he received at Yale from Morgan and Ahlstrom, proved to be a potent combination.[4]

Evidence of this striking balance soon surfaced in Marsden's writings. His first book, *The Evangelical Mind and the New School Presbyterian Experience* (1970), was probably his narrowest, as one might expect from a revised doctoral dissertation. It was the closest thing Marsden ever wrote to denominational history, yet, as Peter Wallace notes in his essay for this volume, it also heralded the great theme of all of Marsden's subsequent work: the evangelical mind. Marsden's authorship of *Fundamentalism and American Culture* (1980) facilitated his first major impact on the discussion of American religion. As Barry Hankins comments, *Fundamentalism and American Culture* almost single-handedly created a new historiography—the intellectual history of American fundamentalism—leaving others to flesh out that history in the three decades since. The book also had impeccable timing, coming out just as the Moral Majority burst onto the American political scene. Finally, it had such a compelling literary quality that many Christian historians recall reading it for the first time as a curious experience, almost like reading one's own life story. While *Fundamentalism* made the persuasive case that fundamentalists had a real intellectual pedigree, *Reforming Evangelicalism: Fuller Seminary and the New Evangelicalism* (1987) revealed the darker side of that pedigree as it generated the wars over biblical inerrancy at Fuller Seminary. Determined to craft an effective sequel to *Fundamentalism and American Culture*, yet equally set on testing different methods and approaches to the writing of evangelicalism's history, Marsden masterfully exploited the internal history of Fuller Seminary—fascinating as it was on its own terms—for fresh reading of the tumultuous theological, cultural, and political forces that reshaped fundamentalism in the post–

World War II years. Though different from *Fundamentalism in American Culture* in its focus and reach, *Reforming Fundamentalism* displayed the same creativity and combination of incisive analysis with compelling prose as its predecessor.

The scale of Marsden's innovation and impact continued to broaden after the publication of *Reforming Fundamentalism*, in part because his own interest in evangelicalism's history assumed broader proportions. Marsden has always worked at a deliberate, methodical pace, publishing major works every half-decade or so; his influence in academic writing has been generated by the weightiness more than the frequency of his published word. This cadence has afforded him the unrushed time needed to turn up new sources and new angles and to open wider intellectual and cultural vistas onto and from which evangelical Protestantism's particular history could be drawn for greater meaning and effect. During the 1990s and 2000s, Marsden's purview turned in a number of new directions, at once backward in time to foundational moments in the nation's pre-twentieth-century sacred past, and beyond the boundaries of evangelical studies to more comprehensive analyses of U.S. religious and cultural history. Marsden's efforts produced several concrete results.

One of the by-products of Marsden's evolving concern was an enlivened reconsideration of American educational history. *The Soul of the American University* (1994) inaugurated Marsden's foray into a corollary concern that has shaped much of the second half of his career: the place of faith in the modern academy. This text featured many of Marsden's finest authorial strategies, including the ironic mode. Working forward from the early national period to the recent past, Marsden tracked a long history in which religion came to be excluded from modern university life, not by some sinister secularist plot or imposition of will by irreligious intellectual elites, but as an unplanned side effect of scientific hegemony. Beginning in the late nineteenth century, he asserted, America's educational leaders started to believe that reliance on the scientific method could lead to both reliable knowledge and the cure of social ills, without cost to the Christian worldview. Over the next few decades such trust in the pedagogics of science deepened among progressive educators even as faith-based knowledge was viewed with greater suspicion. Amid the explosive Cold War period, when government funding of public universities expanded and the country's academicians and administrators began celebrating the virtues of applied sciences, faith found itself relegated to margins. Having welcomed science into their classroom during the late nineteenth century as a complement to Christian training, educators thus approached the late twentieth century trumpeting scientific rationalism and objectivity over the faith claims of yesteryear.

Written as history, in the voice of an informed observer, *The Soul of the American University* nevertheless exhibited a quality rarely highlighted in previous books: open partiality. Hints of his inclinations surfaced in his Postscript, in which Marsden argued for a revisiting of faith's place in the academy. Having made the transition from the modern assumptions of the Cold War academy, in which a confidence in human reason reigned supreme, to the destabilization of the postmodern age, in which certainty about anything seemed lost, Marsden averred that American higher education was ready to reincorporate religion in its curricula. Trading the hat of the historian for that of the pundit, Marsden expanded this argument in his relatively brief follow-up text, *The Outrageous Idea of Christian Scholarship* (1997). Marsden used this short sequel to advance a provocative two-pronged thesis: that philosophical justification no longer existed for excluding faith perspectives from the academy, and that viewpoints of faith could, when applied thoughtfully and responsibly within a transparent context, enrich academic inquiry. With another dash of irony, Marsden referenced the recent advent of postmodern perspectivalism, a trend viewed by some as threatening to religious creeds, as evidence of widespread doubt that knowledge of any kind could be objective. All knowledge, he insisted in concert with cultural critics of the day, was located in specific communities and inseparable from contexts created by confluences of thought, tradition, and circumstance. In Marsden's mind, this suggested at least two new potentials for academia: first, that private religious colleges be allowed to teach in accordance with their theological heritages, and second, that public institutions carve out space for faculty and instruction geared to particular faith commitments. Amid the celebration of postmodern diversity, he asked, why shouldn't "representatives of [religious] subcultures" have "their voices heard within public institutions so long as

[they] respect the reasonable rules necessary to public institutions that serve diverse constituencies"?[5]

A second by-product of Marsden's evolving concern was his turn away from recent historical concerns to their roots in the eighteenth century. Fundamentalism's struggles with liberal trends, evangelicalism's quest for relevance in the modern and postmodern eras, post–Civil War trajectories in higher education: these themes, which Marsden charted in his first four major books (*Outrageous Idea* not included), grew out of his broader interest in the long history of the evangelical mind. In his fifth extensive book—*Jonathan Edwards: A Life* (2003)—he turned to America's finest example of that mind. In some ways this book marked a departure from what he had done before. Turning away from institution-based research and themes, Marsden employed another medium—biography—for entry into the continuities and changes of the Protestant worldview. The medium proved well suited to Marsden's temperament and skill as an author. While delving into the life of this intellectual heavyweight, Marsden was able to write with the empathy and attention to detail evidenced in Edmund Morgan's work as well as the theological thoroughness and intuitive sense of church life seen in Sydney Ahlstrom's treatises. Moreover, in Edwards's life Marsden found a narrative arc full of drama but also profound significance, allowing him to write as he always desired to write: armed with colorful stories of the particular that contained nuggets of universal truth.

Of course *Jonathan Edwards* also marked a culmination of his previous years of labor. On its pages Marsden openly demonstrated respect for this prophet's capabilities but steered clear of the hagiography witnessed elsewhere in Edwards studies, and throughout he portrayed Edwards as a man with forward-looking vision who was nevertheless firmly planted in the limiting contexts of eighteenth-century American culture. He readily conceded Edwards's shortsightedness on topics such as slavery and Christian ecumenism and acknowledged the restraints of Edwards's theology, which in some ways would hinder future development within evangelical Protestantism. Yet at the same time that he played by the rules of professional history laid out by his mentors in graduate school, he also wrote of Edwards out of a deeply personal and publicly stated sense of vocation. In Edwards's life Marsden identified ways that a Christian could fully engage with the intellectual trends of his time and in doing so make a robust defense of orthodox Christianity. And in Edwards's labors Marsden recognized the potential—indeed, necessity—that he had already laid out in his previous studies, of a thoughtful citizenry willing to participate in spirited intellectual exchange, carried out in common respect and humility, for the betterment of church and community. When asked to comment on the origins of his interest in history and commitment to the profession, Marsden once wrote that his was a quest to search out answers for the fundamentals of human experience especially as they related to the individual's search for rootedness, meaning, and cosmic purpose in a world of rapidly increasing plurality and change. Extending his reflections on his own journey out of a protective religious tradition into the highest levels of academia, he wondered aloud how deeply grounded subcommunities of shared values could survive, let alone flourish, in a modern world that encouraged disjuncture and change, and do so in a mode of constructive negotiation without slipping into a state of kneejerk reaction. And he pondered how these subcultures could "pass on from generation to generation assumptions, beliefs, values . . . peculiar to their own heritage at the same time they [were] constantly being shaped by . . . more common cultural outlooks." In Edwards, a man of strong intellect and moral assurance yet sharp awareness of his times, Marsden seemed to find the answer to this query—which is why he wrote with such conviction.[6]

One of the central tasks of this volume's authors is to assess this conviction as it appears in *all of* Marsden's major books; another is to reflect on its wider significance for the historical profession. *American Evangelicalism: George Marsden and the State of American Religious History* intends to facilitate this process by framing Marsden's work in at least three different contexts. First and foremost, it seeks to assess Marsden's work in light of recent evangelical historiography. No one has done more to shape and mainstream the history of evangelicalism than Marsden, which is why this most vital contribution will receive the most attention by the volume's authors. While recognized as the dean of evangelical history, Marsden has also garnered respect for his general contributions to the development of U.S. religious history. A diverse field encompassing scholars from various disciplines and educational settings (religious studies and American studies as well as history, seminaries and divinity schools as well as universities), U.S. religious history has flourished during the past few decades in part because of the friction created by the collision of interpretations, and in part because of constructive exchange across the fields. By virtue of his lofty position in the study of modern evangelicalism—a particularly charged subject in recent years—Marsden has often found himself in the middle of the collisions and collaborations. His work, therefore, needs to be appraised within these broader encounters. A third context in which Marsden's writings will be appraised is the biggest: as manifestations of good writing. Craftsmanship has always meant as much to Marsden as fresh thinking and sound argumentation. His drive to test new methodologies and literary devices and always write well is thus worthy of attention, and this collection of essays will flesh out those distinctive characteristics of Marsden's prose that allowed him to be such an effective author.

This breadth of interests and range of perspectives should indicate that this volume seeks to be something more than a festschrift, a tribute to one historian's illustrious career. Though we certainly want to honor the efforts of a scholar who has fundamentally altered his discipline—his profession—we as editors and essayists also want to use his writings as a launch for wider discussion about past and future trajectories in the history of evangelicalism and American religion, the challenges and opportunities facing the next wave of religious historians, and the unchanging virtues of good historical writing. Accordingly, we hope that readers from various backgrounds will find this volume profitable, not just as a guide to the historiographical terrain of American evangelicalism, but also as an instructive lens onto the curiosities, ambitions, techniques, and intellectual wherewithal that allowed Marsden to write with such immense authority. In a sense, we want this volume to advance yet another of Marsden's legacies, that of effective teaching.

This volume's structure has been designed with these goals in mind. Each of the book's five sections will use one of Marsden's foundational texts as an entry into specific historical stages in the development of American evangelicalism and religion. Moving chronologically from the eighteenth century to the present, the volume will begin by addressing Marsden's study of Jonathan Edwards in light of the nation's "Puritan beginnings," then shift into the nineteenth century with a look at Marsden's early study of New School Presbyterianism. In the third and fourth sections readers will encounter *Fundamentalism and American Culture* and *The Soul of the American University*. Discussion surrounding the former will open up fresh examination of the late nineteenth and early twentieth centuries, while examination of the latter will facilitate broader discussion about secularization, Protestantism, and education in the mid-twentieth century. The fifth section, titled "Pluralism's Blessing," will use *Reforming Fundamentalism* to trigger examination of evangelicalism in the post–World War II period.

The internal logic of these book sections is meant to enable instruction as well. In each section a "state of the field" essay connects Marsden's profiled work to other voices and studies in the relevant historiography, then a brief "scholarship profile" essay assesses the unique substantive and stylistic qualities of the profiled book. Finally, in each of the five sections, one, two, or three "new directions" essays will build on Marsden's corpus and in some cases explore territory in American religious and evangelical history left untouched by Marsden's scholarship. Marsden certainly laid the foundation for the historical study of fundamentalism and evangelicalism, but (thankfully) he left something for others to say. Some of what can and still needs to be said is suggested in these "new directions" chapters.

The volume then ends with Mark Noll's essay on the trajectory of American religious history since World War II, considering how "an evangelical won the Bancroft Prize," as Marsden did for *Jonathan Edwards: A Life*. To be sure, Marsden has reached the upper echelon of academic religious history by working alongside other outstanding scholars in his field, a few of whom have aided in the publication of this volume, including Jon Butler, Nathan Hatch, Mark Noll, Harry Stout, and Grant Wacker. Others such as Catherine Albanese, Catherine Brekus, Richard Bushman, Joel Carpenter, John Corrigan, Jay Dolan, Marie Griffith, David Hall, Paul Harvey, Brooks Holifield, David Hollinger, Laurie Maffly-Kipp, Martin Marty, Colleen McDannell, John McGreevy, Robert Orsi, Amanda Porterfield, Jonathan Sarna, Leigh Schmidt, Ann Taves, and Thomas Tweed (just to name a few) have advanced American religious history in similarly vital ways by training students and writing critical texts that have challenged us to rethink the place of the sacred in this nation's past.

Yet for various reasons Marsden has managed to carve out a résumé that stands apart. Slightly older than most of his contemporaries on this "who's who" list, he was among the first to create and ride the wave of new interest in U.S. religious history. Besides working on the leading edge of the new religious history, he served as a field general of sorts in guiding the historical study of evangelicalism into the academic mainstream. That he did so with an uncanny sense of timing is notable as well; the publication of *Fundamentalism and American Culture* in 1980, at the dawn of the Reagan Revolution, was not only a godsend for a curious public trying to figure out what was happening in Washington, but also for the young historian himself, who wanted (and needed) to write for a wider audience. Marsden's breadth has also made him a leader. By writing about subjects spanning the eighteenth century to the present, Marsden has managed to converse with religious specialists from across the spectrum, thus enhancing the scope of his influence. Still, however much external circumstances have aided his professional profile, Marsden's exceptional career is something that has been generated from within as a product of his own exceptional abilities. In his concluding essay Noll captures a few of the essential qualities that allowed Marsden to excel in his profession *and* aspire to a higher sense of vocation derived from his deep investment in the Christian life of the mind.

NOTES

1. Robert B. Townsend, "A New Found Religion? The Field Surges among AHA Members," *Perspectives on History* 47 (December 2009), www.historians.org/publications-and-directories/perspectives-on-history/december-2009/a-new-found-religion-the-field-surges-among-aha-members.

2. Jon Butler, respondent in "Religion and the Historical Profession," *The Immanent Frame*, http://blogs.ssrc.org/tif/2009/12/30/religion-and-the-historical-profession/, December 30, 2009.

3. Ibid. See also Darren Dochuk, "Searching Out the Sacred in U.S. Political History," *Perspectives on History* 49 (May 2011): 46–49.

4. George Marsden, "Reflections: Doing American History in a World of Subcultures," *Reviews in American History* 37 (June 2009): 303–14.

5. See George Marsden, "A Truly Multicultural Society," e-mail exchange with Wen Stephenson, *Atlantic Online*, October 2000, www.theatlantic.com/past/docs/issues/2000/10/wolfe-marsden.htm.

6. Marsden, "Reflections," 307.

PART I

PURITAN BEGINNINGS

CHAPTER 1

Jonathan Edwards and the Study of His Eighteenth-Century World

George Marsden's Contribution to Colonial American Religious Historiography

DOUGLAS A. SWEENEY

George Marsden has been working on Jonathan Edwards since the time when this was actually a fashionable pursuit. Two of his first publications treated Perry Miller's views of Edwards's Puritan predecessors and Edwards's controversial legacy in the Presbyterian Church. These appeared in 1970, when Miller, though deceased, continued to haunt the guild at large but *The Works of Jonathan Edwards*, founded by Miller, had nearly stalled.[1] Ironically, in the forty years since Marsden's first book, social historians have managed to banish Miller's ghost from the guild, and dead white males have lost preeminence in "the new religious history," but *The Works of Jonathan Edwards* has succeeded beyond belief, fueling an Edwards renaissance in some of the byways of the discipline that evangelical males like Marsden himself have helped to lead.[2]

Books on Christian intellectuals no longer stand near the cutting edge of any field of study—except theology, of course. But the so-called "evangelical surge" in American academe, combined with Edwards's iconic status among the leaders of the surge, has meant that Marsden and his Edwards have played a powerful role in the guild—cutting against the scholarly grain and teaching hundreds of younger scholars to do the same.[3] Who would have guessed that a biography of a W.A.S.P. clergyman and evangelical theologian, *Jonathan Edwards: A Life*, could have taken the Bancroft Prize in 2004?[4] I will plumb this irony further in the latter part of this essay. First, however, I want to offer a word about a few of the less surprising and more practical contributions of Marsden's Edwards: to scholarship on the life of Edwards since the time of Miller; to the field of Atlantic history; to the study of evangelicals; and to our estimation of the place of Christianity in the rise of the American Revolution.

MODERN EDWARDS SCHOLARSHIP

Most of the leading lives of Edwards published during the twentieth century interpret their subject in tragic terms. Ola Winslow painted Edwards as a detached and lonely leader struggling to nurture true religion with an "outworn dogmatic system." Perry Miller depicted Edwards and his work as "an enigma." Though he "speaks from a primitive religious conception which often seems hopelessly out of touch with even his own day," claimed Miller, "yet at the same time he speaks from an insight into science and psychology so much ahead of his time that our own can hardly be said to have caught up with him." As Miller expounded on this elsewhere, "Part of the tragedy of Edwards is that he expended so much energy upon [a theological] effort that has subsequently fallen into contempt." Miller's Edwards was a genius, a literary artist, stuck in the role of a Calvinist pastor in the hinterlands of New England—a pity, to be sure. Patricia Tracy echoed the theme of Edwards's tragic limitations, though in a somewhat different way, interpreting Edwards's pastoral labors in terms of the conflict she perceived between his own patriarchy and the increasingly democratic aspirations of his people—one that ended in Edwards's ejection from Northampton. "The tragedy of . . . Edwards," she concluded, true to form, "was that he was so clearly a product of the changing patterns of authority and community life in eighteenth-century New England."[5]

Marsden resists this chronic temptation to employ the trope of tragedy. He refuses to rehearse the usual biographical data and then make sense of Edwards's life in terms of his failure to transcend his socio-cultural location and anticipate the advances of later American cultural leaders. "In writing this life of Edwards," he announces early on, "one of my goals has been to understand him as a real person in his own time." Marsden reiterates this goal so often that one can hardly miss it. "Our challenge," he explains, "is to try to step into [Edwards's] world and to understand it in terms that he himself would recognize." Again, "My focus is primarily on understanding Edwards as a person, a public figure, and a thinker in his own time and place."[6] As Marsden reflected on this challenge in another publication, he said it required him to struggle "to get beyond Perry Miller, who simultaneously did the most to promote Edwards studies over the past half century and the most to confuse the issues of biography." Miller's tragic, anachronistic, even presentist life of Edwards, he said, "is to Edwards what Shakespeare's *Hamlet* is to the actual Danish prince—a triumph of the imagination."[7] Marsden's Edwards is a triumph of historical understanding.

Indeed, Marsden meets his goal of placing Edwards back in context better than anyone else before. He helps us enter Edwards's world—physically, mentally, and spiritually—and understand his significance as an eighteenth-century leader. He covers all the usual ground, from Edwards's birth in East Windsor, Connecticut, through his study and teaching at Yale, from his pastorates in New York, Bolton, Connecticut, and Northampton through his move to the Stockbridge mission and short-lived presidency of Princeton. He also provides an expert account of Edwards's revivalism.

Along the way, Marsden brings to life a varied cast of characters who were central to Edwards's life but have often been neglected by other scholars: Jonathan Belcher, for example, a crucial friend and supporter who served as Massachusetts's governor and, later, New Jersey's too, becoming president of the board of trustees of the College of New Jersey (Princeton); Abigail Williams Sergeant Dwight, a cousin and nemesis of Edwards who married his predecessor in Stockbridge (the Rev. John Sergeant), became a leader at the mission, and, after her first husband's death, remarried a judge, politician, and British military officer named Col. Joseph Dwight, who joined her family's opposition to Edwards's ministry; and William Shippen, one of the architects of Princeton's old main (Nassau Hall) and the physician who administered the inoculation for smallpox that led to Edwards's death two months after he had assumed the Princeton presidency.

Marsden also covers new ground. He makes extensive use of Edwards's understudied manuscripts, working most closely with correspondence and filling out our estimation of Edwards's everyday affairs. Especially impressive is Marsden's handling of the military context of Edwards's life on the western edge of English Massachusetts, and with Native American Indians. He aids us in imagining the billeting of soldiers in the Edwards parsonage, the outfitting of Edwards's Stockbridge cabin as a garrison, and Edwards's near obsession with the significance—apocalyptic and otherwise—of British fighting against the Roman Catholic French. He thereby highlights Edwards's remarkable composure as a scholar. And he stresses the worldly importance of Edwards's work with Stockbridge Indians.

"The first goal of a biographer," Marsden stipulates, "should be to tell a good story that illuminates not only the subject, but also the landscapes surrounding that person and the horizons of the readers."[8] Marsden tells a wonderful story, enriching his narrative with a wealth of little-known gems from Edwards's world. He also succeeds in shedding new light on the varied landscapes of Edwards's life, inviting his readers to enter them vicariously.

As he acknowledges in his preface, his ability to do this was enlarged exponentially by *The Works of Jonathan Edwards*. For more than half a century, a team of seasoned scholars and employees of "the Edition" has transcribed, annotated, and introduced Edwards's writings, working in recent years especially with unpublished manuscripts. Read in the past only by those who could decipher Edwards's hand (an extremely difficult task that has left many in despair) and could afford an extended stay at Yale's Beinecke Library, these manuscripts—as published in *The Works of Jonathan Edwards*—have revolutionized the field of Edwards studies. It is not exaggeration, in fact, to assert that Marsden's most significant feat in *Jonathan Edwards* is to have written the first biography that comprehends the massive, critical work of the Yale Edition.

Of course, as Edwards has been placed back into his eighteenth-century world, he has proven less attractive to progressive, modern thinkers. Now that Edwards has been shown to be a man of his own time—a supernaturalist, a biblicist, a Calvinist and revivalist, a patriarchal, hierarchical, slaveholding monarchist—many find it difficult to pay him heed today. In the words of Bruce Kuklick, Edwards was far more serviceable to secular intellectuals when portrayed by Perry Miller as "one of us—close to being an atheist for Niebuhr." But now that Edwards has been unmasked—ironically, by Miller's Yale Edition of his *Works*—his thought "is not likely to compel the attention of intellectuals ever again. Indeed," argues Kuklick, "it is more likely to repel their attention."[9] To disinterested observers Kuklick's claim seems hyperbolic. Large numbers of intellectuals remain intrigued by Edwards. Nonetheless, Kuklick's statement represents a common perception that Marsden's eighteenth-century Edwards is not as useful in the public square as Miller's protomodern, enigmatic, artful Edwards.

THE EIGHTEENTH-CENTURY ATLANTIC WORLD

One of the first things Marsden does as he puts Edwards into the setting of his eighteenth-century world is to broaden our understanding of its geography. "The world into which Edwards was born will make a lot more sense," he suggests, furthermore, "if we think of it as British" (i.e., "rather than American").[10] These moves, along with Marsden's later depictions of that world as an international, cosmopolitan, broadly Protestant world, render Marsden's life of Edwards an important contribution to the most popular form of early modern history: the history of the transatlantic world, or the "Atlantic world."

Atlantic history treats the multilateral contacts and exchanges of the peoples, cultures, and merchants near the Atlantic (in western Africa, Europe, and eastern North and South America).[11] For much of the twentieth century, national boundaries shaped and limited the scope of most history and restricted the frames of reference scholars employed. However, during the past couple of decades, rapid globalization of commerce, culture, and even national politics has yielded globalization in

Western history.¹² This trend has gained so much momentum, in fact, that even Atlantic history is often blamed for being parochial (or insufficiently global). Nevertheless, it continues to shape the field of American history. Eighteenth-century American studies often feature cultural commerce—both voluntary and forced—between the ethnic groups that skirt the planet's second largest ocean.¹³

Marsden's life of Edwards is an Atlantic life of Edwards. It foregrounds the fact that although Edwards never traveled beyond Great Britain's American borders he circled the globe with his mind, pen, and legacy. Marsden highlights Edwards's vast array of foreign correspondence. He explains the global context of Edwards's sense of identity, Christian faith and practice, defense of Calvinist orthodoxy, and work with Native Americans. He shows that Edwards was part of the Anglicization of British America—and gentrification of North America's cultural leadership—during the early eighteenth century.¹⁴ He is careful to note the "British or Old World character" of Edwards's life, "evident," he says, "in its rigid hierarchical structures."¹⁵

Most significantly, perhaps, Marsden demonstrates that Edwards was fully engaged with the Enlightenment, the Christian republic of letters, and the world of Western public discourse.¹⁶ He engaged this world primarily in defense of "the Protestant interest," a phenomenon that Thomas Kidd has done so much to explore.¹⁷ Edwards's cosmopolitanism was clearly not an end in itself; it was part of a larger mission to combat the forces of Antichrist and spread the Protestant gospel through revival and reform. Nevertheless, it was significant. No longer does Edwards represent the isolated, archetypal, national man of letters, heading straight for revolution, transcendentalism, and pragmatism, and adumbrating American exceptionalism. Marsden demonstrates that Edwards's Atlantic world was bigger than that.

MODERN EVANGELICALISM

Marsden also contributes, of course, to the field of evangelical studies, a form of scholarship that he has helped to make a cottage industry. With colleagues Mark Noll, David Bebbington, George Rawlyk, Nathan Hatch, and many others, through the Institute for the Study of American Evangelicals (which Marsden helped to found), through a host of books and articles on nearly every period of American evangelicalism, Marsden has elucidated the transatlantic origins, multifaceted character, and international history of the movement. Marsden's Edwards shines yet more light on its early modern founding.[18]

Most who write about evangelicalism treat the "Great Awakening" of the 1730s and '40s as its matrix, or its catalyst, which birthed or sped the development of its global social network and its spirit of enthusiastic, ecumenical mission. And many tie the Awakening to the ethos of the Enlightenment, suggesting that evangelicals share a uniquely modern history that has played a powerful role in shaping modern American culture.[19] Since the early 1980s, however, this story line has been challenged by several highly regarded scholars, along with the nature—and even existence—of the Awakening itself. Jon Butler, Joseph Conforti, Frank Lambert, and their followers have termed the Great Awakening an "interpretative fiction," a socially constructed way of making sense of the conflict, heat, and chaos of the age. Though diverging over the timing of this evangelical construct, the reasons for its appearance, and the uses to which it was put, they agree that the revivals Edwards did so much to shape were not a unitary phenomenon, a massive work of God, or even a "great and general" working out of common religious concerns. They were a loosely tied assortment, rather, of regional anomalies, reducible to social and physiological explanation. The clergy, who were eager to render a spiritual reading of the wonders all around, invented the Great Awakening concept. It should not be taken literally. And its architects should not be seen as Christian nation builders, clearing the way for modern America—certainly not for "Christian America"—with a tidal wave of personal, evangelical conversions.[20]

Marsden treats the Awakening as a great and general work, indeed a transatlantic movement giving rise to evangelicalism. His Edwards was the movement's most important theologian. He was not, however, a protomodern champion of democracy, or even a progressive, ecumenical evangelical who condoned his movement's interconfessional tendencies, but a Janus-faced member of a conservative, Calvinistic, and imperial state church. "Edwards anticipated some traits of later evangelicals, but the facts that he was a Calvinistic thinker, that he was rigorously intellectual, and that he was working in an eighteenth-century context make him very different from his evangelical heirs."[21] Or as Marsden stated elsewhere, Edwards's evangelicalism "had a paradoxical outlook. . . . Aspects of it reflected Reformed establishmentarianism and cultural imperialism. Other aspects were anti-establishment, subversive, and invited individualism."[22] Marsden's Edwards helped to found the modern evangelical movement. He would not have been happy, though, with the way it evolved in later years. Paradoxically, he lived and led as a servant of Protestant Christendom, even as he contributed to its ultimate dissolution. He was never wholly modern, not a product of the Enlightenment. Neither was his evangelical movement.[23]

RELIGION AND THE RISE OF THE AMERICAN REVOLUTION

Similarly, Edwards never intended to ignite a revolution or to sever ties with Britain. These were "not yet on anyone's horizon" in his day.[24] Edwards himself "was an aristocrat," the scion of "an elite extended family that was part of the ruling class" that ran the bulk of Edwards's world.[25] Such elites were hierarchical, monarchical, and loyal—much as Edwards proved to be. But what if Edwards had survived to see the American Revolution? Would he have joined what other clergy called the "the sacred cause of liberty"? The Rev. John Witherspoon, a Calvinist successor in the presidency of Princeton, signed the Declaration of Independence in 1776, becoming a clerical founding father of the new United States. "Edwards surely would not have played that role," Marsden tells his readers. He "probably" would have summoned a "religious rationale" in support of the revolution, but "he would not have been happy to see spiritual concerns submerged amid the political ardor."[26]

Edwards was not a rebel. Nor was he a politician. This is not to say, however, that he had no part in the social transformations of his day. Since 1966, rather, many have said the opposite, suggesting several ways in which the early evangelicals might have hastened revolution—whether intentionally or not. As they called for true conversion and personal moral accountability, gathered true believers into separated cliques, and gained authority and adherents by addressing common people, they gave pro-revival Protestants a sense of spiritual fellowship, identity, and mission with compatriots in places ranging up and down the seaboard. This camaraderie, moreover, relied on voluntary commitment, not inherited establishments. It undercut the status quo by binding people together in the name of reformation, moral earnestness—a new spiritual order for the ages. It was rooted in older, European calls for reformation. But its patrons thought the Reformation churches needed change, indeed a spiritual revolution that would liberate their members from the tyranny of Satan and complacent culture Protestantism. Its leaders founded the first pan-colonial social movement in Great Britain's American colonies, contributing, some contend, to what Jon Butler calls "the revolution before the revolution."[27]

Marsden's Edwards played a conflicted role in this protorevolution. He was a patriarchal leader who professed that rank in the Kingdom of God depended, not on station, but on spiritual transformation. He was a slave master who trained a generation of abolitionists, a racist who devoted the prime of his life to Native Americans. Refusing to learn their language, teaching them English civilization, he insisted they were his siblings in the global family of God—and were morally superior to many of the English. He was traditional *and* modern, conservative *and* progressive, aristocratic *and* egalitarian. For the sake of an old-time gospel, he promoted religious reform that paved the way for revolution and the ultimate disestablishment of America's state churches. He would not have been pleased to know, however, that New Light evangelicalism would play a role in weakening the cultural force of Calvinism at home and around the world.[28]

MARSDEN'S EIGHTEENTH-CENTURY BRITISH, PROTESTANT, EVANGELICAL, TRAGICOMIC EDWARDS FOR THE AGES

Edwards makes good sense when viewed as an eighteenth-century man. He furthers our understanding of the transatlantic world, its late colonial evangelicals, and their varied, paradoxical, conflicted, and ambivalent relationships to the social transformations of their day. He is not a tragic figure, an ingenious disappointment. He is difficult to assess by later modern moral standards. But when viewed beneath the light of the regnant values of his day, he stands out as a specimen of (imperfect) moral rectitude and intellectual acumen.

He also makes good sense when recommended as a model, not for post-Christian public intellectuals in the West, but for still-Christian leaders of the world's evangelical and Reformed churches and schools. Marsden tenders Edwards's insights to anyone who will listen, but he clearly works the hardest to commend them to believers. "As a biographer," he writes,

> I have been working most directly as a cultural historian. Yet I have been doing this always with an eye on the theological question, taking his thought seriously as part of the larger Christian tradition.... My belief is that one of the uses of being an historian, particularly if one is part of a community of faith, is to help persons of such communities better understand what they and their community might appropriate from the great mentors of the past and what is extraneous and nonessential. Everything is, of course, time-bound and there is a danger for us who are so shaped by historical consciousness to dismiss every authority from the past once we have understood the peculiarities of the historical, personal, or theoretical factors that shaped its outlook. A far more profitable approach is to employ historical consciousness for developing more *discriminating* assessments of the wisdom of the past. The point of historical scholarship should not be, as it so often is today, simply to take things apart, to destroy myths, or to say that what looks simple is really quite complex. It should also be to help people see how to put things back together again. We need to use history for the guidance it offers, learning from great figures in the past—both in their brilliance and in their shortcomings. Otherwise we are stuck with only the wisdom of the present.[29]

Accordingly, though Marsden renders Edwards as a finite, fallen sinner, he also highlights what he takes to be the "wisdom" and the "guidance"

Edwards offers to the ages. He lauds Edwards's handling of the pretensions of the Enlightenment. He shows his own hand as he suggests that "liberal modernity" has always been "tragically flawed, and precisely at the point that Edwards . . . said it was," that is, "in its optimism regarding human nature."[30] Marsden notes that Edwards's Calvinism "put him in a position to critically scrutinize" that optimism. It taught him that the "grand ideal" of his ever "hopeful era"—that "humans would . . . establish on scientific principles a universal system of morality that would bring to an end the destructive conflicts that had plagued human history"—was a chimera at its best, deadly arrogance at worst.[31] Marsden ends his book with a paean to Edwards's modern-Augustinian view of God and the meaning of life, leaving sympathetic Christians cheering the power of Edwards's worldview and confident in learning from this "mentor of the past."[32]

He never apologizes for heralding his Edwards as model. He comes from a neo-Calvinist background in which Christians are taught to claim their basic "epistemic rights" (to think and write in a Christian way) without defending such practices on evidential grounds.[33] He also knows that he has a multitude of evangelical readers who applaud his efforts to write against the modern scholarly grain. They are now a small minority in Western academe. They comprise a large percentage, though, of readers in America, a sizable majority of those who read about Edwards.[34] As Marsden has explained to them in his work on the university, the de-Christianization of Western thought is not inevitable. It started on their watch. They failed to stem the tide of secularism that now pervades the academy. The "outrageous idea of Christian scholarship" still beckons today, however, deserving their noblest efforts and a place at any pluralistic academic table.[35]

Not everyone is convinced. Allen Guelzo has no brief against the idea of Christian scholarship (in principle, at least).[36] But he does oppose what he reckons Marsden's Christian special pleading. He accuses Marsden, ironically, of writing like Perry Miller, using Edwards to promote his own perspective on modernity. His "focus," Guelzo claims, "is not the Edwards of the 18th century," as Marsden has professed, "but the evangelicals of the 21st, with Edwards as a stand-in and marker for them." Much like "Miller's Jonathan Edwards, which was less a biography and more of a tract for neo-orthodox times, Marsden's

Edwards will be remembered," Guelzo guesses patronizingly, "less as a biography and more as a period piece from the 'evangelical surge' in American academic culture."[37]

Douglas Winiarski registers even stronger criticism of Marsden's Christian commendation of Edwards. Like Guelzo, and despite Marsden's protests to the contrary, Winiarski claims that Marsden's Edwards resonates with that of Miller and his allies. He agrees that "Marsden's neo-evangelical reading of Edwards's life" belies his stated goal of placing Edwards back in context. More importantly, however, Winiarski disapproves of using Edwards as "a transhistorical critic of modernity." He finds Marsden's "stern critique" of modern America "troubling." In sum, he complains (with ideological transparency and modernistic prejudice), "Marsden's oblique references to the atrocities of the twentieth century and his palpable contempt for the Enlightenment and its more recent historians unmask the contemporary evangelical concerns that shape *Jonathan Edwards: A Life*."[38]

Marsden surely could have done more to help his critics come to terms with his appreciation of Edwards. His tendency has long been to abstract what is best from the materials he writes about and use it to facilitate his readers' understanding of the nature of reality (or to "help people see how to put things back together again"). As he wrote in the book that put him on the academic map,

> Since God's work appears to us in historical circumstances where imperfect humans are major agents, the actions of the Holy Spirit . . . are always intertwined with culturally conditioned factors. The theologian's task is to try to establish from Scripture criteria for determining what in . . . history . . . is truly the work of the Spirit. The Christian historian takes an opposite, although complementary, approach. While he must keep in mind certain theological criteria, he may refrain from explicit judgments on what is properly Christian while he concentrates on observable cultural forces. By identifying these forces, he provides material which individuals of various theological persuasions may use to help distinguish God's genuine work from practices that have no greater authority than the customs or ways of thinking of a particular time and place.[39]

God's goodness, truth, beauty, and will transcend our social locations but are revealed in mundane history in and through our cultural forms. "So the identification of cultural forces . . . is essentially a constructive enterprise, with the positive purpose of finding the gold among the dross."[40] Marsden finds both gold and dross within the story of Edwards's life. He knows that distinguishing the gold is a largely theological task. He refrains from delving deeply into theological arguments. But he sometimes finds it difficult to refrain from making metahistorical judgments altogether. Though he interprets Edwards in context, as an eighteenth-century man, Marsden is not an antiquarian. He also wants to interpret Edwards's importance for his readers. He is aware that some will blame him for departing from "critical history," or for stepping over the boundary between history and theology.[41] Perhaps, then, he should have skipped his Christian commendation. He would have enjoyed a better reception as a historical interpreter if he had spent more time in tracking Edwards's legacy *through* time, restricting claims about the power of Edwards's Calvinistic worldview to descriptive and indicative forms of argument. Or just perhaps—dare I say it?—if he really thinks that Edwards offers gold, or timeless truth, he should have said so more forthrightly and defended his claims with detailed theological discussion (boundary lines be damned).

No matter what people have thought of Marsden's commendation of Edwards, most agree that he has written a truly masterful biography—the best life of Edwards that has ever been produced. He has contributed immensely to colonial American religious historiography. He has earned the right to portray his subject by his own lights. Marsden may well be the most important historian of American religion at work today. He is certainly our most prominent proponent of Christian scholarship. I, for one, am glad that he has demonstrated the courage of his convictions over the years, calling things (for the most part) completely as he sees them. This is not an easy thing for Christian scholars to do today. Many of us are grateful for his help in the formation of "more discriminating assessments of the wisdom of the past."

As Edwards said to the town of Northampton in a tribute to his grandfather, the Rev. Solomon Stoddard, "It was a great price that God put into your hands, by ordering it to be your lot to live under such a ministry. God was nigh to you; you lived under a burning and shining light."[42] I count it a privilege to have grown up under Marsden's scholarly light.

NOTES

1. George M. Marsden, "Perry Miller's Rehabilitation of the Puritans: A Critique," *Church History* 39 (March 1970): 91–105, and *The Evangelical Mind and the New School Presbyterian Experience: A Case Study of Thought and Theology in Nineteenth-Century America* (New Haven, CT: Yale University Press, 1970). Founded in the early 1950s, the Yale Edition of Edwards's *Works* included barely three volumes by 1970. See Stephen D. Crocco, "Edwards's Intellectual Legacy," in *The Cambridge Companion to Jonathan Edwards*, ed. Stephen J. Stein (New York: Cambridge University Press, 2007), 314–19.

2. On the new religious history, see especially Jay Dolan, "The New Religious History," *Reviews in American History* 15 (September 1987): 449–54; Philip R. VanderMeer and Robert P. Swierenga, eds., *Belief and Behavior: Essays in the New Religious History* (New Brunswick, NJ: Rutgers University Press, 1991); and the spate of state-of-the art discussions published in 1997: Harry S. Stout and D. G. Hart, eds., *New Directions in American Religious History* (New York: Oxford University Press, 1997); David D. Hall, ed., *Lived Religion in America: Toward a History of Practice* (Princeton, NJ: Princeton University Press, 1997); Thomas A. Tweed, ed., *Retelling U.S. Religious History* (Berkeley: University of California Press, 1997); and Charles L. Cohen, "The Post-Puritan Paradigm of Early American Religious History," *William and Mary Quarterly* 54 (October 1997): 695–722. The best record of the Edwards renaissance is M. X. Lesser, *Reading Jonathan Edwards: An Annotated Bibliography in Three Parts, 1729–2005* (Grand Rapids, MI: Eerdmans, 2008). On the role of evangelicals in this renaissance, see also Sean Michael Lucas, "Jonathan Edwards between Church and Academy: A Bibliographic Essay," in *The Legacy of Jonathan Edwards: American Religion and the Evangelical Tradition*, ed. D. G. Hart, Sean Michael Lucas, and Stephen J. Nichols (Grand Rapids, MI: Baker Academic Publishing, 2003), 228–47; Kenneth P. Minkema, "Jonathan Edwards in the Twentieth Century," *Journal of the Evangelical Theological Society* 47 (December 2004): 659–87; and Douglas A. Sweeney, "Evangelical Tradition in America," in Stein, *Cambridge Companion*, 229–32.

3. On the place of Marsden's Edwards in the "evangelical surge," see the critical review of *Jonathan Edwards: A Life* by Allen C. Guelzo, "America's Theologian: Piety and Intellect," *Christian Century*, October 4, 2003, 30–31, 34–35. On the surge itself, consult the work of the Institute on Culture, Religion and

World Affairs (CURA), Boston University, which recently sponsored a two-year project on evangelicals making a difference in the secular academy (and as public intellectuals) directed by Timothy S. Shah and Peter L. Berger (www.bu.edu /cura/projects/evangelicalculture/). See also D. Michael Lindsay, *Faith in the Halls of Power: How Evangelicals Joined the American Elite* (New York: Oxford University Press, 2007), 75–113. Marsden's leadership of this surge is symbolized most famously in his book *The Outrageous Idea of Christian Scholarship* (New York: Oxford University Press, 1997).

4. George M. Marsden, *Jonathan Edwards: A Life* (New Haven, CT: Yale University Press, 2003). Marsden recently published another, shorter biography of Edwards: *A Short Life of Jonathan Edwards*, Library of Religious Biography (Grand Rapids, MI: Eerdmans, 2008). But inasmuch as it is based on his more comprehensive biography, it will not receive a separate treatment here. All references in this essay to Marsden's book, *Jonathan Edwards*, refer to the longer *Jonathan Edwards: A Life*.

5. Ola Elizabeth Winslow, *Jonathan Edwards, 1703–1758: A Biography* (New York: Macmillan, 1940), 325–30; Perry Miller, *Jonathan Edwards*, American Men of Letters Series (New York: William Sloane, 1949), xi, xiii; Perry Miller, introduction to *Images or Shadows of Divine Things by Jonathan Edwards*, ed. Perry Miller (New Haven, CT: Yale University Press, 1948), 25; and Patricia J. Tracy, *Jonathan Edwards, Pastor: Religion and Society in Eighteenth-Century Northampton*, American Century Series (New York: Hill and Wang, 1979), 193–94. This and the following six paragraphs are adapted (loosely) from Douglas A. Sweeney, "A More Discriminating Assessment: George Marsden's Tercentennial Look at Edwards," *Evangelical Studies Bulletin* 20 (Spring 2003): 1–5.

6. Marsden, *Jonathan Edwards*, 2, 4, 6.

7. George M. Marsden, "The Quest for the Historical Edwards: The Challenge of Biography," in *Jonathan Edwards at Home and Abroad: Historical Memories, Cultural Movements, Global Horizons*, ed. David W. Kling and Douglas A. Sweeney (Columbia: University of South Carolina Press, 2003), 6.

8. Marsden, *Jonathan Edwards*, 10.

9. Bruce Kuklick, "Review Essay: An Edwards for the Millennium," *Religion and American Culture: A Journal of Interpretation* 11 (Winter 2001): 117, 116.

10. Marsden, *Jonathan Edwards*, 2.

11. Bernard Bailyn has done more than anyone to promote the concept and study of the Atlantic world, primarily through Harvard's International Seminar on the History of the Atlantic World, 1500–1825, which Bailyn directs, and which was founded in 1995 under the auspices of the Charles Warren Center for Studies in American History. But there have been many other programs, workshops, conferences, and books on the Atlantic world as well, most notably at Johns Hopkins and the Omohundro Institute for the Study of Early American History and Culture. See especially the following introductory, programmatic,

and summative works: Jack P. Greene and Philip D. Morgan, eds., *Atlantic History: A Critical Appraisal*, Reinterpreting History (Oxford: Oxford University Press, 2008); Bernard Bailyn, *Atlantic History: Concept and Contours* (Cambridge, MA: Harvard University Press, 2005); Toyin Falola and Kevin D. Roberts, eds., *The Atlantic World, 1450–2000*, Blacks in the Diaspora (Bloomington: Indiana University Press, 2008); Douglas Egerton, Alison Games, Kris Lane, and Donald R. Wright, *The Atlantic World: A History, 1400–1888* (Wheeling, IL: Harlan Davidson, 2007); David Armitage and Michael J. Braddick, eds., *The British Atlantic World, 1500–1800*, 2nd ed. (New York: Palgrave Macmillan, 2009); William O'Reilly, "Genealogies of Atlantic History," *Atlantic Studies* 1, no. 1 (2004): 66–84; Nicholas Canny, "Writing Atlantic History; or Reconfiguring the History of Colonial British America," *Journal of American History* 86 (December 1999): 1093–1114; Wayne Bodle, "Atlantic History Is the New 'New Social History,'" *William and Mary Quarterly* 64 (January 2007): 203–20; Alison Games, "Atlantic History: Definitions, Challenges, and Opportunities," *American Historical Review* 111 (June 2006): 741–57; and Peter Coclanis, "Atlantic World or Atlantic/World?" *William and Mary Quarterly* 63 (October 2006): 725–42.

12. Thomas Bender, ed., *Rethinking American History in a Global Age* (Berkeley: University of California Press, 2002).

13. On the state of the conversation regarding eighteenth-century America, see Michael V. Kennedy and William G. Shade, eds., *The World Turned Upside-Down: The State of Eighteenth-Century American Studies at the Beginning of the Twenty-First Century* (Bethlehem, PA: Lehigh University Press, 2001), which emerged from a series of symposia led by the Lawrence Henry Gipson Institute for Eighteenth-Century Studies, Lehigh University.

14. On Anglicization, gentrification, and the rise of a culture of mass consumption in Edwards's day, see especially Richard Bushman, *The Refinement of America: Persons, Houses, Cities* (New York: Vintage Books, 1993); Cary Carson, Ronald Hoffman, and Peter J. Albert, eds., *Of Consuming Interests: The Style of Life in the Eighteenth Century* (Charlottesville: University Press of Virginia, 1994); Mark Peterson, "Puritanism and Refinement in Early New England: Reflections on Communion Silver," *William and Mary Quarterly*, 3rd ser., 63 (April 2001): 304–46; and T. H. Breen, *The Marketplace of Revolution: How Consumer Politics Shaped American Independence* (New York: Oxford University Press, 2004).

15. Marsden, *Jonathan Edwards*, 2–3.

16. The notion that Christians like Edwards participated in the Enlightenment and the storied republic of letters may sound strange to some readers, but it, too, finds support in recent work on the Enlightenment, which many are now discovering had an important religious dimension. See, for example, B. W. Young, *Religion and Enlightenment in Eighteenth-Century England: Theological Debate from Locke to Burke* (Oxford: Clarendon Press, 1998), which deals with what

its author labels "England's peculiarly clerical Enlightenment" (2); Helena Rosenblatt, "The Christian Enlightenment," in *Enlightenment, Reawakening and Revolution, 1660–1815*, ed. Stewart J. Brown and Timothy Tackett, Cambridge History of Christianity 7 (Cambridge: Cambridge University Press, 2006), 283–301; Constance M. Furey, *Erasmus, Contarini, and the Religious Republic of Letters* (Cambridge: Cambridge University Press, 2006), which focuses on the early sixteenth century but argues that the republic of letters was never entirely secular; Susan Manning and Francis D. Cogliano, eds., *The Atlantic Enlightenment*, Ashgate Series in Nineteenth-Century Transatlantic Studies (Aldershot: Ashgate, 2008), which interprets the Enlightenment in terms of Atlantic history and includes a brief discussion of the "Christian Enlightenment" (61); and David Sorkin, *The Religious Enlightenment: Protestants, Jews, and Catholics from London to Vienna*, Jews, Christians, and Muslims from the Ancient to the Modern World (Princeton, NJ: Princeton University Press, 2008), which presents "an Enlightenment spectrum that, by including the religious Enlightenment, complicates our understanding of belief's critical and abiding role in modern culture" (314).

17. See Thomas S. Kidd, *The Protestant Interest: New England after Puritanism* (New Haven, CT: Yale University Press, 2004), which began as a dissertation under Marsden at Notre Dame. On this theme, see also Carla Gardina Pestana, *Protestant Empire: Religion and the Making of the British Atlantic World* (Philadelphia: University of Pennsylvania Press, 2009), esp. 159–217. Though Pestana's book is far more rudimentary than Kidd's, she too stresses the importance of the Protestant comradeship, anti-Catholicism, and eschatological rhetoric that accompanied and succeeded England's "Glorious Revolution" (a Protestant designation)—playing a powerful role in shaping Atlantic history in Edwards's day.

18. For just a sampling of the work on evangelicals in Edwards's eighteenth-century Atlantic world, see David Hempton, *Methodism: Empire of the Spirit* (New Haven, CT: Yale University Press, 2005); Mark A. Noll, *The Rise of Evangelicalism: The Age of Edwards, Whitefield, and the Wesleys*, History of Evangelicalism (Downers Grove, IL: InterVarsity Press, 2003); Kling and Sweeney, *Jonathan Edwards*; Mark A. Noll, David W. Bebbington, and George A. Rawlyk, eds., *Evangelicalism: Comparative Studies of Popular Protestantism in North America, the British Isles, and Beyond, 1700–1900* (New York: Oxford University Press, 1994); George A. Rawlyk and Mark A. Noll, eds., *Amazing Grace: Evangelicalism in Australia, Britain, Canada, and the United States* (Montreal: McGill-Queen's University Press, 1994); Frank Lambert, *Pedlar in Divinity: George Whitefield and the Transatlantic Revivals, 1737–1770* (Princeton, NJ: Princeton University Press, 1994); Michael J. Crawford, *Seasons of Grace: Colonial New England's Revival Tradition in Its British Context* (New York: Oxford University Press, 1991); Harry S. Stout, *The Divine Dramatist: George Whitefield and the Rise of Modern*

Evangelicalism (Grand Rapids, MI: Eerdmans, 1991); and Susan O'Brien, "A Transatlantic Community of Saints: The Great Awakening and the First Evangelical Network, 1735–1755," *American Historical Review* 91 (October 1986): 811–32. On the Institute for the Study of American Evangelicals, see the organization's website (http://isae.wheaton.edu/).

19. For the most sophisticated version of this story line, see D. W. Bebbington, *Evangelicalism in Modern Britain: A History from the 1730s to the 1980s* (London: Unwin Hyman, 1989); and Mark A. Noll, *America's God: From Jonathan Edwards to Abraham Lincoln* (New York: Oxford University Press, 2002). But note that Noll (along with Bebbington and nearly everyone else who works in the field of American religious history in the academy) opposes the argument that America was founded as an officially Christian nation. See Mark A. Noll, Nathan O. Hatch, and George M. Marsden, *The Search for Christian America* (Westchester, IL: Crossway Books, 1983).

20. See especially Jon Butler, "Enthusiasm Described and Decried: The Great Awakening as Interpretative Fiction," *Journal of American History* 69 (October 1982): 305–25; Joseph Conforti, *Jonathan Edwards, Religious Tradition, and American Culture* (Chapel Hill: University of North Carolina Press, 1995); Frank Lambert, *Inventing the "Great Awakening"* (Princeton, NJ: Princeton University Press, 1999); and Allen C. Guelzo, "God's Designs: The Literature of the Colonial Revivals of Religion, 1735–1760," in Stout and Hart, *New Directions*, 141–72, who discusses this revision in its historiographical context.

21. Marsden, *Jonathan Edwards*, 4.

22. Marsden, "Quest," 9.

23. Here Marsden departs from his colleague David Bebbington's well-known argument that evangelicalism "was created by the Enlightenment." Bebbington, *Evangelicalism in Modern Britain*, 74.

24. Marsden, *Jonathan Edwards*, 2.

25. Ibid., 3.

26. Ibid., 498. See also Marsden, "Quest," 11–12, in which he reiterates his argument that Edwards "was an eighteenth-century British provincial aristocrat—a slaveholding Tory hierarchist—whose social views need to be understood according to the standards of his own day. Modern readers can be put off by his attitudes because they want him to be more of a post-Revolutionary American. Yet his untimely death in 1758 meant that he was entirely a pre-Revolutionary. True, one can find in Edwards the roots of more popular views—such as his spiritual egalitarianism. It is also true that his immediate successors, such as Samuel Hopkins and Jonathan Edwards Jr., turned his theology to the cause of antislavery. It is fair enough to point out these potentialities. Yet we also need to exercise the historical imagination to understand Edwards as a man of his own time, and we should not impose the standards of our time on people of his era."

27. Jon Butler, *Becoming America: The Revolution before 1776* (Cambridge, MA: Harvard University Press, 2000). Alan Heimert and Harry Stout (a student of Marsden at Calvin College) have been the most important proponents of the notion that evangelicals and their so-called Great Awakening paved a way for revolution, though many other scholars have contributed as well to what has become a rich discussion of these issues. See especially Alan Heimert, *Religion and the American Mind, from the Great Awakening to the Revolution* (Cambridge, MA: Harvard University Press, 1966); William McLoughlin, "The Role of Religion in the Revolution: Liberty of Conscience and Cultural Cohesion in the New Nation," in *Essays on the American Revolution*, ed. Stephen G. Kurtz and James H. Hutson (Chapel Hill: University of North Carolina Press, 1973), 197–255; Nathan O. Hatch, *The Sacred Cause of Liberty: Republican Thought and the Millennium in Revolutionary New England* (New Haven, CT: Yale University Press, 1977); Rhys Isaac, *The Transformation of Virginia: Community, Religion, and Authority, 1740–1790* (Chapel Hill: University of North Carolina Press, 1982); John Murrin, "No Awakening, No Revolution? More Counterfactual Speculations," *Reviews in American History* 11 (June 1983): 161–71; Ruth H. Bloch, *Visionary Republic: Millennial Themes in American Thought, 1756–1800* (New York: Cambridge University Press, 1985); Harry S. Stout, *The New England Soul: Preaching and Religious Culture in Colonial New England* (New York: Oxford University Press, 1986); Nathan O. Hatch, *The Democratization of American Christianity* (New Haven, CT: Yale University Press, 1989); Stout, *Divine Dramatist*; Gordon Wood, *The Radicalism of the American Revolution* (New York: Vintage Books, 1993); Susan Juster, *Disorderly Women: Sexual Politics and Evangelicalism in Revolutionary New England* (Ithaca, NY: Cornell University Press, 1994); Guelzo, "God's Designs"; Gordon S. Wood, "Religion and the American Revolution," in Stout and Hart, *New Directions*, 173–205; Philip Goff, "Revivals and Revolution: Historiographic Turns since Alan Heimert's *Religion and the American Mind*," *Church History* 67 (December 1998): 695–721; and Noll, *America's God*. On the roots of evangelicalism in Europe's reformations, see especially Michael A. G. Haykin and Kenneth J. Stewart, eds., *The Emergence of Evangelicalism: Exploring Historical Continuities* (Nottingham: Apollos, 2008), a volume of essays that respond to Bebbington's claim that evangelicalism sprang from the Enlightenment.

28. For more on Edwards's ambivalent roles in antislavery and Indian missions, see Marsden, *Jonathan Edwards*, 255–58, 375–431, and the following work, much of which Marsden used in his biography: Kenneth P. Minkema, "Jonathan Edwards on Slavery and the Slave Trade," *William and Mary Quarterly* 54 (October 1997): 823–34, and "Jonathan Edwards's Defense of Slavery," *Massachusetts Historical Review* 4 (2002): 23–59; Charles E. Hambrick-Stowe, "All Things Were New and Astonishing: Edwardsian Piety, the New Divinity, and Race," in Kling and Sweeney, *Jonathan Edwards*, 121–36; Kenneth P. Minkema

and Harry S. Stout, "The Edwardsean Tradition and the Antislavery Debate, 1740–1865," *Journal of American History* 92 (June 2005): 47–74; Rachel Wheeler, "'Friends to Your Souls': Jonathan Edwards' Indian Pastorate and the Doctrine of Original Sin," *Church History* 72 (December 2003): 736–65; Rachel Wheeler, "Lessons from Stockbridge: Jonathan Edwards and the Stockbridge Indians," in *Jonathan Edwards at 300: Essays on the Tercentenary of His Birth*, ed. Harry S. Stout, Kenneth P. Minkema, and Caleb J. D. Maskell (Lanham, MD: University Press of America, 2005), 131–40; Rachel M. Wheeler, "Edwards as Missionary," in Stein, *Cambridge Companion*, 196–214; and Rachel Wheeler, *To Live upon Hope: Mohicans and Missionaries in the Eighteenth-Century Northeast* (Ithaca, NY: Cornell University Press, 2008).

29. Marsden, *Jonathan Edwards*, 502.

30. Ibid., 458.

31. Ibid., 471.

32. Ibid., 504–5. For more of Marsden's commendation of Edwards's insights to his readers, see George M. Marsden, "Jonathan Edwards in the Twenty-First Century," in Stout, Minkema, and Maskell, *Jonathan Edwards at 300*, 152–64, where he responds to the question, "What can we learn from Jonathan Edwards today?"

33. Alvin Plantinga and Nicholas Wolterstorff, longtime colleagues of Marsden, have performed the heavy lifting for neo-Calvinists who want to claim their epistemic rights to practice scholarship from an unapologetically Christian perspective. See esp. Alvin Plantinga and Nicholas Wolterstorff, eds., *Faith and Rationality: Reason and Belief in God* (Notre Dame, IN: University of Notre Dame Press, 1983); and Alvin Plantinga, *Warranted Christian Belief* (New York: Oxford University Press, 2000). Marsden fleshes out his neo-Calvinist view of history (and Christian scholarship generally) in George Marsden and Frank Roberts, eds., *A Christian View of History?* (Grand Rapids, MI: Eerdmans, 1975); George Marsden, "Common Sense and the Spiritual Vision of History," in *History and Historical Understanding*, ed. C. T. McIntire and R. A. Wells (Grand Rapids, MI: Eerdmans, 1984), 55–68; and Marsden, *Outrageous Idea*.

34. On evangelical interest in Edwards, see Lucas, "Jonathan Edwards," 228–47; Minkema, "Jonathan Edwards in the Twentieth Century," 659–87; R. Bryan Bademan, "The Edwards of History and the Edwards of Faith," *Reviews in American History* 34 (June 2006): 131–49; and Sweeney, "Evangelical Tradition in America," 229–32.

35. George M. Marsden and Bradley J. Longfield, eds., *The Secularization of the Academy* (New York: Oxford University Press, 1992); George M. Marsden, *The Soul of the American University: From Protestant Establishment to Established Nonbelief* (New York: Oxford University Press, 1994); and Marsden, *Outrageous Idea*.

36. Guelzo himself is a Christian scholar who has commended Edwards's labors—and his theological legacy—in a number of publications, such as Sang Hyun Lee and Allen C. Guelzo, eds., *Edwards in Our Time: Jonathan Edwards and the Shaping of American Religion* (Grand Rapids, MI: Eerdmans, 1999), vii, 87–110; and Douglas A. Sweeney and Allen C. Guelzo, eds., *The New England Theology: From Jonathan Edwards to Edwards Amasa Park* (Grand Rapids, MI: Baker Academic Publishing, 2006), 13–24.

37. Guelzo, "America's Theologian," 34, 35.

38. Douglas L. Winiarski, "Seeking Synthesis in Edwards Scholarship," *William and Mary Quarterly* 61 (January 2004): 139–40.

39. George M. Marsden, *Fundamentalism and American Culture*, 2nd ed. (New York: Oxford University Press, 2006), 502, 260.

40. Ibid., 260.

41. See especially Bruce Kuklick, "On Critical History," in *Religious Advocacy and American History*, ed. Bruce Kuklick and D. G. Hart (Grand Rapids, MI: Eerdmans, 1997), 54–64, who argues that a naturalistic notion of critical thought stands "at the core of history as a humanistic pursuit today—for secular liberals, for postmodernists, and for Christians. For Christian scholars it has been a pact with the devil necessary for them to have any credit in the scholarly community, and it has brought about bad faith. On the one hand, Christian scholars must, at bottom, reject the secularism that the critical conception now entails. Yet, on the other, they will get themselves laughed out of the profession unless they adopt a vision of history that they do not believe. They think that their convictions lend some special insight into the study of the past—for them history is, after all, in some measure the revelation of the divine and the eschaton is part of it. But how are Christians to show this? How can they show how God peeps through in history? If Christian convictions lend no such insight, if they are not cashed out, they are worthless" (58–59).

42. Jonathan Edwards, "Living Unconverted under an Eminent Means of Grace," in Jonathan Edwards, *Sermons and Discourses, 1723–1729*, ed. Kenneth P. Minkema, *The Works of Jonathan Edwards*, vol. 14 (New Haven, CT: Yale University Press, 1997), 367.

CHAPTER 2

Jonathan Edwards: A Life

THOMAS S. KIDD

In 1808, in the midst of the Second Great Awakening, the *Connecticut Evangelical Magazine and Religious Intelligencer* offered its readers a biographical sketch of Jonathan Edwards, the great theologian and revivalist of the First Great Awakening. Edwards, the author remarked, was "endowed with powers of mind that are rarely exceeded." But his intellectual capabilities were not what made him great. "His greatest praise was, that he employed these talents to the noblest purpose, that of doing good."[1] To the "New Divinity" publishers of the *Connecticut Evangelical Magazine*, however, it was important to show that Edwards was a fervent but moderate evangelical, not like the wild-eyed, uneducated Baptist and Methodist itinerants loose in early nineteenth-century America. Edwards's sermons were "familiar to the most common understanding, without descending beneath the dignity of the pulpit, or debasing the subject by vulgarity of style." No yelling and gesticulating came from Edwards, for "he had but little gesture—his voice was not strong—his enunciation was distinct and clear.... His manner was grave and solemn, yet easy, natural and animated."[2] Although some itinerants and converts at the time of the First Great Awakening were "undoubtedly led away by enthusiasm," which became an "occasion of reproach" to the movement, Edwards focused on distinguishing "real conversion from counterfeits" and helped save the revivals from the radical abyss.[3]

Since his death in 1758, biographers have put Jonathan Edwards's thought and life to many uses. Americans seemingly have an insatiable appetite for biography, and Edwards is in the second rank of our most popular and enduring American subjects (several founding fathers, as well as Abraham Lincoln, have commanded the interest of many more writers). Nevertheless, Edwards has consistently generated his share of attention since his untimely death in 1758. In recent years, scholarly interest in Edwards has seen quite a renaissance, capped by the recent completion of Yale University Press's monumental *Works of Jonathan Edwards* series, the opening of the Jonathan Edwards Center at Yale University and its online resource collection, and the publication of George Marsden's biography, *Jonathan Edwards: A Life* (2003).

Religious biographers, like the writer for the *Connecticut Evangelical Magazine*, almost always use their subject to advocate, at least subtly, for a contemporary issue or position. But that is not unique, as political and intellectual biographers often do the same, using significant life stories to frame a "usable past." Biographers of religious figures, and religious historians in general, do face a special quandary, however, as they contend with the theological truth-claims made by their subjects. Those theological precepts are viewed as irrelevant, impossible to verify, and out of bounds in academia by many scholars. Although Marsden himself has routinely encouraged historians of faith to operate within the rules of the "guild" and not write providential history, religious biography still implicitly pressures a writer to assess the views held by the subject.[4]

While there are many ways that historians might assess theological beliefs, from relative silence to explicit evaluation, objective description no longer seems a tenable option. Professional historians still endorse the standard of fairness in their writing, but "objectivity" is widely viewed as a rhetorical posture rather than an intellectual reality. When someone like Jonathan Edwards makes precise religious assertions, his biographer must, at some level, contend with whether he or she accepts the subject's ideas, and to what extent and purposes. The special character of theological knowledge puts this enterprise in a different category than, say, evaluating the merits of Abraham Lincoln's views on the Constitution. Although historians often do assess the social effects of religious beliefs, or the logical consistency of them, their ultimate veracity cannot be tested in conventional ways. Edwards, for instance, said that only people with faith in Christ go to heaven, but we cannot demonstrate whether this is the case. We can only believe so, or not.

Because of the epistemological conundrums posed by the history of religion, recent Edwards biographers have become more sensitive to audience in a way that eighteenth- and nineteenth-century writers were not. Twentieth- and early twenty-first century religious biographers must negotiate in a particular way the tensions between an audience of the faithful and a scholarly audience, although there is always some overlap between the two. Academic Christian historians like Marsden gravitate toward subjects like Edwards partly out of religious interest and conviction, but in the "pragmatic academy," like the larger public sphere, one can no longer promote Edwards on the basis that he brilliantly explicated the truths of revealed religion.[5] The authority supporting that argument is not shared by much of the academic audience but is widely accepted by the audience of the faithful.

Historically, Edwards's biographers have mostly fallen into one of four categories: first, those writers who commended him as a man of faith and unique insight into scriptural truth; second, those who found Edwards and his Calvinism deplorable and regressive; third, those who admired some of Edwards's characteristics or the implications of his views but who did not accept his Calvinist theology; and fourth, those like Marsden who believed that Edwards's theology best accounted for the human condition, implying (but not arguing) that the Calvinist system is likely to be true. The first two approaches, which we might call "biblicist" and "Progressive," respectively, have long since fallen out of favor in the academy. The third approach, which we might call "neo-orthodox" because of the theological movement that helped inspire it, chiefly generated the scholarly renaissance in Edwards studies. The fourth approach, which one might call "Reformed academic," has been pioneered by Marsden and other Christian historians who publish with mainstream academic presses. While these Christian historians have demonstrated that one need not hide one's faith commitments in the academy if one accepts the pragmatic rules of the scholarly game, Marsden's advocacy of Christian perspectives in the postmodern academy also opens new possibilities for bridging the gap between scholarly and religious audiences.

Eighteenth- and nineteenth-century American biographers of Edwards, the "biblicists," largely did not face the problem of audience and religious biography because they assumed that most of their scholarly readers also possessed Christian faith. Many prominent colleges retained direct ties with supporting denominations, and many of the most learned public figures were pastors. Edwards's disciple Samuel Hopkins wrote the first biography of Edwards, *The Life and Character of the Late Reverend Mr. Jonathan Edwards* (1765), and understandably painted his mentor as both intellectually powerful and faithful. Just as Hopkins became consumed with defending theological Calvinism against surging Arminianism, so did Edwards possess "remarkable strength of mind, clearness of thought, and depth of penetration" and labor "to vindicate the great doctrines of Christianity." But Edwards's "zeal for God" and "universal obedience" matched his philosophical greatness.[6] Hopkins hoped that by publishing his life and works, "others may hereby be directed and excited to go and do likewise."[7] Hopkins's Edwards served to edify the evangelical Calvinist movement that he helped found.

Edwards's great-grandson Sereno Edwards Dwight took Edwards's reputation to new heights of fame in his *Life of President Edwards* (1829), which established the view of Edwards as a wilderness savant providentially chosen by God to revive the languishing churches and defend key Christian tenets. Although Edwards was "born in an obscure colony in the midst of a wilderness . . . , he discovered, and unfolded, a system of the divine moral government so new, so clear, so full, that . . . it has at length constrained a reluctant world to bow in homage to its truth," Dwight wrote.[8] Dwight's memoir elevated Edwards above all his contemporaries, not only as the chief luminary of the Great Awakening, but as a saint with no equal since the apostolic era. "We know of no writer, since the days of the Apostles, who has better comprehended the WORD OF GOD."[9] Moreover, "We can probably select no individual, of all who have lived in that long period, who has manifested a more ardent or elevated piety towards God . . . one, who gave the concentrated strength of all his powers, more absolutely, to the one end of glorifying God in the salvation of Man."¹⁰ Dwight's reverential biography helped to turn Edwards into a major cultural icon and to invent an Edwardsian theological tradition. By the time that Joseph Tracy published his monumental *The Great Awakening* (1841), it had become conventional to view Edwards, along with George Whitefield, as a chief architect of the "Great Awakening." He had "done more than any other man to awaken the ministry and the churches . . . , and to produce the movement which had now become general," Tracy wrote.¹¹

That Edwardsian Calvinist tradition fell on harder times in the late nineteenth century, as New England theological critics began to abandon Calvinism. Oliver Wendell Holmes Sr., in a biographical essay on Edwards, ridiculed Edwards's defense of the doctrine of original sin, which asserted that all mankind shared in Adam's transgression. "Edwards's system," Holmes wrote, "seems, in the light of to-day, to the last degree barbaric, mechanical, materialistic, [and] pessimistic."¹² Even though Holmes's father had been a Calvinist minister, Holmes declared that "after long smothering in the sulphurous atmosphere of [Edwards's] thought one cannot help asking, Was this or anything like this . . . the accepted belief of any considerable part of Protestantism?" Edwards's thought served to "diabolize the Deity."¹³

But many post–Civil War New Englanders, even those who rejected Calvinism, still cast the Puritans as the original Americans, who valued hard work, discipline, and intellectual rigor. Episcopal theology professor Alexander Allen produced the chief post–Civil War biography of Edwards in 1889. The charitably critical Allen recommended Edwards's stunning intellectual powers, "whatever we may think of his theology."¹⁴ Edwards represented the hardy, active character that made New Englanders, and the Christian West in general, so successful: "He represents the concentrated vitality and aggressiveness of the occidental peoples,—of the Anglo-Saxon race in particular, of which he was a consummate flower blossoming in a new world."¹⁵ To Allen, Edwards possessed remarkable insights into God's character, but his Calvinist emphases on depravity and judgment were lingering falsehoods inherited from his Puritan forebears. Take away the Calvinism, however, and there would "remain an imperishable element which points to the reality of the divine existence, and of the revelation of God to the world."[16] Anticipating the interpretation of historian Perry Miller, Allen painted Edwards as a "forerunner" of the New England transcendental school in his elaboration of a universe suffused with God's glory. Edwards represented a crucial step in theological progress, but the "great wrong which Edwards did, which haunts us as an evil dream throughout his writings, was to assert God at the expense of humanity."[17] Allen's Edwards was a key figure in the rise of a new Christian theological liberalism.

By the time of Allen's biography, critics began to divide between those who saw Edwards as salvageable despite his Calvinism (many of those would soon be affiliated with the "neo-orthodox" movement), and those who dismissed Edwards as fatally flawed because of that theology (the "Progressives"). Many historians of the Progressive Era saw American history as a slow crawl toward democracy and power for the common man. The Puritans stood in the way of democratic progress and foisted an arcane, oppressive theocratic system on the people. Jonathan Edwards, in this view, was the chief proponent of one of history's most antidemocratic creeds, Calvinism. In retrospect, it is striking to note how confidently the Progressives denounced Edwards on theological grounds—his theology presented such a negative image of man that it simply could not be true. Although Edwards's mystical streak and evangelical individualism seemed to portend a better outcome, Progressive historian Vernon Parrington argued, his acceptance of the doctrine of God's sovereignty "led [him] back to an absolutist past, rather than forward to a more liberal future."[18] With "grotesque" logic, Edwards defended predestination, but the Calvinist system was "doomed." "It might still remain as an evil genius to darken the conscience of men and women; but its authoritative appeal was gone," Parrington wrote.[19] Edwards's vivid defense of Calvinism actually hastened its demise by highlighting its morbid irrationality. To Parrington, Edwards was a tragic, conflicted figure, who devoted his "noble gifts to the thankless task of re-imprisoning the mind of New England."[20]

Ola Winslow's Pulitzer Prize–winning biography *Jonathan Edwards, 1703–1758* (1940) dwelt less than other Progressive histories on Edwards's theological deficiencies but still saw Edwards as a man of massive but undeveloped potential. Winslow admired Edwards for how he simultaneously crafted a new theological system and inspired a popular religious movement. He dignified the individual religious experiences of the people. But he led his individualistic spiritual movement by speaking in the idiom of "an outworn, dogmatic system." Calvinism, in Winslow's estimation, "needed to be demolished, most of it thrown away." She wondered why "he could not take the one more step and be free."[21] Her implicit confidence in a benevolent God and noble human beings required no argument. "God must be made more kind and man more worthy,"[22] and so Arminianism inevitably dominated post-Revolutionary evangelicalism. Progressives like Winslow took it as self-evident that Calvinism was not true and that Edwards's uncritical acceptance of it seriously hindered "his greatness as an original thinker."[23]

Although Winslow's biography met with great critical acclaim, it also came toward the end of the Progressive critics' dominance of American historical studies. Even before Winslow's biography, other historians had begun to advance a more charitable assessment of Edwards, including his Calvinism. Many of these historians were inspired by the neo-orthodox theological movement, which tried to reassert the doctrines of sin, inherent human depravity, and a God-centered universe. Some of these historians were believers themselves, while others did not believe but considered themselves fellow travelers with the neo-orthodox. The most celebrated of the latter writers was Perry Miller, the great historian of the American Puritans and the author of the compelling but flawed *Jonathan Edwards* (1949).

Miller's Edwards was a lonely prodigy, grasping as a teenager all the implications of Locke, Newton, and their revolutionary thoughts on science and psychology. To Miller, Edwards "grasped in a flash" the challenge of the Enlightenment to theology and proclaimed sober realism in the face of the cheery individualism emerging in America. No one understood these things like the backwoods genius Edwards.[24]

Miller's Edwards dealt fearlessly with the tragedies and ironies of human existence in a way that liberal individualists never could. This conviction led Miller to include a remarkable, if somewhat opaque, personal reflection on Edwards's brilliance in showing that we are not in control and are not self-made people. The "lust for selfhood insists that men are good or bad according as they do, and wants them praised or blamed proportionably. . . . Arminian rationalism—we would call it liberalism—tries to haggle with life, to purchase life piecemeal; it has no resources for coping with the prospect that God may 'incline to suffer that which is unharmonious in itself, for the promotion of universal harmony,' and when it can no longer ignore the unharmonious, its fabric of experience is shattered. This is sin, the *original* sin."[25] Miller's Edwards was an isolated prophet raging against the pretensions of emergent American culture.

Miller was also general editor of the *Works of Jonathan Edwards* project at Yale University. This series dramatically changed the study of Edwards for a new generation of scholars, beginning with the 1957 publication of *Freedom of the Will* and ending in 2008 with the twenty-sixth and final volume in the series. As Douglas Sweeney points out in his essay in this volume, this collection made available not only scholarly editions of Edwards's published writings but also great numbers of manuscript writings that had languished largely unused. Prior to their publication, many of these required not only a special trip to the archives but the deciphering of Edwards's tiny, inscrutable writing.

Marsden's biography was the most significant scholarly fruit grown from the new soil of *The Works*. Miller and others simply could not have gotten the full picture of Edwards's thought and writing made accessible by these volumes. To his credit, Marsden read widely and diligently in *The Works of Jonathan Edwards* to prepare his book. His biography does not simply synthesize the conclusions of other historians, although one can certainly see the influence of voluminous books and dissertations on Edwards and his world. Marsden dedicated the book "to a generation of Edwards scholars who made this work possible." But Marsden also read Edwards afresh and helped locate him in the eighteenth-century context on a scale that no other scholar had done.

Unlike Miller's biography, which saw Edwards as the isolated genius, Marsden's presented Edwards as heavily influenced by his eighteenth-century setting. Marsden specifically contrasted his approach with that of Miller, "who let his creativity get the best of him in his biography of Edwards."[26] Marsden presented Edwards as a brilliant, yet often typical thinker of eighteenth-century Anglo-America. This context helps explain some of Edwards's perspectives that may seem peculiar now but were common in his time. To cite only two examples, Edwards held views of slavery and Roman Catholicism that may strike even his most ardent admirers as unfortunate and outdated. Edwards typically owned a household slave and believed that the Bible accepted the institution of slavery. There was no direct hint that the Bible condemned slavery, even in Christ's revolutionary moral teachings. The Apostle Paul told slaves to obey their masters, not to rebel against them or to seek their freedom. Edwards expressed concerns about the immorality of slavery *as practiced* in the Atlantic world but did not object to slavery itself.

Similarly, Edwards indulged a conventional but virulent hatred for Roman Catholicism, bred in the imperial wars of the eighteenth century. He identified Catholicism with Antichrist and read the news with an eye toward events signaling the coming apocalyptic destruction of the papacy and its associated political powers, especially France and Spain. He also studied biblical prophecy to try and discern when Catholicism would fall, setting the stage for the eventual return of Christ. In holding these views, Edwards was nothing special: most New England pastors (as well as many in Britain) agreed with him, including his archrival Charles Chauncy, with whom he sparred over the legitimacy of the Great Awakening.

Marsden's Edwards is also fully human. He is given not only to unappealing views on slavery and Catholicism but to personal failings, and yes, even to sin. He especially struggles with vanity, arrogance, and impatience. He did not care for those less committed than him to the cause of revival and Reformed Christianity. Even as a student at Yale he was unpopular, showing trademark irritation with the frivolity of others. These qualities made Edwards a relatively poor pastor, which in time bore ill fruit, as he tried to change his grandfather Solomon Stoddard's open standards for admission to church membership. He so bungled the affair that he got dismissed from the Northampton pastorate. His deep religious principles gave him tunnel vision and an inability to concede to tradition or the sensibilities of his congregants.

Ironically, Marsden's flawed Edwards may prove of greater value to devout readers than a more hagiographical portrait. If Edwards was a struggling man of limited vision in so many ways, yet made such signal contributions to the church and Kingdom, then we can take heart. God indeed uses people like Edwards, so perhaps God can use us too. Marsden's Edwards is, of course, an intellectual giant, and a man of intense discipline and unshakable principle, yet he still seems human. In a literary sense, this balance represents one of the chief accomplishments of the biography.

Despite Marsden's successful efforts to locate Edwards as an eighteenth-century figure and a flawed man, he is drawn to Edwards primarily for theological reasons. Marsden frankly confesses at the outset that his "attitude toward Edwards' theology is more sympathetic than not."[27] We know going into the book that Marsden is coming from a Reformed Christian perspective, but his candor about Edwards's theology is a striking admission for a book published by a top-tier academic press. It becomes even more remarkable when one considers that *Jonathan Edwards: A Life* went on to win the Bancroft Prize in American History, a major honor within the discipline, given by a Columbia University committee with (presumably) no connection to Marsden's confessional sympathies.

The heart of the book is Marsden's lucid explication of Edwards's formidable and sometimes difficult theology. In several discrete chapters toward the end of the book, Marsden explains Edwards's greatest treatises, including *Freedom of the Will, Original Sin, The End for Which God Created the World*, and *The Nature of True Virtue*. Marsden shows how Edwards took on the rising spirit of the age in arguing that individuals were not as free and autonomous as many like to think. The will was not free, as commonly understood; instead, one was only "free to do what one wants to do."[28] One could not determine the inclination of one's own will. Its bent was determined by forces outside one's self, either the sin of Adam or the regenerating power of the Holy Spirit.

Although Marsden does not attempt to defend Edwards against all possible objections to his theology, he insists that Edwards's views are a useful corrective to the dominant free-will individualism birthed by the American Revolution. He was "challenging the project that dominated Western thought, and eventually much of world thought, for the next two centuries."[29] He was challenging the Enlightenment. Marsden believed that the twentieth century's abysmal record of totalitarianism and utopian massacres showed just how flawed Enlightenment optimism was. Edwards also offers us an alternative vision of the God-centered universe whose ultimate meaning is rooted in divine trinitarian love, as opposed to the self-centered universe of modern American and global capitalist culture.

Despite the overall warm praise and multiple prizes that Marsden's book won, its reception was not entirely uncritical. In his review in the *William and Mary Quarterly*, historian Douglas Winiarski highlighted one of the most significant objections to the book. As someone apparently without Marsden's theological predilections, Winiarski found Marsden's concern for the "transhistorical" Edwards ultimately unsatisfying. For Marsden, Edwards is a guide for interpreting our own world, for shaping our own theology. Winiarski thinks that this use of Edwards jeopardizes Marsden's otherwise commendable re-creation of Edwards as a man of his time.[30] But surely we should not reject Marsden's approach simply because he finds Edwards's thought useful and instructive. Marsden stands in a long line of historians looking for a responsible but "usable" past. Perhaps Marsden's usable Edwards is more objectionable because his Edwards is a source of theological truth. To many scholars of American history, of course, theological truth is no longer a legitimate kind of knowledge—inaccessible at best, fraudulent and coercive at worst. Why study Edwards, then? To Winiarski, Edwards is instructive only because he is different from us. We have nothing in particular to learn from him, especially in the realm of theology. But to Marsden, the eighteenth-century Edwards is also a teacher—his ideas give us alternative ways of thinking about ourselves and about God.

Winiarski's own work on Edwards has portrayed Edwards as an evangelical revivalist who at times showed a surprising inclination toward the enthusiasm he later would grow to disdain. Yes, Edwards was a reasoned defender of Calvinism, but he was "an equally powerful revivalist who hovered above contorting bodies and rapturous groans," according to Winiarski.[31] Marsden's Edwards certainly knows about the raptures of many saints—including his own wife—but one hardly gets the idea that his Edwards would encourage evangelical radicalism. Yet Winiarski uncovered a remarkable account of Edwards's 1741 revival at Suffield, Connecticut, a mere two days before preaching "Sinners in the

Hands of an Angry God" at Enfield. At Suffield, hundreds of attendees melted into the torments of conversion, with all manner of crying and screaming, including the "Houlings and Yellings" of those convinced they were destined for perdition. Edwards led the meeting for a full three hours, praying for and with the distressed. Winiarski suggested that some of the Suffield radicals made the trip to Enfield for Edwards's sermon two days later, and Edwards gave them what they wanted: a fervent, awakening sermon that ushered attendees into the ecstasies of the Holy Spirit.[32]

This emphasis on Edwards as evangelical preacher also marked *Jonathan Edwards: America's Evangelical* (2005), by Philip Gura, which appeared shortly after Marsden's book. This excellent book has received less attention than it deserves, perhaps lost in the wake of Marsden's "definitive" biography. But Gura and Winiarski have separately identified the most significant deficiency in Marsden's portrait of Edwards. Marsden's Edwards is primarily a Reformed theologian, but Gura's Edwards is "America's Evangelical." Marsden's Edwards is mainly the author of *Freedom of the Will* and *Original Sin*, while Gura's is the Edwards of *A Faithful Narrative*, *Personal Narrative*, *David Brainerd*, and *Religious Affections*. In terms of sheer cultural impact, Gura's is the better case for what makes Edwards significant. Edwards no doubt still appeals to devotees of his Calvinist theology, but in global terms the evangelical Edwards is more influential. "The cornerstone of Edwards's legacy and his subsequent import for American culture is his writing about personal religious experience," Gura concluded.[33] Around the world, evangelical and Pentecostal leaders read Edwards as a guide to revival and evangelical piety, but many of them have no use for Edwards's Reformed theology.

Marsden accepts Edwards the evangelical, but he loves Edwards the Reformed theologian. By the end of the biography, the Great Awakening has largely faded from view, and all that is left is Edwards's brilliant, moving portrayal of the sovereign God of Christianity. In the conclusion, Marsden's vision and Edwards's merge, and Marsden simply recommends to readers Edwards's "post-Newtonian statement of classic Augustinian themes" as "breathtaking." Marsden posits a future in which, presumably through spreading revivals, the majority of people will finally embrace Edwards's redeemer, Jesus, as the embodiment of grace. "Seeing the beauty of the redemptive love of Christ as the true center of reality, they will love God and all that he has created."[34]

This is quite a way to end an academic biography that won the Bancroft Prize. But Marsden's approach works because he so compellingly describes Edwards's world before he recommends his ideas. A reader does not have to share Edwards's or Marsden's convictions to fully appreciate why Edwards's Christianity made sense. Marsden no doubt hopes that some readers will find themselves not just understanding Edwards's ideas but accepting them. His Edwards is certainly a man of the eighteenth century, but he trafficked in ideas that may yet have relevance. The prospect of relevance does not detract from Marsden's biography; instead, it marks its greatness.

NOTES

1. "Life and Character of Rev. Jonathan Edwards," *Connecticut Evangelical Magazine and Religious Intelligencer* 1, no. 5 (May 1808): 161.

2. Ibid., 165.

3. Ibid., 166; on this *Connecticut Evangelical Magazine* article, see also Joseph A. Conforti, *Jonathan Edwards, Religious Tradition, and American Culture* (Chapel Hill: University of North Carolina Press, 1995), 18.

4. George M. Marsden, *The Outrageous Idea of Christian Scholarship* (New York: Oxford University Press, 1997), 95.

5. Ibid., 49.

6. Samuel Hopkins, *The Life and Character of the Late Reverend Mr. Jonathan Edwards* (Boston: S. Kneeland, 1765), A2.

7. Ibid., A3.

8. Sereno Edwards Dwight, *The Life of President Edwards* (New York: G. & C. & H. Carvill, 1830), 9.

9. Ibid., 624.

10. Ibid., 25.

11. Joseph Tracy, *The Great Awakening: A History of the Revival of Religion in the Time of Edwards and Whitefield* (1841; repr., Carlisle, PA: Banner of Truth Trust, 1976), 213. On Dwight and Tracy's significance, see Conforti, *Jonathan Edwards*, 31–32, 39–40.

12. Oliver Wendell Holmes, "Jonathan Edwards," in *Pages from an Old Volume of Life* (Boston: Houghton, Mifflin, 1892), 395.

13. Ibid., 400. See also Louis Menand, *The Metaphysical Club* (New York: Farrar, Straus, and Giroux, 2001), 6–7; Conforti, *Jonathan Edwards*, 159–60.

14. Alexander Allen, *Jonathan Edwards* (1889; repr., New York: Burt Franklin, 1975), vi; on Allen's biography, see also Conforti, *Jonathan Edwards*, 160–63.

15. Ibid., 7.

16. Ibid., 386.

17. Ibid., 388.

18. Vernon L. Parrington, *Main Currents in American Thought*, vol. 1, *1620–1800: The Colonial Mind* (New York: Harcourt, Brace, 1927), 159.

19. Ibid., 162.

20. Ibid., 165; on Parrington, see also Conforti, *Jonathan Edwards*, 189.

21. Ola Elizabeth Winslow, *Jonathan Edwards, 1703–1758: A Biography* (New York: Macmillan, 1940), 326.

22. Ibid., 328.

23. Ibid., 326; see also George M. Marsden, *Jonathan Edwards: A Life* (New Haven, CT: Yale University Press, 2003), 501.

24. Perry Miller, *Jonathan Edwards* (New York: W. Sloane, 1949), 52.

25. Ibid., 124.

26. Marsden, *Jonathan Edwards*, 60–61.

27. Ibid., 6.

28. Ibid., 440.

29. Ibid., 471.

30. Douglas L. Winiarski, "Seeking Synthesis in Edwards Scholarship," *William and Mary Quarterly*, 3rd ser., 61, no. 1 (January 2004), www.historycooperative.org/journals/wm/61.1/br_3.html, para. 5.

31. Douglas L. Winiarski, "Jonathan Edwards, Enthusiast? Radical Revivalism and the Great Awakening in the Connecticut Valley," *Church History* 74, no. 4 (December 2005): 689.

32. Ibid., 738.

33. Philip F. Gura, *Jonathan Edwards: America's Evangelical* (New York: Hill and Wang, 2005), 229.

34. Marsden, *Jonathan Edwards*, 505.

CHAPTER 3

Jonathan Edwards and Francis Asbury

JOHN WIGGER

Edwards sits hunched over the wheel, watching telephone poles whip by at regular intervals in the morning light. The road stretches out before him to the horizon without end. Asbury is sprawled out on the passenger side, working last month's crossword puzzle. His feet, propped up on the dashboard, are killing him. Two empty coffee cups jiggle in the cup holder. Despite being middle aged, both men are rail thin. Both habitually rise early, anxious to make good use of the day. They have been on the road for hours.

"Help me with this one," says Asbury. "Supreme authority or power, eleven letters, third letter V."

"Sovereignty," Edwards immediately replies.

"Oh, right. Easy for you. How about this, 'God's grace properly understood.' Eleven letters, second letter R, last letter M."

"Second letter R . . ." A moment of concentration flickers across Edwards's face followed quickly by exasperation. "You mean to make me say Arminianism," he snaps.

"I believe I just did," says Asbury.

"Where do you get these wretched puzzles?" asks Edwards.

"The *Arminian Magazine.* Why?"

Edwards groans.

"A little levity is good for the soul, Reverend Edwards," says Asbury. "How about, 'state of Christian perfection, attainable in this life,' fourteen letters, starts with S . . ."

Okay, Jonathan Edwards and Francis Asbury never took a road trip together, never met, for that matter. But if they had, would they have gotten on well? What can we learn about American religion from their differences and similarities? What new directions does a comparison of the two suggest?

DIFFERENCES

Much separated the two. Edwards (1703–58) was born and raised among New England's cultural elite. Family was a consistent presence in his life, beginning with the Stoddard line on his mother Esther's side, anchored by the venerable Solomon Stoddard who was a pastor at Northampton, Massachusetts, for sixty years. Edwards's paternal grandmother was "a scandal and a disgrace," but his father, Timothy, was a Harvard graduate and a respected clergyman. Together Jonathan's parents created a model New England household. Jonathan grew up with four older and six younger sisters. He was raised in a meticulously organized and accomplished family that enjoyed a large measure of respect in the broader community.[1]

Asbury (1745–1816) was born and raised in the West Midlands of England, where his upbringing was decidedly more commonplace than Edwards's. Asbury's father, Joseph, was a gardener and agricultural laborer. If Timothy Edwards and Joseph Asbury had passed on the street, it would have been Joseph who doffed his cap and Timothy who nodded benignly. Joseph also exhibited some kind of moral failing that everyone acknowledged but no records identify. The Asburys lived in a small cottage in the village of Great Barr, about four miles outside Birmingham, England. The cottage was owned by a brewery, indicating that Joseph worked there and suggesting that his problem may have been drinking too much. Though he was generally good-natured, he was also known to squander the family's money, so perhaps gambling, a common component of cockfighting and other popular recreations in the area, was also a problem for Joseph.[2] About 1796, two years before Joseph's death, the American preacher Jeremiah Minter put the following question to Asbury: "Mr. Asbury, I have often heard you mention your Mother, but never heard you mention your Father, is he living or is he dead?" When Asbury did not reply, another preacher answered for him: "It may be that he has no Father."[3] At least not that he cared to discuss. His mother, Elizabeth, was more upright, but not without her share of struggles. She sank into a deep depression following the death of her only other child, Sarah, at age six, when Francis was just three. For years Elizabeth dwelt "in a very dark, dark, dark day and place," Francis later remembered.[4] Perhaps as a result, Elizabeth was possessive of her son and had a hard time letting go.[5]

Edwards and Asbury pursued different paths with regard to marriage, no doubt partly as a consequence of their family life growing up. One was a model to aspire to, the other a warning of what to avoid. While Edwards's marriage to Sarah Pierpont and the family it produced became the social center of his life, Asbury remained single, never owning a home or much more than he could carry on horseback. Sarah Edwards was "renowned as the model wife and caring hostess," writes George Marsden, supplying much of the social grace and domestic sensibility that Jonathan so clearly lacked. In the midst of their raising eleven children and entertaining a steady stream of visitors and boarders, their home was known for its discipline and orderliness. It must have been both hectic and inspiring.[6]

The turmoil of Joseph and Elizabeth Asbury's marriage evidently had much to do with Francis's decision never to marry, as did the unhappy unions of other Methodist preachers, including John Wesley himself.[7] The nature of circuit preaching made it nearly impossible to combine with marriage and family, as Asbury, who averaged at least three thousand miles a year in the saddle for forty-five years, could readily testify. "What right has any man to take advantage of the affections of a woman, make her his wife, and by a voluntary absence subvert the whole order and economy of the marriage state, by separating those whom neither God, nature, nor the requirements of civil society permit long to be *put asunder*?" he wondered in 1804.[8] Most Methodists agreed, for financial reasons as much as anything else. While they believed that marriage was part of God's natural order, Methodists were reluctant to pay for a preacher's wife and children, preferring less expensive single preachers instead. The itinerant Pleasant Thurman learned this lesson when he was appointed to the Edenton Circuit in North Carolina in 1811. That September, Thurman made a motion at the circuit stewards' meeting "that all the residue of the money after the payment of his own board and church expences should be applied to the board & salary of his wife." The stewards rejected the motion "unanimously." When Thurman continued to press his case at the circuit's October 1811 quarterly meeting conference, local leaders affirmed the stewards' decision, noting that "the Society are not bound to support P. Thurman's wife."[9] By the early nineteenth century Asbury had heard dozens of similar cases each year, easing any doubts he may have had about his own choices.[10]

In response to his family history and the pressures of itinerancy, Asbury forswore marriage and sexual romance in a way that Edwards did not. Yet Asbury's life was not emotionally flat, revolving as it did around the relationships he formed with other Methodists. As he traveled the nation year in and year out, the community of Methodist believers became his vast extended family. They welcomed him into their homes, a testament to his easy disposition in small settings. His life in this regard could not have been more unlike Edwards's.

Education and intellectual temperament also separated Edwards and Asbury. Edwards was precocious as a boy and took his schooling seriously. At Yale he lived "like a young monk seeking sainthood in a school of rowdy boys," writes Marsden.[11] Edwards gloried in the life of the mind. Even as a young man he set out to construct a "unified account of all knowledge," encompassing what we think of as natural science and theology.[12] Toward this end he aspired to spend thirteen hours a day alone in his study, forgoing the usual pastoral calls expected of eighteenth-century ministers. "I am fit for no other business but study," Edwards wrote in 1750.[13]

Asbury's schooling was more limited and his intellectual ambitions were more subdued. He was a diligent, but not gifted, student. By age six he could read the Bible, and he attended a charity school at Sneal's Green, about a quarter of a mile from the family's cottage. But, as Asbury later remembered, the school's master was "a great churl, and used to beat me cruelly." His severity filled Asbury "with such horrible dread, that with me anything was preferable to going to school."[14] So he left school at about age thirteen and was soon apprenticed to a local metalworker, slipping into the rapidly expanding metalworking industry that made Birmingham an early center of the industrial revolution.[15] When he had the chance Asbury read voraciously throughout his adult life, but he never published an original book, treatise, or sermon of any note. "I applied myself to the Greek and Latin Testament; but this is not to me like preaching the Gospel," he wrote in March 1778, though he would have said the same at any point in his ministry.[16] Edwards would have seen a stronger link between scholarship and preaching.

Theology also separated Edwards and Asbury. In his student days Edwards questioned the legitimacy of Calvinism, which seemed to unfairly condemn certain people to hell. But he soon reached a point where his "vision expanded to appreciate that the triune God who controlled this vast universe must be ineffably good, beautiful, and loving beyond human comprehension," as Marsden writes.[17] For the remainder of his life Edwards used his considerable intellectual abilities to reconcile God's sovereignty with "modern" ways of thinking that relied more on human reason and stressed "the individual's wholly unfettered free will." Closely tied to these ideas was Edwards's fear and distrust of Arminian tendencies in contemporary theology.[18]

Asbury read either Edwards's *A Faithful Narrative of the Surprising Work of God* or *Some Thoughts Concerning the Present Revival of Religion* (Wesley abridged and published both) while on board a ship to America in 1771. In 1779 Asbury read Edwards's *A Treatise On Religious Affections*, which he admired "excepting the small vein of Calvinism which runs through this book." Asbury had fewer reservations about Edwards's biography of David Brainerd, which he read at least twice, in 1778 and again in 1805. Brainerd was "a man of my make, such a constitution, and of great labours; his religion was all gold, the purest gold." As these comments suggest, Asbury could enjoy Edwards because he was able to focus on something other than Edwards's Calvinism. Asbury cared about theological issues, but not in the way that Edwards or John Wesley did. For Asbury, correct theological interpretations could support faith but never really define it.[19]

Asbury and Edwards also differed in their ability to manage people and organizations. This was not Edwards's strong suit, as events in Northampton reveal at several points. He could be clumsy when it came to mediating disputes, as in what Marsden calls the "'young folks' Bible' case," and could appear highhanded, as in his ongoing disputes with the town over his salary. Worse still was his campaign to abolish Solomon Stoddard's policies regarding the sacraments and church membership in favor of stricter standards that repudiated even the halfway covenant. It seemed suspicious to many in Northampton that Edwards waited to do this until they had given him a generous, fixed salary, making him one of the highest-paid ministers in the region. It also seemed in bad taste that he acted only after the death of Colonel John Stoddard, Solomon's son and Edwards's patron, who would have opposed the changes. Edwards was in fact acting on convictions long held, but once the debate spilled into the messy world of town politics he managed to confuse or alienate just about everyone.[20]

Asbury, on the other hand, was a brilliant administrator. Much has been made of the O'Kelly schism, which split the Methodist Church in southern Virginia and North Carolina in 1792, but the wonder is that it was the only sizable schism in the Methodist movement during Asbury's forty-five years in America. During that time the church expanded from a few hundred members to more than two hundred thousand members and nearly seven hundred itinerant preachers scattered across every state and territory in the nation. Asbury's ability to make it all work was based largely on his detailed knowledge of the church and nation, gleaned from his continuous travels and endless conversations with preachers, members, and people he met on the road. He received and wrote hundreds of letters a year, further expanding his knowledge of people and places. Once he made up his mind on an issue, Asbury cultivated a consensus as he crisscrossed the nation, such that by the time the preachers met at a conference he often needed to say little. "He knew ... the art of governing, and seldom trusted to the naked force of authority. Indeed, the majesty of command, was almost wholly concealed, or superseded by the wonderful faculty, which belongs to this class of human geniuses, and which enables them to inspire their own disposition for action, into the breasts of others," wrote Nicholas Snethen, who observed Asbury at many conferences from 1794 to 1814. This was something of a backhanded compliment from Snethen, who left the Methodist Episcopal Church to help found the Methodist Protestant Church in the 1820s because he did not think that the former was democratic enough. Edwards's opponents would have been less likely to say the same about his administrative skills.[21]

Finally, Edwards and Asbury were different from one another in the way that they related to people in social settings, though in a more ambiguous way than might first seem apparent. Edwards "was not good at small talk, often not of a sociable frame of mind," writes Marsden. He felt that he could communicate most effectively with his pen and tried to save as much time as possible for his study. Sarah shouldered much of the burden of running their household and raising their children. Unlike most men of his social standing, Edwards paid little attention to his crops or cattle.[22] "He kept himself quite free from worldly Cares . . . and entangled not himself with the Affairs of this Life," wrote Samuel Hopkins, Edwards's student and admiring biographer. Hopkins admitted that many found Edwards "*stiff* and *unsociable*," slow to speak in social settings and anxious to avoid verbal disputes. Yet with family and close friends another side of Edwards emerged. "They always found him easy of access, kind and condescending; and tho' not talkative, yet affable and free," writes Hopkins. Edwards was withdrawn because he did not believe that his abilities were put to their best use in idle banter. "He observed, that some Ministers had a talent at entertaining and profiting by occasional Visits among their People. . . . But he looked on his Talents to be quite otherwise," writes Hopkins.[23]

Edwards was not a good judge of human desire. Even in Northampton, where he knew almost everyone, he was unable to comprehend the people's reaction to his attempt to impose a high view of the sacraments, leading to his dismissal as the town's minister in 1750. His aloofness from gritty popular culture allowed him to develop a less conflicted perspective on theological issues, but it also clouded his judgment about local concerns and motivations. Edwards cared about the people in his town, but his first loyalties were clearly elsewhere.[24]

Asbury shared some of these qualities, though he turned them to a much different purpose. Like Edwards, Asbury was not quick on his feet and often felt uncomfortable in large groups. Yet in small groups and one on one he had a way of putting people at ease that inspired confidence and devotion. He had a "superior talent to read men," as Peter Cartwright put it, including a keen sense of what motivated those around him.[25] During his career Asbury traveled at least 130,000 miles by horse and crossed the Allegheny Mountains some sixty times. He knew the back roads and rural corners of America as well as any person of his generation. More people met him face to face than any other national figure. Parents named more than a thousand children after him, and landlords and tavern keepers, not to mention ordinary Methodists, knew him on sight in every region.

Asbury was legendary for his ability to draw people to him in close conversation late at night, or while riding a solitary road. It is remarkable how many people became permanent friends with him after only a single conversation. Asbury often chided himself for excessive "levity," especially late at night, and considered his love of talking in these settings a drain on his piety. In reality it was one of his greatest assets, allowing him to build connections across the Methodist movement and feel closely the pulse of the church and nation. Henry Boehm, who traveled some twenty-five thousand miles with Asbury from 1808 to 1813, recalled that "in private circles he would unbend, and relate amusing incidents and laugh most heartily." "His conversational powers were great. He was full of interesting anecdotes, and could entertain people for hours," wrote Boehm. Nicholas Snethen, who traveled with Asbury for several years beginning in 1800, recalled that "as a road-companion, no man could be more agreeable; he was cheerful almost to gaiety; his conversation was sprightly, and sufficiently seasoned with wit and anecdote." Early Methodists did not associate laughing or even talking very much with the spiritual life, so it is remarkable that this is what people remembered about Asbury. It is difficult to imagine Edwards enjoying and using conversation outside his family circle in the same way.[26]

Asbury's ability to draw others to him is a thread that runs through his entire career. In the early 1770s, before he was recognized as the leader of the Methodist movement in America, he was already developing close relationships with a growing number of young American preachers, particularly in the South. Many of these became lifelong friends and leaders in the church, including John Dickins, Freeborn Garrettson, and William Watters. Asbury took the time to listen to their concerns and eventually came to sympathize with many of their positions. He adapted to the American religious landscape so quickly and so thoroughly because he immersed himself in it so completely. Thomas Rankin, Wesley's head missionary in America before the Revolution, was never as comfortable with American ways, particularly the emotionalism of southern worship. He saw Asbury's growing attachment to the American preachers as a threat to his authority and tried to limit it as much as possible. When Asbury quit writing to the southern preacher Edward Dromgoole in late 1774, Dromgoole feared that he had "offended" Asbury in some way. Asbury finally responded that January, explaining that he had "dropt writing" because "my influence and fellowship among the younger preachers has been much suspected, as stirring them up against those they should be in subjection to." Edwards could at times inspire this kind of loyalty in a small group of friends, but Asbury did it time and time again in countless settings across the nation.[27]

Asbury could also be funny, which further helped him to connect with others. In the summer of 1776 Thomas Rankin made a tour through Virginia during which he was dismayed by the raucous emotionalism of southerners' meetings. At a conference of the preachers soon afterward Rankin launched into a tirade against "the spirit of the Americans," criticizing the preachers for allowing "noise" and "wild enthusiasm" in their meetings and for becoming "infected with it" themselves.[28] As the tension mounted, Asbury "became alarmed, and deemed it absolutely necessary that a stop should be put to the debate," according to Thomas Ware, who witnessed the event. Jumping up, Asbury pointed across the room and said, "I thought,—I thought,—I thought," to which Rankin replied, "Pray . . . what did you thought?" "I thought I saw a mouse!" exclaimed Asbury. This joke "electrified" the preachers, and in the ensuing laughter Rankin realized that he had lost.[29] He could not keep the preachers from laughing even as he lectured them about the dangers of enthusiasm. The result was "alike gratifying to the preachers generally, and mortifying to the person concerned [Rankin]," according to Ware.[30] Asbury clearly knew the American preachers better than Rankin. His timing must have also been perfect to get such a big laugh. One suspects that in this case Edwards would have had more sympathy for Rankin than Asbury.

So it would seem that Edwards and Asbury had almost nothing in common. But there are other ways of looking at the two that make them appear much more alike and that connect them to two important characteristics of American religion.

PIETY

First, Edwards and Asbury shared a core sense of piety and single-minded devotion to God. Edwards lived his life by rule (one might say method) as an expression of his piety. He rose early, usually by 4:00 or 5:00 a.m., and he was "abstemious in eating and drinking," as Samuel Hopkins and others observed. Edwards was steady in his habits, and he saw the long hours he spent in his study as a form of spiritual devotion. But he could also become overwhelmed by spiritual rapture as he prayed and walked alone in the woods. What Edwards admired most about David Brainerd was his spiritual intensity, particularly in prayer. Edwards sought and often obtained this same degree of intensity. As Marsden writes, Edwards "had no middle gears" when it came to seeking after God. For all of Edwards's intellectual brilliance, it is easy to lose sight of how much his reputation for spiritual devotion influenced his contemporaries.[31]

Asbury was equally defined by his piety. He essentially lived as a houseguest in thousands of people's homes across the nation during his forty-five years in America. This manner of life "exposed him, continually, to public or private observation and inspection, and subjected him to a constant and critical review; and that from day to day, and from year to year," wrote Ezekiel Cooper, who knew Asbury for more than thirty years. He had no privacy. If Asbury's spiritual devotion had been half-hearted, it would have been difficult to hide from the tens of thousands that saw him up close. In fact, the closer people got to Asbury, the more they tended to respect him in this regard.[32]

Like Edwards, Asbury usually rose between 4:00 and 5:00 a.m. to spend an hour in prayer in the morning stillness. He also ate sparingly, in part because of frequent illnesses brought on by the beating his body took from exposure to the weather, questionable food, and poor housing, but also as an expression of spiritual discipline. Being a Methodist meant nothing if not holding to a pattern, a method, so as to live a more holy life. This included practicing voluntary poverty. Asbury gave away almost all the money that came his way, often to people he met on the road. Though he spent his life on the road, he insisted on riding unexceptional horses (which he nevertheless named and grew attached to) and using cheap saddles and riding gear. His clothes were generally presentable but also plain, inexpensive, and limited to what he could carry. At times he experimented with using sulkies and other small carriages when his health made riding difficult. From 1793 on he suffered from steadily worsening congestive heart failure probably brought on by streptococcal pharyngitis (strep throat) and rheumatic fever that damaged his heart valves. This led to edema in his feet, among other things, made worse by the long hours on horseback with this feet dangling until they were too swollen to fit in the stirrups. He nevertheless disliked limiting himself only to roads suitable to a carriage, which risked cutting him off from the edges of Methodist growth. During 1809 and 1810, when he was well past his prime but still traveling up to five thousand miles a year, Asbury for a time used a two-wheeled sulky. He had a stiffer shaft installed in April 1809 to take the pounding of backcountry roads, but it broke anyway that July in Pennsylvania and again in Ohio in August. He finally sold the sulky in November 1810 and returned to horseback. "The advantages of being on horseback are: that I can better turn aside to visit the poor; I can get along more difficult and intricate roads; I shall save money to give away to the needy; and, lastly, I can be more tender to my poor, faithful beast," he wrote that November while in Tennessee. Yet perseverance came at a price. Toward the end of his life he often had to be carried from his horse to his preaching appointments because he could not bear the pain of walking. The sight left one observer in "breathless awe and silent astonishment."³³

No one believed that Asbury was perfect, particularly in his administration of the church, but they had a difficult time accusing him of insincerity or love of money. His spiritual devotion produced a "confidence in the uprightness of his intentions and wisdom of his plans, which gave him such a control over both preachers and people as enabled him to discharge the high trusts confided to him," observed Ezekiel Cooper. Even James O'Kelly, who could be a bitter critic, felt compelled to acknowledge Asbury's "cogent zeal, and unwearied diligence, in spite of every disappointment." Much the same could be said of Edwards in his sphere of influence. Though they often fell short of their own expectations, evangelicals, Calvinist and Arminian alike, valued nothing so much as a heart yearning to serve God and his people. This was the foundation on which all of Asbury's and Edwards's accomplishments were built.³⁴

In this regard it is worth considering that neither Edwards nor Asbury was a particularly good preacher. This may sound strange since people often associate Edwards with his sermon "Sinners in the Hands of an Angry God," and Methodist preachers were primarily known for their impassioned extemporaneous preaching. Yet neither Edwards nor Asbury was usually memorable in the pulpit when compared to contemporaries like George Whitefield or the many Methodist circuit riders renowned for their ability to move an audience. Asbury was well known for preaching disjointed sermons that were nearly impossible to follow, and he seldom spoke at the church's annual and general conferences. "This excessive delicacy of feeling, which shuts my mouth so often, may appear strange to those who do not know me," he wrote in August 1806, and it did. Writing on the occasion of Asbury's death in 1816, Nicholas Snethen admitted that people generally did not find Asbury's preaching "edifying." "This was owing, in part, to his laconic and sententious style, and the frequent concealment of his method; and in part, also, to his natural impatience of minuteness of detail, which was always heightened by the pressure of disease." This was more or less what everyone said about Asbury's preaching. Nathan Bangs heard him for the first time at the New York Annual Conference meeting in June 1804. "His preaching was quite discursive, if not disconnected, a fact attributed to his many cares and unintermitted travels, which admitted of little or no study.... He slid from one subject to another without system. He abounded in illustrations and anecdotes." Nonetheless, Bangs left the conference "filled ... with admiration" for Asbury because "he presided with great wisdom" and "treated the young preachers as a father."[35]

MEDIATING IMPULSE

It was not their sermon delivery but their piety and ability to make the gospel relevant in their time and place that drew people to Edwards and Asbury. This mediating impulse is the second thread that connects the two to the broader development of American religious culture. Edwards made a great effort to mediate between Puritan thought and the Awakening in New England, and it was to this element in Edwards's writings that Asbury was drawn. Edwards's great project was to reconcile Calvinist theology with new ways of thinking about reason and individual rights and freedoms. He "was an apologist for 'Calvinistic' theology versus 'the modern writers.' Specifically, he was determined to answer objections to Calvinism based on appeals to the great touchstone of so much of eighteenth-century thought, 'the common sense of mankind,'" writes Marsden.[36] Edwards's ability to connect the evangelical awakening of his day and popular culture was more abstract than Asbury's, but it was no less deliberate. In his time, Boston's Cotton Mather (1663–1728) was as famous as Edwards, but by comparison Mather now seems quaint and irrelevant. While Edwards in some measure bridged the chasm between faith and reason that the eighteenth century opened up, Mather was left stranded on the far side.

In a similar manner Asbury mediated between Wesley's theology and American culture. His annual tours regularly took him from Charleston, South Carolina, to New England to the western frontier and everywhere in between. Asbury used his extensive travels and ability to connect with people to develop a deep understanding of American culture in its various settings. This allowed him to appreciate the vitality of southern worship in the early 1770s when Wesley's other missionaries from Great Britain (like Thomas Rankin) found it distasteful, and to immediately grasp the potential of camp meetings in the early 1800s. Soon after attending his first camp meeting (by that name) in 1802, Asbury began urging his preachers to hold them whenever possible. "They have never been tried without success. . . . This is field fighting, this is fishing with a large net," he wrote to Thornton Fleming, presiding elder for the Pittsburgh District in December 1802.[37] Asbury was usually quick to pick up on these kinds of innovations and to promote them across the church, even when they did not appeal to him personally. He was rarely among the shouters or those who fell at camp meetings.

At the same time, his commitment to working within the broad parameters of American culture could trap him, as it did over the issue of slavery in the South. During the mid-1770s (shortly after he first visited the South) he came to believe that slavery was a moral evil. "I have lately been impressed with a deep concern, for bringing about the freedom of slaves, in America, and feel resolved to do what little I can to promote it. . . . I am strongly persuaded, that if the Methodists will not yield in this point, and emancipate their slaves, God will depart from them," he wrote in February 1779.[38] As a result of these convictions, during the 1780s Asbury backed a drive to exclude slaveholders from the church that was ultimately unsuccessful. By the turn of the century the weight of southern intransigence had pushed him to accept that the church could not remain in the South without accommodating slavery. "We are defrauded of great numbers by the pains that are taken to keep the blacks from us; their masters are afraid of the influence of our principles," Asbury complained in February 1809. "Would not an *amelioration* in the condition and treatment of slaves have produced more practical good to the poor Africans, than any attempt at their *emancipation*?"[39]

Edwards's involvement with slavery was equally shaped by his cultural setting. While Edwards's "hierarchical instincts," as Marsden writes, prevented him from seeing slavery as an absolute moral evil, he nevertheless "regarded Africans . . . as spiritual equals," a typical position among New England Congregationalists of his time.[40]

Cultural accommodation was a double-edged sword, as Asbury and Edwards discovered. Yet both were committed to preserving Christianity's relevance in their time and place. Edwards's writings are a testament to this goal, as is his promotion of the awakening that swept through New England beginning in the 1730s. Asbury pursued a similar goal through his guidance of young preachers and direction of the Methodist Church, which became the largest religious movement between the Revolution and the Civil War. By 1876 American Methodism in all its branches numbered more than forty thousand itinerant and local preachers and more than 2.9 million members.[41]

LEGACY

Edwards and Asbury are arguably two of the most important religious figures in American history. Yet while Edwards is often acknowledged as such, Asbury generally is not, at least not to the same degree. This is all the more ironic since the Congregationalists declined as a percentage of the American population after Edwards's death, while the Methodists expanded into the twentieth century. So why does Edwards get so much more attention? In part because of the skill of historians who have taken an interest in Edwards as an intellectual and theologian, and in part because of the depth of primary sources Edwards left behind. Asbury's journal and letters are not exactly a riveting read. But there is something else going on as well. Historians are often drawn to intellectuals and colorful public figures, good and bad. We have a harder time with people whose significance must be more indirectly observed through their influence on those around them and the institutions they create. Edwards's legacy is primarily in the immense collection of writings he left behind. Asbury's is largely in the thousands of preachers whose careers he shaped one conversation at a time, a much more difficult thing to gauge. Yet we need to understand leaders like Asbury if we want a more complete understanding of the development of American religion.

One of the achievements of Marsden's biography of Edwards is the sense of context it creates. Too often Edwards has been seen as theologically pure while Asbury was merely pragmatic. But once their surprisingly similar approaches to cultural engagement are taken into account, a different picture emerges. Asbury could appreciate Edwards's writings specifically because his theology taught him that there were more important things than disputes over Calvinism. Edwards could accept some degree of enthusiasm in the Awakening because it was indicative of a larger good, as demonstrated in the lives of his people. In this regard Edwards wasn't intentionally any less pragmatic than Asbury or any more pure, though Edwards was certainly more intellectually sophisticated. Only as Edwards becomes someone firmly rooted in his time and place does this become apparent. Perhaps the greatest lesson we can learn from Marsden's scholarship has to do with his subtlety of interpretation, his willingness to begin by stripping away convention. Marsden's Edwards is not only America's greatest theologian but also a complex, flawed, and yet extraordinary human being.

In light of the overarching purpose of this volume, I would like to close with an observation that comes not from Edwards or Asbury but from my association with George Marsden. A few years ago I was on a panel with two other professors about what students could expect in graduate school. My fellow panelists described at some length how deeply demoralizing their graduate school days had been. One shared that graduate school had nearly cost him his marriage, and both seemed to carry deep scars from the whole experience. As I sat listening to them I was struck by how different graduate school had been for me. The years I spent at the University of Notre Dame were among the happiest of my life, in part because of George Marsden's guidance and friendship. Those who have read his books know of his intelligence and insight. But he is also gracious, generous, and quietly tolerant of the failings of others. In many respects he embodies some of the best traits of both Edwards and Asbury. I owe him an incalculable debt, and I'm sure his many other students do as well.

NOTES

Portions of this chapter appear in my book *American Saint: Francis Asbury and the Methodists* (2009) and are used with Oxford University Press's permission.

1. George M. Marsden, *Jonathan Edwards: A Life* (New Haven, CT: Yale University Press, 2003), 11–24, quote on 22.

2. On cockfighting and other popular recreations, see Frederick W. Hackwood, *Old English Sports* (London: T. Fisher Unwin, 1907), 159–66, 186–87, 224–88, 296–325; Robert W. Malcolmson, *Popular Recreations in English Society, 1700–1850* (Cambridge: Cambridge University Press, 1973), 15–88.

3. Jeremiah Minter, *A Brief Account of the Religious Experience, Travels, Preaching, Persecutions from Evil Men, and God's Special Helps in the Faith and Life, &c. of Jerem. Minter, Minister of the Gospel of Christ* (Washington, DC: Printed for the Author, 1817), 26

4. Francis Asbury, *Journals and Letters of Francis Asbury*, 3 vols., ed. Elmer T. Clark, J. Manning Potts, and Jacob S. Payton (London: Epworth Press; Nashville, TN: Abingdon Press, 1958), 1:720.

5. On Elizabeth and on Francis Asbury's upbringing, see David J. A. Hallam, *Eliza Asbury: Her Cottage and Her Son* (Studley, Warwickshire: Brewin Books, 2003), 1–3, 12.

6. Marsden, *Jonathan Edwards*, 251, 322, 323, 363, quote on 320; Samuel Hopkins, *The Life and Character of the Late Reverend Mr. Jonathan Edwards* (Boston: S. Kneeland, 1765), 42–44.

7. On Wesley's marriage, see Henry D. Rack, *Reasonable Enthusiast: John Wesley and the Rise of Methodism* (London: Epworth Press, 1989), 257–69.

8. Asbury, *Journals and Letters*, 2:423.

9. Edenton, North Carolina, Methodist Episcopal Church Papers, Southern Historical Collection, University of North Carolina at Chapel Hill.

10. Many accounts of Asbury's life accept Nathan Bangs's exaggerated claim that Asbury traveled 6,000 miles a year for forty-five years, or 270,000 miles total. During the height of his career Asbury did travel this much, but early and late in his career his annual mileage was often less. For estimates ranging from 4,000 to 6,000 miles a year, see Asbury, *Journals and Letters*, 1:402; 2:541, 556, 566, 708; and 3:197, 198. In 1814 Asbury wrote to a friend that he had "traveled annually a circuit of 3000 miles, for forty-two years and four months." See Asbury, *Journals and Letters*, 3:499; Nathan Bangs, *A History of the Methodist Episcopal Church*, 2 vols. (New York: T. Mason and G. Lane, 1839), 2:399–400; Darius L. Salter, *America's Bishop: The Life of Francis Asbury* (Nappanee, IN: Evangel Publishing House, 2003), 114–15.

11. Marsden, *Jonathan Edwards*, 39.

12. Ibid., 81.

13. Ibid., 362; see also 59–81, 134–35, and Hopkins, *Life*, 40.

14. Asbury, *Journals and Letters*, 1:721; see also George Griffin, *The Free Schools and Endowments of Staffordshire* (London: Whittaker, 1860), 429–31, and Hallam, *Eliza Asbury*, 21.

15. The literature on the early industrial revolution in Britain is, of course, immense. On the water-powered mills and forges near Asbury's home, see D. Dilworth, *The Tame Mills of Staffordshire* (London: Pillimore, 1976), 40–52.

16. Asbury, *Journals and Letters*, 1:264.

17. Marsden, *Jonathan Edwards*, 40, quote on 43.

18. Ibid., 436–38, quote on 438.

19. Asbury, *Journals and Letters*, 1:5, 300; 2:486. Asbury made his most extensive attempt to mediate between Calvinism and Arminianism in January

1779, after reading James Hervey's *Theron and Aspasio: Or, A Series of Dialogues and Letters, Upon the Most Important and Interesting Subjects*, 3 vols. (London: John and James Rivington, 1755). John Wesley was much harder on Hervey's Calvinism than Asbury. See John Wesley, *A Preservative against Unsettled Notions in Religion. By John Wesley, M.A.* (Bristol: E. Farley, 1758), 211–36. Wesley's editions of Edwards's books include *A Narrative of the Late Work of God At and Near Northampton, in New England. Extracted From Mr. Edwards's Letter to Dr. Coleman* (Bristol: Farley, 1743); *Thoughts Concerning the Present Revival of Religion in New-England. By Jonathan Edwards, . . . Abridg'd by John Wesley* (London: Wl Strahan, 1745); *An Extract of the Life of the Late Rev. Mr. David Brainerd, Missionary to the Indians* (Bristol: William Pine, 1768).

20. Marsden, *Jonathan Edwards*, 292–305, 341, 343–55; Hopkins, *Life*, 53–66. Beginning about 1662, the halfway covenant granted partial membership to those who had not experienced conversion but who agreed to own the church covenant and lead upright lives. Halfway members could then have their children baptized, a key aim of provision.

21. Nicholas Snethen, *A Discourse on the Death of the Reverend Francis Asbury* (Baltimore: John J. Harrod, 1816), 6; [Methodist Episcopal Church], *Minutes of the Annual Conferences of the Methodist Episcopal Church, for the Years 1773–1828*, 2 vols. (New York: T. Mason and G. Lane, 1840), 1:282.

22. Marsden, *Jonathan Edwards*, 135, 253, quote from 135.

23. Hopkins, *Life*, 49, 42, 50.

24. Marsden, *Jonathan Edwards*, 345–65.

25. Peter Cartwright, *Autobiography of Peter Cartwright: The Backwoods Preacher*, ed. W. P. Strickland (Cincinnati, OH: Cranston and Curts, 1856), 155.

26. Henry Boehm, *Reminiscences, Historical and Biographical, of Sixty-Four Years in the Ministry* (New York: Carlton and Porter, 1866), 443, 447; Snethen, *Discourse*, 9. For similar assessments of Asbury in social settings, see John Wesley Bond, "Anecdotes of Bishop Asbury, No. 2," Drew University Archives, Madison, NJ; John F. Wright, *Sketches of the Life and Labours of James Quinn, Who Was Nearly Half a Century a Minister of the Gospel, in the Methodist Episcopal Church* (Cincinnati, OH: Methodist Book Concern, 1851), 164, 245; Bangs, *History*, 2:407–8. The Bond manuscript is transcribed in Robert J. Bull, "John Wesley Bond's Reminiscences of Francis Asbury," *Methodist History* 4 (1965).

27. In fact, it was at about this time that Rankin began writing to John Wesley urging him to recall Asbury to England. Asbury, *Journals and Letters*, 3:20.

28. Thomas Ware, *Sketches of the Life and Travels of Rev. Thomas Ware* (New York: T. Mason and G. Lane, 1840), 252, 253.

29. Thomas Ware, "The Christmas Conference of 1784," *Methodist Magazine and Quarterly Review* 14, no. 1 (January 1832): 96–104, quotes from 102.

30. Ware, *Sketches*, 253. See also Jesse Lee, *A Short History of the Methodists, in the United States of America; Beginning in 1766, and Continued till 1809*

(Baltimore: Magill and Clime, 1810), 51–52. This exchange between Rankin and Asbury probably took place at the May 1777 conference at Deer Creek, in Harford County, Maryland. See Asbury, *Journals and Letters*, 1:239; Thomas Rankin, manuscript journal entry, May 18, 1777, Garrett Evangelical Theological Seminary, Evanston, IL, 136–37. On Rankin, also see Thomas Jackson, *The Lives of Early Methodist Preachers*, 3rd ed., 6 vols. (London: Wesleyan Conference Office, 1866), 5:135–217.

31. Marsden, *Jonathan Edwards*, 39, 96, 133, 185, 325, quote from 39; Hopkins, *Life*, 40.

32. Ezekiel Cooper, *The Substance of a Funeral Discourse, Delivered at the Request of the Annual Conference, on Tuesday, the 23d of April, 1816, in St. George's Church, Philadelphia: on the Death of the Rev. Francis Asbury, Superintendent, or Senior Bishop, of the Methodist Episcopal Church* (Philadelphia: Jonathan Pounder, 1819), 21.

33. Quotes from Asbury, *Journals and Letters*, 2:652, and Bangs, *History*, 2:364. See also Asbury, *Journals and Letters*, 2:603, 610, 612, 614, and 3:406, 408, 436. I am grateful to Dr. Marilyn James-Kracke for helping me to work out the connection between Asbury's sore throats, fevers, and heart problems, and to Dr. Louise Thai for helping me to understand the specific connection between streptococcal pharyngitis and rheumatic fever.

34. Cooper, *Substance*, 25–26; James O'Kelly, *Vindication of the Author's Apology, with Reflections on the Reply and a Few Remarks on Bishop Asbury's Annotations on His Book of Discipline* (Raleigh, NC: Printed for the Author by Joseph Gates, 1801), 61.

35. Asbury, *Journals and Letters*, 2:515; Snethen, *Discourse*, 5; Abel Stevens, *Life and Times of Nathan Bangs, D. D.* (New York: Carlton and Porter, 1863), 128; see also Cooper, *Substance*, 120, 121.

36. Marsden, *Jonathan Edwards*, 437.

37. Asbury, *Journals and Letters*, 3:251.

38. Francis Asbury, *An Extract from the Journal of Francis Asbury, One of the Bishops of the Methodist Episcopal Church: From January 1st. 1779, to September 3d. 1780* (Philadelphia: Ezekiel Cooper, 1802), 18. Unfortunately this passage was expunged from the 1821 and 1958 editions of Asbury's journal. Asbury's manuscript journals burned in a publishing house fire in 1836. Also see Frederick E. Maser, "Discovery," *Methodist History* 9 (January 1971): 34–43.

39. Asbury, *Journals and Letters*, 2:591.

40. Marsden, *Jonathan Edwards*, 258.

41. John Wigger, *Taking Heaven by Storm: Methodism and the Rise of Popular Christianity in America* (1998; repr., Champaign: University of Illinois Press, 2001), 175–80; Matthew Simpson, *Cyclopedia of American Methodism* (Philadelphia: Louis H. Everts, 1880), 586–607, statistics from 589.

PART II

PROTESTANTISM'S CENTURY

CHAPTER 4

The Evangelical Mind and the Historians

MARGARET BENDROTH

Calvinism was not on most people's minds in 1970, but it certainly could have been. As George Marsden's *The Evangelical Mind and the New School Presbyterian Experience* came to press, the 1960s were winding down into a series of events that blurred simple lines between good and evil. Idealistic student protests had spiraled into the violent designs of Weathermen and bloodshed at Kent State; the civil rights movement, now bereft of Martin Luther King, found anarchic new voices among radical splinter groups. In Vietnam, what looked like a drawdown of American troops turned out to be a new outbreak of war in Cambodia and Laos. If there were ever a time for some orchestrated brooding about sin and human nature, this would have been it.

George Marsden's study of nineteenth-century Calvinists also came at an important time of transition in the study of American religion. This change began with the grand narrative of American history itself: no longer the epic of a people sharing common ideals and common challenges, the new story incorporated a thousand different accounts of the past, framed by gender, social class, race, and region. The same energy reinvigorated American religious history from a neglected subfield into a robust academic specialty with its own set of tales to tell.

This was the cultural and academic setting for *The Evangelical Mind and the New School Presbyterian Experience*. At the time of its publication, most reviewers welcomed Marsden's book as a solid account of a complex dispute among northeastern Calvinists, people who still occupied a central role in American political, literary, intellectual, and religious history. The broad themes in *The Evangelical Mind*, particularly the interplay between Protestant revivalism and Calvinist orthodoxy, were familiar signposts in the historiography of the nineteenth century.[1] But even by that time, the plotline of American religion and its cast of characters were in the midst of substantial change. Today Presbyterians no longer claim pride of place in the pecking order of American religious bodies, having given way to groups that are not Calvinist, Protestant, or even Christian. White males have similarly ceded space to women and racial and ethnic minorities. Even historians' relatively straightforward methodology of collecting and interpreting sources has been replaced by more intricate modes of analysis coming out of literary criticism and anthropology. Most scholars now exercise a "hermeneutic of suspicion" toward canonical texts and institutions, a move that has forever altered the study of Calvinist theology and the doctrinal woes of Presbyterians.

Even so, *The Evangelical Mind* dealt with some enduring themes in the historiography of American religion and opened lines of inquiry that continue to attract serious scholarly attention. Especially with the relative decline in Puritan studies, the story of the nineteenth century, and in particular the rise of evangelicalism, has become one of the most intensely scrutinized subjects in American religious history. Three themes loom large.

The first of those themes is the role of revivalism, a subject central to Marsden's analysis and one still fraught with knotty questions about theology and the role of the intellect. It touches on the relative power of economic realities and religious ideals and has generated some fundamental questions about how religion "works" in the United States. Were revivals cyclical or a broadly characteristic pattern of American religiosity? Were they an instance of democracy in action or were they, at bottom, mostly about emotional manipulation? Not surprisingly, revivalism is a topic with a long pedigree and significant staying power.

A second theme is the significance of Calvinism in American culture. This may sound like a fairly arcane question, interesting only to a few committed insiders. But it is also a central question about the nature of American Protestantism, in the nineteenth century and today. As we will see, the recent shift of historiographical focus from Calvinists to Arminians has been one of the most important scholarly developments of the past two decades.

The third theme has to do with periodization, one of those issues of perpetual interest to the historians' guild, but also based on fundamental questions about continuity and change: What was the relationship between the intense religiosity of the early nineteenth century—a period often dubbed the "Second Great Awakening"—and American religion today? How did the Civil War affect American morality and religious faith? Does modern-day evangelicalism have a spiritual DNA, and if so, what does this reveal about its basic nature?

AMERICAN CHURCH HISTORY AND THE PROTESTANT CONSENSUS

The best place to begin this discussion is with a quick overview of the scholarly context of the 1960s and early 1970s. There the logical beginning point is Henry May's "The Recovery of American Religious History," presented to a local meeting of the American Studies Association in 1959 and published in the *Journal of American History* some five years later. A highly regarded scholar in American intellectual history at the University of California, Berkeley, May used the occasion to applaud a development that he judged "the most important achievement of the last thirty years" for the study and understanding of American culture. No longer a minor piece in the weighty narratives of a Vernon Parrington or Charles Beard, or a subject fit only for dusty denominational scribes, religion was "a vast and crucial area of American experience" being "rescued from neglect and misunderstanding."[2]

Yet in many ways May's declaration of independence was less radical than it sounded. He was still confident of the need to build "a convincing synthesis" of religious history, a phrase that reflects the concerns of postwar "consensus" historians to build a single American story line;[3] it also, no doubt, reflected the unifying feel of mainline religion in the 1950s. Moreover, as an intellectual historian, May applauded new attention being given to theology, especially among secular thinkers who admired its "complexity and uncompromising intellectual struggle."[4] Most of the theology in question was neo-orthodox, with Reinhold and H. Richard Niebuhr the central figures; the latter's *Social Sources of Denominationalism* had been admired by scholars from a variety of academic disciplines. But, as May also pointed out, most historians of American religion were still housed in mainline Protestant seminaries, men with "impeccable secular academic credentials" as well as theological training, ministerial experience, and an "explicit religious affiliation." This undifferentiated mixture of secular and openly religious scholarship was, in his view, a good thing, since "no one could say with precision where, in religious terms, the best new writing was coming from."[5]

Sidney Mead, teaching at the University of Chicago Divinity School, was prepared to take May a step further. "However necessary it may have seemed a generation ago, to pay . . . homage to the rather presumptuous occupants of university chairs of secular history in order to gain any scholarly recognition and respect at all for the history of religion," Mead declared, "it is not necessary now." He pointedly warned the rising generation of "Church historians" against granting "too much initiative to the unpredictable and transient interpretative vagaries of so-called 'secular' historians."[6] It was time for religious history to chart a separate course.

This emerging scholarly profile of religious historians shaped the historiography of nineteenth-century American religion and, as some critics have charged, its narrative structure. It is hard to deny that the major elements of the story reflect the concerns of Protestant theology—in Jon Butler's words, "Calvinism, evangelicalism, declension, rising secularism, laicization, democracy, and American exceptionalism."[7] Historians' preoccupation with rates of adherence, with a cyclical rise and fall of religious enthusiasm, and of course with Protestant texts and institutions made it difficult to make much sense of other groups, especially Catholics, who by century's end had become the nation's single largest religious group. A great deal of the new energy in the field followed on the heels of Perry Miller's magisterial reworking of the Puritans and the "New England Mind," and many historians were eager to track that legacy into the creation of what they believed were uniquely American institutions. The list of topics under study was therefore almost exclusively Protestant, a fact perhaps best illustrated by Henry May's own opening list of items being "brought out of the attic and put back in the historical front parlor": "Puritanism, Edwardsian Calvinism, revivalism, liberalism, modernism, and the social gospel." Only at the end of the article did he call attention to the relative lack of participation by Roman Catholic or Jewish historians, and he did not even mention the absence of minority faiths.[8]

This would soon change. In the introduction to his comprehensive *Religious History of the American People*, George Marsden's doctoral adviser Sydney Ahlstrom took strong exception to the emerging Protestant consensus May had described so approvingly. Ahlstrom was writing about a decade later, in the early 1970s, keenly aware of the seismic cultural shifts of the 1960s and of the inadequacy of existing scholarship on American religion to even begin to explain these changes. "Our whole view of what is relevant in the past must be revised," Ahlstrom declared. "A new set of circumstances now stands in need of historical explanation. We are driven to an awareness of historiographical crisis by the mere mention of John XXIII and John Kennedy, of Martin Luther King, Malcolm X, and the Beatles, or if we think of the student movement, the environmental awakening, the alleged death of God, and the new mood in which American priorities at home and abroad are being reevaluated." Indeed, any reconstruction of American narratives, religious or not, had to "do justice to the fundamentally pluralistic situation which has been struggling to be born ever since this country was formally dedicated to the proposition that all men are created equal."[9] The old "Protestant synthesis," which Ahlstrom identified with the Chicago historians—Sidney Mead, Martin Marty, Winthrop Hudson, Jerald Brauer, and Robert Handy—needed to be "left to one side," replaced by a new construction of the past that would include Catholics, Jews, and the Eastern Orthodox, "as well as such large nonecclesiastical religious movements as New Thought, Theosophy, and Rosicrucianism."[10]

The Evangelical Mind is a product of this emerging scholarly and social milieu, not just at Yale but also at Calvin College, where Marsden began teaching in 1965. The book's general subject matter is fairly traditional: (male) evangelical Protestants wrestling with Calvinism, set against a fairly spare social canvas. One of the concluding chapters uses Ralph Gabriel's *History of American Democratic Thought*, first published in 1940, to demonstrate the intertwining of New School Presbyterianism and American cultural mores. But the overall message of the book is that New School Presbyterians cut their own path through the pre–Civil War decades and that their story is not a simple subset of political events. Even the ruinous denominational schism in 1837 had relatively little to do with one of the greatest moral issues of that day, the continued existence of slavery. Methodists and Baptists were on the verge of division, and Congregationalists were roiled by moral absolutists in their midst, but Marsden's Presbyterians were wrapped up in a theological debate about divine sovereignty and free will, churchly order and revivalistic excess, that they believed was of utmost consequence.

The book's final chapter sums up the New School Presbyterian experience with language reminiscent of H. Richard Niebuhr's *Christ and Culture*. "In the early decades of the nineteenth century," Marsden writes, "the American Churches clearly represented the Church militant, standing arrayed against a secular nation and challenging its citizens to repent and be saved. But by the end of the Civil War era, though their primary message appeared much the same, the denominations had almost merged with the culture. The Kingdom of God and the nation were virtually equated."[11] It is not hard to imagine this language set against the seismic changes of the 1960s in academia as well as the outside world—as well as many long conversations, laced with cigarettes and strong black coffee, deep in the inner recesses of the Calvin College History Department.

REVIVALISM AND THE LIFE OF THE MIND

By the 1960s, revivalism was already a venerable topic in American religious history. Serious scholarly interest began with William Warren

Sweet, one of the single most important figures in the field up through the mid-twentieth century. Sweet held the Chair of American Church History at the University of Chicago from 1927 to 1946 but viewed his subject matter in the broadest possible terms, straddling the gap between matters religious and secular. His interest in revivals followed a path blazed by Frederick Jackson Turner's "frontier thesis"—the idea that westward expansion was central to the development of American democratic institutions. Fully aware that he was rescuing an old story from years of "cheap debunking," Sweet argued that revivals represented the "Americanization of Christianity," as Protestants adapted to the individualistic drive of a "society in motion."[12]

Sweet's upbeat assessment did not, however, offset the influence of Richard Hofstadter's *Anti-intellectualism in American Life*, published in 1963. Hofstadter dismissed revivals as little more than empty populism, thus reflecting a Cold War–era dis-ease with anything that looked like psychological manipulation—a view that was increasingly shared by many religious historians themselves.[13] According to Sidney Mead, revivalism was primarily responsible for the "anti-intellectual bias in American Protestantism." By the early nineteenth century, the fires of the intellect, once bright in Puritan New England, were burning low across the new nation; as evangelicals "parted company with the intellectual currents of the modern world," a chasm widened "between 'religion' and 'intelligence.'"[14] Not surprisingly, one of the more widely read analyses of revivalism, Bernard Weisberger's *They Gathered at the River* (1958), treated theological doctrines only "very briefly," since the revivalists themselves reduced "doctrines to their barest essentials."[15]

What little attention nineteenth-century theology received was overwhelmingly negative. For many decades the foundational study was Joseph Haroutounian's *Piety versus Moralism: The Passing of the New England Theology*, published in 1932. He depicted the early-nineteenth century heirs of Jonathan Edwards as dry legalists, purveyors of a "bleak and cruel Calvinism." Edwards's theology in his view was an unstable mixture of two essentially irreconcilable truths, God's divine sovereignty and human moral responsibility; his followers "lacked either his profound piety, or his intellectual vigor, or both."[16] Other historians were less kind. To Progressive-era historian Vernon Louis Parrington, the

New Divinity men were "as humorless and ungainly a breed of theologians as ever quarreled over the loving-kindness of God."[17]

By the late 1960s, however, the remarkable popularity of Billy Graham demanded another serious look at revivalism and a more coherent picture of what was broadly called "evangelicalism." William McLoughlin supplied both of these, first with a narrative history entitled *Modern Revivalism* that incorporated a memorable cast of characters into a cyclical model of religious enthusiasm. More important was McLoughlin's seminal essay on "evangelicalism," introducing the anthology of sources he published in 1968. Here he described it as simply "the story of America itself in the years 1800 to 1900"; to understand evangelicalism, he declared, "is to understand the whole temper of American life in the nineteenth century." McLoughlin's essay is still a solid treatment of the subject, outlining both the social and the intellectual dimensions of evangelical faith, which he argued was "the pervasive system behind American philosophic thought" in its early formative stages.[18]

McLoughlin's essay dovetailed with a spate of new works on revivalism that focused on its social role. Over the long haul, one of the most important of these works would prove to be Timothy Smith's *Revivalism and Social Reform*, published in 1957. Smith not only anchored revivalism to urban, East Coast enthusiasm and support but also drew a connection between the moral idealism of Wesleyan theology, especially its optimism about human sanctification, and campaigns against slavery and the exploitation of the poor. In Smith's view, revivalism was neither anti-intellectual nor a cyclical event but a permanent, respectable feature of religion in the United States. Other studies by Charles Cole, John Bodo, and Bertram Wyatt-Brown quietly eroded the populist, frontier image of revivals introduced by Sweet and anchored them in the urban East Coast.[19] Donald Mathews's seminal essay "The Second Great Awakening as an Organizing Process" brought the study of revivalism even further into the mainstream of American social history, demonstrating its central role in forging new community bonds and building national unity.[20]

By 1970, revivalism's intellectual context was still an open question. Marsden's book, which incorporated Miller's "life of the mind" into its title, was "one of the first to confront the mishandling of Evangelicals as intellectual lightweights by their critics."[21] Marsden described an intense and deeply nuanced debate over questions of free will and divine sovereignty among Presbyterians, a debate so fundamental that it temporarily split the denomination in two. Rather than dilute the intellectual firepower of American evangelicals, revivalism energized it, prompting decades of earnest discussion in pulpits, pews, and theological seminaries.

There is no doubt that in the years since Marsden's book the study of American theology has grown in depth and sophistication. No more the remorseless Calvinist theologues of popular legend, the "New Divinity" heirs of Edwards look more and more like men of their time and place. Much of this changing perspective is due to a deeper understanding of Edwards as a theologian more pastoral than rigidly systematic (the subject of another chapter in this volume). It is also the result of new methods of study, using social history to build a richer historical context, and biography to build a more nuanced understanding of Calvinist belief in practice. In his study of pastors and churches in Connecticut, David Kling found both warm piety and an active moral engagement, not the "either/or" originally posed by Haroutounian. Douglas Sweeney's biography of Nathaniel William Taylor has corrected old assumptions that the Yale theologian's Calvinist convictions ultimately tailed off into Arminianism. It now appears that the Edwardsian tradition was both durable and strong, giving "birth to a rich and relatively diverse theological world" central to "the intellectual culture of evangelical America."[22]

Deeper appreciation of common sense rationalism and its impact on American evangelicalism has provided historians with another tool for understanding early nineteenth-century theology. It was perhaps no surprise to discover Marsden's New School Presbyterians applying this category of thought in disputes over the meaning of scripture—Princeton Seminary's debt to Thomas Reid and Dugald Stewart was hard to dispute. But just a few years after Marsden's book, Brooks Holifield and Theodore Dwight Bozeman demonstrated its reach to southern "gentleman theologians" and antebellum scientists.[23] The emerging picture was of a religious culture that was not so much anti-intellectual as absolutely steeped in a particular form of rationalism, based on the thoroughly pragmatic insistence that every human being possesses an intuitive "common sense" that allows a direct, unmediated perception of matters both secular and spiritual.[24]

One result of this advancing understanding of American theology has been broad synthetic analyses of the early nineteenth century. According to Brooks Holifield, author of a definitive history of American theology from the Puritan era to the Civil War, the central problematic of the Protestant tradition was a "preoccupation with the reasonableness of Christianity." This in turn created a uniquely American theology that blended pragmatism with Calvinism, and European and academic thought with popular, homegrown religion.[25] Mark Noll's magisterial *America's God* similarly gathered emerging scholarship on the legacy of Edwards and the rise of "common sense" into a powerful account of theology's central role in the creation of American thought and culture.[26] In contrast to Europe, where Christianity and republican thought parted ways in the late eighteenth and early nineteenth centuries, American Protestants combined the two into a reasonable, democratic faith firmly committed to the common man.

If the intellectual context of Marsden's New School Presbyterians has widened, so have discussions of revivalism. In this case, however, closer scrutiny has brought a more mixed verdict. Back in 1950, Whitney Cross's study of the "burned-over district" in western New York demonstrated a link between successive waves of religious excitement and the expansion of the Erie Canal and westward migration of New Englanders.[27] Methods pioneered by the "new social history" in the 1970s took Cross a step further, using models of economic conflict and social control to unearth, as Paul Johnson put it, the "social origins of revival religion."[28] Social historians like Johnson used data about occupations, economic markets, and urban geography, drawn from focused study of discrete communities, to cement connections between religious rhetoric and emerging middle-class solidarity. During the 1980s, methodologies introduced by cultural anthropology further expanded the view of what were now called "religious revitalization movements" to include Native Americans and mill workers.[29] William McLoughlin's provocative *Revivals, Awakenings and Reform* (1978) used these insights to argue that American "great awakenings" originated during "periods of cultural distortion and grave personal stress" and ended with "basic restructuring of our institutions and redefinitions of our social goals."[30]

These broader approaches to revivalism allowed religious historians to incorporate new characters into the story, including Roman Catholics and women.[31] Studies by Mary Ryan, Keith Melder, Carroll Smith-Rosenberg, and Nancy Hewitt—to name only a few—demonstrated that women played a key role in the success of revival programs. Women's missionary and maternal societies, families, and kinship networks helped organize, finance, and publicize the careers of major figures like Charles Finney and Theodore Dwight Weld.[32] Another spate of studies began to link the women's rights movement with the kind of perfectionist, millenarian piety identified earlier by Timothy Smith.[33]

Despite, or perhaps even because of, all of these new perspectives on a very old issue in American religious history, the current picture of revivalism and the early nineteenth-century "life of the mind" is far more complicated than it was in 1970. Using analytical tools from literary criticism and religious studies, modern-day scholars are interested in not just ideas or social locations but the place where text and audience come together, where ideas and social realities connect. They ask questions not just about the meaning of texts but about how the ways in which audiences actively understood and received them.[34] One result has been a growing gulf between the reigning view of nineteenth-century evangelicals as predominantly female, geographically mobile, and deeply pragmatic, and an ever more sophisticated discussion of post-Edwardsian thought. Did women, the great majority of Protestant church members, also care about Edwardsian theology or denominational turf wars?[35] The more we know about antebellum piety and thought, the deeper the old divide between head and heart seems to become.

CALVINISM AND AMERICAN CULTURE

Debates about revivalism have also altered the Protestant landscape, specifically with regard to Calvinism. In *The Evangelical Mind*, Marsden described New School Presbyterians as a "central and representative" group. "By almost any measure," he wrote, "the New School movement in the Presbyterian Church in the United States stood near the center of American religious life in the first half of the nineteenth century."[36] It "embodied the characteristics that virtually all observers agree were typical of the mainstream of American Protestantism."[37]

This was not a surprising claim. There is certainly long precedent for Calvinism as a central problematic in American culture, a shorthand term for futility in the face of determinism—everything from Captain Ahab's search for the white whale to the losing ways of the Boston Red Sox.[38] Moreover, since the nineteenth century, Presbyterians and other Reformed bodies have rarely seemed to tire of scholarly self-reflection and have produced a large and sophisticated body of work, much of it devoted to demonstrating their quintessentially American character.[39] Though perhaps an "uneasy center," as Paul Conkin has argued in a recent book, the Reformed tradition has enjoyed unusual influence in shaping culture.[40] Certainly anyone interested in the history of American theology would simply have to engage Calvinism and what Brooks Holifield has described as "an extended debate, stretching over more than two centuries" about human nature and free will. Calvinist theology attained such permanence and prestige in the major Protestant seminaries and educational institutions of the nineteenth century that "most subsequent theological movements had to define themselves in relation to the Calvinist traditions. In a history of American theology," Holifield concludes, "the Calvinists loom large."[41]

But as Nathan Hatch argued in 1994, the great "puzzle" of American religious historiography was not the tormented psyches of Presbyterians but the astonishing absence of serious study about Methodists. He took issue with historians' long-standing fascination with the "great tradition of the American churches," a "Puritan-turned mainline" story line that emphasized consensus and the power of ideas. "Until the mid-1960s," Hatch wrote, "it is safe to say, the canon of American religious history was surprisingly uniform and coherent. Its primary institutional base remained divinity schools at elite universities, its institutional focus the intellectual history of American mainline Protestants." To these scholars, Methodism was profoundly uninteresting, "the banal residue" of "what had been the noble and intellectually rich tradition of Puritanism and Edwardsian Calvinism."[42] By that time, however, Hatch's *Democra-*

tization of American Christianity was already revolutionizing the old narrative of the antebellum years into a new one focused on popular religion and its role in establishing the dynamism of American religious culture. Echoing William Warren Sweet, Hatch wrote about frontier preachers and wandering evangelists, people in active rebellion against the high-handed ways of New England Calvinists and their determinist theology.

The scholarly turn toward Methodism gathered increasing momentum with the growing popularity of economic metaphors to explain the persistence and diversity of American religion. Describing the differences that separated "winners" from "losers," Roger Finke and Rodney Stark lauded the organizational simplicity and spiritual earnestness of frontier Methodists and Baptists—qualities in sharp contrast to the apparent elitism of East Coast Presbyterians and Congregationalists. Comfortably ensconced in expensive church buildings and the beneficiaries of equally expensive seminary educations, these old-line ministers would have been "of little worth out where the great harvest of souls was under way, even had they been willing to venture forth."[43]

These changes have involved much more than a simple shift from Presbyterians to Methodists. The popularity of market metaphors and methodologies derived from religious studies and anthropology has also dulled interest in Protestant denominations as a primary subject of study. Religious historians are more attuned to studying large-scale motifs and movements, not the fate of one group within the whole. Although the genre has seen periodic revival, it's not likely to enjoy the preeminence it once did, especially as Protestants themselves—Calvinists and non-Calvinists—have receded from the center stage. This is, I think, unfortunate. Denominational politics are not always edifying and are often dull, but they are also an uncommonly useful means of tracking threads of continuity and change over long periods of time; like it or not, these institutions were (and in many ways still are) places where a great deal of cultural "heavy lifting" gets done.

CALVINISTS AND THE LONG HAUL

In an epilogue to *The Democratization of American Christianity* (1989), Nathan Hatch posited a core connection between the religiosity of early nineteenth-century Methodists and other popular sects with modern-day fundamentalists and Pentecostals. All were part of a "recurring populist impulse," reacting to centralized denominational control and intellectualized approaches to faith. Hatch's suggestion was provocative on a number of fronts; it challenged some of the emerging conventional wisdom not only about Methodism but also about evangelicalism in general. The idea that the evangelical movement of the 1970s and 1980s had a Methodist ancestry made sense but raised as many questions as it answered. Historians had yet to agree on the larger narrative connecting the evangelicals of the early nineteenth century with their late nineteenth- and twentieth-century descendants.[44]

George Marsden's epilogue to the *Evangelical Mind* issued a similar challenge, but some twenty years earlier. Back then, most accounts of Presbyterian history placed the New School in line with twentieth-century Protestant liberalism, since both seemed to share a progressive spirit and commitment to social engagement.[45] Marsden's book, however, argued the reverse, that the New School's greatest affinities were with twentieth-century fundamentalism. In his view, the New School emphases on "revivalism, moralistic reformism, strict Biblicism, a relatively low view of the Church, a form of millennialism, and a tendency to emphasize fundamentalism as a means of unifying the Church against rationalism and corruption—all suggest later characteristics of the fundamentalist movement."[46]

Years later, this is still a striking argument, though not for what it says about Presbyterians. Marsden was really arguing that modern-day evangelicalism was a product of the Protestant mainstream, not an aberration of history. In the early days of the modern evangelical resurgence, and to a young scholar emerging from a small religious community like the Orthodox Presbyterian Church, this was a provocative idea.[47] In effect, Marsden was arguing that even fundamentalism was not a stagnant backwater but possessed a distinct intellectual lineage—an idea being developed at that same time by Ernest Sandeen, whose *Roots of Fundamentalism* also appeared in 1970.

This being said, the larger question of the relationship between the evangelicalism of the antebellum period and its subsequent unfolding after the Civil War is an open one. What happened to the moral absolutism and optimism of reformers and revivalists? Did it resurface in the social gospel movement? Did it die a slower death under the secularizing forces of modern science and social pluralism? Or did it find less public expression in the holiness movement, in smaller groups like the Salvation Army or the Volunteers for America?[48] In 1957 Timothy Smith described the post–Civil War years, and the subsequent unfolding of the fundamentalist saga, as a "great reversal" in which evangelicals forgot how to combine doctrinal orthodoxy with the demand for social justice.[49] This is the central argument of Mark Noll's *Scandal of the Evangelical Mind*, that the people claiming to be evangelicals in the late twentieth century had virtually no connection with the intellectual depth and moral passion of Jonathan Edwards and his heirs.[50]

Part of the answer to the question of periodization has to involve reweaving religious into so-called "secular" political and economic narratives. Recent scholarship on the Protestant churches and the Civil War has made it impossible to leave that event in the background of any nineteenth-century denominational saga. The war left an enormous moral crater in all religious communities, both North and South, that historians have only begun to assess.[51] But for the most part, religious history runs along a parallel track with political elections and the business cycle, a problem that becomes more acute further into the twentieth century. The average survey course in modern America might highlight the Scopes trial or perhaps even Billy Graham but, in contrast to the antebellum period, does not need religion to carry the story forward. Jon Butler describes this phenomenon as "jack-in-the-box religion," "more anomalous than normal and more innocuous than powerful."[52]

Mostly we understand now that the whole picture of evangelical religion in American culture is far more complex and tragic than any single theory or methodology could have accounted for. In that respect, the best place to return is *America's God*. Noll's analysis almost reads like an extended archaeological dig into sources and issues that Marsden identified decades before. Noll explains how the turn toward common sense rationalism and the enthusiastic embrace of democratic political philosophies made evangelicalism a common American faith, and over time a socially impotent force. The implicit connection between the God of scripture and the destiny of the United States ultimately muted

Protestant moral concerns, to the point of their no longer mattering in public discourse. By midcentury, as evangelical scribes from both South and North scoured the Bible for the definitive argument for or against slavery, it was Lincoln, the lapsed Presbyterian, who was able to articulate the moral meaning of the war to save the Union. As Noll tells the story, it seems very clear that by the end of the nineteenth century America's God will have become a fairly dull deity, reigning supreme over denominational bureaucracies and evangelical dinner tables but not much else.

In some ways, judging the scholarly trajectory of Marsden's *Evangelical Mind and the New School Presbyterian Experience* is hardly fair. Over the past forty years, American society and American academia, and evangelical religion itself, have undergone dramatic changes. In this present day, it seems almost perverse to pursue discussion of the evangelical "life of the mind," much less to insist that it had a historical antecedent. Many expressions of religious life today, perhaps especially in the evangelical world, seem nearer to Hofstadter's boisterous anti-intellectualism than to any ideal set forth by earnest, long-dead Presbyterians.

Perhaps that's the reason why books like *The Evangelical Mind* remain important. Marsden's picture of evangelical Protestants deeply engaged in the pursuit of both orthodoxy and social morality is always worth returning to—and not just for the challenges it still poses to scholarly research and writing. It can also provide a means for us to judge the temper of our own times.

NOTES

1. For reviews of Marsden's *The Evangelical Mind*, see Fred Hood, *American Historical Review* 76 (October 1971): 1227; Sidney Mead, *Journal of American History* 58 (September 1971): 454–55; William R. Hoyt, *Church History* 40 (September 1971): 338; Harold Vanderpool, *New England Quarterly* 44 (March 1971): 166–68.

2. Henry May, "The Recovery of American Religious History," *American Historical Review* 70 (May 1964): 79.

3. Ibid., 79.

4. Ibid.; quote on 84.
5. Ibid., 91.
6. Sidney Mead, "Prof. Sweet's Religion and Culture in America: A Review Article," *Church History* 22 (March 1953): 46.
7. Jon Butler, "Historiographical Heresy: Catholicism as a Model for American Religious History," in *Belief in History: Innovative Approaches to European and American Religion*, ed. Thomas Kselman (Notre Dame, IN: University of Notre Dame Press, 1991), 286.
8. May, "Recovery of American Religious History," 79, 90–92.
9. Sidney E. Ahlstrom, *A Religious History of the American People* (New Haven, CT: Yale University Press, 1972), 12.
10. Ibid., 13.
11. George Marsden, *The Evangelical Mind and the New School Presbyterian Experience* (New Haven, CT: Yale University Press, 1970), 241.
12. William Warren Sweet, *Revivalism in America: Its Origin, Growth, and Decline* (New York: Charles Scribner's Sons, 1944), xii, xiv.
13. Richard Hofstadter, *Anti-intellectualism in American Life* (New York: Knopf, 1963). See also Ray Allen Billington, *The Protestant Crusade, 1800–1860: A Study of the Origins of American Nativism* (New York: Macmillan, 1938).
14. Sydney Mead, *The Lively Experiment: The Shaping of Christianity in America* (New York: Harper and Row, 1963), 126, 129; see also Perry Miller, *The Life of the Mind in America: From the Revolution to the Civil War* (New York: Harcourt, Brace, 1965).
15. Bernard Weisberger, *They Gathered at the River: The Story of the Great Revivalists and Their Impact upon Religion in America* (Boston: Little, Brown, 1958), viii.
16. Joseph Haroutounian, *Piety versus Moralism: The Passing of the New England Theology* (New York: Henry Holt, 1932), xxii.
17. Vernon Louis Parrington, *Main Currents in American Thought: An Interpretation of American Literature from the Beginnings to 1920*, 3 vols. (New York: Harcourt, Brace, 1927), 2:323–25, cited in Douglas A. Sweeney, "Edwards and His Mantle: The Historiography of the New England Theology," *New England Quarterly* 71 (March 1998): 106.
18. William G. McLoughlin, *Modern Revivalism: Charles Grandison Finney to Billy Graham* (New York: Ronald Press, 1959) and *The American Evangelicals, 1800–1900: An Anthology* (New York: Harper Torchbooks, 1968), 1, 2, 26. See also Leonard I. Sweet, "The Evangelical Tradition in America," in *The Evangelical Tradition in America*, ed. Leonard Sweet (Macon, GA: Mercer University Press, 1984), 1, 2.
19. Timothy Smith, *Revivalism and Social Reform* (New York: Harper, 1957); Charles Cole, *The Social Ideals of the Northern Evangelists* (New York: Columbia University Press, 1954); John R. Bodo, *The Protestant Clergy and Social Issues*,

1812–1848 (Princeton, NJ: Princeton University Press, 1954); Bertram Wyatt-Brown, *Lewis Tappan and the Evangelical War against Slavery* (Cleveland, OH: Press of Case Western Reserve University, 1969). See also Smith's afterword to the republication of *Revivalism and Social Reform* by Johns Hopkins University Press in 1980, *History, Social Theory, and the Vision of the American Religious Past, 1955–1980*, 249–61.

20. Donald Mathews, "The Second Great Awakening as an Organizing Process, 1780–1830," *American Quarterly* 21 (Spring 1969): 23–43.

21. Sweet, "Evangelical Tradition in America," 26–27.

22. David Kling, *A Field of Divine Wonders: The New Divinity and Village Revivals in Northwestern Connecticut, 1792–1822* (University Park: Pennsylvania State University Press, 1993); Douglas A. Sweeney, *Nathaniel William Taylor, New Haven Theology, and the Legacy of Jonathan Edwards* (New York: Oxford University Press, 2003), 12. Sweeney provides a far more detailed assessment in "Edwards and His Mantle." See also William Breitenbach, "Piety and Moralism: Edwards and the New Divinity," in *Jonathan Edwards and the American Experience*, ed. Harry Stout and Nathan Hatch (New York: Oxford University Press, 1988).

23. E. Brooks Holifield, *The Gentleman Theologians: American Theology in Southern Culture, 1795–1860* (Durham, NC: Duke University Press, 1978); Theodore Dwight Bozeman, *Protestants in an Age of Science: The Baconian Ideal and Antebellum American Religious Thought* (Chapel Hill: University of North Carolina Press, 1977). See also Sidney Ahlstrom, "The Scottish Philosophy and American Theology," *Church History* 24 (1955): 257–72.

24. For an assessment of its role, especially in modern-day evangelicalism, see Mark Noll, "Common Sense Traditions and American Evangelical Thought," *American Quarterly* 37 (1985): 216–38.

25. E. Brooks Holifield, *Theology in America: Christian Thought from the Age of the Puritans to the Civil War* (New Haven, CT: Yale University Press, 2003), 4.

26. Mark Noll, *America's God: From Jonathan Edwards to Abraham Lincoln* (New York: Oxford University Press, 2002).

27. Whitney R. Cross, *The Burned-Over District: The Social and Intellectual History of Enthusiastic Religion in Western New York, 1800–1850* (Ithaca, NY: Cornell University Press, 1950).

28. Paul Johnson, *A Shopkeeper's Millennium: Society and Revivals in Rochester, New York, 1815–1837* (New York: Hill and Wang, 1978), 13.

29. Anthony F. C. Wallace, "Revitalization Movements," *American Anthropology* 58 (1956): 264–81, *Death and Rebirth of the Seneca* (New York: Knopf, 1970), and *Rockdale: The Growth of an American Village in the Early Industrial Revolution* (New York: Knopf, 1978). A series of essays from a summit meeting of historians in 1977 proclaimed anthropologist Clifford Geertz the "patron saint of the conference." See John Higham and Paul Conkin, eds., *New Direc-*

tions in American Intellectual History (Baltimore: Johns Hopkins University Press, 1979), xvi–xvii.

30. William G. McLoughlin, *Revivals, Awakenings, and Reform: An Essay on Religion and Social Change in America, 1607–1977* (Chicago: University of Chicago Press, 1978), 2.

31. Jay Dolan, *Catholic Revivalism: The American Experience, 1830–1900* (Notre Dame, IN: University of Notre Dame Press, 1978).

32. Mary Ryan, *Cradle of the Middle Class: The Family in Oneida County, New York, 1790–1865* (Cambridge: Cambridge University Press, 1981); Keith Melder, *The Beginnings of Sisterhood: The American Women's Rights Movement, 1800–1850* (New York: Schocken Books, 1977); Carroll Smith Rosenberg, *Religion and the Rise of the American City: The New York City Mission Movement, 1812–1870* (Ithaca, NY: Cornell University Press, 1971); Nancy A. Hewett, *Women's Activism and Social Change, Rochester, New York, 1822–1872* (Ithaca, NY: Cornell University Press, 1984).

33. Nancy Hardesty, Lucille Sider, and Donald W. Dayton, "'Your Daughters Shall Prophesy?': Feminism in the Holiness Movement," *Methodist History* 14 (January 1976): 67–92; Donald Dayton, *Discovering an Evangelical Heritage* (New York: Harper and Row, 1976).

34. See, for example, a recent critique of evangelical historiography by John Lardas Modern, "Evangelical Secularism and the Measure of Leviathan," *Church History* (December 2008): 801–76.

35. See Ann Braude, "Women's History *Is* American Religious History," in *Retelling U.S. Religious History*, ed. Thomas A. Tweed (Berkeley: University of California Press, 1997), 87–107.

36. Marsden, *Evangelical Mind*, x.

37. Ibid., x–xi.

38. "Is It Calvinism or Realism?" *Boston Globe*, August 14, 1986, cited in Thomas J. Davis, "Images of Intolerance: John Calvin in Nineteenth-Century Textbooks," *Church History* 65 (June 1996): 234.

39. For an overview of the historiography, see Sean Michael Lucas, "Presbyterians in America: Denominational History and the Quest for Identity," in *American Denominational History: Perspectives on the Past, Prospects for the Future*, ed. Keith Harper (Tuscaloosa: University of Alabama Press, 2008), 50–70; James H. Moorhead, "Redefining Confessionalism: American Presbyterians in the Twentieth Century," in *The Confessional Mosaic: Presbyterians and Twentieth-Century Theology*, ed. Milton Coalter, John Mulder, and Louis Weeks (Louisville, KY: Westminster/John Knox Press, 1990), 83. See also Gary Scott Smith, *Seeds of Secularism: Calvinism, Culture, and Pluralism in America, 1870–1915* (Grand Rapids, MI: Christian University Press, 1985).

40. Paul Conkin, *The Uneasy Center: Reformed Christianity in Antebellum America* (Chapel Hill: University of North Carolina Press, 1995), (oddly)

includes not only Presbyterian bodies but Methodists and Episcopalians under the "Reformed" umbrella. See also assessments by Paul Harvey, "Thoroughly Centered: The Reformed Tradition and American Religious History," *Reviews in American History* 23 (1995): 421–26, and Allen Guelzo's review of Conkin's *The Uneasy Center* in *William and Mary Quarterly* 52 (October 1995): 759–64.

41. Holifield, *Theology in America*, 10.

42. Nathan Hatch, "The Puzzle of American Methodism," *Church History* 63 (June 1994): 176, 77.

43. Roger Finke and Rodney Stark, *The Churching of America, 1776–1990: Winners and Losers in Our Religious Economy* (New Brunswick, NJ: Rutgers University Press, 1992), 103–4, quote on 104.

44. Nathan Hatch, *The Democratization of American Christianity* (New Haven, CT: Yale University Press, 1989). "The Recurring Populist Impulse" is the title of Hatch's epilogue, 210–19.

45. Elwyn Smith, *Presbyterian Ministry in American Culture: A Study in Changing Concepts, 1700–1900* (Philadelphia: Westminster Press, 1962), 264; Edmund Rian, *The Presbyterian Conflict* (Grand Rapids, MI: Eerdmans, 1940), 23; Lefferts Loetscher, *The Broadening Church: A Study of Theological Issues in the Presbyterian Church since 1869* (Philadelphia: University of Pennsylvania Press, 1957), 18.

46. Marsden, *Evangelical Mind*, 246. Marsden's later work, *Fundamentalism and American Culture* (1980), does not press this argument, however, and foregrounds Old School Presbyterians in the development of fundamentalist doctrines, especially the insistence on inerrancy.

47. As Marsden recalled in an interview, even at the very beginning of his college career his fundamental "historical question" had to do with the way his own "Old School Presbyterian outlook" had become "so hopelessly out of date" and culturally irrelevant. See George Marsden, "Doing American History in a World of Subcultures," *Reviews in American History* 38 (2009): 304.

48. Norris Magnuson, *Salvation in the Slums: Evangelical Social Work, 1865–1920* (Metuchen, NJ: Scarecrow Press, 1977).

49. T. Smith, *Revivalism and Social Reform*, 212.

50. Mark Noll, *The Scandal of the Evangelical Mind* (Grand Rapids, MI: Eerdmans, 1994).

51. This literature is becoming fairly vast, but see Harry S. Stout, *Upon the Altar of the Nation: A Moral History of the Civil War* (New York: Viking, 2006).

52. Jon Butler, "Jack-in-the-Box Faith: The Religion Problem in Modern American History," *Journal of American History* (March 2004): 1358. See also Randall Stephens, "More Recovered: A Review of Recent Historical Literature on Evangelicalism in the Late Victorian Era," *Quodlibet Journal* 3 (Winter 2001), www.quodlibet.net/articles/stephens-victorian.shtml.

CHAPTER 5

The Evangelical Mind and the New School Presbyterian Experience

PETER J. WALLACE

While focused on a single denomination (the New School Presbyterians from 1837 to 1869), George Marsden's first book set forth a far broader thesis regarding the importance of religion and theology in American history that would dominate his later works. *The Evangelical Mind and the New School Presbyterian Experience* may have started out as a relatively obscure "case study of thought and theology in nineteenth-century America," but in retrospect it points in the direction of Marsden's later projects. The discussion of evangelicalism and fundamentalism in the book's preface, introduction, and epilogue already discloses the trajectory continued in Marsden's works of the 1980s and 1990s, such as *Fundamentalism and American Culture*, *Reforming Fundamentalism*, and *Understanding Fundamentalism and Evangelicalism*. Likewise, the emphasis on the life of the mind and the book's frequent references to collegiate education bore fruit in *The Soul of the American University*, as well as his more popular work *The Outrageous Idea of Christian Scholarship*. And the roots of New School Presbyterianism are traced back to none other than Jonathan Edwards. Indeed, *The Evangelical Mind* could very well have been included in the title or subtitle of almost every volume Marsden has produced.

Nonetheless, the second half of the title, *and the New School Presbyterian Experience*, should not be shortchanged. After all, Marsden's broader thesis regarding the importance of religion and theology in nineteenth- and twentieth-century society compels historians precisely because of the stories he told. And his first story was a particularly Presbyterian one. Marsden grew up in the Orthodox Presbyterian Church, a denomination that prized the Reformed doctrinal emphases of the Old School tradition versus the broader evangelical tendencies of the New School. Likewise, he attended Westminster Theological Seminary, which considered itself the heir of the "old" Princeton Theological Seminary (having formed after Princeton's reorganization in 1929). Indeed, Marsden has often told the story of how he went to Yale to write a dissertation on the Old School—but that his adviser Sydney Ahlstrom insisted that he write on the New School instead.

Several issues lay at the root of the Presbyterian controversy of the 1830s: (1) the New School's alleged doctrinal deviation from the Westminster Confession of Faith regarding the nature of the atonement and the imputation of sin and grace; (2) the 1801 "Plan of Union" between Presbyterians and Congregationalists, which permitted an easy transfer of ministers and churches between the two denominations (a point that became contested only after the rise of New School theology); (3) the power of voluntary associations such as the American Home Missions Society (for paying church planters in the West), the American Education Society (for training ministers), and the American Board of Commissioners for Foreign Missions—all of which were controlled by an alliance of New School Presbyterians and Congregationalists; and (4) the revivalism of Charles Finney, which the Old School believed was rooted in New School theology. The place of slavery in these debates will be noted below.

ARGUMENT AND APPROACH

Marsden asserts that the purpose of this study was to show how "the Church's persistent tendency to embrace American nationalism and

American middle-class mores in the name of Christianity" found its sources in "the influential middle-class evangelical Protestant establishment of a century ago."[1] Arguing that New School Presbyterians lived at the center of that establishment, Marsden retold the story of the New School as the development of the Evangelical Mind.

But Marsden refrained from a typical "intellectual history" of religion. Insisting that "the life of the mind . . . cannot be understood apart from the activities associated with it" (2), Marsden sought to explain the importance of revivalism and social reform as a "comprehensive program designed to Christianize every aspect of American life—spiritually, morally, and intellectually" (3). Starting with the theology of the New School and the Presbyterian division of 1837, Marsden then dealt with the issues of abolition and social reform, the rise of denominationalism, and the intellectual challenges that arose in science and philosophy.

In these chapters Marsden sketched a narrative of how cooperative evangelicalism became denominational bureaucracies, how calls for moral and social reform were transformed into the union of flag and cross—in short, to paraphrase one of Marsden's chapter titles, how the Kingdom of Christ became wedded to the American Nation.

In the 1830s, New School Presbyterians (with most American evangelicals) embarked with great confidence on their project of Christianizing America and the world. Marsden points out that they had reason for their confidence: they had so successfully resisted the incursion of Deism and "infidelity" that by 1833 Alexis de Tocqueville would declare the United States to be the world's most Christian nation (16). But Marsden points out that the Civil War revealed that the New School identified its "mission to prepare the world for the millennium" with its mission "to call the nation to its covenantal obligations with the patriotic dogmas that the Union must be preserved and slavery abolished" (199). Was this Christianizing America or Americanizing Christianity?

In the middle of the book, immediately after explaining the midcentury challenges in science and philosophy, Marsden included a chapter entitled "The Mediating Theology of Henry B. Smith." This decision to focus a chapter on one individual theologian has the effect of highlighting Smith as the archetypal New School theologian, but also (since the New School did not always follow Smith) as an alternative path, a "middle way" between Princetonian conservatism and German liberalism. Plainly Marsden wishes that the Presbyterian Church had followed Smith!

It would be an understatement to say that *The Evangelical Mind and the New School Presbyterian Experience* has not been the best seller among Marsden's works, but it did lay the foundation for his subsequent productions. Marsden summarized the perils of evangelical success by contrasting the early decades of the nineteenth century, when "the American Churches clearly represented the Church militant, standing arrayed against a secular nation and challenging its citizens to repent and be saved," with the latter decades of the century, when "the Kingdom of God and the nation were virtually equated" (241). While his central thesis remains unchallenged, certain aspects of his argument need to be nuanced—especially his tendency to conflate the views of old Princeton with those of the Old School as a whole.

NEW SCHOOL THEOLOGY AND ANTEBELLUM REFORM

In his introduction Marsden cited numerous versions of the "anti-intellectual" interpretation of revivalism (4–5). Marsden sought to demonstrate that New School Presbyterians maintained an "uneasy" alliance between Reformed theology and revivalism. If anything, Marsden was too cautious in his thesis. As Leo Hirrel has subsequently shown, there was nothing "uneasy" about the relationship between New School theology and the evangelical social agenda of the revivalists. Hirrel pointed out that the New School "combination of Calvinist terminology with rationalist ideas produced a religious outlook that combined a strong fear of human depravity with a belief in human ability to overcome sin."[2] And this outlook fostered the evangelical social agenda, with its crusading zeal against its foes, such as Roman Catholicism, alcoholic beverages, and chattel slavery. Revivalism and the evangelical social agenda were intimately connected with a certain intellectual and theological standpoint.

But here the first problem with Marsden's account emerges. Marsden reports that the New School Assembly of 1840 adopted a resolution endorsing "the only true principle of temperance—total abstinence from everything that will intoxicate" (100). He then claims that Charles Hodge and the majority of the Old School opposed such a denominational stand. But the practice of the Old School General Assembly reveals a very different story. At the time, Charles Hodge was the junior professor at Princeton Theological Seminary, and not yet especially popular in Old School circles. In fact, in the face of Hodge's protests, Old School Presbyterians frequently engaged in the same crusades, especially against Roman Catholicism and alcoholic beverages (and even some against slavery).

The explanation begins three years earlier, at the end of the General Assembly of 1837—the same body that had excised the New School synods. In its annual pastoral letter, approved after two-thirds of the New School delegates had left, the Old School declared its dismay that Presbyterians, even Old School ruling elders, "still manufacture and sell ardent spirits.... No Church can shine as a light in the world, while she openly sanctions and sustains any practices which are so evidently destructive of the best interests of society."[3] Contrary to Marsden's claim, the Old School was just as interested in temperance reform as the New School.

Two of the key leaders of the Old School movement pressed this point home. Robert J. Breckinridge, then pastor of Second Presbyterian Church in Baltimore, and the mastermind of the excision of the New School synods, published (and probably wrote) "A Plea for Total Abstinence from Intoxicating Liquors" in 1840. This pamphlet opposed even temperate drinking on the grounds that total abstinence was the safest way to avoid drunkenness and suggested that every penny gained through the sale of alcohol was "the price of blood."[4] William Swan Plumer, the pastor of the First Presbyterian Church of Richmond, Virginia, and editor of the *Watchman of the South* (a paper he started in order to win over Virginia Presbyterians to the Old School cause), argued that while Christians technically had permission to drink, the course of prudence and safety was to abstain. Indeed, Plumer argued, given the present context of runaway drunkenness, it was imperative for Christians to abstain from alcohol. And "if it be wrong to use ardent spirits except for medicinal purpose, it is certainly wrong to make, or sell, or give it away for other than medicinal purposes. He that aids or abets in the commission of any crime is himself . . . a partaker in the crime," and to furnish an intemperate man with liquor is to kill him by inches.[5] Old School leaders could be every bit as devoted to the temperance cause as New Schoolers, even as they battled against the New School theology that allegedly lay at the root of the temperance reform movement.

In 1843, the Synod of Pittsburgh declared that retailers of alcoholic beverages were guilty of tempting others to sin and therefore should be excluded from the church.[6] The Old School was evenly divided on the wisdom of this course of action. In the end, the Assembly decided that the Synod was wrong to establish this as a test of communion in the church but insisted that each situation be handled on a case-by-case basis (thereby allowing for the possibility that retailers of alcoholic beverages could be excluded from the church).[7] Just five years later, in 1848, the Synod of Cincinnati was not challenged when it determined that retailing alcoholic beverages was grounds to "debar persons so engaged from the communion of the church."[8] Indeed, the 1848 "Narrative of the State of Religion," adopted by the General Assembly, for the first time urged all Old School Presbyterians to "have nothing to do with the traffic in intoxicating liquors, and [to] discountenance in every proper way the drinking usages of society."[9] It is true that Charles Hodge protested against these sorts of statements, but contrary to the popular Princeton-centered interpretation Hodge was often a minority in the Old School.

If, as many writers say, temperance was a pursuit of "individual perfectionism," allied with the "revivalist waves of Methodism, Baptism, and the 'new Presbyterianism,'" than theoretically Old School Presbyterians should have had a large population of antitemperance writers.[10] But in fact, virtually all supported temperance, and a significant majority supported total abstinence. John J. Rumbarger suggests the solution to this seeming contradiction: while the rhetoric of the temperance movement was indeed influenced by the New School/perfectionist wing of the evangelical movement, the goal of temperance reform was the establishment of a "rational social order," and Old School Presbyterians were as fully invested in the market economy of the antebellum era as anyone else, and equally desired social and moral reforms.[11] While some might deplore the "ultra" antialcohol rhetoric of their New School colleagues, they joined the moderate wing of the movement, only to discover that the rhetoric was not an optional feature. After all, if revivalism and the evangelical social agenda were grounded in a New School doctrine of sin and grace (as Hirrel has argued), then Old School Presbyterians who embraced that social agenda were implicitly endorsing New School theology as well.

SLAVERY AND THE DIVISION OF 1837

A second place where Marsden's account may need some revision is the role of slavery in the division of 1837. Prior to Marsden's work, many historians sided with C. Bruce Staiger's claim that the division of the church was the result of a covert deal between the South and northern conservatives to get rid of the supposedly abolitionist New York synods.[12] In response, Marsden explained the connections between six "interrelated issues. . . . (1) the meaning of confessionalism, (2) Presbyterian polity, (3) the relation of the church to the voluntary societies of the "Evangelical united front," (4) methods of revivalism, (5) theology itself, and (6) slavery" (67). Marsden correctly pointed out that the Old School's central concerns focused on the inroads of New England theology and polity into the Presbyterian Church. Marsden's attempt to show that slavery was more of a background issue has found favor from most historians of American religion, though a couple of nuances are needed.[13]

First, Marsden argued that "the Southern vote was indeed the decisive factor" in the Old School's triumph, but Marsden did not correctly represent the precise nature of the southern shift (99). The Presbyterian General Assembly recorded the votes of each commissioner on significant issues, enabling us to trace the voting patterns in different regions of the church. The only regions that saw a significant shift in voting patterns between the pro–New School Assembly of 1836 and the pro–Old School Assembly of 1837 were the synods of Tennessee, Virginia, and New Jersey (outside Charleston, South Carolina, the deep South was firmly in the Old School camp from the beginning). A closer examination of the regional discussions at that time reveals that Tennessee, Virginia, and New Jersey desired to hold the two sides together but that when it became clear that the church would divide, a majority of these synods preferred the Old School to the New School. Therefore they voted with the New School in 1836 when they still hoped for peace but switched to the Old School when forced to choose.[14]

Second, Marsden (with many other historians) errs in arguing that northerners agreed to stop agitating for an antislavery statement from the General Assembly, thereby bringing the southerners on board and giving the victory to the Old School. In fact, it was the other way around. Immediately after the vote on the Albert Barnes heresy trial (where the New School's Barnes, a Philadelphia pastor, had been accused of denying key Presbyterian doctrines regarding original sin and the atonement), the General Assembly turned to a debate over slavery and abolition. One speaker moved that since any action on slavery would likely divide the church, "the whole subject [should] be indefinitely postponed." This motion passed by a vote of 154–87. Marsden explains this by saying that in 1836 the "abolitionists could find only 87 votes" to try to block an attempt to postpone indefinitely any action on slavery, whereas the New School party acquitted Barnes of heresy by a vote of 134–96 (96).[15] In other words, Marsden reads this as a failure on the part of the New School to stand firm on the subject of slavery. But the problem with calling these eighty-seven votes "abolitionist" is that they included forty southern votes, including the whole delegations from the Synod of Virginia and the Synod of South Carolina and Georgia—neither of which favored abolition!

To understand the vote on the motion to "postpone indefinitely," one must understand what was postponed. The proposal on the floor was a statement that the General Assembly had "no authority to assume or exercise jurisdiction in regard to the existence of Slavery."[16] In other words, the Assembly was about to vote on a motion that most *southerners* would have found very congenial! Indeed, many southern commissioners came to the 1836 General Assembly seeking a statement on slavery that would condemn the abolitionist position.[17] Therefore, a vote to postpone the matter indefinitely would kill a prosouthern report.

A closer look at the eighty-seven votes against indefinite postponement reveals that forty came from the South and twenty-two from the synods formed under the Plan of Union (namely, the most "New School" synods in the Presbyterian Church). In other words, the two extremes (abolitionist and proslavery advocates) joined forces in their wish to continue the debate, while the conservatives (both North and South) won the day.

Therefore, while Marsden and other historians have argued that the Old School won the South by agreeing to "shut up" on the matter of slavery, in fact the opposite is true. Most northerners in the Old School had no desire to speak on the slavery question—it was the southerners who agreed to keep quiet for the sake of the peace of the church.

AMERICAN NATIONALISM AND THE CIVIL WAR

As Marsden traced the history of the New School and its relations with the Old School, he concluded that "Civil War patriotism and the southern exodus made the Old School more like the New. Conversely, the New School's strong denominational organization, developed in the antebellum years, gave it a character more like that of the Old" (211). But once again Marsden was operating with a particularly "Princetonian" definition of the Old School. One particular Old School debate in the 1850s is especially helpful for illuminating how the Old School became more like the New School *even before* either Civil War patriotism or the southern exodus. The education debate in the Old School demonstrates that Marsden's thesis regarding the trajectory of the "Evangelical Mind" in the nineteenth century is equally applicable to Old School Presbyterians.

The Old School certainly contained a strong element of confessionalism that wanted to maintain a distinctive Presbyterian identity over and against the evangelical Protestant ethos of antebellum America. This was revealed perhaps most clearly in the efforts of Charles Hodge, Cortlandt Van Rensselaer, and others to establish a system of Presbyterian parochial schools in the 1840s and 1850s—the precise time when most states were developing their own system of common schools.[18] True to the New School concept of catholicity (individual Christians working together across denominational lines), few New School Presbyterians liked the concept of parochial schools. But in 1841 the Old School General Assembly adopted a report encouraging every congregation to have a school for children ages six to ten, and every presbytery to have at least one grammar school or academy. The report suggested that a better educational system would produce greater attachment to the Presbyterian doctrine and hopefully would increase the number of ministerial candidates. Most telling, however, was their conviction that the secularization of public education resulted in the removal of religious content and church control.[19]

But this model called forth stiff opposition from Robert J. Breckinridge, president of Jefferson College in Pennsylvania, who urged the duty of every evangelical denomination to influence the public schools. He claimed that since Presbyterians had an influence in education disproportionate to the church's numbers, it should be the last to withdraw from this general partnership. If the Presbyterian Church "would prosper they must enter heart and hand in the common enterprises of the country, in which they have an interest, and not attempt to set up for themselves."[20]

Two Presbyterian college presidents from the South, Samuel K. Talmage, president of Oglethorpe University in Georgia, and John C. Young, president of Centre College, Danville, Kentucky, immediately rose in defense of parochial education. Young argued that natural religion was insufficient for the education of children. If Presbyterian children were not receiving adequate religious training, then it was the church's fault. Presbyterians could not expect the state to teach the knowledge of God properly to their children. Both in Protestant and in Catholic countries in Europe the church was in charge of overseeing the religious education of the schools. Indeed, he suggested that the states should permit any religious group to draw money from the public fund for their schools. But if the state would not allow Presbyterians a portion of the common funds, then they must follow their own path: "The Free Church of Scotland has taught us that it is not only in established churches that the system of parochial schools is feasible."[21] Charles Hodge hoped that "if the several denominations adopt the plan of parochial schools, the state will soon be forced to the obviously just method of a proportionate distribution of the public funds, whether derived from taxation or lands or a capital stock."²²

Hodge's optimism did not take into account the extent to which anti-Catholicism drove the engine of the common school movement. Robert J. Breckinridge (who in 1847 became the superintendent of public education for the state of Kentucky) and James Henley Thornwell (who in 1852 became president of the South Carolina College) championed the cause of public education. Both had been zealous and prolific writers in the anti-Catholic campaigns of the 1830s and 1840s, and both explicitly argued that public education was necessary to capture the hearts and minds of all Americans for the evangelical Protestant cause.²³

Breckinridge feared that Roman Catholics would use tax money to create a system of schools that would work to subvert not only Protestant religion but also republican institutions. For more than twenty years Breckinridge championed public schools with a distinctively Protestant flavor as the best way to combat Rome.²⁴ Calling his readers to remember the Presbyterian involvement in the American Revolution, he gloried in his vision of Presbyterian catholicity: "Narrow views may be put forth in her name; they are not hers. . . . Weak, timid or selfish counsels may appear for a time to gain her consent, but the calm, final, settled purpose, the true, earnest, cordial action she will take at last, will be in full accord with the spirit of the age." While Breckinridge had been a champion of the Old School against the New School, his view of education shared the New School emphasis on individual cooperation. He decried denominational education as sectarian and bigoted, sacrificing "all hope of the general education of mankind."²⁵ For some, catholicity was developing into a particular form of American nationalism. Indicative of this trend, at the 1850 General Assembly, Breckinridge argued vehemently against parochial schools and also urged the church to present a memorial to Congress on the importance of maintaining the Federal Union. His emphasis on Presbyterian involvement in the public schools was intimately connected with his hope that the Presbyterian Church could help avert the "calamity" of national disunion.²⁶

Thornwell likewise defended the common schools. In a letter to Governor John L. Manning of South Carolina, which was reprinted throughout North and South alike, Thornwell argued that while the state "knows nothing of sects, but to protect them . . . it does not follow that the State must be necessarily godless." While public schools should not be denominational, neither should they be atheistic or un-Christian. "What is wanted is the pervading influence of religion as a life; the habitual sense of responsibility to God and of the true worth and destiny of the soul, which shall give tone to the character, and regulate all the pursuits of the place." He admitted that a state school could not teach religion as a science, or a discipline, but "Let it come in the character of the Professors, let it come in the stated worship of the Sanctuary, and let it come in the vindication of those immortal records which constitute the basis of our faith. Leave creeds and confessions to the fireside and Church, the home and the pulpit. Have godly teachers, and you will have comparatively a godly College." Grant the church control over education, Thornwell argued, and you wind up with a church that intrudes into every aspect of life. "The church is a distinct corporation—with distinct rights and authority. She has direct control over nothing that is not spiritual in its matter and connected with our relations to Jesus Christ."[27] Because of the fragmentation of the church, Thornwell believed that a state education was essential for a well-educated public. Thornwell's doctrine of the spirituality of the church should not be seen exclusively in the light of his desire to avoid the church's involvement in slavery. It also was connected to his desire to avoid the church's involvement in education. But once again the idea of catholicity was transferred from the church to the state. Christian unity was expressed, not in the realm of the church, but in the united action of evangelical Protestants under the aegis of the state.

By the end of the 1850s the parochial school movement was waning in the Old School church. Presbyterian involvement in the common schools was largely taken for granted, and in the 1860s the last vestiges of the parochial schools were swept away. Old School Presbyterians still tended to think of Christianity as the established religion (even if they vigorously opposed the establishment of a single denomination), which encouraged the conflation of catholicity and Protestant nationalism.

After the Civil War, there was hardly any memory of the antebellum debates. In 1870 a column in the *Home and Foreign Record* set forth the official position of the united church. A truly American system of education must be universal, equal, and supported at the public expense. The author suggested that "if 'all men are created equal' and 'endowed by their Creator with certain inalienable rights'. . . so also it is self-evident that the nature, exercise and limits of these rights must be taught in the appropriate period of youth, to each generation. Thus the ends of government are accomplished in the most cheap, effectual, and wholesome way." Further, he argued that while no creed could be taught, "the Bible should be read as an authority, and for its information upon matters of infinite value to the soul of man; a brief prayer, in some simple form if preferred should be offered," juvenile hymns should be sung, and a "spirit of reverence towards God and respect for his truth should pervade the literature and tuition of the school room." In this Protestant vision for the common schools he insisted that "every pastor of a church should feel. . . [that] he is called, by his vows to God, by his professional duty, by his interest in the future of the youth, and by his patriotism to diligently cultivate." Breckinridge and Thornwell had won the day. In the union of Old and New Schools, catholicity had become a particular version of American Protestant nationalism.[28]

The irony of all this is that Breckinridge and Thornwell had been two of the most bitterly anti–New School partisans of the 1830s, while Hodge had played the moderate role—even wondering about the constitutionality of the excision of the New School synods that Breckinridge had engineered. Thornwell also accused Hodge of being a moderate in their debates over Presbyterian polity. But Hodge seems to have been the only one of the three who recognized that the common schools could not carry the load of catholicity. Perhaps his proximity to the common school battles in New York and the 1844 Bible Riots of Philadelphia (where Protestants and Catholics were literally shooting each other in the streets of Philadelphia over the question of whether the Bible should be read in the common schools) helped him to see the frailty of Protestant nationalism, and his broader vision of catholicity (which included Roman Catholicism as a part of the visible church) certainly influenced his attitude toward the role of the Old School Presbyterian Church. Perhaps that is also why Hodge remained one of the few holdouts who believed that reunion with the New School was unwise.[29]

In 1861 the Old School Presbyterian Church divided along the Mason-Dixon line, and within months American and Confederate nationalism had trumped Presbyterian ecclesiology in both halves of the divided Old School. Sectional political ideologies overran the earlier emphasis on catholicity. And perhaps not surprisingly, Robert J. Breckinridge and James H. Thornwell played fundamentally similar parts (though on opposite sides) in voicing the Old School's transfer of the catholicity of the visible church to a Protestant vision of the nation. Thornwell helped author the southern Old School's declaration of loyalty to the Confederacy in 1861, while Breckinridge authored a statement of loyalty of the northern Old School to the federal government in 1862.[30]

Ironically, by identifying their church so closely with the Union, Presbyterians allowed—or even encouraged—the very transference of catholicity from the church to the state. The mystical union that had once defined the church now referred to the nation. Nowhere was this better expressed than by Robert J. Breckinridge in June of 1862. Reflecting on the General Assembly's statement of loyalty to the federal government that he had drafted just weeks before, he declared that no "loyal church" could have done other than to remain "*loyal* to Christ—*loyal* to his truth—*loyal* to the free and noble civil institutions he has given us—*loyal* to the magistrates he has set up over us—*loyal* to the flock committed to her charge—*loyal* to the fallen race it is her sublime mission to evangelize!"[31] Loyalty to Christ and loyalty to the Union had become identical. Certainly the departure of the southern wing of the Old School and the patriotic fervor surrounding the Civil War played a significant role in revealing the similarities between the Old School and the New, but in fact the Old School shared the same vision as the New School for "the Kingdom of Christ and the American Nation" that Marsden outlines in his ninth chapter.

NEW SCHOOL PRESBYTERIANISM AND THE RISE OF FUNDAMENTALISM AND MODERNISM

In his later works, George Marsden developed the further story of the evangelical mind. His 1980 masterpiece, *Fundamentalism and American*

Culture, 1870–1925, expanded the narrative, though largely staying within the Presbyterian and Baptist traditions. Likewise, in 1987 he published *Reforming Fundamentalism: Fuller Seminary and the New Evangelicalism,* telling the story of one of the most prominent evangelical institutions of the mid-twentieth century. In these narratives he continued to unfold the themes that he had developed in the *Evangelical Mind and the New School Presbyterian Experience.* In these new books he suggested a connection between the New School and the rise of fundamentalism and evangelicalism, and he also continued to identify Old School Presbyterianism as a more strictly confessional tradition than it actually was.

In the epilogue to *The Evangelical Mind,* Marsden suggests that the New School should be seen as having both protoliberal *and* protofundamentalist tendencies. One of his few references to the Old School suggests that the large number of early dispensational leaders produced by the Old School may indicate that it had more protofundamentalist tendencies (247–48 n. 5). But at the same time, Old School Presbyterianism could also be seen as contributing heavily to the rise of theological modernism. In fact, the first notorious theological liberal of the Presbyterian Church, David Swing, was an Old School Presbyterian. A student of Nathan L. Rice at Cincinnati Theological Seminary, Swing had been ordained in 1854 by the Old School Oxford Presbytery, while serving as a professor at Miami University. After supplying several Old School churches around Miami during his tenure there, he was called to Westminster Presbyterian Church (New School) in 1866 and so spent only three years in the New School.[32]

Hence Old School Presbyterianism should not be identified with Charles Hodge, or with a strictly confessional tradition, or with the "spirituality of the church" views of a James H. Thornwell. All of these traditions were part of the Old School Presbyterian Church, but the Old School simply viewed itself as the Presbyterian Church—purged, certainly, of the Congregational element that had crept in after the Plan of Union of 1801, but consisting of the entire Presbyterian tradition. As such the roots of both fundamentalism and modernism can be found as easily in the Old School as in the New School, though perhaps in somewhat different ways.

But of course, these caveats to Marsden's reading of the Old School only serve to highlight the accuracy of the narrative he told! After all, the result is to show that what Marsden saw regarding *The Evangelical Mind and the New School Presbyterian Experience* had a far broader currency than he imagined. Nineteenth-century evangelicals of various stripes openly embraced a distinctively American blend of republicanism, common sense thought, and Protestant nationalism in an attempt to maintain evangelical hegemony over the early republic. Ironically, they also sowed the seeds of their own destruction by unwittingly embracing the very forces that would render them impotent. In this respect the central thesis of Marsden's earliest monograph has only been further advanced and supported by works that have appeared since 1970, by James Turner, Nathan Hatch, and Mark Noll, among many others.[33]

NOTES

1. George M. Marsden, *The Evangelical Mind and the New School Presbyterian Experience* (New Haven, CT: Yale University Press, 1970), xii; subsequent citations to this work are given parenthetically in the text.
2. Leo P. Hirrel, *Children of Wrath: New School Calvinism and Antebellum Reform* (Lexington: University Press of Kentucky, 1998), 2.
3. *Minutes of the General Assembly of the Presbyterian Church in the United States of America* (hereafter *Minutes*) (1837), 510.
4. "A Plea for Total Abstinence from Intoxicating Liquors," *Baltimore Literary and Religious Magazine*, June 1840, 510–17, quote on 516. Breckinridge had caused no little controversy when he preached on total abstinence in Baltimore, in spite of the fact that one of the ruling elders in the Second Presbyterian Church was a wine merchant. Edmund Arthur Moore, "The Earlier Life of Robert J. Breckinridge, 1800–1845" (PhD diss., University of Chicago, 1932), 35.
5. "Intemperance," *Watchman of the South*, February 18, 1841; February 25, 1841; March 4, 1841; March 11, 1841.
6. X, "Decision of the Synod of Pittsburgh, on the Question of Continuing the Retailer of Alcoholic Drinks in Church Membership," *Presbyterian and Herald*, December 8, 1842.
7. *Minutes* (1843), 189.
8. L., "New Term of Communion in the Presbyterian Church," *Presbyterian of the West*, November 30, 1848, 38. In the same issue, it was reported that the Synod of New York refused to make temperance a test of church member-

ship. The Synod of Pittsburgh went unchallenged in 1855 when it declared that "members of the Church engaged in the traffic of intoxicating drinks as a beverage are liable to discipline when they sell contrary to the law of the land, or the laws of God." *Presbyterian Magazine*, December 1855, 562.

9. *Minutes* (1848), 168. The committee consisted of ministers Dr. Samuel McFarren, pastor of Congruity, Pennsylvania; Dr. William Smith, editor of the *Presbyterian of the West*; Lancelot G. Bell, pastor of Fairfield, Iowa; and Melanchthon W. Jacobus, professor at Western Theological Seminary, along with elders S. Millspaugh of Hudson Presbytery (New York), Alexander Cromartie of Florida Presbytery (Florida), and C. S. Carrington of West Hanover Presbytery (Virginia). Since committees were usually appointed by the moderator, the fact that the three leading ministers on the committee were members of synods that had taken similar actions suggests that the moderator, Alexander T. McGill of Western Theological Seminary, may have desired some such statement.

10. Joseph R. Gusfield, *Symbolic Crusade: Status Politics and the American Temperance Movement* (1963; repr., Urbana: University of Illinois Press, 1986), 44, 45.

11. John J. Rumbarger, *Profits, Power, and Prohibition: Alcohol Reform and the Industrializing of America, 1800–1930* (Albany: State University of New York Press, 1989), xxii.

12. C. Bruce Staiger, "Abolitionism and the Presbyterian Schism of 1837–1838," *Mississippi Valley Historical Review* 36 (December 1949): 391–414. This was the dominant view in the middle decades of the twentieth century, accepted by Louis Filler, *The Crusade against Slavery, 1830–1860* (New York: Harper and Row, 1960), 185–86; Timothy L. Smith, *Revivalism and Social Reform: American Protestantism on the Eve of the Civil War* (1957; repr., Baltimore: Johns Hopkins University Press, 1980), 185–86; Donald G. Mathews, *Religion in the Old South* (Chicago: University of Chicago Press, 1977), 163–64.

13. James H. Moorhead, "The 'Restless Spirit of Radicalism': Old School Fears and the Schism of 1837," *Journal of Presbyterian History* 78, no. 1 (Spring 2000): 19–34. See also Earl A. Pope, *New England Calvinism and the Disruption of the Presbyterian Church* (New York: Garland, 1987), 5–30; Chris Padgett, "Evangelicals Divided: Abolition and the Plan of Union's Demise in Ohio's Western Reserve," in *Religion and the Antebellum Debate over Slavery*, ed. John R. McKivigan and Mitchell Snay (Athens: University of Georgia Press, 1998), 249–72; Victor B. Howard, *Conscience and Slavery: The Evangelistic Calvinist Domestic Mission, 1837–1861* (Kent, OH: Kent State University Press, 1990), ch. 2.

14. For a detailed analysis of the regional discussions and voting patterns leading up to the split, see Peter J. Wallace, "'The Bond of Union': The Old School Presbyterian Church and the American Nation, 1837–1861" (PhD diss., University of Notre Dame, 2004), ch. 1.

15. Many of the "moderates" in New Jersey, Tennessee, and Virginia were convinced that Barnes was in "error" but that he should only be rebuked, not removed from the ministry.

16. *Minutes* (1836), 271.

17. Editorial, "Slavery," *Southern Christian Herald*, March 23, 1836. This is covered in more detail in Wallace, "'Bond of Union,'" ch. 1.

18. The standard history of education is Lawrence A. Cremin's multivolume study *American Education*. On the antebellum era, see Cremin, *American Education: The National Experience, 1783–1876* (New York: Harper and Row, 1980); Frederick M. Binder, *The Age of the Common School, 1830–1865* (New York: John Wiley and Sons, 1974); Michael Katz, *Class, Bureaucracy and Schools: The Illusion of Educational Change in America* (New York: Praeger, 1975); Donald H. Parkerson and Jo Ann Parkerson, *The Emergence of the Common School in the U.S. Countryside* (Lewiston, NY: Edwin Mellen Press, 1998).

19. Lewis Joseph Sherrill, *Presbyterian Parochial Schools, 1846–1870* (New Haven, CT: Yale University Press, 1932), 8–11. There is a connection between this sort of plan (which would later include a college in each synod) and the secular proposals of Benjamin Rush and Thomas Jefferson forty years before. They have a common source in the educational system of Scotland, where each parish had a school, and each presbytery an academy.

20. Quoted by Charles Hodge, "General Assembly," *Biblical Repertory and Princeton Review* 18 (July 1846): 431.

21. Ibid., 431–38.

22. Ibid., 438. Hodge would lay out his rationale in greater detail in his sermon to the 1847 General Assembly, "The General Assembly," *Southern Presbyterian Review* 1, no. 2 (September 1847). The reviewer, James Henley Thornwell, commented that if the state schools excluded "the distinctive principles of Christianity," then "the church will be driven to establish institutions of her own" (98). Thornwell, however, did not think that the state had excluded Christianity. Others who agreed that Hodge's sermon had been instrumental included Cortlandt Van Rensselaer, *Presbyterian Treasury*, January 1850, 5, and Stuart Robinson, "The General Assembly of 1854," *Southern Presbyterian Review* 8 (January, 1855): 426.

23. See Wallace, "'Bond of Union,'" ch. 3.

24. "Papal Interference with Public Schools," *Baltimore Literary and Religious Magazine*, December 1840, 535–36.

25. Robert J. Breckinridge, "Denominational Education," *Southern Presbyterian Review* 3, no. 1 (June 1849): 18–19.

26. Charles Hodge, "The General Assembly," *Biblical Repertory and Princeton Review* 22, no. 3 (July 1850): 459.

27. James Henley Thornwell, "Does Education Belong to the Church or State?" *Watchman and Observer*, December 22, 1853, 76. Thornwell cites Breckinridge's 1849 article in the *Southern Presbyterian Review* quite favorably.

28. "American System of Education," *Home and Foreign Record* 21 (1870): 221–22.

29. "The Public Schools of Philadelphia," *Presbyterian*, January 21, 1843, 10. The Philadelphia riots of 1844 have been described by Vincent P. Lannie and Bernard C. Diethorn, "For the Honor and Glory of God: The Philadelphia Bible Riots of 1844," *History of Education Quarterly* 8, no. 1 (Spring 1968): 44–106. Binder points out that the grand jury that investigated the riots reported that blame was largely due to "the effort of a portion of the community to exclude the Bible from our Public Schools" (*Age of the Common School*, 69). For Hodge's battle with Breckinridge and Thornwell over the validity of Roman Catholic baptism, see Wallace, "'Bond of Union,'" ch. 3.

30. Thornwell, "Address to All Churches of Jesus Christ throughout the World," in *The Collected Writings of James Henley Thornwell: Theological and Controversial*, ed. John B. Adger and John L. Girardeau (Richmond, VA: Presbyterian Committee of Publication, 1873), 4:454. This statement launched a nine-page defense of slavery, thus forming more than half of the "Address." Erskine Clarke, "Southern Nationalism and Columbia Theological Seminary," *American Presbyterians* 66, no. 2 (1988): 123–33.

31. R. J. B., "The General Assembly of 1862, of the Presbyterian Church in the United States of America," *Danville Quarterly Review* 2, no. 2 (June 1862): 301–70.

32. Marilee Munger Scroggs, *A Light in the City: The Fourth Presbyterian Church of Chicago* (Chicago: Fourth Presbyterian Church of Chicago, 1990), 18–23.

33. James Turner, *Without God, without Creed: The Origins of Unbelief in America* (Baltimore: Johns Hopkins University Press, 1986; Nathan O. Hatch, *The Democratization of American Christianity* (New Haven, CT: Yale University Press, 1991); Mark A. Noll, *America's God: From Jonathan Edwards to Abraham Lincoln* (New York: Oxford University Press, 2002).

CHAPTER 6

The African American Great Awakening and Modernity, 1866–1900

JAY R. CASE

"This has been a year of revivals in Georgia," Henry McNeal Turner reported in November 1866. "I never expected to see such a sight this side of heaven, nor do I believe such a scene was ever witnessed before in America."[1] A minister in the African Methodist Episcopal Church (AME), Turner had come south during the Civil War as the first black chaplain in the Union Army. After a brief stint with the Freedman's Bureau, Turner had been appointed as superintendent of AME missions in Georgia and pastor of the AME church in Macon.[2] In May of 1866 he had launched a series of prayer meetings and nightly revival meetings at his church. After several days, "scores came forward" in response to an invitation for salvation. "From that time till now convert has followed convert, till in every part of the city it looks like a jubilee," he wrote.[3] The conversions extended to other churches in the region, as well, with some churches reporting as many as 450 individuals seeking salvation. In Cuthburt, Georgia, Turner's revival services were so loud that a Freedman's Bureau official sent a man with the message that "it was time to stop that noise!" Indignantly, Turner told the messenger that "he was crazy, and that we were all free people."[4] The meeting continued.

One does not usually think of 1866 as a "year of revivals" for African Americans. This was the year, after all, that the Fourteenth Amendment was ratified, Congress passed a civil rights bill, and race riots broke out in Memphis and New Orleans. Across the South in 1866, freedpeople embraced their newfound liberty by attending school, relocating separated family members, looking for opportunities to grow their own crops, and attending political conventions. Yet they also converted in revivals led by black preachers. Revival reports poured in from regions far beyond Turner's AME circuit in Georgia. "Some of my brethren say they have never witnessed before such an outpouring of the Spirit of God upon the Church," wrote a black pastor from Raleigh, North Carolina. In Texas, an AME minister reported that "the Holy Ghost came down with great power, and many souls were hopefully converted to Christ."[5] The *Christian Recorder*, flagship newspaper of the AME Church, gave news of additional revivals in Louisiana, Missouri, Tennessee, Georgia, South Carolina, North Carolina, Virginia, and Maryland. Men and women, the elderly and youth converted. Revivals took place in city churches, small towns, and "many plantations and secluded spots."[6] Many commented on the unprecedented numbers that responded. "The revival is one such as I have never before experienced," wrote an AME pastor from Norfolk, Virginia, who received more than two hundred members and six hundred inquirers during a ten-week series of daily meetings.[7] A black pastor in Annapolis, Maryland, reported that "the oldest inhabitants say there never was such a time," as the crowds were so big they were "obliged to put some of the mourners in the pulpit."[8]

These evangelical revivals constituted the beginning of a widespread religious movement that might be termed the African American Great Awakening. From emancipation through the end of the century, revivalism swept the black communities of the South, bringing significant growth to black Baptist and Methodist denominations. While historians have explained how black Christians seized the opportunity afforded by emancipation to leave white-controlled denominations, the evangelical growth of independent black denominations in this era has gone largely unexamined.[9] This growth did not simply stem from black Christians switching to new churches. The African American Great Awakening added several million African Americans to the Christian faith and doubled the percentage of American blacks who considered themselves Christian. It was a movement that would have a significant impact on African American culture. In fact, the emergence of independent black churches after emancipation should be seen as a religious movement with important political and civic implications, rather than a political and civic event with religious implications.

The African American Great Awakening also provides a new angle from which to view evangelicalism and its paradoxical relationship to modernity. Emerging in the red-hot forge of Reconstruction and Jim Crow racial tensions, the African American Great Awakening produced a brand of evangelicalism shaped by a deep ambivalence toward American culture. On the one hand, the African American Great Awakening thrived amid some very modern religious arrangements: a sudden disestablishment of former elites, a range of religious options battling in a competitive religious atmosphere, energetic movement-building efforts by democratized leaders, the assertion of institutional autonomy, and the establishment of systematized denominational structures. Yet the evangelical dynamics of the African American Great Awakening also wired the movement with resisters to key aspects of the modern American establishment. African American evangelicalism held tightly to its supernaturalistic and enthusiastic forms of religion, preserved elements of African culture, rejected reigning conceptions of Christian civilization, hammered out a sense of peoplehood that contradicted modern conceptions of identity built upon the nation-state, and tied African American culture to local communities rather than the ideal of the autonomous individual. Amid these modern and countermodern tensions, the critical element of race shaped African American evangelicalism in ways that distinguished it from white evangelicalism.

The African American Great Awakening did not simply replicate the First and Second Great Awakenings. This evangelical movement built itself upon the vibrant, active, and distinctive faith of slave Christianity, playing itself out among newly emancipated freedpeople who found themselves in a unique situation.[10] But like the earlier Awakenings it unfolded as a popular movement, driven by the efforts of ordinary preachers and laypeople, acting in a newly created setting of religious disestablishment. This was no insignificant development. The African American Great Awakening ensured that independent black evangelicalism, with its own paradoxical relationship to American culture, would form the heart of African American life for the century that followed.

AFRICAN AMERICAN EVANGELICALISM AND MODERNITY

Many freedpeople believed that God was moving in a special way in the aftermath of emancipation. African American ministers noted that the revivals brought people into the faith who had not been there before. "Persons who were thought to be immovable, have been brought into the church and powerfully converted, not under me, but under God," Henry McNeal Turner wrote.[11] This is why Turner made a distinction between the 17,000 church membership transfers to the AME church that he had supervised and the additional 14,300 new conversions that occurred under his direction between 1865 and 1871.[12] The two sets of numbers encapsulate the two sides of the African American Great Awakening: the movement of existing black Christians into independent black churches and the addition of new members into the faith. In many places, new converts may have represented as much as half of the members who joined independent black churches.[13] Statistics of the religious adherence of African Americans in the nineteenth century necessarily rely on estimates, but the evidence indicates that there was more going on after emancipation than church switching. The number of black Baptists in the United States increased from around 400,000 in 1860, to about 800,000 in 1882, to 2.2 million in 1906.[14] Black Methodists jumped from 190,000 in 1860, to more than 300,000 in 1876, to more than 1 million in 1906.[15] Some of this increase can be attributed to population growth and the institutionalization of unchurched slaves who had practiced Christianity in secret, but these factors cannot explain all of this growth. The highest estimates for African American Christians in 1860 that include the "invisible institution" under slavery end up at about 22 percent of the black population, up from 4 percent in 1800.[16] By 1900, the estimated percentage of African American Christians had risen to 42 percent.[17] Although the statistics for nineteenth-century black Christians cannot be nailed down with precision, the existence of widespread revivals, reports of "immovable" blacks converting, and the massive growth of recorded black membership all point to large numbers of new converts in the last decades of the century.

This postwar evangelistic growth forms a key chapter in the story of African American Christianity. If it is true, as Sylvia Frey and Betty Wood write, that "the conversion of African Americans to Protestant Christianity was a, perhaps *the* defining moment in African American history," then the African American Great Awakening propelled African Americans into a critical stage in that history.[18] The First Great Awakening, the Second Great Awakening, and antebellum slave religion laid the foundation and erected the framework for African American Christianity. The African American Great Awakening filled in the walls and constructed the design of the edifice.

That design made effective use of the materials that modernity had handed African Americans. While all sorts of new political, economic, and social obstacles hedged in African Americans in the late nineteenth century, black Baptist and Methodist churches thrived. This growth emerged, in part, because the African American Great Awakening took advantage of a religious arrangement quite characteristic of modernity: religious disestablishment. This arrangement was something quite new for the freedpeople. Under the slave system, black Christians usually joined whites in biracial worship settings but sometimes separated themselves in the "invisible institution" they created. As Eugene Genovese has stated, "The whites of the Old South tried to shape the religious life of their slaves, and the slaves overtly, covertly and even intuitively fought to shape it themselves."[19] But even as slaves went to great lengths to shape their religious lives, the reality was that they still worshipped under a de facto religious establishment. Emancipation struck down this racialized religious establishment. Even though whites managed to reassert power in political, economic, educational, and social spheres after emancipation, American society provided whites with very few tools that they could use to control African American religion. The freedpeople had more freedom to form independent black religious bodies, structure worship the way that they wished, and follow black ministers who preached as they saw fit. In fact, during Reconstruction's "Unfinished Revolution," African Americans enjoyed more liberty in the religious sphere than they did in politics, economics, education, or social relations, a pattern that continued well into the twentieth century.[20]

To be sure, Christian slaves had enjoyed a limited amount of religious freedom, particularly in the early nineteenth century. During the era of the Early Republic, much of American Christianity had become democratized in a shifting culture in which old hierarchies had broken down, popular audiences no longer deferred to mediating elites, and religious movements competed against one another for adherents. This religious environment resonated deeply with many African Americans, as democratized Christianity made substantial gains among blacks who joined religious movements shaped by popular leaders.[21]

But slavery prevented democratized Christianity from unfolding among black communities in the same way that it did in white communities. As the slave system expanded and hardened in the nineteenth century, white evangelicals attempted "to take back with one hand what had been granted by the other."[22] Antislavery initiatives in southern Methodist and Baptist churches faded away. White Methodist and Baptist leaders in the South increasingly evoked proslavery arguments and biblical passages urging slaves to obey their masters. The racialized religious establishment reinvigorated itself in the South after 1830, limiting the free exercise of religion among evangelical blacks. A swath of new laws swept the South that, though they varied from state to state, reflected a common desire to prevent black religious movements from challenging the existing order. Many state governments passed laws making it illegal to teach slaves to read and write, undermining a key component of evangelical faith: the ability to read the Bible for oneself. Some slaves still taught one another to read, some whites defied these laws, and some states permitted black literacy, but the vast majority of slaves remained illiterate, with no means to learn. Some states made it illegal to ordain black ministers, and most states made it illegal for slaves to hold religious meetings without white supervision, impeding the evangelical impulse to promote ministers on the basis of their preaching abilities. Many slaveowners would not allow slaves to hold religious services during the week, and some prohibited all religious services among blacks. Meanwhile, southern Methodist, Baptist, and Presbyterian denominations launched missions to the slaves that, though motivated by a sincere concern to bring slaves to the Christian faith, were also designed to police black worship and reinforce the validity of the slave system.[23]

Then the Civil War and emancipation suddenly arrived. The African American Great Awakening swept through black communities in the decades that followed. The evangelical growth of this movement indicates that, contrary to some proslavery arguments, slavery proved to be more of a hindrance to the expansion of Christianity among blacks than the means for its promotion. Statements made by the freedpeople to sympathetic northern missionaries indicate ways that the racialized religious establishment had hindered evangelical faith. Some freedpeople reported that for years they had wanted to be baptized but couldn't get their master's permission. Others explained how slavery had restricted the freedom of black religious leaders. As one freedperson explained, some black slaves were good preachers, but under slavery they "couldn't preach as they want to, must preach as Massah allowed." Even though southern white evangelical ministers often cooperated with black evangelicals in promoting the faith, the slave system placed slaves in a set of social relations that blinded white ministers to the sort of struggles and trials that slaves faced. "We couldn't tell, NO PREACHER, NEVER, how we suffer all these long years," one African American explained to a northern missionary. "He knowed nothing about we."[24]

Emancipation, then, presented the southern blacks with a modern arrangement of religious disestablishment. But in 1866, it was not certain to anybody just what African Americans would do with this new kind of religious freedom. It is easy to assume that the freedpeople were destined to form independent black Baptist and Methodist churches, since these churches became so integral to African American life in the century after emancipation. In reality, a variety of different religious bodies competed for African American attention, each claiming a limited amount of success among African Americans.

An examination of the religious options that African Americans largely rejected helps to bring the modern components of African

American evangelicalism into focus. With numerous religious and cultural options available to them, the freedpeople proved to be quite selective in the religious and cultural institutions they adopted, a selectivity that played itself out in both the new conversions and the church switching of the African American Great Awakening. First of all, as scholars have long noted, a large majority of freedpeople rejected the southern white evangelical bodies that most black Christians had belonged to under slavery. Most Christian slaves had been members of southern Baptist churches and the Methodist Episcopal Church, South. While a small percentage of freedpeople remained in these churches, most black Christians in the first decades after the war voted with their feet and fled their former churches. Despite existing patterns of biracial worship and the existence of postwar revivalism in white churches, these evangelical denominations were unable to hold onto most black members or woo new black converts to their congregations.[25] Slavery had instilled within the freedpeople a deep-seated sensitivity to the structural and institutional forms of racism, a sensitivity that extended to religious life. Many freedpeople who had heard proslavery sermons in white Baptist and Methodist churches happily found preachers with different exegetical perspectives.

Similar dynamics operated in other southern denominations with white leadership. These institutions not only failed to attract large numbers of freedpeople after the Civil War but often lost many that they had. Most of the six thousand blacks in Protestant Episcopal churches surprised their former masters by abandoning Episcopalianism for independent black Baptist and Methodist bodies. The General Assembly of the Southern Presbyterian Church faced a similar problem with its thirty-four thousand former slaves and attempted to stanch the bleeding in 1874 by setting up independent black congregations and presbyteries.[26] About six thousand slaves had belonged to the Roman Catholic Church, which was limited to a few regions in the South such as Louisiana and Charleston, South Carolina. Unlike the Episcopalians and Presbyterians, the Catholic Church made some inroads among African Americans in the late nineteenth century, increasing their numbers to thirty-eight thousand by 1906. Still, this growth paled in comparison to that of black Baptist and Methodist bodies.[27]

While blacks' desire to extract themselves from white southern oversight fits existing historical narratives, it might be less obvious why the freedpeople were not attracted to northern white denominations that competed with white southerners for black allegiance. Represented by the missionaries and reformers who arrived in the South in the wake of Union troops, these religious bodies had fought against slavery, provided educational aid to newly emancipated African Americans, and staunchly supported Radical Republican attempts to refashion southern society. Biracial worship still remained a real option, particularly with white Christians who fought against slavery. Yet even with these civic credentials in their favor, these northern denominations failed to win over most freedpeople.

Essentially, these northerners can be divided into two broad groups, each of which offered the freedpeople religious resources and worldviews embedded in the educational, economic, and social institutions that the missionaries established. The first group, best exemplified by the American Freedman's Union Commission (AFUC), brought liberal theological sensibilities derived from Unitarian, Universalist, Garrisonian, Hicksite Quaker, or freethinker backgrounds. Though they did not promote religious conversion, these AFUC reformers hoped the freedpeople would adopt their cultural vision on the basis of moral instruction, common schools, and liberal theology.[28] The freedpeople flocked to AFUC schools, but they largely rejected the liberal religious vision that accompanied these educational programs. An incident that took place on the Sea Islands of South Carolina during the war illustrates dynamics that would continue in African American religious life in decades to come. Several Unitarian reformers had complained to a Union general that a black congregation, under the direction of a northern Baptist minister, had instituted "closed communion," thereby excluding the non-Baptist teachers and reformers from the sacrament. When the general intervened in the congregation by suggesting to the black elders that perhaps a different minister would be better suited for them, the black elders stood their ground, making the point that their Baptist congregation had the authority to call the minister of their choosing. Union officials responded by pressuring the white Baptist minister out of his position anyway. The AFUC reformers then endeavored to explain Unitarian theology to the black Baptists. Despite, or perhaps because of these attempts at ecclesiastical instruction, the African Americans continued closed communion under the direction of their black elders. The particulars of this incident would not be widely repeated during Reconstruction, but it reflects the independent spirit, cultural selectivity, and desire for evangelical faith that would characterize African American church life in the decades ahead. Very few African Americans throughout the South adopted liberal theological perspectives, even though they came embedded in the moral instruction established by teachers in many of the schools that blacks supported.[29]

Northern white evangelical missionary agencies represented the second group of northern reformers that offered their program available to African Americans. Congregationalists, northern Presbyterians, northern Methodists, and northern Baptists led this effort, well into the early twentieth century. Thanks to their foreign missionary experience, these white northern evangelical agencies carried with them a vision for training non-Anglo preachers and teachers, leading them to establish seminaries and normal schools for African Americans, in addition to Sunday schools and common schools.[30] But even though they resonated more fully with these northern programs, most freedpeople did not throw their lot in with them. By many measures, the Methodist Episcopal Church (MEC) enjoyed more success among African Americans than any northern denomination led by whites. With its antislavery credentials, revivalistic sensibilities, organizational acumen, educational resources, and ties to the northern white establishment, the MEC had a lot to offer to the freedpeople. Indeed, the MEC established numerous elementary and secondary schools for blacks, founded a dozen black colleges and seminaries, and attracted 246,000 African Americans to its congregations by 1890, claiming seven times as many blacks as the next largest white denomination, the northern Baptists.[31] While these instances of biracial cooperation are not insignificant, the MEC numbers were dwarfed by two independent black Methodist denominations, the AME and AME Zion bodies, which drew in three times as many black members as the MEC.[32] Again, African Americans embraced the educational institutions of these northern evangelicals but largely rejected their religious offerings.

The African American Great Awakening, then, flourished in a system of religious autonomy based on black leadership. A northern white official from the American Baptist Home Missionary Society reported from New Orleans in 1870 that the freedpeople were "determined to have pastors and teachers of their own color, and no argument can dissuade them."[33] When Henry McNeal Turner arrived in Lowell, Georgia, in 1866, blacks filled the church so full that scores of people could not get into the building. "The idea of seeing a colored elder among them almost set the people crazy," he explained.[34] With a finely tuned sense of the pervasiveness and subtleties of racism, most African Americans had little interest in simply adopting at face value the religious visions that whites offered them, particularly since these initiatives did not guarantee that whites would share positions of authority equally with blacks. So the northern missionary agencies largely contented themselves with providing education, while African Americans themselves led black congregations and evangelized their fellow freedpeople.

In true democratized fashion the African American Great Awakening swept the South through the efforts of ordinary black believers. African American congregations evaluated black preachers not on the basis of their theological and educational credentials but on the basis of their effectiveness in stirring audiences and their abilities to identify with the spiritual situation of ordinary blacks. During the 1860s and '70s, Turner led the way for the AME Church in mobilizing black preachers, licensing hundreds of illiterate and poorly educated black ministers, asking candidates simply "Can you preach?" and sometimes resorting to "Can you sing and pray?" if they waffled on the first question. He later claimed that he gave each candidate a long examination, but the preaching candidate's desire to evangelize and willingness to undergo future training functioned as the most important qualifications. Turner licensed preachers on street corners and train trips, filling out the preaching certificate on whatever surface lay close at hand.[35] Throughout the South, African Americans responded enthusiastically to the evangelistic efforts of these ordinary African American preachers, who understood the needs and circumstances of their people better than more highly educated white leaders.

COUNTERMODERN CHARACTERISTICS OF AFRICAN AMERICAN EVANGELICALISM

Yet there is more to the story of the African American Great Awakening than religious disestablishment. Historians have long noted that black Baptist and Methodist churches provided African Americans with institutional autonomy, democratized black leadership, and provided the opportunity to make a religious choice that seemed better suited to them than other options. Each of these characteristics fit well with modernity. Yet the very modern structures of the African American Great Awakening simultaneously provided the means for ordinary black Christians to resist other characteristics of modernity that dominated nineteenth-century America. The paradox comes into view with a closer examination of the African American Great Awakening.

Take, for instance, the African American resistance to the religious vision provided by Daniel Alexander Payne, a prominent black leader of the African Methodist Episcopal Church. Payne would seem to be just the sort of evangelical minister that the freedpeople would want to follow. As the most famous bishop of the AME denomination, a champion of abolition, a spokesperson for the independent black church, an erudite theological leader, and an indefatigable promoter of education, Payne embodied key elements of the new society that freedpeople hoped to establish after the Civil War. Indeed, because of his extensive administrative and educational efforts in the late nineteenth century, Payne deserves credit for establishing a great deal of the institutional infrastructure of the AME Church in the South.[36]

But the freedpeople did not embrace Payne's spirituality—or at least, not all of it. Payne and black Yankee ministers like him regularly traveled African American circuits attempting, and often failing, to eliminate certain popular religious practices among ordinary African American Christians. The most famous example comes from a description Payne gave of his response to a ring shout at an AME "bush meeting" in 1878. Payne reported that "after the sermon they formed a ring, and with coats off sung, clapped their hands and stamped their feet in a most ridiculous and heathenish way."[37] Expressing his unhappiness with the "strange delusions that many ignorant but well-meaning people labor under," Payne asked the minister to order the congregation to stop their dancing and clapping and "sit down and sing in a rational manner."[38] He then pulled the minister aside and explained that "it was a heathenish way to worship and disgraceful to themselves, the race, and the Christian name." Later that afternoon the young AME minister approached Payne and defended the practice, arguing that "sinners won't get converted unless there is a ring." Payne replied that this singing would fail to convert anyone because "nothing but the Spirit of God and the word of God can convert sinners." The young minister countered by declaring that "the Spirit of God works upon people in different ways." He explained that "at campmeeting there must be a ring here, a ring there, and a ring over yonder, or sinners will not get converted."[39]

Daniel Alexander Payne's use of the term *heathenish* indicates that he recognized what twentieth-century scholars later demonstrated: the ring shout had some sort of tie to African culture. Elements of African culture, though transformed, had persisted in black evangelicalism. These vestiges of African culture emerged in the shouting, dancing, and rhythmic clapping of black worship, as well as in black perceptions of pervasive supernaturalism, such as the activities of Satan or God speaking though dreams.[40] To Payne, this was a problem. Black Yankee ministers saw themselves working to "uplift" African Americans who had recently emerged from the "degradation of slavery." Accepting the modern claim that civilization had progressed beyond the superstitious ideas of primitive societies, elite black ministers like Payne tended to believe that the highest forms of Christianity and civilization conformed to the standards established by the type of evangelicalism found in the fair environs of New England.[41] Payne proudly declared, in fact, that with abolition, the defeat of the Confederacy, and northern missionaries at work in the South, "New England ideas, sentiments, and principles will ultimately rule the entire South."[42]

The problem was that New England civilization disdained particular practices and conceptions of Christianity that resonated with the freedpeople. Payne's insistence that the congregation "sing in a rational manner" reveals a characteristically modern view of the relationship between spirituality and rationality. Before the Enlightenment, many highly educated Christians had accepted supernatural activity, religious ecstasy, and visible manifestations of God's activities as realities. The Puritans, for instance, found no problem reconciling pervasive supernatural activity with erudite theological reflection.[43] But Enlightenment advocates derided supernatural activity as superstition, clamped down on religious enthusiasm as a threat to social order, and asserted that there was no way to empirically verify any special activity of God. By the nineteenth century, Yankee evangelicals, like many other Christians with ties to the cultural establishment, reshaped their faith to accommodate these beliefs, which they defined as more "rational." Under these modern forces of disenchantment, perceptions of supernatural activity and visible manifestations of divine agency were greatly attenuated.[44] While elite black ministers like Payne adopted this modern way of thinking, most African Americans did not. Forty years after emancipation, the most insightful observer of African American life, W. E. B. DuBois, identified three persistent elements of African American worship. DuBois correctly noted that these worship practices drew from African culture, but it can also be said that they countered Enlightenment claims about the relationship between rationality and religious practice. DuBois famously described "the Preacher," who stirred the congregation into an enthusiastic response to Scripture; "the Music," which evoked both the joyful and doleful realities of the African American situation; and "the Frenzy," a variety of expressive responses grounded in the conviction that "without the visible manifestation of the God there could be no true communion with the Invisible."[45]

Payne's resistance to the ring shout has been well noted by historians wishing to demonstrate that black elites, with their ideals of Victorian respectability, failed because of the class dimensions of their bourgeois chauvinism. As one historian writes, Payne was "swimming upstream in wrestling with the concrete issue of class divisions within the African-based community, expressed in terms of religion."[46] Yet this class-based explanation cannot carry the day. Ordinary African American Christians accepted other middle-class reforms proposed by elite black ministers, such as the use of new hymns and more regularity in service times. Freedpeople throughout the South enthusiastically welcomed and embraced the cornerstone of middle-class Yankee respectability, the common school.⁴⁷ Furthermore, the highest concerns of the young AME minister at the bush meeting did not derive from issues of class, civilization, or black identity. He did not protest to Payne by saying, "This is how common folk do things," or even "This is how we express our Africanness." Instead he said, "Sinners will not get converted" without a ring. This minister had clear evangelical purposes, not class purposes, in mind. Like countless others who participated in the African American Great Awakening, this AME pastor believed that he was part of a movement in which God was working in powerful ways, with the Holy Spirit manifest in visible expressions like the ring shout. The issue was one of correct religious activity, expressed in class and cultural terms, not the other way around. In this sense, the African American Great Awakening repeated a common tension of the Second Great Awakening, with Payne playing the role of Lyman Beecher, warning fellow evangelicals to ignore "Crazy" Lorenzo Dow and other democratized preachers. Payne proved to be just as ineffective on this score as Beecher had been.⁴⁸ In its worship and evangelism, popular black evangelicalism thrived on these countermodern religious practices.

Black evangelical resistance to some forms of modernity also seems to be tied to a conflicted relationship with the American nation-state. The African American Great Awakening emerged right in the thick of racial conflicts that, even amid the joys of emancipation, dampened suggestions that American society would usher in the millennium for blacks. Even during the most optimistic days of Reconstruction, when blacks were elected to state legislatures, schools for black children were being established across the South, and black denominations grew, most African Americans were all too painfully reminded that racism still permeated American society. A report from Henry McNeal Turner in 1866 gives a glimpse of these harsh realities. He wrote that in the middle of the night four whites near Auburn, Alabama, broke into the room of an AME pastor who had just arrived in the area. They beat and stabbed the minister nearly to death, telling him that "no d----d negro schools should be taught there, nor should any negro preacher remain there." During the beating, several black women had rushed to an agent of the Freedman's Bureau for help, but the northern white officer told them he could not do anything and refused to leave his room. "Such conduct is lauded by a certain class here," Turner informed the readers of the *Christian Recorder*, who, like Turner, must have wondered what sort of future lay in store for African Americans, Christianity, the South, and the nation. "O God! where is our civilization?" Turner wrote in closing. "Is this Christendom, or is it hell? Pray for us."[49] In the century to come, of course, violence toward blacks who stepped out of their assigned roles would be repeated countless times. Most African Americans, it seems, would not put as much faith in American civilization as Payne did.

Turner's question of whether this society was Christendom or hell would have seemed ludicrous to most white American Protestants in the nineteenth century. But it reflects another characteristic of popular black evangelicalism in the late nineteenth century: resistance to a type of civil religion that tidily blended Christianity with faith in the progress of the American nation. Given the racial violence, discrimination, and hardships heaped upon them, many African Americans simply could not accept the idea that existing American institutions were specially ordained by God.[50] The racial dynamics here were deeply rooted in a key feature of modern Western culture: the concept of the nation-state. As Allen Dwight Callahan points out, because modernity grounded nationhood in blood and land, African Americans could not claim privileges to either. Modern nation-states tended to locate peoplehood in an ancestry formed around a particular language or culture.[51] Given its ethnic diversity, the United States had a more complicated task than many European nation-states in this regard, but it managed, through the nineteenth century and most of the twentieth, to work out a complicated formula that grounded American peoplehood in a European ancestry, or what some historians call "whiteness." Furthermore, white Americans instinctively denied African Americans access to land, a resource that lay dear to national identity. This impulse ran so deep that liberal and evangelical abolitionists from the North, who sincerely believed they had the best interests of African Americans at heart, saw no inconsistency in rejecting the idea of granting freedpeople "forty acres and a mule" while simultaneously supporting the 1862 Homestead Act, which essentially gave away western land to common white settlers and immigrants. Most northern liberal and evangelical reformers in the Reconstruction South insisted instead that African Americans work for wages on land owned by former slaveowners.⁵² The Fourteenth Amendment granted African Americans citizenship in theory, but actions on the ground proved otherwise. As W. E. B. DuBois famously explained, the black person "ever feels his twoness,—an American, a Negro; two souls, two thoughts, two unreconciled strivings."⁵³

No wonder, then, that African American Christians repeatedly found significance in the verse from Acts 17 that "God hath made one blood of all the nations." No wonder that black Christians mined Exodus, not just for themes of liberation, but for its themes of landlessness and exile.⁵⁴ African American evangelicalism drew upon biblical resources in an attempt to transcend modern conceptions of ancestry grounded in blood and land, challenging modernity to reconfigure its terms.⁵⁵ That battle would last well beyond the end of the nineteenth century.

This struggle placed ordinary African Americans in a conflicted position with the ideal of Christian civilization that dominated the conceptual universe of many white Protestants. It also put them at odds with elite black ministers who often found much to laud in that civilizing ideal. Highly educated black ministers often held out hope that white America would grant blacks equal respect and the full rights of citizenship if blacks demonstrated they were capable of "civilized" behavior. Following in Daniel Alexander Payne's intellectual footsteps, AME bishop Wesley Gaines argued in 1897 that African American progress represented "the outcome of education, as all must admit, and demonstrates how civilization in a short time may convert the slave of centuries into an intelligent, property-holding citizen."⁵⁶ Praising the schoolhouse as "the birth-place of a nation's power, progress and civilization," Gaines upheld Anglo-grounded education as the key to his vision for the black race.⁵⁷ Reflecting the progressive assumptions of the civilizing ideal, Gaines believed that both the African American church and the wider African American community depended upon the presence of an "educated, cultured leadership."⁵⁸ Gaines decried the past failures of African American ministers who had not been properly educated and defended the uplifting effects of highly educated African Americans upon the race. With one eye on the "better class" of whites in the American establishment, Gaines explained that the African Americans aspired to emulate their Anglo brethren.[59]

Even though they nourished a desire for a more just society, most ordinary African Americans remained suspicious of Gaines's faith in Anglo civilization. Many former slaves had heard a similar sort of civilizing concept extolled by the master class. The failure of Reconstruction, the rise of Jim Crow, and the emergence of lynchings in the 1890s made it very difficult to buy into the idea that American society embodied the highest civic ideals of Christianity. Breaking ranks with his fellow elite ministers, Henry McNeal Turner could not accept Gaines's praise of American civilization. Turner had proven himself to be a prime mover in the African American Great Awakening, which had instilled in him a profound respect for the virtues of ordinary African Americans. Unlike Gaines, he expressed a powerful critique of America's refusal to face up to the injustices it perpetuated against blacks. "The white people of this country have no true Christian civilization," he declared in a characteristically blunt statement in 1900. "We are often confronted through the public press with reports of the most barbarous and cruel outrages that can be perpetrated upon human beings, known in the history of the world. No savage nation can exceed the atrocities which are often heralded through the country and accepted by many as an incidental consequence."[60] The placement of the ethics of savagery above that of American civilization was not exactly a modern expression of progressive millennialism.

Finally, the African American Great Awakening resisted particular modernizing trends that eroded the bonds of local communities. In the late nineteenth century, increased industrialization, urbanization, and bureaucratization weakened local community structures. This process combined with existing forces of modernity to promote the ideal of the upwardly mobile, autonomous individual. In the sphere of religion, evangelicalism sometimes aided this process, with a theology of conversion that emphasized individual choice and a disregard for religious tradition. In one sense, the African American Great Awakening fit this modern pattern, for it encouraged black Christians to abandon established congregations and promoted the idea that African Americans could think for themselves, apart from the guiding authority of white elites.[61]

However, the African American Great Awakening used these individualistic means for communal ends, reconfiguring and reconstructing new communities on the foundation of the black church. The communal ethic of the African American black church helps explain why many freedpeople no longer maintained another religious option available to them at emancipation, African folk religion. Ironically, African American evangelicalism ended up, in practice, promoting stronger bonds of community than these traditional practices derived from communal life in Africa. Originally, traditional African religious practices such as *vaudou* had been organically tied to local African communities, but the Middle Passage disrupted their communal dimensions.[62] These religious practices did not simply disappear but adapted to life in the South, evolving into folk practices of voodoo, hoodoo, and conjuring. During the two and a half centuries of slavery in America, many blacks had privately consulted spirit-workers or conjurers. These religious practices persisted through the nineteenth century and into the twentieth, sometimes blending with popular black evangelicalism.[63] But African folk religion ended up serving individualistic ends in the United States, as African Americans turned to these practices in attempts to access individual healing, achieve some sort of personal gain, or assert power over another individual. Often reconstructed as a spiritual technique in the United States, African folk religion did little to forge communal bonds.

On the other hand, the African American Great Awakening thrived, in part, by reconstituting religious communities. In this movement, the communal side of evangelicalism comes into view. Though eager to leave traditional white churches and their racial hierarchies, most black Christians at emancipation did not seem so anxious to embrace the modern ideal of the autonomous individual. Neither did the large numbers who converted to Christianity during the late nineteenth century. Several factors seem to be at work here. By blending traditional African cultural forms with Christian theology, the communal practice of evangelical worship enabled African American to see what they believed to be the hand of God visibly manifesting itself in their congregations. Furthermore, black Baptist and Methodist churches became key institutions whereby African Americans could collectively negotiate the oppression of racism. And the church gave black Americans a foundation on which to establish a collective identity, since the modern nation-state held them at the margins. Finally, through black preaching, music, and worship, the church became the hermeneutic for African American Christians, providing them with a particular means to interpret their role in an often hostile world. This was no insignificant matter. Independent black Baptist and Methodist churches eventually provided a critical base from which the modern civil rights movement would emerge. In the words of Eric Foner, the black church was "second only to the family as the focal point of black life."[64]

THE CULTURAL PARADOX OF EVANGELICALISM

How, then, does the African American Great Awakening affect our understanding of evangelicalism? We owe much to the scholarship of George Marsden, so it is fitting that we consider this question in light of his work. In *The Evangelical Mind and the New School Presbyterian Experience*, Marsden rescued the study of evangelicalism from the hinterlands of American intellectual history, but he did not substantially address issues of race. In that work, Marsden placed New School Presbyterianism in the center of nineteenth-century American religious life, as evangelicalism grew into a movement that closely identified itself with the center of American culture. But this picture of evangelicalism cannot be sustained if African American religious life is taken into account.

Oddly, though, the African American Great Awakening affirms many of Marsden's observations about evangelicalism in *Fundamentalism and American Culture*. While it may seem curious to juxtapose fundamentalism with independent black evangelicalism, both movements drew upon common revivalistic traditions, popular spirituality, and evangelical theological commitments. More significantly, both movements thrived amid cultural ambivalence, as they simultaneously affirmed and countered the surrounding culture. Marsden decisively put to rest the old conception of fundamentalism as a "dying way of life" that could not adjust to modern changes. He demonstrated that even though fundamentalists distrusted particular intellectual developments and sometimes positioned themselves as sectarian "outsiders," they also embraced a modern version of Baconian rationality and sometimes positioned themselves with the "establishment."[65] Independent black evangelicalism, meanwhile, effectively marshaled an ambivalence felt by African Americans, merging modern characteristics of autonomy, democratization, and religious choice with countermodern features such as religious enchantment, African cultural expressions, and a resistance to individualism.

Of course, there were key differences to that ambivalence. While white fundamentalists found themselves moving from a position of evangelical respectability in late nineteenth-century American culture to one of ridicule in the early twentieth century, racism ensured that black evangelicals would not enjoy a position of respectability in American culture at any time in this era. Reaction to the intellectual challenges of evolution and higher criticism played a significant role in the formation and growth of fundamentalism, but these intellectual crises did not animate the growth of independent black evangelical churches. African American evangelicals were negotiating their way through a different set of modern issues, structured around the intractable dynamics of race.

The shared religious dynamics of both movements suggest that evangelicalism may come hard-wired with some level of cultural ambivalence. These cultural tensions may not be quite so evident among New School Presbyterians, apart from the uneasy alliance between Calvinism and revivalism. However, a wider scope of nineteenth-century evangelicalism reveals many more tensions if one includes the African American Great Awakening and movements of other culturally marginal evangelicals. This evangelical ambivalence becomes more apparent when one considers how ordinary black evangelicals refused to fully embrace the program promoted by Daniel Alexander Payne, the black leader who most closely mirrored the cultural spirit of New School Presbyterianism.

The cultural paradox that Marsden first identified in *Fundamentalism and American Culture* may help explain why evangelicalism has grown and persisted in so many different situations in the modern world. Social locations, historical eras, theological challenges, and cultural dynamics may change, but evangelicalism seems to have a knack for identifying existing tensions and forming some sort of religious response that resonates widely.[66] The African American Great Awakening provided the most popular religious response to the particular cultural tensions faced by ordinary blacks in the decades after the Civil War. Independent black evangelicalism thrived, just as other strands of late nineteenth-century evangelicalism thrived, even as it resisted particular cultural visions promoted by other evangelicals.

NOTES

1. *Christian Recorder*, November 24, 1866.
2. Stephen Ward Angell, *Bishop Henry McNeal Turner and African-American Religion in the South* (Knoxville: University of Tennessee Press, 1992), 68–69.
3. *Christian Recorder*, September 29, 1866, 154.
4. *Christian Recorder*, December 1, 1866, 189.
5. *Christian Recorder*, August 18, 1866, 129.
6. *Christian Recorder*, September 29, 1866, 154.
7. *Christian Recorder*, August 4, 1866, 122.
8. *Christian Recorder*, September 8, 1866, 142. For additional reports of revivals among AME churches across the South, see the *Christian Recorder* for the years of 1866 and 1867.
9. The political, economic, social, and cultural issues tied to Reconstruction in the 1860s and '70s and then the emergence of segregation in the 1880s and '90s have quite understandably captured the attention of most historians. These issues have shaped a number of very fine investigations into the African American church in this era, but they have also tended to relegate issues of evangelistic growth to the margins. Clarence E. Walker, *A Rock in a Weary Land: The African Methodist Episcopal Church during the Civil War and Reconstruction* (Baton Rouge: Louisiana State University Press, 1982); William E. Montgomery, *Under Their Own Vine and Fig Tree: The African-American Church in the South, 1865–1900* (Baton Rouge: Louisiana State University Press, 1993); Reginald F. Hildebrand, *The Times Were Strange and Stirring: Methodist Preachers and the Crisis of Emancipation* (Durham, NC: Duke University Press, 1995); James T. Campbell, *Songs of Zion: The African Methodist Episcopal Church in the United States and South Africa* (New York: Oxford University Press, 1995); Daniel W. Stowell, *Rebuilding Zion: The Religious Reconstruction of the South, 1863–1877* (New York: Oxford University Press, 1998); Paul Harvey, *Redeeming the South: Religious Cultures and Racial Identities among Southern Baptists, 1865–1925* (Chapel Hill: University of North Carolina Press, 1997); Edward J. Blum and W. Scott Poole, eds., *Vale of Tears: New Essays on Religion and Reconstruction* (Macon, GA: Mercer University Press, 2005).

10. African Americans, for instance, used the term *revivals* and did not see their movement as one of "awakening" a cold and slumbering church. With a collective consciousness that traced its roots to Africa rather than European Christendom, African American evangelicals worked within a different historical framework than traditional white Protestants, who worked within the Reformation conception of a people reforming a corrupt church.

11. *Christian Recorder*, November 24, 1866.

12. The 14,300 conversions apparently included those that occurred under other ministers that Turner supervised. Angell, *Bishop Henry McNeal Turner*, 79.

13. In Georgia, for example, almost all of the thirty thousand blacks who had been members of the white-controlled Methodist Episcopal Church, South in 1860 had left that denomination by 1871 for independent black Methodist denominations, but they were joined by an additional forty thousand African Americans. These figures come from an analysis made by Daniel W. Stowell. Stowell's calculations would put the number of new conversions at nearly three-fifths of the total number of black Methodists. Steven Ward Angell has a lower number for just the AME Church in Georgia, estimating that two-fifths of those who joined the AME Church between 1866 and 1871 were from conversions. Since the vast majority of freedpeople were illiterate, we simply do not have sources for much of what was taking place in these black churches. However, the reports from literate black ministers combined with the existing statistical evidence point to a very large number of new members in a very short time period, whatever the actual numbers might be. Stowell, *Rebuilding Zion*, 90; Angell, *Bishop Henry McNeal Turner*, 79.

14. The 1860 and 1882 figures are from American Baptist Home Mission Society, *Baptist Home Missions in North America; Including a Full Report of the Proceedings and Addresses of the Jubilee Meeting, and a Historical Sketch of the American Baptist Home Mission Society, Historical Tables, Etc., 1832–1882* (New York: Baptist Home Mission Rooms, 1883), 421; the 1906 figure is from U.S. Census, *Census of Religious Bodies: 1906*, 2 vols. (Washington, DC, 1910), 1:139.

15. Postemancipation growth built upon evangelical expansion among African Americans that had been building throughout the entire century. The overall number of African American church members jumped from 40,000 in 1800, to 635,000 in 1860, to 3,750,000 in 1906. For 1860, the figures (in this note, for African Americans, and in the text, for Methodist Church members generally) are from Mechal Sobel, *Trabelin' On: The Slave Journey to an Afro-Baptist Faith* (Princeton, NJ: Princeton University Press, 1988), 182; the 1882 figures are from Stowell, *Rebuilding Zion*, 94; the 1906 figures are from U.S. Census, *Census of Religious Bodies: 1906*, 2 vols. (Washington, DC, 1910), 1:139.

16. Michael A. Gomez, *Exchanging Our Country Marks: The Transformation of African Identities in the Colonial and Antebellum South* (Chapel Hill: University of North Carolina Press, 1998), 260–61.

17. U.S. Census, *Census of Religious Bodies*, 1:137–39.
18. Frey and Wood, *Come Shouting to Zion*, xi.
19. Eugene D. Genovese, *Roll, Jordan, Roll: The World the Slaves Made* (New York: Vintage Books), 162; Charles F. Irons, *The Origins of Proslavery Christianity: White and Black Evangelicals in Colonial and Antebellum Virginia* (Chapel Hill: University of North Carolina Press, 2008).
20. "Unfinished Revolution" refers to the subtitle of Eric Foner's influential synthesis of the era. Eric Foner, *Reconstruction: America's Unfinished Revolution, 1863–1877* (New York: Harper and Row, 1988).
21. Methodist, Baptist, Church of Christ, and Mormon movements were fashioned to address this new democratized arrangement and exploded in growth, numerically overwhelming older Protestant groups. Nathan O. Hatch, *The Democratization of American Christianity* (New Haven, CT: Yale University Press, 1989); John H. Wigger, *Taking Heaven by Storm: Methodism and the Rise of Popular Christianity in America* (New York: Oxford University Press, 1998).
22. Hatch, *Democratization of American Christianity*, 107; Donald G. Mathews, *Religion in the Old South* (Chicago: University of Chicago Press, 1977).
23. Anne C. Loveland, *Southern Evangelicals and the Social Order, 1800–1860* (Baton Rouge: Louisiana State University Press, 1980); Genovese, *Roll, Jordan, Roll*; Mathews, *Religion in the Old South*; Irons, *Origins of Proslavery Christianity*.
24. These quotes come from the pen of a white northern missionary, A. M. French, who cast the comments in a dialect that often reinforced demeaning stereotypes of blacks. Here the spelling from that quote has been changed but the grammar remains intact. Mrs. A. M. French, *Slavery in South Carolina and the Ex-Slaves: or, the Port Royal Mission* (1862; repr., New York: Negro Universities Press, 1969), 126, 127. See also Rupert Sargent, ed., *Letters and Diary of Laura M. Towne: Written from the Sea Islands of South Carolina, 1862–1884* (1912; repr., New York: Negro Universities Press, 1969), 81; Willie Lee Rose, *Rehearsal for Reconstruction: The Port Royal Experiment* (London: Oxford University Press, 1964), 86–87.
25. Even those blacks who initially remained in the Methodist Episcopal Church South (MECS) formed independent churches in 1870 in a new body, the Colored Methodist Episcopal Church, that worked more cooperatively with the MECS. Montgomery, *Under Their Own Vine*, 121–24; Edward J. Blum, *Reforging the White Republic: Race, Religion and American Nationalism, 1865–1898* (Baton Rouge: Louisiana State University Press, 2005).
26. Montgomery, *Under Their Own Vine*, 125–27; Sobel, *Trabelin' On*, 182–83.
27. Although the Catholic Church did not officially support the Confederacy during the Civil War, southern white Catholics, including most southern priests and bishops, had supported the Confederacy and resented Radical Republican actions during Reconstruction. Furthermore, the Catholic Church,

which did not ordain an African American priest until 1886, did not provide opportunities for black leadership that African Americans found in the Baptist and Methodist churches. U.S. Census, *Census of Religious Bodies*, 1:137; David T. Gleeson, "'No Disruption of Union': The Catholic Church in the South and Reconstruction," in Blum and Poole, *Vale of Tears*, 164–86; Cyprian Davis, O.S.B., *The History of Black Catholics in the United States* (New York: Crossroad, 1990).

28. Rose, *Rehearsal for Reconstruction*, 73–75; Robert C. Morris, *Reading, 'Riting, and Reconstruction: The Education of the Freedmen in the South, 1861–1870* (Chicago: University of Chicago Press, 1981), 61; Foner, *Reconstruction*, 145–47.

29. Rose, *Rehearsal for Reconstruction*, 74, 92–93, 180–81.

30. Jay Riley Case, "From the Native Ministry to the Talented Tenth: The Foreign Missionary Origins of White Support for Black Colleges," in *The Foreign Missionary Enterprise at Home: Explorations in North American Cultural History*, ed. Daniel E. Bays and Grant Wacker (Tuscaloosa: University of Alabama Press, 2003); Joe M. Richardson, *Christian Reconstruction: The American Missionary Association and Southern Blacks* (Athens: University of Georgia Press, 1986), 74.

31. James M. McPherson, *The Abolitionist Legacy: From Reconstruction to the NAACP* (Princeton, NJ: Princeton University Press, 1975), 411–12.

32. Even among the Baptists, whose congregational polity allowed for looser ties, blacks tended to form associations with one another and largely resisted connections with the American Baptist Missionary Union, the northern white Baptist agency. U.S. Census, *Census of Religious Bodies*, 1:139.

33. *Macedonian and Home Mission Record*, May 1870, 17. For other observations by white missionary officials of African American leadership during the African American Great Awakening, see also *The Macedonian and Home Mission Record*, June 1870, 22; July 1867, 26 and 28; October 1869, 37; December 1869, 46; American Baptist Home Mission Society, *Baptist Home Missions*, 405.

34. *Christian Recorder*, December 1, 1866, 189.

35. Edwin S. Redkey, *Black Exodus: Black Nationalist and Back-to-Africa Movements, 1890–1910* (New Haven, CT: Yale University Press, 1969), 30; Angell, *Bishop Henry McNeal Turner*, 72–76.

36. William J. Simmons, *Men of Mark: Eminent, Progressive and Rising* (1887; repr., New York: Arno Press, 1968), 1084; David W. Wills, "Womanhood and Domesticity in the A.M.E. Tradition: The Influence of Daniel Alexander Payne," in *Black Apostles at Home and Abroad: Afro-Americans and the Christian Mission from the Revolution to Reconstruction*, ed. David W. Wills and Richard Newman (Boston: G. K. Hall, 1982), 133–46; Campbell, *Songs of Zion*, 37–39.

37. Daniel Alexander Payne, *Recollections of Seventy Years* (1888; repr., New York: Arno Press, 1968), 253.

38. Ibid., 253, 253–54.

39. Ibid., 254.

40. Albert J. Raboteau, *Slave Religion: The "Invisible Institution" in the Antebellum South* (Oxford: Oxford University Press, 1978), 44–75; Frey and Wood, *Come Shouting to Zion*; Gomez, *Exchanging Our Country Marks*.

41. Similar sort of dynamics appear in many accounts from northern black ministers and missionaries who worked among the freedpeople during Reconstruction. Harvey, *Redeeming the South*, 112; Montgomery, *Under Their Own Vine*; Wilson Jeremiah Moses, *The Golden Age of Black Nationalism, 1850–1925* (Hamden, CT: Archon Books, 1978), 10, 20–23; Edward L. Wheeler, *Uplifting the Race: The Black Minister in the New South, 1865–1902* (Lanham, MD: University Press of America, 1986); Kevin K. Gaines, *Uplifting the Race: Black Leadership, Politics, and Culture in the Twentieth Century* (Chapel Hill: University of North Carolina Press, 1996).

42. Payne, *Recollections of Seventy Years*, 161–65, quote on 163.

43. For a good example of the Puritan supernaturalistic worldview right before the Enlightenment, see David D. Hall, *Worlds of Wonder, Days of Judgment: Popular Religious Belief in Early New England* (Cambridge, MA: Harvard University Press, 1990).

44. Ann Taves, *Fits, Trances and Visions: Experiencing Religion and Explaining Experience from Wesley to James* (Princeton, NJ: Princeton University Press, 1999); Henry F. May, *The Enlightenment in America* (Oxford: Oxford University Press, 1976).

45. W. E. B. DuBois, *The Souls of Black Folk* (New York: Bantam Classics, 2005), 140–41. As Allen Dwight Callahan points out, this was where "the spirit possession of West African religion meets the 'experimental religion' of Evangelical Christianity." Allen Dwight Callahan, *The Talking Book: African Americans and the Bible* (New Haven, CT: Yale University Press, 2006), 62–63; Harvey, *Redeeming the South*, 114–23.

46. Gomez, *Exchanging Our Country Marks*, 270; see also Campbell, *Songs of Zion*, 39–44; Montgomery, *Under Their Own Vine*, 266–68; Moses, *Golden Age*, 41.

47. Harvey, *Redeeming the South*, 108; Heather Andrea Williams, *Self-Taught: African American Education in Slavery and Freedom* (Chapel Hill: University of North Carolina Press, 2005); Richardson, *Christian Reconstruction*; Foner, *Reconstruction*.

48. For an excellent explanation of how democratized Christianity provoked a crisis of authority for New England ministers like Lyman Beecher and Timothy Dwight, see Hatch, *Democratization of American Christianity*, 17–22.

49. *Christian Recorder*, June 23, 1866, 97.

50. Even after emancipation, nineteenth-century African Americans simply could not feel fully at home in the United States. This presented African Americans with a deep-seated conflict as to their identity as Americans, a conflict

eloquently described by W. E. B. DuBois famously as the double consciousness of African Americans. DuBois, *Souls of Black Folk.*

51. Callahan, *Talking Book*, 163.

52. Segregation and miscegenation laws were only the most obvious expressions of how this concept of blood ancestry established itself in American institutions. Tellingly, Irish American immigrants arrived on American shores facing the disadvantages of poverty, poor education, and anti-Catholic hostility but succeeded in claiming a home in America, in part by learning very quickly that it was possible for them to obtain land and claim a white ancestry, while their chief competitors, African Americans and Chinese immigrants, could not. Blum, *Reforging the White Republic*; David R. Roediger, *Working toward Whiteness: How America's Immigrants Became White, The Strange Journey from Ellis Island to the Suburbs* (New York: Basic Books, 2005); Noel Ignatiev, *How the Irish Became White* (New York: Routledge, 1995); Foner, *Reconstruction*.

53. DuBois, *Souls of Black Folk*, 3.

54. Monroe Fordham, *Major Themes in Northern Black Religious Thought, 1800–1860* (Hicksville, NY: Exposition Press, 1975), 139–50; Wheeler, *Uplifting the Race*, 37–51; Daniel Alexander Payne, *History of the African Methodist Episcopal Church* (Nashville, TN: Publishing House of the A.M.E. Sunday-School Union, 1891), 483; Callahan, *Talking Book.*

55. Christianity had already facilitated the formation of African American racial identity. As Michael Gomez explains, those descended from Africans passed through stages of identity, from African ethnicities to African American racial identity. Christianity "ultimately facilitated the transition to race." Gomez, *Exchanging Our Country Marks*, 15.

56. W. J. Gaines, *The Negro and the White Man* (1897; repr., New York: Negro Universities Press, 1969), 138.

57. Ibid., 132.

58. Ibid., 134.

59. Ibid., 147.

60. *Voice of Missions*, August 1900; Edwin S. Redkey, ed., *Respect Black: The Writings and Speeches of Henry McNeal Turner* (New York: Arno Press, 1971), 189.

61. Robert Wiebe, *The Search for Order, 1877–1920* (New York: Hill and Wang, 1967). On the relationship between early evangelicalism and modern ideas of individual autonomy, see George M. Marsden, *Jonathan Edwards: A Life* (New Haven, CT: Yale University Press, 2003), 438–40.

62. All of these African practices underwent some sort of adaptation and change in America, though many characteristics, such as beliefs in specific African gods, did not persist, for the nature of the Middle Passage made a full transplantation of African culture impossible. Raboteau, *Slave Religion*, 75–87; Frey and Wood, *Come Shouting to Zion*, 209–12; Gomez, *Exchanging Our Country Marks*, 54–58; Sobel, *Trabelin' On*, 221–24.

63. Yvonne P. Chireau, *Black Magic: Religion and the African American Conjuring Tradition* (Berkeley: University of California Press, 2003); Raboteau, *Slave Religion*; Sobel, *Trabelin' On*.

64. Foner, *Reconstruction*, 88.

65. George Marsden, *Fundamentalism and American Culture: The Shaping of Twentieth Century Evangelicalism, 1870–1925* (New York: Oxford University Press, 1980), viii, 3–8.

66. This cultural paradox not only seems to animate different forms of evangelicalism in diverse cultures around the world but may be a critical dynamic of Christianity down through history. Andrew Walls has articulated a theological basis for these cultural tensions that applies widely within Christianity down through history and across cultural boundaries. Andrew Walls, "The Gospel as Prisoner and Liberator of Culture," in *The Missionary Movement in Christian History: Studies in the Transmission of Faith* (Maryknoll, NY: Orbis Books, 1996), 3–15.

PART III

PROTESTING MODERNITY

CHAPTER 7

Marsden and Modern Fundamentalism

BARRY HANKINS

At the 2002 biennial meeting of the Conference on Faith and History, Michael Hamilton suggested that the historiography of twentieth-century fundamentalism and evangelicalism had been done in reverse. Rather than a sweeping work of synthesis coming on the heels of a number of narrowly focused biographies and monographs, the synthesis came first in the form of George Marsden's 1980 book *Fundamentalism and American Culture: The Shaping of Twentieth Century Evangelicalism, 1870–1925*. Over the next quarter century scholars have been filling in the details of twentieth-century evangelical history. Several have tweaked Marsden's interpretation, and a few have challenged it directly. Still, in the wake of the twenty-five-year anniversary edition of the book, the Marsden paradigm prevails. This has been a good thing in some respects while problematic in others.

Anyone who has written a dissertation on Protestant fundamentalism knows that the historiography of the movement starts with Stewart Cole's 1931 book *The History of Fundamentalism*, which was written (don't laugh) because fundamentalism had ended and could now be analyzed as a historical relic.[1] Until 1970, with a few notable exceptions, the historiography of religion in twentieth-century America followed a very modern and progressive line of interpretation in which fundamentalism was a dying remnant of a bygone era. In what today sounds like a rank caricature, Richard Hofstadter summarized fundamentalism in his Pulitzer Prize–winning book *Anti-intellectualism in American Life* as variously "frantic," "rhetorically violent," "panic stricken," and "desperate." He lumped fundamentalism with the Ku Klux Klan, the Scopes trial, Prohibition, and the campaign against Al Smith, ignoring that Protestant liberals had often led the fight against both liquor and the Catholic Democratic presidential candidate. Hofstadter's favorite fundamentalists were Billy Sunday, J. Frank Norris, Carl McIntire, and the two Geralds—L. K. Smith, and Winrod. The only mention he made of the scholarly fundamentalist J. Gresham Machen was to say that he had once been associated with McIntire.[2]

As was typical of the interpretation of his time, Hofstadter viewed the twenties as the "waning phase" of fundamentalist history. Hofstadter often took great liberties with historical interpretation and even said in a "Prefatory Note" that his book lacked documentation and was "largely a personal book, whose factual details are organized and dominated by my views." Nevertheless, Hofstadter's view that fundamentalism was on its way out after the Scopes trial summarized essentially the progressive view of traditional religion retained by the consensus historians of the 1950s. As Henry May wrote in 1986, "In the late thirties, when I was in graduate school, the progressive interpretation of American history had the allegiance of nearly everybody I knew. Part of the progressive ideology was the assumption that religion was and must be declining."[3]

Progressive historians believed religion was dying out as secular science became the arbiter of truth. Truths arrived at scientifically would prove superior and more trustworthy than religious belief, freeing people from their need for superstition and supernatural myths. Consensus historians of the fifties differed from progressives in some respects, but they, too, retained the idea that religious myths were giving way to scientific knowledge. As the consensus interpretation went, fundamentalism emerged from "status anxiety" of conservative Protestants who found themselves pushed to the margins of a culture they had formerly controlled. In this interpretation fundamentalist religion was epiphenomenal; fundamentalist status anxiety was real. While historians such as Hofstadter maligned fundamentalism, most simply ignored it. As Ernest Sandeen wrote in 1970, "The fate of Fundamentalism in historiography has been worse than its lot in history."[4]

Perry Miller is often credited as the first historian of the twentieth century to break with the progressive tradition and take religious ideas seriously. In his work on the Puritans and in his 1949 biography of Jonathan Edwards, he sought to understand how New England colonists and their heirs centered their society on religious principles, often with ironic consequences. While Miller did not himself believe in God, he admired the Puritans as people who acted on intellectual convictions, and he explored how their sense of mission helped form the American character. A few scholars did for nineteenth-century evangelicals or twentieth-century fundamentalists what Miller did for the Puritans, among them the aforementioned Sandeen, Timothy Smith, C. Allyn Russell, and Willard Gatewood. Rather than dismissing ideas as a cover for status anxiety and a reactionary longing for rural past, these historians sought to understand the theology of evangelicals and fundamentalists. In his book *The Roots of Fundamentalism: British and American Millenarianism* Sandeen argued that fundamentalism was a combination of dispensationalism and the Reformed theology of the late nineteenth-century Princeton theologians.

Sandeen's book served as a foundation for Marsden but also as his foil. Marsden claimed that Sandeen had found one root of fundamentalism, premillennialism, and mistaken it for the whole tree. Sandeen's error resulted from his starting with millennialism in the nineteenth century and tracing it forward into the 1920s. Marsden suggested in his review of the book that if one started with fundamentalism in the 1920s and traced the movement back into the nineteenth century he or she would find that fundamentalism had more than one root. It was not even one tree. "Rather, it was a complex, though somewhat unified, overgrowth of tangled trees and vines whose roots were also complex and tangled." In his 1971 review of Sandeen, Marsden sketched out *Fundamentalism and American Culture*, which appeared in print slightly less than a decade later.[5]

In the book, Marsden identified a cluster of nineteenth-century ideas that came together to form fundamentalism: Scottish common sense realism, Baconian science, revivalism, holiness impulses, pietism, Reformed confessionalism, Baptist traditionalism, and dispensational premillennialism. These coalesced in the fight against modernism during the first two decades of the twentieth century. When the term *fundamentalism* was coined in 1920 by New York Baptist preacher and journal editor Curtis Lee Laws, the movement was essentially "militantly, anti-modernist, Protestant evangelicalism," as Marsden wrote in his most concise definition. To elaborate, he continued, "Fundamentalists were evangelical Christians, close to the traditions of the dominant American revivalist establishment of the nineteenth century, who in the twentieth century militantly opposed both modernism in theology and the cultural changes that modernism endorsed."[6] Historians of fundamentalism might ponder how many times they have quoted or paraphrased Marsden's definition in article and book introductions. One of the most beneficial attributes of Marsden's interpretation was that he brought together both intellectual and cultural components while at the same time forging a concise and satisfying interpretive definition. He argued persuasively that fundamentalism was a cultural response to change, indeed a militant response, yet that the movement also had a set of coherent ideas. Most of the ideas of fundamentalism had been at the center of American intellectual life as late as the 1870s, but by 1920 they seemed quaint, especially when combined with the militantly antimodernist spirit, which often coalesced around opposition to evolution. As important books usually do, Marsden's successfully combined the sociological and psychological definition of fundamentalism summarized by Hofstadter with the intellectual definition provided by Sandeen.

Marsden's interpretation turned fundamentalism into an important component of historical study, not just of traditional Protestantism or even of religion in America, but also of twentieth-century American culture writ large. Moreover, the book may well have been the most timely ever published, because of cultural conditions far beyond Marsden's control. Neither he nor anyone else could have predicted in the early 1970s when he began work on the book that Ronald Reagan would be elected the same year the book was published. The conservative resurgence that helped elect Reagan was aided by the birth of what is today called the Christian Right. In other words, the book appeared at the exact time fundamentalists and evangelicals made their dramatic reappearance on the stage of mainstream American culture.

THE IMMEDIATE IMPACT OF MARSDEN'S BOOK

For the most part, scholars recognized immediately that *Fundamentalism and American Culture* was a groundbreaking work of scholarship. This was by no means due to the fame of the book's author. When the book appeared in print, Marsden was a forty-one-year-old professor of history at Calvin College, where he had been teaching since the mid-sixties. He had been working on the project for a decade, and its publication was no surprise, but this was only his second book in fifteen years in the academy. Marsden was well known in American religious history circles but by no means an academic star. As he said recently about so ambitious a project, "I, of course, did not know what to expect and [the book] suddenly put me on the map among scholars."[7]

Reviews of the book began appearing in 1981 and continued through 1984. James Findlay's was among the earliest, published in the *American Historical Review*. Findlay called the book "the capstone of more than a decade of work by scholars on the thorny topic of the place of the fundamentalist movement in early-twentieth-century American religious and social history."[8] While lauding the book as a fine study, however, Findlay did not identify *Fundamentalism and American Culture* as a paradigm-creating work of scholarship. He concluded his review tepidly by saying the book was a "superb monograph, to be recommended to all students of early-twentieth-century American culture and religion."[9]

Writing in the *Journal of Southern History*, David Edwin Harrell came closer to identifying the impact the book would have. Echoing Findlay, Harrell wrote that Marsden's book fit into the growth industry of scholarship on American religion, adding, "This book is by all means the most important volume to appear thus far." He concluded by writing that *Fundamentalism and American Culture* had replaced the narrow interpretation of fundamentalism that had reigned previously. That interpretation "made it very difficult to fit all the pegs into the holes,"

Harrell wrote. "Now the puzzle begins to fit together."[10] In retrospect, one might paraphrase Harrell as saying that we are onto something big here, and we can all now start to work on the rest of the puzzle of fundamentalism, adding a piece here and another piece there.

Like Harrell, Russell Richey correctly predicted the effect that Marsden's book would have on the historiography of American religious history. His review appeared in the *Journal for the Scientific Study of Religion* just four months after Harrell's. It began, "Erudite, fulsomely documented, carefully argued, judiciously illustrated, this is now the standard treatment of fundamentalism." Richey noted how Marsden succeeded in writing from a Christian perspective with the sensitivity of an insider while still interpreting fundamentalism from the outside. The result was that he made fundamentalism plausible as he described "the culture of fundamentalism as well as fundamentalism and American culture." Richey predicted that the book would be viewed over against the "the extremes of earlier scholarship" such as Stewart Cole, Norman Furniss, and Richard Hofstadter, as well as eclipsing the "first-rate scholarly expression" of Ernest Sandeen. Citing Marsden's ability to engage in "polite dialogue," Richey said that Marsden's treatment was "too rich and nuanced to summarize adequately here," that it made fundamentalism "a plausible, religious world view," and that in that sense the book "vindicates fundamentalism." "A very important book," Richey concluded.[11]

Later reviewers were able to put the book into the context of the resurgence of fundamentalism in the form of the New Religious Right, as it was called then, and that movement's apparent, if not real, influence on the Reagan administration. Writing in 1983, the eminent historian of American religious history William McLoughlin started his review by saying, "This study provides a new interpretation not only of the fundamentalist movement at the turn of the century but also of the resurgent fundamentalism today." This was important, McLoughlin continued, because consensus historians and sociological analysts had refused to take the doctrinal positions of fundamentalists seriously. Those interpretations "left us confused when the fundamentalist worldview became a live option again after 1960," he wrote.[12] In a similar vein sociologist Roy Wallis wrote in his review that from 1930 to as late as 1970 the notion that conservative evangelicalism would reemerge as a significant political force "must have seemed profoundly unlikely . . . , but by 1980 it became a reality."[13]

One of the earliest reviews of *Fundamentalism and American Culture* was also the longest, most critical, and oddest. Written by (soon-to-be) Harry Emerson Fosdick biographer Robert Moats Miller, the essay bore the title "A Compleat (Almost) Guide through the Forest of Fundamentalism." It appeared in the September 1981 issue of *Reviews in American History* and ran seven pages. Early on Miller wrote, "[This] is a marvelous book, now the finest single volume on the subject." He continued effusively for the first half of his review before turning critical.[14]

As "splendid" as the book was, it was in Miller's estimation "not inerrant," and so he had a duty as a reviewer to point up its shortcomings. In doing so, Miller joked, he would also engage in "an act of charity to save [Marsden] from the sin of pride."[15] Miller then listed several secondary works Marsden had failed to consider but also said that Marsden's review of secondary literature was "masterful."[16] As for primary sources, Miller claimed that in all Marsden's notes "there are merely six archival citations drawn from only four archives," and he described Marsden's handling of denominational controversies as "disappointing." Finally, he noted his interpretive differences with Marsden. Specifically, he counted himself as much more worried about how America would have turned out had the fundamentalists of the twenties actually won, adding parenthetically, "or should they win in the 1980s." Had that been the case, he mused, "the land would have rung with the lyrics, 'Everyday is a lovely day for an auto-da-fé.'" Musing that many of Marsden's fundamentalist subjects would be good candidates for psychobiography, Miller concluded (one is tempted to say schizophrenically), "This is not a great work of original scholarship, but precisely because Marsden stands on the shoulders of other scholars, his vision does have great sweep and clarity. He has given us a superb guide and we are grateful."[17]

Marsden had long forgotten Miller's review, but when prompted to read it again recently he said, "I think my reaction was that I was so pleased by all the superlatives in the first half of the review that I was not much concerned about the criticisms." Marsden was well aware that because he was synthesizing a half century of history he would be open to the type of criticism Miller levied.[18] Still, read today Miller's review leaves a reader wondering if there was something else going on behind the scenes that we do not know about. While acknowledging the book's obvious virtues, Miller seemed reluctant to give an evangelical professor at Calvin College his full due.

TO THE ARCHIVES

Miller was partly correct, however, when he cited all the archives that Marsden could have visited. The book was based largely on research in original yet published fundamentalist sources—books, pamphlets, magazines, and other printed materials authored by nineteenth and twentieth-century revivalists, dispensationalists, Reformed theologians, and the like. As Marsden acknowledged recently, "There were many things I had not looked at or details I might have missed."[19] Thankfully, Marsden had not said everything. This was especially so for graduate students in the 1980s who were interested in fundamentalism and looking for dissertation topics. Marsden's book was part synthesis, part original research, but the book did much more than "stand on the shoulders of others," as Miller wrote. Rather, it provided a paradigm for interpreting fundamentalism within which scholars could maneuver as they tackled more narrowly focused topics. This was the genius of the book. It was definitive without being the last word. Rather than closing off research possibilities, it opened them. Younger scholars might well have rejoiced had they read Miller's review and learned that the archives containing the personal papers of fundamentalists had been relatively untouched. With a clear paradigm in place, graduate students and new PhDs began to fill in the details, especially with biographical, regional, and gender studies that appeared in the 1980s and 1990s.

During the fifteen years following publication of *Fundamentalism and American Culture*, biographies emerged from research in the archives of August H. Strong, William Bell Riley, Billy Sunday, Aimee Semple McPherson, J. Gresham Machen, J. Frank Norris, the Joneses (Bobs I, II, and III), and other evangelical and fundamentalist figures who lived and worked in the period Marsden covered.[20] All the individuals just listed played roles in Marsden's story. The books on Riley,

Machen, Norris, and the Joneses emerged from dissertations that were done in the eighties and early nineties. Along with the biographical aspect of the study of fundamentalism, regional themes also emerged— Riley in the Midwest; Machen on the eastern seaboard, straddling North and South; the Joneses in the South; and Norris in Texas and the Southwest. While the bulk of *Fundamentalism and American Culture* focused on the rise of fundamentalism in the North, Marsden noted at the end of his book that after the Scopes trial the center of gravity began to shift to the South. The South, therefore, became a fertile field in the study of fundamentalism. Along with the biographies of the Joneses and Norris, monographs and edited collections soon appeared devoted to a study of southern fundamentalism.[21]

While the book left the South relatively untouched, Marsden addressed women and fundamentalism not at all. Joining the regional and biographical studies, therefore, were books that addressed gender and fundamentalism.[22] Sociologists as well as historians benefited from the Marsden paradigm, as there emerged a spate of books on the New Religious Right of the 1980s that morphed into the Christian Right of the 1990s. The burgeoning field also saw the publication of ethnographic studies done by sociologists and anthropologists, some of whom did fieldwork within fundamentalist communities as their primary mode of research.[23]

The Scopes trial, of course, looms large in the history of fundamentalism. As Marsden wrote, "It would be difficult to overestimate the 'Monkey Trial' at Dayton, Tennessee, in the transformation of fundamentalism." Marsden's book by no means created or launched interest in fundamentalism and science. Historians such as Ronald Numbers, David Lindberg, David Livingstone, Edward Larson, and others were pursuing fruitful lines of inquiry in the history of science before and after *Fundamentalism and American Culture* appeared. Larson, for example, does not count himself as one of those influenced significantly by Marsden's work and actually found Joel Carpenter's *Revive Us Again* more useful. Nevertheless, Larson read *Fundamentalism and American Culture* for background and utilized the Marsden paradigm in his Pulitzer Prize–winning *Summer for the Gods: The Scopes Trial and America's Continuing Debate over Science and Religion*. Larson views fundamentalism as no more inward looking after Scopes than it was before and in this way resists that part of Marsden's interpretation. Still, Larson views the trial as having exasperated fundamentalists, contributing to the entrenched fundamentalist opposition to Darwinism that continues to our own time.[24]

WHAT WERE YOU DOING WHEN YOU FIRST READ FUNDAMENTALISM AND AMERICAN CULTURE?

Because *Fundamentalism and American Culture* had such a significant impact on scholarship, the book helped clarify the career paths of some aspiring historians. Many scholars have clear recollections of what they were doing and what they thought about when they first read the book.

Darryl Hart was already scheming to write his biography of J. Gresham Machen when he read *Fundamentalism and American Culture* in a Harvard Divinity School seminar he was taking with William Hutchison. Hutchison wrote the most important work on theological modernism, *The Modernist Impulse in American Protestantism*, a book that did for our understanding of modernism almost as much as Marsden's did for our understanding of fundamentalism and evangelicalism. In reading *Fundamentalism and American Culture*, Hart understood immediately that Marsden had provided "a benchmark for interpreting conservative Protestantism in that era of U.S. history" and "the grid for interpreting fundamentalism."[25]

Like Hart, William Vance Trollinger Jr. was already moving toward a dissertation topic when he first read Marsden in the early eighties. Having been left somewhat unsatisfied by the narrowness of Sandeen's interpretation, Trollinger was struck by the breadth of Marsden's approach and the "brilliant way he made the case that fundamentalism shaped contemporary evangelicalism. . . . Thanks to this book, I knew where I was headed in my dissertation," Trollinger said recently.[26] Trollinger speaks for many when he says that virtually all of us who did dissertations in the wake of *Fundamentalism and American Culture* owe a debt to Marsden for virtually establishing the field of evangelical studies and placing our area of interest firmly in the center of American religious history, where it has remained ever since. Moreover, there was a personal element to all of this, as young scholars met Marsden at various conferences. As Trollinger puts it, "On a personal level, as a newly minted Ph.D. I benefited greatly from George's gracious willingness to help me think more clearly about fundamentalism."[27]

While Hart and Trollinger were attracted to topics within the same time frame Marsden covered, at least one graduate student in the 1980s moved his sights to the post-1925 period precisely because of *Fundamentalism and American Culture*. Michael Hamilton read the book in 1987 and believed it was "the last word on fundamentalism." He therefore wrote his dissertation on Wheaton College from 1919 to 1964. Hamilton no longer believes that *Fundamentalism and American Culture* is the last word and offers some helpful lines of inquiry for the future that will be discussed below.

Margaret Bendroth first read *Fundamentalism and American Culture* while in an American history graduate seminar at Johns Hopkins University. The book was virtually the only reading on religion in the seminar. Bendroth had known Marsden for some time through the Christian Reformed Church network and felt a little strange when Marsden rose to academic stardom. It was, she writes, "like somebody I knew suddenly got on television." What was most significant, however, was not that Marsden had become famous but that the book was a turning point. The professor of Bendroth's seminar was the influential cultural historian John Higham, who was duly impressed with Marsden's scholarship. As Bendroth recalls, "It was one of those moments back then when you saw other scholars beginning to take religion seriously." Bendroth also noted, however, that Marsden failed to address gender, so another dissertation was born out of the need to fill in the details of Marsden's synthesis. Bendroth's revised dissertation was published as *Fundamentalism and Gender, 1875 to the Present*.[28]

Across the Atlantic, David Bebbington recalls *Fundamentalism and American Culture* as having an enormous influence in making evangelical history part of mainstream scholarship. The book was his introduction to the evangelical school of religious history. In Britain, the approach was much more institutional or social. By contrast, Bebbington writes,

"Marsden showed that ideas, not extracted from their social context, were the heart of Christian history." This approach confirmed Bebbington's growing view that history could be written with much more attention to theology than had been customary in Britain. That conviction showed in his own account of evangelicalism in Britain, from which he developed his highly influential quadrilateral.[29] Bebbington's four-faceted historical definition sees evangelicals as Protestant Christians marked by their biblicism, crucicentrism (emphasis on Christ's atoning death), conversionism, and activism. This definition and Bebbington's stress on the transatlantic nature of modern evangelicalism moved the conversation forward in helpful ways.

As a friend and former student of Marsden's, Joel Carpenter first read *Fundamentalism and American Culture* in manuscript form as Marsden was writing the book. Carpenter maintains that it would be too much to say that Marsden created the field of evangelical studies. Pioneers such as Timothy Smith, Samuel Hill, Donald Matthews, Ernest Sandeen, Ernest Tuveson, and others had already done much. Still, Carpenter says, like so many others, that *Fundamentalism and American Culture* "was seminal in my own thinking about the origins, character, and legacy of fundamentalism." The book made it possible for Carpenter to write his important sequel *Revive Us Again: The Reawakening of Fundamentalism*, which took up the story where Marsden left off but at the same time took a somewhat different approach—more social and organizational, whereas Marsden had done mostly intellectual history. Still, Carpenter was able to write about the period from 1925 to 1950 and the development of neoevangelicalism without, as he puts it, "having to come up with original arguments about the origins and character of the movement." Carpenter also notes how important it was that the book was published by Oxford University Press, where editor Charles Scott, an Episcopal priest, recognized the importance of Marsden's work. Marsden's subtitle, *The Shaping of Twentieth-Century Evangelicalism*, Carpenter notes, provoked scholars from a variety of Protestant traditions to study their own group's history, in part because they were not shaped by fundamentalism. "They used George's book as a challenge to get out their own stories," Carpenter wrote recently.[30]

For my part, when I first heard of Marsden's book I was attending Fuller Theological Seminary, taking a course called "American Evangelicalism" with historian James Bradley. We did not read the book itself, probably because it was not in print and certainly not in paperback when Bradley set the syllabus. We did, however, read Marsden's critique of Sandeen, and in class Bradley told us that Marsden had been at work on his fundamentalism project for ten years and that with the book's appearance we were going to know more about fundamentalism than ever before. He was certainly correct.

CHALLENGES TO THE MARSDEN PARADIGM AND NEW LINES OF INQUIRY

Not everyone was enamored with Marsden's interpretation of fundamentalism. The first major interpretative critique came from Donald Dayton, who squared off with Marsden in a number of venues during the 1980s and into the early 1990s. *Fundamentalism and American Culture* was in large part an intellectual history of fundamentalism. The pre-Sandeen interpretations had ignored ideas and sought the essence of fundamentalism in status anxiety, a longing for the past, and even psychologically imbalanced hatred for all things modern. Appropriately, Marsden sought to balance those arguments by showing that ideas mattered. Fundamentalism was an understandable militancy in defense of ideas and was therefore heavily doctrinal.

Because Marsden placed Reformed theology of the Princeton theologians near the center of the cluster of ideas that constituted fundamentalism, Dayton called Marsden's interpretation the "Presbyterian paradigm." Over against Marsden, Dayton offered what some have called a "Pentecostal paradigm" but what might better be called a "Wesleyan" or even "Wesleyan-Finneyite" paradigm that is understood to include Pentecostalism. Dayton believes that classical evangelicalism of the eighteenth and nineteenth centuries was conversionist and experiential more than doctrinal and propositional. Moreover, classical evangelicalism was marked by the holiness and Pentecostal spirit of radical resistance to "embourgeoisement," a sort of middle-class, conservative respectability. Dayton sees evangelicalism as "a specific and modern form of Christianity that disrupts the traditional and conservative churches." Classical evangelicalism was more this spirit of resistance than "the orthodoxy from which the mainstream churches have departed."[31]

For Dayton, the evangelical ethos found its center in conversion, an experience of the Holy Spirit, and a deep commitment to social reform. In this interpretation, fundamentalism was not so much an expression of evangelicalism as a reaction against it, and Dayton often bristles both in print and in conversation at the way fundamentalists and neoevangelicals infect Wesleyan and holiness groups. The result is often a turn away from the radical evangelical spirit toward inerrancy and dispensationalism as preoccupations of orthodoxy. In his book *Reforming Fundamentalism: Fuller Seminary and the New Evangelicalism* Marsden interpreted mid-twentieth-century neoevangelicals as the heirs of both nineteenth-century evangelicals and early twentieth-century fundamentalists. Dayton sees prefundamentalist classical evangelicalism and postfundamentalist neoevangelicalism as two different movements. Dayton believes the umbrella term *evangelical*, as it is used to describe a large swath of Christians from the eighteenth century to the present, should be suspended.[32] It seems, however, that the core reason Dayton no longer likes *evangelical* is that he believes the term is often used to co-opt and even subvert the true evangelical spirit, and Marsden's fundamentalists and neoevangelicals are the chief culprits.

One of the ironies of the Marsden-Dayton debate is that Marsden did a good bit of research for *Fundamentalism and American Culture* in Dayton's personal library, with its large collection of sources on holiness evangelicalism. While researching the book Marsden visited Dayton at North Park College and Seminary from time to time, toting off a sack of books after each foray. Dayton also urged Oxford University Press to publish *Fundamentalism and American Culture*.[33]

Like Dayton later, Timothy Smith, in his influential 1957 book on nineteenth-century evangelicalism, *Revivalism and Social Reform*, leaned toward the holiness strain of evangelicalism. Smith made the most important early connection between nineteenth-century evangelicalism and reformist and even radical political and social movements. Carpenter studied with Smith at Johns Hopkins and continues to believe that the Smith-Dayton interpretation of evangelicalism is essentially correct. Carpenter commented recently, "Evangelicalism, over its long and global history, generally looks more like Pentecostalism than fundamentalism."[34]

Leaning on Dayton, Smith, and Carpenter, one can make a plausible argument for a continuous stream of evangelicalism from the nineteenth century (or even eighteenth) that bypassed the forging fires of fundamentalism. Recently, David Bebbington has begun to make rumblings of this sort. He suggested in a 2007 *Books and Culture* article that holiness groups such as the Nazarenes and Salvation Army had appropriated the nineteenth-century evangelical spirit without being part of fundamentalism. Likewise, Methodism in the United States and Britain remained evangelical into the mid-twentieth century without being refracted through the fundamentalist prism.[35]

To these one might add Southern Baptists, who, with the exception of J. Frank Norris and a few others, retained a hearty evangelicalism well into the twentieth century without participating fully in either fundamentalism or, until the 1980s, neoevangelicalism. What passes for Southern Baptist fundamentalism circa 1980 to the present might better be understood as conservative evangelicalism with a militant spirit that manifests itself as much in culture war as in theology. In a new concluding chapter to his twenty-fifth anniversary edition of *Fundamentalism and American Culture*, Marsden has suggested the term *fundamentalistic evangelicals* for those who appropriate the militancy of fundamentalism but not its separatism.[36] As scholars move increasingly toward a global understanding of the history of Christianity, American fundamentalism of the early twentieth century may become less central to the story of twentieth-century evangelicalism. Fundamentalism of the variety covered in *Fundamentalism and American Culture* may be viewed as a side branch of a much broader movement.

Like Bebbington, Michael Hamilton has called the Marsden paradigm into question (see chapter 12 of this book). Rather than seeing fundamentalism as a movement that coalesced and became militant as a result of the controversies of the 1920s, he follows Sandeen in drawing a sharp distinction between the fundamentalist movement and the fundamentalist controversies. On the one hand, the *controversies* consisted of battles for control of large northern Protestant denominations (fought mainly by northern denominational conservatives). The *controversies* also include battles to outlaw evolution in the schools (fought mainly by southern evangelicals). On the other hand, Hamilton argues, the fundamentalist *movement* was actually a new form of interdenominational evangelicalism brought into being by Dwight L. Moody in the late nineteenth century. It was committed to dispensationalism and interdenominationalism, which made it anathema to denominational conservatives; and it was based in the North, which made it foreign to southern evangelicals. Despite these divisions, progressives of the 1920s lumped all three groups together and called them all "fundamentalists," a framework that Marsden adopted. By contrast, Hamilton argues, the Moody coalition stayed on the sidelines of the controversies for the most part because it had no strong desire to wage war against modernism. Moreover, the Moody coalition continued after the controversies with little change to its basic nonmilitant character.[37]

If the Dayton-Bebbington-Hamilton-Carpenter et al. interpretation someday supplants the Marsden paradigm, then fundamentalism will likely be understood as an important movement but one that was never at the center of evangelicalism. In this case, Sandeen's interpretation could actually be revived, especially his argument for the centrality of dispensationalism as the defining feature of fundamentalism. Hamilton and Trollinger have suggested that Sandeen has recently come to make much more sense to them than when they first read Marsden.[38]

THE INFLUENCE OF *FUNDAMENTALISM AND AMERICAN CULTURE* ON CHRISTIAN SCHOLARSHIP

In addition to setting forth the paradigm within which subsequent scholarship on fundamentalism and evangelicalism would take place, *Fundamentalism and American Culture* proved pivotal in shaping scholarship done from a distinctly Christian point of view. In the second paragraph of the first edition of the book, Marsden wrote, "This is an essay in distinctly Christian scholarship, an attempt to present a careful, honest, and critical evaluation of a tradition not far from my own." In his usual winsome way he preceded this statement by acknowledging that, however much Christian scholars might find it difficult to be fools for Christ, they were certainly as adept as others at being merely fools.[39] Long before his more widely discussed postscript in *The Soul of the American University* and his book *The Outrageous Idea of Christian Scholarship*, Marsden explained in the afterword to *Fundamentalism and American Culture* what difference being a Christian made for him as a scholar. He described his Christian view of history as being akin to that portrayed in the fiction of J. R. R. Tolkien. "We live in the midst of contests between great and mysterious spiritual forces," he wrote. We know partially, imperfectly, and only in occasional glimpses the shape that contest takes, and it is therefore incumbent on Christian historians to keep their wits about them and move cautiously and humbly. Moreover, Marsden was willing for the sake of such humility to analyze the visible side of Tolkien's universe. He characterized his methods as largely in sympathy with "the modern mode of explanation in terms of natural historical causation." The Christian historian's modest task, therefore, was to try to understand how cultural forces have promoted or distorted "our understanding of God and his revelation."[40] In other words, Marsden was willing to do history according to the academic rules of the game, what he would later call "methodological secularization." As he wrote in *The Outrageous Idea of Christian Scholarship* nearly two decades later, "Methodological secularization means only that for limited ad hoc purposes we will focus on natural phenomena accessible to all, while not denying their spiritual dimensions as created and ordered by God or forgetting that there is much more to the picture."[41]

Other Christian scholars of Marsden's generation also endeavored to work from a broadly Christian point of view, and Oxford University Press had published works by scholars who self-identified as Christians, usually in church history. Still, *Fundamentalism and American Culture* was a breakthrough piece of Christian scholarship for at least three reasons. First, as we have seen, Marsden outlined his point of view as being explicitly evangelical, not just Christian in the broad sense. As Oxford editor Cynthia Read noted recently, "It probably was a kind of watershed moment for evangelical scholarship."[42] Second, Marsden classed his evangelical approach as part of mainstream history, not church history. And third, the book received instant critical acclaim in the wider academy, as the reviews cited above bear witness. As one reviewer wrote of Marsden's self-identification as a Christian scholar, "A decade or so ago that avowal probably would have relegated the book to the margin of what was considered the mainstream of serious historical scholarship."[43]

During the rest of the century the evangelical approach to scholarship that Marsden outlined became well known in the academy, often referred to informally as the "evangelical school of historians." Marsden, Mark Noll, and Nathan Hatch served as a sort of trinity of well-known scholars sometimes joined by Joel Carpenter, Harry Stout, and Grant Wacker to become the big six. By the nineties Marsden was a fixture on the lecture circuit of conferences organized to promote Christian scholarship across disciplines. Leonard Sweet called him "the closest thing one can imagine to pontiff of evangelical history."[44] Bebbington recalls meeting Marsden for the first time in 1988 at an evangelical conference in Oxford run by the C. S. Lewis Society and attended by Carl F. H. Henry, who had been kicking around the idea of a Christian research university since at least the 1960s. That conference turned Bebbington into an enthusiast for Christian scholarship, which led eventually to his going to Baylor University as a visiting distinguished professor for a semester every other year.[45]

Marsden's influence on Baylor is undeniable. I recall interviewing there in 1996. In provost Don Schmeltekopf's office, at eye level to the side of my head, unshelved and ready for quick reference, sat the book *The Soul of the American University*, and I suspected that Noll's *The Scandal of the Evangelical Mind* was somewhere in the vicinity as well. The year before, Marsden had been a presenter and panelist for one of the conferences held in conjunction with the inauguration of President Robert Sloan, who along with Schmeltekopf launched Baylor 2012, the ten-year vision geared toward ramping up Baylor's research profile while at the same time cultivating the integration of faith and learning.[46] There were many influences along with Marsden, especially among Christian philosophers, who were always a step ahead of historians in the development of distinctly Christian scholarship. Still, it would not be going too far to say that *Fundamentalism and American Culture* was among the earliest and most important books for this movement. Moreover, the book placed Marsden squarely in the center of the debate over the integration of faith and learning, where he has remained ever since.

It would be difficult to identify a twentieth-century work of scholarship more important than *Fundamentalism and American Culture*. Very few books have a shelf life of even a decade, while Marsden's book has served as virtually every scholar's starting point for discussing fundamentalism and evangelicalism for more than a quarter century. This has had its downside, to be sure. A few have noted recently the problems that arise when a field of study is dominated by one interpretation in this way. One historian remarked, "It may not be all that good a thing for the field to have one big icon to agree or disagree with." Yet this historian adds, "I've reread [*Fundamentalism and American Culture*] again just recently, and it is a sophisticated piece of work." Another scholar has mused, "Because Marsden became the Bible, I wonder if his book hurt the development of other approaches to the history of fundamentalism that could have emerged from a host of dissertations and smaller topics." These comments will remain anonymous, but both come from historians who also give the book high praise. Both make an interesting point, especially given that with all of the recent challenges to Marsden cited above, few have made their way into print, even in article form. More importantly, in the three decades since the book appeared, no one has attempted a book-length synthetic interpretation aimed at supplanting the Marsden paradigm.

For a generation *Fundamentalism and American Culture* has reigned as the defining interpretation of fundamentalism while substantially shaping our view of evangelicalism as well. The book inspired other scholars to get busy filling in the details of twentieth-century evangelical studies. Moreover, because the book launched Marsden into the big leagues of American historians, it also moved Christian scholars into the mainstream of the academy. At the same time, the book may have scared off competing interpretations and in that sense blinded us to helpful ways of viewing evangelicalism. As we have seen, a handful of historians now view the interpretation that the book replaced as substantially correct. The next phase of scholarship may bring us full circle back to Ernest Sandeen, even further back to Timothy Smith, or on to new ways of seeing things no one has thought of yet. Such irony might just please or even amuse a historian who says his outlook can be described as a combination of Jonathan Edwards and Reinhold Niebuhr.

NOTES

1. Stewart Cole, *The History of Fundamentalism* (New York: R. R. Smith, 1931).
2. Richard Hofstadter, *Anti-intellectualism in American Life* (New York: Knopf, 1963), 138–39. I have also discussed the Hofstadter view in Barry Hankins, *American Evangelicals: A Contemporary History of a Mainstream Religious Movement* (Lanham, MD: Rowman and Littlefield, 2008), 163.
3. Henry F. May, *The Divided Heart: Essays on Protestantism and the Enlightenment in America* (New York: Oxford University Press, 1991), 18. May first gave this lecture at a conference at the Smithsonian as "Religion and American Intellectual History, 1945–1985: Reflections on an Uneasy Relationship."
4. Ernest Sandeen, *The Roots of Fundamentalism: British and American Millenarianism* (Chicago: University of Chicago Press, 1970), 285, quoted in George Marsden, "Defining Fundamentalism," *Christian Scholars Review* 1, no. 2 (Winter 1971): 141.
5. Marsden, "Defining Fundamentalism," 145.
6. George Marsden, *Fundamentalism and American Culture: The Shaping of Twentieth-Century Evangelicalism, 1870–1925* (New York: Oxford University Press, 1980), 4.
7. George Marsden, e-mail to author, January 6, 2010.
8. James Findlay, review of Marsden, *Fundamentalism and American Culture, American Historical Review* 86 (October 1981): 946.
9. Ibid., 947.
10. David Edwin Harrell, review of Marsden, *Fundamentalism and American Culture, Journal of Southern History* 47 (November 1981): 621–22.
11. Russell Richey, review of Marsden, *Fundamentalism and American Culture, Journal for the Scientific Study of Religion* 21 (June 1982): 178–79.
12. William G. McLoughlin, review of Marsden, *Fundamentalism and American Culture, Review of Religious Research* 24 (March 1983): 278, 279.
13. Roy Wallis, review of Marsden, *Fundamentalism and American Culture, Religious Studies* 19 (September 1983): 422.

14. Robert Moats Miller, "A Compleat (Almost) Guide through the Forest of Fundamentalism," *Reviews in American History* 9, no. 3 (September 1981): 392–97; quote on 392.
15. Ibid., 395.
16. Ibid., 395–96.
17. Ibid., all quotes on 397.
18. George Marsden, e-mail to author, January 5, 2010.
19. Ibid.
20. Grant Wacker, *Augustus H. Strong and the Dilemma of Historical Consciousness* (Macon, GA: Mercer University Press, 1985); William Vance Trollinger Jr., *God's Empire: William Bell Riley and Midwestern Fundamentalism* (Madison: University of Wisconsin Press, 1990); Lyle Dorsett, *Billy Sunday and the Redemption of Urban America* (Grand Rapids, MI: Eerdmans, 1991); Edith Bloomhofer, *Aimee Semple McPherson: Everybody's Sister* (Grand Rapids, MI: Eerdmans, 1993); D. G. Hart, *Defending the Faith: J. Gresham Machen and the Crisis of Conservative Protestantism in Modern America* (Baltimore: Johns Hopkins University Press, 1994); Barry Hankins, *God's Rascal: J. Frank Norris and the Beginnings of Southern Fundamentalism* (Lexington: University Press of Kentucky, 1996); and Mark Taylor Dalhouse, *An Island in a Lake of Fire: Bob Jones University, Fundamentalism, and the Separatist Movement* (Athens: University of Georgia Press, 1996). See also David Edwin Harrell Jr., *Oral Roberts: An American Life* (Bloomington: Indiana University Press, 1985), and *Pat Robertson: A Personal, Religious, and Political Portrait* (San Francisco: Harper and Row, 1987); I should also mention here C. Allyn Russell's *Voices of Fundamentalism: Seven Biographical Studies* (Philadelphia: Westminster Press, 1976). Coming four years before Marsden's book, Russell's book also inspired younger scholars to take up the biographical approach to the study of fundamentalism.

More recent biographies include Matthew Sutton, *Aimee Semple McPherson and the Resurrection of Christian America* (Cambridge, MA: Harvard University Press, 2007); John G. Turner, *Bill Bright and Campus Crusade for Christ: The Renewal of Evangelicalism in Postwar America* (Chapel Hill: University of North Carolina Press, 2009). Turner was a Marsden student.

A recent regional study is Margaret Lamberts Bendroth, *Fundamentalists in the City: Conflict and Division in Boston's Churches, 1885–1950* (New York: Oxford University Press, 2005).

Recent books employing Marsden's "fundamentalism and American culture" approach are Douglas Carl Abrams, *Selling the Old-Time Religion: American Fundamentalists and Mass Culture, 1920–1940* (Athens: University of Georgia Press, 2001); and Tona Hangen, *Redeeming the Dial: Radio, Religion, and Popular Culture in America* (Chapel Hill: University of North Carolina Press, 2002).

21. See, for example, David Edwin Harrell, ed., *Varieties of Southern Evangelicalism* (Macon, GA: Mercer University Press, 1981); William Glass, *Strangers*

in Zion: Fundamentalists in the South, 1900–1950 (Macon, GA: Mercer University Press, 2001); Mary Beth Swetnam Mathews, *Rethinking Zion: How the Print Media Placed Fundamentalism in the South* (Knoxville: University of Tennessee Press, 2006); Darren Dochuk, *From Bible Belt to Sunbelt: Plain-Folk Religion, Grassroots Politics, and the Rise of Evangelical Conservatism* (New York: Norton, 2011). Dochuk was a Marsden student. With his interpretation of the nexus of Reaganite Republicanism, the Christian Right, transplanted southerners, Southern California, and the entire tenor of American conservatism in late twentieth-century America, Dochuk's book may be the most important on evangelicals since Marsden's *Fundamentalism and American Culture*.

22. For examples, see Janette Hassey, *No Time for Silence: Evangelical Women in Public Ministry around the Turn of the Century* (Grand Rapids, MI: Academie, 1986); Betty DeBerg, *Ungodly Women* (Minneapolis: Fortress Press, 1990); Virginia Brereton, *Stories of Women's Conversions, 1800 to the Present* (Bloomington: Indiana University Press, 1991); Margaret Lamberts Bendroth, *Fundamentalism and Gender, 1875 to the Present* (New Haven, CT: Yale University Press, 1993); Susie Stanley, *Feminist Pillar of Fire: The Life of Alma White* (Cleveland, OH: Pilgrim Press, 1993); R. Marie Griffith, *God's Daughters: Evangelical Women and the Power of Submission* (Berkeley: University of California Press, 1997); Susan K. Gallagher, *Evangelical Identity and Gendered Family Life* (New Brunswick, NJ: Rutgers University Press, 2003); Christine Pohl and Nicoloa Hoggard Creegan, *Living on the Boundaries: Evangelical Women, Feminism, and the Theological Academy* (Downers Grove, IL: InterVarsity Press, 2005); Brenda Brasher, *Godly Women: Fundamentalism and Female Power* (New Brunswick, NJ: Rutgers University Press, 1998); and R. Marie Griffith, *Born Again Bodies: Flesh and Spirit in American Christianity* (Berkeley: University of California Press, 2004).

23. For examples of ethnographic studies, see James Ault Jr., *Spirit and Flesh: Life in a Fundamentalist Baptist Church* (New York: Vintage Books, 2004); Nancy Ammerman, *Bible Believers: Fundamentalists in the Modern World* (New Brunswick, NJ: Rutgers University Press, 1987); Alan Peshkin, *God's Choice: The Total World of a Fundamentalist Christian School* (Chicago: University of Chicago Press, 1986); Randall Balmer, *Mine Eyes Have Seen the Glory: A Journey into the Evangelical Subculture in America*, 4th ed. (New York: Oxford University Press, 2006). Balmer is a historian.

For historical and biographical works on the Christian Right, see Harrell, *Oral Roberts* and *Pat Robertson*; L. Edward Hicks, *"Sometimes in the Wrong but Never in Doubt": George S. Benson and the Education of the New Religious Right* (Knoxville: University of Tennessee Press, 1994); Justin Watson, *The Christian Coalition: Dreams of Restoration, Demands for Recognition* (New York: St. Martin's Press, 1997); Susan Friend Harding, *The Book of Jerry Falwell: Fundamentalist Language and Politics* (Princeton, NJ: Princeton University Press, 2000); Axel R. Schafer, *Countercultural Conservatives: American Evangelicalism from the Postwar*

Revival to the New Christian Right (Madison: University of Wisconsin Press, 2011); Daniel K. Williams, *God's Own Party: The Making of the Christian Right* (New York: Oxford University Press, 2012).

Harding's approach is ethnographic. Like the other sociologists/anthropologists cited above, she spent time living among her subjects, in this case at Thomas Road Baptist Church, Lynchburg, Virginia.

For works by sociologists, see William Martin, *With God on Our Side: The Rise of the Christian Right in America* (New York: Broadway Books, 1996); Clyde Wilcox and Carin Larson, *Onward Christian Soldiers? The Religious Right in American Politics*, 3rd ed. (Boulder, CO: Westview Press, 2006); Sara Diamond, *Not by Politics Alone: The Enduring Influence of the Christian Right* (New York: Guilford Press, 1998).

See also Murray Dempster and Augustus Cerillo Jr., *Salt and Light: Evangelical Political Thought in Modern America* (Grand Rapids, MI: Baker, 1989); James Skillen, *The Scattered Voice: Christians at Odds in the Public Square* (Edmonton, AB: Canadian Institute for Law, Theology, and Public Policy, 1996).

Much of the most important sociological work on evangelicals over the past decade and a half has been done by Christian Smith. For examples, see Christian Smith, *American Evangelicalism: Embattled and Thriving* (Chicago: University of Chicago Press, 1998); Christian Smith, *A Christian America? What Evangelicals Really Want* (Berkeley: University of California Press, 2000); Michael Emerson and Christian Smith, *Divided by Faith: Evangelical Religion and the Problem of Race in America* (New York: Oxford University Press, 2000).

Recently books have begun to emerge on the Evangelical Left and the evangelical counterculture. For examples, see David R. Swartz, *Moral Minority: The Evangelical Left in an Age of Conservatism* (Philadelphia: University of Pennsylvania Press, 2012); Larry Eskridge, *God's Forever Family: The Jesus People Movement in America* (New York: Oxford University Press, 2013).

24. Edward Larson, *Summer for the Gods: The Scopes Trial and America's Continuing Debate Over Science and Religion* (New York: Basic Books, 1997), 35, 76, and 232; Edward Larson, e-mails to author, January 12, 2010, and January 19, 2010. See also Paul K. Conkin, *When All the Gods Trembled: Darwinism, Scopes, and American Intellectuals* (Lanham, MD: Rowman and Littlefield, 1998); David N. Livingstone, *Darwin's Forgotten Defenders: The Encounter between Evangelical Theology and Evolutionary Thought* (Grand Rapids, MI: Eerdmans, 1987); David N. Livingstone, D. G. Hart, and Mark A. Noll, eds., *Evangelicals and Science in Historical Perspective* (New York: Oxford University Press, 1999); Ronald L. Numbers, *The Creationists: The Evolution of Scientific Creationism* (Berkeley: University of California Press, 1993); Mark Kalthoff, "The New Evangelical Engagement with Science: The American Scientific Affiliation, Origin to 1963" (PhD diss., Indiana University, 1998); Charles Israel, *Before Scopes: Evangelicals, Evolution, and Education in Tennessee, 1870–1925* (Athens: University of Georgia

Press, 2004); Adam Laats, *Fundamentalism and Education in the Scopes Era: God, Darwin, and the Roots of America's Culture Wars* (New York: Palgrave Macmillan, 2012).

25. Darryl Hart, e-mail to author, December 8, 2009.
26. William Vance Trollinger Jr., e-mail to author, November 16, 2009.
27. Ibid.
28. Margaret Bendroth, e-mail to author, November 11, 2009. See Bendroth, *Fundamentalism and Gender*.
29. David Bebbington, e-mail to author, November 17, 2009. See David Bebbington, *Evangelicalism in Modern Britain: A History from the 1730s to the 1980s* (Grand Rapids, MI: Baker Book House, 1982).
30. Joel Carpenter, e-mail to author, November 17, 2009. See Joel Carpenter, *Revive Us Again: The Reawakening of Fundamentalism* (New York: Oxford University Press, 1997).
31. For an accessible recent summary of the Dayton challenge, see Kenneth Collins, *The Evangelical Moment: The Promise of an American Religion* (Grand Rapids, MI: Baker Academic Publishing, 2005), 64–70. For Dayton's embourgeoisement argument, see Donald Dayton, "The Embourgeoisement of a Vision: Lament of a Radical Evangelical," *Other Side* 23, no. 8 (October 1987): 19. The gist of the Marsden-Dayton debate can be found in *Christian Scholars Review* 23, no. 1 (1993). See also Donald Dayton and Robert K. Johnson, eds., *The Variety of American Evangelicalism* (Knoxville: University of Tennessee Press, 1991).
32. Donald Dayton, "Are Charismatic-Inclined Pietists the True Evangelicals? And Have the Reformed Tried to Highjack Their Movement?," interview, *Modern Reformation* 10, no. 2 (March/April 2001), 40–49, www.modernreformation.org/default.php?page=articledisplay&var1=ArtRead&var2=400&var3=main.
33. Both Dayton and Carpenter have recently told of Marsden's research at Dayton's library, and Dayton recently said in conversation that he urged Oxford to publish Marsden.
34. Carpenter, e-mail to author. Edward Larson also places himself and his book *Summer for the Gods* in the Dayton-Smith-Carpenter camp. Larson, e-mail to author, January 19, 2009.
35. David Bebbington, "Not So Exceptional after All: American Evangelicals Reassessed," *Books and Culture*, May/June 2007, 18.
36. George Marsden, *Fundamentalism and American Culture*, 2nd ed. (New York: Oxford University Press, 2006), 235.
37. Hamilton, "Interdenominational Evangelicalism."
38. Hamilton, e-mail to author; Trollinger, e-mail to author. See also William Vance Trollinger Jr., "How John Nelson Darby Went Visiting: Dispensational Premillennialism in the Believers Church Tradition and the Historiogra-

phy of Fundamentalism," in *Apocalypticism and Millennialism: Shaping a Believers Church Eschatology for the Twenty-First Century*, edited by Loren L. Johns (Kitchener, ON: Pandora Press; Scottdale, PA: Herald Press, 2000), 264–81.

39. Marsden, *Fundamentalism and American Culture* [1980], v.

40. Ibid., 229–30.

41. George Marsden, *The Outrageous Idea of Christian Scholarship* (New York: Oxford University Press, 1997), 91.

42. Cynthia Read, e-mail to author, January 19, 2010.

43. Donald M. Scott, "Review of *Fundamentalism and American Culture*," *Journal of American History* 71, no. 3 (December 1984): 596–98.

44. Leonard I. Sweet, "Wise as Serpents, Innocent as Doves: The New Evangelical Historiography," *Journal of the American Academy of Religion* 56, no. 3 (1988): 398.

45. Bebbington, e-mail to author.

46. For essays on the Baylor endeavor, see Barry Hankins and Donald Schmeltekopf, eds., *The Baylor Project* (South Bend, IN: St. Augustine's Press, 2007).

CHAPTER 8

Fundamentalism and American Culture

WILLIAM L. SVELMOE

It is impossible to say exactly when George Marsden, unassuming Calvin College professor, became George Marsden, unassuming icon in the field of religious history. But it is safe to say that the transformation took place at some point during the years following the publication of *Fundamentalism and American Culture*. Perhaps Marsden's transformation occurred as reviewers weighed its impact and searched for superlatives.[1] Perhaps the transformation was signaled when an NBC crew crowded into Marsden's cluttered office in the basement of the Calvin College library. They had heard that Professor Marsden was the man who might explain for them the people whose votes had carried a B-movie star into the White House. Perhaps the transformation was complete when the heavyweights came calling in the mid-1980s—Yale, Duke, and even Berkeley—all vying for the learned professor's services. Or perhaps the transformation happened far from the centers of power when a young divinity student insisted halfway through the term that his professor add a new book to the course syllabus. "I've found the book that explains me to myself," he might have said. Perhaps it *is* best to find the transformation here, within the evangelical world itself, where Marsden's book served as a guide to the historical and cultural antecedents that had shaped a powerful religious subculture. That he was able to address so many audiences with such remarkable felicity, and that he did so as a self-confessed Christian scholar, is one of the greatest tributes to what remains perhaps his most important book.

ON SUBSTANCE AND STYLE

In 1976 Jimmy Carter reminded America's opinion makers that "born again" religious folk had not retreated to some Appalachian redoubt to lick their wounds after their humiliation at the notorious Scopes trial and that in fact they now gathered in uptown Atlanta and Dallas, where they worked, played, and worshipped in great numbers. The shock on the faces of network anchors was both amusing and instructive. In 1980 a book written by a professor from a midwestern religious college had a similar effect on opinion makers in America's elite academies. Marsden's exploration of Protestant fundamentalism dropped into an academic world devoted to secularization theories, which posited the notion that the disappearance of the kind of folk about whom Marsden wrote was a natural and proper concomitant of modernization. Marsden convincingly argued the opposite. He demonstrated that such religious, even antimodernist, groups were central to the American story. He dared to suggest that they might still have a say in America's future. Later that fall, Americans discovered how right he was.

Marsden's work, while respectful to theology and devotion, was primarily a cultural history. It was also a very American story. He argued that to understand evangelicals and fundamentalists one had to recognize how profoundly the movement had been shaped by a particular stance toward America, its culture and its politics, a stance shaped by the events of the 1870s through the 1920s. Evangelicals, who enjoyed a kind of hegemony over American culture for much of the nineteenth century, now faced a tense, several decades-long "collective uprooting" from their position of dominance.[2] Evangelicals did not go gently into that good night. They fought to retain their position, first in their denominations and missions, and eventually, in perhaps the sorriest and most humiliating episode in their long proud history, on the world stage at Dayton in 1925. This struggle to retain their position gave rise in Marsden's account to what we know today as fundamentalism.

Throughout his book Marsden demonstrated how fundamentalists operated under what he terms the "establishment-or-outsider paradox."[3] At times they felt like part of the establishment. They owned the culture. They argued that America was essentially a God-blessed, God-saturated land. They loved America. "America the Beautiful," they sang with great fervor. At other times they felt like outsiders. The culture they had once owned had disowned them. They argued that America was essentially a God-cursed, God-deserted, and God-deserting land. They despised America. "We Want America Back," they sang with great fervor. This chronological and dialectical movement between insider and outsider became a powerful explanatory device in Marsden's hands for an understanding both of fundamentalism in the early 1900s and of evangelicalism today. And it suggested for readers in the 1980s that evangelicalism's potent mood of aggrieved patriotism might still hold great appeal in American politics at the end of the century.

Marsden both complicated and clarified the historical understanding of fundamentalism. Ironically, however, Marsden's complications actually clarified the picture, while his clarifications led to further complications.

First, the complications that clarified. Where earlier historians of fundamentalism had seen the movement's origins in one or perhaps two religious streams—Ernest Sandeen in premillennialism, for example—Marsden found an entire web of interlocking precursors and fellow travelers.[4] To dispensational premillennialists, Marsden added mainstream nineteenth-century evangelicals from the revivalist tradition, advocates of various strands of the holiness movement, and upholders of traditional faith in the mainline denominations and at Princeton Seminary. His cast of colorful characters included John Nelson Darby, the Plymouth Brethren preacher who can be credited with thinking up dispensationalism; buttoned-down Moody lieutenant R. A. Torrey, who traveled the country in starched shirts converting sinners and railing against liberalism; presidential hopeful William Jennings Bryan, who fought the good fight against evolution; and Princeton theologian B. B. Warfield, who more than likely would have bitterly resented being seen as a fellow traveler with any of the aforementioned characters.

In one of his most fascinating chapters, Marsden emphasized the importance of the commitment by such nineteenth-century evangelicals to an essentially Enlightenment view of science. For much of the eighteenth and nineteenth centuries, science seemed no necessary enemy of religion. This commitment set evangelicals up for a fall when, with the advent of Darwinism, the foundations of Western science shifted beneath their feet. Evangelicals, who for over a century had eagerly embraced scientific discoveries that seemed to demonstrate that an infinitely complex but ordered universe pointed toward a design by an infinite God, suddenly found themselves pitted against their former allies, who now argued that the complexity and raw disorder of the natural world pointed toward more naturalistic explanations of origins.

Evangelicals' view of science had profound implications for scriptural interpretation. Marsden demonstrated how a science built on the theories of the seventeenth-century philosopher Francis Bacon combined with Scottish common sense realism to virtually force evangelicals toward what subsequently became one of their most defining beliefs, the literal interpretation of scripture. Bacon argued that science must be built on purely inductive reasoning from a set of facts. Common sense philosophy argued that average human beings with their innate faculties should be able to ascertain truths about the world from the facts and perceptions before them. When applied to scripture, this seemed to indicate that spiritual truth should be also readily and accurately induced by average minds. If average folk could understand scripture on their own, scripture could not be a collection of esoteric hidden truths. It had to be plain. It had to be simple. It had to be literal.

The next step was to argue that such literal truth was induced from an inerrant text. If God wanted his people to arrive at truth, it made sense that he would have left them an accurate written record. As Marsden wrote, "At Princeton it was an article of faith that God would provide nothing less than wholly accurate facts, whether large or small. Common Sense philosophy assured that throughout the ages people could discover the same truths in the unchanging storehouse of Scripture."[5] Such views on inerrancy hardened as the biblical text was challenged by proponents of new historical-critical methods. One could argue that the defining principle of fundamentalism was thereby clarified, a commitment to a unitary truth capable of being gleaned by regular folk from an inerrant authority. From this inerrant authority a core group of theological and historical statements was inductively arrived at, statements that brooked no argument from reasonable people. To argue was to place oneself outside the camp.

As new views of science took hold in the educated world, evangelicals, instead of adapting as did liberal Christians, decided to fight it out rather than surrender. They felt that under the old rules they were still approaching these questions in a properly scientific manner. In fact, they felt they were doing science even better than the new scientists, because they did not begin with the presupposition that supernatural interpretations were by their very nature out of bounds. If the intervention of the supernatural was the simplest explanation for a phenomenon, whether observed in the natural world or recorded in scripture, then it was only right to accept that explanation. This is what commitments to Baconian science and a common sense philosophy seemed to demand. Having gone "all in" with science when the scientific revolution seemed to support scripture, evangelicals now found themselves in an extremely difficult position when science suddenly went in a new direction. They reacted like a betrayed suitor. It was science that had been unfaithful, and unfaithful to its own agreed-upon method, not scripture. And for evangelicals, this new science had the potential to be extremely destructive.

Marsden then demonstrated how this sense of betrayal united the wildly disparate evangelical movements and galvanized them into a fighting fundamentalist coalition after World War I. Fundamentalists blamed the German war machine on Germany's embrace of this new scientific mistress, with its drift toward rationalism and away from a commitment to supernatural Christianity. Ultimately this led Germany into an evolutionary view of life, and it was plain to fundamentalists the damage that ensued. They feared it might happen in America. In fact, it was happening already in their denominations, their churches, and their schools. They determined to resist the "Germanification" of America. They banded together and fought. They fought for their country, for their lost place in the leadership of their country, and for the honor of God. The fight was brief and bitter. Fundamentalists lost, and their loss resonates throughout the evangelical world to this day.

By the time a reader finished this tour de force, it had become obvious that fundamentalist origins were more complex than the historiography before 1980 had indicated. Many springs fed the fundamentalist pool, not simply one or two. Marsden's gift to his readers was to first reveal this complexity and then clearly demonstrate the forces that united the various factions into a somewhat coherent movement.

Now, the clarification that complicated. After demonstrating just how complex were fundamentalism's roots, Marsden sharply defined fundamentalism itself as a "militant antimodernism" that united these disparate groups in a spasm of activism in the early 1920s.[6] By pushing his definition of fundamentalism to this sharply delineated point, Marsden both clarified the issue and called the question. This clarification has led to subsequent complications as some interpreters have objected to what they see as a too narrow definition of fundamentalism. Others resist the swallowing up of evangelicalism, with its wide range of interests, by the giant of fundamentalism created by Marsden's influential work. Critics of the first persuasion have argued that Marsden's definition leaves out groups such as the Pentecostals, who shared much with fundamentalists except participation in their most militant crusades.[7] Critics of the second have objected that by emphasizing militant antimodernism Marsden neglected the more important fundamentalist and evangelical focus on holiness and evangelism. Mike Hamilton has argued persuasively in this vein.[8] I have argued in another setting that "in studying missions we study the heart of the evangelical impulse." The Moody Bible Institute itself, perhaps fundamentalism's premier institution, argued that the "leading feature" of the school was instruction in missions. It is, therefore, at our peril that we permit a fundamentalist militant impulse to overwhelm our view of the evangelical mainstream.[9]

Marsden acknowledged this tension throughout his work both in the text and in footnotes. He wrote, for example, "When the battles against modernism arose, fundamentalism always retained a tension between an exclusivist militancy and an irenic spirit concerned with holiness and saving souls. These latter elements in the tradition of Moody gave the movement its largest appeal."[10] Marsden was not ungenerous in acknowledging that evangelism was what really concerned the movement most of the time. Perhaps it is a tribute to the power of his work that despite such acknowledgments, "militant antimodernism" became a standard definition of fundamentalism, so that, as with all groundbreaking work, subsequent interpreters have been forced to place their own work in relationship to Marsden. Marsden's clarification has, therefore, given rise to all manner of healthy definitional discussion and complication.

Rereading *Fundamentalism and American Culture* in its new edition today, one is most struck by Marsden's accomplishment as a historian. To grasp the big picture of the roots of American fundamentalism, Marsden had to master a bewildering variety and number of sources. There is simply no way to write a groundbreaking work on the cheap. You have to actually read and digest all that stuff, the stuff of history, the books and magazines in libraries, the letters in archives, the footnote that leads to a book that leads to a footnote that leads to a book that leads to the "aha moment" upon which it all hangs. There is no need to turn to the footnotes and bibliography to recognize what Marsden achieved. The number and richness of Marsden's sources are evident on every page.

Also evident on every page is this: after a vast reading must come a focused synthesis. Hours of research must be turned into a single sentence or paragraph that captures the essence of the insight gleaned during those lonely hours. Marsden wrote with tremendous interpretive confidence, and this confidence is communicated to the reader from the first page. Marsden earns the trust of his readers both with his command of the sources and with the confidence with which he asserted his judgments on those sources. Beginning students can see here the symbiotic relationship between thorough command of the sources and justly forceful arguments that demonstrate that command. And Marsden did all this with startling concision. By rights this ought to be a 600-page book; it covers that much material. Instead it is an astonishingly tight 230-page seminal essay.

Which brings me to a comment on Marsden's writing style. Marsden writes with great care and focus. There are few rhetorical flourishes in his writing. What rhetorical flourishes there are usually serve Marsden's sense of humor. Those who have viewed the caricature of Marsden that hangs in his home, a caricature done in the classic "New York Review" style, will also recognize the sly grin that emerges from time to time in the pages of *Fundamentalism*. Marsden's humor is rarely broad. As broad as it comes was this comment about Henry Ward Beecher: "Although [Beecher] was well informed, he claimed he 'never read a book through' . . . presumably with the exception of those he wrote."[11] With this deft aside, Marsden summed up his attitude toward Beecher's intellectual gifts and discipline. But most Marsden humor is even more subtle: "Strict Calvinists had maintained that the human mind was blinded in mankind's Fall from innocence; in the Common Sense version, the intellect seemed to suffer from a slight astigmatism only."[12] "These courts . . . reduced the chances that Presbyterians would let theological differences coexist, or sleeping dogmas lie." Or so insider that some readers may have missed it entirely: "The 'Shorter' and the 'Larger' catechisms (the 'Shorter' being shorter only relative to the 'Larger') were carefully engraved upon the minds of the young through arduous and awesome processes of memorization."[13] Or even further inside: "According to the dispensationalists, the ten toes [on the image in Daniel's dream] represented the ten European nations whose federation . . . would be the final restoration of the Roman Empire. These nations were increasingly turning to constitutional or 'mixed' democracies, and this was just what the mixture of iron and clay in the dream prophesied."[14] Of course! Rarely have the three words "this was just" been used to more devastating effect. And consequently, rarely has an overreaching scheme of biblical interpretation been dismissed so subtly.

ON CHRISTIAN SCHOLARSHIP

Marsden has been justifiably celebrated for drawing attention to Christian scholarship. He has argued eloquently for the acceptance in the academy of scholarship done by confessed Christians, even as he has raised the question of just what exactly such scholarship might look like. Marsden discussed the role of Christian scholars in the academy at length in 1997 in *The Outrageous Idea of Christian Scholarship*. But as Marsden first raised the issue, at least on a large stage, with this volume, it behooves us to pay some attention to what this high-profile work of Christian scholarship suggested about the question.

In a key paragraph in the preface to the first edition of *Fundamentalism* Marsden laid his religious cards on the table. "While I have attempted to assume a stance of detachment and to avoid using history as a tool for partisan debate," Marsden wrote, "this study represents a definite point of view and set of interests. Since these give it direction, they are best revealed at the outset. This is an essay in distinctly Christian scholarship, an attempt to present a careful, honest, and critical evaluation of a tradition not far from my own." But what does Marsden actually say in his preface about how his Christianity affects his scholarship? He promises a "dispassionate analysis" addressed to "thoughtful Christians" as well as to the scholarly community. He reveals that he admires Jonathan Edwards and Reinhold Niebuhr, perhaps the two most prominent theologian/philosophers in American history. Perspectives associated with these great men can be "found implicitly" throughout his study. He will focus on culture and the "relationship of Christians to it." The questions and themes that shape the study are informed by these interests. Later he thanks friends at Calvin College because "Christian scholarship is essentially a communal enterprise." Marsden's preface is alive with implicit Christian influences that somehow shape the author's enterprise, but it is very difficult to put a finger on exactly what it all means beyond "an attempt to present a careful, honest, and critical evaluation" of a religious tradition, an attempt perhaps instigated by his own religious faith.[15]

We read Marsden's preface now after several decades of discussion about the meaning of Christian scholarship, discussions that have taken place at the very highest level of the academic enterprise. We owe these discussions to George Marsden. With several short paragraphs in a landmark volume, Marsden essentially challenged the academy to open its mind to the fact that Christians could do remarkable scholarly work that would, at least at the level of evidence and interpretation, the level upon which all scholarly work must be judged, be fair and balanced.

Marsden was never defensive about his religious tradition or his personal faith. He demonstrated that a Christian believer could honestly analyze Christians, acknowledging in the analysis both strengths and weaknesses, and all without ever making a single declaration based on faith alone, or on evidence that could not be fairly weighed by any reader, religious or secular.

But Marsden also implicitly understood that he was caught between two audiences. While the initial audience that had to be addressed and persuaded was a secular academic one, eventually the Christian community, an evangelical, even fundamentalist one, might tune in. And the popular evangelical audience, at least, is used to reading its history through a providential lens. They want to know what God is doing in the world. Even if a popular evangelical audience never read *Fundamentalism* in great numbers, Marsden knew that a strong "No" would have to be spoken to this community, and that the academic community would need to hear that "No" before there was much chance it would accept the challenging "Yes" that he laid at its door.

Eventually Marsden addressed these questions in *Outrageous Idea*, a volume that has been criticized for saying more about what Christian scholarship is not than about what it is. As one reviewer wrote, "If there is a flaw in this short volume, it is that Marsden spends more time answering his critics and defining what faith-informed scholarship is not than in delineating what it might have to offer."[16] But perhaps that is the essential truth of the matter. There is simply more to be said about what Christian scholarship is not than about what it is. The greater danger lies in the direction of making too explicit an attempt to mold a positively Christian history. Perhaps there is no such thing. Christian scholarship simply must not be scholarship that attempts to advance the agenda of the subculture in any way. Its role is not to make the subculture feel good about itself and its heroes. Its role is not to somehow bring converts into the kingdom. Christian scholarship must simply be scholarship written by a Christian that attempts to tell the truth. That's it.

Marsden's volume on fundamentalism reveals that this truth telling can have profound implications and consequences. There are rewards for a secular as well as a Christian audience. A secular readership gains insight into religious people and movements from an author who understands how religion works to motivate its members. He accepts the reality and importance of deep religious commitment. He does not attempt to define away religious commitment as something else, as somehow duplicitous or fake. As Marsden notes in his introduction, "Fundamentalism was primarily a religious movement." He goes on, "Unless we appreciate the immense implications of a deep religious commitment to such beliefs . . . we cannot appreciate the dynamics of fundamentalist thought and action."[17] Throughout he works hard to make those beliefs intelligible to all audiences, and by doing so, forces perhaps a grudging respect for at least the coherence and authenticity of fundamentalists' belief. They may have been paranoid, but perhaps, suggests Marsden, they had good reason to be.

It is the task of the scholar with a religious background to write about religious people with the complexity they deserve. Scholars who do not claim religious affiliation or convictions may suspect, even stress, other causes for what they see as strange and irrational behavior. Marsden, on the other hand, understood that fundamentalists acted from a variety of motivations—indeed this was central to his analysis—but he refused to assign primary motivation to forces outside the religious. As he said at one point, "Social factors exert a considerable influence on religious life, and, except for explicitly stated commitments, may provide the best means of predicting religious behavior. It is, however, a mistake to reduce religious behavior to its social dimensions, or to assume that these are usually primary."[18] Marsden demanded that secular scholars attend carefully to religious language and motivations. He demonstrated how to properly weight such factors when analyzing events driven by religious folk. This is perhaps the greatest gift the explicitly religious scholar provides the academy at large.

As crucially important as that function of religious scholarship may be, the religious scholar brings a word to his own community that is equally significant. I suspect that this aspect of Marsden's impact might be shielded from Marsden himself, inasmuch as he was nurtured in a Reformed community that fosters scholarship in ways that the mainstream evangelical community has not always embraced. But many of those most affected by *Fundamentalism* tell stories that approach conversion narratives in their appeal. In a sense the insider is most affected by the flip side of the coin from that which affects the reader from outside the community. Yes, said Marsden, we must respect the religious motivations of our actors, but we must also understand that while social factors must not be the sum total of our interpretation, social factors do in fact "exert a considerable influence on religious life."[19] Readers who grew up in a religious culture in which the authority that circumscribed their lives seemed to exist outside of time were plunged by Marsden back into the stream of history, immersed along with all their religious certainties into a stream of contingencies and the fickle choices of often exceedingly odd human beings. To be faced with the fact that a view of the future that held both fascination and terror for one as a child owed as much or more to a wandering Plymouth Brethren preacher as it did to the Bible is a profoundly enlightening moment. And it is a moment that leads to additional reassessments. It is critical for this insider audience to understand the historical and cultural antecedents for what they believe. It is important that evangelicals be encouraged to step outside their naturally Manichean worldviews and understand just how complex is the relationship of their subculture to the wider world. Religiously committed historians then have a duty to their own community. It is their role to suggest where the thought or action of religious leaders owes more to the frailties of human nature than to divine inspiration, and perhaps to suggest through the story they tell just how difficult it is to know with any certainty what God is up to in the world. Whether intentionally or not, Marsden expertly provided a model for engaging in such scholarship.

In an "Afterword" Marsden picked up these issues again and attempted to articulate how explicitly Christian historians might fit their work into their faith tradition. In language that may have made his secular audience a bit nervous, he sought to balance the Christian view that God is at work in history with a tempered acknowledgment that it is very difficult for human beings to pronounce with any authority on what God is up to. He assured his religious readers that a work of scholarship, which played by the rules of the academy and was thereby bound to explain events "in terms of natural historical causation," did not of necessity negate the reality of supernatural forces that might be at work. Indeed Marsden suggested that the Christian historian was servant to theologians and all who attempt the theological task of distinguishing the genuine works of God from the merely culturally conditioned, or "the gold from the dross."[20]

Here Marsden was perhaps too politic. If indeed a historian with Marsden's skill and integrity plays the servant to theologians, then surely that servant occupies a very special role. Perhaps historians like Marsden play the fool to the theologians' and ministers' king. In ancient courts the fool operated somewhat independently and was the one person who spoke truth to the king. No threat to the king's power, the fool told him what he least wanted to hear. The fool dared to remind the king of his mortality, of his shortsightedness, of his mistaken assumptions. In a subculture whose religious devotees have been prone to hubris when pronouncing on the works of God, whose kings have often operated with virtually unchecked power, wise fools are desperately needed. The role of the Christian historian is simply to speak the truth. By telling a very human story, historians speak caution to a community that too often believes it understands exactly whither the Spirit is blowing.

NOTES

1. See Barry Hankins in this volume (chapter 7) for an excellent summary of the reviews of *Fundamentalism and American Culture*.

2. George Marsden, *Fundamentalism and American Culture: The Shaping of Twentieth-Century Evangelicalism, 1870–1925* (New York: Oxford University Press, 1980), vi.

3. Ibid., 7.

4. Again, see Hankins's chapter for a review of the early literature on fundamentalism.

5. Marsden, *Fundamentalism and American Culture*, 113.

6. Ibid., 4.

7. The Hankins essay is helpful on what might be called the Donald Dayton argument.

8. Michael Hamilton, "Awash in a Sea of Fundamentalisms: Problems in the Literature on American Fundamentalism, 1925–1960," paper presented at

the annual meeting of the American Academy of Religion, November 1998. Hamilton believes that Marsden and subsequent interpreters actually use the term *militant* too loosely, leading to the kind of definitional inaccuracy that permits virtually all evangelicals to be subsumed under the term *fundamentalist*.

9. William Lawrence Svelmoe, *A New Vision for Missions: William Cameron Townsend, the Wycliffe Bible Translators, and the Culture of Early Evangelical Faith Missions, 1896–1945* (Tuscaloosa: University of Alabama Press, 2008), 18–19.

10. Marsden, *Fundamentalism and American Culture*, 39.

11. Ibid., 23.

12. Ibid., 16.

13. Ibid., 109.

14. Ibid., 126.

15. Ibid., v–vi.

16. From Kirkus review of *The Outrageous Idea of Christian Scholarship*, by George Marsden, as quoted on Amazon, www.amazon.com/The-Outrageous-Idea-Christian-Scholarship/dp/0195122909.

17. Marsden, *Fundamentalism and American Culture*, 3.

18. Ibid., 203.

19. Ibid.

20. Ibid., 259–60.

CHAPTER 9

Reorienting American Religious History in the Age of Global Christianity

The Case of Katharine Bushnell

Kristin Kobes Du Mez

With the publication of *Fundamentalism and American Culture* in 1980, George Marsden emerged as one of the leading interpreters of conservative evangelicalism at a time when there was a pressing need for a thoughtful, dispassionate analysis of the roots of contemporary American evangelicalism. Just four years earlier presidential candidate Jimmy Carter had left reporters scrambling to comprehend what he meant when he claimed to be "born again"; evangelicals' presence in American culture and politics was soon undeniable, but many outside of the evangelical fold remained mystified as to the nature of the popular religious movement. At this crucial time, Marsden offered invaluable insight into evangelicalism's often-ambivalent relationship to American culture. In doing so, he not only helped validate the study of conservative Christianity as a legitimate academic pursuit but also elevated the place of American religious history within the historical profession. At the same time, *Fundamentalism and American Culture* modeled the promises of Christian scholarship; writing explicitly as a Christian, Marsden supplied a "usable past" not only for academics but for reflective Christians as well. Ultimately, the contributions he hoped to make were as much theological as historiographical. In his own words, he hoped through his research to help Christians "identify the formative cultural elements that have either properly shaped or distorted our understanding of God and his revelation."[1]

Today American religious history, and the study of conservative evangelicalism in particular, remains a vibrant enterprise, continuing to illuminate powerful currents in American culture and politics. Yet as religious historians search for elusive "new directions" and attempt to speak to the critical issues of the day, and as Christian scholars seek to follow Marsden's example to help distinguish the work of the Spirit from mere custom and cultural tradition, they would do well to look beyond American shores to what is arguably the most significant development in modern religious history: the remarkable growth of the Christian Church in the "Two Thirds World." A few statistics make clear this dramatic expansion of global Christianity in the twentieth century. At the beginning of the century, missiologist Andrew Walls explains, "the heartlands of Christianity lay in Europe and North America. More than 80 per cent of professing Christians lived there; Christianity was both a western religion and the religion of the west." But as of the beginning of the twenty-first century, "well over half of the world's Christians live in Africa, Asia, Latin America and the Pacific; and the proportion is steadily rising."[2] Already Christianity is predominantly a non-Western religion; by the end of the century, two-thirds of the world's Christians may well reside in southern continents. As Philip Jenkins concludes, "The centuries-long North Atlantic captivity of the church is drawing to an end."[3]

This striking demographic shift, which Walls has characterized as "the most staggering development in the church for at least a millennium," has caught many Westerners by surprise.[4] Indeed, as historian Dana Robert explains, as recently as the 1970s world Christianity "seemed in disarray." As decolonization swept the globe in the wake of the Second World War, non-Western churches routinely accused Western missionaries of racism, paternalism, and cultural imperialism.[5]

Indigenous leaders called for a moratorium on missionaries and funding from the West, and many Western intellectuals and mainline church leaders became "highly self-critical and guilt-ridden." But "the irony of world Christianity from the Second World War through the 1970s," according to Robert, "was that even as scholars were writing books implicating Christianity in European imperialism," the Christian Church was expanding rapidly in the global South. The undeniable vitality of indigenous Christianity demonstrated convincingly that the faith was no mere Western import.[6] Indeed, it would not be long before observers would begin to note the influence of global Christianity on Western Christian thought and practice.[7]

These extraordinary demographic developments ought to compel Western scholars, particularly historians of American religion, to address the changing face of Christianity at home and abroad. As Joel Carpenter explains, studies of Christianity in the West can continue, but they must address questions raised by Christianity's new global status.[8] Mark Noll concurs, arguing that there is "a pressing need for new historical perspectives that explore the new world situation." Older histories "remain irreplaceable," but they generally "presume a core Christian narrative dominated by events, personalities, organizations, money and cultural expectations in Europe and North America—and then surrounded by a fringe of miscellaneous missionary phenomena scattered throughout the rest of the globe."[9] As the periphery moves to the center, historical narratives must take a new shape.

Christian scholars, too, who hope through their scholarship to sharpen the church's witness, have compelling reasons to turn their attention to this "southward shift." As Tite Tiénou contends, the future of their faith will depend in part on the guidance they can offer.[10] Carpenter, too, suggests that Christian scholars from the North and the South have a unique opportunity to provide direction and insight at this transitional moment in the history of Christianity. "If we journey much deeper into this new century with our eyes on the North Atlantic shores," Carpenter warns, "we may hinder Christian scholarship's ability to help the church navigate the new global reality."[11]

KATHARINE BUSHNELL AND GLOBAL CHRISTIANITY

The life and work of Katharine Bushnell demonstrate well how one particular topic in American religious history might be reoriented to reflect and address concerns arising from this new era in Christian history. A late nineteenth- and early twentieth-century American social reformer active in the World Woman's Christian Temperance Union and the author of a number of protofeminist theologies, including the book *God's Word to Women*, Bushnell is a fascinating figure in American religious history.[12] Within traditional narratives, her story demonstrates both the vibrancy of late Victorian female biblical interpretation and the challenges she, and other women like her, faced as American Protestantism became increasingly polarized between fundamentalist and modernist camps. But situated globally, Bushnell's story can open up promising new avenues of historical inquiry and bring the past into conversation with the present, with clear consequences for the global church today, North and South.

Bushnell began her career in the 1870s as a medical missionary for the Methodist Episcopal Church in China. Like many Western missionaries, Bushnell was disturbed by the cultural subjugation of Chinese women, and she was convinced that the Christian gospel contained the key to freeing Chinese women from their cultural oppression.[13] What set her apart from the majority of her contemporaries, however, was that she turned her heightened awareness of women's oppression back upon Western, Christian culture. Although she believed that the condition of women was far worse in "heathen" cultures than in the West, she refused to turn a blind eye to the persistent oppression of women even within "civilized" Western societies. For instance, when her experiences on the mission field revealed to her the subjectivity of biblical translations, particularly when it came to passages concerning women, she applied her newfound skepticism to English translations as well, taking up what would become a lifelong investigation of the Christian scriptures. She hoped that by uncovering what she considered the faulty biblical origins of Western patriarchy, she would succeed in reversing centuries of women's oppression.[14] Upon returning to the United States in 1882, Bushnell took up a career in social reform. Under the auspices of the Woman's Christian Temperance Union's social purity department, she led a widely publicized crusade against the "white slave trade" in northern Wisconsin and Michigan. From there she traveled to England, where she worked with Josephine Butler to undertake similar investigations of English military brothels in India. Through her reform work she repeatedly confronted the fact that "Christian" men perpetrated acts of appalling cruelty against women. These observations reaffirmed her conviction that to change men's behavior she must first challenge the religious faith underlying their actions.[15]

In the early twentieth century Bushnell began publishing a series of Bible studies that attempted to identify and rectify male bias against women in the Christian scriptures and tradition. In some ways the motives behind her project were similar to those of Elizabeth Cady Stanton's *Woman's Bible*, but Bushnell's hermeneutical methods were strikingly different. Stanton freely tossed aside passages she found problematic, drawing the ire of conservatives and leading to a powerful backlash against her project and against feminist theologies more generally. Indeed, the legacy of Stanton's *Woman's Bible* persists today among those conservative Christians and secular feminists alike who consider feminism and Christianity incompatible, as well as among historians who presume that the publication of Stanton's *Woman's Bible* brought an end to vigorous theological defenses of women's rights. But unlike Stanton, Bushnell adhered to a more conservative hermeneutic. Pointedly rejecting higher critical methods, she instead insisted that her work "assumes that the Bible is all that it claims for itself"—that it is "inspired," "infallible," and "inviolable."[16] But Bushnell made clear that her commitment to the authority of the scriptures was based, not on the English version, "or any mere version, but [on] the original text."[17] She, and other women like her, continued to construct a theological foundation for women's rights well into the twentieth century.

By retranslating from Hebrew and Greek Bushnell was able to produce radical reinterpretations of the scriptures while maintaining a conservative view of scriptural authority. In her retranslation of the first chapters of Genesis, for example, Bushnell described the fall into sin as resulting not from Adam and Eve's tasting of the forbidden fruit but rather from Adam's choice to blame God for his own transgression ("The woman *you* put here with me made me do it") and Eve's choice to turn away from God to follow her husband out of Eden. Man, then, sinned when he rebelled against God; woman sinned in submitting to her husband rather than to her God.[18] From this foundation Bushnell reexamined the rest of the scriptures. She found in the Old Testament abundant evidence that Adam and Eve's sin had led to the patriarchal overthrow of God's intended matriarchal order.[19] And she found ample confirmation of her suspicions that male translators had erroneously translated numerous passages to the detriment of women by introducing faulty notions of male headship and a separate "woman's sphere," by restricting women's right to teach and preach, and by elevating unrealistic standards of women's virtue and contributing to a sexual "double standard."[20] Verse by verse, she demonstrated how the Victorian social order and traditional Christianity worked together to subjugate women. While maintaining an ardent commitment to the authority of the scriptures, then, Bushnell nevertheless offered a profound reinterpretation of the Christian faith.

Although Bushnell's reform work attracted widespread interest worldwide, her theological writings received far less attention. This was partly because of the piecemeal fashion in which she published her reflections. Without strong connections to prominent American seminaries and publishers, she self-published her Bible studies beginning in 1910. It was not until 1923 that she released a near-final compilation of her Bible studies, at which point developments within American Protestantism inhibited its reception.[21] By the 1920s liberal Protestants and feminists who might once have welcomed a progressive theology of gender had come to put more stock in scientific authorities than in meticulous biblical studies. Meanwhile, conservative Protestants who shared with Bushnell a commitment to the authority of the scriptures had become highly suspicious of modern translations and had also strengthened their commitment to "traditional" gender roles in the face of liberal trends that increasingly seemed to be unsettling American society. To such conservatives, tampering with the mythical Victorian ideal suggested an affinity with modernism of all kinds. Although a small number of women and biblical studies scholars would keep her work alive over the course of the twentieth century, at the time of her death her work seemed to have faded into oblivion. It was "like a rock dropped to the bottom of the ocean," recalled her pastor at the time of her death. "Kerplunk, it was gone, the end of it."[22]

In a fascinating turn of events, however, some of the very factors that conspired to limit the reception of Bushnell's work in her own lifetime have come to facilitate the reception of her work among Christians in the twenty-first-century global South. The efforts of missionaries, together with greater global Internet accessibility, have in recent years fostered a growing interest in Bushnell among women and men in Africa and South Asia. Gladys Masore is one such woman. Masore, together with her husband Zaphania, ministers to women and children in the slums of Nairobi and in neighboring towns and villages. Her ministry offers counseling to women who are hurting or abused, offers food, shelter, school fees, and health care to orphans, and promotes community development projects that empower women to achieve economic security. In Bushnell, Masore has found a theology to combat the patriarchal customs that pervade traditional Kenyan society and that can be found in many traditional interpretations of Christianity as well.[23] As Masore writes, "The word of God is sharper than a double edged sword, when applied it acts."[24] Inspired by Bushnell's work, she has started a "God's Word to Women" group through which she hopes to "reach many women and tell them the truth," to teach a life-changing, liberating Gospel of Christ.[25]

It might at first seem incongruous that a twenty-first-century Kenyan woman would resurrect the work of a nearly forgotten American Victorian, but Bushnell's appeal begins to make sense given striking parallels between their seemingly disparate worlds. Indeed, in his book *The New Shape of World Christianity: How American Experience Reflects Global Faith*, Mark Noll suggests that contemporary world Christianity, with its emphasis on voluntarism, pragmatism, and orientation to the Bible and to individual conscience, reflects in significant ways the Christian faith forged in the American environment.[26] For Noll, then, the history of nineteenth-century American Christianity is vital to understanding the global faith today. Not only did that century witness the emergence of the worldwide missionary movement and the global spread of Christianity, but the social conditions that fostered the emergence of a conversionistic and voluntaristic faith—namely, "social fluidity, personal choice, the need for innovation and a search for anchorage in the face of vanishing traditions"—parallel the experiences of many global citizens today.[27] Given this congruence, Noll argues, historians can explore topics in American religious history with the purpose of providing guidance to a new generation of global believers.

Even before American religious historians had taken note of these similarities, however, women like Masore had already established links between their own circumstances and those of Victorian Christians. What most binds Bushnell and Masore across time and space, it turns out, is a shared concern for a biblical challenge to contemporary gender and family arrangements. Like Victorians, many global South Christians are undertaking a profound reexamination of their cultural inheritance. And just as Victorian Christians like Bushnell looked to their faith to restructure society, global South Christians are searching for biblical foundations upon which they can construct a new social order. As Philip Jenkins explains, the Bible has a vitality and social significance that is lacking in the contemporary West. "In modern Africa and Asia, too," he writes, "whether we are interested in politics strictly defined or in wider social concerns—attitudes to gender and family, wealth and poverty, debt and development—the Bible provides a critical guide to worldly matters, much as it did in Europe in 1600 and the United States in 1850."[28] Mirroring the efforts of Protestant female reformers like Bushnell, many women in the global South today, much like Masore, are looking to Christianity to confront oppressive and often abusive social conventions. They are seeking biblical understanding with which they can empower women, challenge patriarchy, and encourage accountability and responsibility in men. Bushnell's efforts to redefine virtue for women and men, her claims that Christianity and patriarchy are irreconcilable, and her insistence on the biblical sanctioning of women preachers and teachers are valuable tools in the hands of many women in the global church. For these women, Bushnell's biblically based defense of women's rights conforms to their own values and needs far better than do secular Western feminist ideologies. It should come as no surprise, then, that Bushnell's writings are finding an eager new audience nearly a century after their initial publication.

NEW DIRECTIONS

Understanding Bushnell's appeal to women in the global church today is an intriguing project that may well offer the sort of guidance for which Noll and others are calling. A genuine reorientation of conventional historical scholarship, however, promises not only to investigate the ways in which American religious history might be useful to global Christians today but also to open up dynamic conversations between past and present, North and South, kindling new approaches both to traditional historical narratives and to contemporary religious issues.

For instance, the global reach of Christianity today can stimulate new historical inquiries into the profound ways in which Western Christianity has long been shaped by its global context. If we look anew at Bushnell's career, the influences of global Christianity are conspicuous. Indeed, her most innovative theological insights emerged out of her cross-cultural engagements. Her experiences as a missionary in China first revealed to her the possibilities for male bias in biblical translations and helped crystallize her awareness of women's oppression more generally; her work as a social purity activist in India and around the world repeatedly exposed to her the "uncivilized" and "unchristian" behavior of Western Christians. It was these experiences that fueled her desire to expunge misogynistic traditions from the Christian faith.[29]

Although Bushnell's extensive world travels set her apart from many of her contemporaries, she was hardly unique. Indeed, even as nineteenth- and early twentieth-century Protestantism remained resolutely "Western," it evolved in the crucible of dynamic global interactions to an extent often underappreciated by historians of American and British Christianity. Global influences were particularly significant in the religious experiences of many Protestant women. To begin with, Victorian women embraced foreign missions by going abroad in impressive numbers—by 1909 over 1,300 women worked in the foreign mission field on behalf of the major Protestant denominations.[30] Yet this "great uprising of Christian women in behalf of their sex" was not limited to the missionaries themselves; it included as well the tens of thousands of women who faithfully supported their work.[31] These women avidly read women's missionary journals (some boasting circulations approaching twenty-five thousand) to keep abreast of the impact Christianity was making on world cultures.[32] A generation of Protestant women, then, few of whom would travel abroad in their lifetimes, came to understand their faith, and their world, in terms of the female missionary experience. The significance of this particular sort of religious education deserves careful attention. Joan Jacobs Brumberg, for example, posits that through their involvement in auxiliaries and their exposure to a "light infantry of missionary literature" Western women became highly conversant in a "missionary ethnology" that drew sharp distinctions between heathens and Christians, elevating Western values while contributing to the degradation of heathen women. According to Brumberg, this discourse often functioned in a way that reinforced a self-congratulatory ethos that regarded Protestant Westerners as more highly evolved and representing a more advanced civilization.[33] As a result, this cross-cultural exposure ended up encouraging most American women to identify their own positions as "privileged" as compared to the gender and family arrangements of their "degraded" non-Christian sisters.[34] This global framework, then, may have inhibited Western women from identifying and working against their own oppression.

Here, too, Bushnell's career offers a useful study. To a point Bushnell certainly exhibited the sort of ethnocentrism Brumberg describes. Frequently critical of the ways in which "heathen" cultures in India and China denigrated women, Bushnell presumed that, as a Western Christian woman, she could uplift the "heathen." Yet unlike many of the women Brumberg describes, Bushnell was also highly critical of Western Christian tradition. She worked both within and against popular Victorian ideologies, often in surprising ways. Ultimately, her belief system privileged an imagined global Christian sisterhood over any notion of Western "civilization."[35] Her observations of non-Western women's oppression opened her eyes to her own marginalization as a woman in Western society. And as marginalized believers have before and since her time, she found within the Bible powerful means of resistance. Her access to the Christian scriptures—amplified by her knowledge of Hebrew and Greek—provided her with resources for a profound critique of her own cultural and religious inheritance.[36]

One example of the critical vantage point Bushnell was able to attain can be seen in her rejection of evolutionary anthropology, a popular ideology that dominated Victorian intellectual life and increasingly infiltrated Protestant thought as well. Influenced by Darwinian theories, nineteenth-century anthropologists enthusiastically applied models of progressive evolution to their study of cultural development. One of the key consequences of this sociocultural evolutionary point of view was an elevation of contemporary Western "civilization" as the most advanced society ever achieved. Implicit in this belief system was a powerful endorsement of the status quo, particularly with regard to Victorian social, moral, and family structures. In other words, this framework not only placed Western culture above all others but also enshrined patriarchy as the height of civilization.[37] Bushnell, however, strenuously objected to sociocultural evolutionary theory on two counts. Her commitment to the historicity of Genesis (albeit a dramatically revised translation of Genesis) led her to reject the Darwinian assumptions underlying this developmental framework. At the same time, her awareness of the abuses suffered by Western and non-Western women at the hands of Western men compelled her to regard modern patriarchy not as the height of civilization, but rather as the result of sin. Her critique of sociocultural evolutionary theory set her at odds not only with many leading Protestants, but also with many women's rights activists of her day, and it demonstrated a rare willingness to call into question the superiority of Western culture.

It is precisely Bushnell's ambivalent relationship to her inherited traditions—her efforts to turn the Christian scriptures against her own social norms and values—that makes her not only an inspiring figure among Christians in the global church today but also a fascinating study for Christian scholars who seek to follow in Marsden's footsteps by investigating the cultural forces shaping current and historical versions of Christianity. And it turns out that global Christians, together with scholars of global Christianity, have much to offer historians engaged in this endeavor. While the majority of Westerners have long remained oblivious to tensions between Christianity and their own cultural traditions, global Christians have rarely been afforded that luxury.[38] As they embraced Christian teachings, they actively transformed the faith to address their particular social and political circumstances—a process that continues to this day.[39] Western Christians, however, freely expressed alarm at such "syncretism," all the while remaining blind to the many ways in which their own faith had been imbued with Western Enlightenment thinking.[40] Missiologists who have studied the reception of Christianity among global communities have devised useful frameworks with which to examine questions of faith and culture, frameworks that can assist historians in examining the relationship between Christianity and Western culture as well.

Andrew Walls, for example, suggests that "church history has always been a battleground for two opposing tendencies": the indigenizing principle and the pilgrim principle. According to Walls, both tendencies find their origins in the gospel itself. On the one hand, the Christian faith never exists in isolation; it is always inculturated, or indigenized. Christians are always "conditioned by a particular time and place, by our family and group and society."[41] This is true for individual believers and for the church, as believers will make their faith "a place to feel at home." As Walls concludes, "All churches are culture churches." Yet at the same time, Walls explains, this indigenizing principle remains in constant tension with the "pilgrim principle." For while the gospel is always inculturated, it also challenges Christians that faithfulness to Christ will place them out of step with their own culture, "for that society never existed, in East or West, ancient time or modern, which could absorb the word of Christ painlessly into its system."[42] The gospel reminds believers that they are not fully at home within their cultures and carries a transformative potential to reshape culture into a closer representation of the spiritual ideal.

Walls's framework helps him to examine Western influences on global Christianity without diminishing the agency of non-Western Christians—an agency facilitated by direct access to the scriptures in indigenous languages. It also helps explain how, even in an imperialistic context, the Christian faith can provide resources for indigenous empowerment and resistance alongside its imperializing tendencies. Certainly it provides a useful framework within which Bushnell's life and work can be examined, allowing for her own inculturation, ethnocentrism, and cultural prejudices, while also illuminating her prophetic stance against some of those cultural traditions. By offering an analytical frame that considers both inculturation and prophecy, and allows for both oppression and agency, Walls's dueling forces of indigenization and pilgrimage can assist Christian scholars who are attempting to offer meaningful histories to believers today, both in the West and throughout the world. Western historical scholarship, then, might well provide guidance to the developing global church today, but global voices and histories can also powerfully shape Western scholarship by helping to illuminate the indigenizing and the pilgrim principles within Western Christianity.

By revealing the inculturation of Western Christianity in new ways, conversations between Christians in the global South and North may also open up new directions for discussions of Christianity and gender, both scholarly and popular. To begin with, global conversations have already transformed the field of gender studies, as Western feminists have worked (with varying degrees of success) to confront their own Western bias, to privilege the voices of marginalized women, and to reorient their studies to global concerns. And these voices from the margins make clear that Enlightenment values of individualism and secularism are not sufficient to address the concerns of many women in the Two Thirds World. As Western feminists come to terms with the deep religiosity of many women globally, figures like Bushnell who offer religious frameworks for women's rights are attracting renewed interest. In addition, insights from women in the global church have the potential to reframe discussions of gender and Christianity not only in their own communities but in the Western church as well. Despite the long-standing efforts of Christian feminists, it is difficult to ignore the widespread conviction—among American Christians in particular—that Christianity and feminism are irreconcilable. Although historians have offered dozens of histories demonstrating the compatibility of feminist values and the Christian faith, the majority of which focus on the nineteenth-century women's rights movement, many conservative Christians continue to consider "feminism" a secular, twentieth-century movement antagonistic to their religious commitments. But as global conversations develop and deepen, fresh understandings of women's oppression and empowerment are emerging from the global South. Development studies have already made clear the centrality of women's empowerment in lifting societies from poverty; as Christian women in the global South—women like Masore—find within the Christian scriptures sources to combat their own oppression, they may well open Westerners' eyes to new understandings of Christianity, feminism, and the role of women in church and society. Insights from Christian women globally may hold the key to moving conversations about gender and Christianity in the West beyond the impasse that characterizes so many of these discussions today.[43]

In this dynamic time in global religious history, insights and expertise arising from the global South will continue to reshape a wide variety of fields, from gender studies to American religious history. For Christian scholars, this moment is particularly vital, as the nature of these global conversations will shape not only the next generation of scholarship but also the future of the Christian Church. Western Christian scholars eager to enter into conversation with colleagues in the global South at this crucial time, however, would do well to listen to the advice of West African scholar Tite Tiénou. Tiénou urges them to first become good listeners and to be willing to abandon their hegemonic research frameworks.[44] Unless they exhibit such humility, he suggests, they will only perpetuate "intellectual imperialism," while remaining essentially provincial. And, as Tiénou insists, "Authentic Christian scholarship and provincialism are incompatible."[45] True Christian scholarship can take place only in a community of mutual dependence.[46]

The promises of such interdependence, however, are profound. For scholars of all fields, North and South, this is a moment filled with occasions for fresh thinking, new topics, and work of genuine relevance. Christian scholars in particular can seize this opportunity to turn away from the triviality and moral compromise that often plague academia and instead to "return to the ideal of scholarship for the glory of God, a return to the ideal of the academic life as a liberating search for truth."[47] Just as Marsden's *Fundamentalism and American Culture* provided a model of engaged, Christian scholarship that spoke to the pressing issues of its day, researchers today have unprecedented opportunities to forge new intellectual approaches by engaging what may prove to be the most dramatic development in a millennium of Christian history. And, as was Marsden's hope for his own scholarship, this work can ultimately help Christians to better discern their "culturally defined loves, allegiances, and understandings" and to prevent those values from overwhelming and taking precedence over their faithfulness to God.[48]

NOTES

1. George M. Marsden, *Fundamentalism and American Culture* (New York: Oxford University Press, 1980), 230.

2. Andrew F. Walls, "Christian Scholarship in Africa in the Twenty-First Century," *Journal of African Christian Thought* 4, no. 2 (December 2001): 46. See also Joel Carpenter, "The Christian Scholar in an Age of Global Christianity," paper presented at the Conference on Christianity and the Soul of the University, Baylor University, Waco, TX, March 25-27, 2004, www.calvin.edu/nagel/resources/carpenter_bakerpublication.html.

3. Philip Jenkins, *The New Faces of Christianity* (New York: Oxford University Press, 2006), 9. Jenkins offers further statistics: of the approximately 2 billion Christians today, "530 million live in Europe, 510 million in Latin America, 390 million in Africa, and perhaps 300 million in Asia." But the demographic trends are clear: "Between 1900 and 2000, the number of Christians in Africa grew from 10 million to over 360 million, from 10 percent of the population to 46 percent. Already today, Africans and Asians represent some 30 percent of all Christians, and the proportion will rise steadily."

4. Andrew F. Walls, *The Significance of Christianity in Africa*, Friends of St. Colm Public Lecture, 1989 (Edinburgh: St. Colm's College, 1989), quoted in Tite Tiénou, "Christian Scholarship and the Changing Center of World Christianity," in *Christian Scholarship . . . For What?*, ed. Susan M. Felch (Grand Rapids, MI: Calvin College, 2003), 89. See also Carpenter, "Christian Scholar."

5. Dana Robert, "Shifting Southward: Global Christianity since 1945," *International Bulletin of Missionary Research* 24 (April 2000): 52.

6. Ibid., 53. Robert notes that "even during the colonial period, indigenous Christians—Bible women, evangelists, catechists, and prophets—were all along the most effective interpreters of Christianity to their own people" (53). With this appreciation, scholars came to identify the extent to which, even during the

colonial era, believers in the global South had adapted the gospel to their local needs and worldviews. It was this earlier indigenization of the faith that set the stage for the phenomenal growth of global Christianity in the postcolonial world.

7. As Soong-Chan Rah's *The Next Evangelicalism: Freeing the Church from Western Cultural Captivity* (Downers Grove, IL: InterVarsity Press, 2009) makes clear, scholars often fail to appreciate the global nature of American evangelicalism and the flourishing of the faith among immigrant communities.

8. Carpenter, "Christian Scholar."

9. Mark Noll, *The New Shape of World Christianity: How American Experience Reflects Global Faith* (Downers Grove, IL: IVP Academic), 10, 9.

10. Tiénou, "Christian Scholarship," 91. Tiénou quotes Walls in arguing that this scholarship must be "rooted in the soil of Africa, Asia, and Latin America." See Walls, "Old Athens and New Jerusalem: Some Signposts for Christian Scholarship in the Early History of Mission Studies," *International Bulletin of Missionary Research* 21, no. 4 (1997): 153.

11. Carpenter, "Christian Scholar."

12. Katharine C. Bushnell, *God's Word to Women: One Hundred Bible Studies on Woman's Place in the Divine Economy* (1923; repr., Mossville, IL: God's Word to Women Publishers, n.d.).

13. For a brief autobiography of Bushnell, see Katharine C. Bushnell, *Dr. Katharine C. Bushnell: A Brief Sketch of Her Life Work* (Hertford: Rose and Sons, 1932). A more extensive account of her life and work can be found in Dana Hardwick, *Oh Thou Woman That Bringest Good Tidings* (Kearney, NE: Morris / Christians for Biblical Equality, 1995).

14. An account of her encounter with a "sex-biased" translation of the scriptures into Chinese can be found in Bushnell, *Dr. Katharine C. Bushnell*, 20.

15. Ibid., 22.

16. Bushnell, *God's Word*, para. 2. (Bushnell organized her book into numbered paragraphs.) On the inspired nature of the biblical text, Bushnell cited 2 Tim. 3:16; on its infallibility, Isa. 40:8; and on its inviolability, John 10:35.

17. Ibid., para. 5.

18. Ibid., paras. 65–145. For a more detailed discussion of Bushnell's theological innovations, see Kristin Kobes Du Mez, "Leaving Eden: Resurrecting the Work of Katharine Bushnell and Lee Anna Starr," in *Breaking Boundaries: Female Biblical Interpreters Who Challenged the Status Quo*, ed. Nancy Calvert-Koyzis and Heather Weir (New York: T&T Clarke, 2010).

19. Bushnell, *God's Word*, paras. 415–615.

20. Ibid., paras 616–798.

21. For a detailed publication history of Bushnell's numerous editions of this work, see Hardwick, *O Thou Woman*, 86–87.

22. Taken from Ruth Hoppin, "Legacy of Katharine Bushnell," *Update: Newsletter of the Evangelical Women's Caucus* 11 (Winter 1987–88): 5–6. Bushnell's pastor, K. Fillmore Gray, had also written an article about Bushnell four years before her death, which was published in the *Christian Advocate*, January 8, 1942.

23. Masore promotes better nutrition and trains women in "knitting, tailoring, bicycle transportation, handcrafts, dress-making, embroidery, small enterprises and micro-farming agricultural activities, especially horticultural produce." She seeks to "welcome every woman of God" into the faith and to "[tear] down strongholds that divide women racially, denominationally, socially, and economically" ("GWTW Missions: Kenya," God's Word to Women, n.d., www.godswordtowomen.org/mission_kenya.htm [accessed September 4, 2009]).

The tribes to which Masore ministers include the Agikuyu, Meru, Akamba, Abagusii, Mijikenda, Luo, Nandi, and Maasai. Masore notes that because of tribal beliefs "women were not recognized but through God's word to women has helped me to reach many people many tribes to tell them the truth" (Masore, e-mail to author, July 4, 2009).

24. Gladys Masore, e-mail to author, January 25, 2010.

25. Gladys Masore, e-mail to author, July 4, 2009.

26. Noll, *New Shape*, 12–13, 189.

27. Ibid., 43, 116. Noll stresses repeatedly that he is making a case not for causation but rather for correlation.

28. Jenkins, *New Faces of Christianity*, 15–16.

29. As Walls explains, it was often Christian missions that initiated the cross-cultural interactions that began to unsettle the comfortable inculturation of Western Christianity after centuries of isolation. According to Walls, "Christian history indicates that searching, fundamental scholarship arises naturally out of the exercise of Christian mission and especially from its cross-cultural expression. Mission involves moving out of one's self and one's accustomed terrain, and taking the risk of entering another world. It means living on someone else's terms, as the gospel itself is about God living on someone else's terms, the Word becoming flesh, Divinity being expressed in terms of humanity. And the transmission of the gospel requires a process analogous, however distantly, to that great act on which Christian faith depends" (Walls, "Christian Scholarship," 46).

30. Joan Jacobs Brumberg, "The Ethnological Mirror: American Evangelical Women and Their Heathen Sisters, 1870–1910," in *Women and the Structure of Society*, ed. Barbara J. Harris and JoAnn K. McNamara (Durham, NC: Duke University Press, 1984), 110–12. Brumberg tallied female missionaries among Baptists, Congregationalists, Methodists, and Presbyterians; across those denominations, the number of auxiliaries stood at over thirty-four thousand by 1909.

31. The "great uprising" quote is attributed to the Reverend N. G. Clark, an officer of the Congregationalists' American Board of Commissioners for Foreign Missions (Brumberg, "Ethnological Mirror," 110).

32. Ibid., 113.

33. Ibid., 113, 125.

34. Ibid., 115.

35. In her history of women's mission theory, Dana Robert outlines the tensions between notions of a global sisterhood and myths of Western superiority that pervaded "Woman's Work for Woman" among late nineteenth-century missionaries. See Robert, *American Women in Mission: A Social History of Their Thought and Practice* (Macon, GA: Mercer University Press, 1996), 136.

36. On American evangelicals' knack for critiquing the culture in which they found themselves, see Jay Riley Case, *An Unpredictable Gospel: American Evangelicals and World Christianity, 1912–1920* (Oxford: Oxford University Press, 2012).

37. See George W. Stocking, *Victorian Anthropology* (New York: Free Press, 1987); Elazar Barkan and Ronald Bush, eds., *Prehistories of the Future: The Primitivist Project and the Culture of Modernism* (Stanford, CA: Stanford University Press, 1995); and Gail Bederman, *Manliness and Civilization: A Cultural History of Gender and Race in the United States, 1880–1917* (Chicago: University of Chicago Press, 1995).

38. During the Victorian era, the notion of "civilization" powerfully linked Christianity and Western culture, masking tensions between the two and baptizing Western cultural practices as necessarily God-ordained. Christianity, of course, was not originally a product of "Western" culture. But as Andrew Walls explains, for many centuries the faith remained largely a Western phenomenon, becoming "thoroughly accommodated to western culture, and in a process extending over centuries had penetrated deep into its thought, its customs, its laws, its art and literature" (Walls, "Christian Scholarship," 45).

39. See Jenkins, *New Faces of Christianity*, 1, and Carpenter, "Christian Scholar." Over against Western Christians, for example, global South believers are far more likely to emphasize the supernatural elements of scripture, such as healing and exorcism, to hold to literal, authoritative interpretations of the scriptures, and to consider the Old Testament as authoritative as the New. They are more concerned with situating their faith in relation to religious pluralism, including primal religious traditions, than with confronting Western secularism, and they tend to place issues of poverty and social justice at center stage (see Jenkins, *New Faces of Christianity*, 4, and Carpenter, "Christian Scholar").

40. See Noll, *New Shape*, 25.

41. Andrew Walls, "The Gospel as Prisoner and Liberator of Culture," in *The Missionary Movement in Christian History: Studies in the Transmission of the Faith* (Maryknoll, NY: Orbis Books, 2004), 7. This indigenizing principle is

rooted in the gospel since "God accepts us as we are," not as "isolated, self-governing units," but as cultural beings.

42. Ibid., 8.

43. Here Jenkins's cautionary words are in order: "Only when we see global South Christianity on its own terms—as opposed to asking how it can contribute to our debates—can we see how the emerging churches are formulating their own responses to social or religious questions, and how these issues are often viewed through a biblical lens" (*New Faces of Christianity*, 13). Liberals and conservatives, progressives and traditionalists, should not look to the global South to confirm their existing beliefs and gain allies in their ongoing battles. Rather, they should seek greater understanding and new perspectives as they engage in conversations with the global community.

44. Tiénou, "Christian Scholarship," 93–94. Tiénou explains that Western scholars must avoid the temptation to use scholars from the Two Thirds World as "purveyor[s] of exotic raw intellectual material to people in the north." Here Tiénou cites Patrick A. Kalilombe, "How Do We Share 'Third World' Christian Insights in Europe?" *AFER: African Ecclesial Review* 40, no. 1 (1998): 19.

45. Tiénou, "Christian Scholarship," 96. Joel Carpenter writes: "Unless Northern Christian scholars can develop just and reconciling relationships with their Southern colleagues," this reorientation of scholarship "will become yet another occasion for intellectual imperialism" ("Christian Scholar," 7).

46. Tiénou, "Christian Scholarship," 88.

47. Walls, "Christian Scholarship," 48.

48. Marsden, *Fundamentalism and American Culture*, 230.

CHAPTER 10

A Gilded Age Modernist

Reuben A. Torrey and the Roots of
Contemporary Conservative Evangelicalism

TIMOTHY E. W. GLOEGE

The entry for Thursday, July 2, 1882, proceeded like most others in this diary. "Read today in Darwin's 'Descent of Man.' Dorner's System of Christian Doctrine a German poem by Arndt and the Christian Union. Mr. Strong, Mrs. Payne and Gurney came this morning and stayed until after dinner. We had a pleasant teachers meeting & delightful prayer meeting this evening." It was just another day in the life of a liberal Ohio minister. Subsequent entries chronicled more of the same: the books he read (Albrecht Ritschl and Charles Darwin), the sermon topics he selected, his visitation schedules, and later details of his theological studies in Germany. But when the same minister began a second diary in 1889, it promised more excitement. In the intervening years he had exchanged the life of books for faith healing, ecstatic spirit possession, and other miraculous demonstrations. "The Heavenly Father has of late shown me so many evidences of His love & care," he began the first entry, "that it seems as though I ought to keep a record of His many kindnesses to me." What followed was a record of his "living on faith"—that is, his reliance on prayer alone for his financial needs without salary or any requests for money. Tellingly, he used an old ledger book for this diary: for it was to be his literal accounting of God's miraculous provision.[1]

The minister publicly announced his intention to engage in this life of faith at the third annual meeting of the Convention of Christian Workers—a group he had chaired since its beginning in 1886. But this was no holiness revival; rather, it was one of the premier gatherings of socially active evangelicals in the Gilded Age. By this time it had gained the endorsement of Lyman Abbott and Josiah Strong and the active participation of several important figures in the future social gospel movement. Sessions included reports of urban evangelism intermingled with discussions of how best to provide material needs, social services, and wholesome entertainment for the poor. But regardless of emphasis, participants were united in their condemnation of traditional middle-class Protestantism—dogmatic and overly technical theological systems, denominational tribalism, pew rents, and fashionable dress codes. Only a thoroughgoing ecumenical and class-leveling reformation in the church would transform society and help bring the Kingdom of God to fruition.[2]

Higher criticism and ecstatic religious experiences, the social gospel and living on faith: the only thing more surprising than these combinations is that they were found in the life and work of Reuben A. Torrey. Torrey's importance to the early fundamentalist movement is well established. He served as the superintendent of both the Moody Bible Institute in Chicago and the Bible Institute of Los Angeles, helped edit *The Fundamentals* and two other important fundamentalist periodicals, conducted massive worldwide revival tours that spread the fundamentalist message around the globe (while inadvertently cultivating the theological soil for Pentecostalism), and hosted the planning meeting that gave birth to the World's Christian Fundamentals Association. He wrote dozens of books, many of which still guide contemporary conservative evangelicals. Yet the development of Torrey's theology and praxis has remained obscured in his Gilded Age ministry. A lack of source material forced scholars to rely on hagiographic biographical treatments created during his revival campaigns and by later fundamentalist admirers, both of which minimized this key period. Unaware of the degree to which Torrey engaged liberal theology, scholarly consensus presumed Torrey's faith was a simple and naive continuation of old orthodoxies. William McLoughlin (who could not call Torrey "educated" without quotation marks) characterized his ministry as a "defense of evangelical Americanism against all that was modern" and "uncompromisingly 'old-fashioned.'" Martin Marty found Torrey emblematic of the "traditionalist" successors of the revivalist Dwight L. Moody, who were "more inflexible and intransigent" and "use[d] the social Christians as a foil." George Marsden's work, and the scholarship it inspired, has been more charitable to Torrey personally, but it still presumes his theology was a product of an earlier age. He exemplifies prototypical fundamentalist thinking—rooted in the science and philosophy of Bacon, Newton, and Scottish common sense realism, and the theologies of the Puritans, Finney, and Princeton Seminary.[3]

Marsden's essential work tracing the often-tangled roots of fundamentalism into nineteenth-century philosophy and evangelical theology demonstrated that the movement was much more than an irrational, modernity-induced paroxysm; rather, it was the continuation of a once-respectable tradition with a coherent internal logic. But over time this near-exclusive focus on continuity with past forms of Protestantism has led to its own distortions. Fundamentalism is too often equated with "traditional" Protestantism (or worse, an "orthodox" Protestantism that is never defined). The simple equation of fundamentalism with its antecedents distorts both the past and the present, especially when innovations of modern evangelicals are read back into the nineteenth century. Fundamentalists and liberals are dichotomized into nonoverlapping "antimodern" and "modern" camps. This schematic makes it difficult to investigate their shared modern characteristics: traits that distinguish both groups from their nineteenth-century forebears. It also obscures the distinctive lines of continuity to traditional Protestantism preserved by self-identified liberals, traditions from which fundamentalists deviated while acclimating to the modern world.[4]

Torrey's life adds to a growing body of research that challenges the antimodernity of fundamentalism and the surprisingly resilient "two-party" schematic that structures the study of fundamentalism.[5] Though later partisans would rather forget it, scholars, including Marsden, have observed that Gilded Age evangelical networks were a heterogeneous mix of future fundamentalists, Pentecostals, and liberals.[6] Torrey's early life and theological development pushes this research further in two respects. First, it suggests that this was no coalition of convenience; future fundamentalists as much as modernists self-consciously positioned themselves in opposition to traditional, dogmatic Protestantism of the first half of the nineteenth century. Torrey found conservative preoccupations with denominational identity, formal theology, social respectability, and inward-looking piety stifling and largely irrelevant. Torrey also demonstrates that at least one important strand of fundamentalism was rooted squarely in the "modernist impulse" described by William R. Hutchison. Torrey read the same theologians Hutchison credits for the spread of modernism in America, and their fingerprints are found even on his fundamentalist belief and practice. He joined ecumenists in deconstructing traditional theological categories, in seeking a new practical, interdenominational theology reformulated in a modern idiom, and in jettisoning any part of traditional Christianity that he believed would impede its relational essence. He was also driven by the modernist impulses to conflate the natural and supernatural and to promote an activist agenda that would bring the Kingdom of God to earth. Although the beliefs and practices that he developed out of these first principles were ultimately irreconcilable with liberal modernism, Torrey's "old-time religion" bears the marks of modernity.[7]

FROM IRRELIGION TO LIBERALISM, 1856–76

Reuben Archer Torrey was born January 28, 1856, into an elite, non-evangelical family. His father, Reuben Slayton Torrey, was a banker in Hoboken, New Jersey. He suffered heavy losses in the financial panic of 1857 but switched to manufacturing and gained lucrative government contracts during the Civil War that allowed the family to retire to a lavish two-hundred-acre estate in Geneva, New York, in 1867. The Torreys' religious affiliations were typical of American elites. The elder Torrey was a Universalist, while his pious Presbyterian wife, Elizabeth

Swift Torrey, cultivated the family practice of daily Bible reading and prayer. Theirs was a sincere but distinctively nonevangelical Protestantism. Torrey's parents made no attempt to bring him into a converted state—a standard practice among evangelicals—and he claimed he "did not know what it meant to accept Christ" until seminary. He first explored formal religious affiliation, and then rejected it, on his own. "I was thirteen years of age," Torrey later wrote, "in a large room . . . where we put the old books out of the library." Here he noticed a copy of the covenant from his mother's church (tellingly discarded) and "wondered if I could not be a church member." Ultimately, Torrey rejected the idea, since a Christian must submit to the will of God. He decided instead to seek after "a life of pleasure."[8]

Two years later Torrey matriculated at Yale University, where he pursued "the card-table, the theatre, the dance, the horse-race, the champagne supper." His hedonism was enabled by an indulgent father and his ability to "[learn] easily without much study." But during his junior year he had a personal crisis and became deeply depressed. His behavior turned "very wreckless" [sic] and he began "drinking very heavily." At the nadir of this crisis, Torrey recalled, "I awoke one night in awful agony and despair. In desperation I sprang out of bed, rushed to my wash-stand drawer and drew it open to take out of it the instrument that would put an end to the whole business, by committing suicide, but I could not find it and in the dark I dropped on my knees beside the open drawer and promised God that if He would take the awful burden off my heart I would preach the gospel." Torrey incongruously treated this as his conversion experience, despite the fact he had only "settled" that he would become a minister. "I did not accept Christ," Torrey recounted, "nor [decide] that I would become a Christian but that I would preach. I made no change whatever in my life, in fact I think my life, if anything, was wilder after that than it was before." Torrey's Christianity was oriented with neither the head nor the heart; it was a matter of the will—his existential decision to submit himself to God. This "conversion" narrative essentially elevated the will above all other human faculties.[9]

Torrey slowly reformed his conduct over the following year and finally decided to make a confession of faith under the influence of two books, both of which rejected traditional theology and denominational identities. *The Bay-Path* was an unremarkable work of historical fiction by Josiah G. Holland, the editor of *Scribner's Monthly*. Its primary purpose was to critique nineteenth-century Protestant dogmatism and middle-class propriety. True religion, it argued, was based in a love for God and others, demonstrated in pragmatic acts of kindness. Even more important to Torrey's theological development was John R. Seeley's *Ecce Homo*, a British biography of the historical Jesus that helped catalyze the social gospel movement in the United States. Seeley claimed to strip from Christianity the philosophical and dogmatic accretions of the last eighteen hundred years: he accepted only "those conclusions about him [Jesus] . . . which the facts themselves, critically weighed appear to warrant." Seeley defined the Christian faith as "a loyal and free confidence in Christ" rather than a theological system; likewise the church was not an institution but a group of believers who struggled to apply Jesus's teachings to the practical problems of society. Combined, these two books envisioned Christianity as a humanitarian and communal effort to bring good into the world.[10]

Torrey joined Yale's college church his senior year and attempted "to lead a Christian life, making a radical change in my conduct," but he encountered profound doubts upon entering the divinity school in 1876. He blamed his reading of "agnostic literature," including the eighteenth-century historian Edward Gibbon, which "utterly unsettled . . . [his] faith." *The Decline and Fall of the Roman Empire* raised difficulties in Christianity caused by historical consciousness—problems that were particularly troubling to Protestants in the late nineteenth century. Using the techniques of textual criticism and comparative religion, Gibbon undermined the uniqueness and veracity of the biblical record and its moral credentials. The humanitarianism that Seeley and Holland naively presumed to be the core of primitive Christianity evaporated under historical scrutiny. Compounding these doubts was Gibbon's elegant dismantling of cessationism—the means by which Protestants sheltered biblical miracles from critiques of Enlightenment science. "I had not been interested enough in Christianity to be an agnostic before," Torrey recounted; but now, "I was utterly at sea." The dismantling of his initial faith triggered a crisis of religious certainty, common among Gilded Age elites. "I made up my mind to find out to an absolute certainty the truth," Torrey wrote. Christianity for Torrey had been a matter of the will. But now his continuing in the faith hinged on finding adequate answers to three questions: "If the Bible was the Word of God . . . if Jesus Christ was the Son of God . . . [and] whether there was a personal God." He determined that he would "act accordingly" to whatever he discovered.[11]

THE MODERNIST SOURCES OF TORREY'S THEOLOGY, 1876–84

Torrey spent the next seven years struggling to rebuild his faith—a process dominated by liberal influences. "Even after I was saved from agnosticism, I was very liberal," he admitted, "in fact I think I may say that I was the leader of the new theology and destructive criticism wing in the Seminary while I was there." He probably overstated his importance to Yale's liberal community, but there is ample evidence of his solidarity with it. While many seminarians in Torrey's graduating class defended theses such as "The Credibility of Our Lord's Miracles" or "The Relation of Theology to Preaching," Torrey's thesis, in contrast, was "The Work of New England Transcendentalism." "I read a great deal of Unitarian literature and got a great deal of help from it," Torrey recalled, "because Unitarianism was more advanced toward the truth in its thinking than I was at that time." He was "a great admirer" of William Ellery Channing, Theodore Parker, and "others of the same or similar schools." A now-lost manuscript he wrote during this time reportedly espoused the higher critical views of William Robertson Smith. But even after he rejected liberal theology, Unitarian and transcendental categories continued to influence his mature assumptions about the Bible, God, and the divine/human relationship. Like Unitarians, Torrey believed that the Bible should be interpreted independent of any other authority, including theological systems and denominational traditions. Transcendentalism shaped Torrey's understanding of the relationship between the believer and God. He insisted that God interacted directly with an individual believer independent of any mediation except the

Bible. "When you read a verse of scripture hear the voice of the living God speaking directly to you in these written words," Torrey told later readers. "There is new power and attractiveness in the Bible when you have learned to hear a living, present person, God, our Father, Himself talking directly to you in these words." Even as a fundamentalist, Torrey insisted that "William Ellery Channing [was] a great thinker," despite his going "astray in his thinking." The main failing of Unitarians, by Torrey's estimation, was not that they rejected tradition but that "they tried to love God as a matter of duty."[12]

Torrey's time in divinity school was not devoid of conservative influences, but these encounters had little effect at the time. Traditional Congregationalism remained in the academic mix at Yale (though it was increasingly challenged by positivist science and social Darwinism); Torrey simply found it unconvincing. "The professors in Yale Seminary at that time were all orthodox (according to present day test they would have been called extremely orthodox)," Torrey reported, "but I was not." He was also first exposed to the evangelist Dwight L. Moody, who held revival services in New Haven during Torrey's final year at seminary. But Moody's theology was also nontraditional. Raised among New England Unitarians, he formulated a modern Protestantism outside any denominational constraints, combining a "plain meaning" of the Bible and a radically individualized divine-human relationship. Like many evangelical liberals, Torrey was favorably disposed to Moody. He worked at his New Haven inquiry meetings and found this "personal work" deeply satisfying. He later read Charles Finney's *Biography* and *Revival Addresses* and became convinced that "the normal state of a church was revival." But it would be nearly a decade before he accepted many standard conservative tenets like a literal hell.[13]

Torrey's first pastorate in Garrettsville, Ohio, had the hallmarks of a liberal ministry. Upon accepting the call, he sent a letter to gauge his congregation's spiritual condition. Without mentioning a personal conversion experience or the practice of evangelism it emphasized instead "the establishment of His kingdom in the world" and their responsibility "to observe his ordinances and to walk worthy of your calling by a life of piety and benevolence." His diary cataloged a modernist reading list, including Charles Darwin, Ralph Waldo Emerson, the *Christian*

Union (a liberal periodical edited by Lyman Abbott), and the German theologian Isaac A. Dorner.[14] Extant correspondence from this time was a single letter to the liberal clergyman Phillips Brooks acknowledging "the debt I owe you for inspiration in my individual religious experience and in my public word."[15] Torrey's sermon topics were dominated by humanitarian and ethical topics like "How Christians Can Help the Lord," "Fruit Bearing," and "Duties to the State." He only occasionally strayed into subjects like "The New Birth," and was surprised when a sermon entitled "Traditional and Personal Faith" was well received.[16] An early sermon manuscript argued that true religion was simply the teachings of Jesus. "Buddhism, Judaism, Mohammedanism, Confucianism all have some truth in the [*sic*] them; and in so far as they agree with the religion of Christ the Episcopals, Methodists, Universalists, Presbyterians, Congregationalists, Baptists all contain truth. . . . But any person in any of them that places his faith in Jesus Christ, and believes he is the son of God and tries to work out the natural results of his faith will surely be saved." Faith in Christ was essential to salvation, but his amorphous definition of this faith considered a practicing Buddhist who "tries to work out the natural results of his faith" in Jesus to be saved.[17]

If Torrey's primary intellectual influences were secular and liberal, his praxis was affected increasingly by the evangelicalism of his congregation. One member, Clara B. Smith, was particularly influential, especially after marrying Torrey in 1879; but there were others. Torrey's diary was devoid of a personal evangelical piety, but many entries ruminated on his parishioners' relational conception of God. He was taken by one woman's testimony that she had been "in great distress" over not being able to visit her sick father but that after prayer "it seemed to her that God said 'I will hold him in the hallow of my hand' & she felt perfect peace and rest." He occasionally experimented with his own attempts to follow God's direct leading: following random impulses to hold spontaneous prayer meetings in saloons, for example, and various union meetings with the town's other churches.[18]

Torrey's ministry in Garrettsville flourished, but he became increasingly troubled by the dissonance between the supernatural basis of his piety and the naturalistic basis of his theology. In July 1882, he began reading Isaac A. Dorner and quickly became "deeply interested" in his

System of Doctrine.[19] Dorner proposed bridging the natural and supernatural through the "central fact" of Christianity: "Jesus Christ, who is . . . a personal unity of the divine life and the human, the Redeemer and the Perfector of humanity" and "in whom the perfect personal union of the divine and human appeared historically."[20] In August, perhaps inspired by this reading, Torrey contemplated postgraduate study in Germany; in a matter of months, he was on his way to Leipzig, family in tow, to clarify his thinking. Torrey began attending theological lectures in November and quickly acclimated to German university life.[21]

In Leipzig, Torrey studied with several noted biblical scholars but was frustrated by their tendency to separate, rather than unite, the natural and the supernatural. Torrey studied under Franz Delitzsch, who had a reputation early in his career as a "bulwark of conservatism."[22] But by Torrey's arrival, Delitzsch had changed his mind on most issues and maintained his confessional Lutheranism only by imposing a strict separation between personal piety and scholarship—the very gap Torrey was attempting to bridge. After a seminar discussing "the question of the late origin of [the] Day [of] Atonement," Torrey noted with frustration that Delitzsch "seemed to regard it difficult if not impossible—of resolution."[23] His only advice on how to keep "scientific questions of authorship" from disrupting the faith of laypeople was not to bring them up. "We tried to make him understand that in America men investigated these things & the preacher had to deal with them," he wrote, but recorded no satisfactory response.[24]

Around this time, Torrey reported reading a gloss of Edward von Hartmann—a philosopher of science who used modern atomic theory and mathematics to connect mind and matter.[25] This led to ruminations about "the great problem of where the natural passes over into the Supernatural & where natural reason ceases & inspiration begins. Are the dividing lines as clearly drawn as some think?"[26] Torrey's extrapolation of Von Hartmann made the material world radically dependent upon the spiritual—as though the natural order was held together by the abstract mathematics in the mind of God. Torrey's later views of miracles reflect this influence. Responding to the objection that miracles are impossible "if the laws of nature are fixed," he argued that "God is the author of the laws of nature," which merely "indicate God's customary ways of working."²⁷ In other words, a miracle was God's choosing to improvise. And since the world was radically dependent on the mind of God, it followed that humanity might best understand reality—both physical and spiritual—through the Bible, the best representation of God's thoughts. Thus for Torrey, the biblical text became the starting point of all knowledge, to which all other areas must align. "I have come to the fork in the road more than fifty times," Torrey would say in terms unimaginable to most conservative Protestants, "and in every instance where my reason and common sense differed from the Bible, the Bible had proved right and my reason wrong."²⁸

But making the biblical revelation the foundation for all other avenues of rational inquiry required absolute certainty in one's interpretation. And so, with Delitzsch's blessing, Torrey moved to Erlangen to study with Franz H. R. Frank, known for his enterprising theory of Christian certitude.²⁹ He also immersed himself in mediating theology, rereading Dorner in the original German and endorsing it even more enthusiastically as "a work of depth, scholarship & power," which "has opened to me many new vistas of truth."³⁰ Although he grew impatient with Frank's technical theology (he described his mentor's magnum opus as "interesting & instructive" but "written in an exceedingly obscure & wearisome style"), he adopted his and Dorner's underlying premise: that certitude was rooted in personal experience rather than externally verifiable scientific or philosophical evidence.³¹ Frank asserted that God literally recreated the believer's personality and that a comparison of the self before and after conversion would lead the believer to certain knowledge of regeneration. Torrey's later advice for dealing with "honest skeptics" reflected this assumption. Rather than using traditional apologetics, he recommended that the skeptic read the Gospel of John "a few verses at a time" with "a willingness to believe," having first asked God to directly lead them in this reading "and promise[d] to act upon so much as you see to be true." But Torrey went even further, asserting that biblical inerrancy could be known with certitude only through one's personal experience of living as though it were true.³² "I believe that there is a God who answers prayers on the conditions stated in the Bible," Torrey wrote, "I believe this because I have put it to the test of practical experiment."³³ In contrast, he regularly denigrated the usefulness of reason or common sense in biblical interpretation. God required "the unquestioning acceptance of its [the Bible's] teachings when definitely ascertained, even when they may appear unreasonable or impossible."[34] Faith preceded evidence; action came before understanding.

But how were the Bible's teachings to be "definitely ascertained" if not through reason? Part of the solution came from an ingenious, if not entirely faithful, appropriation of the liberal German theologian Albrecht Ritschl. Torrey read *Rechtfertigung und Versoehnung* (*Justification and Reconciliation*) in Erlangen and considered it "an interesting & profitable book, both in what one believes & what he has to combat." Though he dismissed some of Ritschl's exegesis as "absurd," he described other parts as "fresh & convincing," and he concluded, "I do not know when I have had a book from which I have received more profit both by its direct teachings & by lines of thought which it suggested."[35] Torrey was vague on specifics, but one certainly sees Ritschl's desire to reform "Protestant dogmatics on the basis of . . . 'Scripture alone'" and his insistence that the Bible should be "primary source for commentary on itself."[36] Torrey combined Ritschl's biblicism with a second idea from Frank: that in each age of human history God gave specific requirements for a faith community to enter into relationship and associated promises if they faithfully met those requirements. The fulfillment of those promises then ushered in a new era with another set of requirements and promises. This promise/fulfillment structure helped Frank address problems of historical development in ways similar to dispensationalism.[37] Torrey adopted it in part for that reason but also redirected it into a radically individualistic way of reading the Bible. If nineteenth-century evangelicals conceived of the Bible as largely a divine companion to God's revelation in nature, Torrey conceived of the Bible as a collection of legal postulates: a contract consisting of promises and their requirements for fulfillment. And by his reading, almost any verse or phrase might become a promise. The sole verse Torrey wrote in the flyleaf of his personal Bible was "Thou, God, seest me": the words of Hagar that he took as God's personal promise to know and meet his own needs.[38] Biblical promises were given to individuals, not groups; thus Torrey told his readers to search the Bible "for promises and appropriate them as fast as you find them—this is done by meeting the conditions and risking all upon them. . . . This is the key to all the treasures of God's grace."[39]

Torrey left Germany without a degree, but the relational theology he forged there still inspires conservative evangelicals. Once he had formulated it, he exchanged the circuitous route through German theology for a simpler and more biblical justification for his approach. The Bible declared itself not only "God breathed" (which Torrey interpreted as "inerrant") but also "useful" or "profitable."[40] This pragmatism fundamentally transformed the Bible from a theological text (knowledge of God for its own sake) to a success manual for Christians. He would claim the Bible was accurate historically and otherwise, but these concerns were of secondary importance. An interpretation was confirmed primarily by personal experience: by practical and demonstrable results. And the cumulative effects of these results, he believed, would transform the world.

FAITH IN ACTION: TORREY AND THE EARLY SOCIAL GOSPEL MOVEMENT, 1883–89

Torrey returned to America in October 1883 with a new drive to undertake practical Christian work. He accepted a call to the Jefferson Street Church in Minneapolis, a mission plant designed to reach the largely immigrant working classes. The local Congregational newspaper characterized his theology as "more old school than progressive," but it anticipated his being "a great addition to the working force of the city." Soon after, the church opened the Immanuel Mission, which provided a variety of social, educational, and religious services to the surrounding neighborhood. The church began with only eleven members in 1884 but grew eightfold in three years. As urban missions took an ever larger part of his time, he eventually resigned his pastorate and began a nondenominational church designed primarily for working-class converts who had received the cold shoulder in established middle-class churches. Like other congregations in the larger "open" or "free church" movement, they eliminated pew rents (a hindrance to working-class participation) and instead gathered "contributions for church expenses by weekly offerings pledged upon pledge cards."[41]

Like other socially oriented evangelicals, Torrey's life among the poor led to his growing criticism of the "respectable" status quo. His only published article in Minneapolis was a scathing critique of conventional Protestant attitudes toward finances. Taking the words and life of Jesus literally, he condemned the purchase of "magnificent and luxurious homes," acerbically commenting. "If Christ should visit our land to day . . . He would be welcomed in the homes of His followers to elegant suites of apartments finished in costly woods and furnished in the highest style of the upholsterer's art." To this, Torrey contrasted the "homes of earnest Christian men supporting families of six or seven or more upon $1.25 a day in summer and what odd jobs they could pick up in winter." The article reflected Torrey's turn to a woodenly literal and exclusively personal biblical hermeneutic: for example, he asserted that the condemnation of "the one who *hid* his Lord's money in the *ground*" in the Parable of the Ten Talents forbade only "certain forms of real estate investment."[42] But this literalness had prophetic bite. To respectable tithers, he suggested they "give eight-tenths more. Yea, 'sell all that thou hast, and distribute unto the poor, and thou shalt have treasures in heaven.' The spirit of this injunction is binding upon all and a very literal interpretation would be desirable on the part of many."[43]

Torrey's growing social consciousness led to his leadership of the International Christian Workers Association—an important precursor to the social gospel movement started by his Yale classmate John C. Collins. An urban missionary in New Haven, Collins convinced Torrey to chair the annual convention proceedings for the duration of the organization. Topics at the first convention in 1886 ranged from the use of statistical analysis to increase Sunday school attendance, to a defense of "the right of women . . . to preach or be pastors." Josiah Strong—organizer of the Evangelical Alliance—pledged his support and participated in the New York City convention the following year; Lyman Abbott's *Christian Union* gave these meetings extensive coverage. By 1891 the convention was attracting prominent participants like Jacob Riis and Anthony Comstock.[44] Torrey's talks increasingly emphasized evangelism, but of a relational sort such that "no people . . . are to be converted to certain doctrines." When his street preaching was interrupted with a question on the nature of the Trinity on one occasion, he reportedly replied, "Never mind about the blessed Trinity; what we are concerned with here is that you have a soul to be saved." This ecumenism was broad enough that he discouraged "all attacks upon Romanism. 'Let the man be converted, and the doctrines will take care of themselves.'"[45]

The "plain" interpretation of the Bible that fueled Torrey's social concerns also led to expectations of supernatural encounters and miraculous demonstrations. As Torrey searched the Bible for promises to claim (and read holiness writers like Phoebe Palmer), he became convinced that a believer might enter into a heightened state of direct communion with God through a "Baptism of the Holy Spirit." Like other types of religious knowledge, certainty of this experience for Torrey came from first accepting the fact through faith. But after this, the believer would receive empirically verifiable evidence—a "new power, a power not his own, 'the power of the Highest!'"[46] In 1886 Torrey became convinced, on the basis of a passage in the book of James, that this power included physical healing through faith. A brief foray into a faith healing ministry was cut short when his failure to heal a young woman with leukemia led to her mother's attempting a resurrection. He ceased public healings after the grisly incident was reported in several metropolitan newspapers, but he continued the practice privately on his family.[47]

Then in 1888, after reading George Müller's *Life of Faith*, he edged toward a second public experiment with the miraculous. Pairing the biblical requirement "that it was wrong to run in debt to any man (Rom. 13.8)" with the promise "that if we trusted God and took our stand upon his plain word of His He would see to it that our wants were met . . . I resolved to go no further in debt & to pay up the old as fast as possible." After a string of apparent answers to prayer, Torrey decided to run the Minneapolis City Mission and the church as a "faith work." Rather than expecting God to bless human efforts with natural increase, Torrey concluded God would provide directly, in answer to specific petitions, because he "stepped right out to trust the Lord."[48] The early months of these arrangements were exceedingly successful. His unusual stipulation that he would not solicit funds from anyone other than God in prayer attracted coverage in the religious and secular press—and with this attention, unsolicited donations. But as the press lost interest, and unsolicited donations slowed to a trickle, he faced difficult questions—especially when he did not have the funds he needed. Over time, Torrey's prayers were answered through increasingly tenuous accounting tricks, as when he remembered "that we had enough in our S. S. treasury to meet the deficiency" for another part of the mission's budget.[49] Later God's provision came by way of two forgotten silver dollars in his desk—suggesting that better office organization would have made the miracle unnecessary.[50] On another occasion, a gift came after a coworker broke Torrey's ironclad principle never to solicit funds to tell a new convert of the mission's financial need.[51] Even more bafflingly, he once credited God's miraculous provision by way of a gift from his wife Clara.[52]

By the summer of 1889 Torrey's experiment of living on faith teetered on the edge of collapse for reasons both practical and conceptual. Since God's provision was predicated on his avoiding debt, financial difficulties necessarily meant he had somehow (even inadvertently) violated that principle. Torrey's diary oscillated erratically as he tried various combinations of saving and spending to demonstrate his unwavering faith while avoiding debt. He first believed that saving was irrelevant since "God can provide for the future" but then determined to "lay by in store day by day . . . as it seems like running in debt to have your house a month & no provision for the rent," and then later to "pay wholly in advance."[53] But when the promises of God still seemed to be failing he concluded "on thinking it over" that paying his landlord in advance "was putting him in debt to me."[54] The source of the radical conclusion that prepaying (or lending money) was transgressing the principle of indebtedness stemmed from his continuing attraction to John Seeley's vision of the church being an organic, interdependent community.[55] But with his certitude grounded in a direct and radically individualistic relationship with God, his communal proclivities led him into a philosophical cul-de-sac. Indeed, from an interdependent perspective, it was impossible to avoid entanglement in debt—either one was indebted to another or one placed another person in debt. This made the entire modern economy—investments, banks, commodities, and futures—a violation of God's biblical requirements. Rents and wages became an insoluble dilemma: Should payments be broken into hourly, minute-by-minute, or second-by-second rates—to be paid simultaneous with use? No wonder that his final diary entry confessed deep confusion. "I am now in straits personally and so is the work. My rent is due and must be paid. I have not paid in advance. I am not clear about this."[56] What had begun as a bold proclamation of God's faithful personal care independent of natural means had become an ambiguous whisper.[57] He would be forced to choose between individualism and the social, certitude and interdependent community.

FROM SOCIAL GOSPEL TO FUNDAMENTALISM, 1889–1907

Given the difficulties of faith work, it is not surprising that in the fall of 1889 Torrey accepted D. L. Moody's offer to serve as dean of what would become the Moody Bible Institute and a steady salary. Though it is known today for its role in the fundamentalist movement, its beginnings were rooted in a milieu of social activism. Moody began his own career as a city missionary in Chicago and had debated founding a training school since the late 1870s. The Chicago Evangelization Society that he organized in 1887, embodied a business-friendly religious individualism. And given that the trustees of the Institute consisted of Chicago business leaders like Cyrus McCormick, the Moody Bible Institute/Chicago Evangelization Society rejected the structural critiques launched by social gospelers and some working-class Christians. But this did not equal an otherworldly faith; its aims were firmly grounded in this world. Moody and the trustees wanted to efficiently solve the growing social problems of the modern industrial city but through urban evangelism rather than substantial economic reform. Torrey's evangelistic success in Minneapolis, his academic credentials, and his executive skill made him an appealing candidate to head the Institute. Torrey was as eager to start as Moody was to have him; within weeks of a brief interview he moved to Chicago.[58]

Historians have regularly contrasted Torrey's conservative dogmatism with Moody's ecumenical openness; but this characteristic appeared in force only after he came under the influence of conservatives that surrounded the famed revivalist. Torrey's address to the convention of Christian Workers in 1890 provides a striking contrast to his earlier positions. An extensive ten-point "Outlines of Doctrine Essential to Leaders and Teachers in Christian Work," included "the *absolute* and *infallible* authority of the Bible from the first chapter of Genesis to the last chapter of Revelation" and the belief that "the death of Jesus Christ is a substitution for the punishment of man's sin that met all the claims of God and His law against the sinner."[59] Such doctrinal specificity and intense focus on conversion as the catchall solution to complex social problems were in marked contrast to Torrey's views just three years prior. But many of his "essential" doctrines (the most important to him being the baptism of the Holy Spirit) were not traditional orthodoxy. Moreover, he gave pragmatic reasons for their importance; they safeguarded Torrey's relational conception of Christianity, and in each case they brought "power," whereas a deviation from them would impede a worker's effectiveness.[60] And regardless, he continued to cooperate with liberals. The future president of the University of Chicago, William R. Harper, and settlement house advocate Graham Taylor held leadership roles in the Convention of Christian Workers under Torrey. In 1894, he joined arch-liberal David Swing, Rabbi Emil G. Hirsch, and Unitarian minister Jenkin Lloyd Jones in a citywide Federation of Ministers that resulted from British journalist William Stead's critique of Chicago's social conditions catalogued in *If Christ Came to Chicago*.[61]

Though tensions in the Gilded Age evangelical coalition had been building through the 1890s, the definitive break, at least in Moody's circle, was caused by a tragic failure of faith healing. In 1898 Torrey lost his young daughter to diphtheria after shunning the widely available and effective antitoxin for prayer alone. Rumors spread about the circumstances of her death, and soon afterward the Chicago YMCA asked for Torrey's resignation from a weekly teaching engagement. A year later several Chicago newspapers reprinted letters Torrey had sent to the now-notorious faith healer John Alexander Dowie asking for prayer. Moody was horrified by the incident and shifted the Institute to a harder-edged dispensationalism—a system that relegated miracles to the past. But the side effect was that Jesus's social teachings were swept aside with his miracles, despite claims of a literal interpretation of the Bible. Liberals, especially in Chicago, concluded that the tragedy was caused by interpreting the Bible plainly without the guidance of higher criticism and modern science.[62] The heartbreaking and humiliating failure of God's promises in preserving the life of his daughter led Torrey to downplay God's direct intervention, but he continued to insist on its possibility and to root his personal certainty in his past experiences of God's faithfulness. Only now he warned that the Devil might suggest "all manner of difficult or even ridiculous things as the will of God" and that "many an honest soul . . . finds that the thing that he did at great sacrifice he was not called upon to do."[63] However, his only advice for discerning God's voice from the devil's was to "wait for God to make the way perfectly clear." He gave no criteria for evaluating "clarity" other than one's intuition.[64]

Torrey's participation in social activism waned after the turn of the century, and soon his once-cordial relations with liberals soured into sometimes-bitter animosity. But he never abandoned his desire to make the coming of Christ's kingdom a physical reality—even despite his premillennialist convictions. This impulse, combined with disagreements with the Institute's trustees, led Torrey to begin a worldwide revival tour in 1902, stretching from Australia, to China, Japan, and India, before settling into a three-year campaign in the British Isles.[65] His British meetings were more successful numerically than Moody's but also more controversial. Liberals opposed Torrey's teachings on the baptism of the Holy Spirit and his recently adopted conviction that there was a literal hell. His growing combativeness and dogmatism (the dark side of religious certitude) made matters worse. Especially when these were combined with his reliance on personal experience for evidence, it is no wonder that his claims of certitude were interpreted by critics as "audaciousness" and as an overreliance on "his own personal authority."[66] Yet these feelings were not yet universal among liberals; Torrey reportedly received the "unfeigned co-operation" of "some of the most vigorous modern thinkers in the American pulpit" when he returned to the United States in 1906 to conduct meetings in Philadelphia, Toronto, and Atlanta. And more importantly, his new worldwide fame put the faith healing controversy (troubling to conservatives and liberals alike) to rest.[67]

The expanding Pentecostal movement in the early twentieth century ultimately became the wedge that forced evangelicals who wanted to maintain their middle-class respectability to choose affiliation either with the coalition of dispensationalist and denominational conservatives or with modernist liberals and social gospelers. As Torrey circled the globe, working-class and "plain-folk" Pentecostals made the expectation of God's immanent intrusion in the world their own and combined it with distinctive practices like speaking in tongues that contravened "respectable" middle-class mores.[68] Meanwhile, continuing success ultimately convinced Torrey that this worldwide revival interest was part of the "latter rain"—an unprecedented outpouring of the Holy Spirit that would bring about the physical return of Jesus. This phrase soon became associated exclusively with Pentecostalism, as did "the baptism of the Holy Spirit" and other language Torrey used to describe the deeply personal and intuitive relationship between the believer and God.[69] With Pentecostalism following close behind Torrey's meetings, he felt a need to distinguish himself from the movement and to critique—often in harsh terms—what he believed were its excesses. He also presented himself publicly as the dry, scholarly champion of "old-time religion" without Pentecostals' undignified "enthusiasm." But he refused to modify his core beliefs. He was critical of dispensationalists who excluded the possibility of modern miracles—"They are mutilating the Word, and stealing from the greater part of God's children what really belongs to them." Neither did he waver from his conviction that God was immanently present in the world, that the Bible was so miraculously composed that it addressed specific issues in a person's life (without complex interpretive systems), or that the Holy Spirit communicated directly to the believer—in ways that might overrule both common sense and traditional biblical interpretations.[70]

Historian Grant Wacker has noted, in reference to the acrimony between Pentecostals and their conservative evangelical opponents, that "feuds within religious families, no less than within biological families, often prove the bitterest of all."[71] This was certainly true for Torrey's relationship with Pentecostals, but also for his relationship with liberals.

The sources of Torrey's theology and the issues it sought to mitigate bear the stamp of a modern mind, and his claim to have been brought to fundamentalist belief *through* (rather than *despite*) his engagement with liberal sources bears consideration. The animosity of liberals to Torrey might be explained in the same way. Although liberal Protestants ignored the Amish (the true antimoderns) and mocked Pentecostals, they attacked fundamentalists as a potent enemy. To suggest some core similarities between fundamentalists and modernists does not deny the real differences between these groups, but it does challenge the ways we define "modernity" and the sources of the heated religious debates of the 1910s and 1920s.[72] Torrey suggests at once the modernity of Pentecostalism, the social engagement of pietistic fundamentalism, and the literalness of some forms of modernism. His theological development suggests that at least one strand of conservative evangelicalism was more a product of modernity than a reaction to it. His mature theology was conservative to be sure, but it was also distinctively modern.

NOTES

1. Reuben A. Torrey, "Diary, 1882–1883," Collection 107, Ephemera of Reuben Archer Torrey Sr., box 3, folder 1, Billy Graham Center Archives, Wheaton College, Wheaton, IL, July 2, 1882, p. 1; Reuben A. Torrey, "Diary, 1889–1890," Torrey Family Papers, Montrose, PA, April 18, 1889 (personal copies of the Torrey Family Papers are in possession of author). The published form of this diary, released after Torrey's death by the Moody Bible Institute, has significant redactions of the original. On Torrey and spirit possession, see Reuben A. Torrey, *The Person and Work of the Holy Spirit* (1910; repr., Grand Rapids, MI: Zondervan, 1968), 244. For an example of Torrey's practice of faith healing during this time, see "Raising the Dead to Life," *St. Paul and Minneapolis Pioneer Press* (hereafter *PP*), February 12, 1887, 6, and his own recollections in Reuben A. Torrey, *Divine Healing: Does God Perform Miracles Today?* (Chicago: Fleming H. Revell, 1924), 21–24.

2. *Proceedings of the Third Convention of Christian Workers in the United States and Canada* (New Haven, CT: Christian Workers Convention, 1888). On the significance of the International Christian Workers Association (Cambridge, MA: Harvard University Press, 1943), 95.

3. William McLoughlin, *Modern Revivalism: Charles Grandison Finney to Billy Graham* (New York: Ronald Press, 1959), 373; Martin E. Marty, *Righteous*

Empire: The Protestant Experience in America (New York: Dial Press, 1970), 182; George Marsden, *Fundamentalism and American Culture: The Shaping of Twentieth-Century Evangelism, 1870–1925* (Oxford: Oxford University Press, 1980). Two dissertations were written on Torrey. See Roger Martin, "The Theology of R. A. Torrey" (PhD diss., Bob Jones University, 1975), and Kermit L. Staggers, "Reuben A. Torrey: American Fundamentalist, 1856–1928" (PhD diss., Claremont Graduate School, 1986). Martin, a committed fundamentalist, corresponded with Torrey's son and later published the only modern biography. It contains valuable biographical information, despite some interpretive limitations. See Roger Martin, *R. A. Torrey: Apostle of Certainty* (Murfreesboro, TN: Sword of the Lord, 1976).

4. The standard dichotomistic framework is best encapsulated in Martin Marty's "two-party" interpretation of American Protestantism in *Righteous Empire*. Marty posited a long-standing contest between "private" Protestantism—which focuses on personal conversion and the afterlife at the expense of social action—and "public" Protestantism, which is both liberal in its theological proclivities and socially engaged. In fact the source of this theory was theological modernists—whose proponents dominated the major divinity schools in the early twentieth century and, as a result, wrote the first draft of the histories of both fundamentalism and liberalism. This model remains persistent in studies of liberal Protestantism. See, for example, Gary J. Dorrien, *Soul in Society: The Making and Renewal of Social Christianity* (Minneapolis: Fortress Press, 1995). Douglas Jacobsen and William Vance Trollinger, eds., *Re-forming the Center: American Protestantism, 1900 to the Present* (Grand Rapids, MI: Eerdmans, 1998), maintains Marty's basic continuum but argues that most Protestants are found between these extremes.

5. On dispensationalism, see Brendan Pietsch, "Dispensational Modernism" (PhD diss., Duke University, 2011). On Pentecostalism, see Matthew Avery Sutton, *Aimee Semple McPherson and the Resurrection of Christian America* (Cambridge, MA: Harvard University Press, 2007), and Roger Glenn Robins, *A. J. Tomlinson: Plainfolk Modernist* (Oxford: Oxford University Press, 2004). The modernity of fundamentalism and conservative evangelicals after World War II has been well established (especially as it relates to modern business and politics). See Darren Dochuk, *From Bible Belt to Sunbelt: Plain-Folk Religion, Grassroots Politics, and the Rise of Evangelical Conservatism* (Norton, 2011); Bethany Moreton, *To Serve God and Wal-Mart: The Making of Christian Free Enterprise* (Cambridge, MA: Harvard University Press, 2009); John G. Turner, *Bill Bright and Campus Crusade for Christ: The Renewal of Evangelicalism in Postwar America* (Chapel Hill: University of North Carolina Press, 2008); Robert Laurence Moore, *Selling God: American Religion in the Marketplace of Culture* (Oxford: Oxford University Press, 1995); Darren Elliott Grem, "The Blessings of Business: Corporate America and Conservative Evangelicalism in the Sunbelt Age,

1945–2000" (PhD diss., University of Georgia, 2010); Sarah Ruth Hammond, "'God's Business Men': Entrepreneurial Evangelicals in Depression and War" (PhD diss., Yale University, 2010).

6. The heterogeneous nature of socially engaged Gilded Age evangelicalism has been noted with increasing frequency. Abell, *Urban Impact*, first connected future fundamentalists and modernists. Ferenc M. Szasz, "The Progressive Clergy and the Kingdom of God," *Mid-America: An Historical Review* 55 (January 1973): 3–20, also noted "conservative" and "liberal" social gospel involvement but concluded they were "two versions masquerading as one" (6). Grant Wacker, "The Holy Spirit and the Spirit of the Age in American Protestantism, 1880–1910," *Journal of American History* 72 (June 1985): 45–62, asserted that "new theologians and higher life leaders . . . emerged from the same religious womb, and, like biological twins, matured in formally comparable ways precisely because they inherited similar genetic blueprints." Marsden, *Fundamentalism and American Culture*, 27–32, focuses on the Blanchard and Beecher families to represent the early unity of Gilded Age evangelicalism and their later "diverging paths." However both families were largely outside the networks that these other scholars have examined. The sole survey of the Gilded Age to my knowledge that incorporates these findings is Rebecca Edwards, *New Spirits: Americans in the Gilded Age, 1865–1905* (New York: Oxford University Press, 2006), 183. The opponents of this heterogeneous evangelical coalition (the "real" conservatives, in a sense) were the "churchly" Protestants described by James D. Bratt, "The Reorientation of American Protestantism, 1835–1845," *Church History* 67, no. 1 (March 1998): 69–76.

7. William R. Hutchison, *The Modernist Impulse in American Protestantism* (Cambridge, MA: Harvard University Press, 1976), 2, 8–9, 44–48, and 79, 86. By his telling, "modernism" was the "conscious, intended adaptation of religious ideas to modern culture"; the belief that God works immanently in the world (what he calls "cultural immanentism," but a broader rejection of the natural/supernatural distinction that was presumed by Protestant orthodoxy); and finally, "a belief that human society is moving toward realization . . . of the Kingdom of God." That liberal modernism might result in a modern supernaturalism is explored by Robert Bruce Mullin, *Miracles and the Modern Religious Imagination* (New Haven, CT: Yale University Press, 1996).

8. Information on Torrey's family is found in Reuben A. Torrey, "Biographical Notes for The National Cyclopædia of American Biography," Torrey Family Papers; George T. B. Davis, *Torrey and Alexander: The Story of a World-Wide Revival: A Record and Study of the Work and Personality of the Evangelists R. A. Torrey, D.D., and Charles M. Alexander* (New York: Fleming H. Revell, 1905), 19; Staggers, "Reuben A. Torrey," 13–15. The narrative of his religious exploration comes from "Autobiographical Notes for R. A. Torrey," R. A. Torrey Files, Moody Bible Institute Archives, Chicago (hereafter MBI Archives). This

document was created in response to a questionnaire from 1908 by an unknown individual at the Moody Bible Institute (in preparation for its twenty-fifth anniversary). It requested a variety of personal data and information on the early years of the Moody Bible Institute. The document is Torrey's unvarnished personal construction of his life, but it has the typical limitations of autobiographical material. He "omitted three or four [questions] that do not seem important," including "Circumstances of anointing by the Holy Spirit, date," and "Date and circumstances of anointing with 'fire,'" which he answered with a curt "I can hardly give that here." See Dr. R. A. Torrey to Mr. A. P. Fitt, October 23, 1908, Reuben A. Torrey Letters 1907–8, Biographical Files, MBI Archives. Other questions he answered in great detail—attaching several single-spaced typewritten sheets. Overall, the document is striking in the degree to which it ignores important conventions of fundamentalist conversion narratives of the time.

9. Torrey's crisis stemmed from multiple sources. His father's finances took a turn for the worse because of a series of factory fires and the financial panic of 1873. Torrey was rejected from a top academic or social society at Yale. Finally, he claimed he was haunted by the thought he would become a minister. Reuben A. Torrey, *The Holy Spirit: Who He Is and What He Does and How to Know Him in All the Fulness of His Gracious and Glorious Ministry* (Old Tappan, NJ: Fleming H. Revell, 1927), 78; Martin, *R. A. Torrey*, 27–37; Davis, *Torrey and Alexander*, 22; "The Box Factory Fires," *Brooklyn Eagle*, May 14, 1873; Reuben Torrey, *Revival Addresses* (Chicago: Fleming H. Revell, 1903), 105; "Autobiographical Notes for R. A. Torrey."

Torrey regularly referenced this incident as his conversion. "I became a minister of the gospel simply because I had to, or be forever lost," he later recounted. "My becoming a Christian and accepting Him as my Saviour turned upon my preaching the gospel.... The night I surrendered to God I did not say, 'I will accept Christ,' or 'I will give up my sins,' I said, 'I will preach.'" Torrey, *Holy Spirit*, 36. See also Reuben A. Torrey, *How to Pray* (Chicago: Fleming H. Revell, 1900), 11. Staggers, "Reuben A. Torrey," 38, treats this incident as Torrey's conversion to traditional conservative evangelicalism, but this homogenization cannot account for his later agnosticism and liberalism. See Christopher G. White, *Unsettled Minds: Psychology and the American Search for Spiritual Assurance, 1830–1940* (Berkeley: University of California Press, 2008), 126–27, for a similar focus on the will among other religious liberals.

10. J. G. Holland, *The Bay-Path; A Tale of New England Colonial Life* (New York: Charles Scribner, 1864); John R. Seeley, *Ecce Homo: A Survey of The Life and Work of Jesus Christ* (Boston: Roberts Brothers, 1867), 2, 351. Holland helped prepare the way for the practical, antidogmatic, interdenominational Protestantism on which the early social gospel was based. Though he was a social conservative, opposing any substantial economic or political reform, he regularly attacked "the theological rigidities of the denominational 'machines.'"

Robert J. Scholnick, "J. G. Holland and the 'Religion of Civilization' in Mid-Nineteenth Century America" *American Studies* 27, no. 1 (1986): 55–79, quote on 70. Seeley awkwardly combined Christian socialism, romantic primitivism, and an ostensibly scientific positivism, though it largely ignored current biblical scholarship. Deborah Wormell, *Sir John Seeley and the Uses of History* (New York: Cambridge University Press, 1980), esp. 21–40 on *Ecce Homo*; and John Kent, "Religion and Science," in *Nineteenth-Century Religious Thought in the West*, ed. Ninian Smart et al. (New York: Cambridge University Press), 1–36. On Seeley and the social gospel in the United States, see Charles Howard Hopkins, *The Rise of the Social Gospel in American Protestantism, 1865–1915* (New Haven, CT: Yale University Press, 1940), 22–23; Henry F. May, *Protestant Churches and Industrial America* (1949; repr., New York: Harper and Row, 1967), 150.

11. All of Torrey's statements here are from his "Autobiographical Notes"; see also Edward Gibbon, *The History of the Decline and Fall of the Roman Empire*, ed. J. B. Bury, 7 vols. (New York: Macmillan, 1914). Gibbon observed that the most humane aspects of Christianity, like universalism, were recent and controversial additions: the primitive church, for its part, "delivered over, without hesitation, to eternal torture, the far greater part of the human species" (2:28). Of cessationism, he noted that any period chosen to end miracles is contradicted by "the insensibility of the Christians who lived at that time" that miracles no longer occurred (2:33). Any time chosen for cessation would have had Christians who had witnessed authentic miracles; their inability to detect fraudulent miracles, Gibbon argued, suggested that all miraculous claims were suspect. Gibbon's relationship to religion is still a matter of debate, but his historical approach to Christianity was clearly critical. See B. W. Young, "'Scepticism in Excess': Gibbon and Eighteenth-Century Christianity," *Historical Journal* [Great Britain] 41, no. 1 (1998): 179–99. On the crisis of historicism among American Protestants, see Grant Wacker, *Augustus H. Strong and the Dilemma of Historical Consciousness* (Macon, GA: Mercer University Press, 1985). On cessationism, see Mullin, *Miracles*. Torrey insisted, "I was not an atheist but an agnostic, not an infidel but a sceptic [sic]." He made this distinction because his crisis of faith occurred *after* his conversion; he maintained a will to believe, despite being unconvinced of its rational, even ethical, viability. On Gilded Age crises of faith, see James Turner, *Without God, without Creed: The Origins of Unbelief in America* (Baltimore: Johns Hopkins University Press, 1985); Paul A. Carter, *The Spiritual Crisis of the Gilded Age* (DeKalb: Northern Illinois University Press, 1971); James T. Kloppenberg, *Uncertain Victory: Social Democracy and Progressivism in European and American Thoughts, 1870–1920* (Oxford: Oxford University Press, 1986).

12. Torrey's thesis subject found in *The Yale Banner* (New Haven, CT: Tuttle, Morehouse and Taylor, 1878), 46; Torrey, "Autobiographical Notes," 2–3. On Torrey and higher criticism, see Martin, "Theology of R. A. Torrey,"

115. Torrey's son (as Martin reports) claimed Torrey's views mirrored those of William Robinson Smith in Smith's entry "The Bible," in the *Encyclopedia Britannica*, 9th ed. (New York: Charles Scribner's Sons, 1878), 634–48. R. A. Torrey, *How to Study the Bible for the Greatest Profit* (New York: F. H. Revell, 1896); Reuben A. Torrey, *The God of the Bible; the God of the Bible as Distinguished from the God of "Christian Science," the God of "New Thought," the God of Spiritualism, the God of "Theosophy," the God of Unitarianism, the God of "the New Theology," the God of Modern Philosophy, and the God of Modernism in General* (New York: George H. Doran, 1923), 73; Reuben A. Torrey, *Power of Prayer*, 101.

Unitarians were pioneers of the "plain meaning" of the Bible. See Nathan O. Hatch, "Sola Scriptura and Novus Ordo Seclorum," in *The Bible in America: Essays in Cultural History*, ed. Nathan O. Hatch and Mark A. Noll (New York: Oxford University Press, 1982), 59–78. This conviction was reinforced by Albrecht Ritschl, as we will see later. Torrey ties Channing and Parker more closely together than some (though certainly not all) students of transcendentalism would. See Joel Myerson, ed., *Transcendentalism: A Reader* (New York: Oxford University Press, 2000). Torrey also mentioned his appreciation for James Freeman Clarke and Edward Everett Hale (Reuben A. Torrey, *The Christ of the Bible* (New York: George H. Doren, 1924), 74). On the controversy of W. R. Smith, see Mark Noll, *Between Faith and Criticism: Evangelicals, Scholarship, and the Bible in America*, 2nd ed. (Grand Rapids, MI: Baker Book House, 1991), esp. 11–27, and Brevard S. Childs, "Wellhausen in English," *Semeia* 25, no. 1 (1982): 83–88.

13. Torrey, "Autobiographical Notes"; Davis, *Torrey and Alexander*, 23–27. On Moody's Unitarian background, see James Findlay, *Dwight L. Moody: American Evangelist* (Chicago: University of Chicago Press, 1969), 36–38. On positivism at Yale in the 1870s, see Charles D. Cashdollar, *The Transformation of Theology, 1830–1890: Positivism and Protestant Thought in Britain and America* (Princeton, NJ: Princeton University Press, 1989).

14. R. A. Torrey to "Beloved," February 1, 1879, Torrey Family Papers, folder 17. On Torrey's reading habits, see Torrey, "Diary, 1882–1883," July 28, 1882, August 31, 1882, July 20, 1882, July 19, 1882, July 6, 1883, and July 18, 1882. Torrey seriously engaged Charles Darwin's *Descent of Man* and agreed only reluctantly with a critique by George Jackson Mivart (Darwin's most scientifically sophisticated British critic). "Mivart points out [radical] defects in Darwin's Theory which Darwin did not sufficiently notice or seem to apprehend in his later editions," he admitted to his diary, but he noted that "this portion of Darwin's work lacks the acuteness and discrimination of other parts." Staggers argued (in "Reuben A. Torrey") that Torrey's studies with James Dana at Yale led him to accept older forms of scientific inquiry. However, this is based on a misreading of William F. Sanford Jr., "Dana and Darwinism," *Journal of the History of Ideas*, 26, no. 4 (October–December 1965): 531–46. Although Dana was ini-

tially resistant to Darwin, he had accepted the major assumptions of Darwinian evolution by the early 1870s, when Torrey attended Yale. Ronald L. Numbers, *The Creationists* (Berkeley: University of California Press, 1992), 39, suggests that Torrey's connection to Dana led to his later lack of alarm over Darwin.

15. R. A. Torrey to Phillips Brooks, December 3, 1879, quoted in Raymond W. Albright, *Focus on Infinity: A Life of Phillips Brooks* (New York: Macmillan, 1961), 201–2.

16. Titles of Torrey's sermons taken from Torrey, "Diary, 1882–1883," August 27, 1882, August 15, 1882, September 15, 1882, September 3, 1882, and August 3, 1882. On his surprise at the success of his "Traditional and Personal Faith" sermon, see Torrey, "Diary, 1882–1883," August 6, 1882.

17. Torrey's sermon, though undated, seems to have been from Garrettsville or perhaps from seminary. See Reuben A. Torrey, "Jesus the Way, the Truth, and the Life John XIV.6," handwritten manuscript, *Torrey Family Papers*, quote from 15–16. The manuscript has no date, but Torrey refers to "the late war" (11) in reference to the Civil War (after 1898 this would have referred to the Spanish-American War). Torrey reportedly began preaching "entirely extempore" in Minneapolis (*Pilgrim*, February 1884, 12). Finally, the rhetorical style is markedly different from that of his many sermons published after 1889.

18. An example of Torrey's interest in evangelical piety is in "Diary, 1882–1883," August 10, 1882. The absence of evangelical themes is striking when compared with his subsequent diaries after 1889. On Torrey and saloon prayer meetings, see Davis, *Torrey and Alexander*, 29. See also Torrey, *Revival Addresses*, 200–202.

19. Torrey, "Diary, 1882–1883," July 18, 1882, quote from July 25, 1882.

20. I. A. Dorner, *A System of Christian Doctrine*, ed. Alfred Cave and J. S. Banks (Edinburgh: T & T Clark, 1880), 47. See also Hutchison, *Modernist Impulse*, 85.

21. Torrey, "Diary, 1882–1883," August 15, 1882, and August 16, 1882. Torrey tutored students in German to supplement his income in Garrettsville. See, for example, Torrey, "Diary, 1882–1883," July 13, 1882. Torrey's first lecture is recounted in "Diary, 1882–1883," November 15, 1882. "Attended one of Luthardt's lectures & found to my surprise that I could understand almost everything." Torrey's class notes began in a mixture of English and German but quickly switched to all German. Reuben A. Torrey, "German Class Notes," Torrey Family Papers.

22. Crawford Howell Toy, "Delitzsch, Franz," in *The Jewish Encyclopedia*, ed. Isidore Singer and Cyrus Adler (New York: Funk and Wagnalls, 1912), 505.

23. Torrey, "Diary, 1882–1883," January 24, 1883.

24. Torrey, "Diary, 1882–1883," November 28, 1882. Torrey also studied with Christoph Ernst Luthardt. After finishing his "Apologetic," Torrey complained it was "hardly of an apologetic nature." Torrey, "Diary, 1882–1883," December 29, 1882.

25. Torrey's exposure to von Hartmann came through Francis Bowen's popular philosophical textbook, which he designed to inoculate the English-speaking world against the "dangers" of continental philosophy. Francis Bowen, *Modern Philosophy from Descartes to Schopenhauer and Hartmann* (London: Sampson Low, Marston, Searle, and Rivington, 1877), vii, 463–64.

26. Torrey, "Diary, 1882–1883," December 7, 1882.

27. R. A. Torrey, *Practical and Perplexing Questions Answered* (Chicago: Moody Press, 1909), 92.

28. *Southern Cross*, September 10, 1902, 12.

29. On Frank, see Gary W. Davis, "A Critical Exposition of F. H. R. Von Frank's System of Christian Certainty" (PhD diss., University of Iowa, 1972).

30. Torrey, "Diary, 1882–1883," May 11, 1883.

31. Ibid., February 6, 1882 [*sic*; actually 1883]. See Dorner, *System of Christian Doctrine*, 31.

32. Reuben A. Torrey, *How to Bring Men to Christ* (Chicago: Fleming H. Revell, 1893), 121.

33. Reuben A. Torrey, "What I Believe" (n.p., n.d.), 3.

34. Reuben A. Torrey, *How to Study*, 109.

35. Torrey, "Diary, 1882–1883," July 6, 1883.

36. Quotes on Ritschl taken from David W. Lotz, "Ritschl in His Nineteenth-Century Setting," in *Ritschl in Retrospect: History, Community, and Science*, ed. Darrell Jodock (Minneapolis: Fortress Press, 1995), 8–27, and Gerald W. McCulloh, "A Historical Bible, a Reasonable Faith, a Conscientious Action: The Theological Legacy of Albrecht Ritschl," in Jodock, *Ritschl in Retrospect*, 31–50. See also Dan L. Deegan, "Albrecht Ritschl as Critical Empiricist," *Journal of Religion* 44 (April 1964): 149–60.

37. For substantive summaries of Frank's theology, see R. Seeberg, "Franz Hermann Reinhold Von Frank," in *The New Schaff-Herzog Encyclopedia of Religious Knowledge*, ed. Samuel Macauley Jackson (Grand Rapids, MI: Baker Book House, 1977), 4:368–69; D. Ritschel, "Erlangen School," in *The New Catholic Encyclopedia*, ed. William J. McDonald (New York: McGraw-Hill, 1967), 5:515–16.

38. Quote in Torrey's Bible is taken from Gen. 16:13 (Torrey's Bible in Reuben Archer Torrey, Collection 107, box 5, Billy Graham Center Archives).

39. Torrey, *How to Study*, 110–11.

40. 2 Tim. 3:16. This was adopted as the official verse of the Moody Bible Institute while he served as its superintendent. See also *Proceedings of the Third Convention*, 130, for Torrey's use of this passage.

41. *Pilgrim*, May 1884, 3. See also the issues for October 1883, February 1884, March 1884 (where his congregation was described as "largely dependent on wages for their daily bread," at a rate such that "the struggle is to provide food"), and November 1885. The Immanuel Mission eventually developed into

the North East Neighborhood House, an important social service organization in Minneapolis. No records from this early period remain. See "North East Neighborhood House," collection P3, box 1, folder 3, Minnesota Historical Society, St. Paul, MN; *Pilgrim*, November 1886. See *Proceedings of the Third Convention*, 150–54, for Torrey's description of the beginnings and operation of the Open Door Church.

42. The Parable of the Talents, recorded in the Gospel of Matthew, tells the story of three servants who were each given different amounts of money (five, two, and one "talents" respectively) to invest for their master. The two servants with the greater amounts doubled their investments, while the other servant, fearing failure, acted conservatively and buried the talent. The first two servants were commended and given greater responsibility while the other servant had his single talent taken and was "cast into the outer darkness." See Matt. 25:14–30.

43. R. A. Torrey, "How Shall We Invest?" *Pilgrim*, December 1885, 1.

44. On the First Convention of Christian Workers, see *Christian Union*, May 6, 1886, 20; June 10, 1886, 21; June 24, 1886, 6; and October 28, 1886, 6; "The Christian Workers," *Chicago Daily Tribune*, June 20, 1886, 17; on the 1887 convention, see *Christian Union*, August 4, 1887, 112–13; September 29, 1887, 294. A sample of prominent participants can be found in *Christian Union*, November 7, 1889, 574. On the 1891 convention, see *Proceedings of the Sixth Convention of Christian Workers in the United States and Canada* (New Haven, CT: Committee for Christian Workers in the United States and Canada, 1891), 4.

45. *Christian Union*, August 4, 1887, 112–13.

46. On spiritual power after the baptism of the Holy Spirit, see Torrey, *Baptism of the Holy Spirit*, 15, 21.

47. On Torrey's failed healing, see "Minor Mention," *PP*, December 1, 1886, 6; "Raising the Dead to Life," 6; "That Phenomenal Faith," *PP*, February 13, 1887, 6. For national coverage, see "The Faithists. Curious Story of a Partial Resurrection from the Dead," *Philadelphia Inquirer*, February 14, 1887, 7; "Resurrected by Faith," *Boston Daily Globe*, February 13, 1887, 2; "Life in the Dead," *New York Times*, February 13, 1887, 7. Torrey's mature views of faith healing are found in Torrey, *Divine Healing*.

48. On Torrey's faith work, see Torrey, "Diary, 1889–1890," 1, 6. Torrey's mission arrangements were less clear-cut than his diary suggests. See *Northwestern Congregationalist*, November 16, 1888, and December 7, 1888, 9.

49. Torrey, "Diary 1889–90," May 26, 1889. This diary is in the possession of the Torrey Family in Montrose, PA, copy in possession of author.

50. Torrey, "Diary 1889–90," August 12, 1889, 20.

51. Torrey, "Diary, 1889–90," May 26, 1889, 17.

52. Torrey, "Diary 1889–90," June 14, 1890.

53. Torrey, "Diary 1889–90," April 18, 1889.

54. Torrey, "Diary 1889–90," August 12, 1889.

55. Torrey, "Diary, 1889–90," August 12, 1889. This passage rethinking debt in communal terms was expunged from the published version of Torrey's diary.

56. Torrey, "Diary, 1889–90," August 12, 1889. Torrey occasionally tied his difficulties to a lack of faith: "There had been sources where money seemed, sure, money that had really been contributed for us, and I had my eye on them rather than on the Lord Jesus, and so our embarrassment arose" (Torrey, "Diary, 1889–90," April 18, 1889).

57. On Torrey's continuing financial troubles, see *Northwestern Congregationalist*, August 16, 1889, 9.

58. James Findlay, "Moody, 'Gapmen' and the Gospel: The Early Days of Moody Bible Institute," *Church History* 31 (Summer 1962): 322–35; Torrey, "Autobiographical Notes."

59. Reuben A. Torrey, "Outlines of Doctrine Essential to Leaders and Teachers in Christian Work," *Proceedings of the Fifth Convention of Christian Workers in the United States and Canada* (New Haven, CT: Committee for Christian Workers in the United States and Canada, 1890), 292–99, quotes on 293, 294.

60. Ibid., 294 and elsewhere.

61. William T. Stead, *If Christ Came to Chicago! A Plea for the Union of All Who Love in the Service of All Who Suffer* (Chicago: Laird and Lee, 1894), 461–63.

62. Moody asked whether the dispute was caused by Torrey's beliefs on "the Second Coming or Divine Healing?"; D. L. Moody to R. A. Torrey, October 31, 1898. On the faith healing incident, see *Daily Interocean*, October 2, 1899, 4; *Chicago Chronicle*, October 2, 1899, 2; "Rev. R. A. Torrey under Hot Fire," *Chicago Journal*, October 2, 1899, 1; "Will Have a New Teacher: The Rev. R. A. Torrey to Be Relieved of His Connection with Y. M. C. A. Sunday School Work," *Chicago Tribune*, November 4, 1898. For liberal criticism, see, e.g., "Henderson on Faith Cure," *Chicago Tribune*, October 16, 1899, 5; "Disease and the Devil," *Chicago Tribune*, April 2, 1899, 6.

63. R. A. Torrey, "How Can I Know That I Am Led by the Holy Spirit?," in *Traits and Tracts of Torrey: A Fresh Appreciation of a Great Man and Teacher*, ed. Louis T. Talbot (Los Angeles: Bible Institute of Los Angeles, n.d.), 104 and 105.

64. Ibid., 106.

65. On Torrey's worldwide mission, see William T. Stead, *The Torrey-Alexander Mission: The Story of the Men and Their Methods* (London: Review of Reviews Publishing Office, 1905).

66. Various British critiques of Torrey's meetings, led largely by Unitarian ministers, were published in 1904. See Thomas Rhondda Williams, *The True Revival versus Torreyism* (London: Percy Lund, Humphries, 1904). For a typical critique of Torrey, drawing from British critics (and from which the quotations

are taken), see Charles S. Macfarland, "Our Readers' Forum," *Congregationalist and Christian World*, November 11, 1905, 678.

67. On continuing liberal cooperation, see "Dr. Torrey in Atlanta," *Zion's Herald*, August 22, 1906, 1070.

68. On Torrey's contributions to Pentecostal theology, see Donald W. Dayton, *The Theological Roots of Pentecostalism* (Grand Rapids, MI: Francis Asbury, 1987). George Marsden, *Fundamentalism and American Culture*, 94, notes that Torrey inadvertently became "a kind of John the Baptist figure for later international Pentecostalism." German Pentecostals traced their beginnings to when "Torrey . . . prayed that the Holy Spirit might come down upon all who desired him." Walter J. Hollenweger, *The Pentecostals* (Peabody, MA: Hendrickson, 1988), 221–23.

69. The *Institute Tie* (especially 1906 and 1907) contained regular reports of Torrey's revival work and numerous allusions to the "latter rain." On the importance of "latter rain" terminology to Pentecostalism, see Edith L. Blumhofer, "Restoration as Revival: Early American Pentecostalism," in *Modern Christian Revivals*, ed. Edith L. Blumhofer and Randall Balmer (Urbana: University of Illinois Press, 1993).

70. Torrey's blistering critique of Pentecostalism is found in Reuben Archer Torrey, *Is The Present "Tongues" Movement of God?* (Los Angeles: Biola Book Room, 1913). His critique of dispensationalism is found in Torrey, *Divine Healing*, 17–18. Though he did not object to the broad contours of premillennialism, he had little, if any interest in end-time prophecy or the intricacies of dispensationalism. Rather, he used it as a backstop to the problems of historical consciousness, in similar ways to his German mentor F. H. R. Frank. On early Pentecostalism, see Grant Wacker, *Heaven Below: Early Pentecostals and American Culture* (Cambridge, MA: Harvard University Press, 2001); Randall J. Stephens, *The Fire Spreads: Holiness and Pentecostalism in the American South* (Cambridge, MA: Harvard University Press, 2010); Sutton, *Aimee Semple McPherson*; James R. Goff Jr., *Fields White unto Harvest: Charles F. Parham and the Missionary Origins of Pentecostalism* (Fayetteville: University of Arkansas Press, 1989).

71. Grant Wacker, "Travail of a Broken Family: Evangelical Responses to Pentecostalism in America," *Journal of Ecclesiastical History* 47, no. 3 (July 1996): 523.

72. A compelling way forward in the definition of modernism is found in Kathryn Lofton, "The Methodology of the Modernists: Process in American Protestantism," *Church History* 75, no. 2 (June 2006): 374–402. Lofton focuses on modernism as a process, a methodology, or an approach rather than specific conclusions about the world—conclusions, Torrey's life suggests, that were also reached by nonmodernists, but by very different means. For modernists, she explains, "How you believe . . . was your belief" (378).

CHAPTER 11

The Interdenominational Evangelicalism of D. L. Moody and the Problem of Fundamentalism

MICHAEL S. HAMILTON

The 2006 republication of George Marsden's *Fundamentalism and American Culture* marked the twenty-fifth anniversary of a true landmark study in American religious history. Writing in the *Atlantic Monthly* in 2003, Benjamin Schwartz called it "one of the most significant works of cultural history in the past twenty-five years."[1] For Marsden himself, the book was in part an exploration of his own religious heritage. Both his father and his father-in-law had been pastors in the Orthodox Presbyterian Church, founded by conservatives during the fundamentalist-modernist controversies. For journalists and politicians the book helped make sense of head-scratching novelties of the late 1970s like "born-again" presidents and the Religious Right. And for those who study American religion, the book consolidated and supplanted two decades of scholarly rediscovery of fundamentalism.[2]

Marsden drew the interpretive map of fundamentalism that scholars and journalists now rely on, and it became the starting place for a new generation of scholarship on American evangelicalism. His definition of fundamentalism and his story line of its basic trajectory have become the consensus view. So strong is this consensus that Oxford University Press reissued his book unchanged, except for a new chapter on developments since 1980.

Marsden defined fundamentalism as "militantly anti-modernist Protestant evangelicalism."[3] He argued that fundamentalism began at the end of World War I as a coalition drawn from various evangelical Protestant religious movements. Modernism was the attempt to bring Christianity in line with modern thought; the fundamentalist coalition was formed to preserve traditional Christianity in part by waging war against modernism in Protestant denominations and the broader culture.[4] On the ecclesiastical front in this war, the fundamentalist coalition fought two major battles—it tried to force theological liberals out of the Northern Baptist Convention and out of the Presbyterian Church, U.S.A. On the cultural front, the fundamentalist coalition fought one major battle—it attempted to outlaw the teaching of evolution in public schools. In the early 1920s the fundamentalists' chances of winning looked good, but in 1925 the tide turned, and all three battles were lost.

Despite our widespread acceptance of this narrative, it is not without its difficulties. The central unsolved problem is this: What is the relationship of the fundamentalist *movement* to the fundamentalist *controversies*?

The traditional view (formulated, as we will see, by fundamentalism's early opponents) defined fundamentalism as a social movement organized to fight against modernism in religion and culture in the 1920s.

This view was challenged in 1970, when Ernest Sandeen argued that the movement antedated the controversies. In Sandeen's reconstruction, the movement was organized after the Civil War not to fight modernism but to promulgate "millenarianism" (now more commonly called premillennialism). In the 1920s the battles in the denominations and the crusade to outlaw evolution would have happened without the participation of the millenarian movement. However, many of its leaders did participate, and in the process they renamed their movement "fundamentalism." In other words, Sandeen saw no "fundamentalist controversy" in the 1920s. What he saw were three different controversies in which some millenarians—now calling themselves fundamentalists—participated alongside other types of conservatives. After the 1920s the millenarian movement continued forward with much the same character as before the controversies, albeit with a new name.[5]

Ten years later, Marsden's book sidestepped Sandeen's thesis and returned to the traditional interpretation. He took account of Sandeen's millenarian movement (chiding him for reducing its character to its premillennialism) but argued that it was entirely absorbed into a larger antimodernist coalition organized in the late 1910s. Sandeen's millenarian movement was to Marsden a "submovement" that fed into this larger "fundamentalist" coalition. During the controversies of the 1920s, this coalition evolved into "a movement distinct from its antecedents and representing more than just the sum of the submovements that supported it." After defeat, this new "fundamentalist movement" then developed "a distinct life, identity, and eventually subculture of its own." It retreated to the cultural periphery and turned its efforts to building a network of independent religious organizations. Thus barricaded, the movement rebuilt its strength, reemerging in the 1970s in the form of the Religious Right to resume its war against modernism.[6]

A few years later, when Joel Carpenter set out to tell the story of fundamentalism after 1925, he encountered an unsettling fact—the "fundamentalists" of the 1930s and 1940s that Carpenter studied looked awfully similar to Sandeen's millenarian network of the 1880s and 1890s. How then could "fundamentalism" have been created after World War I? And how could its raison d'être be waging war against modernism? So he tried to synthesize the two interpretations. He called Sandeen's millenarian movement an "interdenominational revivalist network that formed around . . . Dwight L. Moody" and, with a nod to Sandeen, allowed that it was the "core of nascent fundamentalism." Then following Marsden, Carpenter argued that this network became militantly antimodernist after World War I and actually took the lead in drawing other conservative Protestants into the antimodernist coalition that called itself "fundamentalism." However, unlike Marsden and similar to Sandeen, Carpenter claimed that what came out of the controversies was not a new coalition movement distinct from its antecedents but a movement "pared back to those whose roots, by and large, were in the older, interdenominational, premillennialist, and 'Bible school' network." But then, like Marsden's new coalition movement,

Carpenter's pared-back movement carried into the 1930s and 1940s not the warm-hearted spirit of the Moody movement but the fighting spirit of militant antimodernism.[7]

What complicates our understanding is that the movement centered on Moody never gave itself a name and historians have yet to figure out what to call it. This is a sure sign that we have failed to bring it into clear view. But the greater problem, and the reason Carpenter's synthesis ultimately breaks down, is how surprisingly vague all the histories have been in making actual connections between the Moody network and the three major battles of the 1920s.

This chapter begins with a backward glance at the Moody movement that would eventually inherit the fundamentalist label, follows it through the controversies of the 1920s, and then proposes reconsideration of four persistent myths about the movement. Along the way the chapter makes six interlocking arguments:

1. There was no single coalition—no single fundamentalist movement—that organized itself in the early 1920s. The three major battles of the fundamentalist-modernist controversies were fought by three separate coalitions that had hardly any overlapping personnel.
2. There was another major battle of the fundamentalist-modernist controversies, one that was resolved before the other three. This was a dispute over the meaning of the term *fundamentalist*. By late 1923 the modernists and their progressive allies had won this fight, developing the definition of *fundamentalism* that we now accept as the scholarly consensus.
3. The fundamentalist battles did not generate a new movement. The popular movement that after 1925 came to be called "fundamentalism"—that is, the movement based in independent Bible institutes, missionary organizations, and large autonomous urban churches—had been organized in the late nineteenth century by Dwight L. Moody and his lieutenants. Before World War I it already had a self-conscious identity, an institutional network, and recognized leaders.
4. Most of the Moody network and its key leaders were never involved in the denominational battles or the battle over evolution in the

schools. The movement as a whole had substantial sympathy for the militant antimodernists, and a very small handful of leaders from the network did become involved in the fights. But most of the network's leaders, institutions, and grassroots constituents remained on the sidelines in the 1920s.

5. The Moody movement did not retreat to the cultural periphery after the battles of the 1920s. Its institutional location in relationship to the rest of American cultural institutions had already been established and locked into place before World War I. Their location in independent parachurch organizations outside the denominational structure did put them farther from American political, educational, and media centers. But it also put them closer to ordinary Americans—at a time when an organizational revolution within the denominations was distancing the denominations from ordinary Americans.

6. The Moody movement was assigned the name *fundamentalist* by those outside the movement. But more often than not these so-called fundamentalists declined to call themselves that, and with good reason. For what Moody midwifed into being was in fact a new form of *interdenominational evangelicalism* that has reshaped American religious life. Moody gave this movement a basic character and structure that, though affected by the fundamentalist-modernist controversies, remained fairly constant through the emergence of Billy Graham in the 1950s.

DWIGHT L. MOODY AND THE CREATION OF INTERDENOMINATIONAL EVANGELICALISM

Evangelist Dwight L. Moody and those around him pulled together this new form of interdenominational evangelicalism in the last quarter of the nineteenth century. Its popular following and its network of interdenominational organizations grew steadily through the first quarter of the twentieth century. In the early years most of those in the Moody network attended denominational churches—primarily Baptist, Presbyterian, and Congregationalist. Over time, however, increasing numbers attended independent nondenominational churches. Regardless of which kind of church they attended, the primary commitments of those in the movement lay not with any denomination but with the movement's unique interdenominational version of Christianity. Its religious signatures were revivalism, dispensational premillennialism, and Keswick holiness pietism. The network was deeply committed to the idea of biblical infallibility, sometimes called "inerrancy" or "verbal inspiration" of the Bible. The institutional signatures of the movement were the independent, interdenominational parachurch organization and the large autonomous urban congregation.[8] Before the controversies of the 1920s the network was already well established and growing above the Mason-Dixon line, and it was expanding to the West Coast.[9] It was not well established in the South, though it had built a few outposts there.[10] The Moody network also had strong ties to what we usually call "conservative evangelicalism" in Canada and Britain—so strong that they are arguably part of the same movement.[11]

The movement was highly decentralized, which has made it difficult for us to see it in focus. Moreover, it never gave itself a name. As a result, we've called it by so many names—the prophecy movement, millenarianism, premillennialism, dispensationalism, conservative evangelicalism, protofundamentalism, or even fundamentalism—that it is not clear we are even speaking of the same movement. All of these names are problematic—they are reductionistic, anachronistic, or imprecise.[12] Historians have paid much attention to the movement's distinctive eschatology, but contemporaries at the time paid just as much attention to its interdenominationalism. Both conservatives and liberals in the denominations often complained that the Moody network people were disloyal. Curtis Lee Laws, a leader of the Baptist traditionalists, had to defend himself repeatedly against Baptist accusations that he was a front for "the interdenominational movement."[13]

We usually assume that in Moody's day this movement was nonmilitant, becoming militant only after World War I. This is an oversimplification that distorts our perception. As we will see, this movement was sympathetic to the militant antimodernists in the three major battles, but few of the movement's leaders participated in the battles. This is because interdenominational evangelicalism was not organized to fight against modernism. Its main purposes were to promote the traditional evangelical agendas of revival, missions, and Bible study, and also the more recent evangelical innovations of dispensational premillennialism, Keswick holiness, and lay leadership.[14] Structurally the movement was designed to bypass the denominations, less because of their modernism and more because of their inertia. Moody was more worried about the denominations' reluctance to innovate and cooperate across interdenominational lines than he was about their modernism. His urgency to spread the gospel and his impatience with the churches' standard way of doing things led him to emphasize lay leadership working through organizations that were independent of the denominations.[15] Lewis Sperry Chafer, founder of Dallas Theological Seminary and protégé of Moody lieutenant C. I. Scofield, believed that evangelicals, to fulfill their calling, had to "be delivered from denominational bondage."[16]

A few of this movement's leaders did participate in the so-called "fundamentalist-modernist" battles, a fact that has led us to mistakenly conclude that the movement as a whole became "fundamentalist." But these leaders were a minority, and they were unsuccessful in persuading the rank and file of the Moody network to follow them into battle. However, the militant minority did have an important impact on the movement. They would bring into interdenominational evangelicalism a strain of militant antimodernism that introduced new tensions into the movement. These would eventually lead to a long, drawn-out schism in the 1940s and 1950s.

OBSTACLES TO ASSEMBLING ANTIMODERNIST COALITIONS IN THE DENOMINATIONS

In the 1920s one could not be both a Baptist and a Presbyterian. This seems like an obvious thing to say, but its significance is often blurred by the way our histories speak of fundamentalism as a single movement. It is important to keep in mind that the battle to purge the Northern Baptist Convention of liberalism and the battle to purge the Presbyterian Church, U.S.A. of liberalism were fought by two different coalitions consisting of entirely different people.

The two coalitions did, however, share a key structural similarity. In each denomination, the antimodernist coalition was drawn primarily from two sectors. The first sector consisted of denominational traditionalists; the second sector consisted of interdenominational evangelicals. At first glance, these seemed like natural allies. They both were orthodox in theology, and they shared much in how they thought about evangelism, piety, and the Bible.[17]

Yet any attempt to draw these two sectors into effective coalitions faced major obstacles. For starters, the traditionalists themselves were handicapped by internal divisions. Baptist traditionalists disagreed on whether establishing a statement of faith to weed out liberals would violate the basic Baptist abhorrence of manmade creeds.[18] Presbyterian traditionalists disagreed on whether revivalism was consistent with a Reformed theology.[19] And among both Baptists and Presbyterians, bitter organizational disagreements divided one conservative from another—disagreements that had commenced before the 1920s and had nothing to do with modernism.[20]

Second, the primary institutional commitments of the traditionalists and the interdenominationals ran in perpendicular directions. The traditionalists cared deeply about the welfare of their denominational organizations, while the Moody network folks were more committed to the welfare of their parachurch organizations. The traditionalists often resented the parachurch agencies as competitors encroaching on their turf. By 1920 some 10 percent of the Northern Baptist pastors had been educated at interdenominational Bible institutes, a fact that was starting to alarm traditionalists.[21] In that year the Northern Baptist Convention appointed a committee of nine conservative clergymen, including William Bell Riley, to investigate Baptist schools. But traditionalists forced Riley to resign, alleging insufficient support for the denomination's schools. Because he was involved in the Moody network they complained that he was "tearing down Seminaries to build up Bible Schools."[22]

Additionally, traditionalists were committed to the historic theologies of their denominations, while the Moody network espoused a sort of "mere Christianity" supplemented by premillennialism and Keswick holiness. These differences made the antimodernist coalitions quite unstable. Many traditionalists considered interdenominationalism and dispensationalism every bit as dangerous as theological liberalism. And the few interdenominationals willing to fight denominational battles bridled at having to mute their dispensationalism.[23]

Another difficulty arose from deep ambivalence in both groups toward forcing the liberals out. The traditionalists opposed liberalism, but many worried that attacking it too aggressively would harm their denomination. Initially they seem to have hoped that the liberals were but a handful of individuals. However, when it became clear that forcing the liberals out might produce a major schism, most traditionalists drew back from the brink. Clarence E. Macartney, a leading Presbyterian traditionalist, illustrates this dynamic. In 1922 he insisted that the liberals were but a "small minority," so few that no banishments would be necessary.[24] After all, the Presbyterian controversies of the 1890s had involved very small numbers of liberals.[25] But by 1924 the situation had changed—over 1,200 ministers signed the liberal-sponsored "Auburn Affirmation," and Henry Sloane Coffin, a liberal leader, threatened schism.[26] This is almost certainly why leading conservatives like Macartney consistently refused to pull the trigger on actions that might split the church.[27]

The Moody network radicals, by contrast, did not fear schism. Their institutional network made them independent of the denominations. But the radicals were few because interdenominational evangelicalism, like Moody himself, was noncontroversialist in character.[28] Since it focused on missions, evangelism, prayer, and personal holiness, since it relied on workers drawn from every denominational tradition, and since it was financially dependent on voluntary gifts, its organizations avoided controversy whenever possible. Most parachurch organizations had supporters on both sides of the denominational battles.[29] Moreover, since the network was outside the denominations, it had no political leverage it could apply in the denominational battles.[30]

THE ATTEMPT TO ASSEMBLE A FUNDAMENTALIST COALITION AMONG NORTHERN BAPTISTS

Shortly after the end of the World War, key Baptist leaders began trying to build a coalition to drive out the liberals. Though the obstacles are perhaps clearer in hindsight, both traditionalists and interdenominationals knew that they had party differences to overcome. As a first step, they decided they needed a new party name that would unify both groups and call them to battle. They chose to call their coalition the "Christian Fundamentals" movement, and they began calling themselves "fundamentalists." This seemed like a promising unifier. The name was owned by neither group, and it suggested that they were fighting for the basics of Christianity.

William Bell Riley's task was to bring the Moody network into the crusade. He was both a member of the Moody network and, as the most powerful Baptist in Minnesota, an important figure in the Northern Baptist Convention. With great fanfare Riley launched the World's Christian Fundamentals Association (WCFA) in May 1919. He almost certainly borrowed this name from the title of *The Fundamentals*, the Moody network's decidedly nonmilitant book series of 1910–15.[31] The initial meeting drew six thousand people, formed five "standing" committees, issued pronouncements blasting modernism, and published a faith statement that included premillennialism and inerrancy. Riley then followed up with a six-week, eighteen-city blitz that sent out fourteen leading speakers and accompanying musicians. The purpose of this ambitious road show was to build local chapters of the WCFA; these in turn were supposed to draw all of interdenominational evangelicalism into a militant crusade against modernism in the denominations and in American culture.[32]

Curtis Lee Laws led the effort to build the coalition from the traditionalist side. Laws was editor of the *Watchman-Examiner*, a widely read independent Baptist newspaper. In 1920 Laws and 154 other signatories called on all Baptist conservatives to unite in a "General Conference on Fundamentals." This led to the formation of a new group dedicated to fighting liberalism in the Northern Baptist Convention. After the first meeting, Laws coined the term *fundamentalist*, explaining that he was searching for a new name that could bring together both Baptist traditionalists and the Moody network premillennialists. At first it looked like the strategy might work. The new group, now called the Fundamentalist Federation, included both traditionalists and interdenominationals.[33]

Yet Riley and Laws failed to build an effective antimodernist coalition. Many histories describe the WCFA as an indicator of the growing strength of fundamentalism, but in reality it flopped.[34] The enthusiasm of 1919 was short-lived, for the WCFA's antimodernist campaign generated little popular support among the interdenominational rank and file. Most of those who played leading roles at the 1919 meeting abandoned the organization within a year or two, leaving it to Riley and a very small handful of militants. Few local chapters materialized. Riley's biographer, William Trollinger, discovered that by 1922—when the antimodernism campaign in the denominations was not even yet at full crescendo—the WCFA "was already displaying signs of collapse." Trollinger shows that "by 1923 at the latest, the World's Christian Fundamentals Association had abandoned its goal of eliminating modernism from the major Protestant denominations."[35]

This is astonishing considering that Riley and the other militant antimodernists in both the Baptist and Presbyterian denominations were still campaigning to purge them of modernism and still had reasonable hope of success. The obvious but overlooked explanation is that the Moody network, though opposed to liberal theology, was unwilling to crusade against it. Riley later attempted to revitalize the WCFA by switching its focus to antievolution, but that would also fail. The organization never sparked a national movement. As one WCFA board member later recalled, "The World Fundamentals Movement was chiefly W. B. Riley and stationery."[36]

THE BATTLE TO DEFINE THE TERM *FUNDAMENTALIST*

Laws's organization fared little better than Riley's. The name Laws hoped would unite traditionalists and interdenominationals instead became one of his greatest burdens. Since *fundamentalist* had no established historical definition, Laws's adversaries moved quickly to seize control of the term. In April 1921 the liberal *Christian Century*, which had been attacking the Moody network and its premillennialism for years, jumped at the chance to discredit Laws's group by equating it with the premillennial movement. "The cult of fundamentalism with its verbal inspiration and infallibility," wrote the *Century*, "is chiliasm or adventism with a new name." In July 1921 the newspaper of the Northern Baptist denominational officials tried to drive a wedge into Laws's coalition by insisting that *fundamentalism* was defined "in its settled, technical sense, as designating the interdenominational movement to disseminate a certain group of theological ideas [premillennialism and infallibility of scripture] and to force a division in the churches along the line of these ideas."[37] Both attacks had one clear objective—to try to keep Baptist traditionalists away from the Fundamentalist Federation by convincing them that it was a front for interdenominational evangelicalism.

These attacks put Laws on the defensive from the beginning. Trying to prevent traditionalist defections, he disingenuously asserted that "our Baptist Fundamentals movement has never had any connection whatever with the interdenominational movement."[38] As a matter of fact, the president of the Federation, J. C. Massee, was a premillennialist with strong connections to the Moody network and was probably chosen for that reason. For the next two years Laws tried in several articles to retain control over the word *fundamentalist*, but to no avail.

His opponents soon laid another charge against fundamentalism—that it was opposed to modern science because it was part of William Jennings Bryan's campaign against evolution. Bryan himself bore some responsibility for this association, for he claimed that evolution led to theological liberalism. Bryan had given his first major address against evolution in the fall of 1920, and because of his commitment to the politics of majoritarianism he insisted that taxpayers had the right to control what was taught in tax-supported schools. When he learned, early in 1922, that the Kentucky Baptist Board of Missions had called for statewide laws against teaching evolution in the public schools, this became the focus of his crusade.[39]

The convergence of three events in early 1922 made it easy for the secular press in the North to associate fundamentalism with antievolutionism and the South. The first bill proposing to outlaw evolution in the schools was introduced in Kentucky, and Bryan vigorously supported it. Bryan's involvement is probably the reason the *New York Times* covered the debate there. At the same time the word *fundamentalist* made its first appearance in the *Times* in a separate group of articles on the impending controversy in the Northern Baptist Convention. Then, within days of these articles, John Roach Straton, a prominent New York City pastor and member of the Fundamentalist Federation's executive committee, announced that he would ask the Federation to crusade against evolution in the schools.[40] For the *Times*, this sealed the connection between the denominational controversies and efforts to drive evolution out of the schools.

What the *Times* failed to report is that the Fundamentalist Federation decided against a public school campaign. Straton carried on his own independent crusade, but it was not part of the Federation's program. Federation president J. C. Massee sometimes talked as though he personally favored legislation against evolution, but when speaking for the Federation he was cool to the idea.[41] Darwinism never did become a significant issue in either the Northern Baptist fight or the Presbyterian controversy. Most denominational traditionalists believed that a crusade against evolution would hamper their efforts to fight liberalism.[42]

They were right about this but it was already too late. An informal alliance of cultural progressives—churchmen, educators, journalists, and social critics—convinced the general public that the effort to challenge liberalism in the denominations was linked to the campaign to outlaw evolution in the public schools. This made it easy to discredit "fundamentalism" as unscientific, medieval, and opposed to truth and liberty. The *Times* lined up with fundamentalism's critics from the very beginning. Not only did the newspaper give plenty of press to liberal attacks on fundamentalism, but its editorials started belittling "fundamentalists" just a few days after the word first appeared in its pages. In the first half of 1922, editorials in the *Times* unfailingly associated "fundamentalism" with the South, anti-Darwinism, ignorance, dogmatism, intolerance, authoritarianism, biblical literalism, premillennialism, and lack of social concern. Perhaps more important than what the editorials said was how they said it—every editorial was written with a wink and a smirk. "Fortunately," wrote one editor, fundamentalism has "so many bigots, and so different, that there is little danger of their being able to unite their forces." The bottom line for the editors of the *Times* was that fundamentalists might be dangerous if they were not quite so ridiculous.[43] It is clear that "fundamentalism" had lost the public relations battle long before the Scopes trial.

In May 1923 Laws's fading hopes of assembling an antimodernist coalition under the name *fundamentalism* were mortally wounded. Riley and other radicals split away from the Federation and formed the Baptist Bible Union (BBU). Riley's schismatics were mostly interdenominationals, leaving the Federation almost completely populated by traditionalists. Behind the division were the incompatibilities between traditionalists and those in the Moody network. Earlier the traditionalists of the Federation had vowed not to split the Northern Baptist Convention, but the Moody network militants were unafraid of schism. Moreover, the Federation had scrupulously avoided tainting itself with inerrancy, premillennialism, and antievolution, but this grated on Riley's sensibilities. So the BBU faith statement promoted inerrancy and premillennialism and opposed evolution. In desperation, Laws insisted that the BBU antimodernists were not true fundamentalists. But trying to say that Riley was not a fundamentalist was as doomed as the campaign against liberalism.[44]

Though conservatives had coined the word *fundamentalism*, by 1923 their opponents had defined it. The progressives developed the concept of fundamentalism as an integrated cultural phenomenon of militant opposition to modernism that had arisen in response to the postwar crisis. In a series of four long articles published toward the end of the year, the liberal churchman-turned-journalist Rollin Lynde Hartt argued that fundamentalism was a diverse alliance of premillennialists, denominational conservatives, and others moved to action by the shocks of the war. Their purpose was to wage "warfare upon modernism," which Hartt defined as higher criticism of the Bible, liberal theology, evolution, and progress in general.[45] Ever since Hartt's articles appeared, militancy against the modern has been ground zero in scholars' understandings of fundamentalism.[46]

By this time Laws was backing away from the battle against liberalism, urging conservatives to recommit themselves to the denomination. Ironically, the Fundamentalist Federation now found itself defending the denomination against the fundamentalist attacks of the BBU. Laws bitterly regretted that the word *fundamentalism* had gotten linked to the antievolution crusade, for he realized that this had crippled his efforts to combat liberalism. Massee's story is even more telling. Sick of the fighting, in 1925 he resigned the presidency of the Federation. He decried the militancy of the BBU and called for an armistice between the warring parties. And where did he go to escape militant fundamentalism? Straight into interdenominational evangelicalism. He spent the last part of his career in the Moody network as a traveling evangelist, Bible conference speaker, and author.[47]

AVOIDING THE TERM *FUNDAMENTALIST* IN THE PRESBYTERIAN BATTLES

While the term *fundamentalist* was failing to hold together a coalition of antimodernist Baptists, it was gaining even less traction among conservatives in the Presbyterian Church, U.S.A. The Presbyterian antimodernists did not try to organize a coalition until the summer of 1922, by which time the progressives were well on their way to gaining control of the term. As a result, none of the antimodernist partisans in the Presbyterian controversy organized themselves under the name *fundamentalist*. Instead, in the Presbyterian battles it was nearly always a term that liberals ascribed to their conservative opponents. Progressives within the church used it to portray conservatives as disloyal to Presbyterianism, while progressives outside the church used it to portray them as ignorant and mean-spirited.

The Presbyterian controversy flared to life in May 1922 when Harry Emerson Fosdick preached his inflammatory sermon "Shall the Fundamentalists Win?" Fosdick was a high-profile liberal Baptist who was minister of the First Presbyterian Church of New York City. He felt goaded to action by antimodernist agitation among China missionaries, by Bryan's campaign for antievolution legislation, and by the impending battle in the Northern Baptist Convention. Fosdick called for greater toleration, but he was spoiling for a fight. His sermon was immediately published in three religious periodicals, and John D. Rockefeller's publicist had it printed as a pamphlet and mailed to every Protestant minister in the nation.[48] Fosdick's sermon solidified the portrait of fundamentalism that was then being worked out by its critics in the pages of the *New York Times* and elsewhere. Fosdick's fundamentalists wanted to pass "laws against teaching modern biology." They demanded belief in an inerrant Bible "dictated by God." They also demanded belief in the premillennial return of Christ—a novel doctrine, one that caused its adherents to "sit still and do nothing and expect the world to grow worse and worse until He comes." To enforce conformity, fundamentalists wanted to set up "a doctrinal tribunal more rigid than the pope's."[49]

Fosdick's provocation was too much for Presbyterian traditionalists. The most famous response was Clarence Macartney's "Shall Unbelief Win?" published in July. Historian Bradley Longfield argues that Macartney, a prominent Philadelphia pastor, was the most representative figure in "Presbyterian fundamentalism."[50] It is therefore striking that Macartney refused to call himself a fundamentalist. Throughout his rejoinder to Fosdick, Macartney placed the word in scare quotes. He made it clear that he preferred to call himself and other antimodernists "conservatives" or "evangelicals." He was not going to call himself a fundamentalist because, like so many other denominational traditionalists, he thought "that in recent years the name has come to be applied to a group . . . whose chief emphasis is the premillennial reign of Christ."[51] Macartney explained that he disagreed with the premillennialists at several points, but he made sure not to offend them. He knew they might be helpful allies.

Macartney was not the only Presbyterian "fundamentalist" who avoided the term. J. Gresham Machen was the last great Princeton Seminary defender of Old School creedal Presbyterianism, and William Jennings Bryan was a politician and social gospel advocate. Both thought that "fundamentalists" were people in the Moody network, though they felt that it was imperative to build alliances with them. On rare occasions they were willing to be called fundamentalists but only for strategic reasons. Machen personally thought that the Moody network's dispensationalism was a serious theological error.⁵² Every time he allowed himself to be associated with "fundamentalism" he sounded as if he was being asked to eat a plate of worms. When the *New York Times* commissioned him to write a three-thousand-word article on fundamentalism, Machen began it with these words: "The term fundamentalism is distasteful to the present writer." Throughout the rest of the piece, he never again used the term.⁵³

The progressives were so successful at associating fundamentalism with controversy, ignorance, and divisive politics that Moody network Presbyterians also tended to avoid the word. Presbyterian evangelist William Biederwolf, a thoroughgoing premillennialist from the Moody network, declined to associate his beloved Winona Lake Bible Conference with fundamentalism: "She is the champion of no particular 'Ism' but 'Evangelism.'"⁵⁴ It was not unusual for speakers at Winona to criticize "fundamentalism" for its unloving and acrimonious self-righteousness.⁵⁵ No wonder that the liberals and their allies, having won the definitional battle, were ever ready to tar any conservative with the fundamentalist brush. This explains why Princeton Seminary president J. Ross Stevenson declared with a straight face that Machen and his allies wanted to swing Princeton "off to the extreme right wing so as to become an interdenominational Seminary for Bible School-premillennial-secession fundamentalism."⁵⁶ As Stevenson surely knew, Machen wanted nothing of the sort, but it speaks volumes that Stevenson thought this the best way to discredit Machen.

One reason the conservatives lost this battle was that they failed to attract much support from the interdenominational sector. Most of the Presbyterians who had strong ties to the Moody network—men like Biederwolf, Chafer, Robert McQuilkin of Columbia Bible School, and William Evans of World Bible Conferences—stayed clear of the fight. A few, like Charles Erdman and Billy Sunday, actually opposed the denominational antimodernist program. To make matters worse, many traditionalists like Macartney and Mark Matthews shifted to an inclusive position before the battle was over. In the end, only a small group led by Machen was militant enough to split the church.⁵⁷ The denomination obliged them by stripping them of their ministerial credentials. Once on their own, the Machenites themselves quickly split along traditionalist and premillennial lines, forming what became the Orthodox Presbyterian Church and the Bible Presbyterian Church.[58]

Looking back at both denominational battles, it is clear that the conservatives lost in part because they failed to build effective coalitions between traditionalists and interdenominationals. Among the Baptists, the strategy of uniting the two factions under the name *fundamentalist* failed when their opponents successfully linked the term with ignorance, intolerance, authoritarianism, premillennialism, antievolutionism, and the South. Progressives then successfully stuck the *fundamentalist* label on Presbyterian conservatives, thereby helping prevent formation of a stable coalition. In the end, only a few interdenominationals were militant enough to join the traditionalists in denominational fights. And when it became clear to the traditionalists that victory, even if possible, could be had only at the cost of major denominational schism, most of them quickly backed off. They had too much investment in the denominations to damage them. Little wonder the modernists were allowed to remain.[59]

WHO AGITATED FOR LAWS AGAINST EVOLUTION IN THE PUBLIC SCHOOLS?

In his 1994 history of creationism in America, George Webb concluded, "Anti-evolution nevertheless represented the issue of greatest interest to the interdenominational fundamentalists. . . . By the early 1920s the topic of evolution had emerged as the prime issue in the fundamentalist-modernist clash, with the fundamentalists' chief concern focused on the passage of state laws to prohibit the teaching of evolution in the public schools. Leaders of the movement accepted this redirection of focus with little difficulty."[60] This argument is significant for two reasons—first, because it represents the consensus view of historians; and second, because every part of it is false.[61] Antievolution was important to interdenominational evangelicalism but was never its main focus. Any perusal of its magazines, journals, and book lists from the mid-1920s will reveal that evolution was but one of many concerns, most of which were purely religious matters like missions, evangelism, Bible teaching, and

Christian living.⁶² More importantly, interdenominational evangelicalism did not agitate for laws against evolution. In that fight, it remained on the sidelines.

Webb was right to exclude denominational "fundamentalists" from his generalization. As noted earlier, most of those who opposed theological modernism in the denominations had little interest in a crusade against evolution. Among Northern Baptists, the Fundamentalist Federation refused to make the issue part of their agenda. Among the northern Presbyterians, Bryan could not even persuade his fellow conservatives to prohibit evolution in *Presbyterian* schools, much less enlist them in his public school campaign.⁶³ Neither Macartney nor Machen favored a public school crusade, and both declined Bryan's request to help him at the Scopes trial.⁶⁴

But neither did the Moody network join Bryan's campaign. In the years leading up to the First World War, interdenominational evangelicalism tolerated a wide range of views on the subject. Its leaders obviously rejected materialistic and antisupernaturalistic forms of evolution—to accept these was, as Charles Hodge had pointed out back in 1874, to embrace atheism.⁶⁵ But varying degrees of theistic evolution coexisted peacefully alongside more definitely antievolution sentiment.

Moody himself was relatively unconcerned about evolution.⁶⁶ He intentionally included both antievolutionists and theistic evolutionists in his vast circle of influence. This was Moody's modus operandi. He had an extraordinary ability to bring together religious leaders who opposed each other on questions related to holiness, dispensationalism, the timing of the millennium, and other matters.⁶⁷ By many accounts the lieutenant who meant most to him personally was Henry Drummond, a Scottish Presbyterian whose two books synthesizing evolution and evangelicalism were best sellers.⁶⁸ Many conservatives on both sides of the Atlantic criticized Drummond's first book, and some of Moody's American lieutenants—C. I. Scofield, William J. Erdman, and W. G. Moorehead—thought that Drummond had gotten far too liberal. But Moody's wife Emma loved Drummond's book, and its nature-spirit analogies were so like those that Moody used in his sermons that historian James Moore has wondered if Drummond might have gotten them from Moody. Despite pressure from his subordinates to exclude Drummond, Moody never ceased inviting him to take a prominent role in his enterprises.[69]

After Moody died in 1899, interdenominational evangelicalism continued for several years to promulgate a range of viewpoints on evolution. Out of ninety essays in *The Fundamentals*, edited and funded by men in the Moody network, only six devoted major attention to evolution. In approach they covered the waterfront from theistic evolution to antievolution. The final two volumes, edited by Moody's chief lieutenant Reuben A. Torrey, included no articles at all on evolution. He had respect for the work of scientists, even Darwin. He was open to the idea of evolution except in the case of human beings. He mainly objected to what he called the "philosophy of evolutionism," exemplified in the "might makes right" theories of German militarists. He continued to maintain publicly, even beyond the Scopes trial in 1925, that orthodox Christians could believe in certain forms of evolution.[70] Most importantly, nothing in *The Fundamentals*—even in the writings of the most vehement antievolutionists—hints at a political campaign against evolution. Historian Ronald Numbers has concluded that those in the Moody network "may not have liked evolution, but at this time few, if any, saw the necessity or the desirability of launching a crusade to eradicate it from the schools and churches of America."[71]

After World War I the attitudes toward evolution in interdenominational evangelicalism did harden in one respect—it became rare to encounter any form of theistic evolution. The unsophisticated thinkers in the movement simply dismissed all forms of evolution as atheistic. The more sophisticated thinkers in the movement were still willing *in private* to distinguish between materialistic and theistic forms of evolution, but they became reluctant to do so publicly.

This is illustrated in a post–Scopes trial exchange between James M. Gray, head of the Moody Bible Institute, and Torrey, who had recently become head of the Los Angeles Bible Institute. Gray's definitive public statement insisted that evolution, properly understood, left no room for God's creation or direction of the universe. Therefore one could not believe in evolution and still be a Christian. Gray chose to define away the possibility of a mediating position that allowed for transmutation of species due to God's direct miraculous intervention—what historian Jon

Roberts has called "progressive creationism."[72] Yet four months later, Gray's magazine published a long letter by Torrey, who wrote, "I can see how a man can believe thoroughly in the absolute infallibility of the Bible and still be an evolutionist of a certain type." In a private letter immediately afterward, Gray agreed that Torrey was right about this but warned his colleague that saying so might lead to misunderstandings among evangelical readers.[73]

It is no surprise that interdenominational evangelicalism's attitude toward evolution narrowed to straightforward opposition. Jon Roberts has discovered that by 1900 the great majority of orthodox Protestant thinkers in America—both inside and outside the Moody network—rejected evolution. They did so not because they were anti-intellectual, or because they were committed to old-fashioned ideas about science, but because they were committed to the idea that the Bible was God's complete revelation. They believed it to be straightforward in meaning and without error in content. Evolution seemed irreconcilable with this view of the Bible, and they had no motivation to revise their view of the Bible to accommodate evolution.[74] Their determination was reinforced by the fact that a number of prominent intellectuals in the era were using science—especially evolution—as a weapon to try to secularize society.[75]

Moreover, in the mid-1920s, evolutionary thinking itself was in disarray. Most scientists had rejected Darwin's mechanism of natural selection. Though they still believed in evolution, they were quite uncertain about how it worked.[76] In 1925 the *Sunday School Times* quoted, with undisguised satisfaction, two eminent British scientists admitting that belief in evolution required the kind of faith usually associated with religion. One of them, William Bateson, a leading figure in research on heredity, told the American Association for the Advancement of Science: "Though our faith in Evolution stands unshaken, we have no acceptable account of the origin of species. . . . Why may we not believe the old comfortable theory in the old way? Well, so we may, if by belief we mean faith, the foundation of things hoped for, the evidence of 'things not seen.'"[77] After the 1940s, the neo-Darwinian synthesis would settle the issue of how evolution worked.[78] But given the scientific uncertainty of the 1920s it is little wonder that conservative Protestants regarded evolution as an unproven hypothesis advanced by scientists as a materialistic alternative to Christianity.

One of the most enduring myths of the historical writing on fundamentalism is that the interdenominational network translated its opposition to evolution into a political crusade. But there is a world of difference between opposing evolution as a set of ideas and trying to pass laws removing evolution from the public schools. Examples of leaders of interdenominational evangelicalism politicizing the evolution issue are so scarce that historians time and again have had to return to William Bell Riley for their evidence.[79] But Riley was an exception. Cast a wider net, and the case for the Moody network participating in the political campaign falls apart.

Take, for example, the curious incident, as Conan Doyle once put it, of the two most important periodicals of the Moody network, the *Sunday School Times* (*SST*) and the *Moody Bible Institute Monthly*. Both, far more than Riley, had enormous influence in the movement, functioning as arbiters of which leaders and parachurch organizations were "in" the network and which were not. The curious incident is this: between the beginning of Bryan's focus on school legislation in January 1922 and the Scopes trial in July 1925, neither periodical called its readers to political action against evolution. They published no editorials favoring legislation, no encouragements to petition legislators, no heroic profiles of antievolution political campaigns, and no support for the few who wanted to go the political route. While both periodicals were friendly to Bryan and publicized his books, both went out of their way to avoid discussing the political part of his program.

If the Moody network were engaged in a political crusade against evolution, one would at least expect the network's press to give significant coverage to the Butler bill, which proposed to outlaw evolution in Tennessee public schools. Yet between January and May 1925, when Bryan was barnstorming for the bill and Tennesseans were debating it, the weekly *SST* never mentioned it once. A reader in this period would have learned more about what was happening in China than in Tennessee.

Instead of supporting the Tennessee antievolution legislation, the *SST* in March 1925 launched a nine-week series by Howard A. Kelly.

Kelly was an internationally prominent surgeon and medical researcher who had long been involved in the Moody network. The secular press often called him a "fundamentalist," but he never used the term of himself. Early in his career he had been active in political causes, but after 1900 he felt that Christians should refrain from promoting legislation.[80] Editor Charles G. Trumbull promoted the series as an exposition of how "a really scientific man" can still be a Bible-believing Christian. Midway through the series Kelly briefly discussed evolution, reasoning that purely materialistic explanations of the origin and development of life strained credulity far more than the Bible's explanation. Kelly briefly affirmed his belief in God's special direct creation of humanity, though he employed a developmental framework for understanding God's purposive work in nature.

Nothing in the series suggested that Christians should crusade against evolution. In fact Trumbull accompanied Kelly's first article with a reminder to readers that it was "disastrous" for Christians to fight "unnecessary battles." Instead, "Christ asks us to let him fight all our battles for us." This was a coded exhortation, well understood in the Moody network at the time, to avoid the temptation of worldly politics. Christ would defeat Satan, Trumbull reminded his readers; the Christian's duty was simply to give witness to the truth. The Kelly series was a big hit with readers. The *SST*'s circulation office was swamped with requests for new subscriptions—29,706 in just a nine-week period. Clearly a huge swath of the evangelical public welcomed a nonconfrontational approach to bridging whatever gap existed between Christianity and science.[81]

The story of James M. Gray and the *Moody Bible Institute Monthly* is similar. In 1925 the February, March, and April issues said not a word about Bryan's crusade or the debates taking place in Tennessee. A March editorial obliquely supported the idea of opposing evolution in public schools but said nothing about how this should be done.[82] In May Gray quoted a call for Christians to give up on the public schools and build their own schools—clearly an alternative to legislation. Gray followed the quotation by noting the practical difficulties of this course of action but allowed that it might one day become necessary.[83]

In the June issue Gray finally turned his attention to the question of evolution in the public schools. The magazine's first-ever news report on Tennessee was near the back of this issue—a short, neutrally written report that Governor Austin Peay had signed the Butler bill.[84] Two feature articles addressed evolution in the schools, but neither advocated legislation. Clara Hall urged parents to monitor the books their children were assigned to read; M. H. Duncan called for a national association of Christian educators to pressure school superintendents to remove anti-Christian teaching from the schools.[85] Gray himself wrote three editorials on the subject. In the first he opposed an Oregon bill that would have foreclosed the Christian school option by requiring all children to attend public schools. The second was mainly a long quotation from a Tennessee Methodist bishop critical of Peay for signing the Butler bill, followed by Gray's comment that of the two of them the governor was "the truer witness for God." The third editorial, just 124 words long, quoted Duncan's article and then tersely concluded, "Governor Peay and the legislature of Tennessee have set them a good example, let them rally to the standard." Who Gray meant by "them," and what he meant by "rally to the standard," are so unclear that the ambiguity was probably intentional.[86] The July issue, which went to press before the Scopes trial began, had one article saying that "materialistic evolutionary thinking" could be eliminated by recruiting more Christian teachers for public schools—yet another alternative to legislation.[87]

In July 1925 the Scopes trial was front-page news for secular newspapers, but the *SST* gave it hardly any coverage. The *SST* printed no reports on the courtroom drama unfolding in Dayton, Tennessee, though it did promise an article by Bryan reflecting on the trial afterwards. Editor Trumbull was more interested in the annual Keswick, England, summer conference than in the Dayton publicity stunt, so he sailed for Europe before the trial ended. When Bryan unexpectedly died a week after the trial, the *SST*'s obituary lauded him for his steadfast faith and his opposition to evolution but tiptoed around his campaign to outlaw evolution. It made but one minor reference to the Scopes trial and never suggested that readers should take up that fight.[88]

As for Gray, he declined Bryan's invitation to come to Dayton, and he published no reports on the trial.[89] However, the cover of his August issue reproduced a passage from a Southern Baptist declaration. It protested antireligious teaching in the schools but rejected a legislated solution. In this issue Gray published his own definitive statement against evolution, and it never mentioned Bryan, the public schools, or anything about politics. It was an ideological manifesto, not a call to arms.[90] Finally, in September editorials, Gray registered his opposition to Bryan's political strategy. "Had our counsel been sought [by Bryan] and taken in advance, the fight would not have occurred in the place and under the circumstances in which it did." Remarkably, Gray spurned Bryan to side with the Roman Catholics. Gray wrote, "We think the editor of *The Catholic Encyclopedia* stated the case as satisfactorily as we have seen it. 'We are not in favor of making laws against the teaching of evolution if it be taught properly.'" By "properly" Gray meant two things—teaching evolution as a hypothesis, and teaching it in a way that did not undermine Christian belief.[91]

While the two most important periodicals of interdenominational evangelicalism were refusing to support Bryan's political campaign against evolution in the schools, William Bell Riley was of course trying to draw the movement into the fight. Most histories suggest that he was successful, but in fact his effort sputtered and died. After the WCFA failed to mobilize the Moody network to fight liberalism in the denominations, Riley tried in 1922 and 1923 to use it to build support for the Bryan crusade. Yet even though Bryan was then at full gallop in his quixotic charge, and even though this was two years before the Scopes trial, the WCFA could build no national constituency around the evolution issue. Its annual meetings degenerated into mere theater, symbolized by the time J. Frank Norris, the renegade Southern Baptist, commandeered the 1923 meeting to stage mock trials of professors at Texas colleges.[92] In the years thereafter Riley sustained the illusion that the WCFA was a national movement by holding his annual conventions at a large urban church with a sympathetic pastor. Riley would bring in a big-name speaker, the local pastor would drum up a crowd, and then Riley would send inflated accounts to Moody network magazines.[93] But in reality Riley's attempt to draw the Moody network into evolution politics diminished his national influence and killed the WCFA. It was, wrote Trollinger, the "final nail in the WCFA's coffin."[94]

The noninvolvement of the Moody network's major periodicals and the demise of the WCFA show that there was little support in interdenominational evangelicalism for a political campaign against evolution in the schools. In addition to the theological concern voiced by Trumbull that these were spiritual battles best left to God, there were practical reasons. The survival of the Moody network's parachurch organizations depended on appealing to a broad spectrum of evangelicals. This meant the organizations had to focus on the things everyone agreed on—evangelism, missions, Bible teaching, prayer, and the like. They usually avoided controversial subjects because these tended to divide their constituents and shrink their support base. This was especially true of politics. The leaders of interdenominational evangelicalism were often willing to comment on politics, but they did not organize for political action.[95] The movement's later politicization originated in the 1930s with growing opposition to New Deal "collectivism" and "statism" and the rising conviction that communism was a real and present danger.[96]

Since attempts to outlaw evolution in the schools received little support from either the northern denominational traditionalists or the Moody network, who then did support them? For decades, scholarship focused on the state level has found that Bryan's national campaign was far less important than locally initiated statewide campaigns. Historian Michael Lienesch recently concluded that the findings of this scholarship still stand—the political campaigns to outlaw evolution in the schools were "home grown, consisting primarily of local preachers leading small but dedicated groups of statewide activists."[97]

The campaigns for antievolution legislation were more widespread and more successful in the South—where the Moody network had little strength.[98] In the South, church life and church political influence were controlled by the state Baptist conventions, the Methodist Episcopal Church (South), and the Presbyterian Church in the United States. They were suspicious of the Moody network because of its base in the urban North, and they actively opposed the spread of its premillennialism and interdenominationalism into their churches.[99] Yet the southern denominational leaders who opposed the encroachments of the Moody network were the people who led the campaigns against evolution in their states. The first successful antievolution law, an Oklahoma prohibition against evolution in textbooks, was initiated by the state's Southern Baptist General Session. (It was passed without Bryan even knowing about it.) The successful citizens' initiative in Arkansas was begun by officials of the state's Southern Baptist convention. The unsuccessful effort in North Carolina was championed by key leaders of the Presbyterian Church. The Moody network was not involved in these contests, and participation of outsiders like Bryan and Riley was incidental.[100]

The primary context for these campaigns was resistance to Progressive educational reforms. All over the nation, Progressives' faith in credentialed experts and centralization was shifting authority in the public schools away from local districts to the state level. This affected everything from teacher credentialing to textbooks to curriculum. In addition, the spread of public high schools increased the years children spent in public school systems and introduced them to more controversial subjects. With school authority now at the state level, disagreements that had previously been settled in local districts now had to be fought out in state legislatures. These changes aroused widespread popular resistance, and not just in the South. Conservative reformers around the country sought legislation restricting the teaching of foreign languages, weeding out political radicalism among teachers, ensuring that history books were sufficiently patriotic and included ethnic Americans, and requiring religious instruction in the schools.[101] In at least two cases—Oklahoma and Tennessee—Progressive governors signed antievolution laws as a trade-off to get the votes they needed for Progressive educational reforms.[102]

The Tennessee law that brought us the Scopes trial illustrates all these themes. Charles Israel's recent history of the politics behind the Butler Act explains that tensions between religion and public education in Tennessee stretched back to Reconstruction. Resentment against federal intrusion and New England missionary teachers had generated stiff resistance to public education. The impasse was finally broken by the "home rule compromise"—local religious and political leaders dropped their opposition to public schools in exchange for a guarantee that the schools would remain under local control. This would ensure that the schools would embody local religious, moral, and segregationist racial sentiments.[103]

But the home rule compromise fell apart when Progressive educational reforms moved control of schools to the state level. Since local school boards could no longer ensure the place of religion in public schools, Tennessee religious leaders pressured the state legislature to act. The first step, which became state law in 1915, was to put religion into the schools by requiring daily Bible reading.[104] The next step was to keep atheism out by prohibiting the teaching of evolution. Israel shows how "the same arguments of majority rule, citizens' rights, and the Christian nation that had been effective in justifying daily Bible reading were quickly employed and equally successful in the campaign to ban the teaching of evolution in Tennessee schools."[105]

Bryan did not instigate this southern crusade against evolution. His contribution was to rally the troops that had already assembled, and in the South he was the perfect man for the job. Every historian has noted that Bryan does not fit a "fundamentalist" profile. He was a postmillennialist social gospeler with few connections to the Moody network. Worse than that, he was a Democrat. As Gray noted in his obituary of Bryan, "We never voted for him for President. His politics were not ours."[106] Gray, like most other Moody network leaders, was a dependable Republican on Election Day. But the Tennessee evangelicals who supported the Butler bill were longtime Bryan Democrats.[107] The idea for laws against evolution in the public schools originated with Kentucky Baptists and found most of its support among Bryan's natural constituency—southern white evangelicals.[108] This, plus southern resistance to Yankee-flavored Progressive educational reforms, explains why only southern states passed laws against evolution. The supplementary efforts of outsiders like Riley and Sunday may have helped the local activists wrap up their legislative victories, but the campaign itself was a native plant, rooted in native soil.

In the final analysis, there is little reason to categorize the campaign against evolution in the schools as part of the so-called "fundamentalist-modernist controversies," for there is no good reason to classify its southern evangelical sponsors as "fundamentalist." Historian Mary Beth Swetnam Mathews has recently found that northern newspapers and magazines invented this idea. They consistently claimed that the South was fundamentalist, writes Matthews, "without regard for evidence—statistical or theological." Their interpretation reflected the northern cultural elite's disinclination to sort out which groups were reacting against which forms of modernity and why they were doing so. Since the northern press aligned itself with critics of these groups, it was simpler and more polemically useful to lump them all together and affix a pejorative label.[109]

FOUR MYTHS RECONSIDERED

Since interdenominational evangelicalism was not deeply involved in the three major battles of the so-called "fundamentalist-modernist" controversies, some other myths about the movement need reconsideration or retirement. First is the myth that after the defeats of the 1920s the movement retreated to the cultural periphery to build a network of independent institutions. A second is that the Moody network embarked on a new wave of separate institution building after their supposed defeats. A third myth, usually implicit, is that the entire Moody network was drawn into the battles of the 1920s. And a fourth is that one of the movement's goals was to retain Victorian manners and morals, especially the ideology of separate spheres for men and women.

The glaring problem with the first myth is that the movement's network of independent institutions was well in place, was thriving, and had a clear sense of group identity *before* the onset of the controversies. The three institutional legs of the Moody network were Bible institutes, independent missionary organizations, and large autonomous urban churches. By 1920 the Moody network had established at least forty interdenominational Bible institutes. It also had organized around forty interdenominational missionary agencies.[110] The Bible institutes gave the Moody network an alternative institutional structure that made denominations unnecessary and gave the network little reason to get involved in denominational controversies. The interdenominational missionary agencies—with strong connections to the Bible institutes—gave greater flexibility and freedom to the network's intense commitment to overseas evangelism.

Interdenominational evangelicalism's network of large urban churches was also well established by 1920. Moody was the pioneer—in 1863 he founded the nondenominational Illinois Street Church (now Moody Memorial) in Chicago. High-profile preachers who followed this pattern included A. J. Gordon and his Clarendon Street Church in Boston (1869), C. I. Scofield and his First Congregational (now Scofield Memorial) Church in Dallas (1882), A. T. Pierson and his Bethany Tabernacle in Philadelphia (1883), and Reuben Torrey and his People's Church in Minneapolis (1886). A. B. Simpson was especially influential. Inspired by Moody and dissatisfied with the suffocating class consciousness of the prestigious New York City Presbyterian church he pastored, Simpson resigned and in 1882 started an independent "Gospel Tabernacle" in a less elite section of the city. This church directly and indirectly begot gospel tabernacles in Buffalo, Chicago, Detroit, Fort Wayne, Minneapolis, Toronto, and many other cities in the United States and Canada.[111]

Reaction against liberalism in the denominations was but a minor reason for the institutional growth of interdenominational evangelicalism.[112] The primary motivation was a desire to be free of denominational constraints. These constraints included the denominations' persistent sectarianism, their resistance to dispensationalism, and their reluctance to adopt new programs and patterns in evangelism and education. Internationally, the interdenominationals deviated from denominational practices by sending missionaries to the interior regions of Asia and Africa, sending them with practical rather than theological training, and relying on "faith" principles for fund-raising—which meant sending missionaries out before all their support money had been raised. Domestically the Moody network emphasized itinerant evangelism, practical training for lay workers, and new kinds of specialized missions, such as those to American Jews. The denominations balked at all these innovations. While the denominations were becoming increasingly centralized, bureaucratic, and reliant on experts, the interdenominational evangelicals were building a decentralized entrepreneurial movement reliant on ordinary laypeople. This was Moody's style, 100 percent. While denominational officials were extending their control over what had been semiautonomous denominational ministries, Moody was urging and inspiring scores of leaders to start independent organizations over which he had no control at all.[113]

Interdenominational evangelicalism built its institutional network in response to perceived need, not in reaction to perceived threat. It tried to work with the denominations but was often rebuffed. For example, the independent mission agencies initially cooperated with the denominational agencies in the Foreign Missions Conference of North America. But in 1911 the denominational agencies unilaterally stripped the independents of membership. This forced the independents to create their own organization, the Interdenominational Foreign Mission Association.[114] Denominational officials also resented Bible institutes and resisted their graduates being hired as pastors.[115] One of the untold stories of the fundamentalist-modernist controversies is how often denominational bureaucrats enforced denominational loyalty by pushing out conservatives who supported the interdenominational parachurch organizations.[116]

There is no hard evidence that the controversies of the 1920s prompted the Moody network to launch a new wave of institution building. By my count, in the fifteen-year period between 1910 and 1924, interdenominational evangelicals founded approximately twenty-eight new Bible institutes. During the fifteen years after the controversies, from 1925 through 1939, they added approximately twenty-eight more Bible institutes.[117] This suggests that the dynamics of institutional growth in the Moody network were largely independent of the controversies and that there was a good deal more continuity between the interdenominational evangelicalism of 1900 and that of 1930 than we have been inclined to think.

Another myth, usually assumed but seldom stated, is that the entire Moody network was sucked into the controversies of the 1920s. Moody himself avoided controversy and counted many liberals as friends, but his younger followers, so the story goes, became militant opponents of modernism. Reuben Torrey is often cited as an example of this change, for he had once written, "We are constantly told in our day that we ought not to attack error but simply teach the truth. This is the method of the coward and trimmer."[118] But it is not quite so obvious that Torrey should be categorized as a militant antimodernist. He did not participate in any of the three major "fundamentalist" battles of the 1920s, nor did he encourage other evangelicals to do so.[119] And he devoted very little effort to attacking modernism. Perhaps two or three of his large body of publications can fairly be categorized as polemical. The majority of his books, before and after the war, are positive statements of Christian doctrine written in the same moderate tone as *The Fundamentals*.[120]

Likewise, recent studies of four major organizational sectors within the Moody network—Bible institutes, foreign missions, missions to Jews, and summer Bible conferences—have found little evidence that its institutions were either involved in the controversies of the 1920s or possessed by the spirit of militant antimodernism. Virginia Brereton's study of Bible institutes shows that militant antimodernism never found a home there. The Bible institutes typically took moderate positions and avoided disputation. They reined in extremists, downplayed theological and ecclesiastical differences, and damped down controversialism. They were against liberal theology, but they stayed out of the denominational battles because their workers and constituents could be found on both sides of the fights. Brereton characterized the period from 1915 to 1930 as one of expansion and consolidation, not one of fights against modernism. The only effect of the battles of the 1920s seems to have been the appearance of doctrinal statements. These were not attacks on modernism but defensive boundary-defining moves designed to reassure themselves and their constituencies that their schools were safe from liberalism.[121]

Edwin Frizen's history of the Interdenominational Foreign Mission Association found that its turning points came in 1911, when the Moody network missions were excluded from the Foreign Missions Conference of North America, and in the early 1940s, when its membership increased and its bureaucracy expanded. The events of the mid-1920s registered little impact. A decade-by-decade study of its main concerns turned up no attacks on denominations or liberal theology. The only noteworthy artifacts of the controversies were a 1932 leaflet highlighting differences between the IFMA and the liberal Layman's Foreign Mission Inquiry, and a 1937 board discussion reaffirming the policy of noncooperation with the Foreign Missions Conference that had been forced on them a quarter century earlier.[122]

One of the signature ideas of dispensational premillennialism was that the Jews were still God's chosen people and would, in the end times, convert to Christianity in large numbers. Many dispensationalists therefore launched ministries to evangelize Jews. Yaakov Ariel's study of these organizations found that they expanded from just one in 1880 to at least forty-five by 1920. The largest and most influential was the interdenominational Chicago Hebrew Mission, founded—of course—by Moody protégés. Some of the missions were independent and others were sponsored by denominations, but all were founded by dispensationalists. As dispensationalism became less welcome in the major denominations, more and more of the missions gravitated into the parachurch world of interdenominational evangelicalism. This process began well before the controversies of the 1920s. The controversies themselves do not seem to have made the missions more militantly antimodernist; in fact, they hardly registered at all. Ariel described the interval from 1920 to 1960 as a "quiet" period, characterized by growth, increasing professionalism, and greater respectability. There was a brief spate of criticism of liberalism during the most heated part of the controversies, but this was because denominational liberals were withdrawing support for Jewish evangelism, not because the missions were becoming more militant.[123]

Another key Moody network institution was the summer Bible conference, dozens of which were scattered all over the country. The most important of them was Winona Lake in northern Indiana. A study of the period 1895 through 1968 found that in the 1920s and 1930s there was little militant antimodernism preached from its platforms. Its directors carefully distanced themselves from militancy: "Others may contend with a belligerent and unkindly spirit; Winona is content with a positive message." Like the Bible institutes, Winona Lake refined its statement of faith to keep theological liberals off the board of directors and to keep overtly liberal doctrines from being preached at the conference. But it did not require its speakers to affirm the statement of faith, and it knowingly invited many speakers whose beliefs diverged from the statement. Moreover, the conference never encouraged attendees to separate from the mainline denominations. Instead it sponsored denominational rallies designed to encourage those who preferred to retain their mainline membership.[124]

Generally, individuals who led the parachurch institutions also stayed out of the controversies. Most heads of the Bible institutes—Gray, Torrey, McQuilkin, Nathan R. Wood of Gordon College, L. E. Maxwell of Prairie Bible Institute, John Brown of John E. Brown College—were opposed to modernism but refrained from militancy.[125] Likewise, the movement's key missionary leaders—Robert Hall Glover, Henry W. Frost, and Joseph A. Davis are typical—participated in no fundamentalist battles. When Lewis Sperry Chafer was ready to start his interdenominational seminary in 1924, he located it in the South, in part to stay out of the northern controversies.[126]

A final myth is that "fundamentalists" tried to preserve Victorian manners and morals, notably the ideology of separate spheres for men and women.[127] One theoretical problem with the historiography making this argument is that it relies on pronouncements about what women's role should be, instead of looking at what women in the movement were actually doing. Another problem is that most studies fail to compare "fundamentalism" to mainline Protestantism at the time. More recent work on the Moody network has found that its imperative to evangelize combined with its entrepreneurial structure unintentionally gave women more, and more varied, opportunities for public ministry than in the mainline Protestant world.[128] W. Cameron Townsend, for example, who founded the Summer Institute of Linguistics in 1934, did not have to convince an entire tradition-bound denominational bureaucracy that women without men could live with indigenous people and do translation work. Once the women themselves convinced him—it took three years—the doors at SIL opened wide.[129]

No part of George Marsden's reconstruction of fundamentalism has proven more enduring than his definition. At the time he was writing the phrase "militant anti-modernism," Islamist revolutionaries were consolidating their first major victory in Iran. To Western intellectuals, the forces unleashed in that revolution were clearly antimodernist and undeniably militant, and so the concept of "global fundamentalism" was born. Throw in the concurrent emergence of America's Religious Right, and Marsden's measured and nuanced reconstruction of the 1920s got caught in a backdraft of politicized reinterpretation. The antimodernists of the 1920s were transformed into the first assault wave in the culture wars of the 1980s. Beaten back temporarily, so the story goes, they retreated and regrouped until ready to mount another offensive.

But if militant antimodernism—as exemplified by the battles of the 1920s—is the hallmark of fundamentalism, then it makes little sense to call the Moody network "fundamentalist" before, during, or after those controversies. The battles of the 1920s were fought not by a movement but by three different groups who shared some ideas and a very small number of common personnel. This fundamentalism was a "movement" only in the eyes of liberal churchmen and their allies and in the wishful thinking of a handful of conservatives. Interdenominational evangelicalism, by contrast, was a genuine popular movement, institutionally grounded in its network of parachurch organizations and autonomous urban churches. It was antimodernist in its beliefs but not militant in behavior.

If there was an American fundamentalism after 1925—and by that I mean a single phenomenon dedicated to militant antimodernism—it was to be found in the small groups of churches that split off from the northern denominations to form new denominations.[130] Having little or nothing in the way of denominational infrastructure, many of these militants attached themselves to the Moody network, which shared their theology if not their militancy. For a while these two groups lived together in an uneasy alliance, with obvious fissures appearing throughout the 1930s. One example: in 1925 Wheaton College hired a young follower of Machen, J. Oliver Buswell Jr., to be president. Though Buswell modernized the academic program, upgraded faculty quality, and saw enrollment increase substantially, his militancy split the college's church and progressively soured relations with multiple other institutions in the Moody network. After one controversy too many, the trustees summarily fired him in 1940, replacing him with V. Raymond Edman—a Moody network man and one of the most nonmilitant, noncontroversial leaders in all of interdenominational evangelicalism.[131]

It was inevitable that these fissures would result in schism between the Moody network and the militant separatists. Institutionally this began in the early 1940s with the formation of two competing umbrella organizations—the militant American Council of Christian Churches and the nonmilitant National Association of Evangelicals. Symbolically the separation was completed when Billy Graham refused the sponsorship of militants for his 1957 New York Crusade.[132] Though Graham was a southerner, his Christianity was formed by the Moody network. As a result he was not in the least militant and was never much of an antimodernist. He always said that Dwight L. Moody was the evangelist he most admired. This is not surprising, for Moody had given his movement a burning desire to spread the gospel combined with a genial "all-things-to-all-people" approach, both of which became Graham signatures. Graham is often interpreted as one who helped produce a "new evangelicalism" that reformed militant fundamentalism. But he was in fact the product of an older "new evangelicalism"—the interdenominational evangelicalism that Moody had brought into being before the close of the nineteenth century.

NOTES

My deepest thanks to Peggy Bendroth, Joel Carpenter, Barry Hankins, Ron Numbers, Rick Ostrander, and Grant Wacker for their helpful comments on this and earlier versions of this chapter.

1. George M. Marsden, *Fundamentalism and American Culture*, 2nd ed. (1980; repr., New York: Oxford University Press, 2006); Benjamin Schwarz, "New and Noteworthy," *Atlantic Monthly*, April 2003, 89–92.

2. Robert Moats Miller, "A Compleat (Almost) Guide through the Forest of Fundamentalism," *Reviews in American History* 9 (September 1981): 392–97.

3. Marsden, *Fundamentalism and American Culture*, 4.

4. William R. Hutchison, *The Modernist Impulse in American Protestantism* (Cambridge, MA: Harvard University Press, 1976), 2–4; W. Clark Gilpin, "Redeeming Modernity: Christian Theology in Modern America," in *American Christianities: A History of Dominance and Diversity*, ed. Catherine A. Brekus and W. Clark Gilpin (Chapel Hill: University of North Carolina Press, 2011), 155–82. Liberalism is an older and broader tradition than modernism—see Leigh Eric Schmidt and Sally M. Promey, eds., *American Religious Liberalism* (Bloomington: Indiana University Press, 2012)—but Protestant modernism was, according to Hutchison, "central to the liberal movement" in the years 1870–1930 (2). Since this is the period under study here, I use the terms *modernism* and *liberalism* interchangeably.

5. Ernest R. Sandeen, *Roots of Fundamentalism: British and American Millenarianism 1800–1930* (Chicago: University of Chicago Press, 1970), xvii–xviii, 246, 248, 256, 260, 263, 266–69.

6. Marsden, *Fundamentalism and American Culture*, 4, 164, 193–95, 205, 231–35; quotations on 164 and 4.

7. Joel A. Carpenter, *Revive Us Again: The Reawakening of American Fundamentalism* (New York: Oxford University Press, 1997), 6–8, 64–69; quotations on 6, 7, and 8.

8. Sandeen, *Roots of Fundamentalism*, xvii–xx; Marsden, *Fundamentalism and American Culture*, 32–39; Carpenter, *Revive Us Again*, 6.

9. Virginia Lieson Brereton, *Training God's Army: The American Bible School, 1880–1940* (Bloomington: Indiana University Press, 1990), 55–84.

10. William R. Glass, *Strangers in Zion: Fundamentalists in the South, 1900–1950* (Macon, GA: Mercer University Press, 2001), 81–133; B. Dwain Waldrep, "Lewis Sperry Chafer and the Roots of Nondenominational Fundamentalism in the South," *Journal of Southern History* 73, no. 4 (November 2007): 807–36.

11. Ian S. Rennie, "Fundamentalism and the Varieties of North Atlantic Evangelicalism," in *Evangelicalism: Comparative Studies of Popular Protestantism in North America, the British Isles, and Beyond, 1700–1990*, ed. Mark A. Noll, David Bebbington, and George A. Rawlyk (New York: Oxford University Press, 1994), 333–50; D. Bruce Hindmarsh, "The Winnipeg Fundamentalist Network, 1910–1940: The Roots of Transdenominational Evangelicalism in Manitoba and Saskatchewan," in *Aspects of the Canadian Evangelical Experience*, ed. G. A. Rawlyk (Montreal: McGill-Queen's University Press, 1997), 303–19; Robert K. Burkinshaw, "Conservative Evangelicalism in the Twentieth-Century 'West': British Columbia and the United States," in *Amazing Grace: Evangelicalism in Australia, Britain, Canada, and the United States*, ed. George A. Rawlyk and Mark A. Noll (Montreal: McGill-Queen's University Press, 1994), 317–48.

12. Sandeen's was the first focused scholarly attempt to describe this movement. He called it the millenarian movement, a name that had the effect of reducing its complexity to a single one of its several distinguishing characteristics. Marsden strongly criticized Sandeen for this—see George Marsden, "Defining Fundamentalism," *Christian Scholar's Review* 1, no. 2 (Winter 1971): 141–51; and Ernest R. Sandeen, "Defining Fundamentalism: A Reply to Professor Marsden," *Christian Scholar's Review* 1, no. 3 (Spring 1971): 227–33. Marsden used various terms, loosely, when he wanted to refer to this movement—*conservative evangelicals, protofundamentalists*, and often, despite his criticism of Sandeen, *premillennialists*. For examples, see Marsden, *Fundamentalism and American Culture*, 141–43. But since Marsden was more interested in ideas than institutions, the movement itself frequently dropped out of sight in his narrative. Carpenter was closer to the mark when he described the movement in its early days as an "in-

terdenominational revivalist network," but the term has not exactly caught on (*Revive Us Again*, 6).

13. Marsden, *Fundamentalism and American Culture*, 169. See also Waldrep, "Lewis Sperry Chafer," 818–19.

14. Marsden, *Fundamentalism and American Culture*, 261 n. 4.

15. Lyle W. Dorsett, *A Passion for Souls: The Life of D. L. Moody* (Chicago: Moody Press, 1997), 410–11.

16. Quoted in Waldrep, "Lewis Sperry Chafer," 827.

17. Marsden, *Fundamentalism and American Culture*, 165.

18. Norman F. Furniss, *The Fundamentalist Controversy, 1918–1931* (New Haven, CT: Yale University Press, 1954), 105.

19. D. G. Hart, *Defending the Faith: J. Gresham Machen and the Crisis of Conservative Protestantism* (Baltimore: Johns Hopkins University Press), 128.

20. Glenn T. Miller, *Piety and Profession: American Protestant Theological Education, 1870–1970* (Grand Rapids, MI: Eerdmans, 2007), 407–37.

21. Ibid., 411.

22. "Dr. Riley's Retirement from the School Committee," *Christian Fundamentals in Church and School*, July–September 1920, 399. See also C. Allyn Russell, *Voices of American Fundamentalism: Seven Biographical Studies* (Philadelphia: Westminster Press, 1976), 120–21, 248 n. 50.

23. Hart, *Defending the Faith*, 64, 162–65.

24. Clarence E. Macartney, "Shall Unbelief Win? An Answer to Dr. Fosdick," part 1, *Presbyterian*, July 13, 1922, part 2, *Presbyterian*, July 20, 1922, republished as a pamphlet in the series For the Faith (Philadelphia: Wilbur Hanf, n.d.).

25. Marsden, *Fundamentalism and American Culture*, 117.

26. Bradley J. Longfield, *The Presbyterian Controversy: Fundamentalists, Modernists, and Moderates* (New York: Oxford University Press, 1991), 100, 152.

27. Ibid., 129, 149, 153.

28. Marsden, *Fundamentalism and American Culture*, 39.

29. Brereton, *Training God's Army*, 139–47.

30. Sandeen, *Roots of Fundamentalism*, 240–43.

31. *The Fundamentals: A Testimony to the Truth*, 12 vols. (Chicago: Testimony Publishing, n.d. [1910–15]).

32. William Vance Trollinger Jr., *God's Empire: William Bell Riley and Midwestern Fundamentalism* (Madison: University of Wisconsin Press, 1990), 37–41, 163.

33. The call to create a Baptist Conference on Fundamentals is reprinted in the introduction to *Baptist Fundamentals: Being Addresses Delivered at the Pre-Convention Conference at Buffalo, June 21 and 22, 1920* (Philadelphia: Judson Press, 1920). Laws's explanation of why he coined the term *fundamentalist* is in

Curtis Lee Laws, "Convention Side Lights," *Watchman-Examiner*, July 1, 1920, 834–35.

34. Marsden, *Fundamentalism and American Culture*, 152, 158; Michael Lienesch, *In the Beginning: Fundamentalism, the Scopes Trial, and the Making of the Antievolution Movement* (Chapel Hill: University of North Carolina Press, 2007), 34–35.

35. Trollinger, *God's Empire*, 41–44, quotations on 41 and 44.

36. William McCarrell to V. Raymond Edman, June 6, 1949, Trustees meetings files, box 1, Wheaton College Archives, Wheaton, IL.

37. Obadiah Holmes, "The Threat of Millennialism," *Christian Century*, April 28, 1921, 10–13, and unsigned editorial, "We Are on the March," *Baptist*, July 9, 1921, 717, both quoted in Marsden, *Fundamentalism and American Culture*, 168; see also 166. *Chiliasm* is a synonym for *millennialism* that uses the Greek root word instead of the Latin root word for the number 1,000.

38. [Curtis Lee Laws], "*The Baptist* on the Rampage," *Watchman-Examiner*, August 4, 1921, 973–74, quoted in Marsden, *Fundamentalism and American Culture*, 169.

39. William Jennings Bryan, "God and Evolution," *New York Times*, February 26, 1922, Special Features Section, 1, 11 (online archives); Michael Kazin, *A Godly Hero: The Life of William Jennings Bryan* (New York: Knopf, 2006), 271–77; Willard B. Gatewood Jr., *Preachers, Pedagogues and Politicians: The Evolution Controversy in North Carolina, 1920–27* (Chapel Hill: University of North Carolina Press, 1966), 56–57; Edward J. Larson, *Summer for the Gods: The Scopes Trial and America's Continuing Debate over Science and Religion* (Cambridge, MA: Harvard University Press, 1997), 43. For an argument that Bryan was responsible for grafting antievolution onto the northern "fundamentalist" movement, see Ferenc Morton Szasz, *The Divided Mind of Protestant America, 1880–1930* (Tuscaloosa: University of Alabama Press, 1982), 107–35.

40. "From Truly 'Dark' Ground," *New York Times*, January 27, 1922, 13; "Darwinian Theory Stirs Up Kentucky," *New York Times*, February 2, 1922, 11; "Concern over Baptist Rift," *New York Times*, February 4, 1922, 3; "Two Factions Seek Baptist Supremacy," *New York Times*, February 5, 1922, 17; "Straton to Fight Darwin in Schools," *New York Times*, February 9, 1922, 9; "Baptists Meditate Anti-Darwin Fight," *New York Times*, February 10, 1922, 3 (all in the online archives of the *New York Times*).

41. Gatewood, *Preachers, Pedagogues*, 50–51; "Baptists Meditate Anti-Darwin Fight," 3; "War on Modernism in Baptist Church," *New York Times*, June 4, 1922, 32 (online archives of the *New York Times*).

42. Marsden, *Fundamentalism and American Culture*, 169, follows other historians in concluding that the denominational opponents of liberalism had little interest in crusading against Darwinism; see Norman Maring, "Conservative but Progressive," in *What God Hath Wrought: Eastern's First Thirty-Five Years*, ed.

Gilbert L. Guffin (Chicago: Judson Press, 1960), 24; and Ronald Nelson, "Fundamentalism and the Northern Baptist Convention" (PhD diss., University of Chicago, 1964), 310–21, both cited in Marsden, *Fundamentalism and American Culture*, 307 n. 24.

43. Quotation is from an unsigned editorial, "The Poisoned Cup," *New York Times*, February 18, 1922, 10. The other *New York Times* editorials from the first half of 1922 critical of fundamentalism by name are "Topics of the Times: Evidently the Man for the Job," February 11, 1922, 12, "The 'Fundamentalists,'" June 15, 1922, 15, and "A 'Radical' Triumph," June 19, 1922, 10 (all from online archives of the *New York Times*). The earliest example of a *Times* article serving as a voice for the antifundamentalists is "Dr. Tyson Criticises [sic] Foes of Evolution," *New York Times*, February 20, 1922, 7 (online archives). Historians often name H. L. Mencken, columnist for the *Baltimore Sun*, as the journalist who led the way in associating fundamentalism with mean-spirited ignorance—see, e.g., Hart, *Defending the Faith*, 61. But the *New York Times* was beating this drum as early as Mencken. For a broader study of how the editorial policy of the *Times* was biased toward progressive religion from 1885 onward, see Richard W. Flory, "Promoting a Secular Standard: Secularization and Modern Journalism, 1870–1930," in *The Secular Revolution: Power, Interests, and Conflict in the Secularization of American Public Life*, ed. Christian Smith (Berkeley: University of California Press, 2003), 395–433.

44. Stewart G. Cole, *The History of Fundamentalism* (New York: Richard R. Smith, 1931), 281–83; Sandeen, *Roots of Fundamentalism*, 262–64; Furniss, *Fundamentalist Controversy*, 106–7. Technically, the BBU statement stopped short of requiring premillennialism, but it did list the dispensationalists' favorite Bible verses, like the Rapture passage in 1 Thessalonians, and said that they were to be taken "at their face and full value." See "Articles Put Forth by the Baptist Bible Union of America, 1923," www.reformedreader.org/ccc/bbu.htm. Most interpretations stress that the main difference between the Federation and the BBU was degree of militancy. This overlooks that the BBU was more militant mainly because of its much weaker commitment to the denomination's preservation and that this weaker commitment was grounded in the fact that the premillennialists who dominated the BBU already had an alternative institutional network in place. See Ernest R. Sandeen, "Toward a Historical Interpretation of the Origins of Fundamentalism," *Church History* 36 (March 1967): 80–81; and Sandeen, *Roots of Fundamentalism*, 264.

45. Rollin Lynde Hartt, "The War in the Churches," *World's Work*, September 1923, 469–77, quotation on 470. The subsequent articles by Hartt are "Down with Evolution!" *World's Work*, October 1923, 605–14; "Fighting for Infallibility," *World's Work*, November 1923, 48–56; and "Is the Church Dividing?" *World's Work*, December 1923, 161–70. Hartt muted his antifundamentalist sentiments in this series, but he freely expressed his contempt two years later

in his coverage of the Scopes trial—see Hartt, "What Lies beyond Dayton," *Nation*, July 22, 1925, 111–12, reprinted in *Monkey Trial: The State of Tennessee vs. John Thomas Scopes*, ed. Sheldon Norman Grebstein (Boston: Houghton Mifflin, 1960), 193–95.

46. See Cole, *History of Fundamentalism* (1931); Ralph Lord Roy, *Apostles of Discord: A Study of Organized Bigotry and Disruption on the Fringes of Protestantism* (Boston: Beacon Press, 1953); Furniss, *Fundamentalist Controversy* (1954); Richard Hofstadter, *Anti-intellectualism in American Life* (1962; repr., New York: Vintage, 1963), 122–29; and of course Marsden, *Fundamentalism and American Culture*. A more recent example is David S. New, *Christian Fundamentalism in America: A Cultural History* (Jefferson, NC: McFarland, 2012), 125–30. Militant opposition to modernism is also central to scholarly understandings of so-called "global fundamentalism"—see, for example, the five massive volumes of *The Fundamentalism Project*, edited by Martin E. Marty and R. Scott Appleby (Chicago: University of Chicago Press, 1991–95), in particular *Fundamentalisms Observed* (1991), ix. Among older works the notable exception to the militant antimodernism interpretation is Sandeen's *Roots of Fundamentalism*. Many newer works are finding that the movement has had a much more complex relationship with cultural modernism—see, for example, Douglas Carl Abrams, *Selling the Old-Time Religion: American Fundamentalists and Mass Culture, 1920–1940* (Athens: University of Georgia Press, 2001); and Timothy E. W. Gloege, "Consumed: Reuben A. Torrey and the Construction of Corporate Fundamentalism" (PhD diss., University of Notre Dame, 2007).

47. Cole, *History of Fundamentalism*, 78; "Baptist Missions in Peril: Dr. Law[s] Fears Controversy Will Wreck Financial Support," *New York Times*, December 19, 1923, 4 (online archives); Sandeen, *Roots of Fundamentalism*, 263; Szasz, *Divided Mind*, 131–32; Russell, *Voices*, 111, 127–29.

48. Longfield, *Presbyterian Controversy*, 9–10; G. Miller, *Piety and Profession*, 425.

49. Harry Emerson Fosdick, "Shall the Fundamentalists Win?" *Christian Work*, June 10, 1922, 716–22, http://historymatters.gmu.edu/d/5070.

50. Longfield, *Presbyterian Controversy*, 227. Longfield did his graduate study with George Marsden.

51. Macartney, "Shall Unbelief Win?"

52. Ned B. Stonehouse, *J. Gresham Machen: A Biographical Memoir* (1954; repr., Philadelphia: Westminster Theological Seminary, 1977), 337–38; Hart, *Defending the Faith*, 63–69.

53. J. Gresham Machen, "What Fundamentalism Stands for Now, Defined by a Leading Exponent of Conservative Reading of the Bible as the Word of God," *New York Times*, June 21, 1925, Special Features section, XX1 (online archives).

54. William E. Biederwolf, "Opening Remarks," in *Winona Echoes: Notable Addresses Delivered at the Thirty-Sixth Annual Bible Conference, Winona Lake, Indiana, August, 1930* (Winona Lake, IN: Winona Lake Institutions, 1931), 6.

55. Michael S. Hamilton and Margaret Lamberts Bendroth, "Keeping the 'Fun' in Fundamentalism: The Winona Lake Bible Conferences, 1895–1968," in *Reforming the Center: American Protestantism, 1900 to the Present*, ed. Douglas Jacobsen and William Vance Trollinger Jr. (Grand Rapids, MI: Eerdmans, 1998), 315.

56. Quoted in Lefferts A. Loetscher, *The Broadening Church: A Study of Theological Issues in the Presbyterian Church since 1869* (Philadelphia: University of Pennsylvania Press, 1954), 143.

57. Longfield, *Presbyterian Controversy*, 149–50, 219–21; Dale E. Soden, *The Reverend Mark Matthews: An Activist in the Progressive Era* (Seattle: University of Washington Press, 2001), 170–82.

58. Charles G. Dennison and Richard C. Gamble, eds., *Pressing toward the Mark: Essays Commemorating Fifty Years of the Orthodox Presbyterian Church* (Philadelphia: Committee for the Historian of the Orthodox Presbyterian Church, 1986).

59. There are also important bureaucratic factors, underexplored in the literature, that aided the liberal cause, but these are beyond the scope of this essay. See G. Miller, *Piety and Profession*, 404–37.

60. George E. Webb, *The Evolution Controversy in America* (Lexington: University Press of Kentucky, 1994), 70.

61. In *Fundamentalism and American Culture*, Marsden argued that for the premillennial branch of fundamentalism by 1921, the "political question" of antievolution "was now virtually its first concern" (170, see also 152–53). This interpretation has been repeated so many times it has taken on the status of unquestioned fact; and it has become the cornerstone of the commonplace argument that the "fundamentalist" crusade to outlaw evolution in the 1920s was a dress rehearsal for the Religious Right of the 1970s. See, for example, Nancy T. Ammerman, "North American Protestant Fundamentalism," in Marty and Appleby, *Fundamentalisms Observed*, 26–27, 38; and Adam Laats, *Fundamentalism and Education in the Scopes Era: God, Darwin and the Roots of America's Culture Wars* (New York: Palgrave Macmillan, 2010).

62. Sometimes Marsden recognized this. See *Fundamentalism and American Culture*, 261 n. 4.

63. Furniss, *Fundamentalist Controversy*, 104; Longfield, *Presbyterian Controversy*, 73–74.

64. Longfield, *Presbyterian Controversy*, 69–72, 154. On Macartney, see Russell, *Voices*, 190–211. On Machen's view of evolution, see Hart, *Defending the Faith*, 84–107.

65. Charles Hodge, *What Is Darwinism?* (New York: Scribners, 1874). Hodge distinguished between evolution, which he thought compatible with Christianity, and Darwinism, which he thought precluded the possibility of God having designed the world for a purpose—see David N. Livingstone, *Darwin's Forgotten Defenders: The Encounter between Evangelical Theology and Evolutionary Thought* (Grand Rapids, MI: Eerdmans, 1987), 100–105.

66. It has entered the literature that Moody preached against evolution, but the evidence for this is a bit trumped up. Marsden makes this assertion on the basis of a very brief passage in one sermon where Moody is warning against the temptation of atheistic philosophies, an example of which is evolution. Moody's exhortation here is to avoid atheism, not to avoid all forms of evolution. See Marsden, *Fundamentalism and American Culture*, 35. Marsden's argument has been picked up by other historians, for example, Michael Ruse, *The Evolution-Creation Struggle* (Cambridge, MA: Harvard University Press, 2005), 154. The Moody passage is in Dwight L. Moody, *Moody's Latest Sermons* (1900; repr., Grand Rapids, MI: Baker Academic Publishing, 1965), 59.

67. Ronald L. Numbers, *The Creationists: The Evolution of Scientific Creationism*, expanded ed. (New York: Knopf, 2006), 24. For an example of how Moody brought together English advocates of Keswick holiness and protesting American dispensationalists, see J. C. Pollock, *The Keswick Story: The Authorized History of the Keswick Convention* (London: Hodder and Stoughton, 1964), 116–17.

68. Henry Drummond, *Natural Law in the Spiritual World* (London: Hodder and Stoughton, 1883), and *The Lowell Lectures on the Ascent of Man* (London: Hodder and Stoughton, 1894).

69. The best account of Drummond's work and his relationship to Moody is James R. Moore, "Evangelicals and Evolution: Henry Drummond, Herbert Spencer, and the Naturalisation of the Spiritual World," *Scottish Journal of Theology* 38 (1985): 383–417, esp. 401–4. See also Ronald L. Numbers, *Science and Christianity in Pulpit and Pew* (New York: Oxford University Press, 2007), 33; and Peter J. Bowler, *Monkey Trials and Gorilla Sermons: Evolution and Christianity from Darwinism to Intelligent Design* (Cambridge, MA: Harvard University Press, 2007), 164–66. Mark James Toone, "Evangelicalism in Transition: A Comparative Analysis of the Work and Theology of D. L. Moody and His Protégés, Henry Drummond and R. A. Torrey" (PhD diss., University of St. Andrews, 1988), is a thorough exploration of the sources relating to Moody, Drummond, and Torrey, though its interpretive value is hampered by its tendencies to dismiss Torrey's testimony on disputed points of fact, to portray Torrey and Drummond as polar opposites, and to conclude that Drummond alone exemplified the true spirit of Moody.

70. *The Fundamentals*; Livingstone, *Darwin's Forgotten Defenders*, 147–54; R. A. Torrey, *What the War Teaches or The Greatest Lessons of 1917* (Los Angeles: BIOLA Book Room, 1918), 9–11; [R. A. Torrey,] "Dr. R. A. Torrey Replies to

Dr. O. E. Brown," *Moody Bible Institute Monthly* [hereafter *MBIM*], December 1925, 162. One exhaustive reading of every article in *The Fundamentals* found that as many as one-fifth of the articles "touched on the issue of evolution" in some way—see Numbers, *Creationists*, 53. However, in the "Indispensable Books" section of vol. 12 of *The Fundamentals* (120–23), none of the nine fifteen-book lists has a single title on evolution or science.

71. Numbers, *Creationists*, 53. Scholars have traditionally interpreted *The Fundamentals* as a "snapshot" from the period 1910–15, showing a range of viewpoints present within conservative sectors of evangelicalism. In addition to Numbers, see Sandeen, *Roots of Fundamentalism*, 188–207; Marsden, *Fundamentalism and American Culture*, 118–23; Livingstone, *Darwin's Forgotten Defenders*, 147–54; and G. Miller, *Piety and Profession*, 410. But more recently Lienesch's *In the Beginning* reads *The Fundamentals* as representing a single viewpoint changing over time. He asserts that the later volumes show "a more pointedly political character," though by this he apparently means they are more polemical, not that they advocate political action—which they do not. He also argues that "when it came to evolution, the authors in these later volumes took an even harder line." This argument seems hard to sustain, given that the final four volumes, published over a four-year span, include not a single essay on evolution. Lienesch himself notes the fact but does not explain how this can be reconciled with his argument—see 8–33, quotations on 24 and 28.

72. James M. Gray, "Why a Christian Cannot Be an Evolutionist," *MBIM*, August 1925, 538–40, quotation on 538; Jon H. Roberts, "Darwinism, American Protestant Thinkers, and the Puzzle of Motivation," in *Disseminating Darwinism: The Role of Race, Place, Religion, and Gender*, ed. Ronald L. Numbers and John Stenhouse (Cambridge: Cambridge University Press, 1999), 155.

73. [Torrey,] "Dr. R. A. Torrey Replies," 161–62, quotation on 162; Numbers, *Creationists*, 359 n. 4.

74. Roberts, "Darwinism, American Protestant Thinkers," 155, 160–63; Jon H. Roberts, *Darwinism and the Divine in America: Protestant Intellectuals and Organic Evolution, 1859–1900* (Notre Dame, IN: University of Notre Dame Press, 2001), x, 209–17; Numbers, *Science and Christianity*, 5. Marsden has argued that it was fundamentalists' commitment to Baconian inductive science and Scottish common sense philosophy that led them to reject evolutionary theory (*Fundamentalism and American Culture*, 214–16), but Roberts thinks that Baconianism was effect, not cause (*Darwinism and the Divine*, 319 n. 3).

75. Numbers, *Science and Christianity*, 54–55; see also Frank M. Turner, *Between Science and Religion: The Reaction to Scientific Naturalism in Late Victorian England* (New Haven, CT: Yale University Press, 1974), esp. p. 16. A contrasting view is Peter J. Bowler's observation that evangelicals, like Gray, who defended creationism had a vested interest in defining all evolution as materialistic and therefore atheistic (*Monkey Trials*, 8).

76. Bowler summarizes what he calls "the eclipse of Darwinism" and its impact on liberal Protestant intellectuals in *Monkey Trials*, 134–88. Fuller accounts are Peter J. Bowler, *The Eclipse of Darwinism: Anti-Darwinian Evolution Theories in the Decades around 1900* (Baltimore: Johns Hopkins University Press, 1983), and Bowler, *The Non-Darwinian Revolution: Reinterpreting a Historical Myth* (Baltimore: Johns Hopkins University Press, 1988).

77. "Scientists' Abandonment of Evolutionary Proof," *Sunday School Times* [hereafter *SST*], February 28, 1925, 130.

78. Bowler, *Monkey Trials*, 192–93.

79. Riley is at the heart of Marsden's argument that the interdenominational wing of "fundamentalism" took up a political campaign against evolution. Of the other leaders he mentions, only A. C. Dixon was an important figure in the Moody network. William Jennings Bryan was involved in the northern Presbyterian controversies, John Roach Straton was involved in the Northern Baptist controversies, and J. Frank Norris was a renegade Southern Baptist, but all of them operated on the periphery of the Moody network (see Marsden, *Fundamentalism and American Culture*, 152–53, 170). Writing seventeen years after Marsden, Edward J. Larson's detailed history of the background of Tennessee's Butler Act and the Scopes trial, *Summer for the Gods*, gives us basically the same leaders—Riley, Bryan, Straton, and Norris—with the addition of the independent southern evangelist T. T. Martin and cameo appearances by Billy Sunday. Writing ten years after Larson, Michael Lienesch somehow concluded that Riley, Straton, and Norris had received too *little* attention in previous histories of the political campaign against evolution, so in this account they were once again the stars of the show (see Lienesch, *In the Beginning*, 3). The literature's excessive focus on Riley has led many good historians astray. For instance, Paul K. Conkin, in *When All the Gods Trembled: Darwinism, Scopes and American Intellectuals* (Lanham, MD: Rowman and Littlefield, 1998), writes that "Riley was arguably the most influential of the early fundamentalist leaders" (68). But the only hard evidence for such an extravagant claim is the first big meeting of the WCFA in 1919. After about 1922 Riley's influence was more regional and denominational than national and interdenominational. He was still sought out as a speaker at major events, but in this regard he was but one of many. The most influential men in interdenominational evangelicalism were those who headed institutions of national and international importance, which Riley did not.

80. Audrey W. Davis, *Dr. Kelly of Hopkins: Surgeon, Scientist, Christian* (Baltimore: Johns Hopkins University Press, 1959), 157–62, 170–71.

81. For the *Sunday School Times*'s lack of interest in the Butler bill as it moved from introduction in the legislature to the governor's signature, see the seventeen weekly issues beginning with January 24, 1925. The Kelly series was an expansion of Howard A. Kelly, MD, "A Personal Testimony," in *The Fundamentals*, 1:123–26. A full-page preview of the Kelly series (source of the "really

scientific man" quotation) appears in *SST*, February 7, 1925, 79. The series begins with Howard A. Kelly, "How I Came to My Present Faith," *SST*, March 7, 1925, 151–52, and continues for a total of nine consecutive weeks. Kelly's discussion of evolution is in "Why I Believe that Jesus Christ Is God," *SST*, April 4, 1925, 223. The editorial is "Unnecessary Battles," *SST*, March 7, 1925, 149. The new subscription figures are reported almost weekly, with the final figures in "To New Subscribers," *SST*, May 2, 1925, 294. Kelly's essays were immediately afterward published in book form: Howard A. Kelly, *A Scientific Man and the Bible: A Personal Testimony* (Philadelphia: Sunday School Times, 1925); Harper and Brothers of New York also published it the same year.

82. [James M. Gray], "Evolution in the Public Schools," *MBIM*, March 1925, 307.

83. [James M. Gray], "Christian Schools," *MBIM*, May 1925, 400.

84. "The State of Tennessee and Evolution," *MBIM*, June 1925, 462.

85. Clara L. Hall, "Evolution in the Primary Schools," *MBIM*, June 1925, 458–59; M. H. Duncan, "A National Association for Christian Education," *MBIM*, June 1925, 459.

86. [James M. Gray], "Oregon School Case," "Bishop Gailer vs. Governor Peay," and "Evolution in the Schools," all in *MBIM*, June 1925, 447–48.

87. G. R. Pease, "A Plea for a Christian Teacher's Agency," *MBIM*, July 1925, 502–3.

88. Advertisement: "Mr. Bryan's Own Impressions of the Tennessee Evolution Trial," *SST*, July 18, 1925, 454; Charles G. Trumbull, "From Philadelphia to Carluke," *SST*, August 1, 1925, 480; Philip E. Howard, "William Jennings Bryan as His Friends Knew Him," *SST*, August 8, 1925, 499.

89. On Gray declining Bryan's invitation, see James Gilbert, *Redeeming Culture: American Religion in an Age of Science* (Chicago: University of Chicago Press, 1997), 23.

90. Front cover and James M. Gray, "Why a Christian Cannot Be an Evolutionist," 538–40, both in *MBIM*, August 1925. On the Southern Baptist Convention's rejection of antievolution laws, see Larson, *Summer for the Gods*, 99.

91. [James M. Gray], "William Jennings Bryan" and "Who Shall Decide It?," both in *MBIM*, September 1925, 3.

92. Furniss, *Fundamentalist Controversy*, 52. Furniss's account of the strength of the WCFA in the 1920s is based on Riley's own self-promoting accounts and therefore unreliable.

93. William McCarrell to V. Raymond Edman, June 6, 1949, Trustees meetings files, box 1, Wheaton College Archives.

94. Trollinger, *God's Empire*, 44–52, quotation on 44; Sandeen, *Roots of Fundamentalism*, 247. Nancy Ammerman also recognized that the WCFA was a failure, but she made a virtue of a necessity by suggesting, incredibly, that premillennialists did not join their main organization dedicated to fighting

modernism and evolution because they were too busy fighting modernism and evolution. Ammerman, "North American Protestant Fundamentalism," 24.

95. Marsden argues that the movement was politicized after World War I, but this interpretation depends entirely on his argument that the movement organized to outlaw the teaching of evolution. See *Fundamentalism and American Culture*, 206–11. The most in-depth study of "fundamentalist" politics in the 1920s found a fair amount of political *commentary*—and that on all sides of most issues—but turned up almost no evidence of political *organization* or *campaigning* on evolution or any other issue. See Robert E. Wenger, *Social Thought in American Fundamentalism, 1918–1933* (1974; repr., Eugene, OR: Wipf and Stock, 2007), 212–88.

96. Darren Dochuk, *From Bible Belt to Sunbelt: Plain-Folk Religion, Grassroots Politics, and the Rise of Evangelical Conservatism* (New York: Norton, 2011); Sarah R. Hammond, "'God Is My Partner': An Evangelical Business Man Confronts Depression and War," *Church History* 80, no. 3 (2011): 498–519; John G. Turner, *Bill Bright and Campus Crusade for Christ: The Renewal of Evangelicalism in Postwar America* (Chapel Hill: University of North Carolina Press, 2008).

97. Lienesch, *In the Beginning*, 115–17, quotation on 115.

98. A helpful discussion of the southern aspects of the antievolution movement of the 1920s is Ronald L. Numbers, *Darwinism Comes to America* (Cambridge, MA: Harvard University Press, 1998), 58–75.

99. Glass, *Strangers in Zion*, 81–133, 137–53; Waldrep, "Lewis Sperry Chafer," 817–29; Paul Harvey, *Redeeming the South: Religious Cultures and Racial Identities among Southern Baptists, 1865–1925* (Chapel Hill: University of North Carolina Press, 1997), 96, 98, 154–56; G. Miller, *Piety and Profession*, 437–38.

100. On Oklahoma, see Edward J. Larson, *Trial and Error: The American Controversy Over Creation and Evolution* (New York: Oxford University Press, 1985), 49–50. On Arkansas, see Virginia Gray, "Anti-evolution Sentiment and Behavior: The Case of Arkansas," *Journal of American History* 57 (September 1970): 355–56. On North Carolina, see Gatewood, *Preachers, Pedagogues*, 87–90; and Christopher P. Tourney, *God's Own Scientists: Creationists in a Secular World* (New Brunswick, NJ: Rutgers University Press, 1994), 149–55.

101. Lienesch, *In the Beginning*, 117–18. On high schools and evolution, see Larson, *Trial and Error*, 15–27. On the history textbook battles, see Joseph Moreau, *Schoolbook Nation: Conflicts over American History Textbooks from the Civil War to the Present* (Ann Arbor: University of Michigan Press, 2003), 175–218. Larson has strongly argued that the campaign to outlaw evolution in public schools was in character with the Progressive movement's legislative efforts (*Trial and Error*, 28–39). This is not inconsistent with the argument that such legislation was also a reaction against the Progressive movement's educational reforms. Larson, quoting Arthur S. Link and Richard L. McCormick, reminds us that "the reformers were a varied and contradictory lot" who shared not an

ideology but an approach to solving social problems" (*Trial and Error*, 29). Progressivism encompassed both secular advocates of the cult of expertise and religious advocates of moral reform, and both groups looked to government to institute their reforms. See Link and McCormick, *Progressivism* (Arlington Heights, IL: Harlan Davidson, 1983).

102. Larson, *Trial and Error*, 51; Conkin, *When All the Gods Trembled*, 82.

103. Charles A. Israel, *Before Scopes: Evangelicalism, Education, and Evolution in Tennessee, 1870–1925* (Athens: University of Georgia Press, 2004), 8, 25–38.

104. Ibid., 9–10, 113–27.

105. Ibid., 10, 128–55, quotation on 138. John Washington Butler, author of Tennessee's antievolution law, had preceded his legislative career by writing numerous newspaper articles critical of trends in public education, including its irreligion (Conkin, *When All the Gods Trembled*, 79–80).

106. "William Jennings Bryan," *MBIM*, September 1925, 3.

107. Israel, *Before Scopes*, 140; Kazin, *Godly Hero*, 279–81.

108. Larson, *Summer for the Gods*, 43; Israel, *Before Scopes*, 141. Like the Moody network, most African Americans opposed evolution, but few favored legislation to outlaw it in the schools. See Jeffrey P. Moran, "The Scopes Trial and Southern Fundamentalism in Black and White: Race, Region and Religion," *Journal of Southern History* 70 (2004): 95–120.

109. Mary Beth Swetnam Mathews, *Rethinking Zion: How the Print Media Placed Fundamentalism in the South* (Knoxville: University of Tennessee Press, 2006), 67–79, quotation on 68. Only recently have historians begun to escape captivity to this partisan labeling of the 1920s and started describing southern Protestants as evangelicals. Edward Larson, in *Summer for the Gods* (1997), calls the Tennessee opponents of evolution "fundamentalists." But Charles Israel's *Before Scopes* (2004) calls them "evangelicals." This is much more accurate for the simple reason that the same Tennesseans who favored antievolution legislation in 1925 had favored daily Bible reading legislation in 1915, before the term *fundamentalist* had been invented. It cannot possibly be helpful to call them "evangelicals" in 1915 and "fundamentalists" in 1925 when they are the same people, making the same arguments, and doing so for the same reasons as ten years earlier.

110. The estimate of the number of interdenominational missionary agencies in existence in 1920 is drawn from three sources: Edwin L. Frizen Jr., *75 Years of IFMA, 1917–1992: The Nondenominational Missions Movement* (Pasadena, CA: William Carey Library, 1992), Appendices D, E, and F, 438–59; Klaus Fiedler, *The Story of Faith Missions: From Hudson Taylor to Present Day Africa* (Oxford: Regnum, 1994), 7–8; and Joel A. Carpenter, "Appendix: The Evangelical Missionary Force in the 1930s," in *Earthen Vessels: American Evangelicals and Foreign Missions, 1880–1980*, ed. Joel A. Carpenter and Wilbert R. Shenk (Grand Rapids, MI: Eerdmans, 1990), 337–42, tables 2 and 4. Agencies were

counted only if they were nondenominational and if it could be ascertained that they were operating in 1920. For a contextual, nonstatistical reconstruction of the precontroversy boom in support for independent evangelical missionary agencies, see Dana L. Robert, *American Women in Mission: A Social History of Their Thought and Practice* (Macon, GA: Mercer University Press, 1996), 188–254. The estimate of the number of Bible institutes comes from Brereton, *Training God's Army*, "Partial List of Bible Schools Founded by 1945," 71–77, and from "Bible Schools That Are True to the Faith," *SST*, February 1, 1930, 63. Schools were counted only if they were nondenominational and if it could be ascertained that they were operating in 1920. For nine schools out of fifty-one on the *Sunday School Times* list of 1930, no founding date could be determined, so these were not counted. It is possible that some of them were in operation in 1920.

111. Carpenter, *Revive Us Again*, 78–79; William G. McLoughlin Jr., *Modern Revivalism: Charles Grandison Finney to Billy Graham* (New York: Ronald Press, 1959), 469. On Pierson, see Dana L. Robert, *Occupy until I Come: A. T. Pierson and the Evangelization of the World* (Grand Rapids, MI: Eerdmans, 2003); on Torrey, see Gloege, "Consumed." Technically Gordon's and Scofield's churches were denominational, but as interdenominational evangelicalism took shape their denominational character rapidly diminished.

112. Sandeen, *Roots of Fundamentalism*, 162, 240–43.

113. On interdenominational evangelicalism's foreign missions, see Joel A. Carpenter, "Propagating the Faith Once Delivered: The Fundamentalist Missionary Enterprise, 1920–1945," in Carpenter and Shenk, *Earthen Vessels*, 92–132. On the organizational revolution that expanded the denominational bureaucracies, see Ben Primer, *Protestants and American Business Methods* (Ann Arbor, MI: UMI Research Press, 1979); J. Michael Utzinger, *Yet Saints Their Watch Are Keeping: Fundamentalists, Modernists, and the Development of Evangelical Ecclesiology, 1887–1937* (Macon, GA: Mercer University Press, 2006); Harvey, *Redeeming the South*, 197–226; and G. Miller, *Piety and Profession*, 412, 432, 445–46. For an example of the denominational bureaucrats reining in specialized ministries, see Patricia R. Hill, *The World Their Household: The American Woman's Foreign Mission Movement and Cultural Transformation, 1870–1920* (Ann Arbor: University of Michigan Press, 1985).

114. Frizen, *75 Years of IFMA*, 89–91.

115. G. Miller, *Piety and Profession*, 417.

116. Carpenter, *Revive Us Again*, 49–53; Waldrep, "Lewis Sperry Chafer," 825–29.

117. Sources for the estimates of the number of Bible institutes are Brereton, *Training God's Army*, 71–77, and "Bible Schools That Are True," *SST*, 63. For the 1910–24 and 1925–39 estimates, schools were counted only if they were

nondenominational and if a founding date could be ascertained. For nine schools out of fifty-one on the *Sunday School Times* list of 1930, no founding date could be determined, so these were not counted. This means that the combined estimate for 1910–24 and 1925–39 is almost certainly too low, as it is unlikely that they were all founded before 1910.

118. Marsden, *Fundamentalism and American Culture*, 43–44, quotation on 43.

119. A characteristic example of how historians have conflated the belief that the ideas of modernism and evolution are wrong and harmful with the belief that it is necessary to fight battles to remove those ideas from church and school can be seen in Joel A. Carpenter, ed., *A Conservative Call to Arms*, Fundamentalism in American Religion, 1880–1950, vol. 21 (New York: Garland, 1988). This volume reprints Torrey's *What the War Teaches or The Greatest Lessons of 1917* (1918), interpreting it as a call to militant action. But it is nothing of the sort. Torrey merely called on evangelicals to do with greater urgency what they had always done—give money to religious causes, pray, evangelize, confess sins, reconcile personal estrangements, and watch for the coming of the Lord (16).

120. G. Miller, *Piety and Profession*, 179, argues that Torrey was no more militant than the other religious figures of the era who held strong opinions—which was virtually everyone on all sides of the debates.

121. Brereton, *Training God's Army*, 78–86, 139–47; cf. Carpenter, *Revive Us Again*, 54.

122. Frizen, *75 Years of IFMA*, 96, 177–94.

123. Yaakov Ariel, *Evangelizing the Chosen People: Missions to the Jews in America, 1880–2000* (Chapel Hill: University of North Carolina Press, 2000), 22–37, 77–82.

124. Hamilton and Bendroth, "Keeping the 'Fun,'" 300–317, quotation on 306. On the Bible conference phenomenon generally, see Carpenter, *Revive Us Again*, 22–23.

125. For example, on Maxwell's nonmilitancy, see John G. Stackhouse Jr., *Canadian Evangelicalism in the Twentieth Century: An Introduction to Its Character* (Toronto: University of Toronto Press, 1993), 71–88.

126. Glass, *Strangers in Zion*, 110.

127. Marsden, *Fundamentalism and American Culture*, 130–31, 202–5; Betty A. DeBerg, *Ungodly Women: Gender and the First Wave of American Fundamentalism* (Minneapolis: Fortress Press, 1990).

128. Margaret Lamberts Bendroth, *Fundamentalism and Gender, 1875 to the Present* (New Haven, CT: Yale University Press, 1993), 73–96; Michael S. Hamilton, "Women, Public Ministry, and American Fundamentalism, 1920–1950," *Religion and American Culture* 3, no. 2 (1993): 171–96. For an example of how this phenomenon worked at Bible institutes, see Brereton, *Training God's Army*, 129–32.

129. William Lawrence Svelmoe, *A New Vision for Missions: William Cameron Townsend, the Wycliffe Bible Translators, and the Culture of Early Evangelical Faith Missions, 1896–1945* (Tuscaloosa: University of Alabama Press, 2008), 266–68.

130. Probably the largest number of churches forming new militant denominations were Baptist. Some of the larger groups were the American Baptist Association and the Baptist Bible Fellowship (which produced Jerry Falwell). Militant groups that attached themselves to interdenominational evangelicalism included the General Association of Regular Baptist Churches, the Independent Fundamental Churches of America, and the Orthodox Presbyterian Church (and its schismatic offspring). The history of fundamentalism from the point of view of these militant groups is told in three books: George W. Dollar, *A History of Fundamentalism in America* (Greenville, SC: Bob Jones University Press, 1973) and *The Fight for Fundamentalism* (Sarasota, FL: pub. by author, 1983); and David O. Beale, *In Pursuit of Purity: American Fundamentalism since 1850* (Greenville, SC: Unusual Publications, 1986).

131. Paul M. Bechtel, *Wheaton College: A Heritage Remembered* (Wheaton, IL: Harold Shaw, 1984), 109–19, 144–53.

132. Graham's role as catalyst of this schism is detailed in William Martin, *A Prophet with Honor: The Billy Graham Story* (New York: William Morrow, 1991), 217–24, 239–41.

PART IV

PLURALISM'S CHALLENGE

CHAPTER 12

Marsden and Secularization

JOHN SCHMALZBAUER

The secularization story line has enjoyed a curious career in the fields of sociology and American history. Long embraced by sociologists, it has also found a place in the historiography of American religion. As recently as 1993, 55 percent of American religion scholars agreed that "secularization remains the dominant trend concerning religion in western societies."[1] The same could not be said today. Few North American religious history textbooks bother to include the term, focusing instead on the mixture of the sacred and the secular in American culture. While many sociologists remain committed to the theory, others have questioned its status as a "disciplinary myth."[2]

One notable exception is scholarship on American higher education, where the secularization concept remains very much in play. Published in 1994, George Marsden's *The Soul of the American University: From Protestant Establishment to Established Nonbelief*, is largely responsible for this debate. Along with an earlier volume, *The Secularization of the Academy*, and 1997's *The Outrageous Idea of Christian Scholarship*, it has spurred a revival of the secularization story line in the historiography of American higher education.[3]

In *The Soul of the American University*, Marsden traced the gradual disappearance of Christian learning from American higher education. Though this work has inspired several parallel studies, not everyone has accepted Marsden's account. Critiquing the literature on the secularization of the university, Martin Marty dismissed it as so many "complaints and whimpers" about "what went wrong with Christian scholarship." Rejecting the secularization story line, some have argued that the marginal place of religious perspectives in American higher education is due to the emergence of specialized academic disciplines, not antireligious animus. Others have recast the story of religion in the academy, emphasizing the *transformation* rather than the *secularization* of American universities.[4] Such scholarship has emphasized the impact of pluralism and diversity on the American academy, arguing that the *de-Christianization* and the *de-Protestantization* of colleges and universities have made room for a host of religious minorities and those with no religious commitments at all.[5] Finally, a number of scholars (including this author) have focused on the *revitalization* of religion in the academy, stressing the resilience of the sacred in the "postsecular" university. Far from monolithic, this revitalization has included some who focus on religion as an object of study and others who (like Marsden) emphasize scholarship grounded in religious traditions. Encompassing believers and skeptics, insiders and outsiders, those who integrate faith and knowledge and those who emphasize the separation of personal commitments from academic scholarship, the return of religion has been realized by diverse groups of scholars with competing conceptions of religion and the academic vocation. From this angle, the visibility of Marsden's work has served as evidence of a comeback, rather than proof of the academy's enduring secularity.[6]

While often agreeing on the facts of particular incidents, scholars have offered conflicting interpretations of the changes in American higher education. If nothing else, these competing accounts have underscored the value-laden nature of historical inquiry. In *The Content of the Form*, Hayden White observed that "narrative is not merely a neutral discursive form" and that it instead "entails ontological and epistemic choices with distinct ideological and even specifically political implications." As White argued in *Metahistory: The Historical Imagination in*

Nineteenth-Century Europe (1973), scholars use the tropes of irony, comedy, tragedy, and romance to convey moral and political meanings.[7] This has certainly been the case in the historiography on religion and American higher education. In the fifties and sixties, liberal consensus historians like Richard Hofstadter and Laurence Veysey depicted the development of the American university in triumphalistic ways, celebrating the victory of academic freedom over the authority of religious tradition. In White's terminology, such accounts exemplified the mode of *romance*, portraying the "triumph of good over evil, of virtue over vice, of light over darkness."[8] By contrast, Marsden employed an *ironic* mode of narration in *The Soul of the American University*, portraying secularization as an unintended consequence of Protestant hegemony. Reflecting on the ethical ambiguities in American history, Reinhold Niebuhr famously described irony as a form of moral criticism. Once called a "technical equivalent for the doctrine of original sin," it has been used to expose the foibles and failures of historical actors. In Marsden's hands, it has served as a tool for critiquing his own religious tradition.[9]

A comparison between historical and sociological approaches reveals equally significant differences. While the sociology of religion has focused on *macro*-level shifts in the structures of entire societies, intellectual and cultural historians have been more attuned to historical actors operating in specific organizations (what sociologists call the *micro*- and *meso*- levels). In the language of literary theorist Kenneth Burke, sociologists have emphasized the *scene* of the social drama, while historians have talked more about *agents*. While historians of higher education have also paid attention to scene (especially the cultural and social context of an era), they have tended to emphasize the local and the particular. In the secularization literature, this has translated into historical accounts foregrounding the decisions of college presidents and sociological accounts analyzing the structural relationship between religious and educational institutions. Because of their disciplinary lenses, both historians and sociologists have missed something the other field has noticed. As Burke noted, "Every way of seeing is also a way of not seeing." Fortunately, some scholars have attempted to combine these approaches, analyzing the interplay between historical actors and structural changes in American higher education.[10]

This chapter provides an overview of the shifting use of the concept of "secularization" in research on American higher education from the 1950s to the present. Exploring the scholarship preceding and following Marsden's *Soul of the American University*, it sketches a map of historical and sociological treatments of religion in the academy, paying special attention to the narratives used to describe the transformation of American higher education. It concludes by suggesting how the study of secularization and higher education might develop in the future, arguing for a combination of historical and sociological approaches.

SECULARIZATION AS ACADEMIC FREEDOM

The postwar period witnessed the publication of several classic histories of American higher education. Though these were written in an ironic age, there was precious little irony in their treatment of religion. By and large, this scholarship framed the secularization of the university in romantic terms, celebrating the triumph of academic freedom over religious tradition.[11]

In her overview of this literature, Linda Eisenmann cited the "long influence of Richard Hofstadter."[12] A professional historian who addressed a wider public, Hofstadter returned again and again to the impact of religion on the American mind, most notably in *Anti-intellectualism in American Life* (1963). An earlier version of the secularization narrative can be found in Hofstadter's *The Development of Academic Freedom in the United States*, coauthored with Walter Metzger. Originally published in 1955, it was released as two separate works in 1961. Written by two Columbia University professors, it was an outgrowth of the university's American Academic Freedom Project, directed by sociologist Robert MacIver and overseen by a blue ribbon panel of advisers, including the presidents of Amherst and Vassar, the director of the New York Public Library, Henry Steele Commager, Iphigene Ochs Sulzberger, J. Robert Oppenheimer, and the Jesuit John Courtney Murray.[13]

In the preface, Hofstadter and Metzger wrote that because "sectarian aspirations did so much to create the restrictive atmosphere of the old college," religion was central to their account. While urging readers not to infer an "aggressive secularism on the part of the authors," they juxtaposed such binaries as tolerance and sectarianism, Enlightenment and retrogression, and searching and conserving.[14] As Joel Carpenter noted in a 1998 review essay, Hofstadter and Metzger cast religion as the "intellectually stultifying villain" of American higher education.[15] While making an effort to "avoid the pitfall of interpreting the past solely from the standpoint of present issues and current anxieties," they reflected the historical context of McCarthyism and postwar liberalism. Part of a generation of American scholars made uneasy by populist anti-intellectualism, they celebrated the triumph of freedom, science, and rationality.[16]

Despite this critique of the denominational college, Hofstadter described a bumpy path to the secular university. Unlike some of his contemporaries, he rejected the "rationalist stereotype" of the Middle Ages "as an age of dogma and suppression," acknowledging the incremental secularization "under way in the Roman Catholic Church." Likewise, his portrait of Puritanism was far from dismissive, drawing on Perry Miller's work on the New England mind and sociologist Robert Merton's account of science in seventeenth-century England. The most extensive treatment of secularization could be found in the chapter entitled "Religion, Reason, and Revolution," a discussion of the eighteenth-century American Enlightenment focusing on such figures as Princeton's John Witherspoon. There Hofstadter described the development of science in the colonial colleges, a first step in the "secularization of learning." Noting an increase in denominational diversity and a shift away from preministerial education, he described a movement toward tolerance and pluralism. This period of liberalization was followed by what Hofstadter dubbed "the great retrogression," an era in which the engines of progress ran backwards. Arguing that the proliferation of small, denominationally controlled institutions hampered the development of academic freedom, he saw few redeeming qualities in nineteenth-century higher education.[17]

In Walter Metzger's second volume of the study, the rise of the modern research university was interpreted as a repudiation of the old-time college and its clergy presidents. Conceiving of the changes in higher education as revolutionary, Metzger described a shift from *conserving* to *searching* institutions. While the former guarded the "knowledge inherited from the past," the latter knew that scholarship was "as fallible as the men who made it." The influence of Darwinism, the German university model, and the elective system were all seen as moving American higher education in a more secular direction. Reflecting a postwar emphasis on the ideology of scientific objectivity, Metzger connected the "value of neutrality" with academic freedom.[18]

Arriving ten years later in 1965, Lawrence Veysey's *The Emergence of the American University* offered a similar narrative of progress. Analyzing "rival conceptions" of higher learning, Veysey isolated four ways of defining colleges and universities. Calling the first model "discipline and piety," he portrayed it as reactionary, intolerant, authoritarian, and insecure.[19] Along the same lines, Frederick Rudolph's *The American College and University* (1962) depicted denominational control as a threat to tolerance.[20]

Shaped by the postwar liberal consensus and its desire to avoid the extremes of the Left and the Right, these classic works defined the emerging historiography of American higher education. Like many works of consensus history, their interpretations have not always stood the test of time. While acknowledging their contributions, contemporary scholars have uncovered a messier reality. Complicating Hofstadter and Veysey's descriptions of nineteenth-century higher education, works by David Potts and Roger Geiger portrayed the old-time colleges in a more flattering light. In a study of sixteen Baptist institutions, Potts demonstrated the importance of such denominational institutions to their local communities, depicting them as vehicles of educational progress. In a review essay on Veysey's classic, Julie Reuben agreed, observing that many innovations in American higher education had their origins in the nineteenth-century college.[21]

In retrospect, the postwar historians failed to do justice to the complex influence of the Enlightenment. Writing at least a decade before Henry May's discussion of the multiple strains of the American Enlightenment, they contrasted a monolithic Enlightenment with a monolithic Christianity. Nowhere was this tendency more apparent than in Richard Hofstadter's section on "the great retrogression." Mourning the changing "intellectual and moral temper of the country," he wrote that "the little candles of the Enlightenment guttered or failed."[22]

Employing the metaphors of light and darkness, Hofstadter and Metzger advanced a simplistic narrative of academic freedom versus denominational control. Recognizing this problem, Hofstadter's biographer called *Academic Freedom in the Age of the College* a "passion play between the forces of pedagogical good and evil." Articulating a similar critique, Joel Carpenter criticized the postwar historians for telling a "triumphal saga" of liberators and victims. As noted above, such polarized narratives exemplified Hayden White's romantic mode of emplotment.[23]

Despite its excesses, there is much to salvage in the postwar historiography on American higher education. While criticizing Hofstadter's portrait of nineteenth-century colleges, Roger Geiger pointed out that the book's chapter on European higher education is "hardly a morality tale," calling it "a subtle dialectic."[24] In spite of their shortcomings, Hofstadter, Veysey, and Rudolph were among the first historians to systematically chronicle the constraints on academic freedom. As noted below, David Hollinger's *Science, Jews, and Secular Culture* (1998) documented the liberating consequences of "de-Christianization" for those outside the Protestant fold. Raised by a Jewish father and a Lutheran mother, Hofstadter was all too aware of the marginal position of Jews in American higher education. According to his biographer, Hofstadter shared the anxieties of his contemporaries about the dangers of populist authoritarianism. As journalist Scott McLemee noted on the fiftieth anniversary of *The Development of Academic Freedom in the United States*, the book was "the closest thing to an official scholarly response to the danger of McCarthyism from the university world." In a world haunted by Joseph McCarthy and a vestigial Protestant establishment, Hofstadter and Metzger recognized the precariousness of academic freedom.[25]

SOCIOLOGISTS AND THE SECULARIZATION OF AMERICAN HIGHER EDUCATION

Missing from most midcentury histories of higher education is any citation of the sociological literature on religion. Focusing instead on the story of specific individuals (college presidents and faculty) in specific institutions (Harvard and Yale), Hofstadter and Veysey did not appropriate the metanarratives of American sociology, eschewing terms like *differentiation* and *modernization*. While they wrote about social institutions and intellectual movements, they focused most of their attention on the local and the particular, neglecting the structural changes in American society. In avoiding the macro level, Hofstadter may have been following the example of Columbia University sociologist C. Wright Mills, a friend and colleague who warned against the dangers of grand theory.[26]

By contrast, sociologists of religion have historically emphasized the importance of large-scale social structures. In the words of Joseph Gusfield, "Culture, social structure, group, and institutions are the scenic essentials of sociological thought." This focus on macro-level social processes helps explain why pioneering works in secularization theory almost completely ignored the literature on American higher education. Originally published in 1967, Peter Berger's *The Sacred Canopy* did not even mention the words *college* or *university*. To be sure, Berger discussed the secularization of "cultural life and of ideation," noting that this "may be observed in the decline of religious contents in the arts, in philosophy, in literature, and most important of all, in the rise of science."[27] Yet the secularization of ideas was just one more example of the impact of the *differentiation* of society into autonomous institutions and the *privatization* of religion in modern societies. Likewise, Robert Bellah's *Beyond Belief* (1970) paid no attention to the secularization of colleges and universities, focusing instead on the evolution of religion over many centuries. Like Berger, Bellah stressed the "gradual differentiation of art, science, and other cultural systems," ignoring the historic shifts in American higher education.[28]

Given the neglect of higher education by secularization theorists, it is not surprising that sociologists Christopher Jencks and David Riesman barely mentioned secularization in their 1968 work *The Academic Revolution*. Despite its focus on the modernization of American colleges and universities, the word *secularization* appeared just twice in a 580-page book. Focusing their attention on the rise of meritocracy, nationalism, and professionalism, they did not put religion at the center of the story. The only hint of the secularization story line was a chapter on Catholic institutions and a section on the "survival of recognizably Protestant colleges."[29]

Not all postwar social scientists ignored the secularization of higher education. In *Religion and Society in Tension* (1965), Charles Glock and Rodney Stark discussed the "incompatibility of religion and science," emphasizing the conflict between rival "images of man." According to Glock and Stark, such differences were evidence of the "tensions between religion and other social institutions."[30] Social scientific surveys from the same period documented the low levels of religious belief and practice among American college and university professors.[31] Along the same lines, a small literature discussed the secular outlook of the college-educated professions (dubbed the "new class" by Peter Berger and Alvin Gouldner), while others explored the impact of secularization on American students.[32]

For the most part, historians of higher education and sociologists of religion did not talk to each other. In the judgment of sociologist Christian Smith, the secularization theorists of the 1960s and 1970s described "transformation without protagonists, action without actors, historical process without agents."[33] Though the secularization literature was growing, it did not combine the story of specific organizations with macrosociological analysis. In the terminology of Kenneth Burke, it was all scene and no agents. By focusing on macro processes like differentiation and privatization, secularization theorists were observing social change from thirty-thousand feet. From such an altitude, the history of American colleges and universities could be dismissed as flyover country.

GEORGE MARSDEN AND THE SECULARIZATION OF THE ACADEMY

In the 1980s, several prominent conservative intellectuals turned their attention to the state of the American university, most notably Allan Bloom in *The Closing of the American Mind* (1987). As Russell Jacoby points out, Bloom's book was the first of "a series of kindred and widely discussed books such as 'Tenured Radicals,' 'Illiberal Education,' 'Killing the Spirit,' 'Dictatorship of Virtue,' 'The Disuniting of America.' These tracts decried the incoherence of higher education; its politicization; political correctness; relativism; and faddishness."[34] Against this backdrop, George Marsden produced his history of religion and American higher education, a "model of judiciousness" compared to such polemical works. His first major statement on the topic came in an edited volume, *The Secularization of the Academy*, published in 1992. Funded by the Pew Charitable Trusts, Marsden's research was rooted in his own experience as an evangelical scholar in the American academy, first at Calvin College and later at Duke University. The book sought to reframe the discussion of religion in higher education. Marsden's opening chapter was a preview of *The Soul of the American University*. The first appearance of a shorter version of this chapter in *First Things*, a neoconservative journal that also published James Burtchaell's articles on the "decline and fall of the Christian college," reflected the ideological context of the secularization debate. Burtchaell and Marsden's critiques of secularization were a good fit for a magazine that lamented what its founder called "the naked public square." By describing the way that religion had been excluded from American higher education, they helped lay the groundwork for its resurgence.[35]

Though Marsden's basic argument is discussed in Stephen Nolt's essay for this volume, several things are worth mentioning in relation to the wider discussion of secularization. First, Marsden consistently ignored the sociological literature on the topic. In this respect, he was in continuity with the postwar historiography on higher education. Though the word *sociology* appeared over twenty times in *The Secularization of the Academy*, it was usually in connection with the history of the social sciences. In *The Soul of the American University* it was mentioned twenty-one times, though never as part of a discussion of secularization theory. The closest Marsden came to the sociological literature was his use of the concept of "methodological secularization," a concept that is very similar to Peter Berger's "methodological atheism." Despite this parallel, *The Sacred Canopy* was never cited. In the introduction to *The*

Secularization of the Academy, Marsden noted the use of the word *secularization* "is a risky business, since it is a word that, once mentioned, can easily lead to a morass of sociological debate."³⁶

Second, Marsden parted company with the postwar historiography by putting secularization at the center of the story. In a 1994 interview, he criticized the absence of religion in Lawrence Veysey's *The Emergence of the American University*, adding that "to the extent that it was there, [Veysey] thought it was a bad thing." In *The Soul of the American University*, he rejected Hofstadter and Metzger's triumphalistic narrative of academic freedom, focusing instead on the gradual disappearance of religion from the American university.³⁷

While quite critical of secularization, Marsden did not mourn the demise of the Protestant establishment. As he noted in the introduction to *The Secularization of the Academy*, "We are not using *secularization* naively as equivalent to *decline*," while acknowledging that most of the contributors to the volume viewed "the change in the role of religion in modern higher education as *in some ways* a loss."³⁸ Though the distinction between loss and decline may seem subtle, it was an important point. Marsden had crafted, not a jeremiad with clear villains and victims, but a tale of unintentional secularization. In this way, he echoed Peter Berger's description of Protestantism as its own gravedigger. Though Marsden's fondness for irony and paradox came from Reinhold Niebuhr, he shared Berger's perspective on religion in the modern world, an outlook ultimately derived from Max Weber.³⁹ In light of Marsden's theological presuppositions, *The Soul of the American University* could be read as a Niebuhrian critique of his own religious tradition. Marsden said as much in his introduction, noting that "it critically analyzes the Protestant heritage to which I am closest." Though some reviews mentioned Marsden's use of irony and paradox, they did not emphasize this aspect of the study.⁴⁰ This is unfortunate. In *The Irony of American History*, Reinhold Niebuhr portrayed irony as a form of contrition. By failing to recognize Marsden's ironic voice, readers have missed his critique of the Protestant establishment.⁴¹

How did an ironic account of Protestant higher education come to be viewed as a narrative of complaint? Most critical reviewers have focused on Marsden's "Concluding Unscientific Postscript," a section that criticized the exclusion of religious viewpoints from contemporary higher education. Had Marsden omitted this critique of "established nonbelief," his book would have been far less controversial. Writing in the *History of Education Quarterly*, Cushing Strout argued that Marsden "is much less convincing" in this part of the book. In a similar way, Mark Schwehn and Dorothy Bass wrote that the "book is controversial both because of its major historical thesis and because of its prescriptions for what ails the modern university." Likewise, sociologist Alan Wolfe criticized Marsden for making white, male Protestants the victims. Some of these reviewers were unhappy with the book's treatment of mainline Protestants. Part of the problem may be that Marsden focused most of his critique on the liberal side of the Protestant house. While Schwehn and Bass wished for a "greater measure of sympathy for the liberal Protestant figures he has studied," Leo Ribuffo wrote that Marsden "sometimes gives them less than their due."[42]

DISESTABLISHMENT AND DE-CHRISTIANIZATION

Several other studies have attempted to provide a more sympathetic account of mainline Protestantism in a century of change. That was the goal of William Hutchison's edited volume *Between the Times: The Travail of the Protestant Establishment in America, 1900–1960* (published in 1989). Avoiding the word *secularization*, Hutchison wrote that "the traditional Protestant denominations, and their influence, have survived better than is commonly supposed." While acknowledging the end of the Protestant establishment "as reality, but even more as rhetoric," Hutchison's contributors did not believe the mainline was dead. Examining the "strategies of Protestant influence" in her chapter on education, Dorothy Bass described the history of denominationally sponsored universities and campus ministries. While characterizing such efforts as a "ministry on the margin," she was more hopeful than Marsden. In a 1986 essay, Hutchison was downright optimistic, arguing that religious liberalism "is doing rather well and does assuredly have a future."[43]

Like Hutchison and Bass, Conrad Cherry articulated a complex view of liberal Protestantism in *Hurrying toward Zion* (1995), chronicling the efforts of mainline leaders to build a pan-Protestant system of education. Discussing the growth of the great mainline Protestant divinity schools, Cherry described how they changed under the influence of specialization, professionalization, and pluralism. In an effort to relate to new constituencies, these institutions gradually adjusted their missions. Accepting a more humble place in the ecology of their universities, they continued to promote the teaching and the practice of religion. Cherry discussed, in place of secularization, the various transformations reshaping Protestant divinity schools.[44]

Taking a very different approach, Douglas Sloan traced the rise and fall of the postwar theological renaissance in *Faith and Knowledge* (1994). Led by Reinhold Niebuhr and Paul Tillich, this movement found expression in a cluster of faculty organizations and journals, generously underwritten by philanthropic foundations. Arguing that the postwar revival never overcame the epistemological divide between faith and knowledge, Sloan ended his story with its collapse, arguing that by the late sixties "the mainstream Protestant churches' scholarly, critical engagement with American higher education was all but over." Along the same lines, D. G. Hart's *The University Gets Religion* (1999) argued that the mainline Protestant effort to engage higher education had ended in failure. Noting the imprint of liberal Protestantism on the postwar field of religious studies, Hart described the emergence of a post-Protestant academy still haunted by theological assumptions. Though framed as declension narratives, neither book embraced the secularization thesis. As Sloan wrote in *Faith and Knowledge*, "While it may make sense in many respects to speak of the growing secularization of higher education, from another perspective this can be very misleading," adding that in "important ways, the university itself became a major religious phenomenon." Likewise, *The University Gets Religion* included only three references to "secularization."[45]

Offering a more critical take on the history of Protestantism in American higher education, David Hollinger replaced the secularization story line with a narrative of "de-Christianization." In *Science,*

Jews, and Secular Culture (1998), Hollinger argued that this process was accomplished by an "informal alliance among liberal Protestants, ex-Protestants, religious Jews and freethinking Jews." Together, they helped bring about the "weakening of the old Protestant cultural hegemony" and the creation of the modern American university. According to Hollinger, the university emerged as an island of openness in a society where Christianity had dominated almost everything else.[46]

Despite their common focus on the post-Protestant academy, these accounts have diverged in important respects. While some scholars (Cherry, Hutchison, and Hollinger) have accepted the place of religion in contemporary higher education, others have been much more critical (Sloan and Hart). In general, their evaluations have reflected their social locations as scholars. As a conservative Protestant in the Calvinist tradition, Hart has criticized the liberal Protestant heritage of religious studies. As the product of a mainline Protestant divinity school who helped shape that field, Cherry has been much more positive. These differences are readily apparent when one reads the way these scholars have written about each other's works. Commenting on *Hurrying toward Zion*, Hart wrote that Cherry's claim that divinity schools practiced unbiased scholarship "would have to be seriously revised." Along the same lines, Cherry accused Hart of letting "dogmatic and supernaturalist convictions" obscure his view of the field. Such disagreements suggest that the historiography of American higher education has continued to be shaped by its cultural and religious context.[47]

ALTERNATIVE NARRATIVES OF SECULARIZATION

Although many scholars have highlighted the post-Protestant and post-Christian character of American colleges and universities, others have focused on different forms of cultural transformation. While calling George Marsden the "leading figure" in the new scholarship, Julie Reuben has emphasized a new set of issues, considering "secularization in the context of the changing position of morality in the university." In *The Making of the Modern University: Intellectual Transformation and the*

Marginalization of Morality (1996), she traced the shifting locus of ethics in higher education.[48]

Taking secularization in new directions, Jon Roberts and James Turner focused on the role of disciplinary specialization in *The Sacred and the Secular University* (2000). Unlike Marsden, they did not uncover significant hostility to religion in the modern American university. According to Roberts and Turner, the marginalization of religious concerns was an unintended consequence of the rise of specialized academic disciplines, a development that generally advanced the progress of knowledge. In the social sciences, the spread of empirical methods narrowed the focus of academic inquiry, excluding larger religious and philosophical issues. Scholars were trained to "think small." In his introduction to the book, John F. Wilson distinguished Roberts and Turner's argument from *The Soul of the American University*, rejecting the notion that Protestantism's "birthright has been stolen." As Wilson noted, the pair advanced an "alternate understanding of how and why religion's relationship to higher education changed," focusing on the processes of "specialization and religious differentiation." Significantly, differentiation has been a central concept in the social scientific literature on secularization, although Roberts and Turner did not cite this scholarship.[49]

By contrast, sociologist Christian Smith grounded his analysis of higher education in the sociological research on social movements. In *The Secular Revolution* (2003), he focused on the role of "power, interests, and conflict in the secularization of American public life," criticizing the lack of attention to human agency and social institutions in the earlier sociological literature. While praising Marsden and Reuben, he focused on a different set of "actors and processes."[50] According to Smith, the "secular revolution succeeded in part because new sources of material resources outside of the control of Protestant authorities became available for secular activists to deploy in the cause of secularization."[51] In Smith's account, the secularization of knowledge was accomplished by an organized network of faculty and administrators, bankrolled by the philanthropy of American businessmen.[52] Though Marsden discussed some of the same figures (Andrew Carnegie) and social processes (industrialization) in *The Soul of the American University*, he did not develop a systematic theory of the secularization of American culture.[53] More than any other work, *The Secular Revolution* has combined the structural focus of sociology with an appreciation for the ways that human beings make history.

By melding historical and sociological approaches, Smith has substantially advanced the discussion. In this way, he has helped overcome the gap between sociology's macro-level orientation and history's focus on agents in particular institutions. In a similar way, Roberts and Turner have paved the way for a rapprochement between history and sociology. Though they do not cite the sociological literature on differentiation, their historically grounded use of this concept is consistent with the work of Berger and other secularization theorists. Despite these interdisciplinary advances, sociologists and historians have continued to ignore each other. This tendency can also be seen in the literature on church-related colleges and universities.

SECULARIZATION NARRATIVES AND THE REVITALIZATION OF CHURCH-RELATED HIGHER EDUCATION

Published in 1998, James Burtchaell's *The Dying of the Light: The Disengagement of Colleges and Universities from Their Christian Churches* applied the secularization concept to the world of church-related higher education. An 868-page book on the erosion of denominational ties, it emphasized the precariousness of religious identity in even the most conservative of institutions. A former provost at the University of Notre Dame, Burtchaell put the blame squarely on the shoulders of college presidents and faculty who "lose their nerve and are intimidated by their academic colleagues." Apart from a discussion of the influence of the professional guild on hiring, sociological explanations took a back seat to Burtchaell's emphasis on careless administrators and the secularizing influence of pietism. Reactions to the book have been mixed.[54]

Funded by the Lilly Endowment, Burtchaell's study was part of a library of foundation-supported works intended to strengthen the identity of church-related higher education. Like *The Dying of the Light*, they have been published by religious journals and presses, especially the William B. Eerdmans Publishing Company of Grand Rapids, Michigan, but also by Oxford University Press and Johns Hopkins University Press. In a survey of over 1,100 individuals who participated during the 1990s in programs funded through Lilly's religion and higher education initiative, 55 percent reported reading at least one of sixteen recently published books on religion in American higher education. Among the most popular titles were *The Soul of the American University* (read by 20 percent of participants), *Exiles from Eden* (13 percent), *Models for Christian Higher Education* (10 percent), and *The Dying of the Light* (9 percent).[55]

The expanding literature on religious colleges also included a bookshelf of denomination-specific titles. While Philip Gleason's *Contending with Modernity: Catholic Higher Education in the Twentieth Century* (1995) traced the accommodation of Catholic institutions to the modern academy, David O'Brien's *From the Heart of the American Church* (1995) celebrated the liberating effects of the "Catholic academic revolution."[56] Joining these works on Catholic higher education were books on Lutheran, Mennonite, Baptist, and Presbyterian colleges.[57]

While many of these works cited Marsden and Burtchaell, not all told a story of declension. Richard Hughes and William Adrian's *Models for Christian Higher Education* (1997) presented case studies from a range of denominational traditions. Rejecting what one contributor calls the "'failure' literature of church-college relations," it offered positive models of church-relatedness.[58] This was the aim of Robert Benne's *Quality with Soul* (2001), an account of "how six premier colleges and universities keep faith with their religious traditions."[59]

Ironically, the widespread dissemination of the secularization story line has motivated efforts to revitalize the religious character of church-related colleges and universities. Like the "secular revolution" chronicled by Christian Smith, these efforts have been accomplished by a network of faculty and administrators supported by strategic philanthropy. They have included new mission statements, cabinet-level positions in mission and identity, greater emphasis on hiring for mission, religion-oriented centers and institutes, and mentoring programs for faculty and staff. Foundation-supported programs like Lilly's $210 million initiative on vocation at religious colleges, denominationally oriented efforts like Collegium and the Lutheran Academy of Scholars, and interdenominational networks such as the Lilly Fellows Program and the Rhodes Consultation have helped to strengthen the religious identity of church-related institutions.[60] In the wake of such activity, even George Marsden acknowledged that religious colleges and universities might not "continue along the slippery slope toward secularism."[61] In many cases, these initiatives have been inspired by Marsden's work on secularization. In at least some church-related institutions, the secularization thesis may turn out to be the gravedigger of secularization.

FUTURE DIRECTIONS IN SECULARIZATION AND AMERICAN HIGHER EDUCATION

Recent scholarship suggests that Marsden may have overstated the extent to which American higher education has marginalized the teaching and the practice of religion. Such research points to the revitalization of church-related colleges, the growth of the academic study of religion, and the vitality of student religious life (see John G. Turner, chapter 14 in this volume).[62] Articles on the return of religion can be found in a dozen disciplines, including art, English, philosophy, music, political science, social work, medicine, history, and sociology. Recently, the American Historical Association reported that religion is the most popular specialization in the field, and America's leading sociology journals are paying more attention to the sacred. Such articles emphasize both religion as an object of study and "pro-religiousness" in the mainstream academy.[63] People of faith are also playing a more visible role in the academy, as witnessed by the growth of such organizations as the Society of Christian Philosophers and the Association of Muslim Social Scientists. While religious topics grace the covers of *Change* and *Academe*, researchers like Alexander Astin (the most cited figure in the literature on higher education) call attention to the importance of spirituality in undergraduate life. Such developments have led some to predict the arrival of a postsecular academy where religion will "succeed high theory and the triumvirate of race, gender, and class as the center of intellectual energy in the academy."[64]

Such comments echo recent debates in the sociology of religion, where scholars have challenged the secularization thesis. Recanting his earlier views, Peter Berger has edited a volume on the "desecularization of the world." Some sociologists have embraced the so-called "new paradigm," attributing America's religious vitality to the ingenuity of savvy congregations and entrepreneurial religious leaders. Others have highlighted the resurgence of public religion, focusing on the *deprivatization* and *dedifferentiation* of religion in politics in the United States and around the world. These discussions have offered conceptual tools for thinking about the comeback of religion in higher education, blending a focus on historical agents with a focus on the American religious scene. While the campus has become a lively religious marketplace, faculty members have gone public with their religious convictions.[65]

At the same time, there are clear limits to the desecularization of the academy. While documenting surprising levels of religious belief and practice, surveys of the professoriate show that faculty remain less devout than the general public. Although professors are more open to religious perspectives than in earlier eras, there are substantial barriers to the integration of faith and knowledge. According to a nationwide survey on students and spirituality, only a minority of faculty explore religious topics in the classroom. Such findings come as no surprise to Robert Wuthnow, who argues that the technocratic character of the American research university has led religion to become a "sideshow in the contemporary academy."[66]

Instead of rejecting the secularization narrative, scholars must develop a more sophisticated understanding of religious change in American higher education. Several recent approaches offer a way forward. First, comparative scholarship offers new insights into the secularization of higher education. Studies of religion in the history of Canadian, German, and British universities complement the existing literature on America. Like sociologist David Martin's comparative work on the secularization of European societies, such works highlight the influence of geography and political traditions on the history of higher education.[67]

A second promising discussion comes from new work in the field of American religious history. In *Culture and Redemption: Religion, the Secular, and American Literature,* Tracy Fessenden situates secularization in the context of "a Protestant ideology that has grown more entrenched and controlling even as its manifestations have often become less visibly religious." In an equally provocative work, John Lardas Modern traces the rise of "evangelical secularism" in nineteenth-century print culture. A similar focus on the interplay between sacred and secular could enrich the study of higher education.[68]

Third, new research on religious diversity in American society is changing the way scholars look at religion and higher education. In an innovative study of Hindu student organizations, sociologist Prema Kurien has explored the efforts of first- and second-generation Americans to find "a place at the multicultural table." Along the same lines, the Education as Transformation Project at Wellesley College has spawned a multivolume series on religious pluralism. More work is needed on this topic.[69]

Last but not least, scholars must break down the walls separating sociological and historical approaches to religion and higher education. For the past fifty years, these two literatures have been largely segregated by discipline. Despite frequent conceptual parallels, sociologists and historians of secularization have rarely cited each other's work. There is no reason why this pattern should continue.

In conclusion, this essay has considered the trajectory of "secularization" in American higher education. Once central to celebratory narratives of academic freedom, the concept was later embedded in more ironic accounts of the marginalization of religion. In recent years, scholars have taken a more balanced approach, acknowledging both the changes in higher education and the resilience of religion in the American academy. As sociologists and historians refine the study of secularization in American higher education, they must learn to work across disciplinary lines. Only then will the fuller potential of this literature be realized.

NOTES

1. Harry S. Stout and Robert M. Taylor Jr., "Studies of Religion in American Society: The State of the Art," in *New Directions in American Religious History*, ed. Harry S. Stout and D. G. Hart (New York: Oxford University Press,

1997), 25. On the changing place of secularization in American religious history, see Clark Gilpin, "Secularism: Religious, Irreligious, and Areligious," The Religion and Culture Web Forum, March 2007, https://divinity.uchicago.edu /sites/default/files/imce/pdfs/webforum/032007/secularism.pdf.

2. Nancy Ammerman calls secularization a disciplinary myth in "Sociology and the Study of Religion," in *Religion, Scholarship, and Higher Education: Perspectives, Models, and Future Prospects*, ed. Andrea Sterk (Notre Dame, IN: University of Notre Dame Press, 2002), 82.

3. George M. Marsden, *The Soul of the American University: From Protestant Establishment to Established Nonbelief* (New York: Oxford University Press, 1994); George M. Marsden and Bradley J. Longfield, eds., *The Secularization of the Academy* (New York: Oxford University Press, 1992).

4. Martin Marty, foreword to *Scholarship and Christian Faith: Enlarging the Conversation*, ed. Douglas Jacobsen and Rhonda Hustedt Jacobsen (New York: Oxford University Press, 2004), vii; Jon Roberts and James Turner, *The Sacred and the Secular University* (Princeton, NJ: Princeton University Press, 2000), 36; Conrad Cherry, *Hurrying toward Zion: Universities, Divinity Schools, and American Protestantism* (Bloomington: Indiana University Press, 1995).

5. David A. Hollinger, *Science, Jews, and Secular Culture: Studies in Mid-Twentieth Century American Intellectual History* (Princeton, NJ: Princeton University Press, 1998); David A. Hollinger, "The 'Secularization' Question and the United States in the Twentieth Century," *Church History* 70, no. 1 (2001): 132–43.

6. John Schmalzbauer and Kathleen Mahoney, "American Scholars Return to Studying Religion," *Contexts* 7, no. 1 (2008): 16–21; Kathleen Mahoney, John Schmalzbauer, and James Youniss, "Religion: A Comeback on Campus," *Liberal Education*, Fall 2001, 36–41; Alan Wolfe, "A Welcome Revival of Religion in the Academy," *Chronicle of Higher Education*, September 19, 1997, B4; Diane Winston, "Campuses Are a Bellwether for Society's Religious Revival," *Chronicle of Higher Education*, January 16, 1998, A60. The last sentence in this paragraph is adapted from John Schmalzbauer and Kathleen Mahoney, "Religion and Knowledge in the Post-secular Academy," in *The Post-Secular in Question: Religion in Contemporary Society*, ed. Philip S. Gorski, David Kyuman Kim, John Torpey, and Jonathan VanAntwerpen (New York: New York University Press, 2012), 216.

7. Hayden White, *The Content of the Form: Narrative Discourse and Historical Representation* (Baltimore: Johns Hopkins University Press, 1973), ix, and *Metahistory: The Historical Imagination in Nineteenth-Century Europe* (Baltimore: Johns Hopkins University Press, 1973), 9.

8. White, *Metahistory*, 9.

9. The trope of irony is discussed at greater length in John Schmalzbauer, *People of Faith: Religious Conviction in American Journalism and Higher Education*

(Ithaca, NY: Cornell University Press, 2003); White, *Metahistory*, 9; Reinhold Niebuhr, *The Irony of American History* (New York: Charles Scribner's Sons, 1952); Martin Marty, "Irony (Fig.) and (Lit.) in Modern American Religion," *Journal of the American Academy of Religion* 53, no. 3 (1985): 187–99; Richard Reinitz, *Irony and Consciousness: American Historiography and Reinhold Niebuhr* (Lewisburg, PA: Bucknell University Press, 1980). The quotation about irony and original sin is from Kenneth Burke, *A Grammar of Motives* (Berkeley: University of California Press, 1969), 515.

10. This discussion of "scene" and "agency" in sociology draws on Joseph Gusfield, "Sociology's Critical Irony: Countering American Individualism," in *Sociology in America*, ed. Herbert J. Gans (Newbury Park, CA: Sage Publications, 1990), 38. See Gusfield's introduction to *Kenneth Burke: On Symbols and Society*, ed. Joseph Gusfield (Chicago: University of Chicago Press, 1989), 1–49; quote from Burke, 8.

11. Godfrey Hodgson argues that the postwar consensus thinkers (including Richard Hofstadter) embraced "irony, paradox, complexity and other safely non-political abstractions." See Hodgson, *America in Our Time: From World War II to Nixon—What Happened and Why* (Princeton, NJ: Princeton University Press, 2005), 93. Yet compared to the rest of Hofstadter's corpus there is little irony in his work on the secularization of higher education. An exception can be found in his discussion of how the Puritan embrace of science led to the unanticipated "decline of orthodoxy." See Richard Hofstadter, *Academic Freedom in the Age of the College* (New York: Columbia University Press, 1961), 201.

12. Linda Eisenmann, "Reclaiming Religion: New Historiographic Challenges in the Relationship of Religion and American Higher Education," *History of Education Quarterly* 39, no. 3 (1999): 297.

13. Richard Hofstadter, *Anti-intellectualism in American Life* (New York: Vintage Books, 1963); Richard Hofstadter and Walter P. Metzger, *The Development of Academic Freedom in the United States* (New York: Columbia University Press, 1955); Hofstadter, *Academic Freedom*; Walter P. Metzger, *Academic Freedom in the Age of the University* (New York: Columbia University Press, 1961).

14. Hofstadter and Metzger, *Development of Academic Freedom*, xi, xii.

15. Joel Carpenter, "Review Essay: Religion in American Life," *Religion and American Culture* 8, no. 2 (1998): 266.

16. Hofstadter and Metzger, *Development of Academic Freedom*, ix. On postwar liberalism and McCarthyism, see David Scott Brown, *Richard Hofstadter: An Intellectual Biography* (Chicago: University of Chicago Press, 2006), 122. On postwar liberalism more broadly, see Hodgson, *America in Our Time*.

17. Hofstadter, *Academic Freedom*, 5, 152–208, 209.

18. Metzger, *Academic Freedom*, 43, 44, 92. See Peter Novick, *That Noble Dream: The "Objectivity Question" and the American Historical Profession* (New York: Cambridge University Press, 1988).

19. Lawrence Veysey, *The Emergence of the American University* (Chicago: University of Chicago Press, 1965), 19, 21–56. See also Julie Reuben, "Writing When Everything Has Been Said: The History of American Higher Education following Lawrence Veysey's Classic," *History of Education Quarterly* 45, no. 3 (2007): 412–19. This suspicious attitude toward religion can also be seen in *The Emergence of the American University*.

20. Frederick Rudolph, *The American College and University: A History* (Athens: University of Georgia Press, 1991). This classic study was originally published in 1962.

21. Roger Geiger, ed., *The American College in the Nineteenth Century* (Nashville, TN: Vanderbilt University Press, 2000); David Potts, *Baptist Colleges in the Development of American Society* (New York: Garland, 1988); Reuben, "Writing," 412–19.

22. Henry May, *The Enlightenment in America* (New York: Oxford University Press, 1978); Hofstadter, *Academic Freedom*, 216.

23. Brown, *Richard Hofstadter*, 81; Carpenter, "Review Essay," 266; White, *Metahistory*, 9.

24. Roger Geiger, introduction to Richard Hofstadter, *Academic Freedom in the Age of the College*, new ed. (New Brunswick, NJ: Transaction, 1995), xiii.

25. Hollinger, *Science, Jews*, 17–41; Brown, *Richard Hofstadter*, 118, 122; Scott McLemee, "Academic Freedom, Then and Now," *InsideHigherEd*, February 17, 2005, www.insidehighered.com/views/mclemee/mclemee62.

26. For a discussion of the metanarratives that have dominated sociological theory, see Margaret R. Somers and Gloria D. Gibson, "Reclaiming the Epistemological 'Other': Narrative and the Social Constitution of Identity," in *Social Theory and the Politics of Identity*, ed. Craig Calhoun (Malden, MA: Wiley-Blackwell, 1994), 37–99. See also Ammerman, "Sociology," 82. On Hofstadter's friendship with Mill, see Brown, *Richard Hofstadter*, 122. Mill's critique of "grand theory" can be found in *The Sociological Imagination* (New York: Oxford University Press, 1959), 25.

27. Gusfield, "Sociology's Critical Irony," 38; Peter L. Berger, *The Sacred Canopy: Elements of a Sociological Theory of Religion* (New York: Doubleday, 1967), 107.

28. Robert Bellah, introduction to *Beyond Belief: Essays on Religion in a Posttraditionalist World*, ed. Robert Bellah (Berkeley: University of California Press, 1970), 16.

29. Christopher Jencks and David Riesman, *The Academic Revolution* (New York: Doubleday, 1968), 330. All word counts in this chapter are taken from Amazon.com or Google Books.

30. Charles Y. Glock and Rodney Stark, *Religion and Society in Tension* (Chicago: Rand McNally, 1965), 262, 289.

31. Rodney Stark, "On the Incompatibility of Religion and Science," *Journal for the Scientific Study of Religion* 3, no. 1 (1963): 3–20; Joseph Zelan,

"Religious Apostasy, Higher Education, and Occupational Choice," *Sociology of Education* 41, no. 4 (1968): 370–79. See also Robert Wuthnow, *The Struggle for America's Soul: Evangelicals, Liberals, and Secularism* (Grand Rapids, MI: Eerdmans, 1989).

32. See the essays in B. Bruce-Briggs, ed., *The New Class?* (New Brunswick, NJ: Transaction, 1979); Alvin Gouldner, *The Future of Intellectuals and the Rise of the New Class* (New York: Seabury Press, 1978); Peter L. Berger, "The Worldview of the New Class: Secularity and Its Discontents," in Bruce-Briggs, *New Class?*, 49–55; Dean Hoge, *Commitment on Campus: Changes in Religion and Values over Five Decades* (Philadelphia: Westminster Press, 1974); James Davison Hunter, *Evangelicalism: The Coming Generation* (Chicago: University of Chicago Press, 1987).

33. Christian Smith, introduction to *The Secular Revolution: Power, Interests, and Conflict in the Secularization of American Public Life*, ed. Christian Smith (Berkeley: University of California Press, 2003), 14.

34. Allan Bloom, *The Closing of the American Mind: How Higher Education Has Failed Democracy and Impoverished the Souls of Today's Students* (New York: Simon and Schuster, 1987); Russell Jacoby, "Ideas: Dissecting the Decade of the Culture Wars," *Newsday*, April 6, 1997, G6.

35. Marsden, *Soul*; Marsden and Longfield, *Secularization of the Academy*; George Marsden, "The Soul of the American University," *First Things*, January 1991, 34–47; James T. Burtchaell, "The Decline and Fall of the Christian College, Part I," *First Things*, April 1991, 16–29, and "The Decline and Fall of the Christian College, Part II," *First Things*, May 1991, 30–38. The "model of judiciousness" quotation comes from Mark R. Schwehn and Dorothy Bass, "Christianity and Academic Soul Searching," *Christian Century*, March 15, 1995, 292. On the biographical influences on Marsden, see Schmalzbauer, *People of Faith*, 73–109. For insight into the vision behind *First Things*, see Richard John Neuhaus, *The Naked Public Square: Religion and Democracy in America* (Grand Rapids, MI: Eerdmans, 1984).

36. Marsden, *Soul*, 156; George M. Marsden, introduction to Marsden and Longfield, *Secularization of the Academy*, 4. Berger discussed "methodological atheism" in *Sacred Canopy*, 100.

37. George M. Marsden, interview by author, Notre Dame, IN, April 1994.

38. Marsden, introduction to Marsden and Longfield, *Secularization of the Academy*, 5.

39. On Marsden's use of Niebuhrian irony, see Schmalzbauer, *People of Faith*. Berger wrote that "historically speaking, Christianity has been its own gravedigger," in *Sacred Canopy*, 129. Weber made this argument in *The Protestant Ethic and the Spirit of Capitalism* (1904–5; repr., London: Blackwell, 2002).

40. Marsden, *Soul*, 8.

41. Niebuhr, *Irony of American History*.

42. Cushing Strout, review of Marsden, *Soul*, *History of Education Quarterly* 35, no. 3 (1995): 322; Schwehn and Bass, "Christianity," 292–96; Alan Wolfe, "Religion and American Higher Education: Rethinking a National Dilemma," *Current*, July 1996, 33; Leo Ribuffo, "God and Man at Harvard, Yale, Princeton, Berkeley, Etc.," *Reviews in American History* 23, no. 1 (1995): 173.

43. William R. Hutchison, "Discovering America," in *Between the Times: The Travail of the Protestant Establishment in America, 1900–1960*, ed. William R. Hutchison (New York: Cambridge University Press, 1989), 308; Dorothy Bass, "Ministry on the Margin: Protestants and Education," in Hutchison, *Between the Times*, 57; William R. Hutchison, "Past Imperfect: History and the Prospect for Liberalism," in *Liberal Protestantism: Realities and Possibilities*, ed. Robert S. Michaelsen and Wade Clark Roof (New York: Pilgrim Press, 1986), 65.

44. Cherry, *Hurrying toward Zion*, 268–300.

45. For Sloan, secularization was not real because the university itself had become a sacred institution. See Douglas Sloan, *Faith and Knowledge: Mainline Protestantism and American Higher Education* (Louisville, KY: Westminster John Knox Press, 1994), 185, 21; D. G. Hart, *The University Gets Religion: Religious Studies in American Higher Education* (Baltimore: Johns Hopkins University Press, 1999).

46. Hollinger, *Science, Jews*, 29; Hollinger, "'Secularization' Question," 132–43. On the legacy of anti-Semitism in higher education, see also Dan A. Oren, *Joining the Club: A History of Jews at Yale* (New Haven, CT: Yale University Press, 2001); Andrew Heinze, *Jews and the American Soul* (Princeton, NJ: Princeton University Press, 2004); Paul Ritterband and Harold S. Wechsler, *Jewish Learning in American Universities: The First Century* (Bloomington: Indiana University Press, 1994); Ritterband and Wechsler, *Jewish Learning*.

47. Hart, *University Gets Religion*, 241; Cherry, review of Hart, *University Gets Religion*, *American Historical Review* 106, no. 2 (2001): 572–73.

48. Julie Reuben, *The Making of the Modern University: Intellectual Transformation and the Marginalization of Morality* (Chicago: University of Chicago Press, 1996), 15.

49. Roberts and Turner, *Sacred and the Secular*, 36; John F. Wilson, introduction to Roberts and Turner, *Sacred and the Secular*, 10. For a discussion of the concept of differentiation in secularization theory, see Olivier Tschannen, "Secularization Theory: A Systematization," *Journal for the Scientific Study of Religion* 30, no. 4 (1991): 395–415.

50. Smith, introduction to Smith, *Secular Revolution*, 14, 98

51. Christian Smith, "Who Paid for Secularization?," *Books and Culture*, May/June 2003, 28

52. Christian Smith, "Secularizing American Higher Education: The Case of Early American Sociology," in Smith, *Secular Revolution*, 97–159.

53. Marsden, *Soul*, 281.

54. James Tunstead Burtchaell, *The Dying of the Light: The Disengagement of Colleges and Universities from Their Christian Churches* (Grand Rapids, MI: Eerdmans, 1998), 851. For contrasting responses to Burtchaell's study, see Ralph Wood, "Rest Not in Peace: The Death and Possible Rebirth of Christian Colleges," *Christian Century*, February 3, 1999, 55–60; Michael Beaty, review of Burtchaell, *Dying of the Light*, *Journal of College and University Law* 26 (1999): 177–91; Richard T. Hughes, review of Burtchaell, *Dying of the Light*, *Catholic Historical Review* 85, no. 4 (1999): 666–69; Raymond Schroth, "Not Dead Just Yet," *National Catholic Reporter*, October 16, 1998, 34–35.

55. The survey was conducted as part of an evaluation of Lilly Endowment's Religion and Higher Education initiative. The results were reported in Kathleen A. Mahoney, John Schmalzbauer, and James Youniss, "Revitalizing Religion in the Academy: An Evaluation of Lilly Endowment's Initiative on Religion and Higher Education," unpublished report to Lilly Endowment, Boston College, Chestnut Hill, MA, 2000. Other results from the survey can be found in Kathleen A. Mahoney, John Schmalzbauer, and James Youniss, "Revitalizing Religion in the Academy: Summary of the Evaluation of Lilly Endowment's Initiative on Religion and Higher Education," Boston College, Chestnut Hill, MA, 2000, www.resourcingchristianity.org/sites/default/files/transcripts/research_article/Mahoney_Schmalzbauer_Youniss_Revitalizing_Religion_Essay.pdf.

56. Philip Gleason, *Contending with Modernity: Catholic Higher Education in the Twentieth Century* (New York: Oxford University Press, 1995); David O'Brien, *From the Heart of the American Church: Catholic Higher Education and American Culture* (Maryknoll, NY: Orbis, 1995), 51. See also John Piderit and Melanie Morey, *Catholic Higher Education: A Culture in Crisis* (New York: Oxford University Press, 2006).

57. Ernest J. Simmons, *Lutheran Higher Education: An Introduction for Faculty* (Minneapolis: Augsburg Fortress, 1998); Keith Graber Miller, *Teaching to Transform: Perspectives on Mennonite Higher Education* (Goshen, IN: Pinchpenny Press, 2000); Duncan S. Ferguson and William J. Weston, eds., *Called to Teach: The Vocation of the Presbyterian Educator* (Louisville, KY: Geneva Press, 2003); Donald D. Schmeltekopf and Dianna M. Vitanza, eds., *The Future of Baptist Higher Education* (Waco, TX: Baylor University Press, 2006).

58. Richard Hughes and William Adrian, eds., *Models for Christian Higher Education: Strategies for Survival and Success in the Twenty-First Century* (Grand Rapids, MI: Eerdmans, 1997); Theron Schlabach, "Goshen College and Its Church Relations: History and Reflections," in Hughes and William Adrian, *Models*, 221. For another book critical of the declension story line, see Jacobsen and Jacobsen, *Scholarship and Christian Faith*.

59. Robert Benne, *Quality with Soul: How Six Premier Colleges and Universities Keep Faith with Their Religious Traditions* (Grand Rapids, MI: Eerdmans,

2001). Several other studies documented the vitality of Christian higher education. See especially Naomi Schaefer Riley, *God on the Quad: How Religious Colleges and the Missionary Generation Are Changing America* (New York: St. Martin's Press, 2003); William Ringenberg, *The Christian College: A History of Protestant Higher Education in America* (Grand Rapids, MI: Baker Academic Publishing, 2006); Samuel Schuman, *Seeing the Light: Religious Colleges in Twenty-First Century America* (Baltimore: Johns Hopkins University Press, 2010); Paul J. Dovre, "Introduction: The Future of Religious Higher Education," in *The Future of Religious Colleges*, ed. Paul J. Dovre (Grand Rapids, MI: Eerdmans, 2002), ix; Mahoney, Schmalzbauer, and Youniss, "Revitalizing Religion" [Summary].

60. Mark Schwehn, "Mark Schwehn on the Heightened Profile of Religion and Vocation within Higher Education," interview by Tracy Schier, October 2001, www.resourcingchristianity.org/sites/default/files/transcripts/interview/MarkSchwehn_Religion_%26_Vocation_Interview.pdf; Paul Dovre, "Reexamination and Renaissance: Lilly-Sponsored Studies at the Turn of the Century," November 2003, www.resourcingchristianity.org/sites/default/files/transcripts/research_article/PaulDovre_Lilly_Sponsored_Studies_Essay.pdf; Alice Gallin, "The Impact of the Lilly-Funded Research on Catholic Campuses," March 2002, www.resourcingchristianity.org/sites/default/files/transcripts/research_article/AliceGallin_Lilly_Funded_Research.pdf.

61. Beth McMurtrie, "Future of Religious Colleges Is Bright, Say Scholars and Officials," *Chronicle of Higher Education*, October 20, 2000, A41.

62. Schmalzbauer and Mahoney, "American Scholars Return," 16–21; Wolfe, "Welcome Revival," B4; Winston, "Campuses Are a Bellwether," A60; Conrad Cherry, Betty A. DeBerg, and Amanda Porterfield, *Religion on Campus* (Chapel Hill: University of North Carolina Press, 2001); Stanley Fish, "One University under God?," *Chronicle of Higher Education*, January 7, 2005, http://chronicle.com/article/One-University-Under-God-/45077/; Damon Mayrl, "Religion and Higher Education: Current Knowledge and Future Directions," *Journal for the Scientific Study of Religion* 48, no. 2 (2009): 260–75.

63. The sentence on the disciplines draws on Schmalzbauer and Mahoney, "American Scholars Return," 16–21. On the discipline of history, see Scott Jaschik, "Religious Revival," *Inside Higher Ed*, December 21, 2009, www.insidehighered.com/news/2009/12/21/religion. Data on the top three sociology journals are presented in David Smilde and Matthew May, "The Emerging Strong Program in the Sociology of Religion," February 8, 2010, Social Science Research Council working paper, http://blogs.ssrc.org/tif/wp-content/uploads/2010/02/Emerging-Strong-Program-TIF.pdf. On proreligiousness, see Smilde and May, "Emerging Strong Program."

64. For an example of Alexander Astin's work on the topic, see *The Spiritual Life of College Students: A National Study of College Students' Search for Meaning and Purpose* (Los Angeles: Higher Education Research Institute, UCLA, 2004).

See also Alexander Astin, Helen Astin, and Jennifer Lindholm, *Cultivating the Spirit: How College Can Enhance Students' Inner Lives* (San Francisco: Jossey-Bass, 2011). According to the Higher Education Research Institute, Astin is the most cited researcher in the field of higher education. On this distinction, see Higher Education Research Institute, "Staff Profile: Alexander Astin," 2014, www.heri.ucla.edu/staff-display.php?staffQry=10. On the postsecular, see Douglas Jacobsen and Rhonda Hustedt Jacobsen, eds., *The American University in a Postsecular Age* (New York: Oxford University Press, 2008). See also Rhonda Hustedt Jacobsen and Douglas Jacobsen, *No Longer Invisible: Religion in University Education* (New York: Oxford University Press, 2012). The quotation is from Fish, "One University under God?"

65. Peter Berger, ed., *The Desecularization of the World: Resurgent Religion and World Politics* (Grand Rapids, MI: Eerdmans, 1999); R. Stephen Warner, "Work in Progress toward a New Paradigm for the Sociological Study of Religion in the United States," *American Journal of Sociology* 98, no. 5 (1993): 1044–93; Jose Casanova, *Public Religions in the Modern World* (Chicago: University of Chicago Press, 1994). See the Social Science Research Council's collection of web forum essays entitled "The Religious Engagements of American Undergraduates," 2007, http://religion.ssrc.org/reforum/. On religious scholars in the academy, see Schmalzbauer, *People of Faith.*

66. Neil Gross and Solon Simmons, "How Religious Are America's College and University Professors?," in Social Science Research Council web forum, "Religious Engagements," February 6, 2007, http://religion.ssrc.org/reforum/Gross_Simmons/; Elaine Howard Ecklund, "Religion and Spirituality among University Scientists," in Social Science Research Council web forum, "Religious Engagements," February 5, 2007, http://religion.ssrc.org/reforum/Ecklund.pdf; Robert Wuthnow, "Can Faith Be More Than a Sideshow in the Contemporary Academy?" in Jacobsen and Jacobsen, *American University*, 31–43.

67. Catherine Gidney, *A Long Eclipse: The Liberal Protestant Establishment and the Canadian University, 1920–1970* (Montreal: McGill-Queen's University Press, 2004); Thomas Albert Howard, *Protestant Theology and the Making of the Modern German University* (New York: Oxford University Press, 2006); David Bebbington, "The Secularization of British Universities since the Mid-Nineteenth Century," in Marsden and Longfield, *Secularization of the Academy*; David Martin, *On Secularization: Toward a Revised General Theory* (Burlington, VT: Ashgate, 2005).

68. Tracy Fessenden, *Culture and Redemption: Religion, the Secular, and American Literature* (Princeton, NJ: Princeton University Press, 2007), 5; John Lardas Modern, "Evangelical Secularism and the Measure of Leviathan," *Church History* 77, no. 4 (2008): 801–76, and *Secularism in Antebellum America* (Chicago: University of Chicago Press, 2011).

69. Prema Kurien, *A Place at the Multicultural Table: The Development of an American Hinduism* (New Brunswick, NJ: Rutgers University Press, 2007). On the Education as Transformation Project's publishing project, see Peter Laurence, "Education as Transformation: History of a Movement," *Spirituality in Higher Education Newsletter*, April 2004, http://spirituality.ucla.edu/newsletter_new/past_pdf/volume_1/vol_1_issue_1/EoT.pdf.

CHAPTER 13

The Soul of the American University

STEVEN M. NOLT

NOTICING THE ABSENCE OF WHAT ISN'T THERE

On a late spring afternoon in 1910 in Paterson, New Jersey, Reverend Clarence Wilmot, the Presbyterian protagonist in John Updike's novel *In the Beauty of the Lilies*, lost his faith.

"The sensation was distinct—a visceral surrender, a set of dark sparkling bubbles escaping upward," as he stood on the first floor of the rectory at the corner of Straight Street and Broadway. But although the Princeton graduate had struggled for years "to maintain [faith] against the grain of the Godless times," his surrender was less a relief than he had expected: "Without Biblical blessing, the physical universe became sheerly horrible."[1] Wilmot recognized that "the depths of vacancy revealed were appalling"[2]—a vacancy that would, as the narrative unfolded, set his grandchildren and great-grandchildren adrift in meaninglessness.

The disappearance of faith and the implications—so obvious to the fictional pastor—were much less plain to most historical actors of his time. If there was slippage in the import or influence of traditional

Christianity among mainline Protestants during the late nineteenth and early twentieth centuries, few were prepared to notice, particularly the leaders of Protestant America's flagship educational institutions. "The Cornell University is . . . a Christian Institution," declared its president, Andrew Dickson White.[3] "Every possible effort has been made . . . to emphasize the fact that the institution is a Christian institution," echoed Chicago's William Rainey Harper, noting that "every faculty meeting in every department has . . . been opened [with prayer]."[4] Trustees in North Carolina asserted that "the aims of Duke University are to assert a faith in the eternal union of knowledge and religion set forth in the teachings and character of Jesus Christ, the Son of God."[5] Even as late as 1952, administrators at Yale proudly publicized that "religious life at Yale is deeper and richer than it has been in many years."[6]

Yet by the late twentieth century many Americans—including students, faculty, and administrators of these same universities—would find it astonishing that these schools had ever, or so recently, framed their purposes in Christian terms. So complete has been the establishment of nonbelief in today's research universities that few academics wonder how God slipped off campus. Secularism is so widely assumed it need not be explained.

What was most remarkable about George Marsden's 1994 book *The Soul of the University: From Protestant Establishment to Established Nonbelief* was not so much the breadth of its inquiry or the strength of its interpretation, impressive as they were. What was most striking was that Marsden's study explored a problem that few other scholars had noticed, let alone thought to question. In doing so, Marsden's scholarship not only delivered a compelling and provoking thesis. It also illustrated its own argument with disarming clarity: religiously informed points of view and self-consciously Christian scholarship can deepen and enrich academic inquiry.

FRAMING THE QUESTION

The question Marsden had noticed was this: How might we explain "the remarkable revolution from a little over a century ago, when

Christianity was a leading force in higher education, to today, when at most it is tolerated as a peripheral enterprise and often simply excluded"?[7] Conventional history of American higher education had been a narrative of free inquiry triumphing over narrow indoctrination, and religion figured only as one of the shackles to be thrown off.[8] Historians might notice that the principles defining American universities were self-consciously Protestant. But scholars accustomed to thinking of religion as epiphenomenal or a cover for some other motive could dismiss educators' religion as a rhetorical flourish. George Marsden refused to do so.

Marsden would later say that the relationship between religion and higher education had been near the center of his thinking from the beginning of his career. "The motive that became a passion to study American history," he reflected, "was my desire to understand two . . . subcultures in which I found myself deeply immersed by my later teens: that of my religious heritage and that of mainstream academia."[9] Those worlds, represented on the one hand by his Orthodox Presbyterian upbringing and Westminster Theological Seminary education, and on the other by his schooling at "impressively humane" Haverford College and Yale University, certainly influenced his early research and writing.[10] But in 1986, when he began teaching at the Divinity School of Duke University, the relationship between faith and learning moved to the head of his scholarly agenda. He set about to understand how and why American universities are defined the way they are with respect to religion. A four-year grant (1988–92) from the Pew Chartable Trusts funded his initial research, aided by Bradley J. Longfield and D. G. Hart, as well as a 1990 symposium on the subject.[11]

As Marsden explored themes and developed arguments that would become *The Soul of the American University*, he refined the scope of his inquiry by delineating what his project was not. American universities' rejection of faith did not mean that people of faith were unwelcome on campus. This was not a history of discrimination against scholars who were Christians, as Marsden took pains to emphasize. Rather, the issue was that modern university life had been constructed in such a way that religious points of view were not deemed reputable bases for intellectual inquiry.[12]

Second, Marsden underscored that he did not wish to offer a wistful lament for some lost golden age when Christians ruled higher education. His would not be a story of declension. The secularization of the academy had entailed both gains and losses. But even more, it involved irony, as a powerful Protestant establishment had sowed the seeds of its undoing, the "unintended consequences of decisions that in their day seemed largely laudable, or at least unavoidable." Framing the story in this way meant that it would be, not a search for culprits, but "an attempt to understand American tendencies toward cultural homogenization and uniformity." Nevertheless, irony left plenty of room for contemporary judgment. "The evaluative question," Marsden announced, "is whether the unintended consequences regarding religion are desirable" and whether it is "not time to reconsider the rules that shape the most respected academic communities."[13]

SEARCHING FOR THE ACADEMY'S SOUL

By almost any measure, *The Soul of the American University* was a major scholarly work. At more than 460 pages, it offered a sweeping yet focused story of the transformation of the academy. The narrative was broad in the sense that Marsden drew on intellectual, cultural, institutional, and religious history, as well as some social and political history. As a result, the book was peppered with cross-fertilized insights. For example, at one point Marsden explored the fact that "the United States is the only modern nation in which the dominant culture was substantially shaped by low-church Protestantism." He then traced the implications of this legacy to a remarkably wide range of characteristics that have come to define American institutions of higher education, including "their pragmatism, their traditionlessness, their competitiveness, their dependence on the market, their resorting to advertising, their emphasis on freedom as free enterprise for professors and individual choice for students, their anti-Catholicism, their scientific spirit, their congeniality to business interests, and their tendency to equate Christianity with democracy and service to the nation."[14]

At the same time, Marsden kept his potentially sprawling subject under control by structuring his narrative around what he called "pace-setting schools" that had come to "define the university in an age of science"—schools such as Cornell, Michigan, and Chicago. These institutions were influential not only because they embodied the new academy but also because they provided graduate training for faculty at other colleges, thus shaping in concrete ways how generations of professors thought about their vocation and about what they expected from their own campuses.[15] Marsden did not discount Roman Catholic, historically black, and women's colleges—and, in fact, he seemed to have a soft spot for their often alternative missions—but the intellectual developments he charted emanated from the pacesetters. Institutions that remained skeptical of trends on elite campuses soon became "outsiders" in the eyes of professional organizations, private foundations, and accrediting agencies.[16]

Most importantly, the narrative Marsden developed was guided by his religious perspective and conviction, including his concern for pluralism and his skepticism of religious and cultural establishments—official and unofficial. A thoughtful review of *The Soul of the American University* would later note that the book "reflects that rejection of consensus, Enlightenment rationalism and the American 'melting pot' which is currently fashionable among American intellectuals" but then mistakenly attributed this orientation to postmodernism.[17] In fact, it was Marsden's formation in the Orthodox Presbyterian tradition that led him to regard cultural consensus as contrived. His faith tradition was one that had jettisoned the assumptions of nineteenth-century "common sense" philosophy "in favor of a sharply pluralistic outlook" championed by Dutch Reformed theologian Abraham Kuyper. According to Kuyper, "Differences in belief were not settled by some neutral standard of rationality, scientific inquiry, or moral intuition, but were determined by 'presuppositions,' that in turn were shaped by pretheoretical dispositions."[18] This was a sophisticated understanding of pluralism, even if the modern academy was largely unfamiliar with it. The position might bear enough similarity to postmodernism to confuse academic reviewers, but Marsden's way of seeing the problem pointed toward different conclusions—conclusions that were, for example, inherently hopeful about the possibility of understanding between and among communities without minimizing real differences. This pluralistic outlook—a gift of religious perspective—was central to the way Marsden analyzed the academy's loss of faith.

THE PROBLEM WITH ESTABLISHMENTS

The Soul of the American University began by outlining a fundamental tension within the American Protestant educational enterprise and offered a cultural context for making sense of that tension. From the founding of Harvard College in 1636, Protestant educators had seen their task in terms of both serving the church in rather particular ways *and* serving all of society in a manner that contributed to the broadest civic good.[19] Although these callings were not necessarily in conflict, and may often have been compatible, a cultural context of Protestant establishment (first legal, later informal) meant that educators did not need to think about the distinction or even contemplate conflict.

Indeed, the power of the Protestant establishment to meld politics, religion, and culture was such that even when critics such as Thomas Jefferson denounced religious dogmatism, Protestant educators could easily construe their faith—and schools—as broadly "nonsectarian," over against Roman Catholicism. Protestantism stood for liberty, the logic ran, and, thus, for free inquiry and republican virtues that stemmed from a godly education.

As the nineteenth century wore on, America's growing diversity—regional, ethnic, religious—might have challenged the de facto Protestant establishment had liberal leaders not been so theologically flexible. Liberal Protestantism maintained hegemony by recasting religion in terms of high moral ideals that were difficult to contest, rather than in terms of traditional doctrine that now persuaded a smaller slice of the population.

Liberal Protestants might have retained their role as cultural custodians, but new intellectual developments were raising questions that liberal Protestant educators were ill equipped to recognize, let alone answer. For years American college curricula had wedded religion and reason by employing a British strain of philosophy known as Scottish common sense. But the rise of scientific naturalism, which promised value-free objectivity, challenged this Enlightenment-era combination. The challenge arose, not from an inherent conflict between religion and science, but from the fact that liberal educators had grown so accustomed to equating progress and Protestantism that they were unable critically to appraise pure naturalism, or to imagine serious alternatives that retained an integral place for some notion of transcendence.

If the intellectual implications of these developments were initially unclear to many participants, their institutional outworking was impossible to miss. In the later nineteenth century, philanthropists launched new universities, and leading colleges reorganized themselves as universities, precisely on the basis of their commitments to scientific naturalism and detached objectivity. The story of these schools, which constitutes Part Two of *The Soul of the American University*, is organized around case studies exploring turning points or conflicts at newly founded Cornell, Johns Hopkins, and Chicago; aspiring state schools in California and Michigan; and the Ivy League's Harvard, Princeton, and Yale struggling to transform themselves from old-time colleges into centers of the new learning. Marsden deftly showed how intellectual and institutional developments on these eight campuses converged to create, often unwittingly, "the dominant university culture that emerged by the early twentieth century."[20]

Two cases seem pivotal—those of Johns Hopkins and Princeton. Hopkins, opened in 1876 under the leadership of Daniel Coit Gilman, epitomized much of the liberal Protestant educational mission. Gilman himself conducted the "nonsectarian" student chapel services during much of his presidency and encouraged student Christian associations. But Hopkins was at the forefront of what Marsden termed "methodological secularization," the process by which academics took the thoroughgoing empiricism of the modern scientific method and turned it into a necessary premise for saying anything meaningful about the world.[21]

Not only did Hopkins disseminate this new academic ideal via its pioneering generations of graduate students, but Gilman and others provided its Christian rationale. Hailing the discoveries of modern science, Gilman reformulated the old coupling of Christianity and civilization as the marriage of Christianity and modern science. Since science promised to distinguish truth from error, improve health, and end human misery, it resonated with Christianity. In fact, science was the most effective tool to advance Christianity, and Gilman cast the university as the harbinger of postmillennial promises. So convincing was this rationale that Hopkins faculty, such as psychologist G. Stanley Hall, could confidently apply the scientific method to religion itself, reducing it to an object that could be understood only in empirical terms. In doing so, Hall and others were persuaded they were furthering the cause of religion.

The situation at Princeton was somewhat different. For a combination of theological, cultural, and institutional reasons, Princeton was unusually resistant to the emerging university model.[22] Under the presidencies of Scotsman James McCosh and Anglo-Bermudian Francis Patton, Princeton maintained a British college ethos and directly challenged the assumptions of methodological secularization without rejecting modern science. McCosh never disallowed evolution, for example, but he rejected the notion that purely naturalistic premises were essential to knowledge. Princeton changed sharply under the presidency of Woodrow Wilson, beginning in 1902, moving quickly to catch up with prevailing university norms.[23] Wilson was a man of conservative theological convictions, but that hardly mattered in an atmosphere where practicing methodological secularization seemed to advance religion more successfully than propagating dogma. Wilson limited Christian teaching in favor of professionalism, substituting civic idealism for any specific religious foundation. By serving the nation, Princeton men would extend (Christian) civilization.

The last third of *The Soul of the American University* is, in a sense, one long dénouement. By equating salvation with social advance, liberal Protestants had long "removed any basis of maintaining a distinction between church and society." And now with social advance measured in purely material terms, the church had become superfluous: "The rest of the twentieth century worked out the inevitable implications of that [new] fusion."[24]

Marsden explored those implications with an insightful review of the origins of academic freedom as freedom from supernaturalism, as well as discussion of changes in student culture and campus ministry that presented new obstacles to maintaining even a private sphere for religiosity in the academy. In a helpful chapter on fundamentalism, he showed how conservative Protestantism did little to threaten the consolidating university ideal, although academics' reaction to fundamentalism trivialized what might have been a serious intellectual discussion about first principles. Lower-profile actors such as the Pension Fund of the Carnegie Foundation for the Advancement of Teaching were more influential than attention-grabbing fundamentalists in the process of sidelining faith. The Pension Fund insisted that participating institutions sever all church ties. Syracuse University, among others, decided it had no choice but to play by the Fund's rules. No aspiring university wanted to be classed with un-American Catholic schools.

By the 1960s the universities' intellectual and moral consensus came under attack. Women and racial minorities, in particular, pointed out that its claims to provide an objective view of the world were hardly value-free; they represented instead the self-interest of the campuses' white, male, and culturally Protestant establishment. Critics called into question the premise of scientific objectivity that had been the foundation of the entire twentieth-century university project. Science, they argued, was not so much a way of really understanding the world as a way of talking about the world from a particular point of view—so why should *its* point of view be privileged? Indeed, any discourse was merely a manifestation of particular groups' power.

As consensus collapsed with no prospect of being replaced, moral discussion on campus became self-evidently hollow. Of course there was no shortage of moral causes on campus, but those who cared had no moral tools with which to work. "The heirs to the liberal Protestant universities still equate all good with the social good," Marsden concluded, with more than a note of sadness. "Yet all they have left is campus politics."[25]

A CONCLUDING UNSCIENTIFIC POSTSCRIPT

Had *The Soul of the American University* ended here, it certainly would have stimulated important discussion. But Marsden went further, adding a gently provocative, twelve-page "Concluding Unscientific Postscript" in which he laid out "how this history bears on some current issues in the light of my own interest." Revisiting the "preeminent evaluative question" with which he had begun the book—"whether, in light of the reasons why American higher education has been defined as it is, there are compelling reasons for perpetuating such strong prejudices against traditional religious viewpoints," he answered bluntly: "I think there are not."[26]

Marsden directly challenged assumptions against granting religious perspectives a place in the academy. He started with an argument that bore some resemblance to postmodern critiques of scientific objectivity. Religious commitments had been excluded from campus because they had not stood up under an early twentieth-century standard of scientific naturalism. But, Marsden pointed out, by the 1990s that standard had become so discredited that it would hardly do to continue to disqualify religious viewpoints because they did not conform to the canons of objectivity. That did not mean that the academy should be a place where "anything goes," he cautioned. Every discipline honors its own procedural rules of inquiry and argument, and those should apply equally to religious and nonreligious perspectives. But religious views should not be dismissed out of hand.[27]

Marsden also dismantled arguments against religion that relied on certain understandings of pluralism, academic freedom, and distinctions between church and state. He called on religious scholars to be clear about their principles and on universities to grant such perspectives a seat at the academic table. Further, he argued that the presence of religious viewpoints would enliven diversity in the face of a deadening "impulse toward homongenization."[28]

In addition to pressing for deeper diversity within academic institutions, Marsden echoed Roman Catholic philosopher Alasdair MacIntyre in calling for institutional pluralism.[29] Not only should religiously informed scholarship receive a hearing in major research universities, he insisted, but academe's gatekeeping and governing agencies should lift their bias against institutions of higher education that prize religious convictions.[30] Surely "it should be recognized that religiously defined points of view can be intellectually as responsible as nonreligious ones," he insisted, so "it follows that religiously defined colleges and universities should have the right, if all else be equal, to be regarded as excellent."[31]

HITTING A NERVE

As intellectual history, *The Soul of the American University* received a warm reception.[32] Reviewers described it as "superb history, richly detailed, comprehensive, stimulating" (*Catholic Historical Review*) and "comprehensively researched and lucidly narrated" (*New York Times Book Review*).[33] Oxford historian Daniel Walker Howe praised the book as "probably the most important work on the history of American higher education since [1965]. . . . It displays a wide range of learning: the history of science, philosophy, theology and biblical criticism are all called upon as required. It is a wise and perceptive book, with much to offer both the specialist and the general reader. While long and fact-filled, it can be read quickly because the author's prose is lucid and engaging."[34]

Criticisms appeared, too, and they fell in two clusters. Some readers faulted the book for focusing on intellectual history to the neglect of other forces shaping twentieth-century campus life. Considered from the distance of more than a decade, these reviewers seem to have wanted a different book and a different research problem.[35]

By far the largest set of criticisms, however, focused on the final pages of the book, the Postscript. The academy might be celebrating perspectivalism and dismissing objectivity, but at the suggestion that religious views should have a place at the table, some reviewers drew a line. Marsden clearly had hit a nerve with his "uncomfortable prescription for changes in the ethos of college and university life."[36] Historian Cushing Strout called the Postscript a "tactical error," wondering aloud if Marsden had thought through the implications of the ideas he presented there. "Freedom, as Marsden insists," he averred, "may have its own limiting framework, but some frameworks are more dogmatic and less capable of revision." Strout "would be proud to have had Reinhold Neibuhr or Will Herberg as theologically-minded colleagues . . . [but] neither of them believed, as fundamentalists do, that biblical truth is analogous to the laws of physics."[37] Some reviewers even drew criticism for not criticizing Marsden sharply enough! The executive director of the American Academy of Religion protested a *New York Times* review that had not sufficiently refuted Marsden's claim that "a largely secular framework has resulted in the removal of religion from the curriculum."[38]

Remarkably, critics of the Postscript rarely had a problem with the historical narrative that preceded it—a narrative shaped by a self-consciously religious point of view. But they reacted strongly against the *idea* of reintroducing religious perspectives into scholarship or the classroom. Marsden himself later wondered "why *advocating* such a program has been less fully accepted in the academic mainstream than has simply doing it."[39] Perhaps the book's publication during the height of the so-called culture wars (or at least a high point in the discussion of cultural polarization) may have added to detractors' ire. Contemporary discussion of an intellectual crisis in American education—with proposals from Stanley Fish to Allan Bloom all afloat—may have raised the stakes as well.[40]

EXPLORING AN OUTRAGEOUS IDEA

If most critics seemed outraged by the notion of approaching scholarship from a religious point of view, one voice offered a different sort of dissent. Duke Divinity School ethicist Stanley Hauerwas praised "this wonderful new book" but then asked whether Marsden practiced the kind of methodological secularization he critiqued. The history was so solid that Hauerwas found "it hard to discover anything in this book that would not make Marsden a well-regarded academic historian." Hauerwas thought a truly Christian perspective would have left the canons of history behind and offered "God's judgment against . . . the vapid character of [liberal] Protestantism."⁴¹ Despite Marsden's assertion that scholars could operate from distinctly religious points of view *and* play within the rules of the scholastic game, it seemed that even a friendly critic was unsure exactly what difference religious perspectives might make. Meanwhile, Marsden had begun to receive a flurry of invitations to speak to academic forums and Christian college faculties about the implications of his call for Christian scholarship. In response to both reviewer criticism and the friendly inquiries, he began to develop the ideas in the Postscript more completely.⁴²

Marsden's exposition, entitled *The Outrageous Idea of Christian Scholarship* (1997), was a concise set of essays running just over one hundred pages. The book expanded on the Postscript's argument that "writing or teaching from a Christian point of view is not really outrageous, so long as one presents that point of view without violating the other usual rules of academia regarding writing or teaching from a point of view." Second, and rather more basically, Marsden explained more fully what he "had in mind by 'Christian scholarship,'" since "many people find this idea strange unless it refers only to theology or to study *about* religious topics."⁴³

Marsden began by describing contemporary university culture, a culture marked by fragmented disciplines and driven by practical applications that give no thought to first principles, all of which left professors with no ability "to produce a compelling basis for preferring one set of principles over another."⁴⁴ Such an environment, Marsden suggested, would benefit greatly from reconsidering perspectives that included transcendence. He advocated opening "the academic mainstream to scholarship that relates one's belief in God to what else one thinks about. Keeping within our intellectual horizons a being who is great enough to create us and the universe, after all, ought to change our perspectives on quite a number of things," he reasoned.⁴⁵ While he urged that "perspectives of [all] religious groups be accepted as legitimate in the mainstream academy," he addressed Christians specifically, "since that is my own faith."⁴⁶

Marsden navigated between two criticisms that his earlier Postscript proposals had engendered. The first was the idea that Christianity was a private conviction that should make no difference in the life of the mind; the other was a view that Christianity so deeply reorders intellectual priorities that believers cannot operate faithfully within conventional academic norms. Rejecting both claims, Marsden drew on Augustinian thought to show that people of faith live simultaneously in two worlds, granting relative respect to different masters.[47]

Often Christians follow the same "rules of the game" as everyone else, he averred. Indeed, "in a pluralistic society we have little choice but to accept pragmatic standards in public life."[48] Using an image popularized by pragmatist philosopher William James, Marsden described the university as like a corridor in a hotel to which many people bring their beliefs and assumptions and commitments from the rooms they inhabit.[49] There is no reason why faith must be kept out of the corridor "so long as one presents that point of view without violating the other usual rules of academia regarding writing or teaching from a point of view."[50] Indeed, everyone would benefit from moving such views from the strictly private sphere to a place where they can be acknowledged, considered, "more rigorously developed," and opened to self-criticism.[51]

At other times, of course, religious commitments make a great deal of difference and *will* radically reshape the way scholars engage their work. "The situation of the religious believer," he explained, "may be analogous to a doctor who is playing softball. So long as she is in the softball game, she tries not to break its rules. If, however, she sees a car accident on a nearby street, she will stop running the bases and go to help. The rules of doctoring take precedence over baseball rules."[52] For Christians, the "rules" include theological commitments with implications for academic life, such as a healthy notion of the human condition—supremely gifted but flawed—that motivates a believer to seek the welfare of the world without falling victim to cynicism when her efforts fall short.[53]

The Outrageous Idea modeled the sort of corridor virtues Marsden championed: a "willingness to listen as well as to speak" and "respect [for] those with whom one differs, even as they may debate their differences." Quoting extensively from critics of *The Soul of the American University*, Marsden uses their criticisms as points of departure (referring to them as "helpful" or "a thoughtful review") and never as straw figures to be dismantled.[54] Although by some measures *The Outrageous*

Idea did not reach as wide an audience as *The Soul of the American University*, the latter book received positive reviews, and Christian scholars, especially, took it as a wise and trusted guide.[55]

But even Christians who appreciated Marsden's seminal contribution also recognized that his project had left some questions unresolved, particularly involving the place of the church. Marsden's use of William James's corridor metaphor assumed vital Christian communities from which Christian scholars emerge into the academic hallway. So although Marsden's aim was to win the secular university's approval, his proposal also raised basic questions of ecclesial practice and priority.

Some evangelical academics, while not dismissing Marsden's call to the corridor, frankly understood their first task as resisting anti-intellectual tendencies and nurturing scholarly sensibilities within their own circles. Churches of Christ historian Richard Hughes, for example, was much less concerned to gain a hearing in secular settings than to show teachers and students from restorationist, holiness, Lutheran, and Anabaptist traditions "how Christian faith can sustain the life of the mind."[56] Meanwhile, from within Marsden's own Reformed tradition, philosopher James K. A. Smith has argued that Christian scholars must offer much more than "a Christian perspective." He urges academics to ground scholarship in worshipping communities, shifting the agenda toward "the formation of a peculiar people." Although such an agenda hardly precludes Marsden's call to corridor conversations, Smith is less sanguine that offering an alternative "point of view," apart from ecclesial formation, will make much difference.[57]

Whatever the measure, it is unclear whether Marsden's arguments have led to greater openness to religious perspectives in wider academe, although any such change is admittedly difficult to document. In 2009 the American Historical Association, a secular professional organization, announced that religion was now the leading research interest of its members. Paul Michaelson, secretary of the Conference of Faith and History, a group founded by evangelical scholars, took that as an encouraging sign that "the misleading dichotomy between sacred and secular spheres is losing some of its recent force in academia."[58] Of course, as Marsden would remind us, studying religion is not the same thing as scholarly inquiry from a religious point of view.

HISTORY WITH SOUL

In 2001 a brief entry on George Marsden appeared in *The Encyclopedia of Evangelicalism*. The sketch summed his groundbreaking scholarship in American religious history but seemed unsure what to make of "five years of research [that] culminated in *The Soul of the American University*," a book that the entry characterized as "an extended jeremiad" and a curious interruption in his scholarly career. So the *Encyclopedia* hurried on: "In the mid-1990s, Marsden resumed his more conventional scholarship with work on a biography of Jonathan Edwards." Apparently, in choosing to write about an eighteenth-century Puritan, Marsden had returned to recognizable history.[59]

Or had he?

Rather than a scholarly diversion, *The Soul of the American University* was as conventional as any history Marsden had ever penned, and it stood in continuity with his earlier and later work, illustrating his scholarly and Christian commitments.[60] *The Soul of the American University* demonstrated the creative power and academic value of working from a particular religious perspective. Marsden had built on a good deal of fairly conventional historiography and had drawn on secondary sources to a degree that his other books had not.[61] What made this study so significant was the fact that he brought new questions to bear on these sources. And those questions were the result of insights born of a particular theological perspective, one that took faith seriously and that took pluralism just as seriously.

His writing also exhibited the gracious characteristics that he had long suggested were distinguishing marks of Christian scholarship: charity and fairness, along with an Augustinian tentativeness that was manifest in humble self-criticism.[62] As he noted near the beginning of *The Soul of the American University*, it was "the Protestant heritage to which I am closest, the Reformed . . . who long set the standards for dominant American education" and "who aspired to dominate the culture" that bore the brunt of his critique.[63] For Christian historians, Marsden showed how writing about one's own tradition was less an apologetic than a call to account—a way of allowing others in the corridor the opportunity to consider and critique alongside the believer.

Certainly one of George Marsden's greatest gifts to the academy was his appealing example and patient argument to broaden the corridor conversations that constitute the contemporary American academy. "Over the past twenty years," Marsden mused in 2008, "change has been taking place quietly, as many talented young people who combine substantive religious commitment with strong scholarship and civility are emerging throughout academia."[64] Characteristically, he took no credit for this remarkable development, but few of those now conversing in the corridor, faith in hand, have any doubt that Marsden played a key role in inviting them to bring their convictions—humbly but confidently—into the conversation.

"If you want to change things," Marsden once observed, ". . . do so by example."[65] With *The Soul of the American University*, Marsden offered an inspiring model of thoughtful, carefully constructed American history. As Christian scholars follow his lead, allowing their religious commitments to shape the questions they pursue with intelligence, clarity, and humility, they enliven the academy and foster authentic conversation. What vocation and calling could be more fulfilling?

NOTES

1. John Updike, *In the Beauty of the Lilies* (New York: Random House, 1996), 5, 6, 7.

2. Ibid., 7.

3. George M. Marsden, *The Soul of the American University: From Protestant Establishment to Established Unbelief* (New York: Oxford University Press, 1994), 116.

4. Ibid., 244–45.

5. George M. Marsden and Bradley J. Longfield, introduction to *The Secularization of the Academy*, ed. George M. Marsden and Bradley J. Longfield (New York: Oxford University Press, 1992), 3.

6. Marsden, *Soul of the American University*, 15.

7. George M. Marsden and Bradley J. Longfield, preface to *Secularization*, v.

8. E.g., Frederick Rudolph, *The American College and University: A History* (New York: Knopf, 1962).

9. George Marsden, "Doing American History in a World of Subcultures," *Reviews in American History* 37 (June 2009): 303.

10. Ibid.

11. Marsden and Longfield, preface to *Secularization*, v, and introduction to *Secularization*, 3–7; Marsden, *Soul*, xi. The grant project was titled "The Religious and the Secular in Modern America," and funding came specifically from the J. Howard Pew Freedom Trust. The conference was held at Duke University in June 1990. Marsden's presentation at that conference, which was chapter 1 of *Secularization*, contained many of the ideas that later appeared in *The Soul of the American University*, including the "Postscript." Marsden developed and tested his ideas with other audiences, including his 1992 American Society of Church History presidential address (see "The Ambiguities of Academic Freedom," *Church History* [June 1993]: 221–36), an invited lecture at the 1993 American Academy of Religion (see report by Peter Steinfels, "Universities Biased against Religion, Scholar Says," *New York Times*, November 26, 1993, A22), and an essay entitled "The Decade Ahead in Scholarship," *Religion and American Culture* 3 (Winter 1993): 9–14.

12. Marsden made this point often, but the quotation is from "Doing American History," 306. For misguided criticism suggesting that Marsden was protesting personal discrimination against scholars who were privately Christians, see Steinfels, "Universities Biased." This criticism was also the main thrust of Randall Balmer at a January 8, 1994, American Society of Church History forum convened in response to Marsden's 1992 ASCH address. See Balmer, "Response to George Marsden," and Marsden's rejoinder, reproduced in "American Society of Church History Papers Presented at the 155th Annual Conference, January 6–9, 1994, San Francisco, California."

13. Marsden, *Soul*, 8, 265; Marsden and Longfield, introduction to *Secularization*, 5–6.

14. Marsden, *Soul*, 239.

15. Ibid., vii, 3–4, 99–100, quotes on vii and 99.

16. Ibid., vii, 13–14, 23, 272–76, 296–97, 357–68, 366–67, 379, 383–84, 401–3.

17. Daniel Walker Howe, review of *The Soul of the American University*, by George Marsden, *Journal of Ecclesiastical History* 47 (April 1996): 399–400. A few reviewers described Marsden's approach as "sectarian," see, e.g., Daniel Sack, review of *The Soul of the American University*, by George Marsden, *Religious Studies Review* 23 (January 1997): 36. This was closer to the mark than crediting postmodernism, but it did not do justice to the nuances of Marsden's thought. See Marsden, *Soul*, 430 and 440 n. 1, for Marsden's discussion of where his religious perspective parts ways with postmodernism. In Marsden and Longfield, introduction to *Secularization*, 41, Marsden used the phrase "unpopular sect" to describe the position of "Christians in the post-modern age."

18. Marsden, "Doing American History," 304: "My peculiar religious heritage made me question claims that the culture ought to be moving toward a consensus." On Kuyper, see John Bolt, *A Free Church, a Holy Nation: Abraham Kuyper's American Public Theology* (Grand Rapids, MI: Eerdmans, 2001).

19. In describing Harvard's ethos in 1654, when Henry Dunster resigned the presidency amid controversy over his questioning infant baptism, Marsden offered a contemporary parallel, explaining that "in the late twentieth [century], it would be like a Harvard president announcing opposition to equal opportunity for women" (*Soul*, 40). As unlikely as such a turn of events may have seemed to readers in 1994, something like this happened in 2006 when Lawrence Summers resigned as Harvard president amid campus furor over his statements that women's "intrinsic aptitude" for math and science was less than men's!

20. Marsden, *Soul*, 100.

21. Ibid., 150–66, but esp. 156–57.

22. Ibid., 196–218.

23. Ibid., 219–35.

24. Ibid., 422.

25. Ibid., 403–4, 423–24, quote from 424.

26. Ibid., 429. Some reviewers mentioned the Postscript title's allusion to Søren Kierkegaard's 1846 *Concluding Unscientific Postscript*, which was an attack on determinism.

27. Marsden, *Soul*, 429–32.

28. Ibid., 432–36, quote from 432. Marsden had been making such points for some time, e.g., "Decade Ahead," 14: "Such discourse would, of course, have to take place within the rules necessary for a diverse scholarly community to proceed civilly. Nonetheless, a great deal more could be accomplished by way of encouraging such true diversity than is now being done in what amounts to a religiously hollow multiculturalism." See also the final pages of Marsden, "Ambiguities of Academic Freedom."

29. Marsden, *Soul*, 436–40; Alasdair MacIntyre, *Three Rival Versions of Moral Enquiry* (Notre Dame, IN: University of Notre Dame Press, 1990), 216–36.

30. Marsden argued that some religiously affiliated institutions suffered discrimination from accrediting agencies and academic honor societies but not that Christian faculty members faced discrimination for their private religious beliefs. (See also Marsden's op-ed "Church, State, and Campus," *New York Times*, April 26, 1994, A23.) A few critics misread this section of the Postscript as a claim that the academy discriminated against scholars who were privately Christian. These critics delighted to saying that such charges must be unfounded because Marsden himself was welcomed to teach in leading schools. See a variation of this theme in Sack, review of Marsden, *Soul*, 37, which states that Marsden believes "the modern university is inherently hostile to Christian scholars" rather than Christian scholarship.

31. Marsden, *Soul*, 437–40, quotes from 439. See also Marsden and Longfield, introduction to *Secularization*, 8 n. 4 and 41.

32. Summary here and below based on reading several dozen of the reviews that appeared in academic history, religion/theology, and education journals.

33. David J. O'Brien, review of *The Soul of the American University*, by George Marsden, *Catholic Historical Review* 82 (April 1996): 307; John Patrick Diggins, "God, Man and the Curriculum," *New York Times Book Review*, April 17, 1994, BR25.

34. Howe, review of Marsden, *Soul*, 399.

35. E.g., Robert L. Johnson, review of *The Soul of the American University*, by George Marsden, *Theology Today* 52 (October 1995): 430–32, which criticized the book's limited discussion of neo-orthodoxy; and Sack, review of Marsden, *Soul*, 37, which criticized the book's focus on pacesetting schools instead of student life and campus ministries across all campuses.

36. Francis Oakley, review of *The Soul of the American University*, by George Marsden, *Journal for the Scientific Study of Religion* 34 (June 1995): 275.

37. Cushing Strout, review of *The Soul of the American University*, by George Marsden, *History of Education Quarterly* 35 (Autumn 1995): 322. Some reviews engaged the Postscript thoughtfully, such as Glenn C. Altschuler's "Schools with Soul," *New England Quarterly* 68 (June 1995): 300–305.

38. Barbara DeConcini, letter to the editor, *New York Times*, May 15, 1994, BR39, letter responding to Diggins's review ("God, Man") in *New York Times Book Review*.

39. Marsden, "Doing American History," 307.

40. During the late 1980s and throughout the 1990s a flood of books dealing with a "crisis" in American education—at all levels—and offering widely varying prescriptions included works by Peter W. Cookson Jr., E. D. Hirsch, Chester Finn, Stanley Fish, Allan Bloom, Paige Smith, Richard Bernstein, Dinesh D'Souza, Richard Kimball, James Traub, and Douglas M. Sloan.

41. Stanley Hauerwas, "Missing from the Curriculum," *Commonweal*, September 23, 1994, 19–20. On method and being a well-regarded historian, see comments in Marsden, "Doing American History," 308–9.

42. George M. Marsden, *The Outrageous Idea of Christian Scholarship* (New York: Oxford University Press, 1997), [v–vi]. See also Marsden, "Doing American History," 306; and George Marsden, "Christian Advocacy and the Rules of the Academic Game," in *Religious Advocacy and American History*, ed. Bruce Kuklick and D. G. Hart (Grand Rapids, MI: Eerdmans, 1997).

43. Marsden, "Doing American History," 306; Marsden, *Outrageous Idea*, [v].

44. Marsden, *Outrageous Idea*, 3.

45. Ibid., 4.

46. Ibid., 8.

47. Ibid., 97–100.

48. Ibid., 46.

49. Ibid., 45–46.

50. Marsden, *Doing American History*, 306.

51. Marsden, *Outrageous Idea*, 55–57, quote from 51.

52. Ibid., 56.

53. Ibid., 83–100.

54. See, e.g., ibid., 51, 53–54, 60. See also Marsden, "Doing American History," 307, in which he did not blame critics who misread his arguments but characteristically took "some of the blame" himself for "inadequacies in my arguments."

55. WorldCat (accessed February 2, 2013) reported that 1,330 academic libraries held copies of *The Soul of the American University* (www.worldcat.org/oclc/28338933&referer=brief_results), while 871 held *The Outrageous Idea of Christian Scholarship* (www.worldcat.org/oclc/34967767&referer=brief_results). *The Outrageous Idea* was also reviewed less widely than the earlier book, and more reviews were in religion-related journals than was true of the earlier book. For one of many examples of the latter book's positive reception, see "Christian Scholarship," chapter reviews by faculty at Abilene Christian University's online forum, 1999, www.acu.edu/academics/adamscenter/resources/faithlearning/christianschol.html.

56. Richard T. Hughes, *How Christian Faith Can Sustain the Life of the Mind* (Grand Rapids, MI: Eerdmans, 2001). Hughes's book is broadly ecumenical, citing Roman Catholic and Reformed examples approvingly, yet the direction of his argument seems couched to appeal most effectively to those outside the Reformed fold. In 1994, when George Marsden published *The Soul of the American University*, Mark A. Noll, the noted evangelical historian and colleague of Marsden, published *The Scandal of the Evangelical Mind* (Grand Rapids, MI: Eerdmans), a lament for what he considered evangelicals' anemic intellectual life. Noll's book provoked wide discussion, and some soul-searching, in evangelical circles.

57. James K. A. Smith, *Desiring the Kingdom: Worldview, Worship, and Cultural Formation* (Grand Rapids, MI: Baker Academic Publishing, 2009), 17, 34, 44 n. 10. Smith's argument in this book is considerably more complex and nuanced than I can suggest here.

58. Robert B. Townsend, "A New Found Religion? The Field Surges among AHA Members," *Perspectives on History*, December 2009, www.historians.org/Perspectives/issues/2009/0912/0912new3.cfm. A survey of AHA members in September 2009 revealed that 7.7 percent of members selected religion as one of their three areas of interest, surpassing cultural history (selected by 7.5 percent), which had been the most popular subject category for more than fifteen years. Michelson quoted in Bobby Ross Jr., "Beyond Believers," *Christianity Today*, March 2010, 14.

59. Randall Balmer, ed., *Encyclopedia of Evangelicalism*, rev. and expanded ed. (Waco, TX: Baylor University Press, 2004), 426.

60. See themes explored as early as Marsden's second book, *A Christian View of History?*, edited with Frank Roberts (Grand Rapids, MI: Eerdmans, 1975).

61. Marsden, *Soul*, ix. The endnotes point to the scholarship of Bruce Kuklick, Dorothy Ross, Richard Hofstadter, Walter P. Metzger, and others. One reviewer, Leo P. Ribuffo, called the book "a synthesis with a message" (*Reviews in American History*, 172).

62. See George M. Marsden, "What Difference Might Christian Perspectives Make?," in *History and the Christian Historian*, ed. Ronald A. Wells (Grand Rapids, MI: Eerdmans, 1998), 11–22.

63. Marsden, *Soul*, 8.

64. Marsden, "Doing American History," 308.

65. Ibid.

CHAPTER 14

More Than a Footnote?

Evangelical Ministries and the Secular University

JOHN G. TURNER

I first encountered *The Soul of the American University* under somewhat unusual circumstances. After hastily submitting my graduate school applications, I traveled to the Philippines for eight months of postcollege volunteer work. Several friends and professors had recommended that I apply to work with George Marsden at the University of Notre Dame. Since I intended to study American Puritanism, I was intrigued by the fact that Professor Marsden was working on a biography of Jonathan Edwards. After gaining admission to Notre Dame, I had a trans-Pacific conversation with George, who offered to expedite me several of his books. Remarkably, given the usually unreliable delivery of international mail on the island, a package arrived several days later.

The Soul of the American University dissipated the intellectual languor induced by tropical weather—it proved both great scholarship and a great read. *Soul* provided a graceful and persuasive explanation of the secularization of American higher education. While tracing the transition from "Protestant establishment" to "established nonbelief," Marsden identified liberal Protestants as the ironic prime movers in this process. Seeking to exclude the "sectarian" viewpoints of evangelicals and Catholics, they molded institutions that eventually proscribed their own brand of Christianity from official university matters as well. In his "Concluding Unscientific Postscript," Marsden critiqued the contemporary state of academia that, under the premise of scientific objectivity, "exclude[s] a priori all religiously based claims on the grounds that they are unscientific," thus ignoring the genuine contributions of Christian intellectual traditions. Even many ostensibly religious institutions of higher education had largely conformed to this posture, he lamented.[1]

Most histories of the relationship between religion and higher education reinforce Marsden's general narrative of secularization, whether they mourn or celebrate this transition and whether they follow the particulars of Marsden's interpretation.[2] More general histories of American higher education typically ignore religion entirely once they reach the twentieth century, with perhaps a passing mention of conflicts between religious dogma and academic freedom in the early 1900s.[3] We are a long way removed from required Protestant chapel services at state and most private universities. Yet, judging by the display booths at student activity fairs, the messages posted in student unions and scrawled on walkways, and the collection of religious centers and churches bordering most university campuses, religion has hardly vanished from American higher education. Evangelical campus organizations have proliferated, mainline campus chapters have staged at least a partial recovery from their nadir in the early 1970s, and Muslim student organizations have grown rapidly.[4] Although Marsden concedes that "the work of campus ministries may provide invaluable compensation for the religious poverty of the rest of the universities," he warns that "as long as the prevailing intellectual outlook of universities is built on community standards antithetical to most traditional religious belief, what goes on in the classrooms will be undermining the outlooks presented in campus religious meetings." "Campus ministries...," Marsden asserts in a footnote to *Soul*, "hardly touch the antireligious heart of modern academia."[5]

The history of Campus Crusade for Christ (or Cru, as the organization renamed itself in 2011) both confirms and challenges Marsden's assertions about evangelical campus ministries. Campus Crusade, founded by Bill Bright in 1951 at the University of California Los Angeles, is currently the largest evangelical parachurch campus ministry in the United States, devoting over $100 million per year and three thousand staff members to collegiate evangelism.[6] While confirming Marsden's broad narrative of religion's relegation to the nonacademic margins of the university, the activities of evangelical campus ministries restored and maintained a visible evangelical presence at American colleges and universities. Indeed, for many students those very margins—the dormitories, locker rooms, and dining halls—constituted something central rather than peripheral to their undergraduate experiences. Thus, while administrators and faculty displaced religion from the lecture halls and collective public life of academia, campus ministries and other religious initiatives created a vibrant spiritual marketplace for American students that mitigated the effects of the academy's secularization.

THE POSTWAR BOOM IN CAMPUS RELIGION

Following his graduation from Oklahoma's tiny Northeastern State College, Bill Bright moved to California, started several businesses, converted to evangelical Christianity at the First Presbyterian Church of Hollywood, and enrolled first in Princeton Theological Seminary and then as part of Fuller Theological Seminary's inaugural class.[7] After struggling with the language requirements and what he considered to be an overly intellectual atmosphere at Fuller, Bright experienced a spiritual vision that led him to found Campus Crusade for Christ. After leaving Fuller, he wrote potential supporters to seek funding for his new organization. Bright asserted that "the average collegian is spiritually illiterate" and "estimated that less than five percent of the college students of America are actively engaged in the church of today." After noting that virtually all American colleges and universities "were founded as Christian institutions," he lamented that "many of our state universities and colleges and other institutions deny the deity of Christ, the Bible as the Word of God, and offer not so much as one Christian course in their curriculum." Furthermore, Bright believed that the campus would resolve the question of "Christ or Communism—which shall it be?" "Communism has already made deep inroads into the American campus," he warned in a bulletin promoting his newly formed organization, "and unless we fill the spiritual vacuum of the collegiate world, the campus may well become America's 'Trojan Horse.'" While Bright's primary focus was evangelism, he viewed the work of Campus Crusade through the lens of Cold War geopolitics. "Win the campus today," Crusade's motto promised, "win the world tomorrow."[8]

Other observers of campus life shared Bright's concerns. Shortly before Bright launched Campus Crusade, William F. Buckley published *God and Man at Yale*, which Marsden spotlights in a prologue to *Soul*. Buckley, a Catholic and a Yale alumnus, portrayed his alma mater as an "institution that derives its moral and financial support from Christian individualists and then addresses itself to the task of persuading the sons of these supporters to be atheistic socialists."[9] Protestant fundamentalists, meanwhile, had been apprehensive about the state of American higher education since the early 1900s. Fundamentalist critics alleged that modernist professors were importing dangerous German philosophies into American lecture halls, turning pious Christian students into what Bob Jones termed "campus shipwrecks" and state universities into—in the words of William Bell Riley—"hot-beds of skepticism." Still, only a small percentage of Americans went to college in the early twentieth century, and most fundamentalists who pursued post-secondary education attended denominational colleges or Bible institutes. By midcentury, however, fundamentalist worries advanced into more widespread evangelical alarm about the state of American colleges and universities. The number of Americans enrolled at institutions of higher education jumped by nearly one million between only 1946 and 1950. Over two million veterans utilized the higher education benefits of the G.I. Bill. As public universities expanded rapidly, their enrollments began to outnumber those of private institutions. This tidal wave of students—many of whom were first-generation collegians—attended universities and colleges that had gradually divested themselves of the most pronounced aspects of their denominational heritage.[10]

Despite his assertions about creeping atheism and communism on the campus, Bright launched Campus Crusade at an auspicious time and place. Crusade's early years at UCLA coincided with a nationwide upsurge in campus religiosity parallel to the more general religious boom of the postwar years. Across the United States, university officials pointed to thriving denominational ministries, the establishment of academic courses in religion, and the success of "religious emphasis" weeks as signs of Christian vitality. Periodicals like *Time* and *Newsweek* maintained that collegians in the 1950s were more religious than their 1920s counterparts.[11] At UCLA, there was considerable evidence of student religiosity. At least ten Christian groups—from the Presbyterian Westminster Club to the pacifist Fellowship of Reconciliation—advertised in the UCLA *Daily Bruin* during the 1951–52 academic year. Thousands of students listened to Billy Graham during the evangelist's October 1951 visit to campus. Louis H. Evans Sr. and Richard Halverson, two ministers from Bright's own Hollywood Presbyterian, addressed UCLA's Westminster Club and InterVarsity chapter, respectively.[12] Such activities, however, do not mean that UCLA was a Christian university, at least not as evangelicals like Bright would have defined the concept.

R. G. Sproul, president of the entire University of California system, commented on the state of religion on campus in conjunction with UCLA's 1953 religious emphasis week. Sproul maintained that the university should encourage "a code of Christianlike behavior" in its students and help them to understand that "there is significance to men's existence." However, Sproul insisted that faith "lives in the hearts of men of a thousand different creeds, and joyously dwells with men who know no creed at all."[13] In short, as Marsden's *Soul* concluded of most universities by the 1950s, UCLA retained the ethical and moral ideals of liberal Protestantism without promoting any particular faith. Yet UCLA had also created an open religious marketplace in which a wide range of groups—including evangelical parachurch organizations—could effectively promote their own brands of religion.

Campus Crusade eagerly took advantage of this marketplace. Crusade targeted prominent student leaders, including fraternity and sorority leaders, student government officials, and athletes. The organization pulled off an early coup when Donn Moomaw, UCLA's All-American linebacker, attended a Crusade meeting and then accompanied the Brights to Hollywood Presbyterian. Bright talked Moomaw through a series of Bible verses about sin and salvation, and Moomaw prayed to "receive" Jesus Christ as his savior. "Because I was high visibility through my athletics," explains Moomaw, "he [Bright] had me going out sharing my conversion experience everywhere." Moomaw and Bright appeared together on Billy Graham's popular *Hour of Decision* television program in 1953. Soon Campus Crusade claimed 250 conversions, "including the student body president, the editor of the newspaper, and a number of the top athletes." Most of the stars on UCLA's 1954 national-championship football team—nicknamed the "Eleven from Heaven"—were outspoken Christians, many of whom made "decisions for Christ" through Bright's influence.[14]

The publicity generated by this early success, combined with Bright's talents for both entrepreneurship and spiritual leadership, helped Crusade rapidly expand its operations. Bolstered by recruits from Christian colleges (especially Bob Jones University) and its own student converts, Crusade established a presence at most state universities in the West and Midwest by the end of the 1950s. The organization utilized several techniques to evangelize collegians, including a "religious questionnaire" designed to identify interested students, Bible studies, newspapers and records, and speaking engagements at Greek houses. However they initiated contacts with students, Crusade staff employed an evangelistic presentation, which culminated in "Are you ready to say 'Yes' to Christ?" Bright streamlined the presentation into a standardized talk entitled "God's Plan for Your Life" and then further condensed it into a pamphlet: *Have You Heard of the Four Spiritual Laws?* "God loves you and has a wonderful plan for your life," began the pamphlet. Like the earlier presentations, it ended by encouraging students to prayerfully tell Jesus: "I open the door of my life and receive You as my Savior and Lord." Bright asked his staff members to use the pamphlet in their attempts at personal evangelism. David Harrington Watt, the most perceptive scholarly critic of the pamphlet, estimated in the early 1990s that "next to the Bible it is the work that contemporary evangelicals are most likely to have encountered."[15]

In its evangelistic presentations, the organization did not attempt to outline a rational or intellectual case for Christianity or relate a relationship with Christ to the academic life of the university. Bright exhibited a strong streak of anti-intellectualism during Campus Crusade's early years. To Bright—and to many evangelicals—intellectual pursuits were luxuries that threatened to distract Christians from more immediate tasks. At training events, Bright told his staff members that they needed to choose between the "simple" and the "scholarly," and he still discerned no positive connection between advanced theological education and effectiveness in ministry. "Some of the most decadent, fruitless people I know," he lamented, "have several degrees." "It's hard [to witness effectively]," he cautioned, "after four years of exegesis, learning the original languages, Hebrew and Greek." He warned potential staff recruits, "The average person to whom you speak, even on the college campus, is not interested in the theology of Barth and Brunner, and Tillich and Niebuhr and the rest." "You must be prepared to communicate in the most simple terms," he challenged them, "and I do not know a more simple way than the Four Spiritual Laws." When Bright explained his Four Spiritual Laws to a group of Berkeley faculty in 1967, a professor asked him how he would present his message to "a genuine intellectual." "Bill said," recollects Crusade staff member Howard Ball, "'I would probably read it more slowly.'"[16]

Such anti-intellectual attitudes did not impede Campus Crusade's growth. Crusade flourished in the 1950s and early 1960s, a time when Greek houses and athletics dominated campus life. Bill Counts, who joined staff in 1960, believes that Crusade effectively reached students because the organization viewed the campus "as a social center" rather than "as an intellectual center." "If you look at where the average student was at a big state university," Counts continues, "they weren't there because they were interested in studying all these academics in depth and they were reading all these books on philosophy. They were there because they were in a fraternity and sorority. They were going to football games." Christianity might have moved from the core to the periphery of campus, but to many students fraternities, locker rooms, and dormitories were the core of college life, and Crusade found ways to penetrate those campus spaces.[17]

CAMPUS CRUSADE AND THE JESUS MOVEMENT

By the late 1960s, Campus Crusade's ministry was at a crossroads. On January 23, 1967, a large crowd of students at the University of California at Berkeley gathered on the Sproul Hall steps to protest Governor Ronald Reagan's dismissal of Clark Kerr, president of the University of California system. They found themselves listening to Christian folk songs performed by the New Folk, a Campus Crusade traveling musical ensemble. Crusade had reserved the area several weeks in advance and refused to allow other student groups to make statements on the Kerr firing. According to Jo Anne Butts, a local InterVarsity staffer, the "mocking in the crowd was almost unbearable as a result." Butts reported that Crusade interpreted the large audience produced by Kerr's dismissal as a divine blessing. Protests aside, most Berkeley students had already moved from folk music into edgier forms of rock and roll. After the New Folk finished its performance, the crowd—at a university where campus life no longer revolved around athletics and the Greek system—heard a football player from a large southern university speak about how Jesus Christ had changed his life. Finally, Jon Braun, Crusade's top university speaker, took the platform and talked about God's love as the only solution for the world's problems. Following the talk, hundreds of Crusade staff and students approached those in the audience and sought to evangelize them using the *Four Spiritual Laws*. It was a rather bizarre encounter between two very different American subcultures: late 1960s Berkeley and evangelical Christianity. In the days that followed, hundreds of Crusade staff evangelized students in what the organization dubbed the "Berkeley Blitz."[18]

At the Berkeley Blitz, Peter Gillquist noticed that "Bill [Bright] stayed in the background, which was unusual for him." "I sensed he almost felt out of his element," Gillquist explains. "This is a white-shirt [man] who wears a suit every day and a necktie, by now all passé on the campus.... I think in the midst of the rabble-rousers he just felt out of place." Initially, Bright struggled to adapt his organization's strategy to a changing campus culture. For example, he forbade his male staff members to grow long hair. "The Apostle Paul," he asserted, "was against long hair [for men] and I don't think you would find any Bible scholar who would say Christ had long hair." Also, Bright agonized about the use of Christian rock music. "The New Folk drifted into hard rock for a while," Bright explained, "but we felt that wasn't for us" because of the complaints of "ex-addicts." Despite Bright's hesitation, Crusade quickly embraced change. The organization still utilized *The Four Spiritual Laws* and its older evangelistic strategies, but Crusade also updated its approach. Bright began portraying Jesus as a "revolutionary," Crusade staff and students picketed New Left and antiwar rallies, and Crusade exhibited a greater awareness of racism and other social problems. Although hardly in the vanguard of the more explicitly countercultural Jesus Movement, Campus Crusade increasingly swam in its wake.[19]

The apogee of Crusade's engagement with the Jesus Movement occurred at the organization's Explo '72 congress in Dallas. That June, Crusade brought nearly one hundred thousand students—high schoolers and collegians—to the Cotton Bowl for a mixture of mass evangelism, door-to-door witnessing, and evangelical revelry. The influence of the Jesus Movement was palpable at Explo. The *New York Times* reported that Explo delegates raised "their arms with clenched fists and the index finger pointed upward as a sign that Jesus is the 'one way'" to heaven. Young people shouted out "Jesus yells" in unison. Every night, the delegates in the Cotton Bowl swayed to Christian rock music—Bright had recognized the evangelistic potential of the new genre—before Bright or Billy Graham took the stage. On Explo's final night, upwards of 150,000 people gathered for a Jesus Music Festival featuring Kris Kristofferson and Johnny Cash.[20]

In the late 1960s and early 1970s, vocal evangelicals like the students and staff of Campus Crusade constituted a decided minority on the campus. Conservatives of all sorts faced an uphill battle on American campuses. Only a small fraction of students—perhaps one-sixth or one-fifth of the overall student population—labeled themselves as "conservative" or "Far Right" in a 1970 survey. Moreover, only 42 percent of American students told Gallup pollsters in 1970 that "organized religion" was a "relevant" part of their lives, far below the response of the general population.[21]

Despite such trends and attitudes, however, religion was not disappearing from campus life. Instead, the locus of campus religiosity was shifting. Mainline campus ministries found themselves less able to attract students to their events than they had been in the 1950s and early 1960s. Some mainline campus ministries, which on occasion still enjoyed tacit support from university administrations, endorsed student protest and sought to align their theologies with current campus politics. Jim Wallis, publisher of the progressive evangelical periodical *Sojourners*, recalls that when he became active in antiwar demonstrations and radical politics leaders of the Wesley Foundation (a Methodist campus ministry) at Michigan State University told him that he belonged to the "real church." Crusade, by contrast, embraced the activism of the student Left but sharply dissented from its political agenda. As Robert Ellwood noted in an early appraisal of the Jesus Movement, the anti-institutionalism of the late 1960s and early 1970s campus ironically worked to the advantage of theologically conservative evangelical organizations rather than the comparatively liberal denominational ministries. Although campuses appeared less hospitable to Christianity in the late 1960s than they had been in the 1950s, Campus Crusade maintained a vigorous ministry at many universities and colleges long after the decline of left-leaning campus activism. Precisely at the time that universities were completing the process of institutional secularization, evangelical organizations were expanding their visibility on the campus.[22]

STAGNATION AND RENEWAL

Between the mid-1970s and 1990, Campus Crusade's campus ministry stagnated, as the organization struggled to attract students and recruit staff. Free-speech platforms and antiwar rallies no longer provided opportunities for Crusade to promote Jesus as history's greatest revolutionary. As campus political activism faded, Crusade needed to once more adapt to changing circumstances. "Christian students are still cause-oriented," commented a Crusade director in 1984. "They just aren't riding a huge cultural wave anymore."[23] Moreover, Crusade staff members found their standard talks on "God's Plan" less welcome at Greek houses. The Greek system and athletics no longer molded a relatively unified campus culture; instead, students at large universities formed many diverse subcultures that required a more flexible approach. "The student culture changed," explains Steve Sellers, who directed Crusade's campus ministry in the 1990s, "I think it took a while for

Campus Crusade and other Christian groups to change with it."[24] Crusade also struggled to reach an increasingly diverse student population with an overwhelmingly white staff. The result of such trends imperiled the future of the campus ministry and the entire organization. In the early 1970s, 700 to 800 American students decided to join Campus Crusade's staff each year. That number gradually declined until only 250 students joined in 1990.[25] Other campus ministries encountered similar obstacles in the eighties. For example, InterVarsity eliminated its operations on scores of campuses during the 1980s. "Traditionally, parachurch ministry has been able to respond to changes almost immediately," stated Gordon MacDonald, the president of InterVarsity. "Perhaps the changes are coming too fast now." *Christianity Today* speculated that "high school and college ministries" had "outlived their purposes."[26]

After this period of stagnation, however, Crusade's campus ministry revived in the 1990s. The organization recommitted itself to its goal of presenting its evangelistic message in a culturally relevant fashion to every student on campuses with a Crusade presence. Local campus directors received greater freedom to design creative evangelistic campaigns, and Crusade speakers no longer relied on the 1960s version of "God's Plan for Your Life." Crusade increased its visibility on campus through a series of high-profile and sometimes controversial advertising campaigns. One poster showed a pair of wedding rings with the message "For the best sex, slip on one of these." Another advertisement pictured a pile of condoms and the banner "Too bad they don't make one of these for your heart." In 1996, during National Coming Out Week, Crusade placed advertisements in university newspapers with testimonies from "former homosexuals"—some newspapers refused to publish the ads and others ran editorial rebuttals. One prominent series of posters highlighted biblical arguments against racism, and another campaign sought to convince African Americans of the African roots of Christianity and the relevance of Jesus to contemporary African American life. The organization also developed an umbrella of niche campus ministries for African American, Latino, and Asian American students, respectively. Crusade's "Impact" ministry to African American students increased the number of black students participating in the organization.[27]

On the campus in the early twenty-first century, Crusaders evangelize students through familiar means and continually experiment with innovative approaches. Staff members cultivate relationships with athletic teams, Greek houses, and other campus groups and invite interested students to Bible studies. At the start of each academic year, Crusaders give incoming students "Freshman Survival Kits" containing Christian books, DVDs, and CDs, all designed to grab students' attention and lead into an opportunity to witness about Jesus. Students who become deeply involved in Crusade activities often attend a spring break or summer project organized by Crusade in popular student destinations, such as Virginia Beach, Daytona Beach, and Mission Beach in San Diego. On summer projects, Crusade students work day jobs, meet for training and Bible studies at night, and spend Saturdays witnessing to vacationers and beachgoers. Typically, Crusaders begin with a "religious survey" and seek to initiate a conversation that leads to *The Four Spiritual Laws*. However, Crusade today places somewhat less emphasis on Bright's booklet, instead encouraging its staff and students to adopt a more conversational approach to evangelism. "Students 'witness' to others," wrote the *Virginian-Pilot* of Crusade's summer project in Virginia Beach, "by sharing their stories of how they came to accept Jesus and how it has affected their lives."[28]

Bright, though hardly a proponent of abandoning *The Four Spiritual Laws*, commented several years before his 2003 death that "this generation is more open to an emotional approach, whereas another generation was open to a logical approach." Crusade published a revised version of the *Four Laws* entitled *Would You Like to Know God Personally?*, which presents "principles" rather than "laws." Although Crusade still engages in aggressive verbal evangelism, the ministry encourages its staff to patiently form friendships with students and to model Christian love as a means of evangelism. "The most powerful thing we can do," stated Bright, "is to reach out in love to our neighbors, our friends and our fellow students on the campus, because love never fails."[29]

Crusade's recommitment to and diversification of its campus ministry increased the ministry's visibility at many colleges and universities. By the early twenty-first century, Crusade maintained active ministries on more than one thousand campuses and counted more than forty thousand involved students annually. Crusade—alongside the Catholic Newman Club—was the largest religious organization at many public universities, particularly in the West, South, and Midwest. In 2005, Campus Crusade's more than five hundred regularly participating students made it the largest student organization of any kind at Ohio State University.[30] Crusade's relatively small presence at the private universities of the Northeast also grew. The *Boston Globe* reported in 2003 that several hundred students were flocking to Harvard's Science Center on Friday nights to sing "praise songs" and hear testimonies about Jesus at Campus Crusade's Real Life Boston, a citywide student ministry.[31] On some campuses today, there are as many as six organizations operating under the umbrella of Campus Crusade: the standard campus ministry, the three ministries geared to minorities, Athletes in Action, and, particularly on the West Coast, Korea Campus Crusade for Christ.

Another measure of Crusade's recent success is its renewed ability to replenish its ranks through new staff recruits from the campus. On this score, Crusade has experienced sharp growth in recent years. After the lull that lasted from the late 1970s through the early 1990s, Crusade has recruited nearly one thousand staff members annually over the past several years. The majority of those recruits have come from the American campus. A variety of other statistics suggests Campus Crusade's current vitality: growing numbers of students involved in campus chapters, expansion to additional campuses, and a massive increase in what Crusade terms "exposures to the Gospel." By "exposures," Crusade means the number of students who have encountered its message of Jesus Christ either at campus events, through conversations with staff and involved students, or through media campaigns, including Crusade's websites. Crusade counted upwards of seven million annual "exposures" between 1998 and 2002.

The large majority of those exposures, however, came through media campaigns rather than through personal contacts. Thus one suspects considerable duplication and superficiality in most recorded "exposures." Indeed, another statistic reveals that Crusade faces great difficulty in its primary mission of "winning the campus for Christ." Between 1994 and 2002, the organization recorded between four thousand

and eleven thousand annual "decisions" for Christ among American college students—an infinitesimal percentage of non-Christian collegians.[32]

There are several reasons for this paradoxical dichotomy of rising participation and staff recruits alongside fewer conversions. In part, the new visibility of campus evangelicalism reflects the upward mobility experienced by evangelicals in recent decades and corresponding changes in the collegiate population. Crusade today encounters fewer first-generation white collegians from small-town Protestant backgrounds—the students of the fifties who had grown up in a Protestant culture and who readily articulated "decisions for Christ." At the same time, contemporary evangelicals are roughly as likely as other Americans to obtain bachelor's degrees, and most evangelical students attend public universities. Today's well-educated and affluent suburban evangelicals are sending children to colleges who have grown up in megachurches and parachurch ministries and who often seamlessly become part of the evangelical subculture on campus. High school students active in Young Life, Student Venture, and Awana Clubs provide a built-in market share for Campus Crusade, InterVarsity, and other evangelical campus ministries, which may partly explain the growing numbers of students participating in such groups.[33]

Crusade, though, faces an uphill battle when it comes to attracting interest from nonevangelical students. R. C. Sproul's affirmation that faith "lives in the hearts of men of a thousand different creeds, and joyously dwells with men who know no creed at all" has become a regnant belief among collegians. The cultural values of liberal Protestantism have survived its disestablishment. According to sociologist Christian Smith, "emerging adults" (including collegians) reflexively affirm values such as "unbounded tolerance" and "epistemological skepticism." While affirming the practical worth of generic religiosity, they express an aversion to "anything 'dogmatic' or committed to particulars."[34] Given this intellectual atmosphere, it is hardly surprising that Campus Crusade struggles to convince students of the *Four Spiritual Laws*' affirmation that "Jesus Christ is God's only provision for our sin." Smith further suggests that only a small minority of those collegians and other young adults who are not already highly committed religionists manifest any noteworthy interest in exploring religious questions and options.[35]

In addition to struggling to convert nonevangelical students, parachurch evangelicalism makes little impact on academic instruction or the institutional values of university culture. Bright himself offered a sober assessment of the state of American higher education shortly before his organization's fiftieth year of ministry. "The philosophy of the classroom . . . ," he charged, "is total decadence, total anti-God, anti-Christ, and anti-Bible. Any person who has anything to do with the secular college or university knows that it's a cesspool." Bright's own assessment—hyperbole aside—indicates that his organization, along with other religious ministries, has made little discernible impact on the overall trajectory of higher education. There are signs that universities are becoming more interested in religion: an increased number of academic articles discussing religion, a proliferation of academic centers studying religion, and the growing willingness of faculty in certain disciplines to articulate their personal religious beliefs. Evangelicals may form a more vocal presence in the ivory tower than in the late 1960s, but particularly in comparison with Crusade's founding years in the 1950s, the secular academy today is at best no more open to traditional religious beliefs in the classroom or other public settings than it was fifty years ago. Few public universities would host a "religious emphasis" week today, as UCLA did in 1953.[36]

Given Bright's repeated incantation of a dictum widely attributed to Abraham Lincoln that "the philosophy of the classroom of one generation becomes the philosophy of government the next," it is surprising that Campus Crusade has never made a concerted attempt to influence "the philosophy of the classroom." The organization has since the mid-1960s operated a small "faculty ministry," and in the 1980s it sought to create a national network of evangelical faculty. Such initiatives, however, have never ranked among the organization's top priorities. Moreover, Crusade's persistent emphasis on direct evangelism as the primary mission of all Christians hardly encourages Crusade staff and students to pursue the vocation of university teaching and scholarship. Walter Bradley, a professor of mechanical engineering at Baylor and a longtime associate Crusade staff member, believes Crusade erred in targeting students while leaving the larger culture of the university intact. "The students are the tourists," explains Bradley. "The faculty and the administrations are the permanent residents." The ministry's "win the campus for Christ" slogan aside, Crusade's mission has actually been to win as many collegians for Christ as possible and to recruit Christian students for evangelical ministries at home and abroad.[37]

The example of Campus Crusade for Christ thus in many respects confirms Marsden's contentions in *Soul* that campus ministries "hardly touch the antireligious heart of academia" and that "as long as the prevailing intellectual outlook of universities is built on community standards antithetical to most traditional religious belief, what goes on in the classrooms will be undermining the outlooks presented in campus religious meetings." However, this is much more likely to be the case at elite institutions whose professors are disproportionately skeptical of traditional Christian doctrines and at which students are more likely to engage intellectual issues raised in the classroom. At nonelite institutions, students pursuing professional degrees rarely pay close attention to whatever ideological messages may be embedded in required core curriculum classes. To paraphrase John Sommerville's recent observation about American society more broadly, large numbers of students ignore "the secularist thrust of the university."[38] Sociologist Christian Smith concludes that university experience is not corrosive of religious faith, as individuals emerge from their college years somewhat more likely to hold religious beliefs and engage in religious practices than their peers who do not attend college.[39] Moreover, the fact that students do not find—and often are not encouraged to find—answers to major philosophical, moral, and religious questions within the classroom creates an opening for evangelical ministries armed with spiritual laws, religious questionnaires, and Freshman Survival Kits. Evangelicals have found space for their message in university dormitories, fraternity houses, and locker rooms—places that are as, if not more, central to the lives of many students as academic classrooms. That Bright succeeded in spreading his ministry across much of the country within several decades testifies not only to his own entrepreneurial genius but also to the ability of evangelical Christianity to thrive in places considered by scholars peripheral to the heart of modern academia.

Despite its struggles to convert non-Christian students and influence the broader trajectory of American higher education, Campus

Crusade helped reestablish evangelicalism as a durable subculture at major American universities. At midcentury, the inchoate efforts of InterVarsity aside, chapel services and mainline Protestant campus ministries constituted the center of Protestantism at American universities and colleges. Today, a plethora of evangelical organizations form the most visible expression of Protestantism at most universities. For example, more than fifty evangelical groups minister to students at both the University of California at Berkeley and UCLA.[40] Betty DeBerg, in a recent study of campus religion, suggests that religious "supply" may well "outstrip" religious "demand" at many universities.[41] With so many different religious organizations operating on some campuses, her observation is probably correct, as a proliferation of religious groups does not necessarily translate into increased student religiosity.

At the same time, such qualifications should not obscure the genuine accomplishments of evangelical campus ministries over the past several decades. When Crusade began its work in 1951, evangelicalism was less prominent on the campus than it is today. American higher education has not returned to the heyday of the YMCA at its most evangelical, and few at Yale would predict a reprise of the 1802 revival that swept through a third of the student body. Partly because of the creative and persistent efforts of organizations like Campus Crusade for Christ, however, it is no longer reasonable to conceive of American higher education as moving inexorably toward a completely secular or post-Christian future. While it may be reasonable to speak of the university's secularization up to the 1960s (with a minor bump during the religious boom of the 1950s), the success of evangelicalism on the margins of the university makes it necessary to question secularization as the fixed end point of this narrative. Furthermore, evangelical campus ministries are only a part of a potentially larger story. At ostensibly secular institutions, Muslim student organizations have grown rapidly in recent decades, mainline campus ministries remain a substantial presence, and university churches of various stripes minister to students.

Too often historians of higher education have equated the academy with the university when the two terms are anything but identical. *The Soul of the American University* persuasively traces the establishment of "nonbelief" through the policies and pronouncements of administrators and faculty. However, scholars of the historical relationship between religion and higher education need to spend more time examining student culture, so that we arrive at a more complete understanding of the ways student religiosity has changed over time. At the same time, historians of higher education who have concentrated on student culture have largely ignored religion. For example, Helen Lefkowitz Horowitz's *Campus Life*, one of the standard works in the field, ignores religion almost entirely.[42] When future scholars write the recent history of religion and higher education, they need to incorporate organizations like the Catholic Newman Club, Hillel, Muslim student organizations, mainline and parachurch Protestant ministries, and ministries of various churches that come onto the campus to minister to students and draw them out to their places of worship. How large have these student movements been over time? How do they structure student religious life? How do they interact with the larger university? Admittedly, the upsurge of religious diversity in American higher education will make it difficult to construct a coherent narrative, but there are many intriguing story lines, such as the relationship between administrations and religious groups or the response of religious groups to issues such as same-sex marriage and transgender identities.

"CONCLUDING UNSCIENTIFIC POSTSCRIPT"

None of these examples of student religiosity obviates Marsden's complaint about the exclusion of religious perspectives from the classroom or the public life of American colleges and universities. Nevertheless, fifteen years after the publication of *Soul* the future for religious perspectives in higher education looks somewhat less bleak. A variety of Catholic and evangelical institutions demonstrate the "pluralism *among* institutions" that Marsden suggested, and even evangelical institutions like Wheaton and Calvin have made progress—demonstrated in favorable coverage in the mainstream media—in what he termed "the right . . . to be regarded as excellent."[43] Moreover, the growth of campus ministries at even the nation's elite secular institutions has attracted the attention of publications as diverse as *Christianity Today* and the *Boston*

Globe.⁴⁴ Campus ministries in and of themselves will not change the institutional culture of secular universities, but they may foreshadow a longer-term trend. Student religiosity may continue the revival of academic interest in religion and foster intellectual forums in which religious perspectives are tolerated or even welcomed. Moreover, a certain percentage of students involved in such ministries or trained at religious colleges and universities will pursue advanced degrees and obtain academic positions in secular institutions. Through his teaching, scholarship, and mentoring, George Marsden has furthered this process for more than four decades. Ironically, given his diagnosis of "the deep-rooted prejudice against substantive religious viewpoints in formerly Protestant universities," he demonstrated that those viewpoints can indeed gain a hearing if presented through careful research and engaging writing.⁴⁵

NOTES

This essay incorporates material from John G. Turner, *Bill Bright and Campus Crusade for Christ: The Renewal of Evangelicalism in Postwar America* (Chapel Hill: University of North Carolina Press, 2008).

1. George Marsden, *The Soul of the American University: From Protestant Establishment to Established Nonbelief* (New York: Oxford University Press), 434.

2. For example, see Jon H. Roberts and James Turner, *The Sacred and the Secular University* (Princeton, NJ: Princeton University Press, 2000); Julie Reuben, *The Making of the Modern University: Intellectual Transformation and the Marginalization of Morality* (Chicago: University of Chicago Press, 1996); Douglas Sloan, *Faith and Knowledge: Mainline Protestantism and American Higher Education* (Louisville, KY: Westminster John Knox Press, 1994); George Marsden and Bradley Longfield, eds., *The Secularization of the Academy* (New York: Oxford University Press, 1992). By contrast, see Douglas Jacobsen and Rhonda Jacobsen, eds., *The American University in a Postsecular Age* (New York: Oxford University Press, 2008); D. Michael Lindsay, *Faith in the Halls of Power: How Evangelicals Joined the American Elite* (New York: Oxford University Press, 2007), chs. 3 and 4; Conrad Cherry, Betty A. DeBerg, and Amanda Porterfield, *Religion on Campus: What Religion Really Means to Today's Undergraduates* (Chapel Hill: University of North Carolina Press, 2001).

3. For example, see John Thelin, *A History of American Higher Education* (Baltimore: Johns Hopkins University Press, 2004), esp. 147–48. See also Christopher J. Lucas, *American Higher Education: A History* (New York: Palgrave Mac-

millan, 2006); Arthur M. Cohen, *The Shaping of American Higher Education: Emergence and Growth of the Contemporary System* (San Francisco: Jossey-Bass, 1998).

4. See John Schmalzbauer, "Campus Ministry: A Statistical Portrait," Social Science Research Council, February 6, 2007, http://religion.ssrc.org/reforum/Schmalzbauer.pdf. On mainline student movements in the 1960s and 1970s, see Sloan, *Faith and Knowledge*, esp. ch. 5.

5. Marsden, *Soul of the American University*, 441 n. 7, 441–42 n. 7.

6. Campus Crusade for Christ, "2008 Annual Report," copy in author's possession. The term *parachurch* refers to organizations that exist alongside (from the Greek *para*) the institutional church (i.e., denominations and congregations). On the role of such "special purpose organizations," see Robert Wuthnow, *The Restructuring of American Religion: Society and Faith since World War II* (Princeton, NJ: Princeton University Press, 1988).

7. Although this essay concentrates on Campus Crusade's "campus ministry," the organization's name became misleading by the 1970s. Bright first exported his campus ministry internationally and then expanded Crusade's national and overseas efforts at evangelism beyond colleges and universities.

8. Campus Crusade for Christ, "Statement of Purpose," enclosed in Bill Bright to John MacKay, April 25, 1951, MacKay Papers, Princeton Theological Seminary Archives, Princeton, NJ.

9. William F. Buckley Jr., *God and Man at Yale: The Superstitions of "Academic Freedom"* (Chicago: Henry Regnery, 1951), xv–xvi. On Buckley, see Marsden, *Soul of the American University*, 10–16.

10. Jones quoted in Joel Carpenter, *Revive Us Again: The Reawakening of American Fundamentalism* (New York: Oxford University Press, 1997), 62; Riley quoted in Adam Laats, "More Than a Monkey Trial: Fundamentalism and American Education in the 1920s" (PhD diss., University of Wisconsin, 2006), 114. Data on the growth of postwar student populations from U.S. Bureau of the Census, *Historical Statistics of the United States, Colonial Times to 1970* (Washington, DC: Government Printing Office, 1975), 383; Diane Ravitch, *The Troubled Crusade: American Education, 1945–1980* (New York: Basic Books, 1983), 14, 183. On earlier fundamentalist worries about American higher education, see George Marsden, *Fundamentalism and American Culture: The Shaping of Twentieth-Century Evangelicalism, 1870–1925* (New York: Oxford University Press, 1980), 141–64; Marsden, *Soul of the American University*, 267–70; Carpenter, *Revive Us Again*, 62–63; Laats, "More Than a Monkey Trial," ch. 4. See also Adam Laats, *Fundamentalism and Education in the Scopes Era: God, Darwin, and the Roots of America's Culture Wars* (New York: Palgrave Macmillan, 2010).

11. *Time*, November 5, 1951, 50–51; *Newsweek*, April 22, 1957, 115–20; *Newsweek*, November 2, 1953, 55.

12. *Daily Bruin*, October 8, 1951, December 12, 1951.

13. *Daily Bruin*, March 21, 1953, and March 12, 1953.

14. Donn Moomaw, interview by author, September 11, 2003; *Hour of Decision*, June 14, 1953, Walter F. Bennet & Company Collection, videotape F 60, Billy Graham Center Archives, Wheaton College, Wheaton, IL.

15. David Harrington Watt, *A Transforming Faith: Explorations of Twentieth-Century Evangelicalism* (New Brunswick, NJ: Rutgers University Press, 1991), 18, 22. As originally published in 1965, the *Four Spiritual Laws* taught: (1) "God loves you, and offers a wonderful plan for your life"; (2) "Man is sinful and separated from God. Therefore he cannot know and experience God's love and plan for his life"; (3) "Jesus Christ is God's only provision for man's sin. Through him you can know and experience God's love and plan for your life"; (4) "We must individually receive Jesus Christ as Savior and Lord; then we can know and experience God's love and plan for our lives." *Have You Heard of the Four Spiritual Laws?* (San Bernardino, CA: Campus Crusade for Christ, 1965). In the era of Rick Warren's *The Purpose-Driven Life* and best-selling fiction like *The Shack*, Watt's observation is probably no longer true of younger evangelicals.

16. Bill Bright, "Witnessing in the Spirit," ca. 1965, personal papers of Dorothy Graham; Howard Ball, interview by author, June 13, 2005. Bright's attitude toward intellectual pursuits largely confirms the observation of Richard Hofstadter in his *Anti-intellectualism in American Life* (New York: Knopf, 1963), 48–49 n. 8. See also the helpful discussion of Hofstadter in Mark Noll, *Scandal of the Evangelical Mind* (Grand Rapids, MI: Eerdmans, 1994), 10–12.

17. Bill Counts, interview by author, January 6, 2004.

18. Jo Anne Butts, "Report on Campus Crusade Invasion," January 29, 1967, Records of InterVarsity Christian Fellowship, box 20, folder 3, Billy Graham Center Archives; Jon Braun, interview by author, January 15, 2004. On Reagan, Kerr, and Berkeley, see Clark Kerr, *The Gold and the Blue: A Personal Memoir of the University of California, 1948–1967*, vol. 2 (Berkeley: University of California Press, 2003), chs. 15–16; W. J. Rorabaugh, *Berkeley at War: The 1960s* (New York: Oxford University Press, 1989), esp. chs. 1–3.

19. Peter Gillquist, interview by author, January 13, 2004. Bright's comments from *Los Angeles Times*, August 8, 1971. On American religion and the counterculture, see Mark Oppenheimer, *Knocking on Heaven's Door: American Religion in the Age of Counterculture* (New Haven, CT: Yale University Press, 2003). For early accounts of the Jesus Movement, see Edward Plowman, *The Jesus Movement in America: Accounts of Christian Revolutionaries in Action* (Elgin, IL: David C. Cook, 1971); Ronald M. Enroth, Edward E. Erickson Jr., and C. Breckinridge Peters, *The Jesus People: Old-Time Religion in the Age of Aquarius* (Grand Rapids, MI: Eerdmans, 1972); Robert S. Ellwood, *One Way: The Jesus Movement and Its Meaning* (Englewood Cliffs, NJ: Prentice-Hall, 1973).

20. *New York Times*, June 16, 1972.

21. Seymour Martin Lipset and Gerald M. Schafflander, *Passion and Politics: Student Activism in America* (Boston: Little, Brown, 1971), 49; George H. Gallup, *The Gallup Poll: Public Opinion, 1935–1971*, vol. 3 (New York: Random House, 1972), 2250.

22. Jim Wallis, interview by author, July 22, 2004. Ellwood, *One Way*, 117. On the trajectory of mainline campus ministries in the 1960s and 1970s, see Phillip E. Hammond and Robert E. Mitchell, "Segmentation of Radicalism: The Case of the Protestant Campus Minister," *American Journal of Sociology* 71 (September 1965): 133–43; Sloan, *Faith and Knowledge*, ch. 5.

23. *Philadelphia Inquirer*, December 31, 1984.

24. Steve Sellers, interview by author, February 11, 2004.

25. Ibid.

26. *Christianity Today*, March 7, 1986, 44, 45. On changes in campus culture during these years, see Helen Lefkowitz Horowitz, *Campus Life: Undergraduate Cultures from the End of the Eighteenth Century to the Present* (Chicago: University of Chicago Press, 1987), chs. 11–12; Murray Sperber, *Beer and Circuses: How Big-Time College Sports Is Crippling Undergraduate Education* (New York: Henry Holt, 2000), 3–11.

27. *Christianity Today*, March 4, 1996, 69.

28. *Virginia-Pilot*, June 17, 2001.

29. *Would You Like to Know God Personally?* (Orlando, FL: Campus Crusade for Christ, 2000); Bright quoted in *National Religious Broadcasters*, November 2000, 24.

30. *Lantern* [Ohio State University newspaper], March 3, 2005.

31. *Boston Globe*, November 30, 2003.

32. Statistics provided by Campus Crusade for Christ, courtesy of Mike Nyfeller. More recent statistics available on Campus Crusade's website suggest a much higher number of such decisions, rising to 110,850 in the 2006–7 academic year. The increased rate of expressed decisions may reflect responses to the organization's larger Web presence. See Campus Crusade for Christ, "U.S. Campus Ministry Statistics Report," http://campuscrusadeforchrist.com/about-us/facts-and-statistics, accessed December 8, 2009.

33. On levels of educational attainment by religion, see Kraid Beyerlein, "Specifying the Impact of Conservative Protestantism on Educational Attainment," *Journal for the Scientific Study of Religion* 43 (December 2004): 505–18. On the growing affluence of evangelicals, see John Schmalzbauer, *People of Faith: Religious Conviction in American Journalism and Higher Education* (Ithaca, NY: Cornell University Press, 2003), ch. 2; *New York Times*, May 22, 2005.

34. Christian Smith with Patricia Snell, *Souls in Transition: The Religious and Spiritual Lives of Emerging Adults* (New York: Oxford University Press, 2009), 288.

35. Ibid., 287–89, 294–95. See also N. Jay Demerath, "Cultural Victory and Organizational Defeat in the Paradoxical Decline of Liberal Protestantism," *Journal for the Scientific Study of Religion* 34 (December 1995): 458–69.

36. Bright quoted in *National Religious Broadcasters*, November 2000, 22–23. For recent statistics on the religious affiliation and beliefs of university professors in the natural and social sciences, see Neil Gross and Solon Simmons, "The Religious Convictions of College and University Professors," in Jacobsen and Jacobsen, *American University*, ch. 2. According to Gross and Simmons, roughly 20 percent of faculty at American universities and colleges describe themselves as "born-again Christians," compared to roughly 40 percent of the general population (20). Schmalzbauer, in *People of Faith*, ch. 3, and Lindsay, in *Faith in the Halls*, ch. 4, suggest that the number and visibility of faculty with strong religious convictions have risen in recent decades.

37. Walter Bradley, interview by author, July 21, 2003.

38. C. John Sommerville, *The Decline of the Secular University* (New York: Oxford University Press, 2006), 59.

39. Smith, *Souls in Transition*, 248–51.

40. Rebecca Y. Kim, *God's New Whiz Kids? Korean American Evangelicals on Campus* (New York: NYU Press, 2006), 1.

41. Conrad Cherry, Betty A. DeBerg, and Amanda Porterfield, *Religion on Campus* (Chapel Hill: University of North Carolina Press, 2001), 282.

42. Helen Lefkovitz Horowitz, *Campus Life: Undergraduate Cultures from the End of the Eighteenth Century to the Present* (New York: Alfred A. Knopf, 1987).

43. For example, see the *Boston Globe*'s largely sympathetic portrait of Wheaton College in its November 14, 2005, issue. Quote from Marsden, *Soul of the American University*, 439.

44. *Boston Globe*, November 30, 2003; *Christianity Today*, September 2005, 64–69.

45. Marsden, *Soul of the American University*, 439.

CHAPTER 15

The Southernization of the Evangelical Mind

RICK OSTRANDER

In April 2006, the International Forum on Christian Higher Education, sponsored by the Council for Christian Colleges and Universities (CCCU), took place at the Gaylord Texan Resort and Convention Center in Dallas, Texas. Nearly 1,300 delegates from CCCU members and affiliates around the world traveled to this vast convention center to discuss the status of Christian higher education in the twenty-first century. The conference featured the announcement of a new president, former U.S. assistant attorney general Paul Corts, and guest speakers such as best-selling author Rick Warren. It was a grand event for this organization of private, generally small evangelical colleges, which, half a century ago, many scholars believed were destined for extinction.

Indeed, these are heady times for the CCCU. Membership in the organization has grown from 27 institutions in 1976 to 118 today. Moreover, enrollment at member institutions grew 67 percent in the decade from 1992 to 2002, compared to just 2 percent for all educational institutions in the United States.[1] The Gaylord Texan, moreover, was an apt setting for the lofty ambitions of the delegates. Putting "resort" on a Texan scale, the Gaylord's vast glass atrium spans over four and a half acres of lush indoor gardens. Restaurants and shops dot the various corridors, and an indoor artificial river provides visitors with the feeling of being transported to San Antonio's River Walk a few hundred miles to the south—without the inconvenience of the blistering Texas sun. And considering the additions of several Texas universities to the CCCU in recent years, the Dallas location was very fitting. In 2002, *Christianity Today* writer Edward Gilbreath trumpeted Dallas as the "New Capital of Evangelicalism." In light of the events at the Gaylord Texan, one could conclude that Dallas—and by extension the American South—represents the future of evangelical higher education as well.[2]

Historians have recently begun taking the role of the South in American evangelicalism more seriously. In 1984, Grant Wacker alerted fellow historians to the significance of the South to twentieth-century evangelicalism. Wacker described the resurgence of evangelicalism in the late twentieth century and related much of it to the "cultural diaspora" of southern evangelicals such as Billy Graham, Pat Robertson, Jerry Falwell, and Bill Bright. Wacker challenged historians of evangelicalism to understand the ways that the southern religious subculture "has overflowed its sectional boundaries and permeated the mainstream" of modern evangelicalism. Other historians such as William Glass, Barry Hankins, and Darren Dochuk have also explored the interaction between northern evangelicals and southern Protestants. Dochuk, for example, analyzes evangelicals in Southern California and chronicles how the region not only became the incubator of conservative Christian politics but profoundly influenced modern evangelicalism through organizations such as Focus on the Family, the megachurch phenomenon (Chuck Smith's Calvary Chapel and more recently Rick Warren's Saddleback Church), and even the rise of contemporary Christian music.[3]

Now that the South's impact on American evangelical culture is generally recognized, it is time to consider that the future of evangelicalism's intellectual and educational life may be shaped by this region as well. Consider the makeup of the CCCU itself. This organization was founded in 1976 under the leadership of northern and northeastern colleges, many of whom were emerging from the shadows of fundamentalist anti-intellectualism. Of the original twenty-seven colleges, seventeen came from the North. Of the four California schools, three—Biola, Simpson, and Westmont—had strong ties to midwestern evangelicalism. The leading schools in the group were the traditional northern colleges such as Wheaton, Taylor, and Gordon.[4]

By 1984, the membership of the CCCU had grown to seventy-one, but only twenty-four of those institutions hailed from the South. This geographical distribution, however, changed dramatically in the 1990s. CCCU membership continued to expand, but primarily through the addition of members from the South. From 1993 to 2005, twenty-two of the twenty-four institutions that joined the CCCU came from southern states. By 2005, the CCCU included 102 member institutions, nearly half of which came from the South. Texas itself is a microcosm of these changes. While no institutions from Texas belonged to the CCCU in 1984, by 2012 eight Texas universities were members, including some of the largest in the organization, such as Abilene Christian and Dallas Baptist. Moreover, if one includes CCCU "affiliates" as well as members, the list would include southern heavyweights such as Baylor, Pepperdine, and Samford.[5]

Student populations at Christian colleges have also shifted south and west, which is what one would expect given the demographic trends in the past half century. In 1950, residents of the South and Southwest made up 44 percent of the nation; in 2000, they constituted 58 percent of the population. Since the 1990s, the demographic contrasts have been even more dramatic. During the 1990s, the population of the South and Southwest increased by over twenty-five million, while that of the North and Northeast grew by only six million. Since 2000, nine of the ten fastest-growing cities in the United States have been in the Sun Belt states of Arizona, California, Florida, Nevada, and Texas.[6]

Christian college enrollment reflects this trend. In terms of size and influence, Calvin College, in Grand Rapids, Michigan, historically has figured quite prominently. Calvin's student population has hovered around 4,000 for the past thirty years (4,108 students in 1980, 4,092 in 2009). During the same time span, Wheaton College's enrollment has remained around 2,500 students. Meanwhile, Wheaton's peer institutions in Southern California, Biola and Azusa Pacific, have experienced steady growth. Biola began the 1980s with a student population of 2,286 students; in 2009 the university had expanded to nearly 6,000. Azusa Pacific's growth has been more dramatic, from 1,196 in 1980 to 8,000 in 2009. The trend has been similar at other southern institutions. Union University in Jackson, Tennessee, for example, has seen its enrollment jump from 1,900 in 1996 to about 4,000 in 2009. When one includes the large Texas institutions such as Dallas Baptist and Abilene Christian, it becomes clear that the majority of students attending CCCU schools today do so in the South or Southwest.

So what does all of this mean for evangelical intellectual life? Can the region that northerners typically associate with NASCAR and country music also serve as the future of evangelical higher education? At the very least, I would suggest that the South offers new opportunities in terms of resources and energy. But as recent events indicate, simply grafting the traditional evangelical paradigm of "recovery" onto southern institutions may prove to be problematic. That is because Christian colleges in the South do not always share in the metanarrative with which historians have generally described Protestant higher education in America. That story has been formed in such works as George Marsden's *The Soul of the American University* (1994) and *The Outrageous Idea of Christian Scholarship* (1997), Mark Noll's *The Scandal of the Evangelical Mind* (1994), William Ringenberg's *The Christian College* (2006), James Burtchaell's *The Dying of the Light* (1998), and Alan Wolfe's *Atlantic Monthly* article "The Opening of the Evangelical Mind (2000)."

It goes something like this: by founding Harvard College in 1636, the Puritans established higher education in American on a solid Christian foundation. Other colonial colleges followed suit in being established on firmly Christian principles, and they enabled Protestants to set the intellectual and cultural agenda in colonial America. In the wake of the Second Great Awakening in the early 1800s, American Protestants founded Christian colleges by the hundreds, and even public universities displayed a strongly Protestant ethos. Indeed, before the Civil War it would be difficult to find many American colleges that were not overtly Christian. The late nineteenth century, however, represented a sea change in Christian higher education. More critical approaches to scientific inquiry left little room for the older Christian enterprise of discerning divine design in the workings of nature and society. Scholars sought to divest themselves of any prior assumptions such as belief in God or the historicity of the Bible. For two centuries, Protestant educators had trumpeted the need for scholarly inquiry to be "nonsectarian" even while their Protestant assumptions dominated the culture. Now they found their nonsectarian guns turned against themselves. New secular universities armed with new financial resources—either from state governments or from private entrepreneurs such as Ezra Cornell and Leland Stanford—supplanted Protestant colleges as culture-shaping institutions. Leading universities such as Harvard and Yale adapted to the changes and became proponents of the secular model, even while preserving in some form (through campus ministries or undergraduate education) a concern for Christian values broadly defined.

Conservative evangelicals, however, took another road. As their church colleges retreated into a cultural backwater, they abandoned the attempt at scholarly engagement. In the wake of secularization, conservative Christians transformed existing institutions or established "Bible institutes" to preserve their educational values. Fearful of modern scholarship, these institutions typically displayed a deep anti-intellectual bias against academic inquiry. Students were instructed in "practical" religious topics in order to prepare for careers in full-time Christian service. Moreover, belief in the imminent end of the world and the return of Jesus nurtured an otherworldly outlook that steered fundamentalists away from politics, social thought, economics, and other so-called "secular" topics. The result of this trend was, in Noll's estimation, the "intellectual disaster of fundamentalism" and the "scandal of the evangelical mind." Dragged down by their anti-intellectualist past, late twentieth-century evangelicals displayed an inability to think deeply and critically about politics and science, resulting in the simplified rhetoric of the Religious Right and attempts to prove scientifically a recent, six-day creation of the world. Meanwhile, claimed Marsden, in the larger academic world, the notion of Christian scholarship came to be seen as "outrageous."

Modern evangelicals in higher education, therefore, are engaged in a project of recovering and renewing the evangelical mind. Noll ends his pessimistic work with indications that an evangelical renaissance may be under way. Ringenberg titles his chapter on the second half of the twentieth century "The Reconstruction of Christian Higher Education." Important to this enterprise have been two institutions in particular, Calvin College and Wheaton College. Abraham Kuyper, a late nineteenth-century Dutch Reformed theologian and politician, articulated an approach to learning in which Christian truths were integrated into all academic disciplines. Kuyper indirectly influenced American Christianity through the vehicle of Calvin College, a Dutch Reformed school founded in 1876 in Grand Rapids, Michigan. When the Christian College Coalition was formed, Calvin College exerted substantial intellectual influence on other institutions. For Christian liberal arts colleges seeking some distance both from secular universities and from Bible colleges, Kuyper's "integration" model seemed particularly attractive. By the end of the 1970s, therefore, the integration of faith and learning had become a mantra among Christian colleges—especially as popularized in Wheaton College philosopher Arthur Holmes's *The Idea of a Christian College* (1975), which became standard reading at CCCU institutions.[7]

Over the past twenty years, then, Christian colleges have been successful in recovering one aspect of Protestant higher education: many small, private, residential Christian colleges are well equipped to nurture Christian character and educate young Christian minds in an atmosphere of academic quality. The number of CCCU schools that pepper the *U.S. News and World Report* rankings would seem to indicate a modest but healthy dose of academic quality in American evangelicalism. Wheaton, for example, typically ranks among the top sixty national liberal arts colleges. Most CCCU institutions are classified as regional baccalaureate colleges, and some of them rank well in their regions. Messiah College in Grantham, Pennsylvania, ranks in the top five in the northern region, and Taylor ranks first in the Midwest. Some CCCU schools in the South and West also tend to fare well. In the southern region, Ouachita Baptist, John Brown, and Covenant consistently rank high in their peer groups, and in the West, Seattle Pacific and Abilene Christian rank in the top twenty.

Evangelical scholars, however, are after bigger game than quality undergraduate Christian colleges. Notes Marsden, "While Protestants support educational institutions at every other level, they have almost nothing to offer at the highest levels of scholarship and graduate training." Christian liberal arts colleges are doing well, echoes Noll, but "they were not designed to promote thorough Christian reflection on the nature of the world, society, and the arts. It is little wonder that they miss so badly that for which they do not aim." What is needed, they believe, is a first-rate Protestant research university—an "evangelical Notre Dame," so to speak—that can produce Christian scholarship of the first order.[8]

Of course, creating a research university presents a significantly greater challenge than building a quality small college. It takes money, and plenty of it. One must recruit scholars through good salaries, and one must pay them to sit in an office and write books rather than teach freshman composition. Such an enterprise lies far beyond the means of the typical small Christian college of the CCCU. No wonder, then, that Marsden laments, "There are no Protestant research universities that approach anything like the first rank. Although there has been talk for two generations about founding a major Protestant university, the obstacles are formidable."[9] One could say that the enterprise requires a Texas-sized ambition and Texas-sized resources—which is where Baylor University, in Waco, Texas, comes into the story. Recent years have witnessed an attempt by northern evangelicals to utilize the resources of the South to build the Protestant research university. This has demonstrated the difficulty of grafting a northern branch onto a southern stalk.

Founded in 1845, Baylor University has been the premier university for Texas Baptists—the "crown jewel" of Baptist educational life, in the words of longtime president Herbert Reynolds. In 1990, President Reynolds, fearful that conservative activists in the Texas Baptist Convention could undermine the stability of the university, orchestrated a charter change that effectively ended the Convention's direct control over the institution. The charter change raised questions of Baylor's religious and educational identity. Without a direct connection to Southern Baptists, what was to keep Baylor a Baptist university, or even a Christian university? What sort of institution should Baylor become?[10]

It was at this point that Baylor's trajectory and the scholarly ambitions of northern evangelicals began to intersect. From the perspective of northern evangelicals, Baylor offered the opportunity that they had been waiting for. With over fourteen thousand students and $750 million in endowment, it offered the institutional heft needed to attract Christian scholars and support quality Christian scholarship. President Reynolds hired Donald Schmeltekopf as chief academic officer in 1991, and the latter interpreted that charter change as an opportunity for Baylor to grow into a world-class university that was "both intellectually enlightened and religiously faithful." Coincidentally, Marsden's "The Soul of the American University" thesis was first published in article form in the same year by *First Things*. It was reprinted in the fall 1991 edition of the Baylor *Faculty Dialogue*. President Reynolds forwarded a copy of the article to Provost Schmeltekopf. With an asterisk by Marsden's name, Reynolds wrote, "Get him here . . . ," followed by a bulleted list of options such as a semester, one year, or lectures.[11]

Schmeltekopf and others believed that Baylor could become to the Protestant world what Notre Dame was to the American Catholic community. References to the flagship Catholic university became common. David Solomon, a Baylor graduate and director of the Center for Ethics and Culture at the University of Notre Dame, gave a paper at a Baylor colloquium in 1995 entitled "What Baylor and Notre Dame Can Learn from Each Other." Remarked Solomon: "Baylor alone among major Protestant universities has a chance both to become a research university of the first rank and also to maintain rich ties to its Protestant tradition."[12]

In 1995, the Baylor campaign took on added momentum when Robert Sloan succeeded Reynolds as president. Under Sloan's direction, the campus adopted a new 2012 vision statement that declared Baylor's intention to "enter the top tier of American universities while reaffirming and deepening its Christian mission." The first of the ten supporting assumptions of the vision was to "encourage the integration of Christian faith and the intellectual life." This was accomplished in part by the establishment of an Institute for Faith and Learning to help new and current Baylor faculty become more intentional about relating Christian faith to academic inquiry. From Marsden's *Soul of the American University* and Burtchaell's *The Dying of the Light*, Sloan concluded that the key to maintaining and strengthening Baylor's Christian academic vision was to hire faculty who were loyal to the Christian tradition and intentional about integrating faith and learning.[13]

Thus began a hiring process in which Baylor recruited northern scholars, many with Wheaton or Calvin connections. C. Stephen Evans, a distinguished professor of philosophy, came from Calvin College. Fellow philosopher Robert Roberts came from Wheaton. Other Christian scholars came from outside the evangelical fold. For example, Thomas Hibbs, a Roman Catholic, came to Baylor from the philosophy department at Boston College; Rodney Stark, a well-known sociologist, came from the University of Washington. In 2000, Sloan hired David Jeffrey, a Wheaton undergraduate and Princeton PhD who had chaired the English department at the University of Ottawa. Soon thereafter Jeffrey replaced Schmeltekopf as the person primarily responsible for implementing the Baylor 2012 vision.

From a northern perspective, then, the Baylor project seemed both natural and, to many, attractive. For many traditional Baylorites, however, that was not the case. President Sloan encountered intense opposition among traditional Baylor faculty and alumni to his campaign to revolutionize Baylor. Particularly controversial was Sloan's hiring of outsiders and his personal interviews of faculty candidates for appropriate Christian fit, something that struck moderate Southern Baptists as overly invasive. After years of controversy and a series of no-confidence votes by the faculty, President Sloan stepped down in 2005. Six months later, David Jeffrey was dismissed as provost. John Lilley, an ordained Baptist minister with a reputation as a peacemaker, was named president in 2006 but was fired two years later. After two years with an interim president, Baylor appointed Ken Starr as president in 2010.

A closer look at Baylor indicates that the Texas soil was not as fertile for growing the great evangelical research university as had been thought. The campus layout, for a start, is a hodge-podge of buildings and architectural styles spread across the Texas plain with seemingly no underlying unity. A visitor is hard pressed to determine where the center of the university lies. It seems as if Baylor's landscape itself gives testament to the independent, decentralized ethic of Southern Baptists. It stands in stark contrast to Notre Dame, with its uniform tan brick architecture centered on the Golden Dome. There was another way in which the physical landscape of the Baylor campus boded ill for the Baylor 2012 vision. The campus of Baylor, Texas's oldest educational institution, is perhaps one of the most memorialized in America. Plaques and statues commemorating Baylor and Texas history sprinkle the campus. The memorials extend even to the campus lampposts, each of which is dedicated to a particular Baylor graduate who died in a war. And to some extent, this devotion not only to Baylor but to Texas and Southern Baptist culture aroused opposition to the Baylor vision.

The word *evangelical* itself was taboo for many Baylor Baptists, partly because of the Southern Baptist conflicts of the 1980s and 1990s. In particular, the events at Southern Baptist Theological Seminary in Louisville, Kentucky, in the early 1990s shaped moderate Southern Baptist stereotypes of northern evangelicals. In the wake of the conservative resurgence in the denomination, leaders at Southern Seminary in 1992 began implementing a kind of "affirmative action" plan to hire evangelical professors—primarily northerners—to diversify the faculty. What began as a moderate transition, however, changed drastically when Al Mohler, a hard-line Southern Baptist conservative, assumed the presidency in 1993. Mohler interpreted his hiring as a mandate from the trustees to take the seminary in a much more conservative direction. Mohler began applying strict doctrinal tests to faculty hiring on such issues as women in ministry. When Diana Garland, the dean of the Carver School of Social Work, objected to the new standards, she was fired and the Carver School was eventually closed. The event sparked a faculty-administration showdown that resulted in the departure of several professors. Ironically, some of Mohler's harshest critics among the faculty at Southern were northern evangelicals who had been hired in recent years. As Barry Hankins observes, the events at Southern revealed a deep divide between two different types of evangelicals, centrist "*Christianity Today*" evangelicals and more conservative "*World Magazine*" evangelicals. Such nuances, however, were lost on moderate Southern Baptists in general, for whom Southern Seminary came to represent what happens when Yankee-influenced evangelicals run the show.[14]

The events at Southern Baptist Seminary, therefore, strengthened among moderate Southern Baptists an instinctive antipathy to anything smacking of northern evangelicalism, with important ramifications for Baylor University. David Lyle Jeffrey was attracted to Baylor because, he says, it offered "a way of realizing the kind of integration of faith and learning that evangelicals once talked about but that had been largely forgotten." In retrospect, however, he believes that Sloan and others seriously underestimated the imperviousness of the local culture to perceived outsider influences. Jeffrey remarked, "No word excites the animosity of traditional Baylorites more than 'northern evangelical.'" Paradoxically, the new Baylorites' understanding of a Christian university was at once broader and more sectarian than that of the traditional Baylor Baptists. The 2012 campaign recruited Catholic scholars, and President Sloan invited the Catholic public intellectual Richard John Neuhaus to give the plenary address at his inauguration. Yet Sloan's attempt to scrutinize faculty candidates for Christian commitment smacked of fundamentalism and conflicted with the traditional Baptist habit of not probing into questions of personal faith. Ultimately, for traditional Baylor moderates, behind the evangelical visage lurked the specter of fundamentalism. As one of them put it at a faculty discussion, evangelicals were "fundamentalists in suits."[15]

The location of Baylor University in the South also meant that the concern for integrating faith and learning often fell on deaf ears and was associated with "northern" values. The notion of integration was rooted, in part, in the historical experience of northern evangelicals who had witnessed the secularization of the academy. Integrating faith and learning, they believed, was the key to maintaining the Christian character of the university; the failure to do so, history seemingly taught, resulted in secularization. Integration, however, was not part of the rhetoric of Southern Baptists. Like Protestant universities in the North in the nineteenth century, Baylor and other Southern Baptist universities such as Wake Forest and Samford had constituted the educational establishment in the Bible Belt. Thus they had been more lax about the need to integrate Christianity and academics. Baylor University, its leaders had traditionally stated, "provides an excellent education in a Christian environment," meaning that Baylor's academic component was manifested in quality education, while the Christian element provided for a caring community and extracurricular opportunities. In the parlance of northern evangelicals, this was the "separate spheres" approach to faith and learning that should be abandoned in favor of integrating Christianity and one's academic field. The new Baylorites' attempts to inspire more robust versions of integration, therefore, were viewed by traditional Baylor professors as closet fundamentalism. For many traditional Baylorites, Jeffrey says, "a Christian university is a contradiction in terms," and the Institute for Faith and Learning was simply "a Bible College in disguise."[16]

For a variety of reasons, then, turning Baylor into the "evangelical Notre Dame" proved more difficult than originally thought. So does the Baylor vision still exist despite the departure of Sloan and the demotion of Jeffrey? The answer to that question depends on whom one asks. Margaret Tate, a "2012" hire who came to Baylor after receiving a PhD from Notre Dame, believes that Baylor is permanently divided between two cultures, new Baylorites and old Baylorites. While the divisions are less public than they were under Sloan's tenure, she says, they still exist. Professors socialize with their particular group and display a clannish mentality. In the faculty dining room, for example, a professor associated with the "new" Baylor would rarely join a table occupied by old Baylorites. The two camps generally have their own churches and social networks.[17]

Many of the newer Baylorites seem to be disillusioned with the events of the past few years. David Jeffrey left the provost's office to join the Honors College and focus on his research. In general, the Baylor 2012 hires seem to have given up on transforming the entire institution and instead focus on building their particular departments into beacons of Christian scholarship. Thomas Kidd, for example, another hire from Notre Dame who studied under George Marsden, teaches American history at Baylor. A native of South Carolina with a southern drawl, Kidd had little difficulty in adapting to Waco culture; yet his Notre Dame pedigree aroused suspicion among old Baylorites. Not one given to controversy, Kidd spends most of his time in a musty basement office churning out impressive monographs on American religious history.

With three books published in the past three years and two more on the way, Kidd has little time to worry about the fate of 2012 in general. Philosophy in particular has become a flagship department for the 2012 vision, and it competes with Notre Dame in attracting bright Christian students. C. Stephen Evans, for example, is dismayed by the recent events at Baylor, yet when asked why he stays, he displays a list of stellar graduate students slated to begin studies at Baylor the following fall.[18]

There have been some "conversions" from traditional Baylorites to the 2012 vision. Anne-Marie Bowery, a philosophy professor hired in the early 1990s, was skeptical at first, but she attended faculty seminars on integration of faith and learning and claims to have benefited from them. Bowery believes that northern emigrants tended to have their own stereotypes of the South. They underappreciated the academic quality of the institution that already existed and tended to be condescending to the old Baylorites. Nevertheless, she has seen improvements to the department and to her own scholarship as a result of the Baylor 2012 endeavor. Having served on the tenure committee over the past year, she has witnessed firsthand the impressive scholarly production of some of the 2012 hires. She now describes herself as having "a foot in both camps."[19]

Larry Lyon, dean of the Graduate School and a Baylor alumnus, supports 2012 for philosophical and pragmatic reasons. There are plenty of very bright college undergraduates and professors out there who are committed Christians, he notes, but "there are not many fishing lines in that pool." One of the pleasant surprises about 2012, he discovered, was the advantage that it gave him in recruiting these bright graduate students and professors to Baylor. In general, the strengthening of Baylor's Christian identity and academic reputation has boosted student interest. Despite a significant increase in student tuition, enrollment is at an all-time high and the university is more selective than ever before in the students that it brings in. According to Lyon, the 2012 initiative has enabled Baylor to occupy a unique niche in the burgeoning market of evangelical students interested in becoming Christian scholars, and the institution has benefited accordingly. It's difficult to argue with success.[20]

In the long run, an optimistic view of the 2012 campaign may be justified. Douglas Henry, an associate professor of philosophy and a

Sloan hire, is cautiously optimistic. He points out that under Sloan's tenure approximately 250 new professors were hired. "The number of faculty who have been hired over the years bodes well for the future," Henry says. "Those faculty members are the ones who will be at Baylor for the long haul." Simple demographics, therefore, would indicate that, barring a drastic change of course by subsequent leadership, the future may be on the side of the new Baylorites. If the 2012 hires can be retained (and that is a big *if*), then one would expect at least some parts of the 2012 vision to continue at Baylor. For the short term, however, David Jeffrey's description of a "balkanized" university seems more appropriate. The creation of the "evangelical Notre Dame" at Baylor University remains in doubt.[21]

Of course, Texas is not the entire South. Other southern universities, growing in both size and scholarly vision, give indications that the recovery of the evangelical mind in the South and Southwest may proceed regardless of the outcome at Baylor. Two institutions at opposite ends of the Sunbelt, Union University in Jackson, Tennessee, and Azusa Pacific University in Southern California, illustrate the different trajectories of evangelical education in the South.

Established in 1823 as Jackson Male Academy, Union University has a Southern Baptist pedigree that rivals that of Baylor. Yet it has made impressive strides academically in the past decade by incorporating northern evangelical elements. David Jeffrey predicts that Union will become the "Wheaton of the South." With an enrollment that has far surpassed Wheaton's and with lofty scholarly aspirations, however, Union may more likely represent a hybrid of the Wheaton and the Baylor models. With an endowment of only $23 million, Union obviously lacks Baylor's financial resources. But it does have an institutional culture united around the pursuit of scholarly excellence and seemingly no reservations about northern evangelicalism. Much of that is due to the leadership of president David Dockery, who was vice president and dean of the faculty during the debacle at Southern Baptist Seminary in Louisville in the mid-1990s. In 1995, Dockery left Southern to assume the presidency of Union, and he took six Southern professors with him, including well-known ethicist David Gushee. Upon coming to Union, Dockery began implementing his plan to make Union a bastion of evangelical scholarly excellence built on the explicitly integrationist model that had become so controversial at Baylor.[22]

For example, Dockery's "Union 2010" strategic plan calls for Union to "prioritize the importance of the Christian intellectual tradition across the curriculum" and for professors to "think Christianly" in their respective academic fields. Remarks Carla Sanderson, Union's provost, "The most significant change in the role of the Union University faculty over the last decade is the expectation for scholarship and the encouragement that scholarly work in the discipline be thoroughly Christian." As a result, Union actively recruits professors who can build a strong record of Christian scholarship. Also reminiscent of Baylor, Union has established a Center for Faculty Development that conducts faculty workshops and maintains a bibliography of written works on integration in various fields. Union faculty have also published collaborative works under Dockery's inspiration on Christian scholarship, such as *Shaping a Christian Worldview: The Foundations of Christian Higher Education* (2002) and *Renewing Minds: Serving Church and Society through Christian Higher Education* (2007).[23]

Union's approach can best be described as inspired by the evangelical ideals of Wheaton and Calvin but flavored by its southern heritage. It has a number of Wheaton alumni on the faculty, and Union professors regularly participate in faculty summer institutes held at Calvin College. Recent faculty workshops have been led by Wheaton president Duane Litfin and former Calvin provost Gordon Van Harn. Union also has endowed faculty chairs in honor of northern evangelical luminaries Carl F. H. Henry and Charles Colson. Nevertheless, says Provost Sanderson, "Union's approach is distinctive, influenced by our regional and denominational identity." The institution is, to use Dockery's phrase, "Baptist by tradition, evangelical by conviction." Furthermore, Union's Sunbelt location and growth trajectory would seem to put it on a different track from that of midwestern colleges. If Union University can harness Southern Baptist resources to its evangelical scholarly vision, it may provide a strong southern regional hub for an evangelical scholarly renaissance.[24]

A different model characterizes Azusa Pacific University in Southern California. APU began as a Bible college, the Training School for

Christian Workers, in 1899. In the 1960s it merged with Los Angeles Pacific College and Arlington College and moved to a new campus in Azusa, twenty-six miles northeast of Los Angeles. Its enrollment has mirrored the growing population of Southern California in general, and it now has 4,564 full-time students and another 4,000 part-time students. APU also has scholarly aspirations, as indicated by its Vision 2014 strategic plan, which emphasizes, among other things, "transformational scholarship." In it the university pledges to strengthen faculty scholarship and to "create an environment that supports and develops recognized researchers and excellent teachers." It also requires professors to intentionally integrate Christian faith into their scholarship and their teaching.[25]

Azusa Pacific's location in the Los Angeles area, however, has produced a different educational culture. Craig Boyd, director of Faith Integration at APU, graduated from Greenville College in Illinois and spent fifteen years in the Midwest before moving to APU. He remarks, "The multicultural environment forces APU to take seriously the many dimensions of God's communication to diverse populations (both Christian and non-Christian). It makes us more tolerant of others' perspectives, I believe." According to Boyd, Wheaton and Calvin, having been influenced by midwestern culture and a conservative Reformed heritage, are too "sectarian" to serve as models of intellectual leadership for institutions such as Azusa Pacific. Having been conditioned by a more diverse Southern Californian environment, APU professors would find it difficult to function at Wheaton or Calvin, where they would have to sign statements that reject Catholicism as a legitimate form of evangelicalism, affirm a historical Adam and Eve, or affirm the Synod of Dordt. Such statements, believes Boyd, are "either outdated concepts or merely cultural elements of Midwest evangelicalism." Boyd displays a certain Californian self-assuredness when he remarks, "Evangelical education in the Midwest is usually about ten years behind what it is on the coasts with regard to addressing important trends in higher education."[26]

Azusa Pacific University may see itself as ten years ahead of Wheaton educationally, but with only $50 million in endowment it is far behind its midwestern rival in terms of endowment. In other words, for all of its scholarly aspirations and statistical growth, APU is not far along in being able to realize what evangelical scholars envision when they talk about a Protestant research university. This leads to two concluding observations. First, despite the demographic shifts in recent decades, northern institutions still assert significant influence in the CCCU and will continue to do so in the foreseeable future. Wheaton College, simply by virtue of its name appeal and resources (its $300 million endowment dwarfs that of Azusa Pacific and most other Christian colleges), continues to attract the best and brightest evangelical students and professors. Calvin College continues to serve as a model for other Christian colleges in producing and reflecting upon Christian scholarship. Its Summer Seminars in Christian Scholarship, for example, attract Christian professors from all over the United States.

The support of intellectual life, after all, is not just about numbers but also about culture. Wheaton and Calvin are embedded in communities that tend to value purely academic pursuits, something that may not be as feasible in the fast-paced lifestyle of Southern California or the pragmatic educational culture of the Old South. In the wake of the Civil War, conditions in the South favored the development of more practical vocational colleges such as John Brown University and Tuskegee University. This pragmatic orientation helps explains Baylor University's historic strengths in professional areas such as law and medicine, which, from David Jeffrey's perspective, have been an obstacle to the success of Baylor 2012. While demographic trends clearly favor southern institutions, a culture that values scholarship for its own sake may have a more difficult time taking root in southern soil.

Second, for all the talk of building an "evangelical Notre Dame," evangelical scholars in the South and elsewhere will have to content themselves with more modest goals for the foreseeable future. And they would do well to abandon the Notre Dame motif as a realistic vision for evangelicalism. The University of Notre Dame seeks to serve the Catholic Church, in part by supporting scholarship. However, for Notre Dame, that mission does not entail hiring only Catholic professors. Rather, states Notre Dame president John Jenkins, the university seeks to maintain "a preponderance" of Catholic faculty. Professors from other faith traditions, as well as secular scholars, "are indispensable to the life and success of Notre Dame" in that they provoke debate and provide a diversity of perspectives. It is unlikely that an "evangelical Notre Dame" would seek to resemble Notre Dame in this aspect. The Catholic Church, several centuries old and a billion members strong, has the institutional size and self-assurance to tolerate non-Catholics and perhaps even anti-Catholics in her midst in a way that Protestant colleges typically do not. In the parlance of former Wheaton College president Duane Litfin, Notre Dame exemplifies an "umbrella" model of a Christian college by having its faith identity characterize the institution but not necessarily permeate every level. Evangelical institutions, in contrast, typically pursue a "systemic" model in which Christian faith is intended to flavor every aspect of the institution. A requirement for membership in the CCCU, in fact, is that colleges hire only Christian professors.[27]

Furthermore, as Notre Dame seeks to become a top-tier research university, maintaining Catholic dominance may prove to be increasingly difficult. As Mark Roche, dean of the College of Arts and Letters, observed, "The academic marketplace cannot replicate the number of Catholics who are retiring from the University." Thus, in the 2005–6 academic year, only 35 percent of Notre Dame's faculty hires were Catholics, and in the 2006–7 year, 42 percent were Catholic. Hardly a "preponderance." But the goal of becoming a top-tier research university increases the pressure to hire the best possible candidate regardless of that person's religious orientation, in some cases by generalizing the meaning of "Catholic." In other words, one finds a situation reminiscent of that described by Marsden at late nineteenth-century Protestant institutions, ironically at Marsden's own former institution. For example, Carolyn Woo, dean of the College of Business, interprets the Catholic mission of the institution broadly by expecting every faculty hire to embrace "Catholic" concepts such as social justice and the inherent dignity of the individual. That is a road that northern Protestants traveled over a century ago, and modern evangelicals have little desire to walk it again.[28]

Evangelical colleges find themselves in a different situation. For one thing, having had few intellectual stars over the past century, evangelical colleges are not pained to replace retiring scholars in large supply (George Marsden being one of the few exceptions). Furthermore, as

Mark Noll relates in *Scandal,* an increasing number of bright young Christian college graduates are pursuing scholarship as a Christian calling and finding financial support for graduate study from initiatives such as the Harvey Fellows Program and the Lilly Fellows Program. Thus the pipeline of prospective evangelical scholars should continue to produce a healthy flow.[29] Nevertheless, if Notre Dame, with its brand appeal and $3.5 billion endowment, finds it difficult to build a research university with Catholic scholars, one may well wonder whether any Protestant university could do the same.

Even if an ample supply of evangelical scholars exists, attracting those scholars to one particular Protestant research university—especially one in the South—will be difficult. Those scholars who joined Baylor under Sloan's tenure typically did so because of the excitement of the Baylor 2012 vision, not because of any attraction to central Texas. One does not need to cast aspersions on Waco to point out that the city lacks the robust intellectual culture found in New Haven, Ann Arbor, or Berkeley. Whether Waco culture can attract and retain the kind of scholars Baylor needs to become a premier research university remains to be seen. And at any rate, American evangelicals are much too diverse to unite behind a single flagship university the way that American Catholics have rallied behind Notre Dame. Perhaps a really good Protestant football team would help. But the failure thus far of Jerry Falwell's Liberty University football team to crack the big time has shown that prospect to be unlikely.[30]

George Marsden, noting modern evangelicalism's disunity, compares the movement to the feudalistic system of the Middle Ages, with its assorted collection of "superficially friendly, somewhat competitive empires," all united by allegiance to a common ruler.[31] In terms of evangelical higher education, one could take Marsden's metaphor a step further and compare the situation to that of the Holy Roman Empire that spanned central Europe for centuries. The feudalism metaphor implies a collection of roughly equal and loosely independent fiefdoms. The Holy Roman Empire, by contrast, was a loose religious confederation containing a wide variety of political units, some large and some small; some unified and some fractious; some wealthy and some poor; some connected to outside entities and some largely independent. In the same way, evangelical higher education varies widely in size, organization, and quality. Some institutions function as imperial cities, answerable to no one but the emperor himself; others receive support (and obligations) from a denomination. The territories of the Holy Roman Empire were united by a religious/political vision that was, as Voltaire famously observed, neither Holy, nor Roman, nor an Empire. Evangelical colleges are united by a scholarly vision that is hopefully more substance than myth.

Despite the chaotic structure of the Holy Roman Empire, a few territories gave rise to some of the leading universities of the early modern era, such as Heidelberg and Leipzig. They also produced figures such as Goethe, Kant, and Hegel, who generated some of the most brilliant and influential ideas of the day. Perhaps some of the principalities of modern evangelicalism in the South and elsewhere can do the same. If so, that would be cause for an even bigger celebration at the Gaylord Texan.

NOTES

1. William Ringenberg, *The Christian College* (Grand Rapids, MI: Baker Academic Publishing, 2006), 209.

2. Edward Gilbreath, "The New Capital of Evangelicalism," *Christianity Today*, May 2002.

3. Grant Wacker, "Uneasy in Zion: Evangelicals in Postmodern Society," in *Evangelicalism and Modern America*, ed. George Marsden (Grand Rapids, MI: Eerdmans, 1984), 17–28; William Glass, *Strangers in Zion: Fundamentalists in the South, 1900–1950* (Macon, GA: Mercer University Press, 2001); Barry Hankins, *Uneasy in Babylon: Southern Baptist Conservatives and American Culture* (Tuscaloosa: University of Alabama Press, 2002); Darren Dochuk, *From Bible Belt to Sunbelt: Plain-Folk Religion, Grassroots Politics, and the Rise of Conservative Politics* (New York: Norton, 2011).

4. Ringenberg, *Christian College*, 198–201.

5. Ibid., 198; Council for Christian Colleges and Universities, "Members and Affiliates," n.d., www.cccu.org/members_and_affiliates (accessed January 14, 2014).

6. Demographic statistics are drawn from National Atlas, "Population Change and Distribution, 1990–2000," n.d., www.nationalatlas.gov/articles/people/a_popchange.html; Forbes, "Fastest Growing Cities in the U.S.," n.d., accessed March 19, 2014, www.forbes.com/pictures/edgl45ffh/introduction-6/.

7. See James Bratt and Ronald Wells, "Piety and Progress: A History of Calvin College," in *Models for Christian Higher Education*, ed. Richard Hughes and William Adrian (Grand Rapids, MI: Eerdmans, 1997), 143.

8. George Marsden, *The Outrageous Idea of Christian Scholarship* (New York: Oxford University Press, 1997), 102; Mark A. Noll, *The Scandal of the Evangelical Mind* (Grand Rapids, MI: Eerdmans, 1994), 16.

9. Marsden, *Outrageous Idea*, 102.

10. Michael Beaty, "The Charter Change: An Uncertain Future," in *Baylor beyond the Crossroads: An Interpretive History, 1985–2005*, ed. Donald Schmeltekopf and Barry Hankins (Waco, TX: Baylor University Press, 2006), 53–57.

11. Hunter Baker, "The Struggle for Baylor's Soul," in Schmeltekopf and Hankins, *Baylor beyond the Crossroads*, 125.

12. Ibid., 124; Solomon quoted in Beaty, "Charter Change," 70.

13. Baylor University, "Pro Futuris: A Strategic Vision for Baylor University," 2012, www.baylor.edu/vision/pdf/vision_full.pdf, 1–2; Baker, "Struggle for Baylor's Soul," 129.

14. Hankins, *Uneasy in Babylon*, 74–106.

15. David Jeffrey, interview by author, January 22, 2007; Margaret Tate, interview by author, January 22, 2007.

16. Beaty, "Charter Change," 54; Jeffrey, interview.

17. Tate, interview.

18. Thomas Kidd, interview by author, January 22, 2007; C. Stephen Evans, interview by author, January 22, 2007.

19. Anne-Marie Bowery, January 22, 2007, interview by author.

20. Larry Lyon, January 22, 2007, interview by author.

21. Douglas Henry, January 22, 2007, interview by author.

22. Hankins, *Uneasy in Babylon*, 98.

23. Union University, "2010 Vision Statement," www.uu.edu/Union2010/overview/priorities.cfm; Carla Sanderson, e-mail interview by author, April 25, 2007.

24. Sanderson, interview. According to Sanderson, President Dockery has recently begun articulating more forcefully the "Baptist" side of Union's heritage. For instance, the title of Dockery's Fall 2006 convocation address was "Between Galatians and Colossians: A Renewed Vision for Baptist Higher Education" (www.uu.edu/dockery/fall2006-convocation.pdf)—his first public address on Union's Baptist heritage in his eleven-year tenure at Union. It is not clear, however, how this Baptist vision will differentiate Union from other CCCU institutions. Union, Dockery states, is about "Christian thinking and thinking Christianly, learning to think carefully, critically, and creatively, engaging the culture and engaging the academy" (12). Such rhetoric could aptly characterize the intentions of most CCCU schools, Baptist or otherwise.

25. Azusa Pacific University, Office of the President, "Academic Vision," 2014, www.apu.edu/president/vision/.

26. Craig Boyd, e-mail interview by author, March 12, 2007.

27. Father John Jenkins, "The Mission," *Notre Dame Magazine*, Winter 2006–7, 37–39; Duane Litfin, *Conceiving the Christian College* (Grand Rapids, MI: Eerdmans, 2004), 14–17.

28. Roche and Woo quoted in Richard Conklin, "How Catholic the Faculty?," *Notre Dame Magazine*, Winter 2006–7, 40–43.

29. Noll, *Scandal of the Evangelical Mind*, 218–39.

30. Liberty University, founded by Falwell in Lynchburg, Virginia, also aspires to be an evangelical Notre Dame. But in the short run, at least, the prospect that Liberty will become an academic powerhouse seems unlikely. The fall 2009 entering class of freshmen had an ACT composite score of 22, well below the standards of a Baylor or a Notre Dame (John Kennedy, "Liberty Unbound," *Christianity Today*, September 2009).

31. George Marsden, "The Evangelical Denomination," in Marsden, *Evangelicalism and Modern America*, xiv.

PART V

PLURALISM'S BLESSING

CHAPTER 16

Marsden and Fundamentalist Resurgence

GARTH M. ROSELL

The publication of George Marsden's *Reforming Fundamentalism: Fuller Seminary and the New Evangelicalism* in 1987 marks an important historiographical watershed in the study of the modern evangelical movement. In contrast with the relative paucity of good research that Leonard I. Sweet had lamented in 1984, the years following the publication of *Reforming Fundamentalism* seemed to have come alive with fresh interest and scholarly attention.[1] New bibliographies devoted exclusively to the American evangelical movement were published,[2] collections of primary documents became available,[3] the Institute for the Study of American Evangelicals continued its important work,[4] new dictionaries and encyclopedias made their way into print,[5] and scores of new articles and monographs were published.[6] Much as the 1980 publication of his *Fundamentalism and American Culture* had helped to spawn dozens of new studies of the early twentieth-century religious landscape, Marsden's study of Fuller Theological Seminary seems in turn to have helped to launch a new "cottage industry" of scholarly research on mid-twentieth-century evangelicalism.

In a sense, of course, *Reforming Fundamentalism* was essentially a continuation of *Fundamentalism and American Culture*. While Marsden was considering a possible "sequel" to his earlier work, as he phrased it in his preface to *Reforming Fundamentalism*, the president of Fuller Theological Seminary asked him if he "might be willing to write the history of that institution." Marsden responded that he would be interested in such an assignment provided that he be allowed to use the seminary "as a window through which to focus my study of recent evangelicalism and fundamentalism."[7] Assured that the seminary would welcome such an approach, Marsden accepted the assignment. The result was that the *particular* became the vehicle whereby the *universal* could more clearly be seen. While such an approach has its limitations, to be sure, it seems especially useful in this instance, since Fuller Theological Seminary so fully embodies the core values and theological tendencies of the tradition that gave that institution its birth.

Like the modern evangelical movement itself, with its roots in the great spiritual awakenings of the eighteenth century, Fuller Theological Seminary has historically centered its educational identity on the cross of Jesus Christ, reflecting evangelicalism's deep and continuing conviction that "God so loved the world that he gave his one and only Son, that whoever believes in him shall not perish but have eternal life."[8] Around the cross, and flowing out from the historic teachings associated with it, are four additional convictions that more than any others have characterized both the evangelical movement and the many institutions it helped to establish: namely, a shared authority (the Bible); a shared experience (conversion); a shared mission (worldwide evangelization); and a shared vision (the spiritual renewal of church and society). Taken together, these five distinguishing marks have provided the theological and practical glue that has held the constantly shifting coalition called "evangelicalism" together for nearly three centuries, even though the movement can claim no geographical center, no normative theological formulation, and no authoritative voice.[9]

Indeed, the twists and turns of Fuller's history, as Marsden's work so persuasively suggests, reflect in microcosm not only the joys and sorrows of a single theological institution but also many of the interpretative challenges, historical developments, and research interests of a much larger set of contexts, historical events, and community concerns. Among the more significant of these, it would seem, are a reengagement with culture, the renewal of church and society, the return to intellectual respectability, the spread of the gospel around the globe, and a thirst for a genuine spiritual awakening. "We surely need prayer and guidance that no mistakes may be made in this stupendous undertaking," Charles E. Fuller confided in a letter to Harold John Ockenga in 1947. "I do believe that God is bringing this school into being to train men and empower them to meet conditions at a particularly needy time in the world's history."[10]

A REENGAGEMENT WITH CULTURE

The founding of Fuller Theological Seminary in 1947, as Charles E. Fuller had astutely observed, took place within an unusual period of world history. Two world wars had not only claimed thousands of human lives but also helped to foster a renewed global consciousness for the nation as well as the church. The devastating depression of the 1930s, moreover, with its dust bowls and bread lines, had helped to replace the optimism of an earlier era with a more realistic assessment of dangers and risks. Yet despite these difficulties, exciting technological innovations in such areas as travel, communication, agriculture, medicine, and entertainment were also opening a world of new and previously unimaginable possibilities.

The old fundamentalist and modernist coalitions, whose bitter battles so profoundly shaped America's religious landscape during the 1920s, were of course still very much alive. The intervening decades, however, had helped to temper their perspectives and transform their strategies. "During the 1930s and 1940s," as Joel Carpenter suggested in his superb study *Revive Us Again: The Reawakening of American Fundamentalism*, fundamentalists began "to establish their identity, consolidate an institutional network, and rethink their mission to America." While they continued to critique their theological opponents, to be sure, they "were also retooling their evangelistic techniques and seizing upon inviting cultural trends to mount a renewed public presence."[11]

"The evangelical defense of the faith theologically," argued Harold John Ockenga, pastor of Boston's historic Park Street Church and the first president of Fuller Theological Seminary, "is identical with that of the older fundamentalists."[12] Evangelicals and fundamentalists differ, however, on matters of style and strategy. In the heat of battle, Ockenga believed, fundamentalists had tended to turn inward, to circle the wagons so to speak, and to adopt a strategy of withdrawal. Fearing that their sons and daughters would lose their faith, for example, many parents had pulled their children out of the increasingly liberal universities, enrolling them instead in Christian liberal arts colleges or Bible schools. Many others, discouraged by what they believed to be the growing strength of modernism in the mainline denominations, chose to sever their ties with those bodies and to seek more like-minded fellowship in evangelically oriented congregations. Those who had once been participants in the ecumenical revolution now found themselves increasingly estranged from its structures and programs. Still others, sensing what they believed to be the moral and cultural decay within America's institutions, withdrew from the public square.

In contrast with this strategy of withdrawal, the founders of Fuller Theological Seminary began to call upon a whole new generation of leaders to infiltrate the very institutions that so many of the old stalwarts had felt compelled to abandon. Evangelicals, Ockenga was convinced, needed to realize that the modernists had been using a strategy of infiltration for years. "They have infiltrated our evangelical denominations, institutions and movements, and then have taken over control of them." Therefore the time has come "to join hands with evangelicals everywhere in testimony and in action" and to seize the opportunity to infiltrate those same denominations, institutions, and movements with the salt and light of biblical Christianity.[13]

Rather than fully embracing Ockenga's bold new strategy, however, as Marsden reminds us in *Reforming Fundamentalism*, the new evangelicals increasingly turned their attention to the task of institution building. If evangelicals were really convinced "that the mainstream denominations were not apostate," Marsden asked, why did they seem to avoid working "through the denominational agencies" and instead invest such enormous energy in the creation of a whole new set of "transdenominational evangelical agencies" such as Fuller Theological Seminary, the National Association of Evangelicals, and *Christianity Today*?[14] When confronted by such questions, Ockenga would respond that when great movements of God's Spirit take place within human history, such as the Protestant Reformation of the sixteenth century, the Wesleyan revival of the eighteenth century, or the evangelical resurgence in the twentieth century, there is often the need for "new wineskins." Old structures are not always adequate to contain the new movements of God. While we should take care that existing structures are not abandoned too quickly, Ockenga cautioned, there are unique moments in human history when new theological movements require new institutional expressions to undergird and support them. The 1940s was precisely such a time, he believed, and organizations such as the National Association of Evangelicals and Fuller Theological Seminary were precisely such wineskins.[15]

The new evangelicals' call to reengage the culture not only gave shape and direction to Fuller Theological Seminary and to the larger movement whose core values it so diligently sought to emulate but also helped to spawn dozens of scholarly projects—including Marsden's *Reforming Fundamentalism*—specifically designed to explore the complex relationships between the evangelical mission and its surrounding cultural contexts. "Renewing the Evangelical Mission," for example, a conference held in 2009 at Gordon-Conwell Theological Seminary in honor of David F. Wells, attracted hundreds of attendees to hear papers by ten noted scholars, all of whom had been engaged in various ways with the interactions between evangelicalism and culture.[16] Dozens of additional conferences, workshops, special lectureships, and scholarly research projects have also helped to focus attention on the relationships between modern evangelicalism and politics, economics, religion, society, education, and the arts. Scores of books and articles have already found their way into print, and it is likely that many additional studies in these important areas will be produced during the coming decades.[17]

RENEWING THE CHURCH AND SOCIETY

A second major theme emerging from Marsden's work, namely the renewal of church and society, seems also to be capturing the attention of growing numbers in the academy. During its first several decades, as

Marsden suggested in *Reforming Fundamentalism*, Fuller Theological Seminary aspired to be nothing less than "a force for renewal" and "a beacon signaling a new stage in world civilization." Such a breathtaking mission, its leaders were convinced, called for the establishment of "a large middle ground" between the "strict fundamentalists" on one side and the "Protestant liberals" on the other—indeed, it called for the building of "a healthy third force in Protestantism" that "could operate between the separatist fundamentalists and the modernists."[18] In addition to reengaging the culture and its institutions, they believed, such a strategy would also enable the new evangelicals to work for the transformation of the church and the society. Such a vision was hardly new. As Timothy L. Smith suggested in his pioneering study *Revivalism and Social Reform: American Protestantism on the Eve of the Civil War*, eighteenth- and nineteenth-century evangelicals had been at the forefront in promoting issues of ecumenical unity and social justice.[19] Smith's argument, as I suggested in the foreword of this edition of his influential work, was deceptively simple: America's mid-nineteenth-century religious revivals, reinforced by a passionate quest for personal and corporate holiness, unleashed a flood of evangelical social activity, mobilizing tens of thousands of new recruits for the battles against slavery, poverty, and greed. Far from abandoning their long-standing commitment to sound theology, biblical authority, personal holiness, and the missionary mandate, these evangelicals believed that it was precisely because of those commitments that they were obligated, to borrow the words of the prophet Micah, to "act justly and to love mercy and to walk humbly" with their God.

In light of their historic commitment to both evangelism and social justice, how is it possible to explain modern evangelicals' seeming lack of interest in the latter? The answer, according to sociologist David O. Moberg, can be found in what Timothy Smith called the "Great Reversal."[20] As modernism became increasingly identified with the social gospel during the early twentieth century, many fundamentalist preachers abandoned the language of reform, choosing rather to concentrate their attention on the important tasks of promoting personal piety and evangelistic outreach. Such a bifurcation between evangelism and social action, to say nothing of the abandonment of one of the movement's key historic commitments, left many evangelicals with a somewhat truncated understanding of biblical Christianity. Not until 1947, with the publication of Carl F. H. Henry's influential little book *The Uneasy Conscience of Modern Fundamentalism*, was the problem systematically addressed by the mid-twentieth-century evangelicals. "Why must the church be on the wrong side of every major social issue," Harold John Ockenga was once asked. "If the Bible-believing Christian is on the wrong side of social problems such as war, race, class, labor, liquor, imperialism, etc.," Ockenga responded, than "it is time to get over the fence to the right side. The church needs a progressive Fundamentalism with a social message."[21] Despite such affirmations, however, modern evangelicalism's recovery of its social justice heritage has been exceedingly slow. Happily, the situation seems to be changing. A fresh interest in such matters appears to be emerging within the scholarly community as growing numbers of researchers turn their attention to a study of these themes.[22] Interest in social reform and the promotion of biblical justice has not been confined to the academy, of course. Many teachers and pastors, in classrooms as well as pulpits, have noticed a significant increase of interest and involvement in these matters among a new generation of students. Those who once might have used their vacations for a week in the sun or their newly graduated status as a time to search for higher-paying jobs, for example, are now routinely volunteering to build houses for the needy, to plant new churches in declining neighborhoods, to establish "new monastic" communities in urban centers, to help find lodging for the homeless, or to teach poor children in a mission school.

A RETURN TO INTELLECTUAL RESPECTABILITY

A third major theme, running like a silver thread through the early history of Fuller Theological Seminary, is the evangelical quest for intellectual respectability. While evangelicals have often excelled in such tasks as "organizing, instituting, building constituency, recruiting, mobilizing, or fund-raising," as Mark A. Noll suggested in his influential 1994 study *The Scandal of the Evangelical Mind*, they have not always pursued the life of the mind with the kind of patience and perseverance that is required for intellectual leadership.[23] The founders of Fuller were determined to address that very problem. Our students, wrote Charles E. Fuller in a letter to the seminary's Board of Trustees, should have "the same caliber of training 'in the Gospel' as West Point makes available for students in Military Science or Caltech provides for those who wish to study engineering." While the seminary must remain "truly orthodox" in theology, it must also reflect "a high scholastic standard."[24]

The establishment of Fuller Theological Seminary, as Noll has reminded us, was part of an important awakening of the evangelical mind that took place during the 1940s and 1950s. The leaders of new evangelicalism, including Harold John Ockenga, Edward John Carnell, Carl F. H. Henry, and Billy Graham, not only promoted "an intellectually responsible evangelicalism" but also participated actively in countering any real or perceived anti-intellectualism within the movement.[25] With its well-trained and carefully selected faculty, Fuller Theological Seminary was positioned to become an important leader in this burgeoning evangelical renaissance, and it has increasingly made good on that original promise. Fuller was not alone. New centers of learning, informal as well as formal, were also emerging within the evangelical movement, and taken together they are beginning to change the intellectual landscape. While it would have been relatively unusual for an evangelical student to pursue a doctoral degree during the 1940s, for example, literally hundreds of bright young evangelical men and women are doing so today. Some of these, following the lead of pioneers such as Timothy L. Smith, were eventually able to secure faculty appointments at major universities. Many of the students they helped to train are now themselves teaching. Indeed, it is probably worth noting in a volume such as this, as we rightly celebrate the publications of one who stands very much in the tradition of Timothy L. Smith, that Marsden's greatest scholarly contribution might well turn out to be the students he has helped to train.

Whether or not such a conclusion is eventually confirmed, certainly evangelical interest in the study of higher education, including that carried out in theological seminaries such as Fuller, has seldom been stronger. Encouraged by generous grants by the Pew Charitable Trusts and the Lilly Endowment, and perhaps as a result of the reception afforded publications such as *Reforming Fundamentalism*, a treasure trove of important new studies began to emerge in the 1990s. Among these were Glenn T. Miller's *Piety and Intellect* (1990), Marsden and Longfield's *The Secularization of the Academy* (1992), Marsden's *The Soul of the American University* (1994), Conrad Cherry's *Hurrying toward Zion* (1995), and Arthur F. Holmes's *Building the Christian Academy* (2001).[26]

More local studies of individual educational institutions, such as Margaret Lamberts Bendroth's *A School of the Church: Andover Newton across Two Centuries* (2008), are now needed to fill out the story of theological education.[27] Furthermore, many more critical analyses of the role that education has played within the larger American culture, such as the publications of older scholars like Lawrence A. Cremin, Bernard Bailyn, Timothy L. Smith, and Nathan M. Pusey, will be essential if we are to understand the complex interactions between education and society.[28] And, of course, far more attention will need to be given to the actual practice of classroom teaching and learning, such as that provided so helpfully in Malcolm L. Warford's *Practical Wisdom* (2004).[29] Until the early 1990s, with the possible exception of teacher training centers, relatively little evangelical attention seems to have been given to such studies as those identified above. With the publication of books like Marsden's *Reforming Fundamentalism*, *The Soul of the American University*, and *The Outrageous Idea of Christian Scholarship*, however, evangelical scholars are now giving fresh attention to these important areas of research.[30]

THE SPREAD OF THE GOSPEL AROUND THE WORLD

A fourth issue, the spread of the gospel around the world, has also been central to the story of Fuller Theological Seminary. "Over the past century," Philip Jenkins observed in his influential book *The Next Christendom: The Coming of Global Christianity*, "the center of gravity in the Christian world has shifted inexorably southward, to Africa, Asia, and Latin America." Drawing upon statistical studies published in the *World Christian Encyclopedia*, Jenkins presented a persuasive case for concluding that "the era of Western Christianity has passed within our lifetimes, and the day of Southern Christianity is dawning."[31] There can be little question, it would seem, that the largest number of Christians—indeed the largest number of evangelical Christians—are currently living outside the geographical boundaries of Europe and North America.[32]

Such a conclusion should hardly come as a surprise. The missionary mandate, after all, was not only one of the most distinctive features of the evangelical movement as a whole but also one of the two central emphases at Fuller Theological Seminary throughout the 1950s: namely, as Marsden reminds us, the importance of "being a center for apologetic scholarship and a training base for sending out spiritually empowered missionaries."[33] During its first thirteen years, in fact, 100 of Fuller's 570 graduates became missionaries.[34] Unlike some of their more isolationist contemporaries, many of the mid-twentieth-century evangelicals seem to have shared a global perspective from their earliest years. When Youth for Christ was founded in the mid-1940s, for example, its members chose to call themselves "Youth for Christ, International," and their programmatic outreach to young men and women was from the beginning both local and global.[35]

"Mission history prior to World War II was largely a denominational affair," observed historian Dana Robert in her insightful historiographical survey of American Protestant Missions since the 1940s. Since the 1980s, however, there has been "an explosion of renewed scholarly interest in the history of American Protestant missions" not only among the so-called "mainline" denominations but among "ethnic Americans, women, assorted subcultures, and Roman Catholics as well. From the ashes of 'mission' reemerged 'missions,'" Robert suggests, "a lively and diverse enterprise, no longer able to fit comfortably into the outgrown garb of denominational history, Christian unity, or American identity."[36]

The scholarly results of this renewed interest have been impressive. Mission study centers, such as the Overseas Ministries Study Center in New Haven, Connecticut, and the Centre for the Story of World Christianity at the University of Edinburgh, have attracted academics from around the world to explore missionary-related issues. Moreover, the work of such gifted scholars as Andrew Walls, Jonathan Bonk, Peter Kuzmic, Dana Robert, Ralph D. Winter, Timothy Tennent, Harold A. Netland, Todd Johnson, and a host of others has greatly advanced the understanding of missionary history, theology, and practice. Much work remains to be done. "Freed from its prison as a subject of interest only in theological seminaries and Bible colleges," Professor Robert suggests, "the history of Protestant missions needs to be taken in new directions," some of which are already being pursued.[37] Mission history can become "a bridge to Asia, Africa, and Latin America," with a "potential to enliven numerous other fields of inquiry and to provide an entree into nonwestern Christianity. At last the historiography of Protestant foreign mission is maturing, growing through adolescence into adulthood," Robert concludes, moving "through and beyond missions to perspectives that may reveal the global historical significance of American Protestant foreign missions for the first time."[38]

THE THIRST FOR A GENUINE SPIRITUAL AWAKENING

Since the modern evangelical movement had its beginnings in the spiritual awakenings that swept across Europe and North America during the eighteenth century, it is hardly surprising to discover a hunger for revival near the center of institutions such as Fuller Theological Seminary. "From the outset," as Marsden has reported, the Fuller faculty "worried that in the high-powered intellectual atmosphere the spiritual life of their students might languish."[39] Such a potential imbalance between head and heart, created in part by what Marsden called Fuller's "heady intellectual atmosphere," could prove damaging not only to the seminary's reputation but also to its efforts at student recruitment.

The reason was quite clear. Many of Fuller's students had come to Christian faith through the ministry of organizations such as the Navigators, Youth for Christ, Young Life, InterVarsity Christian Fellowship, and Word of Life. Scores of such organizations, geared primarily to the tasks of evangelizing and making disciples of young men and women, had been established throughout North America during the decades between World War I (1914–18) and World War II (1939–45), and tens of thousands of young people had been swept into the Christian faith as a result of their combined ministries. The burgeoning youth rallies of the 1940s, while largely forgotten today, not only prepared the way for the well-known citywide evangelists of the 1950s but also seemed to provide a foundation for what J. Edwin Orr liked to call the "Mid-Twentieth Century Awakening."[40] Fuller Theological Seminary was founded, like scores of evangelical educational institutions before it, in the midst of a surge of religious revival, and its history can scarcely be understood without the inclusion of the American revival tradition as part of the story.

An important aspect of that spiritual awakening, of course, was the exploding growth of the worldwide Pentecostal movement—an enormously important development that had its modern beginnings, at least symbolically, in the great Azusa Street revival of 1906 and the remarkable ministry of William J. Seymour.[41] Despite the divisions that had emerged in the 1920s between the fundamentalists and the developing Pentecostal denominations, Fuller Theological Seminary was well positioned to take advantage of the enormous growth in this expanding wing of world Christianity. With his Methodist upbringing and Wesleyan convictions, Harold John Ockenga not only had encouraged groups such as the Assemblies of God to join the National Association of Evangelicals but was inclined to welcome students from Pentecostal churches to enroll at the seminary. "Fuller did deeply wish to cultivate its ministry to the pentecostal and charismatic wings of evangelicalism," Marsden observed in *Reforming Fundamentalism*, and one evidence of that interest "was the establishment in 1958 of the David J. du Plessis Center for Christian Spirituality," named after a widely respected leader of mid-twentieth-century Pentecostalism and designed to foster research in Pentecostal studies.[42]

Important new research is currently being pursued on a variety of themes, issues, and personalities connected with the development of worldwide Pentecostalism and its holiness roots, as evidenced by the wide array of papers presented at meetings of the Society for Pentecostal Studies and the Wesleyan Theological Society. With rare exceptions, however, courses on such matters have been remarkably slow in making their way into the curricula of universities and seminaries. Given the enormous growth and influence of these movements, such relative neglect is difficult to understand.

FUTURE PROSPECTS

In briefly introducing these five themes—a reengagement with culture, the renewal of church and society, the return to intellectual respectability, the spread of the gospel around the globe, and a thirst for genuine spiritual awakening—we have of course only begun to explore the scores of important issues that emerge from the pages of *Reforming Fundamentalism*. Like his other major writings, it would seem, Marsden's publication in 1987 of the history of Fuller Theological Seminary has not only raised a multitude of important questions for his readers but also helped to foster additional research in related areas. One can scarcely ask more of a book than that.

The history of any living institution remains a "work in progress." Just as there is always a "history before the history," as Marsden titled one of his early chapters, there is always also a history after the history. Indeed, the future prospects of the movement that gave birth to the seminary are themselves a matter of considerable discussion. While admitting that there is substantial "evidence of weakness and complacency" within evangelicalism, Alister McGrath was still prepared to suggest in 1995 that "the future of Christianity" seems to belong to the movement.[43] Others like Douglas A. Sweeney, while recognizing the movement's "sins and other shortcomings" and its need to regain its "spiritual bearings," observed in 2005 that evangelicals were "bursting at the seams—so much so that we are finding it hard to keep ourselves together or to distinguish ourselves from some of the many cultures we have imbued."[44]

Historians, even those as gifted and perceptive as George M. Marsden, are seldom also prophets, of course, and history has its own unique way of thwarting even the best informed of predictions. Yet those who are privileged to earn their livings looking primarily backward can take some comfort in the realization that more research will always need to be done and more chapters will always need to be written. As future historians take up those tasks, it is good to know that there are competent guides such as George Marsden to help them.

NOTES

1. Leonard I. Sweet, ed., *The Evangelical Tradition in America* (Macon, GA: Mercer University Press, 1984), 2.

2. See, for example, Norris A. Magnuson and William G. Travis, *American Evangelicalism: An Annotated Bibliography* (West Cornwall, CT: Locust Hills Press, 1990); Edith L. Blumhofer and Joel Carpenter, *Twentieth-Century Evangelicalism: A Guide to the Sources* (New York: Garland, 1990); and Robert D. Shuster, James Stambaugh, and Ferne Weimer, *Researching Modern Evangelicalism: A Guide to the Holdings of the Billy Graham Center, with Information on Other Collections* (New York: Greenwood Press, 1990).

3. See, for example, Joel A. Carpenter, ed., *Two Reformers of Fundamentalism* (New York: Garland, 1988) and *A New Evangelical Coalition: Early Documents of the National Association of Evangelicals*, both in Garland's facsimile series Fundamentalism in American Religion, 1880–1950.

4. The Institute for the Study of American Evangelicals was founded at Wheaton College in 1982 as a center for research on the evangelical movement. Dozens of books and articles have been published as a result of studies, conferences, and lectures sponsored by the Institute.

5. See, for example, Daniel G. Reid, ed., *Dictionary of Christianity in America* (Downers Grove, IL: InterVarsity Press, 1990); Randall Balmer, *Encyclopedia of Evangelicalism* (Louisville, KY: Westminster John Knox Press, 2002); and Timothy Larsen, ed., *Biographical Dictionary of Evangelicals* (Downers Grove, IL: InterVarsity Press, 2003).

6. See, for example, David W. Bebbington and Mark A. Noll, eds., *A History of Evangelicalism: People, Movements and Ideas in the English-Speaking World* (Downers Grove, IL: InterVarsity Press, 2003), a magisterial five-volume study of the movement; and Douglas A. Sweeney, *The American Evangelical Story: A History of the Movement* (Grand Rapids, MI: Baker Academic Publishing, 2005).

7. George M. Marsden, *Reforming Fundamentalism: Fuller Seminary and the New Evangelicalism* (Grand Rapids, MI: Eerdmans, 1987), vii–viii.

8. For a discussion of the roots of modern evangelicalism, see Mark A. Noll, *The Rise of Evangelicalism: The Age of Edwards, Whitefield and the Wesleys* (Downers Grove, IL: InterVarsity Press, 2003), 18–19.

9. This particular listing of core values is taken from Garth Rosell, *The Surprising Work of God* (Grand Rapids, MI: Baker Academic Publishing, 2008), 25–27. Similar listings can be found in Garth Rosell, "Charles G. Finney: His Place in the Stream of American Evangelicalism," in Sweet, *Evangelical Tradition*, 132, and Garth M. Rosell, ed., *The Evangelical Landscape: Essays on the American Evangelical Tradition* (Grand Rapids, MI: Baker Book House, 1996), 9. David Bebbington's well-known quadrilateral, in his *Evangelicalism in Modern*

Britain (Grand Rapids, MI: Baker Academic Publications, 1992), 2–3, remains the most familiar listing of evangelical characteristics.

10. Charles E. Fuller to Harold John Ockenga, July 17, 1947, Harold John Ockenga Papers, Gordon-Conwell Theological Seminary, South Hamilton, MA.

11. Joel A. Carpenter, *Revive Us Again: The Reawakening of American Fundamentalism* (New York: Oxford University Press, 1997), xii.

12. Harold John Ockenga, "Resurgent Evangelical Leadership," *Christianity Today*, October 10, 1960, 13.

13. Ibid., 15.

14. Marsden, *Reforming Fundamentalism*, 95. For a discussion of these "transdenominational" agencies, see Wesley K. Willmer and J. David Schmidt, *The Prospering Parachurch: Enlarging the Boundaries of God's Kingdom* (San Francisco: Jossey-Bass, 1998).

15. See, for example, Harold John Ockenga, "The Distinctives of Seminary Education," lecture, October 5, 1971, Harold John Ockenga Papers, Gordon-Conwell Theological Seminary, South Hamilton, MA.

16. The conference "Renewing the Evangelical Mission" was held October 13–15, 2009, on the campus of Gordon-Conwell Theological Seminary. Participants included Tite Tiénou, Os Guiness, Mark Noll, Miroslav Volf, Cornelius Plantinga, Bruce McCormack, Kevin J. Vanhoozer, Michael S. Horton, Gary Parrett (substituting for J. I. Packer), and Lauren Winner. For a collection of papers from the conference see Richard Lints, ed., *Renewing the Evangelical Mission* (Grand Rapids, MI: Eerdmans, 2013).

17. See, for example, Molly Worthen, *Apostles of Reason: The Crisis of Authority in American Evangelicalism* (New York: Oxford University Press, 2014); Soong-Chan Rah, *The Next Evangelicalism: Freeing the Church from Western Cultural Captivity* (Downers Grove, IL: InterVarsity Press, 2009); Brian Stanley, *The Global Diffusion of Evangelicalism* (Downers Grove, IL: InterVarsity Press, 2013); Christian Smith, *American Evangelicalism: Embattled and Thriving* (Chicago: University of Chicago Press, 1998), 291–304; Jon R. Stone, *On the Boundaries of American Evangelicalism: The Postwar Evangelical Coalition* (New York: St. Martin's Press, 1997), 203–220; Magnuson and Travis, *American Evangelicalism*; and the listings on the website of the Institute for the Study of American Evangelicals. For an example of the kind of in-depth work that has already taken place, see the five perceptive and interrelated studies by David F. Wells: *No Place for Truth* (1993), *God in the Wasteland* (1994), *Losing Our Virtue* (1999), *Above All Earthly Powers* (2005), and *The Courage to Be Protestant* (2008), all published by Eerdmans.

18. Marsden, *Reforming Fundamentalism*, 67.

19. Timothy L. Smith, *Revivalism and Social Reform: American Protestantism on the Eve of the Civil War* (Eugene, OR: Wipf and Stock, 2004), 3–6.

20. David O. Moberg, *The Great Reversal: Evangelism and Social Concern*, rev. ed. (Philadelphia: Lippincott, 1977).

21. Carl F. H. Henry, *The Uneasy Conscience of Modern Fundamentalism* (Grand Rapids, MI: Eerdmans, 1947). Ockenga's comment can be found in his introduction to the book.

22. See, for example, Peter Heltzel, *Jesus and Justice: Evangelicals, Race, and American Politics* (New Haven, CT: Yale University Press, 2009).

23. Mark A. Noll, *The Scandal of the Evangelical Mind* (Grand Rapids, MI: Eerdmans, 1994), 243–53.

24. Charles E. Fuller to Trustees of Fuller Theological Seminary, undated six-page letter (probably written in the autumn of 1961, since the letter makes mention "that our beloved school is starting its 15th year"), Harold John Ockenga Papers, Gordon-Conwell Theological Seminary.

25. Noll, *Scandal of the Evangelical Mind*, 212–14.

26. Glenn T. Miller, *Piety and Intellect: The Aims and Purposes of Ante-bellum Theological Education* (Atlanta, GA: Scholars Press, 1990); George M. Marsden and Bradley J. Longfield, eds., *The Secularization of the Academy* (New York: Oxford University Press, 1992); George M. Marsden, *The Soul of the American University: From Protestant Establishment to Established Nonbelief* (New York: Oxford University Press, 1994); Conrad Cherry, *Hurrying toward Zion: Universities, Divinity Schools, and American Protestantism* (Bloomington: Indiana University Press, 1995); Arthur F. Holmes, *Building the Christian Academy* (Grand Rapids, MI: Eerdmans, 2001).

27. James H. Moorhead, *Princeton Seminary in American Religion and Culture* (Grand Rapids, MI: Eerdmans, 2012); Gregory A. Wills, *Southern Baptist Theological Seminary* (New York: Oxford University Press, 2009); John Hannah, *An Uncommon Union* (Grand Rapids, MI: Zondervan, 2009); Margaret Lamberts Bendroth, *A School of the Church: Andover Newton across Two Centuries* (Grand Rapids, MI: Eerdmans, 2008).

28. Lawrence A. Cremin, *Traditions of American Education* (New York: Basic Books, 1976); Bernard Bailyn, *Education in the Forming of American Society* (New York: Vintage Books, 1960); Timothy L. Smith, *Uncommon Schools: Christian Colleges and Social Idealism in Midwestern America, 1820–1950* (Indianapolis: Indiana Historical Society, 1978), originally a paper presented at Wabash College in 1976; and Nathan M. Pusey, *American Higher Education* (Cambridge, MA: Harvard University Press, 1978).

29. Malcolm L. Warford, ed., *Practical Wisdom on Theological Teaching and Learning* (New York: Peter Lang, 2004).

30. George M. Marsden, *The Outrageous Idea of Christian Scholarship* (New York: Oxford University Press, 1997).

31. Philip Jenkins, *The Next Christendom: The Coming of Global Christianity* (New York: Oxford University Press, 2002), 2–3. See also Todd M. Johnson and Sandra S. Kim, "The Changing Demographics of World Christianity," a special report on global Christianity prepared for the inauguration of a World Chris-

tianity group at the 2006 American Academy of Religion meetings in Washington, DC; and Todd M. Johnson and Kenneth R. Ross, *Atlas of Global Christianity: 1910–2010* (Edinburgh: Edinburgh University Press, 2010).

32. For a helpful study of evangelicalism's global expansion in the twentieth century, see Donald M. Lewis, ed., *Christianity Reborn: The Global Expansion of Evangelicalism in the Twentieth Century* (Grand Rapids, MI: Eerdmans, 2004).

33. Marsden, *Reforming Fundamentalism*, 83–93, quote from 83.

34. Ibid., 238.

35. For example, Billy Graham, one of Youth for Christ's first staff members, spent a substantial portion of his time working in the British Isles.

36. Dana Robert, "From Missions to Mission to beyond Missions," in *New Directions in American Religious History*, ed. Harry S. Stout and D. G. Hart (New York: Oxford University Press, 1997), 362–93, quotations from 363 and 364.

37. Ibid., 381.

38. Ibid., 381, 383.

39. Marsden, *Reforming Fundamentalism*, 87–89, quote from 87.

40. J. Edwin Orr, *The Second Evangelical Awakening in America* (London: Marshall, Morgan and Scott, 1952), 202. See also Rosell, *Surprising Work of God*, 107–59.

41. See Grant Wacker, *Heaven Below: Early Pentecostals and American Culture* (Cambridge, MA: Harvard University Press, 2001); Cecil M. Robeck Jr., *The Azusa Street Mission and Revival: The Birth of the Global Pentecostal Movement* (Nashville, TN: Nelson, 2006); Vinson Synan and Charles R. Fox Jr., *William J. Seymour: Pioneer of the Azusa Street Revival* (Alachua, FL: Bridge Logos Foundation, 2012); Vinson Synan, *The Holiness-Pentecostal Tradition* (Grand Rapids, MI: Eerdmans, 1997).

42. Marsden, *Reforming Fundamentalism*, quotes from 294, 294–95. While some have questioned whether Pentecostal/charismatic Christians should be included as part of the evangelical movement, most seem to agree with Mark Noll's conclusion that "modern-day Pentecostals must be considered part of the broader evangelical family since they are descended from nineteenth-century leaders who emphasized holiness and the work of the Holy Spirit, and who were themselves decisively shaped by the teaching of several important leaders of the eighteenth-century revivals, especially John and Charles Wesley." See Noll, *Rise of Evangelicalism*, 18.

43. Alister McGrath, *Evangelicalism and the Future of Christianity* (Downers Grove, IL: InterVarsity Press, 1995), 11, 10.

44. Sweeney, *American Evangelical Story*, 185.

CHAPTER 17

Reforming Fundamentalism

DARREN DOCHUK

Who knew the history of a seminary could be so scintillating? Fortunately for students of American religious history, George Marsden did. Wanting to write a suitable follow-up to his groundbreaking *Fundamentalism and American Culture* (1980), yet also test new ways of writing evangelicalism's history, Marsden settled on the story of Fuller Seminary. The result was *Reforming Fundamentalism: Fuller Seminary and the New Evangelicalism* (1987), a brilliant achievement that combined meticulous research with forceful narrative about American evangelicalism's post–World War II ascent.

Brilliant, of course, is a term scholars throw around loosely, sometimes to pat the back of a respected colleague (in hopes they will pat back), but in the case of *Reforming Fundamentalism* Marsden earns the designation honestly. Several exceptional qualities make this study worthy of such praise, one of which Garth Rosell has already highlighted in this volume's chapter 16. Writing as an accomplished professor of church history at Gordon-Conwell Theological Seminary, with firsthand insight into the peculiar challenges that schools like Fuller face, Rosell zeroes in on the didactic dimensions of *Reforming Fundamentalism* and applies them to his own context of Christian vocation.

At Fuller between the 1940s and 1960s, he underscores, "New Evangelicals" embarked on a quest to reengage culture, renew church and society, attain intellectual responsibility, spread the gospel around the world, and "thirst" after "a genuine awakening." Fifty years later, Rosell intimates with a pastor's touch, church folk would do well to follow Fuller's lead. An important work of history certainly, *Reforming Fundamentalism*, he emphasizes, is also an invaluable handbook for devout Christians desiring to retool their faith traditions for effective witness in the new century.

Rosell, it is worth noting, is not the only seminarian to cite the prescriptive qualities of *Reforming Fundamentalism* as among its best. In fact, as much as new evangelicals of Rosell's ilk have held this book up as a blueprint for how to turn their congregations, parachurch ministries, and schools into spiritually revived and culturally engaged forces, critics of the new evangelicalism have used it as a dire warning of what can happen to "the church" when it veers too sharply in that direction. Indeed, for fundamentalists set on reifying rather than retooling the evangelical tradition, Marsden's text amounts to a treatise of *what not to do* when trying to build and sustain institutions of faith. Armed with *Reforming Fundamentalism* as their proof text, fundamentalist pastors and professors have taught their parishioners and students about the perils of accommodation with the world: start the theological slide toward permissive thinking as Fuller did in the 1940s, they assert, and one will quickly assume the worldview Fuller embraced in the 1970s, one compromised by theological temerity, loose biblical standards of worship and Christian witness, and a confused and ambiguous sense of mission to the lost.[1]

Regardless of their theological perspective, then, ardent new evangelicals and staunch fundamentalists alike have heralded *Reforming Fundamentalism* as pedagogy for the saints, yet one does not need to be an evangelical "insider" to appreciate many other striking qualities of Marsden's text. Revered by some for its incisive theological lessons, *Reforming Fundamentalism* can and should be viewed by a broader scholarly community as an arresting example of *good religious history*. From its commitment to painstaking primary research to its adroit handling of a vast secondary literature, from its structural integrity and analytical precision to its remarkable creativity and commanding authorial voice, *Reforming Fundamentalism* displays a level of craftsmanship to which all historians should strive. What makes this book even more extraordinary is that Marsden openly addresses the challenges that come when one is pursuing this lofty ideal. In the extensive scaffolding that buttresses his book's central narrative—its "Preface to the First Edition," "Preface to the Paperback Edition," "Introduction," "Epilogue," and "Sequel"—he openly wrestles with the difficulties of writing engaging but responsible history for an audience with myriad theological, intellectual, and political convictions. In fact, more so than anywhere else in his published work, Marsden emerges from this book's pages not just as an expert of evangelical history but also as an artist who is striving to perfect his craft, in spite of the many vicissitudes that accompany this task. It is this unique blend of virtuosity and vulnerability, I would argue, that stands out as *Reforming Fundamentalism*'s most important and enduring legacy.

So what makes this book's ingenuity so transparent? Several of its features stand out, but none are more important than its structural design, which stems from the author's respect for the fundamentals of institutional history. Studying institutions, whether congregations or schools, parachurch ministries or missionary agencies, is hardly novel in religious history. Quite the opposite: this strategy has long been the life source of the discipline, stretching back generations. William Warren Sweet's prolific career at the University of Chicago during the 1930s and 1940s revitalized the study of American religion in part by placing stories of local institutions at its heart.[2] Sweet's legacy lived on in the historians that followed his lead, including Jerald Brauer, Robert Handy, Winthrop Hudson, Martin Marty, and especially Sidney E. Mead, who collectively spurred what Henry F. May described in 1964 as a "veritable thirty-year 'renaissance' in the writing of American church history."[3] Amid the unsettledness of the 1950s and the cultural revolutions of the 1960s, these historians looked for ways to account for the remarkable diversity of American religion without losing sight of its consistency, durability, and Protestant core. Even as they began casting their gaze on the ethnic Catholic or Jewish experience, or tried to make better sense of black spirituality or the non-Western religious traditions that were flourishing in their time, these scholars singled out the local religious body as the essential glue that held people and communities—hence their histories—together.

Marsden's own mentor, Sydney Ahlstrom, was a master of this approach. In his epic, award-winning text *A Religious History of the American People*, Ahlstrom achieved a level of analytical and historical breadth that was truly staggering. He explained his ambition at his book's very beginning. "Religious history as a field of study must be placed not only spatially but theoretically within the larger frame of world history," he charged. Moreover, the concept and study of American religion had to expand "to include 'secular' movements and conviction," account for the "radical diversity of American religious movements," and be closely attuned to the social contexts—"demographic, economic, political, and psychological"—in which all of these strands of spirituality were nurtured.[4] It would be difficult to imagine a bigger canvas on which to paint the history of American religion, yet Ahlstrom managed this task by staying close to the rooted stories of religious institutions—those "churches, sects, cults, and denominations" that have always existed as "human communities" set apart from but also contributing to the life of American society.[5] What sustained these religious institutions and made them so integral to America's religious experience, Ahlstrom charged, was their ability to frame modes of abstract thinking about the universe in concrete, worldly terms, and to connect "a transcendent" realm above with "mundane considerations" below.[6] It was the religious institution, Ahlstrom asserted, that kept America's dizzying expressions of faith moored to a foundation of civility and common purpose and, at the same time, mediated devout citizens' encounters with the material and secular.

Marsden's Ahlstrom-like appreciation for institutional life in American religious and cultural contexts frames his study of Fuller Seminary.[7] Through a close reading of Fuller's campus happenings between the 1940s and the early 1970s, he is able to portray the evangelical seminary as a robust and complex organism whose day-to-day operations draw meaning from a blend of interests, ranging from the fiscal to the operational, the theological to the political. The internal workings of an institution—however quirky or quotidian—are important enough to be studied on their own terms, Marsden suggests, but if approached carefully they also offer the historian of religion a much broader perspective on near-universal patterns of change. Indeed, the biography of a church or seminary is not so different, in this regard, from the biography of a pastor or theologian, something Marsden stresses in his text. "Though I hope that no one has claimed that all history is institutional history, the story of an institution does have some of the same potential that good biography does. This may not seem readily apparent, since institutions are usually a lot duller than individuals are. Nonetheless, institutions stand midway between the people who run them and the larger movements and cultural trends in which they participate" (*RF,* 8). "As well as being important in themselves," Marsden adds in this regard, "institutions can be means through which to look at both the more particular and the more general" (8).

Marsden's effort to blend the "particular" and the "more general" is indeed impressive, evidenced first in his foray into the realm of ideas, his comfort zone. As he states in his opening section, his is an attempt to build an expansive narrative of theological contestation out of Fuller Seminary's idiosyncratic endeavors to make fundamentalism more progressive. This initiative meets with resounding success, thanks in large part to Marsden's unmatched ability to untangle the knotty threads of mid-twentieth-century liberal, conservative, reformed, and neo-orthodox theologies that Fuller's famous professors wrestled with regularly. In Marsden's account, we learn how cerebral and at times highly abstract disputes over premillennialism, dispensationalism, biblical inerrancy, and literalist readings of scripture—touchstones of classical fundamentalist theology—defined the seminary's early years, creating crises of conscience that split the staff into multiple camps. During their school's infancy, Fuller's leadership team, headed by Harold Ockenga, sought to "reform" fundamentalism in at least two ways, first by encouraging a greater flexibility of belief under the rubric of evangelical doctrine, and second by endorsing a "Reformed" view of the world as it was articulated by Abraham Kuyper and J. Gresham Machen.[8] Nudged along these paths by the likes of revered evangelical theologian Carl Henry, Fuller's willing progressives "found in Kuyperian thought" a "twentieth-century conservative Christian articulation of a point that had been part of the reformist side of the American evangelical heritage but which had diminished severely in fundamentalism since the 1930s. The point was the broadly Calvinistic vision that the Christian's mission involves not only evangelism but also a cultural task, both remaking the mind of an era and transforming society" (*RF,* 79). Henry's cohort met resistance at each turn. With each step toward inclusivity, some Fuller faculty members looked to firm up the boundaries of classical fundamentalist thought: they vociferously argued for the inerrancy and infallibility of scripture, emphasized the virtues of dispensational eschatology, and reaffirmed a separatist ideology, which required church folk to steer clear of any cultural accommodation. Eventually disagreement led to schism in Fuller Seminary, after which supporters of fundamentalism directed their loyalties elsewhere.

But even after surviving this initial storm, internal divisions at Fuller surfaced in other forms, including among the school's powerful progressives. If Fuller had "reformed" itself in the first meaning of the term, how "reformed" should it become in the second? This was the question that split progressives, according to their stance for or against Reformed theology. While some wholeheartedly embraced the teachings of Kuyper and Machen, others shifted into more radical neo-orthodox ideas that allowed for a wider ecumenism in thought and association than Henry believed beneficial for the church. As Marsden guides his reader into the later chapters of his book, it becomes evident that the tension between the radical and centrist elements in Fuller's progressive new evangelicalism was never solved. Rather, it was accentuated as the seminary's curriculum expanded in the late 1960s and 1970s to include innovative teachings about missionary outreach, church-growth strategies, and charismatic renewal. What becomes apparent through Marsden's sophisticated but accessible treatment of Fuller's competing theological trends, then, is that the intellectual project this school assumed at its birth was truly ambitious but always fraught with a discord that assumed epic proportions. Amid post–World War II America's ebullience and "boundless religious freedom" (*RF,* 152), when the nation's future seemed bright but also up for grabs, Fuller's battle for the evangelical mind came to be interpreted by its staff as a life-and-death struggle, with "the future of Western civilization at stake" (61).

Ideas always matter, something Marsden has made perfectly clear in his career-long study of American Protestantism, but in Fuller Seminary's case they proved to be all consuming and profoundly disruptive.

As focused as he is on these purely academic contests, Marsden also shows that they did not play out in an ivory tower vacuum. The evangelical seminary, like evangelicalism in general, is highly democratic and decentralized and therefore prone to the push-pull forces of the religious marketplace. Fuller's physical location in the heart of Southern California, "a land renowned for restlessness," Marsden writes, made it all the more vulnerable to the winds of controversy and change (*RF,* 52). So even as he fleshes out the substantive qualities of Fuller's intellectual community in relation to day-to-day functions of the institution, he also carefully measures their connection to wider exigencies beyond the school's Pasadena home. Harold Ockenga's vision of a new, irenic, interdenominational evangelicalism, we learn for instance, came with a price in the realm of Southern California Presbyterian politics. Rent with discord between an ambitious liberalism and a staunch conservatism, Southern California Presbyterianism saw Fuller Seminary as a potentially dangerous wedge that would drive these two sides farther apart. The Presbytery of Los Angeles, seeking to prevent Fuller from playing such a role, "declared war on the new seminary" and, by doing so, placed Ockenga—a Presbyterian minister—in a tenuous spot (*RF,* 64). After stoking the fires further with criticism of California Presbyterians' theological laxity, Ockenga back-peddled by stressing the "positive" role Fuller Seminary could play *within* California Presbyterianism as a middle ground and by repudiating fundamentalist "come-out-ism" (64). Ockenga's actions eased relations with the liberal camp but raised the ire of fundamentalist Presbyterians, who followed Carl McIntire's lead in demanding separation from all denominational apostasy. Through thick description of Ockenga's—hence Fuller's—early difficulties with California's denominational politics, Marsden thus opens up a more expansive view of a church schism with regional and ultimately national repercussions.

He creates the same effect when assessing the theologies of Wilbur Smith and Béla Vassady. Fuller's hire of the former was seen as a victory for classical fundamentalism; Smith's biblical literalism and premillennial dispensationalism harkened back to this movement's golden years (1880–1920s) when prophecy, Bible teaching, and regular revivalism animated the church. His calls for evangelicals to avoid the trappings of politics and "dwell in Christ, and witness for the Lord" were also typically pre–World War II fundamentalist in tone (*RF*, 74). Yet Smith also spoke with the lilt of a pacesetter. He championed the intellectualism to which new evangelicals aspired, and he encouraged a respect for classical thought that was seen as a worthy attribute for the emerging cosmopolitan Christian. He was, in this way, "a transitional figure between Charles Fuller's original vision of a missionary training school" and the seminary's "younger founders' vision of a great center for new evangelical thought" and, in no small degree, for new evangelical engagement with contemporary American conditions, social and cultural as well as political (*RF*, 69). Through Marsden's nimble handling, Smith's liminality becomes a litmus test for American evangelicalism as a whole. In each of Smith's frustrations with the new order we bear witness to an entire generation of fundamentalists' wariness of social change and yearning for a bygone era. Yet with each of Smith's endorsements for Fuller's innovations we also see how this institution's momentum for change was infectious and unyielding, and difficult to resist.

Through Vassady, Marsden underscores the limits of this momentum. Neo-orthodox to the core, Vassady was recruited by Ockenga in the late 1940s to illustrate Fuller's ecumenical and international aspirations, major impulses at that time in American society. As Marsden writes, "though not simply an attempt to cultivate an image and to gain an entrée into the mainline denominations," Vassady's hire in 1948 "had the conspicuous attraction of being a way to do just that" (*RF*, 97). But his place on Fuller's faculty was troublesome from the beginning. Ockenga saw in the Romanian "a man of internationally established credentials"; Fuller's fundamentalist supporters saw a "wolf of modernism dressed in the clothes of the Lamb" who taught Karl Barth's neo-orthodoxy and endorsed the World Council of Churches (*RF*, 98). Vassady's third failing, in fundamentalists' eyes, was the most egregious: his refusal to sign Fuller's statement of faith because of its strict stand on biblical inerrancy (*RF*, 114). Through his examination of the subsequent controversy that led to Vassady's ouster, Marsden effectively charts the tumult of American religion's midcentury turn within an emerging new global order. "The point tested in Vassady's appointment to Fuller," he writes, "was whether the fundamentalist movement could sustain the openness now being proclaimed by some of its younger leaders. Could the unity that seemed theoretically possible through emphasizing the positive aspects of the gospel transcend the heritage of division, suspiciousness, and theological causation fostered by the disputes of the 1920s and 1930s?" (98). Marsden's answer is "no." "Whatever its hopes and rhetoric," the Vassady affair proved that new evangelicalism "had not blossomed far from its fundamentalist roots" (98).

Coursing through Marsden's account of all three men and the controversies they helped incite is sensitivity to one other critical dimension of institutional life: money. The genius of *Reforming Fundamentalism* is that even as it gives so much credence to ideas and their expression by Fuller's esteemed faculty, it is just as attentive to the mundane matters of finance. This is as it should be, for as historians have pointed out, fundamentalism has always been attuned to the business ethic, by necessity as much as ideological accord. As Timothy Gloege underscores in his scholarship (part of which appears in this volume), since its creation in the late nineteenth century conservative evangelicalism has structured itself according to the principles of modern capitalism; while its executives have translated corporate models of organization to the church and its concomitant institutions, its rank-and-file members have expected a consumer-based system of ministry in which the empowered individual enjoys the abundance of choice that comes with participation in a free market of Christian goods and services. Moreover, when it has come to the actual "funding of fundamentalism" and each of its institutional arms—print media and communication systems, missionary agencies and parachurch organizations, churches, Bible schools, and seminaries—a dominant role has been played by corporate executives, whose commercial success has afforded them the privilege (God-given, in their estimation) of financing the religious endeavors of their choosing.[9] This was the blueprint for classical fundamentalism in the Victorian era, and it remained so for the new evangelicalism of the post-1940s period. The challenges facing evangelicals in their movement's former dispensation remained the same for those in the latter: how to minimize the destructive excesses of the free market while maximizing its potential for institutional growth and proliferation of the gospel.

Marsden teases out this conundrum. To be sure, his intention is not to offer a critique of evangelical capitalist assumptions but rather to show how any evangelical institution's dependency on corporate and consumptive modes creates as many challenges as possibilities. Fuller Seminary's financial ebbs and flows, extremely volatile at times, stand out as evidence. Throughout *Reforming Fundamentalism* we see a school desperately wanting to "brand" itself as an appealing commodity to a buying evangelical public, while constantly dodging bankruptcy and collapse. Early on in Fuller's history, school officials leaned on their founder for a hopeful economic future and enjoyed the payout. Charles Fuller, Marsden describes, was a "self-made man" who rose to elite status in his church and Los Angeles' corporate sector as the consummate booster: while constructing a fortune in ranching, orange groves, and even oil, he also built a legacy as a radio preacher whose "disarmingly simple" appeal came from his "haunting power of transparent sincerity" (*RF*, 15).[10] Fuller's buoyant outlook, bolstered by the confidence of his prosperity, was shared by some of his seminary's first faculty members, including Ockenga and Smith, whose own optimism for ministry was bankrolled by several wealthy donors (*RF*, 29). In the late 1940s and early 1950s, a consensus opinion seemed to exist that "the freedom and the resources" (*RF*, 29) at Fuller Seminary promised the creation of something special; all Fuller faculty needed to do "was seize the opportunity" (*RF*, 30) and this fledgling school would become the "Cal Tech of the evangelical world" (*RF*, 53). Such was the heady promise of an entrepreneurialism cut loose from the constraints of any governing body, secular or sacred.

This same promise of short-term success, however, came with a price: vulnerability over the long term. Even as they settled into their plush new offices in the heart of Pasadena, where mountain views, palm trees, and the charming aesthetics of arts and crafts architecture seemed all around, Fuller's professors entered into a cycle of trying times. During the 1950s, Charles Fuller's wealth began dwindling at an alarming rate, largely because of mismanagement. In keeping with the spirit of the wildcat oilman he had just become (he formed Providential Oil

Company in the early 1950s), Fuller rode the turbulent waves of speculative capitalism, enjoying a boom in one instance, then suffering a bust in the next. Gradually the busts erased any positive gains made during the booms. As corporate losses increased, Fuller tried to stem the tide by investing from his own personal fortune, and "good money went after bad" (*RF*, 178). As Marsden explains, the more Fuller "tried to recover, the more embarrassing the situation became. He could not understand 'why the dear Lord has permitted adverse results.' Only the Lord knew 'why almost overnight salt water was permitted to enter certain wells and make them worthless'" (*RF*, 179). With an intractable financial picture now fully in view, Fuller's leading administrators were forced out onto the road to sell their school's wares to potential donors. Marsden's description of Edward Carnell and his colleagues' efforts to recruit cash, drawn from their own words, is layered with rich description and analysis. "They called on some very wealthy cattlemen, dealers in rice and cotton, ranchers, oilmen, and custodians of foundations. He [Carnell] 'kissed babies, inspected turkey hatcheries, rode around vast ranches, listened to small talk, and sat hours in an unventilated room with children who were in the last stages of Asian flu.' Despite all this, 'we [Carnell and colleagues] brought no direct gifts into the Seminary.' The fact was, 'Fuller Seminary has no real constituency.' It was not connected with a denomination or anything else, and 'the wealthy have no conception of the new evangelicalism'" (*RF*, 180). Making matters worse was that the one constituency to which Fuller Seminary could lay claim—classical fundamentalists who revered Charles Fuller's "old time gospel"—became increasingly suspicious of a school that looked to trim traditions from its statement of faith. Indeed, with every turn in Fuller Seminary's financial development came a reaction by those who, amid the school's economic woes, increasingly controlled the purse strings—theologically and politically conservative trustees who in accordance with their business-friendly worldviews demanded a bottom line of strict adherence to fundamentalist codes (*RF*, 226–27). As Marsden shows, Fuller's faculty did not appreciate such unbending corporate logic and reacted in unflinching fashion.

The resulting clash in fact serves as a critical turning point in Marsden's text, revealing yet another one of its obvious strengths: sensitivity to plot. Throughout his book, Marsden carefully unpacks the complicated workings of new evangelical ideas, organizational apparatuses, and economics—essentials to good religious institutional history—but never at the cost of drama, a literary quality that he takes seriously. Art must meet scholarship, Marsden believes, and he applies this maxim in two ways, first through close attention to character development. An institutional history in design, *Reforming Fundamentalism* also reads as collective biography, a compelling narrative pieced together by the emotional life stories of Fuller Seminary's leading lights. Marsden treats this host of characters in an incisive but playful, critical but respectful way. In his book's earliest pages we encounter the Fuller family—Charles, Grace, and Dan—and learn of a mother's abiding wish for her son to follow in his father's steps. The son would follow, but not in a way Charles or Grace might have expected; rather than extend the legacy of Charles's orthodoxy, Dan would become one of Fuller Seminary's leading progressives. Then, during his treatment of the school's identity crises in the 1950s, Marsden guides his readers through the mix of angst, anger, insecurity, arrogance, and depression that clouded the lives of Fuller's most accomplished academicians, from Carl Henry and Wilbur Smith to Harold Lindsell, George Ladd, and Edward Carnell. Toward the end of the book we see signs of a new forward-looking institutional agenda, rooted in the upbeat personalities of Dan Fuller and David Hubbard, who would steer Fuller toward new prominence in the 1970s. Paradox and pathos, personal triumph amid trial and the pain and joy of unintended consequences: these are the elements of a good story, and thanks to Marsden's graceful touch we find them aplenty in *Reforming Fundamentalism*.

The second way Marsden instills drama in his institutional history is by pausing his analysis for rich description of key events. One exemplary passage illustrates this skill, and it has to do with the brass tacks of boardroom politics that drove faculty and trustees apart amid financial duress. Tucked away in the heart of a chapter titled "The Crisis and the Turning" is a section subtitled "Black Saturday." "At this juncture" in December of 1962, Marsden writes, "came the most dramatic moment in the seminary's history. The tensions over the struggles for control and the parallel tensions over differing views on Scripture suddenly erupted in a scene that left everyone shaken. After 'Black Saturday,' as the incident came to be called, little hope remained for reconciliation" (*RF*, 208). The incident itself was complex and involved several dimensions: the search for a new presidency, the fiscal foundations of the school, and the nature of Fuller's theological mandate. Over a three-day stretch, congregated in the Huntington Sheraton Hotel, Fuller's faculty, administrators, lay supporters, and board of trustees wrestled with these complicated issues, which they saw as three parts of one overriding problem: Fuller Seminary's cloudy future as a center of conservative evangelical instruction. With care and patience, and an eye for colorful quotes, Marsden tracks the sequence of emotional confrontations that culminated on "Black Saturday" (December 1), starting with the contested hiring of David Hubbard as Fuller's new president. Though stellar in his credentials as an evangelical, Hubbard raised suspicions in Fuller circles for his coauthorship of a text that downplayed (and in part denied) the inerrancy of scripture. Fuller's faculty members quickly picked sides in the debate, with Dan Fuller leading Hubbard's defense, and joining them were the seminary's principal executives and backers, including Charles Fuller, Harold Ockenga, financier and board of trustees member C. Davis Weyerhaeuser, and Billy Graham. Even as the problems of Hubbard's candidacy were being ironed out, emotions boiled over during a "ten-year planning" session that was held on Saturday, December 1. At issue were the seminary's statement of faith and the strictness of stand on inerrancy. In Marsden's hands the daylong proceedings assume the guise of a bloody battle, with champions of change (Dan Fuller) confronting defenders of the old gospel (Edward Carnell). Descriptive flourishes, like the following exchange between Carnell and Fuller, show Marsden's ability to bring theology alive:

> At this point, Carnell jumped in with considerable irritation . . . [and] opened up his rhetorical guns on Dan Fuller. He was convinced that a purely inductive defense of the truth of Scripture was philosophically disastrous. Rather, one should come to the Bible with the hypothesis that it was indeed the word of God. Only then do we frankly admit that we have some unsolved problems. "My list of discrepancies is longer than yours, Dan Fuller," Carnell insisted.

But that did not matter, because if we come to the Bible as the verbally inspired word of God we find that we have fewer major problems with our system than with any competing system. By this time, almost everyone was ready to join in the fray. (*RF,* 212)

The back-and-forth grew more intense, and understandably so, Marsden allows, for dogma in this setting was no dull or tangential thing. "Inerrancy itself was a deeply important subject to everyone, but at Fuller it could never be discussed as an isolated intellectual question. In this setting it was always tied to political, personal, and other doctrinal concerns" (213).

Over the course of this and coming days, solutions would be reached, though not to the satisfaction of all. Hubbard would gain the presidency, inerrancy would be stricken from the seminary's statement of faith, and Fuller Seminary's progressives would win the day, leaving them in charge of the school's future. A few of those present for Black Saturday were not convinced that this was "what the Lord had willed" (*RF,* 219). Others seemed oblivious to it all. Having built narrative tension throughout this entire section, leading to the climactic showdowns at the Huntington Sheraton, Marsden draws the thread to an end with a touch of comedic release. On Sunday, December 2, conferees congregated for breakfast, still numb from the infighting of the day before and exhausted from a restless night. "The only relief," Marsden writes, "was that Wilbur Smith finally bustled in late and was asked to give the opening prayer. Having missed the entire disruptive proceeding, Smith thanked the Lord for the harmony that had prevailed at the conference thus far. He was quickly filled in and joined in the alarm" (215). Understated, and no doubt delivered with a wry grin, Marsden's brief depiction of an esteemed professor of theology praying in ignorance is emblematic not just of the light touch with which he seeks to write but also of the healthy pace he strives to maintain. Throughout his account of "Black Saturday" he keeps his larger, substantive paragraphs weighted with rich description of big-picture dynamics, his shorter ones spiced up with brief and specific yet lively anecdotes, and his entire narrative sequence connected to a subtle and never-overbearing line of reasoning. Analysis never smothers plot, allowing the audience to remain emotionally invested as much as intellectually challenged, and always eager to read on.

Marsden's pivotal chapter about Fuller Seminary's decisive turn toward a progressive evangelicalism is also representative of a final exceptional quality of Marsden's religious history, that being a bold yet judicious authorial voice. As we witness in his treatment of Black Saturday's central voices, Marsden writes in a playful but never edgy tone. In *Reforming Fundamentalism*'s "Preface to the Paperback Edition," Marsden addresses the initial criticism of David Hubbard, Fuller's president at the time (and the man who commissioned the book), who worried at first that the manuscript's emphasis on controversy overshadowed the school's more vital track record of quietly training "men and women to serve God in ministries all over the world" (viii). While acknowledging Hubbard's valid point, Marsden ably defends his strategy by saying that there was no way to incorporate Hubbard's emphases on Fuller's ministerial focus and reach without compromising "the intrigue of the history of controversy that holds the main plot together" (viii). Marsden the author needs his narrative tension and is unwilling to sacrifice it for the sake of coverage demanded by the antiquarian. Though limited in its documentation of Fuller's full offerings in ministry and service, *Reforming Fundamentalism* offers the reader just enough information about the school to make its impact on modern evangelicalism clear, and just enough action and emotional effect to make this information digestible. A seasoned historian, Marsden clearly understands how to instruct and entertain his audience at the same time, and knows that if one of these elements is shortchanged, both are shortchanged.

Moreover, even in his penchant for the theatrical, Marsden always remains respectful in spirit and tone; his quest for drama never comes at the cost of empathy for his subjects. He applies a number of strategies in service of this goal. At each dramatic crescendo in his text, for instance, Marsden relies more heavily on his primary sources—correspondence, institutional reports, firsthand accounts—to flesh out the lines of friction. Conjecture and sensationalism have no place in his approach, only close, careful reading of original "texts." In this same vein, he lets his subjects speak for themselves at those precise moments when their words, not his, are most needed, for the sake of both clarity and evenhandedness. Direct quotes, capturing the exact tenor of a thought or moment, are employed at junctures in the story that are particularly freighted with meaning but also vulnerable to misrepresentation. Sometimes these are lengthy, revealing the full flavor of a private moment that has larger significances (as evidenced in Grace Fuller's correspondence with Dan Fuller), at times they are short and crisp, and meant to express a single emotion (Harold Ockenga's "indignation" toward Dan Fuller during Black Saturday, for instance), but they are always substantial for the way they ascribe agency to the people who populate the text and relegate the author to a supportive role (*RF*, 212). Finally, Marsden always errs on the side of mercy when characterizing his primary subjects, be they Fuller Seminary as a whole or the individual faculty members that make it up. As others in this volume have stressed when appraising his many works, Marsden approaches his central characters as he would want them to approach him were they to tell his life story: as individuals who, within the limits of their time and place and the exigencies of human nature, are trying to do the best they can. Full of wit and humor and never devoid of criticism, *Reforming Fundamentalism* is at the same time always empathetic and generous in spirit.

One telling example of this is Marsden's treatment of Edward Carnell, Fuller's most tragic figure. Carnell's role in Fuller's development took on unexpected importance in 1954, when, in the wake of Harold Ockenga's decision to decline the school's presidency, he found himself designated as the seminary's next boss. Carnell lacked experience in administration, yet he accepted the post, in part out of an insatiable desire to head this emerging theological powerhouse. It was a fateful decision. Carnell's brief presidency produced some high points for the school but also some dark times for the headman himself. Suffering from insomnia and depression, and profound insecurities, Carnell constantly battled his demons but fell short of conquering them. The first defeat came during his formal inaugural speech in 1955, when, after underscoring the theological orthodoxy of his seminary, he wandered into murky waters (for fundamentalists, at least) by arguing for a "spirit of tolerance." As Marsden skillfully explains it, Carnell's words exposed much about the man and his faith community.

The Carnell who displayed this immense confidence in human rationality, the Carnell whose trust in his own logical powers had led him to develop his own apologetic system and to outdistance his colleagues at a school where apologetics was the king of the sciences, lived with a deep sensitivity to the inadequacy of himself and his movement in embodying the spirit of Christ. He had written dissertations refuting Reinhold Niebuhr and Søren Kierkegaard as not being rational enough. Yet he knew that they represented aspects of the great Christian tradition that he did not often see around him at Fuller Seminary. As preachers do, he preached as much to himself as to his colleagues. (*RF,* 148)

The new president immediately lost the confidence of his cohort, especially those who already harbored doubts about his leadership abilities, and with subtle challenge to his authority came a steadier questioning of himself. Carnell pressed on, but by the late 1950s "he was exhausted from constant tension and inability to sleep," and tired of trying to rehabilitate the fundamentalist heritage into which he had been born (*RF,* 173). In large, block quotes from Carnell's correspondence, offered with little commentary, we learn of the president's inner decline: "I am feeling somewhat better, thanks to sleeping pills every night. I hope to find relief from the tension in this office some time next summer. I am a misfit as president, that is the trouble." "If I could get out of this job gracefully, I would do it with no small joy" (173).

Even after finally escaping the chains of administration, Carnell's personal journey brought little joy, and Marsden tracks the emotional breakdown that ensued. Despite his best efforts to author a text that would change evangelicalism's core doctrines, Carnell fell short, and with each failure in his profession he lost further ground in his personal life, leaving him grasping for help through various therapies (including shock treatment). Carnell finally ran out of solutions. In 1967 he died in a hotel room of an apparent drug overdose. Marsden's handling of the theologian's life and death is testament to his own theology of grace. Instead of sensationalizing Carnell's demise, Marsden uses it as an opportunity to critique—even chastise—evangelicals for their opinions about psychology and mental health. Many members of Fuller's faculty, he points out, suffered psychological crises—Carnell's case was simply the most publicized. And evangelical responses (or lack thereof) to these strains, coupled with the community's obsession with Carnell's purported suicide, he intimates, are tragic in their own way, for they ignore the realities of mental disorder. "The issue of suicide is moot," he declares. "Carnell died as the result of acute depression that one way or another overwhelmed his rational control. He was in a state in which desperation could have obliterated normal categories of intention. If his death was in any sense willed, it was not premeditated. It had none of the Carnell organization. The overdose was 'moderate,' and the room showed signs that the seizure was unexpected" (*RF,* 258). Marsden's description of Carnell's death curiously becomes a tribute of sorts, as well as an important lesson about the human condition. After reading the account of Carnell's career—so accomplished and influential, despite debilitating self-doubt—one is left with a sobering sense that we are all frayed and broken, and exceedingly susceptible to the fragilities of life. This is a poignant take-home message that Marsden delivers with searing effect.

At its essence, Marsden's treatment of Carnell is also further proof of why institutional studies have much to offer religious history. The rise and fall of this theologian is, of course, inextricably linked to the successes and failures of the school to which he dedicated his life. Marsden makes it clear that it is impossible to understand the shapers of the new evangelicalism without fully appreciating the institutional pressures that shaped them and gave their ideas and personas traction in a broader world. Institutions, in short, define the parameters in which religious persons imagine, encounter, articulate, debate, and defend their faith. This is something Marsden's mentors realized in the 1960s, and it is something that students of religious history continue to recognize today, to the benefit of the field. Yet beyond the philosophical stands the practical. Marsden is a master practitioner of his craft, an artist who wants to be read and enjoyed, not simply cited, and the institutional approach gives him the leeway to achieve this outcome. In Fuller Seminary he finds a perfect vehicle—grounded and contained, yet ripe with metaphor, illustration, and meaning—for extracting universal meaning from the particular and making people inside and outside the academy take notice. In the paperback version of his book he jokes at the outset that this is the only one of his manuscripts to garner close attention from his wife, Lucie. "The pages of my first copy are still warped from when she took it into the bathtub. That was my greatest literary triumph" (*RF*, vii). Tongue-in-cheek, Marsden would rather poke fun at himself than draw attention to the truth in his statement. *Reforming Fundamentalism* is his greatest literary triumph.

NOTES

1. This observation stems from firsthand experience. I came to appreciate the way fundamentalist Protestants appropriated *Reforming Fundamentalism* while talking with a young divinity student at Master's College in Southern California, during a brief research visit. Upon hearing that I was a student of George Marsden's, the seminarian proceeded to tell me how much he and his peers had learned from Marsden's history of Fuller Seminary, a text they had studied closely and carefully in class as an example of how evangelical institutions can easily stray from the fundamentals of the faith. Later, when hearing of my encounter, Marsden said that he was well aware of his book's classroom applications in conservative seminaries around the country. He touches on this in the preface to the paperback version of his book. See George M. Marsden, *Reforming Fundamentalism: Fuller Seminary and the New Evangelicalism* (Grand Rapids, MI: Eerdmans, 1987), xiii; subsequently cited parenthetically in the text as *RF*.

2. William Warren Sweet, *The Story of Religion in America* (New York: Harper and Brothers, 1950).

3. As quoted and paraphrased in Sydney E. Ahlstrom, *A Religious History of the American People* (New Haven, CT: Yale University Press, 1972), 11. This generation's exemplary works include Jerald C. Brauer, *Protestantism in America: A Narrative History* (Philadelphia: Westminster Press, 1953); Edwin Gaustad, *A Religious History of America* (New York: Harper and Row, 1966); Robert T. Handy, *A Christian America: Protestant Hopes and Historical Realities* (New York: Oxford University Press, 1971); Winthrop S. Hudson, *American Protestantism* (Chicago: University of Chicago Press, 1961) and *Religion in America* (New York: Charles Scribner's Sons, 1965); Martin E. Marty, *Righteous Empire: The Protestant Experience in America* (New York: Dial Press, 1970); Sidney E. Mead, *The Lively Experiment: The Shaping of Christianity in America* (New York: Harper and Row, 1963); David O. Moberg, *The Church as a Social Institution: The Sociology of American Religion* (Englewood Cliffs, NJ: Prentice-Hall, 1962).

4. Ahlstrom, *Religious History*, xiv.
5. Ibid.
6. Ibid.
7. It is worth noting that another leading historian of modern evangelicalism, Joel Carpenter, whose history of the movement in the early twentieth century serves as a prehistory to Marsden's *Reforming Fundamentalism*, also focuses on the life of the faith-based institution as a window into broader religious and cultural trends. See Joel A. Carpenter, *Revive Us Again: The Reawakening of American Fundamentalism* (New York: Oxford University Press, 1997).
8. Robert W. Shinn nicely outlines Marsden's two-pronged use of the term *reforming* in his review of *Reforming Fundamentalism*, Church History 58 (December 1989): 536–37.
9. See Timothy E. W. Gloege, "Consumed: Reuben A. Torrey and the Construction of Corporate Fundamentalism" (PhD diss., University of Notre Dame, 2007). Other recent insightful works that highlight the connections between modern evangelicalism and business include D. Michael Lindsay, *Faith in the Halls of Power: How Evangelicals Joined the American Elite* (New York: Oxford University Press, 2007); Larry Eskridge and Mark Noll, eds., *More Money, More Ministry: Money and Evangelicals in Recent North American History* (Grand Rapids, MI: Eerdmans, 2000); Bethany Moreton, *To Serve God and Wal-Mart: The Making of Christian Free Enterprise* (Cambridge, MA: Harvard University Press, 2009). Two remarkable dissertations speak to the future potential of this analysis: Darren Grem, "The Blessings of Business: Corporate America and Conservative Evangelicalism in the Sunbelt Age, 1945–2000" (PhD diss., University of Georgia, 2010), and Sarah Hammond, "'God's Business Men': Entrepreneurial Evangelicals in Depression and War" (PhD diss., Yale University, 2010).
10. See also Philip Goff, "Fighting Like the Devil in the City of Angels: The Rise of Fundamentalist Charles E. Fuller," in *Metropolis in the Making: Los Angeles in the 1920s*, ed. Tom Sitton and William Deverell (Berkeley: University of California Press, 2001), 220–51.

CHAPTER 18

Missionary Realities and the New Evangelicalism in Post–World War II America

KATHRYN T. LONG

The history of evangelical reengagement with American culture during the years following the Second World War usually is told as a story of the innovations and cultural creativity of a loose coalition of moderate fundamentalists within the United States. Youth for Christ rallies, Charles Fuller's *Old Time Revival Hour*, and, most important, Billy Graham and his crusades serve as familiar markers pointing toward renewed evangelical visibility and potential influence in American public life.[1] The contribution of conservative Protestant missions to this domestic resurgence of evangelicalism has received little attention. Yet missions did play a role in changes on the home front. During a brief but significant period from about 1956 to 1966, evangelical missionaries enjoyed widespread sympathy, attention, and publicity in mainstream America. They were supported by influential figures from the world of popular media. What seemed like an improbable alliance between secular media and conversionist Protestants reflected evangelicalism's compatibility with the cultural consensus of the time. It also reinforced the idea that evangelicals had assumed a new place in national life.[2]

From the evangelical side, two factors were crucial to popular interest in conservative Protestant missions that began during the mid-1950s. First was the national response to the deaths in January 1956 of five young American missionaries during an unsuccessful attempt to make peaceful contact with the Waorani people (then known as "Aucas") in the isolated rain forest of Amazonian Ecuador. Second was the public relations acumen of W. Cameron Townsend, founder of the Wycliffe Bible Translators (WBT) and its sister organization, the Summer Institute of Linguistics (SIL).[3] Historian Bill Svelmoe has suggested that Townsend was "the highest profile North American missionary in the twentieth century."[4] He also was an inveterate entrepreneur and a promotional genius.

The daring efforts by Jim Elliot, Peter Fleming, Ed McCully, Nate Saint, and Roger Youderian to evangelize the Waorani, as well as their tragic deaths—speared to death by the people they sought to befriend—were featured in print and broadcast media nationwide. Newspapers, *Life* magazine, the *Reader's Digest*, and best-selling books all told the story outright, while the popular television program *This Is Your Life* offered a sequel. Townsend, in turn, built on the interest and sympathy engendered by these reports to tell Americans about the need to translate the Bible into the languages of indigenous people in Latin America and around the world. While many evangelicals were cautious in their engagement with American culture during the 1950s, Townsend acted with a genial brashness, buttonholing anyone he thought would help to further his Bible translation goals. The results sometimes backfired, but they also paved the way for the familiar public relations efforts of later humanitarian-oriented Christian NGOs, such as World Vision and Habitat for Humanity.

Popular media embraced the Ecuador missionary martyr story in part because Americans were fascinated by the lives of the five, clean-cut, dedicated young missionaries and their families, as well as by the exotic and violent Waorani. The missionaries were portrayed as heroic and inspiring figures against the backdrop of Cold War fears. Their story appeared during the same year that Americans first learned about the exploits of a young Catholic "jungle doctor," Thomas A. Dooley, who would become a folk hero for his humanitarian service in Vietnam and Laos. Within five years, John F. Kennedy would authorize the Peace Corps as an opportunity for youthful volunteers to become "missionaries" for their country.[5] In addition, the publicity reflected an increased awareness on the part of mainstream media that conservative Protestantism appealed to a broad segment of the American public. Some of the same outlets that marketed Thomas A. Dooley and his more distinguished predecessor Albert Schweitzer featured Billy Graham and the Ecuador missionaries as well.

Evangelicals actively cultivated national publicity. Missionaries gained attention in part because they made strategic contacts in major media outlets.[6] Less recognized but no less essential was the role of these contacts. A number of outstanding communicators in the world of print and of television helped to promote the Ecuador story and evangelical missions more broadly. Most important were Magnum photographer Cornell Capa; *Reader's Digest* editor and writer Clarence Hall; Harper and Brothers' religion editor Melvin Arnold; and television producer and host Ralph Edwards. Understanding the part each played clarifies how and why a modest missionary project in the jungles of Ecuador with an apparently tragic ending captured the attention of some of the most powerful media outlets in the United States and touched the lives of millions of Americans.

CORNELL CAPA, MAGNUM PHOTOS

Perhaps the single most significant figure and the one who most directly facilitated secular interest in missionaries and the Waorani was photographer Cornell Capa (1918–2008). A Hungarian by birth, Capa was the child of "non-practicing, assimilated Jewish parents" who sent their young son to the *Evangelisches* School in Budapest, a choice Capa later saw as foreshadowing his involvement with missionaries.[7] The decision by the editors of *Life* magazine to send Capa to Ecuador when the five men were killed was itself a product of evangelical/secular networking. Sam Saint, an aviation consultant in Washington, D.C., was an older brother of pilot Nate Saint, one of the slain missionaries. Sam knew Jerry Hannifin, a *Time* magazine correspondent. When Hannifin saw an early Associated Press bulletin from Quito announcing that five missionaries were missing, he called *Life* and spent hours convincing editors to cover the story. Hannifin also used his Washington contacts to get authorization for Capa to board U.S. military planes. Leaving New York City on Thursday, January 12, 1956, Capa landed in a U.S. Army helicopter on the banks of the Curaray River in the rain forest of eastern Ecuador twenty-four hours later. There he joined and photographed a search party recovering and burying the bodies of the missionaries killed by the Waorani.

From the first, this Hungarian American who had never before met an evangelical missionary was fascinated by the people he encountered in the jungles of Ecuador. In the evening after the men had been buried, Capa sat in the darkness of a remote, makeshift camp in the forest while armed guards kept watch against a possible Waorani attack. He listened to a spontaneous prayer by missionary Don Johnson, a member of the ground party that had come to recover the men's bodies. Surrounded by jungle and against a cacophony of unfamiliar night sounds, Capa found the simple conversation with God strangely moving. Once back at the mission station, he was taken by the faith and dignity of the widows. They had experienced great loss, and they responded with "fortitude and acceptance of God's will." Some of Capa's most powerful photographs were of the missionary men who participated in the search party and of the widows and their children.[8]

Capa returned to New York with his own photographs, as well as film taken by Nate Saint before his death. The widows provided excerpts from their husbands' diaries. Sam Saint, who had also gone to Ecuador after news of his brother's death, flew to New York City to act as consultant for the *Life* story. Capa wrote, designed, and edited it, drawing heavily on the dead men's own words. Ten pages long, it was the lead news story in the January 30, 1956, issue of the magazine.[9] Readers praised the story as "the most inspiring article ever in *Life*," and "*Life*'s greatest reporting *feat*."[10] Capa himself described it as the story of a lifetime. It was, he later said, as if someone had given him the key to the door of a new world. He spent a significant portion of his professional life during the next eight years taking photographs of missionary work among indigenous people in Latin America.

Capa also served as a booster for missionaries and their stories to Harper's publishers. In late 1956, with some trepidation, Harper's religion editor Mel Arnold brought missionary Elisabeth Elliot, Jim Elliot's widow, to New York City to write a book about her husband and his friends. It would become the best seller *Through Gates of Splendor* (1957). Capa would stop by Elliot's hotel room each day as she sat at the typewriter, look over her shoulder, and read her work. He would then reassure Arnold that the manuscript was "terrific." The photographer and his wife, Edie, also rescued Elliot from the isolation of the hotel, taking her to plays and movies.[11] Capa volunteered to be the photo editor for *Through Gates of Splendor*, lending his prestige to the volume. In addition to Elliot's text, the book included forty-one Capa photographs, as well as photos taken by the missionaries themselves. The success of Elliot's book plus Capa's enthusiasm led Harper's to launch what came to be known as the "Harper Missionary Classics," a series of sixteen missionary adventure books published between 1957 and 1966. Capa was photo editor or contributed pictures to four of the books.[12]

During a subsequent trip to Ecuador after Elliot had returned to her mission assignment, Capa taught her to take pictures. Elliot proved an apt pupil, and the result was *The Savage My Kinsman* (1961), a book-length photo essay in collaboration with Capa, telling the story of Elliot's peaceful contact with the Waorani in 1958 and her first year living among them. In the quality and sensitivity of the photographs, it is one of the finest examples of twentieth-century American missionary photography.[13] When Elliot had decided to take her three-year-old daughter, Valerie, and together with missionary Rachel Saint to live among the people who had killed their loved ones, she signed an exclusive contract with *Life* for rights to the story via Magnum Photos, Capa's agency. Capa and Sam Saint also encouraged Elliot to secure exclusive rights to her story in *Time* and selected foreign publications. *Life* published two essays with Capa's and Elliot's photos: "Child among Her Father's Killers: Missionaries Live with Aucas" (1958) and "Widow's Jungle Life amid Husband's Killers" (1961).[14] These essays emphasized the strength and courage of families in overcoming tragedy, reflecting the editorial priorities of *Life* and of publisher Henry R. Luce. Images of middle-class families represented the American way of life at its best. The appeal of these missionary essays centered on the presence of a young widow and her small, blonde daughter among fearsome "savages" in Amazonia.[15]

In 1961, the same year *The Savage My Kinsman* appeared, Capa and writer Matthew Huxley traveled to the tropical jungles of Peru to do a book-length study of the Amahuaca people, *Farewell to Eden* (1964). The overt focus of the book was humanitarian, to raise awareness of the cultural threat faced by indigenous peoples as modern Peruvian culture intruded on their traditional ways of life. At the same time, *Farewell to Eden* documented the work of SIL translator Robert Russell and suggested that, because of their altruistic as well as religious concerns, members of the SIL were best equipped to help the Indians negotiate the pressures of modernity. The book caused some controversy within the SIL, in part because writer Matthew Huxley was the son of *Brave New World* author Aldous Huxley and a member of a noted British family with a history of skepticism toward evangelical Christianity.[16] Although he was careful to qualify his endorsement of the book in some circles, Cameron Townsend liked *Farewell to Eden* and extended his friendship to "Max" Huxley.[17] Townsend distributed complimentary copies to members of the U.S. Congress and other officials as part of lobbying efforts to make surplus federal property available for nonprofit use abroad.[18]

In short, Cornell Capa used his photography and his professional contacts to promote positive images of evangelical missionaries in American popular culture between 1956 and 1966. Why? In part, because he was fascinated by visually compelling stories and by the adventure of jungle photography. Photographing tribal peoples in the rain forests of Ecuador and Peru was heady stuff for a man whose previous knowledge of Amerindians had been limited to the Hungarian translation of James Fenimore Cooper he had read as a child.[19] On a personal level, he valued his friendships with Elisabeth Elliot and William Cameron Townsend. In part, too, Capa had a strong humanitarian bent, extended to indigenous people and missionaries alike. He was enthralled by what he viewed as the beauty and integrity of an "Eden" that was rapidly disappearing. He admired Elliot's courage and unwavering desire to live peacefully among her husband's killers. He photographed SIL linguist Will Kindberg in Peru as an example of "a frontiersman of the New Breed," carrying "the work and purpose of his generation . . . [beyond] the borders of the U.S."[20]

At the same time Capa realized that these young Americans represented the arrival of a modernity that would change irreparably the lives of remote jungle tribes, no matter how carefully the linguists tried to mediate or moderate the changes. Caught in the dilemma, Capa cultivated an identity as a "concerned photographer," one who cared deeply about the imperfect world he sought to chronicle.[21] Through the pages of *Life* and of books published by Harper's, he communicated that concern to the American public. Capa's images of evangelical missionaries and indigenous peoples reflected the same empathy as his photographs of Adlai Stevenson, John F. Kennedy, and Robert Kennedy, the politicians of the 1950s and 1960s he most admired.[22]

CLARENCE HALL, *READER'S DIGEST*

In contrast to Capa, *Reader's Digest* senior editor Clarence W. Hall (1902–85) was familiar with American religion and missionaries. Hall began his journalistic career in the 1930s, writing articles for religious periodicals. In February 1946, he became associate editor of the *Christian Herald*, an interdenominational family magazine based in New York City that managed to appeal to Protestants in both mainline and fundamentalist churches. In 1952, he was named executive editor.

Hall wrote on a range of subjects but specialized in inspirational personality profiles, usually biographical sketches of Christians expressing their faith in practical ways. Before World War II, he wrote about such figures as James L. Kraft, of Kraft cheese fame; Henry Ford; and Marion Grace ("Tiny") Seagrave, gutsy ambulance driver on the Burma Road and wife of Gordon S. Seagrave, legendary Baptist missionary doctor in Burma. Hall's first article for the *Herald* after the war featured the Christian heritage of Cold War architect John Foster Dulles. During the late 1940s and the 1950s, Hall was staunchly anticommunist and attuned to the values of the cultural mainstream. He supported the United Nations and the World Council of Churches, opposed pornography, and chastised "morally loose" movie stars while still backing the film industry.[23]

Beginning in 1947, several of Hall's articles were condensed for publication in *Reader's Digest*, a natural choice, since the writing style and practical focus of the *Herald* and the *Digest* had much in common. Hall's views of Christianity and American life also were similar to those espoused by the *Digest*. In a 1951 book, *Protestant Panorama: A Story of the Faith That Made America Free*, Hall summarized the "Big Idea" of Protestantism in a single word: "freedom." He argued that the ideal of individual freedom at the heart of Protestantism—in contrast to Catholic authoritarianism—was the only effective response to the threat of communism in the United States and around the world.[24] Hall combined such sentiments with support for conversionist Christianity and enthusiasm for foreign missions. Protestant missionary expansion was "the amazement of the modern world, and . . . our best hope in the war against Communism and all other atheistic and inhuman ideologies."[25]

The man who better than anyone else understood the appeal of these ideas to ordinary Americans was DeWitt Wallace, a Presbyterian preacher's kid and founder and publisher of a twentieth-century phenomenon, the *Reader's Digest*. Although he never went to church or affiliated with a particular congregation or denomination, Wallace approved a kind of upbeat, nondenominational Protestantism for the pages of the *Digest*. It was a gospel of hope and inspiration, told through stories of individual triumph, and often related to themes of patriotism and anticommunism.[26] In 1956 he hired Clarence Hall as a senior editor.

In December 1955, shortly before Hall joined the *Digest*, the senior editors met with a charismatic young navy lieutenant, Thomas A. Dooley. Dooley held the group spellbound with tales of his heroism in a massive effort to relocate Vietnamese refugees, many of them Catholic, from North to South Vietnam after the country was partitioned in 1954. The *Digest* agreed on the spot to feature Dooley's book, *Deliver Us from Evil*, as the "condensation" in its April 1956 issue, even though the actual manuscript still was in draft form and the book had no publisher. The *Digest*'s influence and formidable editorial resources overcame the obstacles. The condensed version of *Deliver Us from Evil* told the dramatic story of "an idealistic, devoutly religious American . . . who was single-handedly holding back the Red sea in Southeast Asia with his thumb."[27] It catapulted Dooley to the fame he would enjoy and cultivate until his death from cancer in 1961.

Historians have suggested that the *Reader's Digest* created Dooley's public persona. Dooley biographer James T. Fisher described the condensation "Deliver Us from Evil" as "a work of propaganda, pure and relatively simple." It was also a *Reader's Digest* editorial "masterpiece" that introduced Americans to a place called Vietnam and to a young humanitarian who bucked military bureaucracy to offer refugees medical aid and religious freedom, even if his actual contributions were greatly exaggerated.[28] Dooley became an early symbol of the nation's concern for Southeast Asia. He was a "missionary for Americanism" who wore his Catholic faith sincerely but lightly in public and thus prepared the way for other young Catholics, such as John F. Kennedy, to find a place at the center of American culture.[29] All this happened despite the many layers of complexity and contradiction in Dooley's own life, including the ways he may have been used by the CIA and his barely concealed identity as a gay man.

Less than a month after Dooley's first meeting with the *Digest*, the five Protestant missionaries in Ecuador were speared to death by the Waorani. Their story was splashed across the front pages of U.S. newspapers even before Capa's photo essay appeared in *Life*. In a move initiated by DeWitt Wallace himself, the *Digest* contacted the widows and learned they had selected Abe Van Der Puy to write a book about the slain men. Field director of the HCJB missionary radio station in Quito, Van Der Puy had prepared news releases that were distributed in response to the media interest surrounding the missionaries' efforts to contact the Waorani and their deaths. However, Van Der Puy's early draft for the *Digest* was not the dramatic adventure the magazine wanted.[30] With deadlines looming, Clarence Hall was called in as ghostwriter. Van Der Puy offered his notes and research, and the widows supplied their husbands' journals. Hall wrote the *Digest* piece, which was published in August 1956 as a twenty-page book condensation under Van Der Puy's name and using the title he had chosen.[31] Even though the fine print at the beginning of the article promised a forthcoming book from Harper and Brothers, the book manuscript had yet to be written. Wallace paid the missionaries $20,000 for their story, twice the normal rate.

The *Digest* version of "Through Gates of Splendor" presented a heroic missionary epic where the tragedy of the men's deaths was overshadowed by the inspiration of their lives. Nate Saint and his four colleagues were exactly the kind of young Americans who were the nation's best ambassadors abroad. The isolated Waorani had no direct connection with the worldwide spread of communism, so "Through Gates of Splendor" focused on the spiritual rather than the political. Nonetheless, the reaction to the men's deaths a few months earlier by Daniel Poling, longtime editor of the *Christian Herald*, suggested an additional layer of meaning *Digest* readers might give to the story. "No braver answer to the blatant denials, the blasphemous physical and mental tortures of atheistic Communism has been offered in our time than the martyred dying of these five young Americans for the One Whom they adored and to Whom they gave that last full measure," Poling wrote.[32]

The role of the *Reader's Digest* in shaping the legend of Tom Dooley raises the question of the extent to which Hall and other editors might have done the same for the five missionaries in "Through Gates of Splendor." Certainly both stories fit the magazine's formula for adventure and inspiration. However, there were clear differences in the ways the articles were written and edited. "Deliver Us from Evil" was overtly pro-American and anticommunist, a tract for the Cold War enlivened by a good story. Even before his relationship with the *Digest*, Dooley and the early drafts of his manuscript were caught up in political intrigues. "Through Gates of Splendor," in contrast, was a modern version of missionary hagiography that gained cultural impact from its publication in the *Digest*. Although "Through Gates of Splendor" burnished the images of the five men and ignored cultural or spiritual complexities, it contained nothing like the overstated claims in "Deliver Us from Evil."

In large part the *Digest* article was a paraphrase of the slain missionaries' own words, framed by Hall's triumphalism. The account promised readers "one of the most daring Christian missionary exploits of modern times," the story of a missionary campaign "to win . . . one of the most feared and savage Stone Age tribes left on earth." Hall described the five young Protestants as "Christian pioneers" who "in a spirit lifted right out of the Acts of the Apostles, fashioned their bold odyssey to the Aucas [sic]."³³ He was able to write a dramatic account of the four-month effort to establish peaceful relations with the Waorani largely because the men themselves kept detailed records. Missionary pilot Nate Saint, who was involved in the project every step of the way, left a chronicle of more than thirty single-spaced, typewritten pages. Hall simply positioned himself as narrator and dramatized Saint's words.

It is difficult to evaluate reader response to "Through Gates of Splendor," since the *Digest* did not print letters to the editor. However, the magazine published eight additional missionary stories, all written by Clarence Hall and set in Asia, Africa, and Latin America, during 1956 and 1957. In August 1957, after SIL missionary Rachel Saint appeared on national television (see below), Hall wrote Cameron Townsend, suggesting an in-depth piece on the Wycliffe Bible Translators. The result, *Two Thousand Tongues to Go*, appeared under Hall's byline as a book condensation in *Reader's Digest*, August 1958, even though once again the book was written later.³⁴

In *Adventurers for God* (1959), a collection of Hall's missionary stories, the writer acknowledged DeWitt and Lila Wallace for their "unfailing encouragement, editorial stimulation and abiding interest in Christian missions."³⁵ In the book's introduction Hall emphasized the character, courage, and talent of the missionaries he had profiled. He believed that they modeled what it meant for the American nation to lead the free world. Missionaries had prepared the way for the United States to move from "isolationism into world responsibility."³⁶ Hall clearly saw himself and his work for *Reader's Digest* as part of a project with national and even international significance.

MELVIN ARNOLD, HARPER AND BROTHERS

In November 1956, twenty-nine-year-old missionary Elisabeth ("Betty") Elliot went to New York City to help with the final editing of the book-length version of "Through Gates of Splendor." Aware of some of the problems with the original *Reader's Digest* essay, she still thought Van Der Puy had completed a book manuscript. When Elliot arrived at the office of Harper's associate book editor Mel Arnold (1913–2000), he pointed her toward a typewriter and told her to write something. Surprised, Elliot asked Arnold what he wanted her to write. It didn't matter, Arnold responded, anything would do. Elliot complied, providing a vivid description of her adventures on a bus trip in Ecuador. Arnold pulled the sheet from the typewriter and read it. He informed Elliot that Harper's did not yet have a manuscript telling the story of her late husband and his friends but that during the next six weeks she would write it. The publisher would provide a suite in a nearby hotel and editorial assistance.[37]

While Elliot needed longer than six weeks to complete a final manuscript, she finished in time for a May 1957 publication date. With permission from the *Digest*, the book used the same title as the Hall/Van Der Puy article, but the text was Elliot's own. The book, *Through Gates of Splendor*, was an immediate best seller and has remained in print for more than half a century. A firsthand account, it became the authoritative version of the lives and deaths of the five Ecuador missionaries and the archetypal narrative of missionary sacrifice and heroism for evangelicals during the second half of the twentieth century. The dust jacket promised to give "millions of readers stirred by the articles and pictures in *Life* and *Reader's Digest* . . . the whole story told in full detail." The success of *Through Gates of Splendor* launched a decade of collaboration between the religious division at Harper's and conservative evangelical missionaries.

Mel Arnold was no stranger to religious books, although when he met Elliot he was still in his first year with Harper and Brothers, one of the most respected names in American publishing and a company in the midst of postwar expansion. Arnold had come to Harper's after a successful decade in Boston as the first director of Beacon Press, the Unitarian publishing house. There he had played a major role in moving Beacon from a denominational publisher of Unitarian materials to a press that saw itself as a voice for "liberal religion" and the "liberal spirit" more broadly.[38] As part of that effort Arnold established a series of books by and about Albert Schweitzer that introduced the doctor's work in what was then French Equatorial Africa to a new generation of Americans.[39] The fourteen books in Beacon's Schweitzer series, all but one published between 1947 and 1954, might be seen as a precursor to the Harper Missionary Classics, Arnold's later series of inspirational missionary adventure books anchored by *Through Gates of Splendor*.

More controversial was Arnold's role in Beacon's decision to publish Paul Blanshard's *American Freedom and Catholic Power* (1949), described by a Beacon insider as a "bold and pioneering critique of the Roman Catholic Church" but viewed by the less sympathetic as an anti-Catholic tract. In the same vein, under Arnold's leadership, Beacon published books challenging both McCarthyism and Soviet totalitarianism, editorial decisions reflecting a postwar American liberalism that was quick to link such works with fears of Catholic power.[40] Despite the flap over Blanshard's book, Arnold was credited with creating the modern Beacon Press and steering it in a generally progressive direction.[41]

Arnold joined Harper's in January 1956, just as the young missionaries engaged in "Operation Auca" were establishing the camp on the bank of the Curaray River where they would lose their lives. Because of the outpouring of interest in the men and their mission when their story became known, and because of the diaries and journals they had left, the widows began talking almost immediately about publishing a book. Conservative missionary heroes or martyrs traditionally had been memorialized by religious publishers, but the widows wanted to extend the reach of their husbands' lives. They intentionally sought a secular publisher with proven promotional capabilities.[42] Rather than speaking only to the faithful, in death the men would become missionaries to the broader American culture.[43] A contract with Harper's had been signed by the time the *Reader's Digest* version appeared in August.[44]

Arnold clearly was nervous about the project, an unease not helped by the difficulties at the *Digest* with Van Der Puy's initial draft. Harpers had published books by Harry Emerson Fosdick, Kenneth Scott Latourette, Helmut Thielicke, Dorothy Day, Paul Tournier, and Martin Luther King Jr., but not by an unknown missionary widow. However, Elisabeth Elliot was perfect for the assignment. She was heir to a family tradition of religious writers that stretched back to before the Civil War. She had grown up in a cultured Philadelphia home steeped in missionary lore. While she idealized her husband and his friends, she abhorred the sentimentality and saccharine tone of much religious biography.[45]

She had a clear sense of the story she wanted to write: an account of young missionaries who were models of true Christianity, their lives characterized by dedication, joy, obedience, and self-sacrifice. The narrative also offered readers a jungle adventure and conveyed the men's sense of excitement as modern missionary pioneers.[46]

Arnold initially found it difficult to approve the unabashed spiritual emphasis of *Through Gates of Splendor*. He was more comfortable with the Schweitzer style of missionary literature—books that focused on the humanitarian and ethical sides of Christianity. Taking turns with Cornell and Edie Capa, Arnold and his wife, Valerie, frequently invited Elliot out to dinner. Mel and Elisabeth would discuss the manuscript, and Elisabeth, well known in the Ecuador missionary community for her independent spirit, stood her ground. It would be her book, as she wrote it, or no book. With Cornell Capa's support and Arnold's unwillingness to start over again or to lose the manuscript to another publisher, Elliot prevailed. Subsequent sales proved her right.[47]

Arnold, who also had experience as an account executive in an advertising agency, recognized an untapped market and moved quickly to capitalize on it. The initially reluctant publisher brought out Elisabeth Elliot's second book, *Shadow of the Almighty* (1958), the biography of her husband, Jim, less than a year later. By then Arnold had contracts for two more books. One, *Jungle Pilot* (1959), was Nate Saint's story, and the other, *Two Thousand Tongues to Go* (1959), as noted above, had grown out of a *Reader's Digest* feature. All this reflected a symbiotic relationship: evangelicals wanted the financial returns and cultural influence represented by Harper's; and the publishing house had come to recognize that "theologically conservative Protestants . . . know how to write books that attract wide readership."[48]

The pursuit of additional manuscripts took Arnold to Ecuador in December 1958 to meet with Elliot and with Rachel Saint. The two recently had come out of the jungles after having established peaceful contact with a group of Waorani. It was the same year that *The Ugly American*, a scathing condemnation of American Foreign Service personnel, had been published. Elliot and Saint stood in striking contrast to the Americans parodied and critiqued in that novel. The two women had risked their lives to live among the people they hoped to serve, to learn their language, and to appreciate their culture. As missionaries, they were motivated by evangelical priorities, but their actions seemed to represent the best of American values as well. Arnold sought exclusive rights to any books they might write. He returned with a commitment from Elliot for an "Auca Notebook," which became *The Savage My Kinsman*, and from Saint for *The Dayuma Story*, a biography of the Waorani woman who played a key role in helping the women gain access to her people.⁴⁹ Published in March 1960, *The Dayuma Story* sold an impressive fifty-three thousand copies by the end of that year. *The Savage My Kinsman* was less successful, although a *Library Journal* review suggested the book be required reading for Peace Corps candidates.⁵⁰ Books by conservative Protestants in the Missionary Classics series remained a prominent part of Harper's religious book list until Arnold left the division in 1966. Within a few years, Harper's began to sell its line of inspirational missionary books to a number of increasingly influential evangelical publishers.

RALPH EDWARDS, *THIS IS YOUR LIFE*

In effect, Wycliffe/SIL founder Cameron Townsend recruited television producer and program host Ralph Edwards (1913–2005) to present a new chapter in the missionary/Waorani story. From the time the five men were killed in Ecuador, Townsend was convinced that their sacrifice and the publicity surrounding it should not be in vain. Instead, the apparent tragedy could be used by God to introduce Americans to the need for Bible translation among indigenous people like the Waorani.⁵¹ However, Townsend was in an awkward position. His organization had not been involved in this specific missionary venture. None of the dead men was an SIL worker. How could he take advantage of the heightened media interest without appearing to be capitalizing on the tragedy and spiritual heroism that rightly belonged to other mission agencies? His response was to focus on the solid connection the WBT/SIL did have: Rachel Saint. Rachel, affiliated with the SIL since 1948, was Nate Saint's older sister. In October 1955, when Nate and the others first launched their project to evangelize the Waorani, Rachel already was living in a jungle hacienda in Ecuador, trying to learn the difficult Wao language from Dayuma, a young woman who had fled the tribal violence. Afraid of interference from "Sis" and her group, the five men kept their plans a secret. After their deaths, however, Rachel seemed destined to fulfill her brother's dream (and her own) to contact the Waorani.

Townsend emphasized this angle, plus a few others, in a letter to Ralph Edwards, suggesting Rachel Saint as a subject of *This Is Your Life*.[52] The program, which Edwards first developed for radio, moved to television in 1952. By 1957, it aired weekly on NBC before a national audience of some thirty million people. The format was simple. Edwards would surprise an unsuspecting guest—sometimes a celebrity, sometimes an ordinary person—with the words "This is your life." He then spent the rest of the program telling the subject's story by dramatically introducing people from his or her past. An early example of "reality TV," the program offered viewers an intimate, sentimental look at another person's past, presented within a moralistic framework. Critics suggested that the show could be voyeuristic and exploited private emotions, but audiences loved it.[53]

When Townsend contacted him, Edwards and his Emmy Award–winning program were at the height of their popularity. Edwards also was legendary as an early celebrity fund-raiser. In the 1940s and 1950s, he pioneered cause marketing, using his own fame and his entertainment programs to promote the American Heart Association and the March of Dimes in addition to lesser-known charities.[54] *This Is Your Life* seemed an ideal venue to give the WBT/SIL a national profile. Although Edwards's rise to Hollywood fame and fortune had been rapid, he was a small-town boy from a staunchly Methodist home. He had spent his first eleven years in the farming community of Merino, Colorado, where neighbors remembered the way his mother, Minnie Mae Edwards, loaded her three sons—Ralph, Paul, and Carl—into a buggy every Sunday and drove them to church. As an adult, Ralph remained a loyal churchman and tried to translate his moral and spiritual values into the world of network television. He once said that the theme of *This Is Your Life* was "Love thy neighbor."[55] The program could be described as a thirty-minute, secularized "testimony meeting," full of stories about people overcoming adversity or helping others.

Edwards understood the appeal of Protestant missions, particularly the "inspiring story" of a forty-two-year-old missionary linguist from Philadelphia who "used to cringe at the sight of the tiniest, harmless spider." Yet she overcame her fears to brave the jungles of Peru and Ecuador to bring Christianity to "primitive people in their own native tongue."[56] He scheduled Rachel Saint for the June 5, 1957, broadcast of *This Is Your Life*. At the time, Saint was only in the initial stages of language study, so Townsend gave Edwards a number of ideas to liven up the program. These included bringing Dayuma, Saint's Waorani language helper, to California, along with Carlos Sevilla, owner of the hacienda where the two women were living. He was, Townsend wrote, the "Daniel Boone of Ecuador." Townsend did not mention that Dayuma's status as an Indian worker at Sevilla's jungle ranch amounted to de facto slavery. Including Sevilla on the television guest list ensured Dayuma's presence as well. It also was a part of quiet efforts by the WBT/SIL to free her from hacienda servitude.

To round out the cast, Townsend suggested flying in another linguist and a native family from among the Candoshi-Shapra speakers of Peru, where Saint had served for two years. Edwards agreed, and "This Is Your Life, Rachel Saint," became a somewhat chaotic mix of Saint family members, missionaries, and stunned indigenous people, trying to communicate with each other in four different languages. However, Edwards managed to hold the program together, and audiences saw missionaries and indigenous people not in photographs or church basement slide shows but live from Hollywood, broadcast into their living rooms. They heard the Shapra leader, Tariri, explain through a translator that "his heart was happy after he had received Jesus." Rachel Saint's willingness to risk her life for violent tribal peoples, including those who had killed her brother, was, Edwards told her, "love for your fellow man in its truest form."[57] As the program concluded, Edwards gave his imprimatur to the Wycliffe venture. He promoted the organization and informed viewers that Rachel and Dayuma would follow their television appearance with a speaking tour in major American cities. As Townsend had hoped, "This Is Your Life, Rachel Saint" and the admiration for missions it engendered helped to usher in a "period of unprecedented publicity for Wycliffe."[58]

* * *

Such overt idealization of missionaries in American public life ended with the Vietnam War and the cultural crisis of the late 1960s, although evangelical missions themselves continued to flourish. Efforts to secularize the public square in the 1960s and the rise of the Religious Right in subsequent decades polarized the culture in such a way that it would become difficult for social liberals in the tradition of a Melvin Arnold or a Cornell Capa to champion conservative Protestant missionaries. At the same time, criticism of traditional missionary work, a characteristic of liberal Protestantism since at least the 1930s, spread to the broader culture. The rise of nationalist movements in Latin America and around the world, radical shifts in anthropology, and the 1971 Barbados Declaration condemning missionary activity among indigenous people as inherently imperialistic all contributed to a more negative view. Such ideas spilled over into popular culture in the form of books and movies such as *At Play in the Fields of the Lord* (1965) and *The Mosquito Coast* (1982).[59]

These changes, however, should not obscure the reality that during the 1950s and the early 1960s conservative missionaries were featured, even celebrated, in some of the most influential media outlets in the United States. Missionaries represented a faith shared by millions of Americans and one that was respected, or at least tolerated, by cultural elites. Publishers DeWitt Wallace and Henry R. Luce, for example, were sons of conservative Protestants of an earlier era. Although their interests were cultural and profit driven, they understood the deep audience appeal of missionary spirituality. They also realized that, in addition to faith and inspiration, missionaries embodied values important in the context of the Cold War. Earnest young men and women taking the gospel to the jungles of South America symbolized the goodness and innate decency of ordinary Americans as the nation's true ambassadors. Missionaries epitomized the strength of American families and the ultimate triumph of those who sacrificed for others and who followed the dictates of their own consciences. Their stories reinforced an American national identity that was "rational, generous, and benevolent."[60] Conservative missionaries benefited from a cultural consensus in the 1950s that viewed them as antidotes to American hubris abroad, not as expressions of it.

Through their efforts on film, in print, and on television, Cornell Capa, Clarence Hall, Melvin Arnold, and Ralph Edwards communicated the story of the missionary-Waorani encounter in Amazonian Ecuador to millions of Americans. They did so for a variety of reasons—humanitarian, religious, political, and commercial—although each also experienced a personal connection with the drama of the people and events involved. The influence and efforts of these four men, the energy and talent of missionaries such as Elisabeth Elliot and W. Cameron Townsend, and the power of the Ecuador narrative itself all contributed to the new evangelicalism's increasingly visible place at the center of American culture.

NOTES

I am grateful to David Heim and to Sarah Miglio for their comments on earlier versions of this chapter and to Michael Parks for his help with research on Clarence Hall and the *Reader's Digest*.

1. For example, Joel A. Carpenter, *Revive Us Again: The Reawakening of American Fundamentalism* (New York: Oxford University Press, 1997), 226–34; Patrick Allitt, *Religion in America since 1945: A History* (New York: Columbia University Press, 2003), 12–16; George M. Marsden, *Fundamentalism and American Culture*, 2nd ed. (New York: Oxford University Press, 2006), 232–36. Mark A. Noll, "Where We Are and How We Got Here," *Christianity Today*, October 2006, 42–49, includes missions and other factors. I am indebted to his emphasis on the innovation and "cultural creativity" of evangelicals. William Lawrence Svelmoe, *A New Vision for Missions: William Cameron Townsend, the Wycliffe Bible Translators, and the Culture of Early Evangelical Faith Missions, 1896–1945* (Tuscaloosa: University of Alabama Press, 2008), 318, notes the influence of missionaries in the emergence of the new evangelicalism.

2. I use *conservative Protestant* and *evangelical* interchangeably. The missionaries featured in this essay were members of faith missions and shared a fundamentalist heritage. However, their irenic spirit and rejection of fundamentalist separatism place them alongside Billy Graham in the group most often called "evangelicals" or "new evangelicals." See Marsden, *Fundamentalism*, 233–35.

3. The SIL is now known as "SIL International" and the WBT as "Wycliffe International." SIL International is an NGO dedicated to Bible translation, language research, literacy, and literature development. It is not incorporated as a religious organization, nor is it legally connected to Wycliffe International, an

overtly religious group, although the two organizations maintain close ties. In the past, the lines between the two entities were much less clear, and I refer to the SIL/WBT in the way it historically functioned, as a single large organization focused on linguistics and Bible translation, viewed by American evangelicals as a missionary agency. For a balanced introduction to the SIL that uses Mexico as a case study, see Todd Hartch, *Missionaries of the State: The Summer Institute of Linguistics, State Formation, and Indigenous Mexico, 1935–1985* (Tuscaloosa: University of Alabama Press, 2006).

4. William Lawrence Svelmoe, "A New Vision for Missions: William Cameron Townsend in Guatemala and Mexico, 1917–1945," vol. 1 (PhD diss., University of Notre Dame, 2001), 5.

5. Gerard T. Rice, *The Bold Experiment: JFK's Peace Corps* (Notre Dame, IN: University of Notre Dame Press, 1985), 2.

6. Carpenter, *Revive Us Again*, 212, 228.

7. Cornell Capa and Richard Whelan, eds., *Cornell Capa Photographs* (Boston: Bulfinch Press, 1992), 15, 152.

8. Cornell Capa, "'Go Ye and Preach the Gospel': Five Do and Die," *Life*, January 30, 1956, 18. This and the previous paragraph are also based on Capa's "The Death of Missionaries in the Ecuadorian Jungle," unpublished typescript, Magnum Photos, February 1, 1956, copy in the author's possession.

9. Capa, "'Go Ye.'"

10. Andrew Heiskell, "Publisher's Preview: Danger and Dedication," *Life*, May 13, 1957, 187.

11. Based on the author's interview with Elisabeth Elliot, June 27, 2001, Magnolia, MA.

12. For a list of the books in the series, see the frontispiece of Jean Dye Johnson, *God Planted Five Seeds* (New York: Harper and Row, 1966). The list may be missing a few additional books occasionally included in the series, sometimes called the Harper Jungle Missionary Classics.

13. Elisabeth Elliot, *The Savage My Kinsman* (New York: Harper and Brothers; London: Hodder and Stoughton, 1961). For more on Capa, Elliot, and missionary photography, see Kathryn T. Long, "Cameras 'Never Lie': The Role of Photography in Telling the Story of American Evangelical Missions," *Church History* 72, no. 4 (December 2003): 841–51.

14. "Child among Her Father's Killers: Missionaries Live with Aucas," *Life*, November 24, 1958, 23–29; Elisabeth Elliot, "Widow's Jungle Life amid Husband's Killers," *Life*, April 7, 1961, 118–33. *Life* also published two other Capa photo essays featuring evangelical missionaries: "The Martyrs' Widows Return to Teach in Jungle," May 20, 1957, 24–33, and "Bring the Word," September 14, 1962, 76A–80.

15. Norman Schreiber, "The Concerns of Cornell Capa," *Camera Arts*, November/December 1980, 35.

16. Matthew Huxley, Cornell Capa, *Farewell to Eden* (New York: Harper and Row, 1964). The book was the brainchild of New York financier Samuel Milbank, who helped fund it, in part through contributions to the SIL. See Samuel R. Milbank to Harold Goodall, April 22, 1960, doc. 14524, Cameron Townsend Archive, Jungle Aviation and Radio Service Headquarters, Waxhaw, NC (hereafter "Townsend Archive"); Harold Goodall to Samuel R. Milbank, May 5, 1961, doc. 20582, Townsend Archive; also Patricia Sullivan, "Author, NIMH Epidemiologist Matthew Huxley Dies at 84," *Washington Post*, February 17, 2005, www.washingtonpost.com/wp-dyn/articles/A31009-2005Feb16.html. The most serious dispute over the book was between Robert L. Russell, an SIL linguist working among the Amahuaca, and the WBT/SIL leadership. Russell felt the published text contained significant errors. Robert L. Russell to Board of Directors of WBT-SIL, May 23, 1965, doc. 23250, Townsend Archive.

17. "Max" Huxley in Townsend to Samuel Milbank, March 24, 1961, doc. 19950, and Townsend to Dear Friends, n.d. [1965], doc. 22260, both in Townsend Archive.

18. Garner E. Shriver to Townsend, June 14, 1965, doc. 22846, Seymour Halpern to Townsend, June 22, 1965, doc. 22778, and Cornell Capa to Ben Elson, September 16, 1965, doc. 23142, all in Townsend Archive.

19. Capa and Whelan, *Capa Photographs*, 152.

20. Cornell Capa, "Bring the Word," *Life*, September 14, 1962, 76B.

21. Capa coined the phrase "concerned photographer" in 1966, only two years after *Farewell to Eden* was published. See Harvey V. Fondiller, "ICP: Photography's Fabulous New Center," *Popular Photography*, April 1975, 53.

22. Capa and Whelan, *Capa Photographs*, the sections "American Politics," 86–121, and "Indians and Missionaries," 152–67.

23. Clarence W. Hall and Desider Holisher, *Protestant Panorama: A Story of the Faith That Made America Free* (New York: Farrar, Straus and Young, 1951), 171, 176; "21 Back U.N. Flag for City Schools," *New York Times*, December 7, 1950, 26; "Newsstand Filth in City Is Charged," *New York Times*, January 6, 1956, 20; Greg Linnell, "'Applauding the Good and Condemning the Bad': The Christian Herald and Varieties of Protestant Response to Hollywood in the 1950s," *Journal of Religion and Popular Culture* 12 (Spring 2006): para. 17.

24. Hall and Holisher, *Protestant Panorama*, 3, 4, 29, 175.

25. Ibid., caption, 162. In later years, Hall became shriller in his anticommunism, particularly in two articles attacking the World Council of Churches and misusing the *Christian Century* to do so. See Clarence W. Hall, "Must Our Churches Finance Revolution?" *Reader's Digest*, October 1971, 95–100, "Which Way the World Council of Churches?" *Reader's Digest*, November 1971, 177–84, "In-Digest-ible Charges," *Christian Century*, October 20, 1971, 1219, and "Attention, 'Digest': Stop Stealing Century Prestige!" *Christian Century*, November 17, 1971, 1342.

26. John Heidenry, *Theirs Was the Kingdom: Lila and DeWitt Wallace and the Story of the Reader's Digest* (New York: Norton, 1993), 52, 252–53.
27. Ibid., 323. My account of *Deliver Us from Evil* is based on Heidenry and on James T. Fisher, *Dr. America: The Lives of Thomas A. Dooley, 1927–1961* (Amherst: University of Massachusetts Press, 1997), 70–81.
28. Fisher, *Dr. America*, 74–77.
29. Ibid., 41, 56, 108.
30. Writing for the *Digest*, probably the most heavily edited publication in the country, was a daunting task for even established authors. Heidenry, *Theirs Was the Kingdom*, 111, 399.
31. Despite qualms, Van Der Puy allowed the use of his name at the *Digest*'s request in order to get the story out. He openly acknowledged Hall's authorship. Abe C. Van Der Puy, interview by author, June 27, 2000, Keystone Heights, FL. The title came from the fourth stanza of a hymn the men had chosen as a theme for their venture. See Edith G. Cherry, "We Rest on Thee, Our Shield and Our Defender," in *Hymns: The Hymnal of Inter-Varsity Christian Fellowship*, comp. and ed. Paul Beckwith (Downers Grove, IL: InterVarsity Press, 1952), 9.
32. Daniel A. Poling, "My Faith Today: Five Heroic Martyrs," 12 February 1956, typescript, V. Raymond Edman Papers, RG/02/004, box 11, folder 11, Wheaton College Archives and Special Collections, Wheaton, IL.
33. Abe C. Van Der Puy [actually written by Clarence W. Hall], "Through Gates of Splendor," *Reader's Digest*, August 1956, 56, 57.
34. James Hefley and Marti Hefley, *Uncle Cam* (Waco, TX: Word Books, 1974), 197–99. *Two Thousand Tongues to Go*, written by Ethel Wallis and Mary Bennett, was published in December 1959.
35. Clarence W. Hall, *Adventurers for God* (New York: Harper and Brothers, 1959), 9.
36. Ibid., 17.
37. Elliot, interview by author, 2001.
38. Ed Darling, Arnold's first assistant at Beacon, quoted in Susan Wilson, "Beacon's Modern Era: 1945–2003," *Journal of Scholarly Publishing* 35 (July 2004): 201.
39. Alexandra Arnold Lynch, "Melvin Arnold: Publisher, 1913–2000," n.d., www.harvardsquarelibrary.org/unitarians/arnold.html (accessed June 7, 2007).
40. John T. McGrevy, *Catholics and American Freedom: A History* (New York: Norton, 2003), 167.
41. Wilson, "Beacon's Modern Era," 202, 203; Allitt, *Religion in America*, 288; Martin E. Marty, *Modern American Religion*, vol. 3, *Under God, Indivisible, 1941–1960* (Chicago: University of Chicago Press, 1996), 158, 159.
42. Abe C. Van Der Puy to Sam Saint, February 21, 1956, copy to Charles Mellis, Mission Aviation Fellowship, collection 136, box 59, folder 31, "Voice of the Andes 1956–1963," Billy Graham Center Archives, Wheaton College, Wheaton, IL.

43. Dana L. Robert, "The Influence of American Missionary Women on the World Back Home," *Religion and American Culture* 12 (Winter 2002): 62, makes this point in the context of Harriet Newell's death.

44. The contract was with Abe Van Der Puy. It later was cancelled and a new contract extended to Elisabeth Elliot. Van Der Puy also gave up his rights to the title. Elisabeth Elliot to "Dear Mother" [Katherine Howard], December 12, 1956, Papers of Elisabeth Howard Elliot, collection 278, box 4, folder 4, Billy Graham Center Archives, Wheaton, IL. The recent release of this and other correspondence in collection 278 provided additional information surrounding the publication of *Through Gates of Splendor* but did not change the interpretation of events in this essay.

45. "Interview of Elisabeth Howard Gren by Robert Shuster," March 26, 1985, Collection 278, tape #T2, Billy Graham Center Archives, Wheaton College, Wheaton, IL; see also Elliot, interview by author, 2001.

46. Elisabeth Elliot, *Through Gates of Splendor* (New York: Harper and Brothers, 1957), 95. See also Kathryn T. Long, "In the Modern World, but Not of It: The 'Auca Martyrs,' Evangelicalism, and Postwar American Culture," in *The Foreign Missionary Enterprise at Home*, ed. Daniel H. Bays and Grant Wacker (Tuscaloosa: University of Alabama Press, 2003), 232–35.

47. Arnold-Elliot exchange based on Elliot interview, 2001. At one point, Arnold asked an editor to rewrite Elliot's draft manuscript, but Elliot, the other widows, and Sam Saint refused to accept the changes. *Through Gates of Splendor* sold one hundred thousand copies in ten months. Eugene Exman, *The House of Harper: One Hundred and Fifty Years of Publishing* (New York: Harper and Row, 1967), 286.

48. Exman, *House of Harper*, 286.

49. Ethel Emily Wallis, *The Dayuma Story: Life under Auca Spears* (New York: Harper and Brothers, 1960). Wallis wrote the book in collaboration with Saint and Dayuma. RGS [Robert G. Schneider] to WCT [Townsend], December 9, 1958, doc. 14940, and RGS to WCT, December 10, 1958, doc. 14934, both in Townsend Archive.

50. Mel Arnold to Dr. Townsend, December 8, 1960, doc. 18708, Townsend Archive. LaVerne Kohl, "Review of Elliot, Elisabeth, *The Savage My Kinsman*," *Library Journal*, May 1, 1961, 1779.

51. Townsend to R. W. Wyatt, June 1, 1957, doc. 12878, cf. Townsend to Bill Wyatt, May 10, 1957, doc. 12917, and Townsend to Bob Schneider, November 23, 1957, doc. 57112, all in Townsend Archive.

52. Townsend to Ralph Edwards, December 3, 1956, doc. 11945, Townsend Archive.

53. Jack Gould, "TV's Misery Shows," *New York Times*, February 7, 1954.

54. "Sermon on the Air," *Time*, February 16, 1953, 49.

55. Fredda Balling, "The World Is His Neighbour," *TV-Radio Mirror*, June 1959, 30, quoted in Mary Desjardins, "Maureen O'Hara's 'Confidential' Life," in *Small Screens, Big Ideas: Television in the 1950s*, ed. Janet Thumin (London: I. B. Tauris, 2002), 120.

56. "This Is Your Life, Rachel Saint," June 5, 1957, video recording.

57. Ibid. As a backdrop, the program also included stock film clips of "savage" jungle peoples with drumbeats as audio, much to the embarrassment of some Wycliffe staff.

58. Hugh Steven, *Yours to Finish the Task: The Memoirs of W. Cameron Townsend from 1947–1982* (Orlando, FL: Wycliffe Bible Translators, 2004), 193.

59. Peter Matthiessen, *At Play in the Fields of the Lord* (New York: Random House, 1965); Paul Theroux, *The Mosquito Coast: A Novel* (Boston: Houghton Mifflin, 1982). *At Play* was released as a motion picture in 1991 and *Mosquito Coast* in 1986. Stewart M. Hoover, "Christianity and the Media: Accommodation, Contradiction, and Transformation," in *American Christianities: A History of Dominance and Diversity*, ed. Catherine A. Brekus and W. Clark Gilpin (Chapel Hill: University of North Carolina Press, 2011), 369, also notes the rise of televangelism in the 1970s as a major factor in the shifting media landscape, contributing to the increasing polarization.

60. Catherine A. Lutz and Jane L. Collins, *Reading National Geographic* (Chicago: University of Chicago Press, 1993), 46, make this point for the kind of stories in the *Geographic* during the same period.

CHAPTER 19

The Evangelical Left and the Politicization of Evangelicalism

DAVID R. SWARTZ

In 1970 Mark Hatfield, a Republican U.S. senator from Oregon and noted critic of the Vietnam conflict, gave the commencement address at Fuller Theological Seminary in Pasadena, California. Expecting to find seminarians who would view war in Vietnam as a holy cause against godlessness and communism, Hatfield was shocked by shows of solidarity with his own dovish stance. During the processional, students in the balcony unfurled a banner that read, "We're with you, Mark." Two-thirds of the seminary graduates marching forward to receive their diplomas wore black armbands over their gowns in protest against the war. Hatfield wrote later that for the first time he sensed that "there were countless evangelicals, who because of their faith in Christ, could not condone the immoral and barbarian violence our nation was inflicting throughout Indochina."[1]

George Marsden's 1987 history of Fuller, *Reforming Fundamentalism*, though it ends before the Hatfield episode, traces the beginnings of a moderate evangelicalism in the 1950s and 1960s. Other scholars note Billy Graham's integrationist impulse, plain-folk evangelical support for the New Deal in California, and the cautious support for Jimmy Carter by Campus Crusade staffers. In many of these cases, however, the story line focuses on the eventual—even inevitable—merging of politically conservative activism and evangelicalism. The story of Hatfield and the Evangelical Left of the 1970s adds to this scholarship's recovery of a richly textured postwar evangelical politics. At Fuller and elsewhere, an emerging Evangelical Left held to a progressive politics, experimented with egalitarian sensibilities, agitated for minority and women's rights, and denounced American foreign policy in Southeast Asia. During the volatile 1970s, before the emergence of the Moral Majority, they sought to direct a remarkably fluid evangelical politics toward the political left.[2]

ORIGINS

As Hatfield's story suggests, most in the Evangelical Left emerged from a constellation of northern and western evangelical institutions, among them Wheaton College, *Christianity Today*, InterVarsity Christian Fellowship, Billy Graham, and Fuller Theological Seminary. This new evangelical infrastructure was growing and substantial. Charles Fuller's *Old Fashioned Revival Hour*, for example, enjoyed a nationwide audience of over twenty million listeners over 456 stations on the Mutual System by the 1940s. Youth for Christ, a high school–age parachurch ministry, filled up Madison Square Gardens at rallies in the 1950s. In the same decade *Christianity Today* shot ahead of mainline periodical *Christian Century*'s 37,500 subscribers and emerged immediately as the preeminent and most read evangelical journal in the nation. Billy Graham, who helped launch *Christianity Today*, drew millions to his evangelistic crusades around the world.[3]

These impressive numbers, however, remained largely unnoticed by the political mainstream. Part of the reason, according to historian Joel Carpenter, was that new evangelicals carried on a rather unambitious social and political agenda. They remained preoccupied with holy living and evangelism, nurturing a passive social conservatism. Among this apolitical sector, stirrings were under way. Theologian Carl F. H. Henry ratcheted up his theological case for social relevance and political involvement in a tract entitled *The Uneasy Conscience of Modern Fundamentalism* (1947). "There is no room here," he wrote, invoking John the Baptist, Jesus, and Paul, "for a gospel that is indifferent to the needs of the total man nor of the global man." Many evangelicals needed no such exhortation. A rabid anticommunism obsessed some; others, growing in wealth and education, were developing cultural and economic tools necessary to "go public" with the social implications of their faith. As the 1960s approached amid the domestic and global ferment of the Cold War, there was a complex unfurling of political interests, institutions, and activities across the evangelical spectrum. Tension and contestation characterized evangelicals and their leaders in the 1960s, with a range of political ideas, agendas, and interests always in play and open to scrutiny.[4]

The Evangelical Left that soon emerged only added to the dynamic nature of evangelical politics in the postwar era. Evidence of political activism on the left centered on civil rights and first appeared on evangelical college campuses in the early 1960s. Dissatisfied with their parents' hesitance to join the civil rights movement, students viewed apoliticism as a posture that served only to buttress existing racial inequalities. Billy Graham, for instance, held integrated crusades in the South, yet he remained conspicuously absent from freedom rides and initially appeared wary of Martin Luther King Jr. Evangelical students found this gradualist approach untenable. One student at Calvin College, a Christian Reformed–affiliated school, wondered how his parents could criticize King. How, the student tearfully asked his philosophy professor Richard Mouw, could they "be like that?" After all, they were the ones who had taught him to sing "red and yellow, black and white; they are precious in His sight. Jesus loves the little children of the world." How could Christians follow a God of love, yet claim states' rights in the face of downtrodden African Americans? Students from many of the one hundred evangelical colleges such as Wheaton (Illinois), Asbury (Kentucky), Trinity (Illinois), Westmont (California), and Gordon (Massachusetts) that would eventually join the Christian College Coalition echoed these plaintive questions.[5]

This youthful angst combined with the growing sociopolitical sensibility of the new evangelicalism. A significant minority of students enthusiastically supported King and sounded a more pronounced rhetoric of integration and racial justice. At Wheaton College, a school that, according to Marsden, stood "at the center of one of the most influential networks of organized evangelical leadership," a group of students picketed a Barry Goldwater rally on campus. The presidential candidate had rented the college's football stadium for a 1964 campaign event that sparked reaction from all sides of the civil rights debate. Goldwater's racial politics were complex. He supported racial integration and called for racist hearts to be transformed. His western libertarianism and fear of communism, on the other hand, directed him away from forced integration by the federal government. Many students interpreted Goldwater's states' rights rhetoric—"Enforcement of the law is a state and local responsibility. There is no room in this country for a federal police force"—on Wheaton's campus as unconscionable. Fifty of them protested Goldwater's denunciation of forced integration and held aloft "LBJ-USA" banners to a chorus of catcalls and boos from Goldwater supporters. Kenneth Landon, one of the protest ringleaders, mourned the opposition he felt while holding his pro-Johnson sign: "I came away from that unbelievable night sorrowing for America, with a fear, not of Goldwater, but of the well-dressed, middle-class suburbia, as well as the crowd-following type who kicks from behind—who cry together, 'For Goldwater and God!'" Many more came to Landon's aid in the following weeks. A week before the election, a half-page "Johnson for President" ad signed by 120 Wheaton students and faculty appeared in the student newspaper.[6]

At Calvin College, nearly three hundred students marched to protest the 1963 bombings of black churches in Birmingham, and in 1965 over two hundred students braved a bitterly cold day in Grand Rapids to protest the death of Boston minister James Reeb, who had been beaten to death in Selma, Alabama. Students within InterVarsity, an evangelical student organization with chapters at hundreds of state universities, favored federal intervention in southern states by an overwhelming majority, and cheered on InterVarsity leader Ruth Lewis as she attempted to integrate the University of Alabama–Birmingham campus. InterVarsity's magazine alone reached a constituency of twenty-six thousand students in over 850 chapters across the nation with pro–civil rights books, magazines, and sermons. Evangelical student newspapers, reaching far fewer readers, likewise faithfully covered the civil rights movement, sympathetically tracking desegregation attempts in the South throughout the early 1960s and editorializing in favor of the Civil Rights Amendment. It is difficult to ascertain the proportion of evangelical students engaged and sympathetic to the civil rights movement, given the range of political interests contested by evangelical youth (in a straw poll of Wheaton students, Goldwater won by a vote of 805–518). Clearly, though, antisegregation sentiment dominated the published discourse on evangelical college campuses.[7]

As the sixties wore on, black evangelicals decisively pushed progressive evangelicals toward the civil rights movement. Tom Skinner, a former Harlem Lords gang leader, launched his vibrant evangelistic career in the early 1960s. In 1962 Skinner, preaching sermons entitled "The White Man Did It" and "A White Man's Religion," converted 2,200 people in a sensational crusade at the Apollo Theater. Skinner quickly catapulted to prominence among white evangelicals with an unusual blend of conversionist piety and increasingly sharp racial rhetoric. In his 1970 book *How Black Is the Gospel?* Skinner urged a return to "that masculine, contemporary, revolutionary Jesus." Skinner's Jesus called racist whites a "brood of vipers." In a 1970 speech before twelve thousand evangelical students at InterVarsity's triennial Urbana convention at the University of Illinois, Skinner renounced "Americanism" in a searing critique of racial prejudice. Skinner's contentious language, sanctioned by numerous key new evangelical institutions (he was a featured speaker at the 1969 U.S. Congress on Evangelism, enjoyed "great respect" from Campus Crusade for Christ president Bill Bright, and traveled with Graham as an associate evangelist), sensitized an emerging Evangelical Left to racial issues.[8]

The entrance into the civil rights fray, though tardy, did awaken progressive evangelicals to the salience of social structures. In the early 1960s most evangelicals defined racism solely in terms of willful individual oppression. The best way to stop lynchings, segregation, and the abuse of black protesters was to spiritually transform southern white racists. But some evangelicals began to doubt the efficacy of evangelism to spark social change. For a case in point, they had only to look at the racial consciences of born-again believers all around them. Too many of the converted evangelicals they knew best—Baptists in the South, people in their own congregations, even their parents—seemed flagrantly racist in their opposition to King. At the same time, progressive evangelicals were encouraged by the flurry of civil rights legislation, activism, and literature. *Soul on Ice* (1967), Black Panther Eldridge Cleaver's collection of lyrical essays on racial liberation; *The Other America* (1962), Catholic socialist Michael Harrington's exposé on poverty in the United States; and the Kerner Report (1968) on race riots each suggested the need for corporate, not merely personal, responsibility. By the early 1970s *The Other Side*, an evangelical magazine in Philadelphia with a subscription base of thirteen thousand at its height, had evolved from a singular preoccupation with racism to a willingness to lobby government on a broad range of concerns such as poverty and gender. Other progressive evangelicals began to speak of "cultures of poverty" and institutional racism. From an emphasis on individual actions emerged a holistic effort to improve the psychological, economic, and political health of a race and a society.[9]

The Vietnam War extended this new attention to social structures and brought in a larger evangelical constituency. The most concentrated antiwar activity initially took place at evangelical colleges, particularly at Wheaton, the only evangelical college to administer a Reserve Officers' Training Corps (ROTC) unit. A compulsory program for male students in their freshman and sophomore years, Wheaton's ROTC unit encountered stiff opposition from students. In 1965, a poll showed that 72 percent of Wheaton male students opposed compulsory ROTC. After one Veterans' Day chapel service in which 550 cadets marched into Edman Chapel in full military dress, a student wrote that it was "an example of this continual attempt to condition our decision—so that it is hardly a decision at all. God and country are whispered to us in the same breath. We march, guns in hand, to 'Onward Christian Soldiers.'" Another student, comparing their parade to those in the Soviet Union, provocatively asked, "You know where else they have May-day military exhibitions?" From 1966 on, battles between protesters and conservative stalwarts enveloped the campus. If patriotism on campus was strong—in late 1965, 937 students signed a petition at the Veterans' Day service in favor of U.S. foreign policy to President Lyndon Johnson—so was dissent. Just two years later, only 330 students (a drop of nearly 600) signed a similar petition. Dan Reigle, elected student government president in 1967, fomented much of this protest. Several antiwar clubs—Students Concerned about Vietnam and Americans for Democratic Action—formed and rallied students on behalf of peace candidate Eugene McCarthy in the 1968 presidential election. By 1969, ferment peaked as parallel antipathies toward the Vietnam War and mandatory ROTC merged into a single protest. Students began to reenact death scenes from Vietnam, carry coffins to the city's draft board office, mock cadet rifle drills with displays of toy machine guns, offer bitter commentary on President Armerding's support for the war, and wear nooses over their heads at demonstrations. Students also held conscientious objection drives and joined the nationwide Moratorium Day protests. For the next five years, antiwar protests fell into a regular rhythm: before and after Veterans' Day chapel services at Edman Chapel in the fall and during the annual ROTC review at the football stadium in the spring. If the protesters were only a minority on campus, as they were in civil rights agitation, they nonetheless dominated student government and the pages of the student newspaper.[10]

Dissenting students enjoyed support from Senator Mark Hatfield, the most prominent politician at midcentury who identified with the new evangelicalism. A longtime opponent of intervention in Southeast Asia, Hatfield made President Richard Nixon's "enemies list" for voting to repeal the Gulf of Tonkin Resolution. In 1970 Hatfield and Democratic senator George McGovern sponsored an "amendment to end the war" that pledged to withdraw from Cambodia in thirty days, remove troops from Vietnam by June 30, 1971, and limit military expenditures to the systematic withdrawal of troops. At Fuller Seminary in 1970, Hatfield's very public positions galvanized the student body, some of whom marched on the post office in Pasadena and wrote petitions against the war. At Wheaton, Hatfield received a standing ovation after giving an antiwar speech. The student newspaper headlined their report, "He Came; He Spoke; and We Were Conquered." Hatfield developed an even closer relationship with Jim Wallis, a former Students for a Democratic Society organizer, and a band of dissenting Trinity Seminary (Illinois) students. The "Post-Americans," as they called themselves, later moved to Washington, D.C., partly on the basis of Hatfield's advice. The senator in turn introduced legislation suggested by the group, which renamed itself Sojourners in 1975. That Hatfield continued to be a welcome presence by many in the Wheaton-Fuller-*Christianity Today* network speaks to the dynamic presence of a liberal activist faction within evangelicalism in the late 1960s and early 1970s.[11]

Concerns about the Vietnam War and civil rights led some evangelicals to wonder more broadly about the nature of U.S. social structures. As Wallis pored over analyses of Vietnamese and American history in leftist journals, he decided that the Vietnam War was not an "aberration, but in fact only the most current example of a long and bloody record of U.S. interventionism." At the heart of American imperialism was not a principled opposition to communism but instead a disturbing commitment to unlimited growth buoyed by big business, the media, and government bureaucracy. A member of the Christian World Liberation Front, an evangelical student organization in Berkeley, California, colorfully described this "technocracy," writing, "And then there's Uncle Sam. The only concern he has for me is where I could kill (or be killed) best that week—South Viet Nam, Laos, Cambodia, Thailand. . . . Uncle Sam would be there waiting again, waiting to make me a first class tin soldier so I could protect the 'Interests' of all the money grabbers in this nation." Technology—new materials, machines, and products—gave the "powers and principalities," as Wallis called governments, corporations, and other brokers of power, an insidious means of wielding control over "the people." Liberalism, inextricably tied to the technocracy, was just as responsible as conservatism for the ponderous pace of desegregation and the sorry state of American society. Wallis and others in the Evangelical Left, given their roots in antimodernist fundamentalism, were in fact nicely positioned to find this critique plausible. Like the New Left, fundamentalists nurtured a profound distrust of big government and skepticism of science and rationality.[12]

A Church of the Brethren veteran of the civil rights and antiwar movements offered the clearest example of this attempt to merge the "old, old story" with the New Left. Art Gish, in the aptly titled *The New Left and Christian Radicalism*, argued that Vietnam, racism, and poverty were merely "manifestations of our problem." An "evil system that forces men to do evil deeds" lay at the root. "We reject," wrote Gish, "the bourgeois liberal contention that all change must be rational, orderly, and within the limits of the present system." Gish proposed that Anabaptist theology was the best Christian analogue of the New Left. Each rejected top-down reform, centralized power, and capitalism. To be sure, only a minority in the Evangelical Left, itself a minority within evangelicalism, held to Wallis and Gish's radical politics. Though some young evangelicals spoke derisively of "Amerika" and the "American Way of Death" and many readily appropriated elements of the New Left's political critique, only a few actually joined Students for a Democratic Society, the most important New Left organization of the 1960s. Many, in fact, condemned the movement's spiritual vacuity, propensity to violence, and abandonment of participatory democracy.[13]

Evangelical radicals nonetheless carried two impulses from the New Left that would come to characterize broader evangelical politics in the late 1970s and 1980s. First, they began to embrace a more contentious style of dissent. This was most evident at Explo '72, a youth rally at the Cotton Bowl in Dallas, Texas. All sides showed up in Dallas to proclaim their vision for a new evangelical politics. Staged by the conservative student ministry Campus Crusade, Explo attracted nearly eighty-five thousand high school and college students. Signs of the establishment predominated. President Nixon tried to attend, according to Campus Crusade historian John Turner, out of fear that Democratic nominee George McGovern "might compete effectively for the moderate and conservative Protestant vote." Campus Crusade, not wanting to explicitly politicize the "Jesus Woodstock" event, instead read a telegram from the president. Students attended seminars like "How to Live with Your Parents," listened to speakers Bill Bright and Billy Graham, and joined in patriotic rituals. A minority of Explo participants, despite their comfort with Campus Crusade's spirituality, viewed the patriotic spectacle with distaste. The surge of patriotism, even as a heavy bombing campaign in Vietnam was in full swing, prompted Jim Wallis to join forces with the Christian World Liberation Front (CWLF), a Campus Crusade chapter turned evangelical commune. During a military ceremony, they stood under the stadium's scoreboard, unfurled a banner—"Cross or Flag, Christ or Country," and chanted "Stop the War!" At their conscientious objector counseling booth, the Post-Americans and the CWLF enjoyed hearing many "right ons" from Explo participants. The CWLF, with a diverse constituency of converted leftists, hippies, and evangelical college students, had been pioneering this colorful, confrontational style of protest on the sidewalks of Bancroft and Telegraph Avenues in Berkeley. Situated on the front lines of the counterculture and the Jesus Movement in California, the CWLF mediated leftist politics for thousands of evangelical students across the nation and introduced demonstrative methods of the counterculture such as guerrilla theater, picketing, and leafleting.[14]

Second, evangelical radicals embraced a theology and rhetoric of moral absolutism. This absolutist sensibility, embedded in two significant sources of the Evangelical Left—fundamentalism and the New Left—demanded total commitment, divided the world into light and darkness, and employed a rhetoric of good and evil in its denunciations of segregation and the Vietnam War. "Racism is satanic, and I knew it would take a supernatural force to defeat it," argued southern black activist John Perkins. "New birth in Jesus meant waging war against segregation just as much as it meant putting the honky-tonks and juke joints out of business." Jim Wallis used absolutist language to condemn the Vietnam War. It wasn't a "mistake" or a "blunder," as liberals often argued. It was a "lie . . . a crime and a sin . . . that continues to poison the body politic." This rhetoric contrasted sharply with the measured, respectable style of the new evangelicalism and prefigured the style of the Religious Right.[15]

By the early 1970s, however, leftist political activists, evangelical and secular alike, were despairing over their apparent defeat. Big business remained big. The Vietnam War continued. Racial conflagration persisted. Poverty was rampant. Richard Nixon coasted to a second easy victory. Radical and traditional methods for political change had been exhausted, yet the technocracy continued to reign unimpeded. Evangelist Tom Skinner explained that he had never seen someone actually get in the system, work themselves way up to a position of power, and then effect change. "By the time you've done that," said Skinner, "you've had to prostitute yourself on the way up and you forgot what you came there for. . . . You see, the system is essentially too evil to change—it cannot change." Society needed "radical, revolutionary" efforts to defeat the technocracy. The New Left approach, however, was no more an option than reformist liberalism. Despite Skinner's affinity for the radical social critique and the participatory democracy of the New Left, he questioned its more recent affinity for violence—to "blow the whole system up, just bomb it out, pick up guns, take to the streets and wipe out the entire establishment and start all over."

Disavowing both liberal and New Left approaches, Skinner proposed a "third way" that would sweep aside established political categories and strategies. The third way would create microcosmic communities of authenticity, peace, and justice. "Have some people who can get together and begin to produce live models of what the world ought to be," suggested Skinner. Such a community would be a "new order," a "beloved community," a "forever family" that would shine a light into a dark world and inspire it to build a new society itself. This third way of a spiritual community of love would offer a theologically and socially legitimate repudiation of the technocracy's dehumanizing forces. Inspired by the zeitgeist of the era and Skinner's vision of a new order, evangelicals established dozens of intentional communities. In the 1970s George Marsden lived in such a community in Grand Rapids, Michigan, as a young professor of history at Calvin College. Worden Street Community, located in a lower-income neighborhood facing white flight, consisted of half a dozen homes whose residents shared communal meals and Bible studies twice a week.[16]

Worden Street Community—and more prominent groups such as the CWLF in Berkeley, the Post-Americans in Chicago, and Patchwork Central in Evansville, Indiana—sought to combat the technocracy through spiritual fervor, egalitarianism, and simple living. If third-way evangelicals extended the cultural boundaries of evangelicalism through more exuberant worship styles and more casual dress and language, they remained theologically conservative and identified themselves as evangelical. Biblical allusions and spiritual disciplines coursed through third-way communities. Feeling a deep existential sense of human sin and depravity in the midst of an evil war and a bureaucratic society that was failing to stamp out poverty and racism, third-way evangelicals looked for Christ as the bridge between the depravity on earth and the integrity of the divine. "Christians derive strength in the inevitability of Christ's victory," wrote Post-American Dennis MacDonald. They were fully committed to a spiritual vision that implicitly opposed the rationalism and bureaucracy that pervaded the midcentury liberal consensus.[17]

Many third-way evangelicals argued that only communal living—with its intimate relationships, egalitarian temper, simple living, and ecological sensitivity—could challenge the life-draining technocracy. True fulfillment and reversal of technocratic bigness, authoritarianism, and consumerism, they resolved, came from the "do-it-yourself" approach of forming food cooperatives, tilling gardens, and, most of all, fully participating in community life. "Community," wrote the CWLF's Jack Sparks, was possible and "actually represents the only effective way to fight the bondage of the economic bureaucracy." Third-way young evangelicals posited that a host of small-scale insurgencies, in the form of models of internal justice rather than traditional politics, was the only way to battle the technocracy with spiritual integrity.[18]

To be sure, there were limits to community: the logistical challenges of maintaining the CWLF's geographically sprawling and organizationally complex community, the exhaustion of egalitarian processes, self-referentialism, and struggles over the common purse. Nevertheless, many third-way evangelicals seemed to find authentic relationships and a fulfilling spirituality in their protest against a technocratic American culture. Many communities, despite intermittent tension, in fact enjoyed surprising staying power. Despite their ultimate failure in sparking a large-scale swell of small communities, these evangelical communities typically outlasted the thousands of irreligious utopian communities that fizzled within months or years of conception.

THE CHICAGO DECLARATION AND THE PROMISE OF A UNITED PROGRESSIVE FRONT

As a swell of third-way communities failed to materialize in the mid-1970s, many evangelicals, still hoping for a way to stimulate large-scale change, began to temper their strictures of idealism. At the same time, a group of Reformed evangelicals previously ensconced in the Dutch enclaves of western Michigan had begun to interact with Billy Graham–style evangelicalism. Academicians from Calvin College and Seminary and the *Reformed Journal* led a movement around principles of reform and realist politics rather than revolution. These evangelicals carried impressive academic credentials and an openness to liberal change based on expertise and technology. James Daane of Calvin, for example, exulted in the potential of automation, suggesting that "the potential wealth of the world is for all practical purposes infinite. For the first time in history it is technically possible to eliminate poverty on a world scale." To implement these technical solutions, evangelicals needed to work within the system, to practice a "progressive realism," in the words of Stephen Monsma, a political scientist at Calvin College and a Democratic member of the Michigan House of Representatives. In 1972 Edward Loucks, a California government researcher, wrote, "The Christian has certain political responsibilities which he cannot justifiably shirk. . . . He *must* participate meaningfully in the political process because he is scripturally obligated to *care* for his neighbor." By 1973 a book called *Political Evangelism* by Richard Mouw had come to typify the approach of a new guard of young evangelicals who saw politics as a legitimate, even divinely appointed office. Even evangelical radicals such as Jim Wallis, fired by anger toward Nixon, began to devour government reports on social problems and campaigned on behalf of George McGovern in 1972. Fellow Post-American Wes Michaelson wrote, "Essentially, there is no difference between what is a political task and a spiritual one. The two are really the same. To pretend they are separate and different things results in amoral politics and irrelevant religiosity." Concerned by sexism, continued fighting in Vietnam, environmentalism, and poverty, a growing movement of nonrightist, reformist evangelicals inaugurated a new era of evangelical electoral engagement.[19]

The early 1970s were heady years for the Evangelical Left. The flashy protests of evangelical radicals and the rigorous communities of third-way evangelicals combined with the technical, politically conventional approach of progressive realists. A series of conferences and statements—the Congress on the Church's Worldwide Mission in 1966; the U.S. Congress on Evangelism in Minneapolis in 1969; the Calvin College Conference on Christianity and Politics in 1973—helped bring diverse evangelicals into the same orbit. Dozens of books—in 1972 alone, evangelical publishers released *Evangelicalism and Social Responsibility, The Great Reversal, The Cross and the Flag, A Christian Political Option*, and *Politics: A Case for Political Action*—fleshed out their new social vision. A set of periodicals—*The Post-American* (55,000 at its highest circulation), *The Other Side* (13,000), *Eternity* (46,000), *Vanguard* (2,000), *Right On* (65,000), *HIS* (90,000), *Wittenburg Door, Inside*, and others—kept up a running commentary on current political developments from a progressive perspective. (Periodicals toward the political right, such as *Christianity Today* with over 100,000 readers, enjoyed a higher circulation. Yet even these magazines consistently printed articles by evangelical progressives.) And a flood of new urban congregations and social service agencies, many listed in a *Post-American* monthly feature called "Signs of a New Order," gave the new movement momentum. By 1972 evangelicals of many stripes were merging into a small, but hopeful and growing movement structured around the organization Evangelicals for McGovern (EFM) and a striking document called "The Chicago Declaration," both of which disclaimed the passive conservatism of midcentury evangelicalism. This explosion of political thought and activism would never gain the traction of the Religious Right. But in the 1970s amid very porous boundaries between left, right, and center evangelicalism—and the consequent ferment of a fluid evangelical politics—the Evangelical Left held very real potential for political impact.[20]

EFM's fund-raising efforts on behalf of the Democratic presidential candidate and vitriolic tone toward President Nixon stunned the mainstream and evangelical media alike. Led by Anabaptist and Messiah College professor Ron Sider, EFM criticized Nixon for his failure to maintain civil rights progress, particularly in his southern-strategy campaign saturated with "law and order" rhetoric; for perpetuating tax loopholes for the rich; and for extending the Vietnam War. EFM's most impressive feat came not in fund-raising—*Newsweek* reported that EFM had received only $3,500 from about 220 contributors within a month of its launching—but in its engineering of a McGovern appearance at Wheaton College just a month before the election. Before an overflow crowd of over two thousand, McGovern stressed that his father was a Wesleyan Methodist pastor who had graduated from the evangelical

Houghton College. Speaking fluently in evangelical language learned as the child of an evangelical pastor and from a brief stint as a seminarian, McGovern sprinkled his Wheaton speech with biblical passages and allusions. He finished with a call for moral and spiritual leadership, quoting John Winthrop on the *Arabella* in 1630 about founding America "as a city upon a hill." "The wish of our forebears," concluded McGovern, "was to see the way of God prevail. We have strayed from their pilgrimage, like lost sheep. But I believe we can begin this ancient journey anew." The overarching theme, pitched perfectly to a newly politicizing evangelicalism, was that faith should shape politics.[21]

EFM, however, fared as poorly among evangelicals as McGovern fared among the general electorate. EFM raised only $5,762 from only 358 supporters, and evangelicals voted overwhelmingly for Nixon. The cause had been taken up too late by too many graduate students and young professors, who lent their moral support but sent very little money. Despite the disheartening loss, the Evangelical Left remained upbeat. They had garnered considerable press and launched the first explicitly evangelical political organization in the twentieth century intended to elect a president.[22]

EFM was a mere prelude to a more significant venture by a growing progressive front whose members were beginning to find each other in diffuse outposts of the evangelical world. A year after Nixon's reelection they converged at the YMCA Hotel on Chicago's South Wabash Street for a series of "Thanksgiving Workshops" organized by EFM founder Ron Sider. The location itself was a fitting site to declare evangelicalism's return to social justice. The hotel featured many accoutrements of the new evangelical progressivism. Its dingy, inexpensive trappings testified to simple living. Its urban location testified to rejection of suburban living and an embrace of social concern. As Paul Henry, Calvin professor and candidate for the U.S. House of Representatives, declared that evangelicals "dare no longer remain silent in the face of glaring social evil," the echoes of stray gunfire from the rough neighborhood outside rang through the hall.

After several days of intense discussion, the group emerged with the 470-word "Chicago Declaration," an evangelical manifesto against racism, sexism, economic injustice, and militarism. It called not for revolution but for reform of social systems. Even for the young proponents of the third way congenitally disinclined to compromise, the weekend was a heartening moment. Twenty-five-year-old Jim Wallis saw hope for the future of evangelicalism as he watched an elder evangelical leader re-sign the document after removing his signature once in a pang of inner anguish over how his constituents might respond. The young man and older man then embraced. Divergent groups disenchanted with both conservatism and apoliticism appeared to be coalescing within broader evangelicalism. They rallied around the assertion that "God lays total claim upon the lives of his people. We cannot, therefore, separate our lives from the situation in which God has placed us in the United States and the world." Signers of the Declaration were claiming that politics, along with prayer, was now a spiritual discipline. As Post-American Jim Stentzel watched the media in the mid-1970s document the Evangelical Left's growing numbers, proliferating literature, and political activities, he wrote, "If the connection between the Bible and the nation's alienation is made, things will start popping. Fifty million 'born-again' Christians could be one hell of a political force."[23]

LEFT BEHIND

As it turned out, the apparent consensus among Declaration signers was really more a negative statement against Nixon and political conservatism than it was authentic agreement for an innovative evangelical politics. There were clear signs, even in the first Thanksgiving Workshop, of cleavages within the nascent Evangelical Left. The first evidence of dissension came from African American participants who perceived hints of "evangelical triumphalism" in Ron Sider's opening remarks at the workshop. How could celebratory rhetoric be sounded, they asked, by a tradition that had failed to embrace the civil rights movement? Very quickly, Sider recalled, "the lid blew off." Black participants sharply attacked the committee for including only one black on the committee. Then, over a separate lunch of turnip greens and ham hocks prepared "for atmosphere," they drew up an alternative statement more radical than the original. Palpable tension permeated the workshop through the first evening. When delegates entered the dark streets after the day's final session in search of a snack, they traveled in two groups, one all white, the other all black, both venting their "frustration in angry separation." Though participants approved section after section of the reworked document the next day, the tone had been set.[24]

Women also raised objections. In a workshop dominated by high-powered evangelical executives and scholars, one woman felt as if "she had walked into an Eastern men's club." "The men," noted Trinity College's Nancy Hardesty, "tended to be insensitive to women as people." Specifically, "Dr. Ruth Bentley" was listed as a participant, but as chairperson for an afternoon session she became "Mrs. William Bentley." Even worse, the CWLF's Sharon Gallagher complained, women were "commanded to speak and then expected to shut up when the men felt the issue had been covered. It seemed easier for the establishment men to be gracious toward the blacks they probably rarely had to deal with, than with status changes that might affect women." When Gallagher and Hardesty, coauthor of the first book-length evangelical feminist tract *All We're Meant to Be* (1975), discovered that there was no mention of sexism in the first draft of the Declaration, they caucused the five women present. Delegates in the plenary sessions mostly affirmed their demands. Though some balked at women's ordination, delegates quickly condemned sexism and affirmed the Equal Rights Amendment.[25]

Pacifists also hijacked the workshop schedule and Declaration drafts. John Howard Yoder, president of Goshen Biblical Seminary, said, "Blacks have a paragraph they can redo; women have a word they can redo; but there is nothing at all about war. It contains something about the military-industrial complex being bad for the budget, but nothing about it being bad for the Vietnamese." Yoder, supported by Sider, on the faculty at the Brethren in Christ–affiliated Messiah College; Jim Wallis, editor of the *Post-American*; Dale Brown, former moderator of the Church of the Brethren; and Myron Augsburger, president of Eastern Mennonite College, persuaded the delegates to insert the following: "We must challenge the misplaced trust of the nation in economic and military might—a proud trust that promotes a national pathology of war and violence which victimizes our neighbors at home and abroad."[26]

Sider, the organizer of the workshops, worked hard to accommodate these diverging interests. But the emerging sexual, racial, and theological identities continued to produce clashes, leaving questions as to whether the Evangelical Left was a viable enterprise. In 1975 the *Moody Monthly* reported that "the mood of many workshop participants was not amenable to 'integration' or 'cooperative ministry.'" By the late 1970s, women in the Evangelical Left were channeling much of their energy into the growth of the Evangelical Women's Caucus, which grew to over a dozen regional chapters with periodic national conventions that attracted nearly one thousand delegates. African Americans cordoned themselves off in the National Black Evangelical Association, Anabaptist progressives in Evangelicals for Social Action, Anabaptist radicals in *Sojourners*, and Calvinists in the Association for Public Justice. Political engagement, racial justice, and a moderate feminism, while key planks in the Evangelical Left's platform, nonetheless contributed to its demise by stripping the movement of much-needed resources. Identity politics, a powerful impulse in American society more broadly, profoundly damaged the progressive coalition.[27]

In 1976 Jimmy Carter offered one last hope. If ever the Evangelical Left could launch a successful movement, this would seem to be the moment. It could follow the momentum of a Democratic candidate who was the first outspokenly born-again candidate since William Jennings Bryan in 1908. Carter, a folksy candidate from peanut country, could bring along the demographic weight of a rising evangelical South. Most evangelicals, even future luminaries of the Religious Right such as Jerry Falwell and Pat Robertson, supported Carter's presidency, believing that Christians brought resources to political office unavailable to nonbelievers.

Several years into Carter's presidency, however, evangelical dissenters emerged with force. Evangelical radicals, some from InterVarsity and many from Sojourners, felt that Carter "wasn't doing enough." In neglecting to take a stand against harsh capitalism and nuclear proliferation, he was failing to rigorously apply his faith to politics. The Moral Majority echoed this charge from the right. They accused Carter of softness toward the ERA, abortion, gay rights, school busing, and high taxes. Personal faith, they seemed to conclude, was not enough. Within evangelicalism, Carter's presidency marked a critical shift toward emphasizing policy over personal piety. Evangelical support for the devout Jimmy Carter in 1976 fell precipitously by 1980. Many sided instead with Ronald Reagan, a nominal churchgoer. A more activist conservatism, catalyzed by the issue of abortion, was co-opting the Evangelical Left's use of activism and moralistic language.[28]

The rise of the Religious Right put the Evangelical Left in a quandary. Even the most outspokenly radical of the Evangelical Left identified with conservative theology; their radicalism was essentially an enlivened, culturally progressive repackaging of conservative values. Moreover, the Political Left, suspicious of the new coalition's conservative theology and Puritan sexuality, remained unimpressed and indifferent toward the Chicago Declaration. The liberal coalition, believed many evangelicals, in fact seemed to go to great lengths—by promoting a libertine sexuality, endorsing abortion rights, and giving a very prominent voice to activist secularists—to alienate a potentially helpful constituency.

This political displacement exacerbated the corrosive effect of identity politics on the Evangelical Left. Some potential and card-carrying members of the Evangelical Left joined the Religious Right. Others, unwilling to concede Jerry Falwell's claim that the Right had successfully "hijacked the evangelical jumbo-jet," remained committed to their progressive political agenda. In the late 1970s, *Sojourners* printed a nine-page investigative article entitled "The Plan to Save America," alleging that certain evangelical leaders, among them Campus Crusade's Bill Bright, were pursuing "an ultraconservative political agenda" that "dangerously distorts the fundamental meaning of the Gospel." The feud between *Sojourners* and Bright, according to Jim Wallis, culminated in a threat from Bright—"If you write this article, I have some power in the churches. . . . I will destroy you"—and a near fistfight between Bright and Tom Skinner at an evangelical event preceding the presidential prayer breakfast in 1977. In the 1980s the Evangelical Left attempted to mobilize against Reagan's welfare cuts, military spending, and military interventions in Latin America. Led by Ron Sider, progressive evangelicals also rallied around a "consistently pro-life" mantra. This new agenda, however, did not fit the platforms of hardening political structures. Evangelical Left politics, left behind by the Political Left and the Religious Right, thus remained highly unsettled.[29]

THE LIMITS OF EVANGELICAL POLITICS

Even as the Evangelical Left succumbed to political trends beyond its control, the movement contributed to the politicization of broader evangelicalism. During a time of heightened fluidity and uncertainty, when evangelical politics ranged from hard-edged anticommunist superpatriotism to political apathy, the Evangelical Left consistently pushed toward political activism. Evangelical new leftists, civil rights activists, and Reformed progressives encouraged engagement of political structures with one's spiritual commitments. Evangelical radicals in the late 1960s and early 1970s prefigured the contentious tactics and absolutist rhetoric of the Religious Right. Evangelical moderates managed to generate remarkable levels of debate on college campuses, at seminaries, and ultimately in the pews.

And yet, if the overarching narrative of postwar evangelicalism is growing politicization, the story of the Evangelical Left also points to the limits of evangelical politics. An inherently diffuse tradition, evangelicalism consists of thousands of large and small congregations, colleges, denominations, and social service agencies—not to mention grassroots movements such as the Evangelical Left. The long history of evangelicalism since the Great Awakenings, chronicled by George Marsden in works on Jonathan Edwards, turn-of-the-century fundamentalism, and Fuller Theological Seminary, points to the tradition's persistent fragmentation.

Thus the caricature of evangelicalism as a monolithic bloc gripped by just a few moral and political issues was, and is, inaccurate. Polls showed that through the 1980s and 1990s around 30 percent of evangelicals voted Democratic—a significant number, even considering both black and southern white Democrats. Since 1980 evangelicalism has only rarely enjoyed successful political mobilization. Even political lobbying by the Religious Right has resulted in only limited achievements in policy change. The Moral Majority and the Christian Coalition, two of the most robust evangelical political organizations of the 1980s and 1990s, enjoyed rather short lives. Critiques of the Religious Right have proliferated as well, showing that the Evangelical Left is still a live option for contemporary evangelicals. Given evangelicals' disordered ecclesiology, their many nonpolitical churchly priorities, and their racial, theological, and political diversities, their political muscle on the left and on the right has been, and is likely to remain, exaggerated.[30]

NOTES

1. Mark Hatfield, *Between a Rock and a Hard Place* (Waco, TX: Word Books, 1976).

2. On Fuller, see George M. Marsden, *Reforming Fundamentalism: Fuller Seminary and the New Evangelicalism* (Grand Rapids, MI: Eerdmans, 1987). For the impressive developing historiography on the rise of evangelical politics in the postwar era, see John G. Turner, *Bill Bright and Campus Crusade for Christ: The Renewal of Evangelicalism in Postwar America* (Chapel Hill: University of North Carolina Press, 2008); Steven P. Miller, *Billy Graham and the Rise of the Republican South* (Philadelphia: University of Pennsylvania Press, 2009); Darren Dochuk, *From Bible Belt to Sunbelt: Plain-Folk Religion, Grassroots Politics, and the Rise of Evangelical Conservatism* (New York: Norton, 2011).

3. On the growth of the new evangelicalism, see Joel A. Carpenter, *Revive Us Again: The Reawakening of American Fundamentalism* (New York: Oxford University Press, 1997), 24.

4. For Henry's call for social relevance, see Carl F. H. Henry, *The Uneasy Conscience of Modern Fundamentalism* (Grand Rapids, MI: Eerdmans, 1947).

5. Richard Mouw, interview, July 12, 2006, Pasadena, CA.

6. On Wheaton's place in evangelicalism, see George M. Marsden, *Evangelicalism and Modern America* (Grand Rapids, MI: Eerdmans, 1984), xv. On Goldwater and pro–civil rights sentiment at Wheaton, see Dan Kuhn, "Kuhn Explains Convictions behind Civil Rights Picketing," *Wheaton Record*, October 8, 1964, 4; Paul Henry, "De Jure," *Wheaton Record*, October 4, 1962, 2; "Mississippi Profs Leave University as a Result of Integration Dispute," *Wheaton Record*, February 7, 1963, 5; "Midwest Students Critically Discuss Civil Rights Acts," *Wheaton Record*, December 3, 1964, 4; "Johnson for President," *Wheaton Record*, October 23, 1964, 12.

7. On Calvin, see Lois Short, "Students Join March to Protest Civil Rights Death," *Chimes*, March 19, 1965, 3; Robert VanDellen, "Just How, Senator?" *Chimes*, October 2, 1964, 2; Mark Wageneveld, "Neighborhood Association Copes with Area Racial Problems," *Chimes*, October 2, 1964, 1; and Marlin

VanElderen, "The Anti-social Gospel," *Chimes*, October 1, 1965, 3. On InterVarsity, see letters to the editor in the May 1963 issue of *HIS* magazine; Ruth Lewis, "New Face at Alabama," *HIS*, May 1964, 11–13; Keith Hunt and Gladys Hunt, *For Christ and the University: The Story of InterVarsity Christian Fellowship* (Downers Grove, IL: InterVarsity Press, 1991), 306.

8. On international pressure, see David Howard, "Cartenega: Mirror for Missions," *HIS*, January 1968, 3. On black evangelicals, see Tom Skinner, *How Black Is the Gospel?* (Philadelphia: Lippincott, 1970), 69, 90; Mildred Mellors, "Reactions to Urbana," *Vanguard*, December 31, 1970, in folder 68:7: "Urbana 1961–1974," InterVarsity Collection, Billy Graham Center Archives. On Skinner in the new evangelical world, see Mrs. G. J. Griswold to Roswell Vaughan, May 19, 1971, in "Tom Skinner" folder, Archer Weniger Collection, Bob Jones University.

9. Even black evangelicals in the early civil rights movement emphasized the inequities of individual more than structural racism. See C. Herbert Oliver's *No Flesh Shall Glory* (Nutley, NJ: Presbyterian and Reformed Publishing, 1959). On the influence of civil rights and social scientific literature, see Don and Madelyn Powell, "We Stayed in the Inner City," *HIS*, November 1969, 18–19; *Post-American* bibliography in box VII7, folder "People's Christian Coalition, Trinity," Sojourners Collection, Wheaton College Archives and Special Collections (WCASC).

10. See Kent Walker, "Conditioned Patriotism," *Wheaton Record*, November 18, 1965, 3; Art Wassmer, "Does Traditional Review Leave ROTC Red-Faced?" *Wheaton Record*, May 4, 1967, 3; Jay Hakes, "Needed: Soph Action on Compulsory ROTC," *Wheaton Record*, May 6, 1965, 2; "Poll Exposes Student Views on ROTC Program Efficacy," *Wheaton Record*, April 29, 1965, 8; Rich Bard, "Campus Political Climate—a Radical Change?" *Wheaton Record*, April 5, 1968, 3; "Funeral March Highlights Moratorium Observance," *Wheaton Record*, November 21, 1969, 1; "ROTC Protest Goes Smoothly; Dr. Armerding Holds Front Campus Talk," *Wheaton Record*, May 14, 1971, 2; notes of Dan Reigle's February 16, 1968, speech in folder "Vietnam," Vertical File, WCASC.

11. Jim Bourgoine, "He Came, He Spoke, and We Were Conquered," *Wheaton Record*, February 22, 1974, 3.

12. For "long and bloody record," see Wallis, *Revive Us Again*, 52–53; Jill Shook, "Vietnam Today," *Right On*, July–August 1974. For "Uncle Sam," see "Reach Me," *Right On*, April 24, 1970, 2. A telling 1975 series in the *Post-American* retrospectively charted the political position the young evangelicals had staked in the late 1960s. The first article, by a professor at the evangelical Malone College, critiqued the conservative evangelical journal *Christianity Today* for its anti–civil rights and prowar positions. See John Oliver, "A Failure of Evangelical Conscience," *Post-American*, May 1975, 26–30. Its companion piece chastised the liberal mainline journal *Christian Century* for never understanding

"the depth of rage and anguish involved in those who broke with the mainstream of American politics because of Vietnam. The protests of the New Left were never taken seriously.... 'America is sick' it [the *Christian Century*] editorialized in 1967, but it never recognized that the end of the war might not restore its health." Even after the war, the *Post-American* observed, the *Century* remained "subdued but unchanged in its support of the American covenant." See Dale Suderman, "A Failure of Liberalism," *Post-American*, October–November 1975, 24.

13. Art Gish, *The New Left and Christian Radicalism* (Grand Rapids, MI: Eerdmans, 1971), 47, 66, 71. One of the more striking ironies of recent scholarship is that the historiography of a movement dedicated to ground-level participatory democracy has been dominated by the study of white, male, elite university students. But New Left impulses were nurtured by more than just Students for a Democratic Society and were located in more places than elite university campuses. Evangelical radicals also questioned "the unholy alliance" of capitalism, democracy, technology, and government bureaucracy. The activism of Jim Wallis, the Post-Americans, and other evangelical radicals suggests that boundaries established by scholars of the New Left might require expansion. For a fuller articulation of this point, see David R. Swartz, "The New Left and Evangelical Radicalism," *Journal for the Study of Radicalism* 3, no. 2 (Fall 2009): 51–80. For a similar critique, see Douglas Rossinow, *The Politics of Authenticity: Liberalism, Christianity, and the New Left in America* (New York: Columbia University Press, 1998).

14. On Explo, see Turner, *Bill Bright*, 138–46.

15. Perkins quoted in Charles Marsh, *The Beloved Community: How Faith Shapes Social Justice* (New York: Basic Books, 2005), 170–72. Wallis quoted in Allan C. Carlson, "Radical Evangelicals and Their Anticapitalist Crusade," *Gazette Telegraph*, November 8, 1981, 11AA.

16. Tom Skinner quoted in Bill Milliken, *So Long, Sweet Jesus* (Buffalo, NY: Prometheus Press, 1973), 12–13.

17. Dennis MacDonald, "Christian Transcendence: Dope or Hope," *Post-American*, Winter 1972, 8–9.

18. On simple living, see January 28, 1974, weekly memorandum of the CWLF and "Peoples Medical Handbook," box 2, "Jill Shook, Jack Sparks," Graduate Theological Union Archives; Arthur G. Gish, *Beyond the Rat Race* (Scottdale, PA: Herald Press, 1973); Doris Janzen Longacre, *More with Less* (Scottdale, PA: Herald Press, 1976); Doris Janzen Longacre, *Living More with Less* (Scottdale, PA: Herald Press, 1980); Ronald J. Sider, *Living More Simply* (Downers Grove, IL: InterVarsity Press, 1980). The *Post-American* and *Vanguard* carried monthly columns on recycling, preparing inexpensive but nutritious food, and fixing up homes. For "bondage of the economic bureaucracy," see review of Richard Goodwin's *The American Condition* by Jack Sparks on a peach-

colored leaflet in box 2, "Jill Shook, Jack Sparks," CWLF Collection, Graduate Theological Union Archives.

19. James Daane, "The War on Poverty Can Be Won," *Reformed Journal* 14, no. 4 (April 1964): 3; Edward A. Loucks, "Deciding How to Vote," *Other Side*, September–October 1972, 25; Richard Mouw, *Political Evangelism* (Grand Rapids, MI: Eerdmans, 1973); Jim Wallis, "The Issue of 1972," *Post-American*, Fall 1972, 2–3; Wes Michaelson, "Politics and Spirituality," *Post-American*, April 1974.

20. See, for example, David O. Moberg, *Inasmuch: Christian Social Responsibility in Twentieth-Century America* (Grand Rapids, MI: Eerdmans, 1965); Foy Valentine, *The Cross in the Marketplace* (Waco, TX: Word Books, 1966); Robert G. Clouse, Robert D. Linder, and Richard V. Pierard, *Protest and Politics: Christianity and Contemporary Affairs* (Greenwood, SC: Attic Press, 1968); Sherwood Wirt, *The Social Conscience of the Evangelical* (New York: Harper and Row, 1968); Vernon Grounds, *Evangelicalism and Social Responsibility* (Scottdale, PA: Herald Press, 1969); Carl F. H. Henry, *A Plea for Evangelical Demonstration* (Grand Rapids, MI: Baker Book House, 1971); David O. Moberg, *The Great Reversal: Evangelism versus Social Concern* (Philadelphia: Lippincott, 1972); Bob Goudzwaard, *A Christian Political Option* (Toronto: Wedge, 1972); Charles Y. Furness, *The Christian and Social Action* (Old Tappan, NJ: Fleming H. Revell, 1972); Robert G. Clouse, Robert D. Linder, and Richard V. Pierard, eds., *The Cross and the Flag* (Carol Stream, IL: Creation House, 1972); Wesley G. Pippert, *Faith at the Top* (Elgin, IL: David C. Cook, 1973); Robert D. Linder and Richard V. Pierard, *Politics: A Case for Christian Action* (Downers Grove, IL: InterVarsity Press, 1973); Paul B. Henry, *Politics for Evangelicals* (Valley Forge, PA: Judson Press, 1974); Stephen Wesley G. Pippert, *Memo for 1976: Some Political Options* (Downers Grove, IL: InterVarsity Press, 1974); William R. Coats, *God in Public: Political Theology beyond Niebuhr* (Grand Rapids, MI: Eerdmans, 1974); Richard J. Mouw, *Political Evangelism* (Grand Rapids, MI: Eerdmans, 1974); Ronald J. Sider, ed., *The Chicago Declaration* (Carol Stream, IL: Creation House, 1974).

21. On the formation of the EFM, see Ronald J. Sider, "A Short Unscientific Sketch of ESA's History," speech given at the Thirtieth Anniversary Celebration of Evangelicals for Social Action, August 24, 2003, 1, copy of manuscript in the Evangelicals for Social Action Archives, Palmer Theological Seminary, Wynnewood, PA (ESAA). For criticism of Nixon, see Clark Pinnock, "Election Reflections," *Post-American*, January–February 1973, 2–3. For McGovern's speech at Wheaton, October 11, 1972, see transcript, Evangelicals for McGovern Collection, ESAA.

22. Sider to Stephen Charles Mott, November 14, 1972, box 1, folder 4: Evangelicals for McGovern: Correspondence, Evangelicals for Social Action Collection, Billy Graham Center Archives, Wheaton, IL (ESAC).

23. Ron Sider, "An Historic Moment," in *The Chicago Declaration*, ed. Ron Sider (Carol Stream, IL: Creation House, 1974), 25, 29. Stentzel quoted in John Junkerman, "Voice of the Evangelical Left," *Madison Press Connection*, November 5, 1979, 7, copy in folder IV3—News Releases and *Post-American*, Sojourners Collection, WCASC.

24. Speech by M. VanElderen at Calvin Theological Seminary, December 5, 1974, folder 13: Thanksgiving Workshop, Evangelicals for Social Action (1974): Reportage; December 1974–January 1975; box 3, ESAC; Sider, "Historic Moment," 26–28.

25. Nancy Hardesty, "Reflections," in Sider, *Chicago Declaration*, 123; Sharon Gallagher, "Radical Evangelicalism: A Conference Report," 61–65, copy in "1973 Thanksgiving Workshop media" folder, ESAA; Nancy Hardesty and Letha Scanzoni, *All We're Meant to Be: A Biblical Approach to Women's Liberation* (Waco, TX: Word Books, 1975).

26. Sider, "Historic Moment," 27.

27. James Mathisen, "Evangelical Racism—A Goose in a Bottle?" *Moody Monthly*, July–August 1975, 12–13. On the Anabaptist-Calvinist dispute, see Jim Wallis, *Agenda for Biblical People: Gospel of a New Order* (New York: Harper and Row, 1976); Isaac C. Rottenberg, "The Shape of the Church's Social-Economic Witness," *Reformed Journal* 27 (May 1977): 16–19; Jim Wallis, "What Does Washington Have to Say to Grand Rapids?" *Sojourners*, July 1977, 3–4; Nicholas P. Wolterstorff, "How Does Grand Rapids Reply to Washington?" *Reformed Journal* 27 (October 1977): 10–14. On the rise of evangelical feminism, see Pamela Cochran, *Evangelical Feminism: A History* (New York: NYU Press, 2005). On the black new evangelicalism, see William H. Bentley, *The National Black Evangelical Association: Reflections on the Evolution of a Concept of Ministry* (Chicago: William H. Bentley, 1979).

28. For Evangelical Left criticism of Carter, see John A. Bernbaum and Steve Moore, "Should the U.S. Boycott Ugandan Coffee?" *HIS*, November 1978, 6–9; Bernard Zylstra, "Jimmy Carter Is the Issue," *Vanguard*, September–October 1980, 4. On the Religious Right's criticism of Carter, see Erling Jorstad, *Evangelicals in the White House: The Cultural Maturation of Born-Again Christianity, 1960–1981* (New York: E. Mellen Press, 1981), 150.

29. On the "evangelical jumbo-jet," see Jerry Falwell, *The Fundamentalist Phenomenon: The Resurgence of Conservative Christianity* (New York: Doubleday, 1981). On the Wallis-Bright feud, see Jim Wallis and Wes Michaelson, "The Plan to Save America: A Disclosure of an Alarming Political Initiative by the Evangelical Far Right," *Sojourners*, April 1976, 4–12; Turner, *Bill Bright*, 164–65. On the consistent prolife campaign, see "Magazine Is Pro-Life," *Chicago Tribune*, November 22, 1980, W18; Ron Sider, *Completely Pro-Life: Building a Consistent Stance* (Downers Grove, IL: InterVarsity Press, 1987).

30. On evangelical voting trends, see Stephen D. Johnson and Joseph B. Tamney, "The Christian Right and the 1980 Presidential Election," *Journal for the Scientific Study of Religion* 21, no. 2 (June 1982): 123–31; James K. Guth, "New Christian Right," in Liebman and Wuthnow, *New Christian Right*, 37; and Robert Booth Fowler, "The Failure of the Religious Right," in *No Longer Exiles: The Religious New Right in American Politics*, ed. Michael Cromartie (Washington, DC: Ethics and Public Policy Center, 1993), 57–74. For evangelical critiques of the Religious Right, see Charles W. Colson, *Born Again* (Old Tappan, NJ: Chosen Books, 1976); Cal Thomas and Ed Dobson, *Blinded by Might: Why the Religious Right Can't Save America* (Grand Rapids, MI: Zondervan, 1999); J. David Kuo, *Tempting Faith: An Inside Story of Political Seduction* (New York: Free Press, 2006); Amy Sullivan, *The Party Faithful: How and Why Democrats Are Closing the God Gap* (New York: Scribner, 2008).

Conclusion

How an Evangelical Won the Bancroft Prize

MARK NOLL

Shortly after Yale University Press in 2003 published George Marsden's compelling biography of Jonathan Edwards, the prizes began to roll in. In short order, this book won awards from the American Society of Church History, the Organization of American Historians, the Historical Society, and the group that picks an annual award in Christian biography. In 2004 the book was named co-winner of the Bancroft Prize from Columbia University, the most distinguished honor given to books published in American history; shortly thereafter the University of Louisville gave this same book the Grawemeyer Award in Religion, the nation's most distinguished honor for religious scholarship. Never before had a book by a self-identified evangelical Christian received this kind of recognition.

Marsden's biography did not, however, simply fall from the skies. It was, rather, only the most notable and widely recognized example of scholarship by evangelical historians that for nearly fifty years had been steadily increasing in academic quality, intellectual self-confidence, and public recognition. In 1957, the Nazarene scholar Timothy L. Smith had published a revision of his Harvard dissertation that was entitled *Revivalism and Social Reform in Mid-Nineteenth-Century America*.[1] Smith's work, which itself won several awards, can be viewed as beginning the process that led to the recognition of Marsden's biography almost a half century later.

Over that period of time, historical scholarship produced by self-consciously evangelical authors and encouraged by several networks either guided by evangelicals or friendly to evangelicals has come into its own. This chapter tries to say a little more about the contemporary situation for evangelical historians and evangelical historical scholarship before outlining in some detail the history of recent evangelical history writing in order to explore causes and reasons for the existence of serious scholarship done by evangelical historians. The primary intention, however, is not simply to present a history of historians for other historians. Instead, the purpose of this exercise is to highlight factors that might be pondered by professed Christian scholars in all fields of endeavor as they seek to honor God with the fruits of their academic labor. In particular, what this history of evangelical historians reveals for all who would practice Christian scholarship is that the process takes time, progress requires cooperative exertions at many levels, and success depends as much on God's providential direction as on the efforts made by the scholars themselves.

The current situation for evangelical historians is relatively good. The "relatively good" must be stressed in order to avoid deceptive triumphalism. We must, in other words, be realistic and not get carried away. Evangelicals do not by any stretch set the general agenda for professional historical scholarship in the United States; responsible evangelical interpretations of American and world history do not dominate academic or popular venues; academic evangelical historians have not done a particularly good job at communicating their work in the evangelical churches themselves; and evangelical historians have not made serious contributions to first-level theoretical discussions about the nature of historical knowledge. Comparatively speaking, evangelical historians have not done nearly as much to shape broader historical study as Christian philosophers have done to shape the modern study of philosophy.

Still, the record of evangelical historical scholarship is now reasonably strong. For some years, evangelical students have been regularly admitted into the nation's best PhD programs in history; some of these students are winning distinction by their superlative work (e.g., a recent Nevins Prize for the best dissertation in American history, a recent award by the Harvard History Department for that year's best dissertation);[2] Christian colleges and evangelical seminaries can draw on an increasing pool of well-trained history PhDs to staff their programs; a number of self-consciously evangelical historians are employed at research universities; a few evangelical historians occupy strategic positions in historical associations (e.g., Donald Yerxa of Eastern Nazarene University as the editor of *Historically Speaking*, a publication of the Historical Association); the Conference on Faith and History enrolls an increasing number of members who take part in its public meetings and support its publications; and some professional groups, like the American Society of Church History, have turned increasingly to evangelicals for leadership of their societies. In addition, books by evangelical historians—often, but not always, on evangelical subjects—now proliferate from the best university presses: Cambridge, Cornell, Harvard, North Carolina, Oxford, Princeton, Yale, and more. Less often, books by evangelical historians are even being published by widely recognized commercial presses. Some of these books, like Marsden's biography of Edwards, are winning considerable recognition and notable prizes. The picture for evangelical historians, in other words, is reasonably propitious.

How did this reasonably propitious situation come about? What in the recent past can be highlighted as the reasons or causes to explain why in 1950 there were virtually no professional evangelical historians known outside of narrow evangelical circles, while today there are many who testify to the recent surge in evangelical historical scholarship at all levels?

To explain what has happened I would like to isolate a number of events, forces, influences, and conditions that have created the current situation.

(1) The first was the general improvement in American economic life after World War II, which included an improved economic position for many evangelical families. Without the social mobility undergirded by increased economic opportunity and then the expansion of

American higher education, it is unlikely that evangelical academic life could have improved. Since the more sectarian evangelicals were concentrated in middle and lower-middle classes, the rising economic tide, and especially the GI Bill, made higher education possible for many who would otherwise not have had the chance. Rising aspirations for professional and social advancement probably played a disproportionately important role for evangelicals, in light of where they began after the Depression and World War II. Expanded opportunity is never by itself the key to stronger intellectual life, but stronger intellectual life for evangelicals would not have occurred had there not been an expanding economic base.

(2) It is a story that has now been told often, but the determination of a younger generation of fundamentalists in the 1930s and 1940s to push beyond the limits of fundamentalism is another important background factor for the history of evangelical historians. The leaders of what became known as "neoevangelicalism" were well-known figures who combined many roles as scholars, pastors, educators, and publishers. Their ranks included the theologian and editor Carl F. H. Henry, the theologian Bernard Ramm, the theologian and seminary president E. J. Carnell, the pastor-entrepreneur John Harold Ockenga, and many more from a broad range of denominations and regions. The long-lasting impact of their work was to reengage contemporary society, including intellectual life, with a traditional gospel. Their own efforts at seeking higher education, founding or strengthening evangelical institutions of higher learning, publishing serious-minded books, and encouraging others to take up cultural as well as directly spiritual vocations all helped push evangelical movements as a whole toward more responsible scholarship. The fact that many of the neoevangelical intelligentsia maintained close ties with the evangelist Billy Graham showed that they understood how important it was for advances in Christian thinking to be matched by continued promotion of distinctly spiritual goals. If the early neoevangelicals underestimated the difficulty in recovering responsible intellectual life, their work was nonetheless crucial for opening doors through which later generations could walk.

(3) For the future of evangelical history, however, it was critical that the historians did not follow closely in the train of the neoevangelical

innovators. The neoevangelical leaders were mostly theologians whose thinking moved most naturally to prioritize theological reasoning. By contrast, evangelical professional historians of the last two generations have chosen to let theology function in the background. To be sure, their subjects have often been related to the churches or church-connected issues. But they have generally treated events, people, and problems in the history of Christianity through broad-ranging research intended for general audiences rather than particular faith communities. This kind of history is aimed at audiences where theological or ideological convictions are looser rather than tighter, broad rather than specific, ecumenical rather than sectarian. In theological terms, this kind of history emphasizes more the secondary causes through which God governs the world than his primary and immediate moving of events.[3]

In short, recent evangelical history mostly takes for granted a practical treaty of peace with the intellectual conventions of the Enlightenment. Evangelical historians have mostly accommodated themselves to the focus on nature, this-worldly causes and effects, and universal human values that has characterized Western thought since the eighteenth century. Yet they are also easily distinguished from secular historians guided by non-Christian convictions. The evangelical historians do feature interpretations drawing on intellectual, economic, cultural, social, and political factors, but they do not reduce religious motives and practices to supposedly more real spheres of human existence. They likewise treat their subjects, both Christian and non-Christian, as creatures of dignity made in the image of God. While their published works are not overtly dogmatic or evangelistic, they are often easily perceived to reflect a Christian frame of reference. They let their Christian subjects speak for themselves; they interpret the factors that shape their subjects as penultimate rather than ultimate realities; and they acknowledge their own respect for (or even adherence to) Christian beliefs.

This kind of history can be called softly providential, in contrast to the sharp providentialism that is naturally prominent in most kinds of evangelical theology. Its practitioners often indicate that they are carrying on their historical work with procedures made possible by God and with conclusions describing a world in which God is an ever-present reality. But they do not require belief in God or in an evangelical bill of particulars as a prerequisite for engaging with their work.

One fortunate by-product of this broader approach to providence is that evangelical historians have by and large escaped the theological infighting that still prevails in many evangelical communities. Maybe we historians are just cowards at heart, but by choosing to write "natural history," even if it is a history in which Christian belief is an overarching reality, we have found it possible to write and teach primarily for insight and information, and less directly for conversion and ultimate commitment. The result, again, has been to open a space for fitting into the academy while keeping foundational Christian commitment alive.

(4) The nonconfrontational style that most evangelical historians have adopted has been effective in the broader history profession because professional history in America has been relatively tolerant, relatively nonideological, and relatively open. American historians of many kinds have often been ready to acknowledge the importance of religion in American history as well as the history of other world regions. The general historical profession has been less antagonistic toward scholarship on religious movements and scholarship emphasizing Christian values than have other disciplines in the American academy. So long as the historical scholarship is done well, with careful research and thoughtful presentation of evidence, there has been ample opportunity for evangelicals to work on subjects of religious interest. Perhaps because the history written by evangelicals has not been trying to make universal or metaphysical claims, it has been accepted without a great deal of controversy in the modern academy.

For their part, leaders of the historical profession have usually not looked kindly on the most radical or the most postmodern theories about knowledge, power, and the human person. As a result, the historical realism that most evangelical historians take for granted synchronizes fairly well with the epistemological standards that prevail in the profession as a whole.

(5) Another background factor that has made it easier for evangelical historians to make their way in the academy is the relative decline of mainline Protestant institutions and perspectives. So long as a large

and vibrant mainline establishment prevailed in private higher education and in American public space as a whole, there was not much room left over for fundamentalists, neoevangelicals, Pentecostals, holiness advocates, or other "sectarians" to promote their approaches to learning. Yet since the time of Reinhold Niebuhr, only a few mainstream Protestant voices, perspectives, or institutions have had a commanding presence. Instead, mainline educational ventures have sometimes drifted away from earlier Christian commitments, or they have suffered a loss of constituencies, or they have been preoccupied with divisive internal squabbles. The taken-for-granted centrality of mainline Protestants throughout much of American history no longer exists. As a consequence, evangelical historians have increasingly become the ones with something definite to say about the religious past and the bearing of that past on the present. And since religion remains an obviously important theme in all the world, as well as for history of almost every kind, evangelicals now perform at least some of the public functions that once were exercised by representatives of the mainline denominations.

(6) To this point I have spoken mostly about background conditions lying behind the emergence of a strong cadre of evangelical historians. The work of important evangelical forerunners or pioneers brings us closer to the active factors that promoted viable evangelical historiography. For this purpose, the most significant pathbreaking work was undertaken by the two scholars already mentioned, Timothy L. Smith and George Marsden.

Smith's Nazarene family provided a strong encouragement for higher education, which he pursued through his doctoral work under Arthur Schlesinger Sr. at Harvard. Smith's study of nineteenth-century revivalism as a socially progressive force greatly altered the standard picture that prevailed in the 1950s of religion as a bland, reactionary, or inherently conservative social force. On the basis of his book about nineteenth-century Protestantism, and then a steady stream of diligently researched articles and chapters, Smith was soon widely recognized as an important interpreter not only of holiness and Methodist movements but of women in American religion, of religious reform movements, and of religion in immigrant communities. Because of the high esteem in which his scholarship was held, Smith won an appointment at the University of Minnesota, and then at Johns Hopkins University. In those positions, and also through his works, Smith encouraged a variety of scholars, especially from holiness and Pentecostal backgrounds, and helped train many young evangelical historians who magnified his influence many times over. His own wide-ranging research, the high standards he maintained for historical writing, and his peripatetic lecturing combined to lend new visibility to evangelical questions and evangelical scholars in the American historical profession.

Smith, however, retained a distinctly Nazarene, or holiness, identity. While he readily volunteered to participate in generic evangelical enterprises, his own commitment to the Church of the Nazarene, which he served as a minister while carrying out his academic tasks, remained preeminent. George Marsden, who came along about a decade and a half after Timothy Smith and so was able to benefit from doors that Smith had opened, enjoyed a different self-identity. Although Marsden was a member of conservative Presbyterian and then Christian Reformed congregations, his primary identity from the start was generally evangelical. Perhaps it is fair to say that the breadth of Marsden's interests (a colonial Congregationalist, nineteenth-century Presbyterians, fundamentalism, Fuller Seminary, Christian scholarship) reflected a broader evangelical self-understanding in the way that Smith's stronger concentration on holiness themes and the Nazarene denomination reflected his self-understanding.

Marsden's doctoral work at Yale with Edmund Morgan and Sydney Ahlstrom was also significant. The fact that his Yale degree was in American studies, and that he studied with Ahlstrom as Ahlstrom was completing his wide-ranging history of religion in American life, may explain Marsden's sensitive attention to the cultural contexts of his subjects. It is noteworthy that he featured "culture" in the title of his second book, which indicated a desire for broad contextual understanding that was a prime goal of the early years of the American studies movement. Marsden's time at Yale also exposed him to the best American historians of his generation and helped him internalize the high standards for careful research and narrative verve that have marked his work from the publication of his doctoral dissertation in 1970 to his Edwards biography and beyond. That dissertation dealt creatively with a significant strand of nineteenth-century Presbyterian intellectual life as it developed in the churches and as it interacted with broader American society.[4] It was a book that did not have particularly broad popular appeal but that did alert many of Marsden's younger peers, including myself, that intellectual history on Christian themes and engaged with Christian questions could become a fruitful calling as well as an intellectually bracing contribution to the academy.

Then in 1980 Marsden published that second book, a major study with Oxford University Press entitled *Fundamentalism and American Culture, 1875–1925*. It was a prize-winning volume that began with research undertaken long before the resurgence of the New Christian Right but was published just as Jimmy Carter's born-again Baptist faith and Ronald Reagan's successful appeal to conservative Christians were making "fundamentalism" into a hot topic of public attention. This book was important, first, for laying out sympathetically, but also with critical acumen, the deep backgrounds of conservative Protestant movements that had seemed to disappear in the 1930s but that in reality had only gone underground for regrouping and renewal. But *Fundamentalism and American Culture* was also important as an example of a well-researched and carefully argued book from a Christian perspective about a Christian subject. It showed other academic historians and other university presses how rewarding it could be to study such subjects and write such books. In the wake of its appearance the revolution in scholarly publishing began that has opened many doors for many evangelical scholars and that seems to open more and more every year.

Like Timothy Smith, Marsden amplified the effects of his example, first by teaching undergraduates—at Calvin College—several of whom have themselves become prominent historians—and then by guiding PhD students at Duke University and the University of Notre Dame. Visiting appointments at the University of California at Berkeley and the Harvard Divinity School amplified his influence. Also like Smith, Marsden, through his wide-ranging writing projects and many speaking engagements, has served as a beacon for younger evangelicals who aspire to make a difference with their chosen subjects as Marsden has done with his.

The labors of Timothy Smith and George Marsden have been significant because they were of such intrinsically high quality, because these two men did such a good job at illuminating the subjects they chose to study, because they worked so selflessly as mentors for their own students, and because they offered so much encouragement to so many younger scholars who were not personally their students. Evangelical history would doubtless have matured to some degree without the presence of Smith and Marsden, but their work made a very great difference in speeding up the process by which evangelical historians moved from the margins of the academy to become substantial contributors and gain some recognition.

(7) But of course leading scholars like Timothy Smith and George Marsden were never alone. Along with the general resurgence of evangelical energy after the Second World War came a resurgence of evangelical higher education. Older institutions like Calvin College and Goshen College, which had been isolated from the intellectual marketplace by their immigrant status; Gordon College and Wheaton College, which had been isolated by their fundamentalist status; and Asbury College and Eastern Nazarene University, which had pursued holiness objectives almost entirely foreign to the broader academy—these schools and many others blossomed in the 1960s and the following decades as vibrant institutions of higher learning. To be sure, they were small, they were all underfunded to one degree or another, and for the most part they were not able to sponsor a great deal of first-level research. Nevertheless, they excelled at preparing graduates for honorable service in society, advanced professional education, and—significantly—graduate study in the arts and humanities.

A related series of developments transformed a number of evangelical seminaries from tiny, isolated outposts into some of the country's largest and most vibrant centers of theological education. Usually the graduates of Asbury, Fuller, Gordon-Conwell, Trinity, Westminster, and other evangelical seminaries have pursued ministerial or theological careers. But more than a handful of students trained at such institutions have also caught the bug for historical study and joined the growing numbers from the rejuvenated Christian colleges and universities who pursue professional study in history.

(8) An important supplement to rejuvenated Christian colleges and evangelical seminaries has been provided by the striking growth of Christian ministries on secular campuses. At such campuses the number of openly Christian faculty has been increasing steadily, as has the number of Christian study centers where students find friendship, spiritual support, and sometimes intellectual stimulation. Especially visible since the 1960s have been the many campus ministries that encourage evangelical spiritual life. Campus Crusade for Christ, the Navigators, and several denominational ministries have been effective in nurturing evangelical students on their campuses. With its major commitment to its graduate and faculty ministry, InterVarsity Christian Fellowship has been especially important for providing Christian nurture and intellectual networks for students and teachers who might otherwise feel isolated as believing scholars.

(9) When the Christian colleges, evangelical seminaries, and campus parachurch ministries generated increasing numbers of students interested in professional careers in history, many of them found a relatively receptive welcome at PhD-granting universities. Sometimes evangelicals like Timothy Smith and George Marsden provided the instruction at these universities. More often, aspiring evangelical historians studied with scholars who were nonevangelical but were willing to work with them and able to help them develop their own interests. Thus numerous evangelical students did their graduate work with William Hutchison at Harvard, Sydney Ahlstrom at Yale, Martin Marty at Chicago, and several more at other institutions. Hutchison, Ahlstrom, and Marty sustained many of the values that had energized the twentieth century's pioneering church historians, preeminently William Warren Sweet of the University of Chicago, whose obvious affection for his Kansas Methodist roots preserved considerable space for exploring evangelical aspects that had once been prominent among mainline Protestants. From such accommodating scholars, aspiring evangelical historians received solid grounding as professional historians, but they also learned something about how to navigate as Christian believers in worlds of higher learning more generally. The availability of several reasonably attentive mentors at a number of graduate schools gave younger evangelical historians the academic launch they needed to function as historians themselves.

(10) As evangelical movements moved beyond fundamentalism and sought to engage the broader culture, they still faced the challenge of articulating Christian motives and Christian understandings for their academic tasks. In this effort, different evangelical traditions provided various answers, but some of the most influential assistance came from the theological tradition associated with Abraham Kuyper and the Christian Reformed Church. Kuyper was the Dutch pastor, newspaper editor, theologian, educator, politician, and general whirlwind of activity who in the late nineteenth century led an important conservative movement in the Reformed Church of his native Holland and also eventually served a term as prime minister of the Netherlands. Kuyper was strongly shaped by pietist movements that shared some things with American revivalism, but he also promoted a revived Calvinist theology that provided much encouragement for academic activity. The key was balancing two theological principles. One he called "the antithesis," which stressed the clear separation between anything that was of Christ and everything that was of the world. The other principle he called "common grace," which stressed God's general providential blessing that allowed Christian believers to make full use of learning, art, culture, politics, and much else from the world at large. In a famous address at the opening of the Free University of Amsterdam in 1880 Kuyper laid out the agenda for his new institution of higher learning by stating, "There is not a square inch in the whole domain of our human existence over which Christ, who is Sovereign of *all*, does not cry 'Mine.'"[5]

Kuyper's theology, combining as it did a strongly evangelical sense of separation from the world with a strongly proprietary sense of engagement with the world, became especially important in the reawakening of American evangelical intellectual life. The Kuyperian position was maintained in varying degrees of strictness by scholars from Calvin College, but it was communicated more widely as scholars associated with Calvin—especially George Marsden, Richard Mouw, Nicholas Wolterstorff, and Alvin Plantinga—showed the way as leaders of the evangelical intellectual resurgence. The general position of confidence in Christ's saving work combined with confidence in Christ's rule over the world could be matched in general terms by theological emphases in other evangelical traditions. The theology of Abraham Kuyper became especially important for encouraging evangelical historians, however, because it led the way out of fundamentalist disengagement toward Christian engagement with scholarship.

(11) Just as important as any one specific theological influence was a broader willingness of evangelicals from widely different backgrounds to work with each other on projects of mutual historical interest. For that labor, yet another foreign influence was important, this time from the Anglican literary scholar C. S. Lewis. Lewis's winsome presentation of "Mere Christianity" announced a program for which many American evangelicals seemed to be waiting.[6] Lewis's articulation of a basic Christian faith that emphasized more what traditional Christians held in common than where they differed was particularly welcomed in the circles that contributed most to the nurture of evangelical historians. My own case might not be entirely representative, but the fact that in working on tasks of Christian history I've been materially assisted by conservative Presbyterians and pacifist Mennonites, Pentecostals and Baptists, members of the Salvation Army and the Seventh-day Adventist Church, and many more suggests something of the contribution that a pan-Christian evangelicalism has made to the efforts of evangelical historians.

(12) As much as developments within the evangelical world have been essential for the rise of evangelical historians, so also has much help been required from the outside. In particular, a great deal of financial assistance from interested philanthropies has been critical for evangelical historical scholarship. Funds from these philanthropies—especially the Lilly Endowment and the Pew Charitable Trusts—have bought time, facilitated meetings, nurtured connections, supported publications, encouraged younger scholars, and stimulated interest in new subjects of inquiry.

For philanthropy to work, however, it has been necessary for two factors to come into play. First has been the funding itself, which derives from the confidence at the foundations that projects organized by evangelicals could make a significant contribution. Second has been wisdom in organizing, directing, and finishing the projects for which funding is secured. Of particular note in these activities was the leadership for many years of Nathan Hatch and Michael Hamilton at the University of

Notre Dame, who in league with Joel Carpenter at the Pew Charitable Trusts mounted a series of projects designed to help evangelical scholars at all levels from undergraduates to senior researchers. The number of academic careers these projects helped launch and the number of scholarly works they helped finish made this program the single most important stimulus ever seen in American history for promoting better Christian thinking among evangelicals. In the Notre Dame programs and many less ambitious efforts, evangelical historians were in the forefront of those who benefited.

(13) Another important feature of recent historical practice has been the broad and fruitful networks on which evangelicals could draw. Friendly relations have existed ecclesiastically, with evangelicals of many types working with each other, with representatives of mainline churches, increasingly with Catholics, and often also with scholars of no known religious commitments. The relationships have also been international, with especially fruitful connections among Canadians, Britons, and Americans, but with networks drawing in evangelical historians, at least on some projects, from Australia, New Zealand, South Africa, the Netherlands, France, and even further afield. Organizations like the Conference on Faith and History have played a decisive role in building these networks, which often begin in fellowship and end in scholarly activity. Additional stimulus for productive cooperation has come from a number of ad hoc projects, such as those sponsored by the Institute for the Study of American Evangelicals at Wheaton College, Gordon College's Center for Faith and Inquiry, and similar centers at several other institutions. Historians have been much enriched by the breadth and depth of these networks.

(14) A last factor returns to background conditions that are not in the control of evangelicals themselves. The emergence of conservative religion as a political force in American public life has certainly involved complications for all evangelicals, but it has also created unusual opportunities. Publishers have put out the welcome mat not only because they have recognized good work but also because evangelical historians are the ones best positioned to provide information and perspective on religious movements that have become important in contemporary

American political life. If American politics should turn away from its recent engagement with religiously charged issues, the open door for evangelical historians may begin to swing in the other direction.

If these fourteen factors do in fact identify some of the events, conditions, and people leading to a relatively strong position for evangelical history, the broader question then arises as to what this history of historians offers for Christian scholars who are not historians.

The first and most obvious is to note that the development of Christian scholarship takes time. The pioneering work of Timothy Smith in the 1950s and of George Marsden in the 1960s, along with the intellectual quickening of Christian colleges, evangelical seminaries, and parachurch campus ministries, eventually produced a numerous cohort of active evangelical historians. But it did not happen overnight, it did not happen as a result of the efforts of any one organization, and it did not transform the university world all of a sudden.

An even longer time frame was involved for the rise of distinctly Christian philosophy in the American academy.[7] Immigrant Protestant scholars providing instruction to handfuls of students in non-English languages was taking place more than a century ago. At the same time Roman Catholics were promoting neo-Scholastic Thomism in institutions that almost no one in the broader world of American academia attended to at all. This situation continued for decades until—after the Second World War, after the Second Vatican Council, and after weaknesses of secular philosophies became more apparent—a vibrant network of Christian philosophers began to make its mark. As with the historians, this process involved distinguished forerunners, active journals, and a little help from funding agencies. But Christian philosophy as a recognized academic enterprise was the result of much faithful, unacknowledged work in a number of out-of-the-way institutions for a long time.

Similarly, for evangelical historians it took several decades of faithful, unnoticed, consistent effort before a critical mass was reached. Christians in other fields who want something similar to happen might take to heart injunctions arising from the history of historians: get to work right now, but be prepared to be patient.

A second observation is that patient, diligent, conscientious, and even exemplary Christian scholarship may not make a noticeable impact unless times and conditions in the broader world are propitious. *Christian scholarship* is an ambiguous term, but whether as sympathetic attention to Christian populations and themes, academic approaches self-consciously guided by overtly theological principles, or efforts to answer normative questions from believing perspectives, for many decades after World War II there was not much of it in American intellectual life. That intellectual situation has, however, changed. Recognizable evangelical history, as an instance, emerged at a time of faltering confidence in the historical profession as a whole. General confidence in the grand narrative of democratic progress, American innocence, and secular advance was severely shaken by the traumas of the 1960s that included the civil rights movement, the Vietnam War, and the rise of feminism. As that confidence faltered, something approaching a critical mass of evangelical historians was at hand to take advantage of uncertainties in how to frame major questions of good and evil in the American past. Later, when politics became culture wars, and culture wars became religious, there was a sudden demand for reliable interpretations of the religious groups and religious issues that were now important in the body politic. Again, a cadre of well-trained evangelical historians was at hand to provide some historical perspective for present concerns. Service rendered for that cause, in turn, opened up further opportunities for other evangelical historians to disseminate their research and to express their perspectives on other matters not so obviously caught up in contemporary culture wars.

The word for evangelical scholars in disciplines other than history might be phrased as "Work hard, but don't hold your breath." The presence of a critical mass of active Christian scholars and the desire to do academic work with skill unto God are certainly preconditions for full-scale Christian learning. But they are not by themselves sufficient. Timing, over which only God is sovereign, plays a critical role as well.

A final lesson that others may take from this brief history of evangelical historians concerns missiological principles as applied to the intellectual domain. The success of works like Timothy Smith's *Revivalism and Social Reform*, George Marsden's biography of Jonathan Edwards, and now many other less noteworthy but no less serious works is not an accident. Such works succeed, at least in part, because they have embodied biblical wisdom—for example, about the mixed character of human nature as profoundly good and profoundly evil, or the possibility of hope in the darkest regions of despair, or the humbling realization that even the most extensive human understanding cannot comprehend the ultimate mystery of the universe. But biblical wisdom, unless it is adapted to the shape of a particular culture, remains chimerical. The way Smith, Marsden, and others of the same ilk have done their work as believers is to treat Christian subjects as first-order concerns but to offer their historical treatments in the conventional terms of the modern academy. They do not pretend to write as though they were inspired authors of scripture who can interpret worldly events as episodes in the history of salvation. Evangelical historians do believe in the history of salvation, but that belief functions as a background framing for work researched and narrated in accordance with conventional historical practice. This approach takes for granted the cultural situation of the modern West, where believers are called to live in a world defined by the intellectual agenda of the Enlightenment while not allowing themselves to be captured by that world. And it can be described as a missiological approach, as Christian insights are communicated in accord with the conventions of a specific cultural environment. The work of Smith, Marsden, and others of their sort exemplifies the dual character of Christian existence suggested by the missiologist Andrew Walls, who has described Christianity as a force adapting to the forms of culture, even as it calls every culture to repentance and an awareness of the universality of Christianity.[8] Translating this missiological insight into modern historical terms means paying special attention to the records of churches, Christian believers, and Christian enterprises, but also studying them with the conventions that general revelation has supplied to the culture as a whole.

This approach to historical practice tries to balance Abraham Kuyper's principles of antithesis and common grace. Holding to the antithesis preserves Christian integrity; holding to common grace makes possible participation in the historical profession at large. The balance may seem too religious for secularists and too worldly for some believers. But it is a balance that has served evangelical historians well.

The last word is to remind all who labor in Christian academic life about the great privileges and significant responsibilities of our calling. Both privilege and responsibility stem from recognizing that the source of our academic vocations is the same source that makes possible all Christian exertions. Believers worship the one who, in the words of the Apostle Paul from Colossians, chapter 1, "is the image of the invisible God, the first born of all creation"; the one "in whom all things in heaven and earth were created"; the one "for" whom all things were created; and the one "who is before all things and in [whom] all things hold together." The Christ in whom we have redemption is the Christ who upholds all things, "whether thrones or dominions or rulers or powers"—that is, the very things that historians and other academics devote their lives to studying. Whatever the stage of development or recognition in any particular field of endeavor, believers may rest assured that the calling of Christian learning is a worthy calling, because it originates in Christ and finds its culmination in him.

NOTES

An earlier version of this chapter was presented at Indiana Wesleyan University on March 27, 2008, and is revised here with the permission of Jerry Pattengale and Indiana Wesleyan University.

1. The original publication was by Abingdon (New York); it was subsequently republished in an expanded version as *Revivalism and Social Reform: American Protestantism on the Eve of the Civil War* (Baltimore: Johns Hopkins University Press, 1980).

2. Those books have now been published as Darren Dochuk, *From Bible Belt to Sunbelt: Plain-Folk Religion, Grassroots Politics, and the Rise of Evangelical Conservatism* (New York: Norton, 2011); and Matthew Lundin, *Paper Memory: A Sixteenth-Century Townsman Writes His World* (Cambridge, MA: Harvard University Press, 2012).

3. The suggestions in the next paragraphs are expanded in Mark A. Noll, *Jesus Christ and the Life of the Mind* (Grand Rapids, MI: Eerdmans, 2011), ch. 5, "Christology: A Key to Understanding History."

4. George Marsden, *The Evangelical Mind and the New School Presbyterian Experience: A Case Study of Thought and Theology in Nineteenth-Century America* (New Haven, CT: Yale University Press, 1970).

5. Abraham Kuyper, "Sphere Sovereignty (1880)," in *Abraham Kuyper: A Centennial Reader*, ed. James D. Bratt (Grand Rapids, MI: Eerdmans, 1998), 488.

6. For an appreciation, see Mark Noll, "C. S. Lewis's 'Mere Christianity' (the Book and the Ideal) at the Start of the Twenty-First Century," *Seven* 19 (2002): 31–44.

7. This paragraph summarizes Mark A. Noll, "History: Made and Making" (on Al Plantinga's retirement), *Center for Philosophy of Religion Newsletter*, Spring 2011, 2–4.

8. See Andrew F. Walls, *The Missionary Movement in Christian History* (Maryknoll, NY: Orbis, 1996) and *The Cross-Cultural Process in Christian History* (Maryknoll, NY: Orbis, 2002).

APPENDIX

George Marsden's Doctoral Students and Their Dissertations

Bademan, Bryan. "Contesting the Evangelical Age: Protestant Challenges to Religious Subjectivity in Antebellum America." PhD diss., University of Notre Dame, 2004.

Bergler, Thomas E. "Winning America: Christian Youth Groups and the Middle-Class Culture of Crisis, 1930–1965." PhD diss., University of Notre Dame, 2000.

Brodrecht, Grant R. "Our Country: Northern Evangelicals and the Union during the Civil War and Reconstruction." PhD diss., University of Notre Dame, 2008.

Butler (Bass), Diana Hochstedt. "Standing against the Whirlwind: The Evangelical Party in the 19th-Century Protestant Episcopal Church." PhD diss., Duke University, 1991.

Case, Jay Riley. "Conversion, Civilization and Cultures in the Evangelical Missionary Mind, 1814–1906." PhD diss., University of Notre Dame, 1999.

Conkin, Jeffrey Bain. "Religious Practices in Nineteenth-Century Louisville, Kentucky." PhD diss., University of Notre Dame (in progress).

Den Hartog, Jonathan J. "'Patriotism and Piety': Orthodox Religion and Federalist Political Culture." PhD diss., University of Notre Dame, 2006.

Dochuk, Darren. "From Bible Belt to Sun Belt: Plain Folk Religion, Grassroots Politics, and the Southernization of Southern California." PhD diss., University of Notre Dame, 2005.

Du Mez, Kristin Kobes. "The Forgotten Woman's Bible: Katharine Bushnell, Lee Anna Starr, Madeline Southard, and the Construction of a Woman-Centered Protestantism in America, 1870–1930." PhD diss., University of Notre Dame, 2004.

Flipse, Scott E. "Bearing the Cross of Vietnam: Humanitarianism, Religion, and the American Commitment to South Vietnam, 1952–1975." PhD diss., University of Notre Dame, 2003.

Gloege, Timothy E. W. "Consumed: Reuben A. Torrey and the Construction of Corporate Fundamentalism." PhD diss., University of Notre Dame, 2007.

Gottwig, Danielle Du Bois. "Before the Culture Wars: Conservative Protestants and the Family, 1920–1970." PhD diss., University of Notre Dame (in progress).

Grow, Matthew J. "'Liberty to the Downtrodden': Thomas L. Kane, Romantic Reformer." PhD diss., University of Notre Dame, 2006.

Hamilton, Michael S. "The Fundamentalist Harvard: Wheaton College and the Continuing Vitality of American Evangelicalism, 1919–1965." PhD diss., University of Notre Dame, 1994. Nathan O. Hatch, adviser.

Jordan, Frederick W. "Between Heaven and Harvard: Protestant Faith and the American Boarding School Experience, 1778–1940." PhD diss., University of Notre Dame, 2004.

Kidd, Thomas Saunders. "From Puritan to Evangelical: Changing Culture in New England, 1689–1740." PhD diss., University of Notre Dame, 2001.

Long, Kathryn. "The Revival of 1857–58: The Power of Interpretation." PhD diss., Duke University, 1993.

Longfield, Bradley. "The Presbyterian Controversy, 1922–1936: Christianity, Culture, and Ecclesiastical Conflict." PhD diss., Duke University, 1988.

Miglio, Sarah. "Civilizing the World: Practical Christianity from Chicago to the Middle East, 1890–1925." PhD diss., University of Notre Dame, 2012.

Nolt, Steven M. "German Faith, American Faithful: Religion and Ethnicity in the Early American Republic." PhD diss., University of Notre Dame, 1998.

Ostrander, Richard. "The Life of Prayer in a World of Science: Protestants, Prayer, and American Culture, 1870–1930." PhD diss., University of Notre Dame, 1996.

Peterson, Kurt W. "Constructing the Covenant: The Evangelical Covenant Church and Twentieth-Century American Religious Culture, 1920–1970." PhD diss., University of Notre Dame, 2003.

Scott, David Hill. "From Boston to the Baltic: New England, Encyclopedics, and the Hartlib Circle." PhD diss., University of Notre Dame, 2003.

Svelmoe, William Lawrence. "A New Vision for Missions: William Cameron Townsend in Guatemala and Mexico: 1917–1945." PhD diss., University of Notre Dame, 2001.

Swartz, David R. "Left Behind: The Evangelical Left and the Limits of Evangelical Politics, 1965–1988." PhD diss., University of Notre Dame, 2008.

Turner, John G. "Selling Jesus to Modern America: Campus Crusade for Christ, Evangelical Culture, and Conservative Politics." PhD diss., University of Notre Dame, 2005.

Van Dyken, Tamara J. "Singing the Gospel: Evangelical Hymnody, Popular Religion, and American Culture, 1870–1940." PhD diss., University of Notre Dame, 2008.

Wallace, Peter J. "'The Bond of Union': The Old School Presbyterian Church and the American Nation, 1837–1861." PhD diss., University of Notre Dame, 2004. James Turner, adviser.

Wigger, John H. "Taking Heaven by Storm: Methodism and the Popularization of American Christianity, 1770–1820." PhD diss., University of Notre Dame, 1994. Nathan O. Hatch, adviser.

SELECTED BIBLIOGRAPHY OF GEORGE MARSDEN'S WORKS

BOOKS

The Evangelical Mind and the New School Presbyterian Experience: A Case Study of Thought and Theology in Nineteenth-Century America. New Haven, CT: Yale University Press, 1970. New ed., Eugene, OR: Wipf and Stock, 2003.

A Christian View of History? Edited with Frank Roberts. Grand Rapids, MI: Eerdmans, 1975.

Fundamentalism and American Culture: The Shaping of Twentieth-Century Evangelicalism, 1870–1925. New York: Oxford University Press, 1980. New ed., New York: Oxford University Press, 2006.

Eerdmans Handbook to the History of Christianity in America. Edited with Mark A. Noll et al. Grand Rapids, MI: Eerdmans, 1983.

The Search for Christian America. Coauthored with Mark A. Noll and Nathan O. Hatch. Westchester, IL: Crossway Books, 1983. Rev. ed., Colorado Springs: Helmers and Howard, 1989.

Evangelicalism and Modern America. Edited. Grand Rapids, MI: Eerdmans, 1984.

Reforming Fundamentalism: Fuller Seminary and the New Evangelicalism. Grand Rapids, MI: Eerdmans, 1987.

Religion and American Culture. Harcourt Brace Jovanovich, 1990. 2nd ed. New York: Harcourt College Publishers [now Wadsworth], 2000.

Understanding Fundamentalism and Evangelicalism. Grand Rapids, MI: Eerdmans, 1991.

The Secularization of the Academy. Edited with Bradley J. Longfield. New York: Oxford University Press, 1992.

The Soul of the American University. New York: Oxford University Press, 1994.

The Outrageous Idea of Christian Scholarship. New York: Oxford University Press, 1997.

Jonathan Edwards: A Life. New Haven, CT: Yale University Press, 2003.
A Short Life of Jonathan Edwards. Grand Rapids, MI: Eerdmans, 2008.
The Twilight of the American Enlightenment: The 1950s and the Crisis of Liberal Belief. New York: Basic Books, 2014.

BOOKLETS

The American Revolution. Christian Perspectives on History Series. Grand Rapids, MI: National Union of Christian Schools, 1973.
The Evangelical Task in the Modern University. Theology in the University Series. Pittsburgh, PA: Association of Theological Schools, 1995.

BOOK CHAPTERS

"A Christian Perspective on the Teaching of History." In *A Christian View of History?*, edited by George Marsden and Frank Roberts. Grand Rapids, MI: Eerdmans, 1975.
"From Fundamentalism to Evangelicalism: A Historical Analysis." In *The Evangelicals*, edited by David F. Wells and John D. Woodbridge. Nashville, TN: Abingdon, 1975.
"The American Revolution: Partisanship, 'Just Wars,' and Crusades." In *The Wars of America: Christian Views*, edited by R. A. Wells. Grand Rapids, MI: Eerdmans, 1982.
"America's 'Christian' Origins: Puritan New England as a Case Study." In *John Calvin: His Influence in the Western World*, edited by W. S. Reid. Grand Rapids, MI: Zondervan, 1982.
"Everyone One's Own Interpreter? The Bible, Science, and Authority in Mid-Nineteenth-Century America." In *The Bible in America*, edited by Nathan O. Hatch and Mark A. Noll. New York: Oxford University Press, 1982.
"The Era of Crisis: From Christendom to Pluralism" [six chapters]. In *Eerdmans' Handbook to Christianity in America*, edited by Mark A. Noll et al. Grand Rapids, MI: Eerdmans, 1983.
"Preachers of Paradox: The Religious New Right in Historical Perspective." In *Religion and America: Spirituality in a Secular Age*, edited by Mary Douglas and Steven M. Tipton. Boston: Beacon Press, 1983.

"Understanding Fundamentalist Views of Society." In *Reformed Faith and Politics*, edited by Ronald H. Stone. Washington, DC: University Press of America, 1983.

"Understanding Fundamentalist Views of Science." In *Science and Creationism*, edited by Ashley Montagu. New York: Oxford University Press, 1983.

"The Collapse of American Evangelical Academia." In *Faith and Rationality*, edited by Alvin Plantinga and Nicholas Wolterstorff. Notre Dame, IN: University of Notre Dame Press, 1984. Reprinted in *Reckoning with the Past: Historical Essays on American Evangelicalism from the Institute for the Study of American Evangelicals*, edited by D. G. Hart (Grand Rapids, MI: Baker Books, 1995), 221–66.

"Common Sense and the Spiritual Vision of History." In *History and Historical Understanding*, edited by C. T. McIntire and R. A. Wells. Grand Rapids, MI: Eerdmans, 1984. Also published as "The Spiritual Vision of History," *Fides et Historia* (Fall 1981).

"The Evangelical Denomination." In *Evangelicalism and Modern America*, edited by George Marsden. Grand Rapids, MI: Eerdmans, 1984. Reprinted in *Piety and Politics: Evangelicals and Fundamentalists Confront the World*, edited by Richard J. Neuhaus and Michael Cromartie (Washington, DC: Ethics and Public Policy Center, 1987).

"Evangelicals, History, and Modernity." In *Evangelicalism and Modern America*, edited by George Marsden. Grand Rapids, MI: Eerdmans, 1984.

"Understanding Fundamentalist Views of Science." In *Science and Creationism*, edited by Ashley Montagu. New York: Oxford University Press, 1984.

"Reformed and American." In *Reformed Theology in America: A History of Its Modern Development*, edited by David F. Wells. Grand Rapids, MI: Eerdmans, 1985.

"Are Secularists the Threat? Is Religion the Solution?" In *Unsecular America*, edited by R. J. Neuhaus. Grand Rapids, MI: Eerdmans, 1986. Also published in *This World* 11 (Spring/Summer 1985) as "Secularism and the Public Square." Reprinted in *The Best of This World*, edited by Michael A. Scully (Lanham, MD: University Press of America, 1986).

"A Case of the Excluded Middle: Creation vs. Evolution in America." In *Uncivil Religion: Interreligious Hostility in America*, edited by Robert W. Bellah and Frederick E. Greenspahn. New York: Crossroad, 1987. (Expansion of article from *Nature*, listed below.)

"The Evangelical Denomination." In *Piety and Politics*, edited by Richard John Neuhaus and Michael Cromartie. Washington, DC: Ethics and Public Policy Center, 1987.

"Why No Major Evangelical University? The Loss and Recovery of Evangelical Advanced Scholarship." In *Making Higher Education Christian: The History and Mission of Evangelical Colleges in America*, edited by Joel A. Carpenter and Kenneth W. Shipps. Grand Rapids, MI: Christian University Press, 1987.

Introduction to *The Fundamentals* (1910–15), edited by Joel A. Carpenter. Fundamentalism in American Religion, 1880–1950. New York: Garland, 1988.

"Reply to William Lee Miller, 'Religion and the Constitution.'" In *Religion and the Public Good*, edited by William L. Miller. Macon, GA: Mercer University Press, 1988.

"Evangelicals and the Scientific Culture: An Overview." In *Religion and Twentieth-Century American Intellectual Life*, edited by Michael J. Lacey. Cambridge: Cambridge University Press, 1989.

"Religion and Politics in America: In Search of a Consensus." In *Religion and American Politics*, edited by Mark A. Noll. New York: Oxford University Press, 1989.

"Unity and Diversity in the Evangelical Resurgence." In *Altered Landscapes: Christianity in America, 1935–1985*, edited by David W. Lotz, Donald W. Shriver Jr., and John F. Wilson. Grand Rapids, MI: Eerdmans, 1989.

"Afterword: Religion, Politics, and the Search for an American Consensus." In *Religion and American Politics*, edited by Mark A. Noll and Luke E. Harlow. New York: Oxford University Press, 1990.

"Defining American Fundamentalism." In *The Fundamentalist Phenomenon*, edited by Norman J. Cohen. Grand Rapids, MI: Eerdmans, 1990.

"Fundamentalism and American Evangelicalism." In *The Variety of American Evangelicalism*, edited by Donald W. Dayton and Robert K. Johnston. Knoxville: University of Tennessee Press, 1991.

"The Soul of the American University." In *The Secularization of the Academy*, edited by Bradley J. Longfield. New York: Oxford University Press, 1992.

"Contemporary American Evangelicalism." In *Southern Baptists and American Evangelicals: The Conversation Continues*, edited by David S. Dockery. Nashville, TN: Boardman and Holman, 1993.

"Fundamentalism as an American Phenomenon: A Comparison with English Evangelicalism." In *Fundamentalism and Evangelicalism*, edited by Martin E. Marty. Munich: K. G. Saur, 1993.

"The Religious Right: A Historical Overview." In *No Longer Exiles: The Religious New Right in American Politics*, edited by Michael Cromartie. Washington, DC: Ethics and Public Policy Center, 1993.

"What Can Catholic Universities Learn from Protestant Examples?" In *The Challenge and Promise of a Catholic University*, edited by Theodore M. Hesburgh, C.S.C. Notre Dame, IN: University of Notre Dame Press, 1994.

"By Primitivism Possessed: How Useful Is the Concept, 'Primitivism,' for Understanding American Fundamentalism." In *The Primitive Church in the Modern World*, edited by Richard T. Hughes. Urbana: University of Illinois Press, 1995.

"Fundamentalism as an American Phenomenon." In *Reckoning with the Past*, edited by D. G. Hart. Grand Rapids, MI: Baker House, 1995.

"Theology and the University: Newman's Ideas and Current Realities." In *The Idea of a University*, edited by Frank M. Turner. Rethinking the Western Tradition. New Haven, CT: Yale University Press, 1996.

"Christian Advocacy and the Rules of the Academic Game." In *Religious Advocacy and American History*, edited by Bruce Kuklick and D. G. Hart. Grand Rapids, MI: Eerdmans, 1997.

"Newman, Theology and the Contemporary University." In *Rethinking the Future of the University*, edited by David Lyle Jeffrey and Dominic Manganiello. Ottawa: University of Ottawa Press, 1998.

"What Difference Might Christian Perspectives Make?" In *History and the Christian Historian*, edited by Ronald A. Wells. Grand Rapids, MI: Eerdmans, 1998.

"Matteo Ricci and the Prodigal Culture." In *A Catholic Modernity: Charles Taylor's Marianist Award Lecture*, edited by James L. Heft, S.M. New York: Oxford University Press, 1999.

"The Meaning of Science for Christians: A New Dialogue on Olympus." In *Evangelicals and Science in Historical Perspective*, edited by David N. Livingstone, D. G. Hart, and Mark A. Noll. New York: Oxford University Press, 1999.

"Beyond Progressive Scientific Humanism." In *The Future of Religious Colleges*, edited by Paul J. Dovre. Grand Rapids, MI: Eerdmans, 2002.

"Religious Scholars in the Academy: Anachronism or Leaven?" In *The Future of Religious Colleges*, edited by Paul J. Dovre. Grand Rapids, MI: Eerdmans, 2002.

"Challenging the Presumptions of the Age: The Two Dissertations" [from a chapter in *Jonathan Edwards: A Life*]. In *The Legacy of Jonathan Edwards: American Religion and the Evangelical Tradition*, edited by D. G. Hart, Sean Michael Lucas, and Stephen J. Nichols. Grand Rapids, MI: Baker Academic Publishing, 2003.

"The Quest for the Historical Edwards: The Challenge of Biography." In *Jonathan Edwards At Home and Abroad*, edited by David W. Kling and Douglas A. Sweeney. Columbia: University of South Carolina Press, 2003.

"Jonathan Edwards in the Twenty-First Century." In *Jonathan Edwards at 300: Essays on the Tercentenary of His Birth*, edited by Harry S. Stout, Kenneth P. Minkema, and Caleb J. D. Maskell. Lanham, MD: University Press of America, 2005.

"Human Depravity: A Neglected Explanatory Category." In *Figures in the Carpet: Finding the Human Person in the American Past*, edited by Wilfred M. McClay. Grand Rapids, MI: Eerdmans, 2007.

ARTICLES

"Did Success Spoil American Protestantism?" *Christianity Today*, September 29, 1967, 4–7.

"Kingdom and Nation: New School Presbyterian Millennialism in the Civil War Era." *Journal of Presbyterian History* 46 (December 1968): 254–73.

"Perry Miller's Rehabilitation of the Puritans: A Critique." *Church History* 39 (March 1970): 91–105. Reprinted in *Marrow of American Divinity*, edited by Peter Charles Hoffer (New York: Garland, 1988), and in *Reckoning with the Past: Historical Essays on American Evangelicalism from the Institute for the Study of American Evangelicals*, edited by D. G. Hart (Grand Rapids, MI: Baker Books, 1995), 23–38.

"The New School Heritage and Presbyterian Fundamentalism." *Westminster Theological Journal* 32 (May 1970): 129–47. Reprinted in *Pressing toward the Mark: Essays Commemorating the Fifty Years of the Orthodox Presbyterian Church*, edited by Charles G. Dennison and Richard C. Gamble (Philadelphia: Committee for the Historian of the O.P.C., 1986).

"Evangelical Social Concern: Dusting Off the Heritage." *Christianity Today*, May 12, 1972, 8–11.

"Evangelicals in Wonderland: The Problem of Nonsense." *Christianity Today*, October 12, 1972, 4–6.

"The Gospel of Wealth, the Social Gospel, and the Salvation of Souls in Nineteenth-Century America." *Fides et Historia* 5, no. 1 (Fall 1972): 10–21.

"Christians and the Teaching of History." *Christian Scholar's Review* 2, no. 4 (1973): 311–24.

"Fundamentalism as an American Phenomenon: A Comparison with English Evangelicalism." *Church History* 46 (June 1977): 215–32. Reprinted in

D. G. Hart, *Reckoning with the Past: Historical Essays on American Evangelicalism from the Institute for the Study of American Evangelicals* (Grand Rapids, MI: Baker Books, 1995), 303–21.

"J. Gresham Machen, History, and Truth." *Westminster Theological Journal* 42 (Fall 1979): 157–75.

"The Spiritual Vision of History." *Fides et Historia* 14, no. 1 (Fall/Winter 1981): 55–66.

"A Law to Limit the Options: Creationists Are Fighting the Right Battle, but on the Wrong Front." *Christianity Today*, March 1982, 28–30.

"Of [Norman] Mayer and Monuments." *Reformed Journal* 33, no. 1 (January 1983): 2.

"The War on Secular Humanism." *Reformed Journal* 33, no. 5 (May 1983): 5–6.

"A Wonderful Plan." *Reformed Journal* 33, no. 8 (August 1983): 3–4.

"Creation versus Evolution: No Middle Way." *Nature* 305, no. 5935 (October 13, 1983): 571–74.

"America's 'Good Old Days': Were They Really?" *Christianity Today*, November 25, 1983, 60.

"The American Hero." *Reformed Journal* 33, no. 12 (December 1983): 5–6.

"Perspective on the Division of 1937." *Presbyterian Guardian*, January–April 1984. Reprinted in *Pressing toward the Mark: Essays Commemorating the Fifty Years of the Orthodox Presbyterian Church*, edited by Charles G. Dennison and Richard C. Gamble (Philadelphia: Committee for the Historian of the O.P.C., 1986).

"Harvey Cox's Conversion." *Reformed Journal* 34, no. 5 (May 1984): 3–4.

"Francis A. Schaeffer (1912–1984)." *Reformed Journal* 34, no. 6 (June 1984): 2–3.

"Evangelicalism in the Sociological Laboratory." *Reformed Journal* 34, no. 6 (June 1984): 20–24.

"God as Political Wildcard." *Reformed Journal* 34, no. 9 (September 1984): 2–3.

"Secularism and the Public Square." *This World*, Spring/Summer 1985, 48–62.

"The Problem with Being a Christian in Congress." *Reformed Journal* 35, no. 5 (May 1985): 2–4.

"Playing Dirty for the Lord." *Reformed Journal* 35, no. 10 (October 1985): 5–7.

"Evangelicalism and Fundamentalism." In *The Encyclopedia of Religion*, edited by Mircea Eliade. New York: Macmillan, 1986.

"Secular Humanism within the Church." *Christianity Today*, January 17, 1986, 14–15.

"Where Have All the Theologians Gone?" *Reformed Journal*, 36, no. 4 (April 1986): 2–4.

"Our 350th." *Reformed Journal* 36, no. 10 (October 1986): 4.

"Pat, Jesse, and a Principle." *Reformed Journal* 36, no. 11 (November 1986): 2–4.
"Let the Church Be a Sect." *Reformed Journal* 37, no. 2 (February 1987): 2–3.
"Irony of Ironies: Evaluating the Moderns." *Christian Century*, April 1987, 359–61.
"Star Wars in Beulah Land." *Reformed Journal* 37, no. 4 (April 1987): 2–4.
"Scalia, Rehnquist, and Free Exercise." *Reformed Journal* 37, no. 7 (July 1987): 2–4.
"The State of Evangelical Christian Scholarship." *Reformed Journal* 37, no. 9 (September 1987): 12–16.
"Fundamentalism." In *Encyclopedia of Religion in America*, edited by Charles H. Lippy and Peter W. Williams. New York: Scribner's, 1988.
"The New Paganism." *Reformed Journal* 38, no. 1 (January 1988): 2–4.
"The Plight of Liberal Protestantism." *Fides et Historia* 20, no. 1 (January 1988): 45–50.
"The State of Evangelical Christian Scholarship." *Christian Scholars Review* 17, no. 4 (June 1988): 347–60. Reprinted in *Perspectives on Science and Christian Faith: Journal of the American Scientific Affiliation* 40, no. 3 (September 1988).
"Politics and Religion in American History." *Reformed Journal* 38, no. 10 (October 1988): 11–16.
"Does Evangelicalism Have a Future?" *Reformed Journal* 39, no. 4 (April 1989): 2–3.
"Understanding J. Gresham Machen." *Princeton Seminary Bulletin*, n.s., 11, no. 1 (February 1990). Frederick Neumann Lecture for 1989 at Princeton Theological Seminary.
"Pursuing Trivial Suits." *Reformed Journal* 40, no. 6 (July/August 1990): 3–4.
"Christian Schooling: Beyond the Multiversity." *Christian Century*, October 7, 1992, 873–75.
"The Decade Ahead in Scholarship." *Religion and American Culture* 3, no. 1 (Winter 1993): 9–15.
"The Ambiguities of Academic Freedom." *Church History* 62, no. 2 (June 1993): 221–36.
Response to Donald Dayton, "'The Search for the Historical Evangelicalism': George Marsden's History of Fuller Seminary as a Case Study." *Christian Scholar's Review* 23, no. 1 (September 1993): 34–40.
"God and Man at Yale (1880)." *First Things*, April 1994, 39–42.
"Church, State, and Campus: Trampling Religion in the Name of Pluralism." *New York Times*, April 26, 1994, A23.

"Faith and Learning on the Catholic Campus." *Commonweal*, November 18, 1994, 36–38.

"Women's Ordination for Conservative Biblicists." *Perspectives*, May 1995, 3–5.

"The Intellectual Task of a Theological Seminary." *Review and Expositor* 92, no. 3 (Summer 1995): 351–57.

"A New Dialogue on Olympus: Science, Religion, and the State." *Books and Culture*, September/October 1995, 16–18.

"Mainline Protestantism and Higher Education: Two Perspectives." *Christian Scholar's Review* 25, no. 3 (March 1996): 356–59.

"Collapse of Culture." *Nature* 382, no. 6588 (July 18, 1996): 218–19.

"Science and Salvation." *Nature* 388, no. 6637 (July 3, 1997): 38–42.

"The Way We Were and Are." *Books and Culture*, November/December 1997, 18–20.

Rejoinder to "Review Symposium: The Outrageous Idea of Christian Scholarship." *Bulletin of the Council of Societies for the Study of Religion* 27, no. 3 (September 1998): 64.

"Liberating Academic Freedom." *First Things*, December 1998, 11–14.

"Christianity and Cultures: Transforming Niebuhr's Categories." *Insights*, Fall 1999, 4–15.

"Jonathan Edwards, American Augustine." *Books and Culture*, November/December 1999, 10–12.

"Response to McKenzie." *Fides et Historia* 32, no. 2 (Summer/Fall 2000): 16–18.

"The Incoherent University." *Hedgehog Review* 2, no. 3 (Fall 2000): 92–105.

"The Rise and Decline of the Modern Liberal Arts Ideal in the U.S.A." *Conversation on the Liberal Arts* (Gaede Institute, Santa Barbara, CA), 2001, 3–8.

"Reformed Strategies in Christian Scholarship: A Response to Robert Sweetman." *Perspectives: A Journal of Reformed Thought* 16, no. 7 (August/September 2001): 20–23.

"On His Own Terms." *Christian History* 22, no. 1 (2003): 44–46.

"Jonathan Edwards: The Missionary." *Journal of Presbyterian History* 81, no. 1 (Spring 2003): 5–17.

"Can Jonathan Edwards (and His Heirs) Be Integrated into the American Historical Narrative." *Historically Speaking* 5, no. 6 (July/August 2004): 13–15.

"Response to McClay and Kuklick." *Historically Speaking* 5, no. 6 (July/August 2004): 19–20.

"Charles Hodges Revisited: A Critical Appraisal of His Life and Work." *Church History* 75, no. 1 (March 2006): 212–13.

"Pulpit Imperfect." *Wall Street Journal*, July 13, 2006, D10.

"The Born-Again Mind." *Christian History and Biography* 92 (Fall 2006): 36–38.
"The Surprising Work of God: Harold John Ockenga, Billy Graham and the Rebirth of Evangelicalism." *Christianity Today*, August 2008, 57–58.
"Doing American History in a World of Subcultures." *Reviews in American History* 37, no. 2 (June 2009): 303–14.
"Fundamentalism." In *Dictionary of Christian Theology*, edited by S. B. Ferguson and D. F. Wright. Leicester: Inter-Varsity Press, forthcoming.

LIST OF CONTRIBUTORS

MARGARET BENDROTH is Executive Director of the American Congregational Association and Director of the Congregational Library in Boston. A doctoral student of Timothy Smith at the Johns Hopkins University, she has written extensively on a variety of topics in American religious history. Her books include *Fundamentalism and Gender, 1875 to the Present* (Yale University Press, 1993), *Growing Up Protestant: Parents, Children, and Mainline Churches* (Rutgers University Press, 2002), and *Fundamentalists in the City: Conflict and Change in Boston's Churches, 1885–1950* (Oxford University Press, 2005). She was Professor of History at Calvin College from 1998 to 2004.

JAY R. CASE is Professor of History at Malone University. He is the author of *An Unpredictable Gospel: American Evangelicals and World Christianity, 1812–1920* (Oxford University Press, 2012). Other publications include "And Ever the Twain Shall Meet: The Holiness Missionary Movement and the Birth of World Pentecostalism, 1870–1920," *Religion and American Culture* (2006); and "The American Baptist Reaction to Asian Christianity," in *The Changing Face of Christianity: Africa, the West and the World.*, edited by Lamin Sanneh and Joel Carpenter (Oxford: Oxford University Press, 2005).

DARREN DOCHUK is an Associate Professor at the John C. Danforth Center on Religion and Politics and in the History Department at Washington University in St. Louis. He has published extensively on the history of modern evangelicalism, religion, and politics. He is author of *From Bible Belt to Sunbelt: Plain-Folk Religion, Grassroots Politics, and the*

Rise of Evangelical Conservatism (Norton, 2011) and coeditor of *Sunbelt Rising: The Politics of Space, Place, and Region* (University of Pennsylvania Press, 2011).

TIMOTHY E. W. GLOEGE is an independent scholar based in Grand Rapids, Michigan. As a graduate student he received the Charlotte Newcombe Dissertation Fellowship and, upon its completion in 2007, the Edward Sorin Postdoctoral Fellowship. Two forthcoming publications are "The Trouble with *Christian History*: Thomas Prince's Failed 'Great Awakening'" (*Church History*) and "Faith Healing, Medical Regulation, and Public Religion in Gilded Age Chicago" (*Journal of Religion and American Culture*). His current book project, under contract with the University of North Carolina Press, examines how consumer capitalism and class identity shaped the early fundamentalist movement.

MICHAEL S. HAMILTON is Associate Professor and Chair, Department of History, Seattle Pacific University. He is the author of numerous articles on American fundamentalism and evangelicalism and is currently writing a history of Calvin College. He also consults frequently for colleges and foundations on matters relating to Christianity, scholarship, and higher education, most recently for the Calvin Seminars in Christian Scholarship program.

BARRY HANKINS is Professor of History and Graduate Program Director in the History Department at Baylor University. He is the author of six books and editor or coeditor of four others. His biography *Francis Schaeffer and the Shaping of Evangelical America* (Eerdmans, 2008) received the 2009 John Pollock Award for Christian Biography. His most recent book is *Jesus and Gin: Evangelicalism, The Roaring Twenties, and Today's Culture Wars* (Palgrave Macmillan, 2010). Hankins's articles have appeared in the journals *Church History, Religion and American Culture, Journal of Church and State, Fides et Historia*, and others.

THOMAS S. KIDD teaches history at Baylor University and is Senior Fellow at Baylor's Institute for Studies of Religion. He is the author of *The Protestant Interest: New England after Puritanism* (Yale University

Press, 2004), *The Great Awakening: The Roots of Evangelical Christianity in Colonial America* (Yale University Press, 2007), *The Great Awakening: A Brief History with Documents* (Bedford/St. Martins, 2007), *American Christians and Islam: Evangelical Culture and Muslims from the Colonial Period to the Age of Terrorism* (Princeton University Press, 2008), *God of Liberty: A Religious History of the American Revolution* (Basic Books, 2010), *The Founding Fathers and the Debate over Religion in Revolutionary America: A History with Documents* (coedited with Matthew Harris, Oxford University Press, 2011), and *Patrick Henry: First among Patriots* (Basic Books, 2011). He won a 2006–7 NEH Fellowship for his research on the Great Awakening.

KRISTIN KOBES DU MEZ is an Associate Professor of History at Calvin College in Grand Rapids, Michigan. Selected publications include "The Beauty of the Lilies: Femininity, Innocence, and the Sweet Gospel of Uldine Utley," in *Religion and American Culture* (2005), and "Leaving Eden: Resurrecting the Work of Katharine Bushnell and Lee Anna Starr," in *Breaking Boundaries: Female Biblical Interpreters Who Challenged the Status Quo* (T&T Clark, 2010). In 2010 she received a Louisville Sabbatical Research Grant to complete her book *The Forgotten Woman's Bible: Katharine Bushnell and the Problem of Christian Feminism* (Oxford University Press, forthcoming). Her current research explores the intersections of gender, militarism, and American Protestantism.

KATHRYN T. LONG is an Associate Professor of History at Wheaton College (Illinois), where she also served for nine years as department chair. She is an expert on revivalism and on evangelical missions in Latin America. Her publications include "Cameras 'Never Lie': The Role of Photography in Telling the Story of American Evangelical Missions," *Church History* (2003); and "In the Modern World, but Not of It: The 'Auca Martyrs,' Evangelicalism, and Postwar American Culture," in *The Foreign Missionary Enterprise at Home: Explorations in North American Cultural History*, edited by Daniel H. Bays and Grant Wacker (University of Alabama Press, 2003). Her book *The Revival of 1857–58: Interpreting an American Religious Awakening* (Oxford University Press, 1998) was awarded the Brewer Prize from the American Society of Church History (outstanding manuscript in church history for a first book). She was awarded a Pew Evangelical Scholars Research Fellowship and a summer stipend from the Louisville Institute for the Study of American Religion for a current book-in-progress, *God in the Rain Forest: Missionaries and the Waorani in Amazonian Ecuador*.

MARK NOLL is the Francis A. McAnaney Professor of History at the University of Notre Dame. He is the author of numerous books, the most recent of which include *Protestantism—A Very Short Introduction* (Oxford University Press, 2011); *God and Race in American Politics: A Short History* (Princeton University Press, 2008); *The Civil War as a Theological Crisis* (University of North Carolina Press, 2006); *America's God, from Jonathan Edwards to Abraham Lincoln* (Oxford University Press, 2002); and as coeditor, *Religion and American Politics: From the Colonial Period to the Present*, 2nd ed. (Oxford University Press, 2007). He is a member of the American Academy of Arts and Sciences and recipient of the National Endowment for the Humanities Medal. He is currently writing a multivolume history of the Bible in American history.

STEVEN M. NOLT is Professor of History at Goshen College, Goshen, Indiana. He is an expert on Mennonites, Amish, and German American religion. His books include *The Amish* (Johns Hopkins University Press, 2013); *Mennonites, Amish, and the American Civil War* (Johns Hopkins University Press, 2007); *Plain Diversity: Amish Cultures and Identities* (Johns Hopkins University Press, 2007); and *Foreigners in Their Own Land: Pennsylvania Germans in the Early Republic* (Pennsylvania State University Press, 2002).

RICK OSTRANDER earned his PhD in American history from the University of Notre Dame in 1996 and currently serves as Provost of Cornerstone University in Grand Rapids, Michigan. He is the author of *The Life of Prayer in a World of Science: Protestants, Prayer, and American Culture, 1870–1930* (Oxford University Press, 2000) and *Head, Heart, and Hand: John Brown University and Modern Evangelical Higher Education* (University of Arkansas Press, 2003). In spring 2004, Dr. Ostrander served as a Fulbright Senior Scholar in Wurzburg, Germany, where he taught courses in American history and lectured on American higher education. His most recent book is *Why College Matters to God: Academic Faithfulness and Christian Higher Education* (Abilene Christian University Press, 2009), which is currently in its second edition as a textbook for Christian college students.

KURT W. PETERSON is Director of Development at Loyola University Chicago. He received his PhD from the University of Notre Dame in 2003 with a dissertation titled "Constructing the Covenant: The Evangelical Covenant Church and Twentieth-Century American Religious Culture." His publications include "American Idol: David Barton's Dream of a Christian Nation," *Christian Century* (2006); with R. J. Snell, "'Faith Forms the Intellectual Task': The Pietist Option in Christian Higher Education," in *The Pietist Impulse in Christianity*, edited by Christian T. Collins Winn et al. (Pickwick, 2011); "Transforming the Covenant: The Emergence of Ethnic Diversity in a Swedish-American Denomination" (*Covenant Quarterly*, 2009); and "A Question of Conscience: Minnesota's Norwegian American Lutherans and the Teaching of Evolution," in *Norwegians and Swedes in the United States: Friends and Neighbors*, edited by Philip J. Anderson and Dag Blanck (Minnesota Historical Society Press, 2011).

GARTH M. ROSELL is Professor of History at Gordon-Conwell Theological Seminary in South Hamilton, Massachusetts. He is the author of *The Surprising Work of God: Billy Graham, Harold John Ockenga and the Rebirth of Evangelicalism* (Baker Academic Publishing, 2008) and *Boston's Historic Park Street Church: The Story of an Evangelical Landmark* (Kregel, 2009); the coeditor (with Richard A. G. Dupuis) of *The Memoirs of Charles G. Finney: The Complete Restored Text* (Zondervan, 1989); the coeditor (with Ronald C. White Jr. and Louis B. Weeks) of *American Christianity* (Eerdmans, 1986); and the editor of *Commending the Faith: The Preaching of D. L. Moody* (Hendrickson, 1999).

JOHN SCHMALZBAUER is Associate Professor and Blanche Gorman Strong Chair in Protestant Studies in the Department of Religious Studies at Missouri State University. His book *People of Faith: Religious*

Conviction in American Journalism and Higher Education (Cornell University Press, 2003) explores the role of religion in the careers of forty prominent journalists and academics. He is completing a book on the return of religion on campus with historian Kathleen Mahoney. He is also co-investigator on the National Study of Campus Ministries. His commentary and reviews have appeared in the *Wall Street Journal*, the PBS NewsHour's Patchwork Nation Project, and the Social Science Research Council's *Immanent Frame* blog. Recent publications include chapters for the *Blackwell Companion to Religion in America*, edited by Philip Goff (Wiley-Blackwell, 2010) and *The Post-Secular in Question*, edited by Philip S. Gorski et al. (NYU Press, 2012).

WILLIAM L. SVELMOE is Professor of History, Saint Mary's College, Notre Dame, Indiana. Recent publications include *A New Vision for Missions: William Cameron Townsend, the Wycliffe Bible Translators, and the Culture of Early Evangelical Faith Missions, 1896–1945* (University of Alabama Press, 2008); with George Marsden, "Evangelical and Fundamental Christianity," in *The Encyclopedia of Religion*, 2nd ed., edited by Lindsay Jones (New York: Macmillan Reference, 2005), and "Evangelism Only? Theory versus Practice in the Early Faith Missions," in *Missiology: An International Review* (2003). His novel *Spirits Eat Ripe Papaya* was published in 2010 by Wipf and Stock.

DAVID R. SWARTZ is Assistant Professor of History at Asbury University. He is the author of *Moral Minority: The Evangelical Left in an Age of Conservatism* (University of Pennsylvania Press, 2012). He has also published articles in the *Journal for the Study of Radicalism, Communal Societies, Books and Culture, Mennonite Quarterly Review*, and *Religion and American Culture*.

DOUGLAS A. SWEENEY is Professor of Church History and the History of Christian Thought and Director of the Jonathan Edwards Center at Trinity Evangelical Divinity School. A former editor of *The Works of Jonathan Edwards* (Yale University Press), he is the author or editor of numerous works on Christian history and theology, including *Nathaniel Taylor, New Haven Theology, and the Legacy of Jonathan*

Edwards (Oxford University Press, 2003), *Jonathan Edwards at Home and Abroad* (University of South Carolina Press, 2003), Edwards's *Miscellanies 1153–1360* (Yale University Press, 2004), *The New England Theology* (Baker Academic Publishing, 2006), *Jonathan Edwards and the Ministry of the Word* (IVP Academic Publishing, 2009), and *After Jonathan Edwards* (Oxford University Press, 2012).

JOHN G. TURNER is Assistant Professor of Religious Studies at George Mason University. His first book, *Bill Bright and Campus Crusade for Christ: The Renewal of Evangelicalism in Postwar America* (University of North Carolina Press, 2008), won *Christianity Today*'s 2009 award for best History/Biography. His most recent book is *Brigham Young: Pioneer Prophet* (Harvard University Press, 2012).

PETER J. WALLACE is Pastor of Michiana Covenant Presbyterian Church in Granger, Indiana, and Adjunct Professor of Church History at Mid-America Reformed Seminary, in Dyer, Indiana. He received his PhD in American history from the University of Notre Dame in 2004 with a dissertation entitled "'The Bond of Union': The Old School Presbyterian Church and the American Nation, 1837–1861." His publications include "The Doctrine of the Covenant in the Elenctic Theology of Francis Turretin," *Mid-America Journal of Theology* (2002); "History and Sacrament: John Williamson Nevin and Charles Hodge on the Lord's Supper," *Mid-America Journal of Theology* (2000); and "The Defense of the Forgotten Center: Charles Hodge and the Enigma of Emancipationism in Antebellum America," *Journal of Presbyterian History* (1997). He is currently at work on a biography of Robert Jefferson Breckinridge.

JOHN WIGGER is Professor and Chair of the History Department at the University of Missouri. His books include *American Saint: Francis Asbury and the Methodists* (Oxford University Press, 2009), *Taking Heaven by Storm: Methodism and the Rise of Popular Christianity in America* (Oxford University Press, 1998; paperback, University of Illinois Press, 2001), and *Methodism and the Shaping of American Culture* (Kingswood Books, 2001), edited with Nathan Hatch.

INDEX

Abbott, Lyman, 200, 207, 212
Abilene Christian University, 360, 362
Adventurers for God, 428
African American Christians/
 Christianity, 113–14, 128–29
African American churches
 Baptist, 113, 116–17, 121, 128
 Methodist, 113, 116–17, 121, 128
African American Great Awakening,
 110–14, 117, 120, 124, 127–31
African Methodist Episcopal Church
 (AME), 110–11, 120–24, 126
Ahlstrom, Sydney, 4, 75, 401, 475, 478
Allen, Alexander, 40
American Council of Christian
 Churches, 265
American Freedman's Union
 Commission (AFUC), 118
American Historical Association, 1,
 300, 326
Americans for Democratic Action,
 448
Anabaptists, 326, 450, 455, 459
anti-Catholicism, 101, 315, 317
anti-evolution, 240, 243–44, 247–48,
 255
antimodernism, 144, 171–72, 201,
 231–33, 243, 263–64
antiwar movement, 342–43
Ariel, Yaakov, 262

Arminianism, 39, 42, 50, 66, 79
Arnold, Melvin, 420, 422, 429–32,
 435–36
Asbury, Francis
 administrative skills of, 55–56
 biography, 51–54, 58–59
 comparison with Jonathan
  Edwards, 51–65
 poor health of, 60
 social skills of, 56–57
 theology, practice, and piety of,
  54–55, 59–62
 views of slavery, 63
Asbury College, 477
Association for Public Justice, 459
Astin, Alexander, 300
Athletes in Action, 346
Atlantic world (studies of), 19–20
Azusa Pacific University, 359–60,
 371–73

Bacon, Francis, 169
Bancroft Prize, 16, 45, 451, 468
Baptist Bible Union (BBU), 243
Baptists, 76, 105, 234–37, 240, 480
 African American denominations,
  111, 113–17, 121, 128–29
 American Baptist Home Missionary
  Society, 120
 anti-evolution position of, 254–57

Baptists (*cont.*)
  antislavery position of, 116
  interdenominational activism of, 234–35, 239–40
  internal divisions among, 237, 241–44, 247–48, 365–67
  missionaries, 424
  Northern Baptist Convention, 119, 231, 237–39, 242–45, 248
  organizational methods and strength of, 83, 288
  politicians, 476
  preachers/preaching, 36, 118, 144, 365
  proslavery position of, 115
  Southern Baptist Convention, 115–18, 155, 254–56, 363, 365–67, 370–71, 447
  in Texas, 363
Barnes, Albert, 98
Barth, Karl, 340, 405
Bass, Dorothy, 294
Baylor University, 158, 348, 362–75
Beacon Press, 429–30
Beard, Charles, 73
Bebbington, David, 20, 151–52, 155–56, 158
Beecher, Henry Ward, 173
Berger, Peter, 290, 292–93, 301
Berkeley Blitz, 341–42
Biederwolf, William, 246
Biola, 359–60
Black Saturday, 409–12
Blanshard, Paul, 430
Bloom, Allan, 291–92, 323
Bowery, Anne-Marie, 369
Boyd, Craig, 372
Bradley, James, 153
Brauer, Jerald, 400
Braun, Jon, 341
Breckinridge, Robert J., 95, 100–104
Brereton, Virginia, 261

Bright, Bill, 335–52, 446–47, 460
Brooks, Phillips, 207
Brown, John E., 263
Brumberg, Joan Jacobs, 189
Bryan, William Jennings, 168, 242, 244–45, 248, 251–57, 459
Buckley, William F., 337
Buddhism, 207
Burke, Kenneth, 285, 291
Burtchaell, James, 292, 298–99, 362, 364
Bushnell, Katherine, 183–90, 192
Buswell, J. Oliver, 264
Butler, Jon, 1, 21, 23, 74, 85
Butler bill, 253, 256
Butts, Jo Anne, 341

Calvin College, 76, 145, 148, 166, 174, 292, 351, 359–62, 365, 373, 444–45, 452–54, 476–77, 479
Calvinism, 23, 25, 38–42, 46, 54, 62–64, 71, 73–77, 79, 80–83, 173
Campus Crusade for Christ, 335–36, 338–52, 446, 450, 460, 478
Capa, Cornell, 420–24, 431, 435–36
Carnell, John Edward, 388, 408–11, 413–15, 471
Carpenter, Joel, 152, 154–56, 182, 232–33, 287, 289, 383, 443
Carter, Jimmy, 167, 180, 459–60
Catholicism, 44, 74–75, 94–95, 103, 317, 372
  and African Americans, 117
  anti-Catholicism, 18, 94–95, 101, 315, 320, 430
  Bible Riots (1844), 103
  educational endeavors of, 100, 291, 299, 316, 335, 337, 346, 351, 364–65, 373–74, 481–82
  missionaries, 419, 425–26
  political views and engagement, 2, 142, 254, 317, 320, 447

scholars and scholarship, 321, 367, 373, 390, 400, 447, 481
secularization, 287, 291
women, 81
youth, 346, 425–26
Catholic Newman Club, 346, 351
Chafer, Lewis Sperry, 236, 246, 263
Cherry, Conrad, 295–96
Chicago Declaration, 455–59
Chicago Evangelization Society, 215
Chicago Hebrew Mission, 262
China, 183, 188–89, 217, 244, 251
Christian Century, 241
Christian Coalition, 461
Christian Herald, 424, 427
Christianity, global, 181, 187–92
Christianity Today, 351, 366, 384, 443
Christian World Liberation Front (CWLF), 449–50, 452–53
Church of the Nazarene, 475
civil rights movement, 445–46
Civil War, 73, 76, 80, 84–85, 93, 99, 102, 104, 110, 116–17, 121, 131, 202, 231, 360, 373, 430
Cleaver, Eldridge, 447
Coffin, Henry Sloan, 238
Cold War, 6, 77, 337, 419, 424, 427, 435, 444
Cole, Stewart, 141, 146
common sense philosophy (Scottish), 169, 173, 318
communism, 255, 336–37, 425, 427, 442, 444–45, 449
Confederacy, 104, 122
Conference on Faith and History, 141, 326
Conforti, Joseph, 21
Congregationalists, 63–64, 76, 83, 92, 105, 206, 211, 235, 259, 475
Convention of Christian Workers, 200, 216
Cooper, Ezekiel, 59–60

Cornell, Ezra, 361
Cornell University, 313, 318
Council for Christian Colleges and Universities (CCCU), 357
C. S. Lewis Society, 158

Daane, James, 454
Dallas Baptist College, 359–60
Dallas Theological Seminary, 236
Darby, John Nelson, 168
Darwin, Charles/Darwinism, 150, 169, 189–90, 199, 206, 242, 249–51, 288
Dayton, Donald, 153–56
Dayuma, 432–34
Dockery, David, 370–71
Dooley, Thomas A., 419–20, 425–27
Dorner, Isaac A., 207–8
Dowie, John Alexander, 216
Drummond, Henry, 248
DuBois, W. E. B., 123, 126
Duke Divinity School/University, 292, 313
Dwight, Sereno Edwards, 39

Ecuador, 418–42
Edman, V. Raymond, 264
education
  African American investment in, 121, 126
  and anti-slavery activism, 118–20
  Christian higher education, 357–76, 382, 392
  crisis within, 323
  curriculum disputes, 256–57
  fundamentalist critiques of, 337, 348
  higher education, 6–7, 284–302, 313, 318, 321–22, 471, 474, 477
  historiography and study of, 5, 285–302, 314–17, 350–51, 388–89

education (*cont.*)
  and impact on denominational life, 99–100
  intellectual developments and trends, 82
  parochial education, 100–102
  public education, 101–2, 256
  and race, 114–15, 120
  reform movements within, 118, 256–57
  role and influence of ministers within, 83
  and role of the state, 102
  and role of women, 189
  secularization, 283–302, 334
  as setting for study of religion, 8
  as site of evangelization, 349
  as site of political advocacy and protest, 444
Edwards, Jonathan
  life and career of, 7–8, 15–16
  Marsden treatment of, 26–27, 43–45
  subject of literary and scholarly analysis, 16–17, 19, 23–24, 36–42, 77
  The Works of Jonathan Edwards, 18–19
Edwards, Ralph, 420, 432–36
Elliot, Elisabeth, 422, 428–32, 436
Elliot, Jim, 419
Ellwood, Robert, 343
Enlightenment, xi, 20–22, 25–26, 42, 45–46, 123, 169, 192, 204, 287–88, 316–18, 484
Episcopalians, 40, 117, 152
Erdman, Charles, 246
Erdman, William J., 248
Evangelical Alliance, 212
evangelicalism, 2, 21–22, 39, 41–42, 79, 81, 84–85, 91, 96, 105–6, 112, 129, 146, 154, 167–70, 231, 383–84, 391–92, 398
  African American, 112–17, 119, 121–22, 124–31
  approach to scholarship, 158, 177, 292, 369–71, 389, 468–85
  campus organizations, 335–36, 342, 347–52, 445–62, 478
  compare and contrast with fundamentalism, 144–45, 150, 155, 171, 384
  definition, 151–52
  entrepreneurship of, 339
  in Gilded Age, 202, 216
  and higher education, 100–101, 337, 348–51, 360–62, 372, 388, 404, 407, 470–73
  historiography and study of, 5, 8–11, 15–16, 20–21, 26, 72, 74, 78, 141, 143, 149, 151–52, 157, 181, 326, 381
  interdenominationalism of, 234–65
  international dimensions of, 390
  Jonathan Edwards, 20–26, 36, 39, 41, 46, 61–62
  and the life of the mind, 4, 85–86, 93, 360, 388, 479
  missionary work, 171, 349, 418, 435–36
  new evangelicalism, 26, 154, 265, 385–88, 399, 403, 405–6, 408–10, 415, 448, 471–72
  in the nineteenth century, 210
  northern varieties, 119, 123, 363–70
  parachurch organizations within, 338
  and political left, 443–62
  and politics, 1–2, 444
  publishing, 339, 343

relationship to American popular culture, 180, 201, 385, 418, 420, 432, 436
relationship to the state, 102
represented in Moody network, 206, 234–65
and secularization, 302
social agenda, 94, 97, 200
southern varieties, 117, 156, 357–76
support of revivals, 111, 144
ties to Pentecostalism, 153–55, 218
Evangelical Left, 443–44, 446, 449–51, 454, 457, 459–61
Evangelicals for McGovern (EFM), 455–56
Evangelicals for Social Action, 459
Evangelical Women's Caucus, 459
Evans, C. Stephen, 369
Evans, Louis H., Sr., 338
Evans, William, 246
evolution, 130, 144, 156, 168, 190, 231, 233, 240–44, 248–57, 319
Explo '72, 342, 450

Falwell, Jerry, 459–60
Farewell to Eden, 423
feminism, 192–93, 475, 483
Findlay, James, 145
Finney, Charles, 81, 92, 201, 206
First Great Awakening, 21, 47–48
First Things, 292
Fish, Stanley, 323
Fleming, Peter, 419
Foreign Missions Conference of North America, 260–61
Fosdick, Harry Emerson, 147, 242–45, 430
Four Spiritual Laws, 339–42, 345, 347
Frank, Franz H. R., 209–10
Frizen, Edwin, 261

Fuller, Charles E., 383, 388, 405–10, 418, 443
Fuller, Dan, 409, 410–13
Fuller Seminary, 336, 381–82, 384–93, 398–416, 442
fundamentalism, 84, 129, 143–44, 154, 169–72, 176, 231–34
and challenges to liberalism and secularization, 7, 402–3
compare and contrast with evangelicalism, 91, 384, 387
and education, 367–68, 402–3, 475
encounters with modernism, 201–2, 263–64, 449
entrepreneurship of, 406
historiography and study of, 141–44, 146–53, 155–60, 168, 230, 263–64
intellectual, 4, 84, 367, 471, 475
origins, 105, 130, 168–69, 241–44, 246
Fundamentalist Federation, 244, 248
Fundamentals, The, 239, 249, 261

Gabriel, Ralph, 76
Gaines, Wesley, 126–27
Gallagher, Sharon, 458
Genovese, Eugene, 114
German education, 208–10
Gibbon, Edward, 204
Gillquist, Peter, 341
Gilman, Daniel Coit, 318
Gish, Art, 449–50
Gleason, Philip, 299
Goldwater, Barry, 445
Gordon, A. J., 259
Gordon College, 477
Gordon-Conwell Theological Seminary, 385, 398, 477
Goshen College/Biblical Seminary, 458, 477

Index

Graham, William (Billy), 78, 85, 265, 338, 388, 410, 418, 420, 443–44, 447, 453, 471
Grawemeyer Award in Religion, 468
Gray, James M., 249–50, 252–54, 256
Guelzo, Allen, 25
Gura, Philip, 47

Habitat for Humanity, 419
Hall, Clarence, 420, 424–28, 436
Halverson, Richard, 338
Hannifin, Jerry, 420–21
Hardesty, Nancy, 458
Haroutounian, Joseph, 77, 79
Harper and Brother's (Harper's), 420, 422, 426, 429–30
Harrell, David Edwin, 145–46
Harrington, Michael, 447
Hart, Darryl G., 150, 295, 314
Hartt, Rollin Lynde, 243
Harvard College/University, 317–18, 360–61
Hatch, Nathan, 21, 82–84, 158
Hatfield, Mark, 442–43, 448–49
Hauerwas, Stanley, 323–24
Henry, Carl F. H., 158, 371, 387–88, 402, 409, 443–44, 471
Henry, Douglas, 369–70
Higham, John, 151
higher criticism, 130, 200, 205, 210–11, 217, 243
Hillel, 351
Hirrel, Leo, 94
Hodge, Charles, 95, 99–103, 105, 248
Hofstadter, Richard, 77, 86, 142, 285–90
Holifield, Brooks, 79–80, 82
holiness movement, 85, 153–55, 168, 171, 200, 213, 248, 392, 474–75, 477
Hollinger, David, 2, 289, 295–96

Hollywood Presbyterian Church, 338
Holmes, Arthur, 362
Holmes, Oliver Wendell, Sr., 40
Hopkins, Samuel, 39
Howe, Daniel Walker, 322
Hubbard, David, 409–12
Hughes, Richard, 326
Hutchison, William, 150, 202, 294, 478
Huxley, Matthew, 423

India, 188, 217
Institute for the Study of American Evangelicals, 481
Interdenominational Foreign Mission Association, 261
interdenominationalism, 235, 238, 255, 259–60, 264
International Christian Workers Association, 212
International Forum on Christian Higher Education, 357
InterVarsity Christian Fellowship, 338, 341, 391, 443, 445–46, 478
Israel, Charles, 256

James, William, 325–26
Jeffrey, David, 365, 367
Jenkins, Philip, 181, 389–90
Jesus Movement, 342–43, 451
Jewish history and scholarship, 75, 289, 296
Jews, 2, 259, 261–62, 400, 420
Jim Crow, 112, 127
John Brown University, 362, 373
Johns Hopkins University, 3, 151, 155, 299, 317–19, 475
Johnson, Don, 421
Johnson, Lyndon, 447
Johnson, Paul, 80
Jones, Bob, 337

Kelly, Howard A., 251–52
Kennedy, John F., 75, 420, 424, 426
Kerr, Clark, 341
Keswick movement, 235–36, 238, 253
Kindberg, Will, 423–24
King, Martin Luther, Jr., 71, 75, 430, 444–47
Kling, David, 79
Kurien, Prema, 302
Kuyper, Abraham, 316, 362, 402–3, 479, 484

Ladd, George, 409
Lambert, Frank, 21
Landon, Kenneth, 445
Larson, Edward, 149–50
Laws, Curtis Lee, 235, 239–41, 243
Lewis, C. S., 480
Lienesch, Michael, 255
Life, 420–21
Lilly Endowment, 298–300, 388, 480
Lindsell, Harold, 409
Longfield, Bradley, 314
Luce, Henry R., 422, 435
Lyon, Larry, 369

Macartney, Clarence E., 238, 245–246
MacDonald, Dennis, 453
Machen, J. Gresham, 148, 150, 245–246, 402–403
MacIntyre, Alasdair, 321–322
Marsden, George
  and Alasdair MacIntyre, 321
  and background in Orthodox Presbyterian Church, 92, 314, 316
  biography and career, 3–5, 7–11, 76, 92, 381–82, 401, 452, 468–70, 475–77
  Calvinist thought of, 71–72, 479
  definition and assessment of evangelicalism, 154, 230–31
  definition and assessment of fundamentalism, 143–44, 154, 167, 168, 176, 201, 230–31
  on Francis Asbury, 64–65
  impact on academy and academicians, xi–xii, 6, 145–53, 158–59, 190, 194, 263, 313, 328, 364, 385, 390, 393, 475–84
  and Reformed theology, xii, 45, 92, 153, 176, 316, 326–27
  on Reinhold Niebuhr, 174
  religious background of, 176, 230, 314, 316
  on revivalism, 78–79, 93
  scholarly approach of, 8, 37, 65, 157–58, 167, 174–78, 180, 194, 293–94, 313, 316, 327–28, 352
  scholarly critiques of, 25–27, 46–47, 147–48, 153–56, 201, 296–97, 322–26
  on slavery, 97–99
  study of Calvinism and Presbyterianism, 71–72, 79–81, 91–106, 129
  study of education, 91, 313–18, 321–22, 327, 334–35
  study of evangelicalism and fundamentalism, 84–86, 93–106, 129, 141–45, 167–78, 180–81, 201–2, 230–32, 263, 381–85, 398–400
  study of higher education, 283–86, 292–302, 313–22, 338, 349–51, 361–63, 385, 391–92
  study of Jonathan Edwards, 15–25, 37–38, 43–48, 52–64, 174, 327
  study of revivalism, 72, 461

Marsden, George (*cont.*)
  study of secularization, 157,
    283–86, 292–300, 313–15,
    318–19, 323, 334–35
  writing style, 5–6, 18, 172–78, 293,
    400–416
Martin, David, 301
Marty, Martin, 201, 284, 400, 478
Masore, Gladys, 186–87, 193
Masse, J. C., 241
Mathews, Donald, 78, 152
Mathews, Mary Beth Swetnam, 257
Matthews, Mark, 246
Maxwell, L. E., 263
May, Henry, 73–75, 142, 288
McCarthy, Eugene, 448
McCarthyism, 287–89
McCosh, James, 319
McCully, Ed, 419
McGovern, George, 450, 454–56
McGrath, Alister, 393
McIntire, Carl, 142, 404
McLoughlin, William, 78, 80, 146, 201
McPherson, Aimee Semple, 148
Mead, Sidney, 74, 77, 400
Messiah College, 362, 458
Methodist Church
  and evangelicalism, 155
  general, 76, 83
  membership, statistics of, 64
  Methodist Episcopal Church, 56, 183
  Methodist Episcopal Church (South), 117, 255
  missionary work, 183
Metzger, Walter, 286–88
Michaelson, Paul, 326
Miller, Perry, 2–3, 15–17, 19, 25,
    41–43, 75, 143, 287
Miller, Robert Moats, 147–48
Mills, C. Wright, 290

Minneapolis City Mission, 212–13
Modern, John Lardas, 302
modernism, 26, 104–5, 144, 150, 171,
    185, 202, 219, 231–32, 236–40,
    243, 248, 260–63, 384, 386, 405
Mohler, Al, 366
Monsma, Stephen, 454
Moody, Dwight L., 155–56, 201, 206,
    215–17, 232–37, 265
Moody, Emma, 248
Moody Bible Institute, 215, 249
Moody Bible Institute Monthly, 251–52,
    459
Moody movement and network,
    233–36, 238–65
Moomaw, Donn, 338
Moorhead, W. G., 248
Moral Majority, 4, 443, 459, 461
Morgan, Edmund, 3, 7, 475
Mouw, Richard, 444, 454, 479

National Association of Evangelicals
    (NAE), 265, 384–85, 392
National Black Evangelical
    Association, 459
Navigators, 391, 478
Neuhaus, Richard John, 367
New Left, 342, 452
Niebuhr, H. Richard, 74, 76
Niebuhr, Reinhold, 160, 174, 285,
    293, 295, 414, 474
Nixon, Richard, 448, 450–51, 455
Noll, Mark, 3, 20, 80, 85–86, 106,
    158, 182, 186–88, 360–61, 363,
    375, 387–88
Norris, J. Frank, 142, 148–49, 155,
    254, 274
Numbers, Ronald, 249

Obama, Barack, 2
Ockenga, Harold John, 383–88,
    392–93, 404–7, 413, 471

Ohio State University, 346
Open Door Church (Minneapolis), 213–14
Operation Auca, 430
Orr, J. Edwin, 392

Park Street Church, 383
Parrington, Vernon, 41, 73, 77–78
Payne, Daniel Alexander, 121–23, 126, 130
Peace Corps, 420
Peay, Austin, 253
Pentecostal/Pentecostals/
    Pentecostalism, 47, 84, 153, 155, 171, 200, 202, 218–19, 392, 474, 475, 480
Perkins, John, 451
Pew Charitable Trusts, 292, 314, 388, 480–81
Pierson, A. T., 259
Plantinga, Alvin, 479
Plumer, William Swan, 95–96
pluralism, 85, 284, 287, 295, 302, 316–17, 320–22, 327, 351
Plymouth Brethren, 168, 177
Poling, Daniel, 427
Post-American, The, 458
Post-Americans, 448–49, 452, 457
postmodernism, 6–7, 39, 316, 321, 473
Prairie Bible Institute, 263
premillennialism, 143–44, 168, 217, 231–32, 235–36, 238–39, 241–43, 245–47, 262, 402
Presbyterianism, 15, 72, 82–84, 234–37, 240, 247
    Bible Presbyterian Church, 247
    debates within, 79, 98, 103–4, 231, 236–48
    education, 299
    First Presbyterian Church of Hollywood, 336–38
    intellectual life of, 476

New School, xi, 10, 72, 76, 79–80, 83–84, 91, 93–106, 129–30
    northern, 119
Old School, 92–106, 245
Orthodox Presbyterian Church, 3, 84, 92, 230, 247, 314, 316
Presbyterian Church, U.S.A., 237, 244, 255
Presbyterian paradigm, 153
Southern California, 404
Southern Presbyterian Church, 117, 255–56
Princeton College/University/
    Seminary, 17–18, 22, 79, 92–96, 143, 153, 168–69, 201, 245–46, 287, 312, 318–19, 336, 470
Protestantism
    conservative and traditional forms, 144, 202, 320, 435
    liberal, 41, 84, 168, 237–44, 254, 259, 261, 294–95, 317–18, 320, 334, 404, 435
    mainline, 82, 263, 294–95, 313, 350, 474
Puritanism, 2, 15, 40–42, 62, 72, 75, 77, 80, 82, 123, 143, 201, 287, 327, 334, 360, 460

Rankin, Thomas, 58–59, 63
Rawlyk, George, 20
Reader's Digest, 420, 425–26
Reagan, Ronald, 11, 341
Reconstruction (era), 112, 115, 119, 124–26, 256
Reformed Journal, 454
Reformed theology, 22, 24, 47, 82, 92, 94, 143–44, 148, 153, 176, 316, 326, 362, 372, 444, 452–53, 461, 479
Religious Right/Christian Right, 146, 149, 230, 263, 361, 435, 451, 460–61

Reserve Officers' Training Corps
(ROTC), 447–48
Reuben, Julie, 296–97
revivalism, 17, 72–82, 84, 92–94, 97,
111, 117, 130, 144, 235, 237, 405,
474, 479
Reynolds, Herbert, 363–64
Ribuffo, Leo, 294
Richey, Russell, 146
Riley, William Bell, 148, 237, 239–40,
243, 250, 254, 257, 337
Ritschl, Albrecht, 210
Robert, Dana, 181, 390–91
Roberts, Jon, 249–50, 297–98
Robertson, Pat, 459
Russell, Robert, 423

Saint, Nate, 419, 421, 427–28,
432
Saint, Rachel, 428, 431–34
Saint, Sam, 420–21
Sandeen, Ernest, 84, 143–44, 146,
150, 152–53, 155–56, 160, 168,
231–32
Sanderson, Carla, 371
Savage My Kinsman, The, 422, 432
Schmeltekopf, Donald, 364
Schwehn, Mark, 294
Schweitzer, Albert, 420, 429
Scofield, C. I., 236, 248, 259
Scopes trial, 168, 243, 249, 251
Second Great Awakening, 36, 73, 78,
112, 114, 124, 360
Second Vatican Council, 482
secularization, 1–2, 10, 25, 157, 167,
283–87, 290–302, 315, 318–19,
323, 334–36, 343, 349–50, 361,
367
Seymour, William J., 392
Sider, Ron, 455–60
Simpson, A. B., 259
Skinner, Tom, 446, 451–52

slavery
African American Christians,
church handling of, 115–19, 122,
386
antislavery activism, 78, 86, 94–95,
98–99, 115–16, 119
Christian and other religious
practice within, 113, 115–17, 128
and Ecuador, Protestant missions,
434
as moral issue, 76
sectionalism and southern secession
because of, 92–93, 97–99
theological debate over, 7, 44, 63,
92–93, 99, 102, 116
Sloan, Douglas, 295, 367
Smith (Torrey), Clara B., 207, 214
Smith, Christian, 291, 297, 349
Smith, James K. A., 326
Smith, Timothy, 3, 78, 81, 143, 152,
154, 160, 386–88, 468, 474–77,
481, 484
Smith, Wilbur, 404–5, 411
social gospel movement, 75, 85, 200,
204, 212, 215, 218, 245, 257
Sojourners, 449, 459–60
Sojourners, 459–60
Solomon, David, 364
Sparks, Jack, 453
Sproul, R. G., 338, 347
Staiger, C. Bruce, 97
Stanford, Leland, 361
Stanton, Elizabeth Cady, 184
Starr, Ken, 365
Stentzel, Jim, 457
Stevenson, J. Ross, 246
Stout, Harry, 158
Straton, John Roach, 242
Strong, Josiah, 200, 212
Strout, Cushing, 322–23
Students Concerned about Vietnam,
448

Summer Institute of Linguistics
  (SIL), 419, 423, 432
Sunbelt, 359, 370
Sunday, Billy, 142, 148, 246, 257
Sunday School Times, 251–52
Sweet, William Warren, 77, 83, 158,
  381, 400, 478
Swing, David, 105
syncretism, 191

Tate, Margaret, 368
Taylor University, 361–62
temperance reform movement, 95–96,
  183–84
This Is Your Life, 432–34
Thornwell, James Henley, 101–5,
  108
Through Gates of Splendor, 422, 429
Tiénou, Tite, 182, 193
Tolkien, J. R. R., 157
Torrey, R. A., 169, 200–219, 249,
  259–61
Townsend, W. Cameron, 263, 419,
  423, 432–34, 436
Trinity College/Seminary, 477
Trollinger, William Vance, 150–51,
  240, 254
Trumbull, Charles G., 252
Turner, Henry McNeal, 110–11, 113,
  120, 124–25, 127
Turner, James, 297–98

Union University, 360, 370–71
Unitarianism, 118–19, 205–6
University of California, Berkeley,
  340–41, 350
University of California, Los Angeles
  (UCLA), 335, 337–38, 348, 350
University of Chicago, 77, 216, 313,
  318, 400
University of Notre Dame, 298, 334,
  363, 373–75, 481

Van Der Puy, Abe, 426
Vassady, Béla, 404–6
Veysey, Laurence, 285, 288, 293
Victorian Christianity, 184–88, 263
Vietnam War, 448–49, 451, 455
Von Hartmann, Edward, 208–9

Wacker, Grant, 158, 218, 358
Wake Forest University, 367
Wallace, DeWitt, 425, 428, 435
Wallace, Lila, 428
Wallis, Jim, 343, 449, 450–51, 457–58
Walls, Andrew, 181–82, 191–92, 484
Waorani ("Aucas"), 419, 421, 436
Warfield, B. B., 168
Warren, Rick, 357–58
Watt, David Harrington, 339
Webb, George, 247
Weisberger, Bernard, 77
Wells, David F., 385
Western civilization, 189–90
Westminster College, 477
Westminster Theological Seminary,
  92
Wheaton College, 264, 351, 359, 362,
  365, 371–74, 443–48, 455–56,
  477, 481
White, Hayden, 284–85
Wilson, John F., 297
Wilson, Woodrow, 319
Winiarski, Douglas, 26, 46–47
Winona Lake Bible Conference, 246,
  262
Winslow, Ola, 41–42
Winthrop, John, 456
Witherspoon, John, 22, 287
Wolfe, Alan, 294, 360
Woman's Christian Temperance
  Union (WCTU), 184
Woo, Carolyn, 374
Wood, Nathan R., 263
Worden Street Community, 452

World Magazine, 366
World's Christian Fundamentals
  Association (WCFA), 200,
  239–40, 254
World Vision, 419
World War I, 170, 233, 235, 248
World War II, 418, 470, 482–83
World Woman's Christian Temperance Union (WWCTU), 183–84
Wuthnow, Robert, 301

Wycliffe Bible Translators (WBT), 419, 432

Yale University, 203–6, 313, 318, 361, 475
Yale University Press, 468
Yerxa, Donald, 470
Yoder, John Howard, 458
Youderian, Roger, 419
Youth for Christ, 390–91, 418

www.ingramcontent.com/pod-product-compliance
Lightning Source LLC
Chambersburg PA
CBHW071431300426
44114CB00013B/1387